THE LATIN INSCRIPTIONS OF ROME

THE LATIN INSCRIPTIONS OF ROME

A Walking Guide

TYLER LANSFORD

THE JOHNS HOPKINS UNIVERSITY PRESS

BALTIMORE

© 2009 The Johns Hopkins University Press
All rights reserved. Published 2009
Printed in the United States of America on acid-free paper

2 4 6 8 9 7 5 3

The Johns Hopkins University Press
2715 North Charles Street
Baltimore, Maryland 21218-4363
www.press.jhu.edu

Library of Congress Control Number: 2008934997

ISBN 13: 978-0-8018-9149-6 (hc), ISBN 10: 0-8018-9149-3 (hc)
ISBN 13: 978-0-8018-9150-2 (pbk), ISBN 10: 0-8018-9150-7 (pbk)

A catalog record for this book is available from the British Library.

The maps in this book were drawn by Michael Southern.

Supplementary phonetic and epigraphic glyphs were created for this book
by Ralph Hancock.

The engravings at the beginning of each chapter are taken from Giovanni Battista
Cipriani, *Itinerario figurato degli edifizi più rimarchevoli di Roma* (Rome, 1835).
The illustrations of papal arms on page xxiii are adapted from *Kunstführer Rom*,
5th ed., by Anton Henze, Kunibert Bering, and Gerhard Wiedmann, with
Ernest Nash and Hellmut Sichtermann (Reclam, 1994).

Special discounts are available for bulk purchases of this book. For more information,
please contact Special Sales at 410-516-6939 or specialsales@press.jhu.edu.

The Johns Hopkins University Press uses environmentally friendly book materials,
including recycled text paper that is composed of at least 30 percent post-consumer
waste, whenever possible. All of our book papers are acid-free, and our jackets and
covers are printed on paper with recycled content.

PARENTIBVS
OPTIMIS
CONIVGI
OPTIMO

QVACVMQVE ENIM INGREDIMVR IN ALIQVA HISTORIA
VESTIGIVM IMPONIMVS

Wherever we step, we tread on one or another scene of history.

— *Cicero,* De Finibus 5.5

CEDIT ENIM RERVM NOVITATE EXTRVSA VETVSTAS
SEMPER ET EX ALIIS ALIVD REPARARE NECESSE EST

The old order ever passes, thrust out by the new,
and one thing must needs be made afresh from others.

— *Lucretius,* De Rerum Natura 3.964–965

Contents

Preface

PERHAPS THE MOST IMPRESSIVE FEATURE of the city of Rome is the simultaneous presence of all her eras. What more eloquent witness to that simultaneity than the prospect from Piazza Venezia? The panorama there unfolded comprehends the monuments of two millennia. The shortest list must include the sepulcher of Bibulus, the Column of Trajan, the Basilica of San Marco, the Church of Santa Maria in Aracoeli, Palazzo di Venezia, Piazza del Campidoglio, and the monument of Vittorio Emanuele. Piazza Venezia is Rome writ small; at every turn, the fundamental oneness of the city's history is declared in the promiscuous confusion of her fabric. To privilege any part is to do violence to the whole. The purpose of the present book is to give sustained expression to this old idea from a novel point of view.

Rome's sheer magnitude defies comprehensive treatment. To fashion a tapestry of her long story, one must discover a thread of continuity—a thread sufficiently robust to set a warp spanning the millennia, yet fine enough to weave a weft that will pick out the detail of individual episodes. One such thread (unbroken and peculiarly Roman) consists in the Latin language itself: Rome's oldest surviving Latin inscription dates perhaps to the sixth century BC, while at the time of the present writing the most recent major specimen was mounted in 2006—a span of more than two and a half thousand years. Over the course of the city's history, Latin has been the vehicle of messages ranging from graffiti and epitaphs to the dedications of temples, arches, basilicas, and obelisks. As a result, the inscriptions furnish the ideal material for an integral if desultory conspectus of her history as a whole—ancient and modern, public and private, sacred and secular.

This book features the texts of more than 350 inscriptions ranging in date from the first century BC to AD 2006; all are equipped with translations and notes. Though most of them celebrate popes and emperors, a few—particularly epitaphs—record the doings and dyings of humbler folk. Taken together, they afford a kind of pointillist entrée into the city's history. The selections are arranged in fifteen itineraries or tours. A topographical approach seems to follow naturally from the view that Rome is best approached as a unitary phenomenon.

Because the book includes both Latin texts and English translations, I hope that it will prove useful to a broad spectrum of readers. On the right-hand page, students of Roman history, of the church, of art and architecture, of urban planning, and of the alphabet and lettering will find the historical and cultural information necessary for understanding the inscriptions; students of Latin—a narrower readership—will find linguistic assistance on the left. I will be gratified if the presence of the Latin text stimulates the general reader's interest in the language and, conversely, if readers of Latin derive pleasure and profit from an excursion beyond the confines of Antiquity.

The definition of 'inscription' proposed by the Italian paleographer Armando Petrucci is admirably complete: 'a text, typically of limited compass, that serves to commemorate, declare or designate; that is incised (but sometimes painted or executed in mosaic); that is of set purpose precise and deliberately solemn; that is realized in a durable medium (marble, stone, more rarely metal) or on objects of various types (paintings, hangings, jewelry, and so forth); and which is displayed for contemplation and reading by the public in an enclosed space (church, chapel, palace) or in the open (square, street, cemetery)'.[1]

Mosaics and metalwork excepted, the specimens included here are artifacts produced by the action of hammer and chisel; their character is determined by an elemental if antagonistic collaboration of steel and stone. For my own part, I find an inexhaustible fascination in the vari-

---

1 'un testo di natura commemorativa, enunciativa o designativa, di solito di non lunga estensione, inciso (ma a volte anche dipinto o eseguito a mosaico) con propositi di accuratezza ed intenzioni di solennità su un supporto di material dura (marmo, pietra o più raramente metallo) o su oggetti (dipinti, arredi, oreficerie, e così via), ed esposto alla pubblica visione e lettura in un luogo chiuso (chiesa, cappella, palazzo) o all'aperto (piazza, via, cimitero)'. Armando Petrucci, *Medioevo da Leggere* (Einaudi, 1992), p. 38.

ety of incised letter forms—their shape and size and, most important, the effect of the play of light on their beauty and legibility. I cherish the paradoxical hope that the use of this book will lead to a realization of the inadequacy of the printed page to convey the experience of observing incised stone.

Obviously an 'omnium gatherum' of the present type can lay little claim to originality. The translations apart, its chief distinction lies in bringing between two covers a thousand scraps of information hitherto dispersed in handbooks, journals, and encyclopedic works of reference. More obviously still, no individual could pretend to familiarity with— let alone mastery of—the numerous academic specialties here represented; for this reason, I shall welcome advice of my blunders from the many scholars into whose fields I have trespassed. Professional students of Rome will appreciate the extent to which I have pillaged the work of my predecessors, in particular that of Ferdinand Gregorovius, whose prose epic *Geschichte der Stadt Rom im Mittelalter* remains fundamental for a sympathetic grasp of the city's historical development.

I have many people to thank for their generous support of my endeavor. At the University of Washington in Seattle, Professors James Clauss, Alain Gowing, and Stephen Hinds read portions of the work in draft and made valuable suggestions for its improvement. To Paul Pascal, Professor Emeritus of Classics at the University of Washington, I owe a special debt of gratitude for sharing with me his wide and multifarious erudition. Such sense as I have wrung from the medieval verse inscriptions is due largely to his acumen; his too are the rogue textual emendations occasionally ventured in the notes on those entries. Elsewhere, Leofranc Holford-Strevens generously provided trenchant and indispensable criticism, as did Margaret Brucia and Sean Cocco. Richard Burgess and John Dillon offered welcome assistance with particular problems. The introductory essays have benefited by the scrutiny of my father, Henry Lansford.

In Rome, I have especially to thank Fabrizio Alessio Angeli and Elisabetta Berti, whose knowledge of medieval Rome is rivaled only by their kindness. I am grateful to architect Riccardo D'Aquino and archeologist Marco Brugia for a private visit to Santo Stefano Rotondo while it was under restoration, as I am to Father Remato Sanges of the Padri Stimmatini for a pleasant and informative discussion of epitaphs at Sant'Agata dei Goti. Father Reginald Foster OCD read and commented on a portion of the work. Jennifer Wilkin of the University of Washington Rome Center has offered support both moral and material over the whole period of the book's gestation.

Those custodians of the Foro Romano will naturally prefer to remain unnamed who permitted me an early-morning foray out of bounds that would have cost considerable time and effort to arrange through official channels; likewise the indulgent employees of the Pontificia Commissione di Archeologia Sacra who granted me ad hoc authorization to make photographs at the Cemetery of San Callisto.

Garrett Boge of Seattle, Matthew Carter of Boston, and Ralph Hancock of London rendered invaluable assistance with challenges of typography. Marc Mariani, my generous colleague at Seattle Language Academy, bore my prolonged distraction in good part. Sharon Carson, who tills a field remote from those explored in this book, took a keen and sympathetic interest in the project from its inception. The mention of these individuals' names is intended as an expression of gratitude only and in no way implies their endorsement of the book.

I would also like to express gratitude to the Johns Hopkins University Press and to my editor, Michael Lonegro, for their faith in an unconventional project and an untried author. Anne Whitmore, my copyeditor at the press, deserves special thanks for the extraordinary care she gave to this complex and difficult project.

I dedicate the book to my parents, who have lavished on me all the love and support that any child could desire, and to Douglas Arbuthnot, companion of my Roman explorations—as of all else—for as long now as Peter pontificated.

Introduction

THE SELECTION OF INSCRIPTIONS included in the present book has been guided by three criteria: presence *in situ*, accessibility, and historical or linguistic interest. Although I have taken pains to ensure that the major public inscriptions of Rome are included, the selection of those found in churches has been determined in some degree by the simple question of accessibility over the years that I compiled my material. As visitors quickly realize, the opening hours of the smaller churches of Rome can be capricious; in any given month a substantial minority will be under restoration. On the other hand, given that the city's Latin epitaphs and minor commemorative stones run to the tens of thousands, the present collection is as likely to be representative of the whole as any of similar size would be. However that may be, with respect to the minor inscriptions, I regard the book as a point of departure for further exploration. On the basis of the items treated here, the persistent explorer should be able to make headway with most of the inscriptions likely to be encountered in the city.

The selection is to a certain extent personal, favoring themes and episodes that particularly appeal to my own imagination. Its principal limitations should be readily apparent: only epigraphical material is treated, and only a small fraction of the material available. Although I have attempted in the introductions and notes to set the inscriptions in context, in no sense does the work pretend to offer a survey of the historical topography of the city of Rome, much less of her artistic, social, political, or cultural history. Such information as is furnished is intended merely to illuminate the inscriptions featured in the itineraries. Further, although I have spared no pains in the effort to assemble a selection that respects the whole history of the city, the paucity of material—or at least of material *in situ*—deprives large and important periods of her history of a representation equal to their importance. Thus, the late Empire, the Renaissance, and the Baroque loom disproportionately large by comparison with the Republic and the Middle Ages.

TRANSLATIONS

As a translator, my chief goal has been to render the Latin as accurately as possible within the confines of tolerably idiomatic English. Since one of the aims of the collection is to address the needs of the Latinless reader, I have preferred to err on the side of overtranslation in the attempt to bring out a sense that may be only implicit. In nearly all cases, moreover, that aim motivated me to convey the gist of the text in phrasing more congenial to English than to Latin; in many cases, it also entailed a throughgoing rearrangement of the ideas. In reformulating the contents, I have nevertheless labored to avoid breaking the English into more sentences than the Latin uses, except in cases where this would have led to gross infelicity or sheer incoherence. It is my hope that the strategy of allowing myself a certain license within this larger constraint has produced versions that reflect something of the complexity of the original syntax while hewing to a respectable standard of fluency in the English.

Like all translators, I have been torn by the competing requirements of fidelity and grace. The complementary aims of euphony and sound idiom have moreover conspired to produce minor inconsistencies in the translation of certain Latin words and constructions. An example: the Ciceronian language affected in many Neo-Latin inscriptions is incorrigibly partial to the superlative degree of the adjective. As this predilection is alien to the spirit of English prose, I have sometimes attempted to convey the force of a Latin superlative by employing a stronger English synonym. Thus, at 1.6F I render the adjective *sacratissimus* ('most sacred') by 'hallowed'. I have in general made a point of avoiding the archaic and unidiomatic, but where biblical texts are quoted or paraphrased, I have invariably adopted the language of the Authorized Version. I have also admitted obsolete diction in cases where it appeared to render the Latin more exactly or to achieve a marked improvement in the cadence of the English. For example, the archaic 'bade' always seemed to represent *iussit* better than 'ordered'. In one or two instances where 'truly' or 'forever' seemed impossibly awkward, I have ventured to write 'forsooth' or 'aye'.

NUMBERING & NOMENCLATURE

In the numbering of the items in the itineraries, each number corresponds to a single monument, be it basilica, obelisk, or fountain. The subdivisions A, B, C, etc., correspond to the several items to be found within a single monument—for example, the epitaphs in a church. The subdivisions i, ii, iii, etc. correspond to the several parts of a single item—for example, the texts on the base of an obelisk.

In the chapter introductions, references to the inscriptions in that itinerary are set in SMALL CAPITALS with initial capitals, and the number of the inscription appears in the outside margin of the page.

Ancient monuments apart, I have preferred to use current Italian names: I write 'Pons Fabricius' for the ancient bridge at the Tiber Island but 'Ponte Sisto' for its modern neighbor upstream.[1] Exceptions to my general practice will be found in occasional references to the Basilica di San Pietro in Vaticano as 'St. Peter's' and to the Basilica di San Giovanni in Laterano as 'St. John Lateran'. In the interest of brevity, I have sometimes written 'Spanish Steps' instead of 'Scalinata della Santissima Trinità dei Monti'.

TEXTS & TRANSCRIPTIONS

Strange as it may seem, it is notoriously difficult to make an accurate transcription. In some cases this difficulty is due to inadequate light, in others to the distance of the inscribed object, in others again to the poor condition of the monument. Those who consult such collections as the *Corpus Inscriptionum Latinarum, Inscriptiones Christianae Urbis Romae Septimo Saeculo Antiquiores*—and others whose name is legion—may be surprised to find that my texts occasionally diverge from the standard

---

1. *The Italian names of the obelisks that appear in this book are as follows: Obelisco Agonale (Piazza Navona), Obelisco Campense (Piazza di Montecitorio), Obelisco Esquilino (Piazza dell'Esquilino), Obelisco Flaminio (Piazza del Popolo), Obelisco Lateranense (Piazza di S. Giovanni in Laterano), Obelisco Macutèo (Piazza della Rotonda), Obelisco Minerveo (Piazza della Minerva), Obelisco Quirinale (Piazza del Quirinale), Obelisco Sallustiano (Piazza della SS. Trinità dei Monti), Obelisco Vaticano (Piazza di San Pietro in Vaticano).*

editions. Such divergences are due either to deterioration in a monument's condition over the time that has intervened since the text was transcribed or to errors of a sort inevitable in the compilation of an encyclopedic collection. For my own part, I have spared no pains to ensure the highest attainable degree of accuracy.

My choices in the typographical presentation of the material have been determined by the anticipated needs of a nonspecialist readership. In producing a scholarly edition, the professional epigrapher brings to bear a complex and finely tuned apparatus for representing such features as the speculative restoration of lost text or of text deliberately effaced and the reading of characters imperfectly legible. Since the modest ambition of the present book is to facilitate the comprehension and enjoyment of the inscriptions on site, it seems right to make use of such instrumentation only insofar as it serves this purpose. In particular, the layout of the text on the page follows that of the original. Where the length of the line renders this impracticable, prose texts are broken over as few lines as the page will permit (e.g., 2.15) and verse texts printed so as to show the metrical scheme (e.g., 5.1).

The text of the inscriptions is set in SMALL CAPITALS. Both vocalic and consonantal U appear as V unless (as in 7.4E, 9.5D, and 10.9) they are distinguished on the stone. In lowercase text, U replaces V: thus VETVSTATE and uetustate. Those portions of text set in lowercase type and enclosed in [*square brackets*] are restorations. In many cases, such portions amount to a few characters easily inferred from context (e.g., 8.8A, lines 1–3); in others, the text has been restored using transcriptions made when the monument was intact (6.9); in yet others, a considerable part of the restoration is conjectural (1.6B).[2] In a very few cases, an entire inscription is restored (3.4D, 11.31). Portions enclosed in ⟦*double brackets*⟧ represent restorations, either by conjecture or through literary trans-

---

2. *In all cases of the last type, the restorations appearing in my texts are based on readings proposed in authoritative scholarly editions.*

mission, of deliberately effaced text. Portions enclosed in ⟨*angle brackets*⟩ have been inscribed on the stone in place of text that was deliberately effaced.[3]

Because of their many ligatures and abbreviations, medieval inscriptions resist typographical expression. Not wishing to revive the anachronistic practice of representing epigraphical features by the use of special characters, I have resolved, or separated, all ligatures except Æ and Œ, traditional in European typography, and have pruned the exuberance of medieval abbreviation to a pair of conventional symbols: the suprascript stroke (e.g., DN̄O = *dominō*) and the apostrophe (e.g., LOCV′ = *locus*). This expedient admittedly results in the blurring of certain paleographical distinctions: in this book, P′ stands for both ꝑ (= *prō*) and ꝑ (= *per*). For the present purposes, however, this compromise seemed better than spelling out abbreviations within the text itself or clotting the page with a profusion of bizarre and inscrutable ligatures. Another medieval convention that I have expressed in type is the suprascript character representing a grammatical desinence: v° = *quīntō* and v¹ = *quīntī*.

NOTES

Even the very accomplished amateur Latinist may stumble at elementary difficulties when on unfamiliar terrain, yet even rather technical linguistic material can be not only digestible but often of absorbing interest to students in the early stages of their study. I have therefore annotated every feature of the Latin that I suspected might provoke either bewilderment in the neophyte or curiosity in the seasoned veteran.

In the notes, both Classical suspensions and medieval abbreviations are completed in parentheses: TI(beriō) and S(ān)C(t)O. Whereas long vowels are indicated in completions, in restored text they are left unmarked: TI(beriō) CLAV[dio drusi f cai]SARI. As a convenience to those readers who are best familiar with Latin in its Classical form, I include

---

3. *I employ this convention only where the original reading can be restored at least in part and not—as at 2.1 and 4.4—where it has been totally effaced.*

the macron over vowels whose quantity is known to be long even when such notation is patently anachronistic. In verse inscriptions, I have noted deviations from Classical metrical schemes by calling out the syllable that exhibits false quantity: the note 'Scans *iŭbilaei*' indicates that the word *iūbĭlaeī* here scans *iŭbĭlaeī*. Where a late spelling may be confusing, I have clarified it (e.g., *hec = haec*) and referred the reader to the note where the phenomenon is explained. In a given entry, only the first instance of this or that orthographical irregularity is noted. The notation 'Sic' calls attention to inadvertent errors, while the sign '=' marks spellings that deviate regularly from Classical Latin orthography. To encourage reading aloud, I have spelled out all numerals. For the sake of consistency, I have used the form *-ēsimus* rather than *-ēnsimus* for ordinal numerals throughout.

In the translation notes, key non-English names and terms are distinguished typographically and ordinarily defined at first use. Words printed in SMALL CAPITALS with initial capitals in the translation notes are defined in the Glossary. These entries furnish information on topics that require more elaborate treatment than can be accommodated in the notes. Following the Glossary are a conspectus of the metrical schemes that appear in the verse inscriptions, an index of first lines, and an index of sites of the inscriptions. Cross-references in the notes that are introduced by 'see' provide substantive information on the topic at hand; those introduced by 'cf.' include material which, while not directly relevant, may yet prove of interest.

In glossing Latin words, it was necessary to establish some common point of departure: The notes assume that the reader has access to *Cassell's Latin Dictionary*, compiled by D. P. Simpson. Its accurate and concise definitions apart, Cassell's has the merit of providing coverage of historical, mythological, and geographical names. I have glossed all words not appearing in Cassell's, including every ecclesiastical term except *cardinālis*: unlike *ecclēsia*, *episcopus*, *apostolus*, or *papa*, *cardinālis* is a native Latin word requiring no explication for the reader of the Classical language. In cases where a classical word is used in a sense that Cassell's does not address, I have furnished a definition.

Books of the Bible are cited by the abbreviations of *The Oxford Dictionary of the Christian Church* (third edition) and Classical authors by those of *The Oxford Classical Dictionary* (third edition).

PERIODIZATION OF LATIN

Old Latin (OL) and Classical Latin (CL) are familiar and uncontroversial designations signifying, respectively, the language as used from its beginnings to about 90 BC and from 90 BC to about AD 120. Beyond these, the categories adopted in this book are conceived less as fixed chronological limits than as useful ways of characterizing the language in various historical contexts.

I use the term Later Latin (LL) to refer broadly to the language of about AD 120 to 500, though in a more general sense it includes all post-Classical usage. For example, the title *Vir Clārissimus* (roughly, 'His Excellency') is peculiarly evocative of the later Empire, when Rome—and Latin—would have been quite foreign to Cicero but were not yet medieval. The CL *dux* ('leader, general') was already 'duke' by the Byzantine period and continues in that sense; it may thus be considered a specimen of LL usage in the wider sense.

The designation Medieval Latin (ML) is reserved for that subset of Later Latin characteristic of the period between about AD 500 and 1400. It is typified both by lexicon and syntax. The term *camerārius* ('chamberlain'), for example, makes its first appearance with Gregory of Tours in the sixth century and was in universal use through the end of the Middle Ages. The construction of noun clauses with such conjunctions as *quod* and *quia* is likewise characteristic of medieval Latin.

At Rome, the advent of Pope Martin V in 1420 makes a neat if artificial caesura between the Middle Ages and Renaissance. The designation Neo-Latin (NL) refers in general to the language as used after about 1400, while Renaissance Latin (RL) refers in particular to the self-consciously Classicizing idiom that may be seen as defining itself in reaction to ML over the two centuries from 1400 to 1600, when ML terms were more or less systematically replaced by their Classical equivalents; its influence remains pervasive in the Ecclesiastical Latin of subsequent periods.

The designation Ecclesiastical Latin (EL) calls attention to elements within Later Latin that are peculiar to the Christian church: *episcopus* ('bishop'), *diāconus* ('deacon'), and *presbyter* ('priest') are among the many. In RL, some such lexical items as these tended to linger on as technical terms. For example, though the formulation *purpurātī patrēs* ('Purple-clad Fathers') may occur in a general context as a Classicizing equivalent for *cardinālēs*, a title such as *Sānctae Rōmānae Ecclēsiae Camerārius* ('Camerlengo of the Holy Roman Church') was stubbornly resistant to modification or substitution.

PRACTICAL ADVICE

Besides binoculars, the reader using this book in Rome will require a reliable guidebook. Currently, the most useful general guide to Rome in English is the relevant volume in the 'Blue Guides' series, published by W. W. Norton in the United States and by A&C Black in the United Kingdom. Filippo Coarelli's *Rome and Environs: An Archeological Guide* (English translation by James J. Clauss and Daniel P. Harmon) furnishes an outstanding introduction to the ancient city. In Italian, the volume *Roma* published by TCI (Touring Club Italiano) can be counted on for a wealth of detailed information in a modest compass. The compact street atlas of Rome published by Michelin (*Roma: Atlante Tascabile*) makes an invaluable supplement to either.

The reader should bear in mind that opening hours of buildings are often unpredictable: at the present writing, for example, the cloister of SS. Apostoli is open only on the mornings of the second and fourth Tuesday of each month. A current guidebook will therefore prove indispensable in planning visits. It is also important to remember that, although the itineraries set out in this book are conceived as walking tours, those terminating at the extramural basilicas are rather long and can at points be downright gritty; public transportation is recommended for all but the most stout-hearted. In any case, the reader who intends to walk the itineraries would be well advised to plot the journey in advance with the help of map and guidebook.

DATES

In a book in which nearly every date is introduced by some such formula as 'In the year of the Lord' or 'In the year of Christian Salvation', I hope that I may be excused for preferring the traditional abbreviations BC and AD to the widely current BCE and CE ('before the Common Era' and 'Common Era').

Arms of Selected Popes

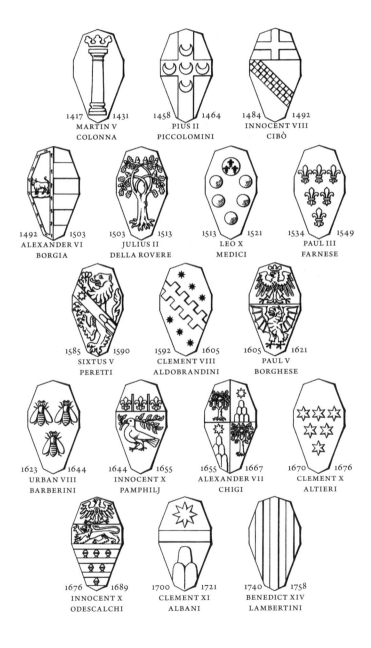

1417 · 1431
MARTIN V
COLONNA

1458 · 1464
PIUS II
PICCOLOMINI

1484 · 1492
INNOCENT VIII
CIBÒ

1492 · 1503
ALEXANDER VI
BORGIA

1503 · 1513
JULIUS II
DELLA ROVERE

1513 · 1521
LEO X
MEDICI

1534 · 1549
PAUL III
FARNESE

1585 · 1590
SIXTUS V
PERETTI

1592 · 1605
CLEMENT VIII
ALDOBRANDINI

1605 · 1621
PAUL V
BORGHESE

1623 · 1644
URBAN VIII
BARBERINI

1644 · 1655
INNOCENT X
PAMPHILJ

1655 · 1667
ALEXANDER VII
CHIGI

1670 · 1676
CLEMENT X
ALTIERI

1676 · 1689
INNOCENT X
ODESCALCHI

1700 · 1721
CLEMENT XI
ALBANI

1740 · 1758
BENEDICT XIV
LAMBERTINI

General Abbreviations and Symbols

Abl. = ablative

Abs. = absolute

Acc. = accusative

Act. = active

AD = anno Domini

Adv. = adverb

App. = appositive, apposition

BC = before Christ

Bl. = Blessed

AUC = anno urbis conditae (*in the year of the founding of the city*)

BVM = Beata Virgo Maria (*Blessed Virgin Mary*)

c. = circa (*about*)

cf. = confer (*compare*)

CL = Classical Latin

Conj. = conjunction

d. = died

Dat. = dative

Def.Art. = definite article

Dep. = deponent

Dir. = direct

E = east(ern)

EG = Ecclesiastical Greek

EL = Ecclesiastical Latin

Eng. = English

Fem. / f. = feminine

Fig. = figurative(ly)

fl. = floruit (*flourished*)

Fr. = French

Fut. = future

Fut.Pf. = future perfect

Gen. = genitive

Ger. = German

IE = Indo-European

Imp. = imperative

Impf. = imperfect

Ind. = indirect

Indic. = indicative

Inf. = infinitive

Intrans. = intransitive

Ital. = Italian

L = left

Lit. = literal(ly)

LL = Later Latin

Loc. = locative

m = meters

Masc. / m. = masculine

ML = Medieval Latin

mod. = modern

MS, MSS = manuscript(s)

N = north(ern)

Neut. / n. = neuter

NL = Neo-Latin

Nom. = nominative

NT = New Testament

Ob. = object(ive)

OL = Old Latin

Part. = participle

Pass. = passive

Pers. = person

Pf. = perfect

Pl. = plural

Plupf. = pluperfect

Prep. = preposition

Pres. = present

R = right

r. = reigned

Rel. = relative

RL = Renaissance Latin

S = south(ern)

S. = San, Santo, Santa, Sant'

sc. = scilicet (*supply*)

Sg. = singular

Sp. = Spanish

S.P.Q.R. = Senate and People of Rome

SS. = Saints / Santi / Santissimo, -a, -i, -e
St. = Saint
Sub. = subject(ive)
Subj. = subjunctive

Subst. = substantive
Trans. = transitive
Voc. = vocative
W = west(ern)

EPIGRAPHICAL SYMBOLS

| = *The line of text breaks in the original*
¬ = *The line of text continues unbroken in the original*
[abc] = *Text accidentally lost is conjecturally restored*
⟦abc⟧ = *Text deliberately effaced is conjecturally restored*
⟨abc⟩ = *Text replaces other text deliberately effaced*

HISTORICAL-LINGUISTIC SYMBOLS

* = *The form is reconstructed by historical linguistics*
× = *The form is spurious*
> = *The form develops into . . .*
< = *The form derives from . . .*

PHONETIC SYMBOLS

ŋ = NG *as in English 'sing'*
ɲ = Ñ *as in Spanish 'doña'*
e = *closed* E
ε = *open* E

o = *closed* O
ɔ = *open* O
ʃ = SH *as in English 'shout'*
: = *long vowel* (/diːkoː/ = dīcō)

Latin and Greek Abbreviations

A = annō
AD = annō dominī
AED PL = aedīlis plēbis
AET = aetātis
A F R = ā fascibus renovātīs
AN = annō
ANN = annō
ANNOR = annōrum
AN SAL = annō salūtis
ANT = Antōnīnus
AP = apostolus, apostolicus
ARCHIEP = archiepiscopus
A S = ā sōlō
ATQ = atque
A V C = ab urbe conditā
AVG, AVGVST = Augustus
AVGG = Augustī
B = beātus
BAPT = baptista
B M = bene merentī
BRITAN = Britannia
C = Christus, Gāius
CAES = Caesar
CAESS = Caesarēs
CAMER = camerārius
CAR, CARD = cardinālis
CENS = cēnsor
CHR = Christus
CLA = Claudia
CN = Gnaeus
COM = comes
COS = cōnsul, cōnsulēs
COS DESIG = cōnsul dēsignātus
COSS = cōnsulēs
D = diēs, dīva, dīvus
D D = dōnum dedit, dōnō dedit
DD NN = dominī nostrī

DDD NNN = dominī nostrī trēs
DECEMB = Decembris
DEP = dēpositus
DI = deī
DIAC CARD = diāconus cardinālis
D N = dominus noster
DNI = dominī
DNIC = dominicus
D N M Q E = dēvōtus nūminī
    māiestātīque eōrum
DNO = dominō
DO = deō
D O M = deō optimō maximō
DOMIN = dominicus
DS = deus
E = est
ECCL = ecclēsia
EID = Eidūs
EP, EPI = episcopus
EVANG = evangelista
F = fīlius, fīlia
FEB = Februārius
FL = Flāvius
FMC = Frātrēs Minōrēs Conventuālēs
FRANC = Francia
GALL = Gallia, Gallus
GERM = Germānicus
HIBERN = Hībernia
HISP = Hispānia, Hispānus
IAN = Ianuārius
ID = Īdūs
IHV = Iēsū
I L = iūre licitō
IMP = imperātor
IMPP = imperātōrēs
INC = incarnātiō
IND, INDICT = indictiōnis

IN HON = in honōrem
IOHS = Iohannēs
IT = iterum
IVB = iūbilaeī
IVL = Iūlia, Iūlius
IVN = Iūnius
KAL, KL = Kalendae
L = lībertus, Lūcius
LATERAN = Laterānēnsis
M = magnus, Mārcus, mēnsis
MA = magnus
MAGR = magister
MAI = Māius
MART = Mārtius, martyr
MAX = maximus
MON = monumentum
N = nepos, noster
NAT = nātus
NON = Nōnae
NOVEMB = Novembris
OCTOB = Octōbris
OPT = optimus
ORD PRAED = ōrdō praedicātōrum
P = posuērunt, posuit, Pūblius
PAENIT = paenitentiārius
PALAT = Palātium
PAROCH = parochia
PARTH = Parthicus
PASS = passūs
P C = post cōnsulātum
P F = pius fēlīx
P M = pontifex maximus
POB = Poblilia
P O M = pontifex optimus maximus
POMP = Pompēius
PONT = pontificātus
PONTIFF = pontificēs
PONT MAX = pontifex maximus

PONTT MAXX = pontificēs maximī
POS = posuit
POSS = posuērunt
PP = papa, pater patriae, posuērunt
PR = praetor, presbyter
PRAEF = praefectus
PBR = presbyter
PRESB CARD = presbyter cardinālis
PRESBB CARDD = presbyterī
  cardinālēs
PRID = prīdiē
PRINC = prīncipātus
PRINCI = prīncipī
PROCOS = prōcōnsul
P S = posterīsque suīs
PVB = pūblicus
QVINT = Quīntīlis
Q = que, Quīntus
REG = rēgiō
REP SAL = reparātae salūtis
REST = restituit
RO, ROM = Rōmānus
S = sacrum, sānctus, sāncta, suus
SAC = sacer
SAL = salūtis
SARM = Sarmāticus
S C = senātūs cōnsultum
SCA = sāncta
SCI = sānctī
SCO = sānctō
SCORVM = sānctōrum
SEMP MEM = sempiternae memoriae
SEN = senātus
SENT = sententia
SEPTEMB = Septembris
SER = sāncta ecclēsia Rōmāna
S P Q R = senātus populusque Rōmānus
S R E = sāncta Rōmāna ecclēsia

S R I = Sacrum Rōmānum Imperium

SS = sānctī, sānctae, sānctissimus,
   sānctissimae

T, TIT = Titus

TI = Tiberius

TIT = titulus

TPRE = tempore

TRIB POT = Tribūniciā potestāte

TR PL = Tribūnus plēbis

TT = titulus

V A = vīxit annōs

V C = vir clārissimus

V E = vir ēgrēgius

V I D = utrīusque iūris doctor

VIRG = virgō

VRB = urbī

VV CC = virī clārissimī

XPIANVS = Christiānus

XPS = Christus

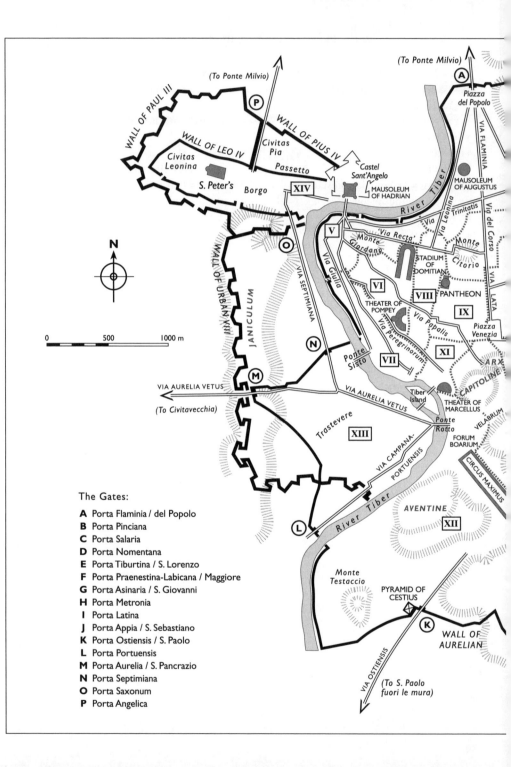

The Gates:

A Porta Flaminia / del Popolo
B Porta Pinciana
C Porta Salaria
D Porta Nomentana
E Porta Tiburtina / S. Lorenzo
F Porta Praenestina-Labicana / Maggiore
G Porta Asinaria / S. Giovanni
H Porta Metronia
I Porta Latina
J Porta Appia / S. Sebastiano
K Porta Ostiensis / S. Paolo
L Porta Portuensis
M Porta Aurelia / S. Pancrazio
N Porta Septimiana
O Porta Saxonum
P Porta Angelica

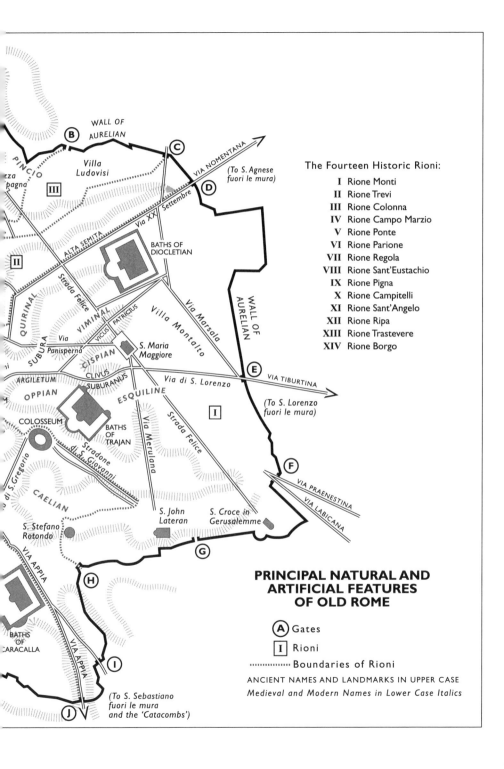

WALL OF
AURELIAN

Ⓑ

Ⓒ

Villa
Ludovisi

VIA NOMENTANA

(To S. Agnese
fuori le mura)

Ⓓ

zza
bagna

III

PINCIO

Via XX Settembre

ALTA SEMITA

BATHS OF
DIOCLETIAN

II

Strada Felice

QUIRINAL

VIMINAL

VICUS PATRICIUS

Via Marsala

Villa Montalto

WALL OF
AURELIAN

SUBURA

Via
Panisperna

CISPIAN

S. Maria
Maggiore

ARGILETUM

CLIVUS
SUBURANUS

OPPIAN

ESQUILINE

Via di S. Lorenzo

Ⓔ   VIA TIBURTINA

(To S. Lorenzo
fuori le mura)

COLOSSEUM

BATHS
OF
TRAJAN

Via Merulana

Strada Felice

I

Stradone
di S. Giovanni

di S. Gregorio

CAELIAN

Ⓕ

VIA PRAENESTINA

VIA LABICANA

S. Stefano
Rotondo

S. John
Lateran

S. Croce in
Gerusalemme

VIA APPIA

Ⓗ

Ⓖ

The Fourteen Historic Rioni:

   I   Rione Monti
  II Rione Trevi
 III Rione Colonna
 IV Rione Campo Marzio
  V Rione Ponte
 VI Rione Parione
VII Rione Regola
VIII Rione Sant'Eustachio
 IX Rione Pigna
  X Rione Campitelli
 XI Rione Sant'Angelo
XII Rione Ripa
XIII Rione Trastevere
XIV Rione Borgo

**PRINCIPAL NATURAL AND
ARTIFICIAL FEATURES
OF OLD ROME**

Ⓐ Gates

I Rioni

·············· Boundaries of Rioni

ANCIENT NAMES AND LANDMARKS IN UPPER CASE
Medieval and Modern Names in Lower Case Italics

BATHS
OF
CARACALLA

Ⓘ

VIA APPIA

Ⓙ

(To S. Sebastiano
fuori le mura
and the 'Catacombs')

THE LATIN INSCRIPTIONS OF ROME

PIAZZA DEL CAMPIDOGLIO

Michelangelo's renovation of Piazza del Campidoglio for Pope Paul III (r. 1534–1549) celebrates the triumph of the papacy in its long struggle to dominate the civil government of Rome. The equestrian statue of Marcus Aurelius at the center of the piazza aptly symbolizes the earthly dimension of papal claims, while the sunburst pattern of the pavement evokes Apollo, interpreted in the Renaissance as an image of Christ. Taken as a whole, the ensemble bodies forth the universal pretensions of a Counter Reformation papacy striving to amalgamate the spiritual power of a high priest with the temporal suzerainty of a king.

I. The Capitoline Hill

ABOUT TWENTY KILOMETERS FROM THE SEA, the Tiber encounters the western rim of the Campagna plateau; at the site of Rome, the river valley narrows from approximately four kilometers to about one. Where it meets the broad plain of the Campus Martius, the stream swings abruptly towards the Vatican, on its right bank; at the foot of the Janiculum it loops back around the bulge of the Campus, on its left. Along the eastern margin of the Campus, fingerlike spurs protrude from the hinterland: these are the hills of Rome. The spurs were formed by minor tributaries that seamed the steep sides of the Tiber valley on their downward course to the river. It is only from the perspective of the valley bottom that they appear as hills; from a higher point of vantage they are seen in their true guise as the westernmost outcroppings of the Campagna. Below the city the plateau retreats; the river flows broad and unimpeded to its mouth at Ostia. The ford at the Tiber Island is the last point on its course where it can be crossed on foot.

In the late Iron Age—perhaps around 675 BC—a visitor to the hills of Rome would have beheld a thriving proto-urban amalgam already several centuries old. Defended by a palisade, an intensively developed nucleus on the Palatine Hill dominated the site. Beyond, a large and diffuse aggregate of huts, gardens, groves, and pastures sprawled over the surrounding hills, across the marshy Forum valley and down to the busy river port. The huts clustered most densely on the sites of the ancient hilltop villages that had coalesced to form the fledgling city. A network of sinuous footpaths—the ancestors of Rome's streets—hugged the contours of steep and wooded valleys. The numerous watercourses that rendered the valley bottoms difficult to traverse for much of the year presented a formidable impediment to communications. Surprisingly, perhaps, there were as yet no temples; the worship of the gods was conducted in ritually demarcated precincts on hilltops, at springs, and in caves. The Capitoline Hill, focus of the community's principal cult, was crowned by the sacred oak and smoking altar of Jove.

3

For a millennium the religious and political life of Rome centered on the Capitol, terminus of splendid triumphal processions and scene of the annual investiture of the consuls. Towards the end of the sixth century BC, the open-air altar gave way to the mighty temple of Jupiter Optimus Maximus, which in its most magnificent instantiation boasted columns of Pentelic marble and a roof of gilt-bronze tiles. On the hill's smaller northerly eminence rose the temple of Juno Moneta; this was the *Arx*, Rome's sacred citadel, not unlike the Acropolis at Athens. From here, where there was a clear view along the Sacra Via to the Alban Mount, the Roman augurs took their auspices. The temple of Juno Moneta was vowed by Marcus Furius Camillus in 345 BC; its name was held to derive from the Latin verb *monēre* ('to warn'). After the state mint was installed in the temple precinct, the epithet *Moneta* passed into use as a synonym for 'coin'—hence such terms as the Italian *moneta*, French *monnaie*, and the colloquial German *Moneten*.

As Antiquity gave way to the Middle Ages, the city's great public buildings collapsed in ruin. By the Renaissance, scarcely a vestige survived of the Capitol's proud monuments, which had fallen victim to earthquake, fire, decay—and the unflagging industry of the *calcarari* ('lime makers'), who systematically plundered and burned the marble of ancient buildings to produce lime for mortar. The humanist scholar Poggio Bracciolini, who employed his ascent of the Capitoline in 1430 as the point of departure for a meditation, *De varietate fortunae* ('On the Vicissitudes of Fortune'), likened the erstwhile seat of empire to 'a gigantic cadaver, rotten and everywhere eaten away'. Populated chiefly by livestock, the hill had by Poggio's day earned the moniker *Monte Caprino* ('Goat Mountain').

1.1   The SEPULCHER OF GAIUS PUBLICIUS BIBULUS, which dates to the first century BC, is among the few relics of Antiquity surviving *in situ* on or around the Capitoline. The tomb has always been exposed: Petrarch tells us that he penned one of his sonnets while resting against it. When first constructed at the northwest foot of the hill, just outside the republican city wall, the sepulcher marked the head of the Via Flaminia. By law, all Roman gravesites had to be located outside the *pomerium* ('sacred boundary') of the city: the situation of this tomb serves as a reminder that in ancient times the Campus Martius—the large floodplain to the northwest of the Capitoline in which medieval Rome was to take shape—lay outside the city proper. The only other considerable remains from Antiquity to be seen on the Capitoline comprise the foundations of the TABULARIUM, erected in 78 BC by Quintus Lutatius Catulus, parti-   1.7B san of the dictator Sulla.

Today the northwest side of the hill is dominated by the elephantine bulk of the MONUMENT TO KING VICTOR EMANUEL II, enlivened by   1.2 a handful of laconic inscriptions that celebrate the unification of Italy in 1870. The erection of this vast memorial between 1885 and 1911 entailed the destruction of the medieval convent of Santa Maria in Aracoeli and of the Renaissance *Torre Belvedere* of Pope Paul III, a lofty square tower on the hill's northwestern brow which commanded a panoramic view over the Campus Martius and the Vatican beyond. Long after 1870, the Church continued to resist the ideals of national unity and civic liberty enshrined in the Victor Emanuel monument. It is hardly surprising that the nation's fathers chose to situate their monument in such a way as to mutilate and occlude these potent symbols of ecclesiastical domination. Later, in order to enlarge the area of Piazza Venezia before the *Vittoriano*, an entire quarter consisting of densely packed streets, palaces, houses, and churches was likewise razed; Palazzetto Venezia—which had formed the backdrop to Piazza Venezia—was dismantled and shunted off to the side.

To complete the isolation of the Capitoline and thereby promote his vision of Ancient Rome Renewed, Mussolini drove two mighty thoroughfares through the heart of the medieval quarters that yet remained to the northeast and southwest of the hill: Via dei Monti (later Via dell'Impero, today's Via dei Fori Imperiali) and Via del Mare (Via di Teatro di Marcello). The construction of the former obliterated the Velia, a ridge connecting the Palatine and Esquiline Hills that beneath its medieval streets harbored irreplaceable evidence of Rome's Iron Age beginnings; construction of the latter resulted in the erasure of the ancient Piazza dell'Aracoeli, which had served as the intimate and indispensable antechamber to Piazza del Campidoglio.

In the Middle Ages, the Capitoline Hill was the subject of a body of rich and fantastic legend. This venerable eminence, from which it was imagined that an all-wise senate had governed the world, was remembered as the *Capitolium Aureum*, the Golden Capitol, for in wisdom and beauty it had surpassed all the realms of the earth. It was thought to have included a gallery of statues representing the various subject nations of the Empire, each fitted with a bell. Whenever a rebellion broke out, the bell of the relevant statue would sound spontaneously. The Piazza del Campidoglio of medieval times amounted to little more than a muddy and irregular depression between the two summits of the hill. Fringed by a disorderly assemblage of nondescript structures, it was overshadowed by the imposing fabric of the Church of Santa Maria in Aracoeli. At the order of Pope Paul III (r. 1534–1549), Michelangelo undertook the renovation of the site. The result is Rome's only fully planned Renaissance piazza and a brilliant gem of urban design. Executed over a period of some 120 years, Michelangelo's scheme underwent a number of modifications without suffering radical deviations from his fundamental vision.

1.3   At the head of Michelangelo's *cordonata*, twin STATUES OF CASTOR AND POLLUX serve as sentinels to the piazza. Excavated in the 1550s at the site of the ancient Circus Flaminius, the figures were erected
1.4   here in 1583. On the balustrade to either side are mounted the 'TROPHIES OF MARIUS', which are representations of barbarian arms dating to the reign of the emperor Domitian. At the center of the piazza, on an oval pavement completed in 1940 to Michelangelo's design, rises
1.5   the celebrated equestrian statue of the emperor MARCUS AURELIUS, brought from the Lateran in 1538 to inaugurate the renovated Capitol of Paul III. The present statue is a copy; the original is housed indoors to

protect it from damage caused by air pollution—as well as from attacks such as that of 1991, in which a bomb was detonated near the statue. The fact that the monument was available as a target is in itself a minor miracle. It owes its existence to the misapprehension that it represented the Christian emperor Constantine I the Great: it would have been impious to consign so illustrious an effigy to the melting pot in which all but a handful of ancient bronze statues were destroyed for their metal.

The transformation of the Campidoglio under Paul III represents the fruition of the popes' century-long struggle to assert their hegemony at the nerve center of the Roman Commune. Following the return of the papacy after its seven-decade Babylonian Captivity at Avignon (1309–1377), successive pontiffs had made a priority of manifesting their temporal pretensions on the Capitol—emblem of republican liberty and focus of popular agitation against papal rule. As early as the 1420s, Martin V (r. 1417–1431) fortified PALAZZO SENATORIO; in the 1450s, following the conspiracy of Stefano Porcari, Nicholas V (r. 1447–1455) built PALAZZO DEI CONSERVATORI to its southeast side. Two decades later, in an act fraught with unmistakable significance, Sixtus IV (r. 1471–1484) caused the celebrated *Lupa Capitolina,* or Capitoline she-wolf—a venerable emblem of papal authority—to be mounted above the very portal of the conservators' palace. With the installation of the statue of Marcus Aurelius under Paul III, the victory was complete. The symbolism of the emperor's statue is particularly pregnant: its transfer from the Lateran suggested that the imperial power of the papacy had now possessed the Campidoglio to fix its gaze on the Vatican, source and fountainhead of its legitimacy.

The origins of the Church of Santa Maria in Aracoeli, which impends over the piazza on the site of the temple of Juno Moneta, are lost to us. Possibly the site of a Greek monastery in the eighth century, it passed eventually into the hands of the Benedictines. In 1246, Innocent IV (r. 1243–1254) assigned Aracoeli and its convent to the Franciscans, who

1.7

1.6

are responsible for the present structure. The church is heavy with history. Upon the reestablishment of the Roman Senate in 1143, it became the effective town hall of Rome, where law was debated and justice dispensed. Here, on 21 June 1265, Charles D'Anjou was installed as Senator of Rome. In 1348, Cola di Rienzo, would-be founder of a resuscitated

1.8A Roman Republic, inaugurated the magnificent ARACOELI STAIR. In March of 1442, St. Bernardino, that eloquent friar, preached here, kindling the hearts of the faithful. In the pious fervor that ensued, the accused witch Maria Funicella was burned, and many Jews were baptized. On 21 November 1571, a triumph was held for Marcantonio Colonna to

1.8B celebrate the victory of the Holy League over the Turks at the BATTLE OF LEPANTO. And it was here, on 15 October 1764, that Edward Gibbon first conceived the project of chronicling Rome's decline and fall as he sat 'musing amid the ruins of the Capitol, while the bare-footed fryars were singing vespers'.

The twenty-two columns lining the nave of the church are all *spolia*—the technical term for materials pillaged from ancient buildings.

1.8C The third on the left bears the inscription A CVBICVLO AVGVSTORVM ('from the bedchamber of the Caesars'), in evident allusion to the medieval legend of the church's founding. In a sixth-century version of that legend, the emperor Augustus (r. 27 BC–AD 14) made inquiry of the Delphic Sibyl to learn who would succeed him; on hearing that it would be a Jewish youth, he erected an altar to the First-born of God. This 'Eastern' version coheres with the tradition that the first monastery on the site was founded by Greek monks. According to the later Roman variant, it was the Sibyl of Tibur to whom the emperor applied, and in this account, the interview took place in the bedchamber of Augustus, fancied to have been situated on the Capitoline. No sooner had the Sibyl made her response than the Virgin Mary appeared to the emperor in glory holding

1.8F the Christ Child; the ALTAR in the chapel of St Helen marks the spot where the vision occurred. It has been suggested that the memory of the *auguraculum*—the platform on the Arx from which the ancient augurs took the auspices—could have played a role in the story's development, that the tale of the apparition represents a conscious baptizing of the *signa ex caelo* ('heavenly portents') for which the augurs scanned the skies.

Two of the church's numerous monuments are consecrated to the memory of famous Renaissance popes: LEO X (r. 1513–1521), who excom- 1.8G municated Luther, and PAUL III (r. 1534–1549), the Capitol's great reno- 1.8D vator.

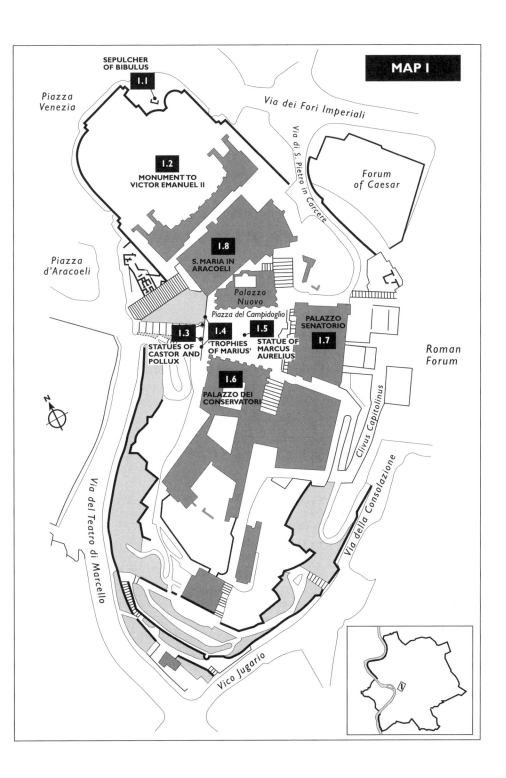

1.1 Epitaph of Gaius Publicius Bibulus

C PO[p]LICIO L F BIBVLO AED PL H[onoris]

VIRTVT[is]QVE CAVSSA SENA[t]VS

CONSVLTO PO[pu]L[i]QVE IVSSV LOCV[s]

MONVMENTO QVO IPSE POSTEREIQVE

5   EIVS INFERRENTV[r pu]BLICE DATVS EST

1. C(āiō) : *The letter* C *originally did duty in the Latin alphabet for both the voiceless velar plosive /k/ and its voiced counterpart /g/. The name* Gāius, *always pronounced with initial /g/, continued to be abbreviated by* C *even after the introduction of the letter* G *(probably in the third century* BC). — PO[p]LICIO : *The* CL *form of the name* Poplicius *is* Pūblicius *(by assimilation to* pūblicus < pūbēs, *'youth'). The portions of the inscription enclosed in brackets represent restorations of lost text (see 1.6B, line 1).* — L(ūcī) F(īliō). — AED(īlī) PL(ēbis).

2. CAVSSA = causā : *According to the grammarian Quintilian, this spelling was current as late as the age of Cicero (106–43 BC).*

4. QVO : *Adv. introducing a final clause whose verb is* INFERRENTVR *(line 5).* — POSTEREIQVE = posterīque : *The inherited* IE *Masc.Nom.Pl. desinence* *-oy *(cf. the equivalent Greek* -οι*) progressed in* OL *to* -ei *and in* CL *to* -ī.

1.2 Monument to Victor Emanuel II: Dedication

i.   *ii.*

PATRIAE VNITATI   CIVIVM LIBERTATI

LABORVM OPVS   ARMORVM VIS

PATRIAM   PATRIAM

SERVAT AVGET   TVETVR EXTOLLIT

i.4. SERVAT AVGET : *The asyndeton strikes a pompous rhetorical note consonant with the spirit of the monument. Asyndeton (Greek ἀσύνδετον, 'want of connection') is the omission of a conjunction. The mannerism is repeated in* TVETVR EXTOLLIT *(ii.4).*

Lawn N of the Monument to Victor Emanuel II

By decree of the Senate and enactment of the People[a]
this place was granted at the public expense
to Gaius Publicius Bibulus,[b] *son of Lucius, Plebeian Aedile,*[c]
by reason of his merit and valor, for a monument
wherein he himself and his descendants might be laid to rest.

a. I.e., by a statute carried in an assembly of the Roman people.

b. The present Bibulus has not been securely identified. Linguistically, the Latin is consistent with a date around 200 BC; as the sepulcher, on the other hand, can be dated on archeological grounds to the first century BC, it must be a reconstruction of the original structure. When it was first erected, the tomb stood on the NW side of the Via Lata just beyond the Porta Fontinalis of the republican city wall. Like all ordinary Roman tombs, therefore, it stood outside the pomerium (*see 13.1, note b*).

c. In origin, the aediles were two officials subordinate to the tribunes of the plebs (*see* TRIBUNICIAN POWER) and charged with supervising the shrine (aedes) and cult of Ceres; in the later Republic, the aediles had charge of temples, markets, and other public buildings. With the addition in 367 BC of two patrician aediles, the original officials were distinguished as 'plebeian'.

Façade, L and R

Left	*Right*
To the unity of the nation.[a]	*To the liberty of the citizens.*
The fruit of toils	*The force of arms*
preserves and increases	*guards and exalts*
the nation.	*the nation.*

a. Begun in 1885 and not finally completed until 1935, the present memorial honors Victor Emanuel II (r. 1861–1878), first king of a united Italy. For the construction of the monument and 'isolation' of the Capitoline Hill, the ancient quarter centering on Piazza di Venezia was systematically destroyed between 1885 and 1932.

1.3 Statues of Castor and Pollux: Dedication by S.P.Q.R.

S P Q R

SIMVLACRA CASTORVM

RVDERIBVS IN THEATRO POMPEI

EGESTIS REPERTA RESTITVIT

5   ET IN CAPITOLIO POSVIT

(Names of Magistrates)

ANNO SALVTIS CIƆ IƆ LXXXIII

1. s(enātus) p(opulus) q(ue) r(ōmānus).
6. CIƆ IƆ LXXXIII : Mīllēsimō quīngentēsimō octōgēsimō tertiō. *The notation* CIƆ IƆ *substitutes* CL *usage for the later* M D. *The figure 1,000 was originally represented by the Greek* Φ, *later domesticated as* CIƆ; *the half of* Φ *(represented as* IƆ) *was adopted for the half of 1,000 (i.e., 500). As well as* CIƆ, *such forms as* CXƆ *are found.*

1.4 'Trophies of Marius': Dedication by Sixtus V

SIXTI V PONT MAX AVCTORITATE

TROPHAEA C MARII VII COS DE TEVTONIS

ET CIMBRIS EX COLLE ESQVILINO ET RVINOSO

AQVAE OLIM MARCIAE CASTELLO

5   IN CAPITOLIVM TRANSLATA ERECTIS BASIBVS

ILLVSTRI LOCO STATVENDA CVRAVERE

(Names of Magistrates)

AN SALVT MDXC

1. SIXTI V : Quīntī. — PONT(ificis) MAX(imī).
2. TROPHAEA = tropaea (< τρόπαιον). — C(āiī). — VII : Septiēs. *To be distinguished from* septimum *or* septimō ('*for the seventh time*'; *cf. 1.6B, line 3*). — CO(n)S(ulis). — DE TEVTONIS : *Both* Teutonī *and* Teutonēs *appear in* CL. *Victory over an opponent is expressed by* dē + *Abl.; here the verbal idea is implicit in the word* trophaea.
4. CASTELLO : *Among other things,* CL castellum *is used of the cistern at the terminus of an aqueduct.*
6. CVRAVERE = cūrāvērunt.
7. AN(nō) SALVT(is) MDXC : Mīllēsimō quīngentēsimō nōnāgēsimō.

Balustrade of Piazza del Campidoglio: Base of Statues, N and S

The Senate and People of Rome
restored these effigies of the Castors,[a]
discovered upon the clearing of the rubble
in the Theater of Pompey,[b]
and placed them on the Capitol.

(Names of Magistrates)
in the year of Salvation 1583.

a. *Fathered on Leda by Zeus in the form of a swan, Castor and Pollux were*
   known as the Dioscuri ('Sons of Zeus') or as the Castores ('Castors'). In
   mythology, Castor was mortal and Pollux immortal.
b. *The figures were discovered in 1561, not in the area of Pompey's theater but*
   at Monte Cenci on the site of the ancient Circus Flaminius, where a temple
   of the Dioscuri is known from literary sources to have stood.

Balustrade of Piazza del Campidoglio: N and S Sides

By authority of Sixtus the Fifth,[a] Supreme Pontiff,
(Names of Magistrates)
undertook to have the trophies of Gaius Marius,[b]
seven times Consul, granted for victories over
the Teutoni and Cimbri, transported to the Capitol from the ruined cistern
formerly of the Aqua Marcia[c] on the Esquiline Hill and,
once bases had been erected, to have them set up in a distinguished spot
in the year of Salvation 1590.

a. *Pope Sixtus V Peretti (r. 1585–1590).*
b. *Gaius Marius served as* CONSUL *in 107, 104–100, and 86 BC. In 102 he*
   defeated the Teutones at Aquae Sextiae and in 101 the Cimbri at Vercel-
   lae. The trophies date not to the time of Marius but to that of the emperor
   Domitian (r. 81–96).
c. *The cistern in fact served a branch of the Aqua Julia. At the seventh mile-*
   stone of the Via Latina, the course of the Aqua Julia merged with that of
   the older Aqua Marcia, the bulk of whose remains was quarried away
   1585–1587 for the construction of the Acqua Felice under Sixtus V (see 4.5
   and 8.6).

1.5 Statue of Marcus Aurelius: Dedication by Paul III

i.

IMP CAESARI DIVI ANTONINI F DIVI HADRIANI

NEPOTI DIVI TRAIANI PARTHICI PRONEPOTI DIVI

NERVAE ABNEPOTI M AVRELIO ANTONINO PIO

AVG GERM SARM PONT MAX TRIB POT XXVII

5 IMP VI COS III P P S P Q R

1. IMP(erātōrī). — DIVI : *See 2.4, line 1.* — F(īliō).
3. M(ārcō).
4. AVG(ustō) GERM(ānicō) SARM(āticō) PONT(ificī) MAX(imō). — TRIB(ūniciā) POT(estāte) XXVII : Vīcēsimum septimum.
5. IMP(erātōrī) VI : Sextum. — CO(n)s(ulī) III : Tertium. — P(atrī) P(atriae). — s(enātus) P(opulus) Q(ue) R(ōmānus).

ii.

PAVLVS III PONT MAX STATVAM AENEAM

EQVESTREM A S P Q R M ANTONINO PIO ETIAM

TVM VIVENTI STATVTAM VARIIS DEINDE VRBIS

CASIB EVERSAM ET A SYXTO IIII PONT MAX AD

5 LATERAN BASILICAM REPOSITAM VT MEMO

RIAE OPT PRINCIPIS CONSVLERET PATRIAEQ

DECORA ATQ ORNAMENTA RESTITVERET

EX HVMILIORE LOCO IN AREAM CAPITOLINAM

TRANSTVLIT ATQ DICAVIT

ANN SAL M D XXXVIII

1. PAVLVS III : Tertius. — PONT(ifex) MAX(imus).
2. s(enātū) P(opulō) Q(ue) R(ōmānō). — M(ārcō).
4. CASIB(us). — SYXTO IIII : Quārtō. *On the spelling* SYXTVS, *see 3.4D, line 4.* — PONT(ifice) MAX(imō).
5. LATERAN(ēnsem) : *See 7.4A, line 1.* — MEMO|RIAE.
6. OPT(imī). — PATRIAEQ(ue).
7–8. ATQ(ue)—ATQ(ue).
9. ANN(ō) SAL(ūtis) M D XXXVIII : Mīllēsimō quīngentēsimō trīcēsimō octāvō.

Piazza del Campidoglio: Base of Statue

South

*The Senate and People of Rome to Imperator Caesar Marcus Aurelius
Antoninus Pius Augustus Germanicus Sarmaticus,^a* son of the Divine
*Antoninus, grandson of the Divine Hadrian, great-grandson of the Divine
Trajan Parthicus, great-great-grandson of the Divine Nerva, Supreme Pontiff,
vested with the Tribunician power for the twenty-seventh time, acclaimed
Imperator for the sixth, Consul for the third, Father of his Country.*

> a. *The emperor Marcus Aurelius (r. 161–180). Marcus took the title* Germani-
> cus *in 172 and* Sarmaticus *in 175. He assumed the* Tribunician Power
> *for the twenty-seventh time on 10 December 172, was saluted as* Impera-
> tor *for the sixth in 170 or 171 and became* Consul *for the third on 1 Janu-
> ary 161. He was made* Supreme Pontiff *on his accession and took the
> title 'Father of his Country' in 166 (see* Pater Patriae*).*

North

*Paul the Third,^a Supreme Pontiff, that he might foster
the memory of the best of emperors ^b and restore to the nation
its glories and honors, transferred from a lowlier site to Piazza del
Campidoglio the bronze equestrian statue erected by the Senate and People
of Rome to Marcus Antoninus Pius in his own lifetime, later overthrown
in the course of the City's sundry calamities and set up again
at the Lateran Basilica by Sixtus the Fourth,^c Supreme Pontiff,
and dedicated it in the year of Salvation 1538.*

> a. *Pope Paul III Farnese (r. 1534–1549). Paul engaged Michelangelo to reno-
> vate the irregular medieval complex that had grown up on the Capitoline
> Hill. The statue of Marcus Aurelius served as an apt emblem of the papal
> claim to temporal authority over the city. Both of the present inscriptions
> date to 1538, the year in which the statue was erected.*
> b. Optimus Princeps *('Best of Emperors') was an honorific title borne by
> Trajan (see 13.5.i, note a); here it is applied to Marcus.*
> c. *Pope Sixtus IV della Rovere (r. 1471–1484). Sixtus had the statue restored
> and set up in a new location. Before its transfer to the Capitol, it had stood
> at the Lateran for some thirteen centuries.*

1.6A Palazzo dei Conservatori: Dedication by S.P.Q.R.

i.

S P Q R

MAIORVM SVORVM PRAESTANTIAM

VT ANIMO SIC RE

QVANTVM LICVIT IMITATVS

5   DEFORMATVM INIVRIA TEMPORVM

CAPITOLIVM RESTITVIT

(*Names of Magistrates*)

ANNO POST VRBEM CONDITAM

CX⊃ CX⊃ CCCXX

1. s(enātus) p(opulus) q(ue) r(ōmānus).
4. QVANTVM : *Acc. of Extent in Degree* (*analogous to Acc. of Extent in Space or Extent in Time*).
7. POST VRBEM CONDITAM : *On the construction, see 1.7A, lines 2–3.*
8. CX⊃ CX⊃ CCCXX : *Bis* mīllēsimō trecentēsimō vīcēsimō. *On the notation, see 1.3, line 6.*

ii.

S P Q R

CAPITOLIVM PRAECIPVE IOVI

OLIM COMMENDATVM

NVNC DEO VERO

5   CVNCTORVM BONORVM AVCTORI

IESV CHRISTO

CVM SALVTE COMMVNI SVPPLEX

TVENDVM TRADIT

ANNO POST SALVTIS INITIVM

10   MDLXVIII

1. s(enātus) p(opulus) q(ue) r(ōmānus).
6. IESV CHRISTO : *The* EL Iēsūs *transliterates the biblical name* Ἰησοῦς; *it declines thus:* Iēsūs, Iēsū, Iēsū, Iēsum, Iēsū. *The* EL Christus *transliterates Greek* Χριστός (*'anointed', then* EG *'Anointed One', 'Messiah'*).
10. MDLXVIII : Mīllēsimō quīngentēsimō sexāgēsimō octāvō.

Entryway

Left

The Senate and People of Rome,
imitating insofar as possible
in deed as in spirit
the excellence of their forbears,
restored the Capitol,
disfigured under the assault of time,
(Names of Magistrates)
in the year 2320
after the founding of the City.[a]

a. *The year 2320 AUC (anno urbis conditae) corresponds to 1568, the year in which the renovation of Palazzo dei Conservatori was completed, substantially to Michelangelo's design, by Giacomo della Porta (see 1.6A.ii). This reckoning respects the era of the Capitoline Fasti, whose epoch corresponds to 752 BC, rather than to the more familiar Varronian era, whose epoch corresponds to 753 BC.*

Right

The Senate and People of Rome
now humbly commend together with the common welfare
the Capitol, once dedicated
first and foremost to Jupiter,[a]
to the keeping
of the true God,
Jesus Christ,
author of all good things,
in the year 1568[b]
after the commencement of Salvation.

a. *According to tradition, the first temple dedicated on the Capitoline Hill— and, indeed, at Rome—was that of Jupiter Feretrius, founded by Romulus himself after his victory over Acron of Caenina (see 13.5.vi, note b).*

b. *See 1.6A.i, note a. The dating by the year of salvation implicitly corrects that by the founding of the city.*

1.6B Triumphal Arch of Claudius: Dedication by S.P.Q.R.

TI CLAV[dio drusi f cai]SARI
AVGV[sto germani]CO
PONTIFIC[i maxim trib potes]TAT X̄Ī
COS V̄ IM[p X̄X̄II cens patri pa]TRIAI
5   SENATVS PO[pulusque] RO[manus q]VOD
REGES BRIT[annorum] XI D[iebus paucis sine]
VLLA IACTVR[a deuicerit et regna eorum]
GENTESQVE B[arbaras trans oceanum sitas]
PRIMVS IN DICI[onem populi romani redegerit]

1. TI(beriō) CLAV[dio : *The portions of the inscription enclosed in brackets represent conjectural restorations of lost text. Because Roman conventions for abbreviating both personal names and political offices were remarkably uniform, these portions can be restored with a high degree of confidence.*
— f(īliō) cai]SARI = Caesarī : *As restored, the name shows the archaizing orthography found in other Claudian inscriptions (cf. 7.5A, line 1, and 13.1, line 2). The spelling may reflect the emperor's antiquarian bent (/ai/ is the OL form of the diphthong /ae/). Since Claudius is known to have taken an interest in spelling reform (see 13.1, line 9), it may rather represent an attempt to fortify the distinction between /ae/ and open /ɛ/, which already in the first century of the present era had begun to fall together in pronunciation; the result can be seen in the parallel development of LL praemiu(m) > Ital. premio and LL pretiu(m) > to Ital. prezzo (cf. 1.8B, line 5).*

3. maxim(ō). — trib(ūniciā) potes]TAT(e) X̄Ī : Ūndecimum. *When an ordinal numeral was used adverbially in the sense 'for the Nth time' (rather than 'N times'), the ordinary practice of the ancients was to mark it with a supralinear bar.*

4. CO(n)S(ulī) V̄ : Quīntum. — IM[p(erātōrī) X̄X̄II : Vīcēsimum secundum. *As Claudius was saluted as* imperātor *for the twenty-second through twenty-fourth times in the year 51, the true reading may be* X̄X̄II, X̄X̄III *or* X̄X̄IV. — cens(ōrī). — pa]TRIAI : *On the spelling, see* cai]SARI *(line 1).*

5–7. q]VOD . . . deuicerit : *The Subj. in the causal clause signals the attribution of the motive for the dedication to the SPQR. This 'virtual' indirect discourse is common in dedicatory inscriptions.*

6. XI : Ūndecim, *the cardinal number (cf.* X̄Ī = ūndecimum, *line 3).*

Palazzo dei Conservatori: Court, NW Wall

The Senate and People of Rome
to Tiberius Claudius Caesar
Augustus Germanicus,[a] *son of Drusus, Supreme Pontiff,*
vested with the Tribunician power for the eleventh time,
Consul for the fifth, acclaimed Imperator for the twenty-second,
Censor, Father of his Country, for having with no losses
defeated eleven kings of the Britons, and for having been the first
to bring their kingdoms and the barbarian nations domiciled across the ocean
under the sovereignty of the Roman people.[b]

a. *The emperor Claudius I (r. 41–54). Tiberius Claudius Nero Germanicus was proclaimed emperor by the Praetorian Guard on 25 January 41. He assumed the* TRIBUNICIAN POWER *for the eleventh time on that date in 51, became* CONSUL *for the fifth and final time on 1 January 51, and was saluted as* IMPERATOR *for the twenty-second time in 51. Like all the successors of Augustus, he was granted the office of* SUPREME PONTIFF *on his accession; among other emperors, the office of* CENSOR *was borne only by Vespasian, Titus, and Domitian. The title 'Father of his Country' was accepted by Augustus in 2 BC and assumed by almost all his successors (see* PATER PATRIAE).

b. *Claudius participated in the invasion of Britain (*AD *43), which established the first permanent Roman presence on the islands (the expeditions of Caesar in 55 and 54 BC had amounted to little more than forays). He celebrated a triumph for the victory in 44. The identity of most of the 'kings' is uncertain, but one of them—Caratacus, son of Cunobelinus (Shakespeare's 'Cymbeline')—was eventually handed over to the Romans and had his life spared. The date of the inscription, eight years after the invasion and four years after the conquest was completed, is perhaps to be associated with the exhibition of Caratacus to the Roman people following his surrender in 50. As it is mounted on an arch that served to carry the Aqua Virgo over the Via Lata (the modern Via del Corso), it is as likely that the delay resulted from the emperor's wish to dedicate the arch at the same time as the aqueduct, which he restored. We learn in a second inscription (9.6) that the arcade of the Aqua Virgo had been demolished by Claudius' predecessor Gaius ('Caligula'), presumably with a view to rebuilding it.*

1.6C Head of Constantine: Dedication by Magistrates

CAPVT EX COLLOSSO COM

MODI ANT AVG ALT TRICENVM

CVBITVM INTER RVINAS TEM

PLI PACIS IN MVLTA FRVSTA RE

5 PERTO CONSPICIENDVM CŌSER

VATORES VRB RO HEIC IVSSER

(Names of Magistrates)

1. COLLOSSO = colossō. — COM|MODI ANT(ōnīnī) AVG(ustī).
2. ALT(itūdinis) : *Gen. of Measure.* — TRICENVM = tricēnōrum : *The use of a distributive numeral instead of a cardinal is typical of verse. The Gen. Pl. in -um is a genuine archaism (see 15.3A, line 3a).*
3. CVBITVM = cubitōrum. — TEM|PLI.
4. RE|PERTO.
5–6. CO(n)SER|VATORES : *In* RL, *cōnservātor represents the Ital.* conservatore. — VRB(is) RO(mae). — HEIC = hīc : *A genuine archaism. In the course of the second century* BC, *the pronunciation of the diphthong* /ei/ *merged with that of the vowel* /i:/ *(e.g.,* OL deicō > CL dīcō). — IVSSER(unt).

1.6D Foot of Constantine: Dedication by S.P.Q.R.

S P Q R

APOLLINIS COLOSSVM A M LVCVLLO

COLLOCATVM IN CAPITOLIO

DEIN TEMPORE AC VI SVBLATVM EX OCVLIS

5 TV TIBI VT ANIMO REPRAESENTES PEDEM VIDE

ET ROMANAE REI MAGNITVDINEM METIRE

(Names of Magistrates)

1. S(enātus) P(opulus) Q(ue) R(ōmānus).
2. M(ārcō).
4. TEMPORE AC VI : *Probably hendiadys ('by the violence of time' rather than 'by time and violence'; see 3.2B, line 6).*
6. ROMANAE REI : *See 13.5.iii, line 6.* — METIRE : *The verb is* mētīrī. *The Pres.Sg.Imp. of deponent verbs looks like an Inf.Act.* (cōnāre, verēre, sequēre, potīre).

Palazzo dei Conservatori: Court, SE Wall

The Conservators[a] of the City of Rome
bade the head from the thirty-cubit colossus
of Commodus Antoninus Augustus,[b]
found in many fragments
amid the ruins of the Temple of Peace,[c]
to be displayed in this place.
(Names of Magistrates)

a. With the senator and the caporioni, the CONSERVATORS headed Rome's municipal administration under the popes.

b. The emperor Commodus (r. 180–192). Commodus was elder son of Marcus Aurelius (see 1.5.i, note a). The fragments in fact pertain to the colossal statue of the emperor Constantine I (r. 306–337) that formerly occupied the W end of the BASILICA begun by Maxentius and completed by his victorious rival (see 2.11A.i, note a).

c. Until the beginning of the nineteenth century, the Basilica of Constantine on the Velia was erroneously identified as Vespasian's Temple of Peace (cf. 2.14, note c).

Court, SE Wall

The Senate and People of Rome:
That you may bring before your mind's eye
the colossus of Apollo[a]—
placed by Marcus Lucullus[b] on the Capitol,
later hidden from sight by the violence of time—
behold this foot and gauge the greatness of the empire of Rome!
(Names of Magistrates)

a. The fragments in fact pertain to the statue of Constantine once housed in the BASILICA bearing his name (see 1.6c, note b).

b. Marcus Licinius Lucullus is said by the elder Pliny to have transported a colossal statue of Apollo from Apollonia to Rome following a military campaign in Thrace (72–71 BC). Marcus was brother to the more famous Lucius Licinius Lucullus, whose proverbially extravagant mode of life inspired the epithet 'Lucullan'.

1.6E Hand and Foot of Constantine: Dedication by Magistrates

VRBANO VIII P O M

PEDEM ET MANVM EX APOLLINIS COLOSSO

XXX CVBITORVM ALTITVDINIS

AB APOLLINEA PONTI VRBE ROMAM ADVECTO

5   DIV HVMI NEGLECTO

IN ANTIQVAE MAGNIFICENTIAE ARGVMENTVM

HONORIFICENTIVS HIC COLLOCARVNT

(Names of Magistrates)

ANNO DOMINI M DC XXXVI

1. VRBANO VIII : Octāvō. — P(ontifice) O(ptimō) M(aximō).
3. XXX : Trīcēn(ōr)um (*on the form, see. 15.3A, line 3a*).
7. COLLOCARVNT = collocāvērunt.
8. M DC XXXVI : Mīllēsimō sescentēsimō trīcēsimō sextō.

1.6F Commemoration of European Constitution

DIE XXIX MENSIS OCTOBRIS A D MMIV

IN HOC SACRATISSIMO CAPITOLINO COLLE

ALMAE VRBIS ORBISQVE TERRARVM ARCE

IN PRAECLARA AVGVSTAQVE EXEDRA

5   AB HORATIIS ET CVRIATIIS NVNCVPATA

NATIONVM IN VNIONE EVROPAEA CONIVNCTARVM

SVMMI MODERATORES

FOEDVS DE CIVITATIS FORMA CONSTITVENDA

VT EVROPAE GENTES IN POPVLI VNIVS CORPVS COALESCERENT

10   VNO ANIMO VNA VOLVNTATE VNO CONSILIO

OBSIGNAVERVNT

1. XXIX : Vīcēsimō nōnō. — OCTOBRIS : *See 1.6G, line 11.* — A(nnō) D(ominī) MMIV : Bis mīllēsimō quārtō.
8. CIVITATIS FORMA : *I.e., 'constitution'. The phrase* fōrma cīvitātis *is Ciceronian.*
10. VNO ANIMO VNA VOLVNTATE VNO CONSILIO : *The asyndeton strikes a note of solemnity (cf. 1.2.i, line 4).*

Palazzo dei Conservatori: Court, SE Wall

During the reign of Urban the Eighth,[a]
supreme and most excellent pontiff,
(Names of Magistrates)
as proof of the grandeur of Antiquity
placed here in more dignified state
the foot and hand from the thirty-cubit colossus of Apollo,[b]
brought to Rome from Apollo's city in Pontus [c]
and long neglected on the ground,
in the year of the Lord 1636.

a. *Pope Urban VIII Barberini (r. 1623–1644).*
b. *See 1.6D, note a.*
c. *Apollonia Pontica (mod. Sozopol) was a coastal city of Thrace. The toponym 'Pontus' refers to the Black Sea.*

Court, SW Wall, in Portico

On the twenty-ninth day of the month of October,
in the year of the Lord 2004,
on this hallowed Capitoline Hill,
citadel of the kindly City and of the world,
in the famous and majestic hall
named after the Horatii and Curiatii,[a]
the supreme leaders of the nations
joined together in the European Union
signed the treaty adopting a constitution,
that with a single mind, a single will, a single purpose
the nations of Europe might merge as the body of a single people.[b]

a. *The hall's frescoes depict the legend of the two trios of brothers who fought to decide whether Rome or Alba Longa should rule Latium (Livy 1.24–26).*
b. *The original treaty establishing the European Community was signed in the hall on 25 March 1957. Representatives of the twenty-five states of the European Union convened in Rome to sign the (abortive) constitution approved in June of 2004 by the Union's Intergovernmental Conference.*

1.6G Capitoline Museum: Dedication by Sixtus IV

SIXTVS IIII PONT MAX

OB IMMENSAM BENIGNITA

TEM AENEAS INSINGNES STA

TVAS PRISCAE EXCELLENTIAE

5   VIRTVTISQVE MONVMEN

TVM ROMANO POPVLO

VNDE EXORTE FVERE RESTI

TVENDAS CONDONANDAS

QVE CENSVIT

(Names of Magistrates)

10   A̅NO SALVTIS NOSTRE M CCCC

LXXI XVIII KL IANVAR

1. SIXTVS IIII : Quārtus. — PONT(ifex) MAX(imus).

2. BENIGNITA|TEM.

3. INSINGNES : *Sic* (= īnsīgnēs). *The error reflects an Italianate pronuncia-tion* /in'siɲɲes/. *The ancient Roman pronunciation was almost certainly* / iːnˈsiŋneːs/, *with* GN *as in English 'wing-nut'*. — STA|TVAS.

5. MONVMEN|TVM.

7–9. EXORTE FVERE = exortae fuērunt : *In* CL, exortae sunt *would be the more usual form of the tense. On the analogy of such expressions as* cārus est, *in* LL *the periphrastic form* amātus est *came to signify 'he is loved'; the form* amātus erat (*or* amātus fuit) *correspondingly signified 'he was loved'. On the spelling of* EXORTE, *see* 1.8B, line 5. — RESTI|TVENDAS CONDONANDAS|QVE : *The expression forms a kind of hendiadys (see* 3.2B, line 6) *in that the statues were returned and presented to the Roman people in a single act.*

10. A(n)NO. — NOSTRE = nostrae. — M CCCC|LXXI : Mīllēsimō quadringentēsimō septuāgēsimō prīmō.

11. XVIII : Duodēvīcēsimō. — K(a)L(endās) IANVAR(iī) : *In* CL, *the names of months are adjectives (e.g.,* XVIII Kalendās Iānuāriās); *in* LL, *they are Masc. nouns.*

Palazzo dei Conservatori: L of Entry to Sala degli Orazi

Sixtus the Fourth,[a] Supreme Pontiff,
on account of his boundless good will,
decreed that these
outstanding bronze statues,[b]
a monument
of antique eminence and worth,
should be restored in gift
to the people of Rome
whence they originated.
(Names of Magistrates)
In the year of our Salvation 1471,
on the fifteenth of December.[c]

a. *Pope Sixtus IV della Rovere (r. 1471–1484). A keen urban planner, Sixtus made many improvements to the infrastructure of the city with a view to accommodating the influx of pilgrims anticipated for the* JUBILEE *of 1475. These included the construction of Ponte Sisto (14.1) to link Trastevere with the Campus Martius. Sixtus was an energetic nepotist, appointing numerous nephews as cardinals: The most famous were Giuliano della Rovere—the future Pope Julius II—and Raffaele Riario, who built Palazzo della Cancelleria (see 13.3).*

b. *The initial donation of Sixtus IV comprised five ancient bronzes formerly housed at the Lateran and made over to the municipality. These include the Capitoline she-wolf, formerly reckoned a masterpiece of archaic bronzework but now dated to the Carolingian era; the figures of the twins were added in 1473 by the Florentine painter and sculptor Antonio Pollaiuolo (see 3.4A). The others are the* spinario *(boy plucking a thorn from his foot), the* camillus *(sacrificial assistant), the colossal head of the emperor Constantius II, and the globe originating from the same statue. The gift betokened less the pontiff's 'boundless good will' than his wish to underscore the seigneurial nature of his relationship with the communal authorities (see* CONSERVATORS*).*

c. *Lit., 'on the eighteenth day before the Kalends of January'.*

1.6H   Fragments of Arco di Portogallo: Dedication by Magistrates

MARMOREAE QVAS VTRINQVE

SPECTAS IMAGINES ALTERA

MARCI AVRELII POPVLVM

ALLOQVENTIS ALTERA FAVSTINAE

5   VETERI SVPERSTITIONE INTER

DIVAS AD COELVM ELATAE

EX RECENTIORI ARCV DIRVTO

VVLGO PORTVGALLIAE

QVI VIAM FLAMINIAM VRBIS

10   HIPPODROMVM IMPEDIEBAT

NOVIS CONSERVATORVM

AEDIBVS EXORNANDIS

SVB ALEXANDRO VII PONT MAX

AD CAPITOLIVM TRANSLATAE

15   VETVSTATE SQVALENTES HIC

RECENTI NITORE PRAEFVLGENT

QVARVM NE MEMORIA

EXCIDERET LAPIDEM POSVERE

(Names of Magistrates)

1. QVAS : *The antecedent is* IMAGINES *(line 2), qualified by* MARMOREAE. — VTRINQVE = utrimque : *On the spelling, see 9.2B, line 8.*

6. DIVAS : *The title* dīva *answers to the Masc.* dīvus *(see 2.8, line 2).* — COELVM = caelum : *On the spelling, see 1.8B, line 5.*

11–12. NOVIS . . . AEDIBVS EXORNANDIS : *Dat. of Purpose. The logical form of the expression is* exōrnandō novās aedēs *('for adorning the new palace'). When the gerund ideally governs a Dir.Ob., however, Latin prefers to cast the whole phrase into the case of the gerund's construction (here Dat.) and to convert the gerund into a gerundive showing formal but illogical agreement with its object (the Fem.Pl.* aedēs*). Thus* exōrnandīs novīs aedibus *(Dat.Fem.Pl.).* — CONSERVATORVM : *See 1.6C, lines 5–6.* — AEDIBVS : *In* RL, aedēs *(Pl.) regularly represents Ital.* palazzo.

13. ALEXANDRO VII : Septimō. — PONT(ifice) MAX(imō).

18. POSVERE = posuērunt.

Palazzo dei Conservatori: L of Entry to Sala degli Orazi

The marble images
that you behold on either side—
one of Marcus Aurelius[a] *addressing the people,*
the other of Faustina,[b]
according to ancient superstition
taken up into heaven among the goddesses—
from the lately demolished arch
popularly called 'di Portogallo'[c]
that formerly encumbered
the Via Flaminia,
racecourse of the City,[d]
transferred to the Capitol
under Alexander the Seventh,[e] *Supreme Pontiff,*
to adorn the Conservators' new palace[f]
and foul with age,
now gleam here with fresh splendor.
(Names of Magistrates)
placed this stone
lest memory of them should lapse.

a. *The relief depicts not Marcus Aurelius but Hadrian (r. 117–138), seen de-livering the eulogy for his wife Sabina. The panels have been moved since their installation in the seventeenth century.*

b. *The younger Faustina was wife of Marcus Aurelius. The subject of the relief is not however Faustina but Sabina, wife of Hadrian.*

c. *So called from the neighboring residence of the Portuguese ambassador in Palazzo Fiano, Arco di Portogallo was a late Roman monument of uncer-tain identity. It was demolished in 1662 (see 9.7).*

d. *In 1466, Pope Paul II (r. 1464–1471) transferred the horse races associated with the Roman Carnival from Monte Testaccio to Via del Corso so that they terminated beneath the windows of Palazzo Venezia, the residence that he had built while* CARDINAL.

e. *Pope Alexander VII Chigi (r. 1655–1667).*

f. *See* CONSERVATORS. *Palazzo dei Conservatori had been completed in 1568 (see 1.6A.i, Note a).*

1.61 Commemoration of the Conversion of Queen Christina

CHRISTINAE

SVECORVM GOTTHORVM

ET VANDALORVM

REGINAE

5   QVOD INSTINCTV DIVINITATIS

CATHOLICAM FIDEM REGNO AVITO PRÆFERENS

POST ADORATA SS APOSTOLORVM LIMINA

ET SVBMISSAM VENERATIONEM ALEXANDRO VII

SVMMO RELIGIONIS ANTISTITI EXHIBITAM

10 DE SEIPSA TRIVMPHANS IN CAPITOLIVM ASCENDERIT

MAIESTATISQVE ROMANAE MONVMENTA

VETVSTIS IN RVDERIBVS ADMIRATA

III VIROS CONSVLARI POTESTATE ET SENATVM

TECTO CAPITE CONSIDENTES

15   REGIO HONORE FVERIT PROSECVTA

VIII EID QVINCTIL AN M DC LVI

S P Q R

(Names of Magistrates)

2–3. SVECORVM GOTTHORVM | ET VANDALORVM : *The Latin names are* Suēcī, Gotthī, *and* Vandalī.

5–10. QVOD . . . ASCENDERIT : *On the construction, see 1.6B, lines 5–7.* — INSTINCTV DIVINITATIS : *Compare the phrasing of 2.11A.i, line 3.*

6. CATHOLICAM : *The EL Adj.* catholicus *transliterates Greek* καθολικός *('universal', then EG 'catholic').*

7. POST ADORATA . . . LIMINA : *On the construction, see 1.7A, lines 2–3.* — SS = sānctōrum. *In abbreviations, doubled letters indicate a plural, as here, or a superlative.* — APOSTOLORVM : *The EL* apostolus *transliterates Greek* ἀπόστολος *('envoy', then EG 'apostle').*

8. ALEXANDRO VII : Septimō.

9. ANTISTITI : *In EL,* antistes *is 'bishop' (see 3.3C, line 13).*

13. III VIROS = trēsvirōs : *In Latin, boards are regularly so designated.*

15. FVERIT PROSECVTA : *On the tense, see 1.6G, line 7.*

16. VIII : Octāvō. — EID(ūs) QVINCTIL(īs) = Quīntīlis : Eidūs *is archaic for* Īdūs *(cf.* HEIC, *1.6C, line 6).* — AN(no) M DC LVI = Mīllēsimō sescentēsimō quīnquāgēsimō sextō.

17. S(enātus) P(opulus) Q(ue) R(omānus).

Palazzo dei Conservatori: Sala dei Magistrati

The Senate and People of Rome
to Christina,[a]
Queen of the Swedes, Geats and Wends,[b]
because on 8 July 1656,[c]
at divine prompting,[d]
setting the Catholic faith before her ancestral realm,
after she had venerated the threshold of the Holy Apostles[e]
and offered humble obeisance to Alexander the Seventh,[f]
Supreme Bishop of the religion,
in triumph over herself she ascended the Capitol[g] and,
having marveled at the monuments of Rome's grandeur
in the ancient ruins,
attended with royal honor
the Board of Three vested with consular authority[h]
and the Senate, convened with covered heads.
(Names of Magistrates)

a. *Christina, queen of Sweden (1626–1689). Known for her intellectual prowess as the 'Minerva of the North', Christina abdicated her throne in 1654 and converted to Catholicism. In 1655 she settled in Rome (cf. 10.1C).*

b. *The Swedes are the inhabitants of Svealand, the ancient core of the Kingdom of Sweden. The Geats are the inhabitants of Götaland in southern Sweden, incorporated by the fourteenth century. The Wends were Slavs living in the region of Pomerania on the southern shore of the Baltic Sea.*

c. *Lit., 'on the eighth day before the Ides of Quintilis'. In 44 BC the month was renamed Iulius in honor of the Dictator.*

d. *The language is borrowed from 2.11A.*

e. *A frequent periphrasis for the BASILICA of St Peter.*

f. *Pope Alexander VII Chigi (r. 1655–1667).*

g. *The Capitol was the terminus of ancient triumphal processions.*

h. *A Classicizing periphrasis for CONSERVATORS (cf. 1.6C, note a).*

1.7A   Commemoration of Exploits of Clement VIII

CLEMENTI VIII PONT MAX

POST GALLIAE REGNVM RECONCILIATO REGE

HENRICO IV CONSTITVTVM

PANNONIAM ARMIS AVXILIARIBVS SERVATAM

5   STRIGONIVM A TVRCAR TYRANNIDE VINDICATVM

RVTHENOS ET AEGYPTIOS RO EC RESTITVTOS

PACEM COMPOSITIS REGVM MAXIMOR DISCORDIIS

CHRISTIANAE REIP REDDITAM

FERRARIAM PETRI ALDOBRANDINI CARD DVCTV

10   FERRO INCRVENTO RECEPTAM

SANCTISSIMAQ PRAESENTIA CONSTABILITAM

OPTATO REDITV IN VRBEM PVB HILARITATIS

SECVRITATISQ   REDVCTORI

1. CLEMENTI VIII : Octāvō. — PONT(ificī) MAX(imō).

2–3. POST . . . REGNVM . . . CONSTITVTVM : *Where English would use an abstract noun ('after the settlement of the realm'), Latin prefers a participle (Lit., 'after the realm settled'). This is the ab urbe conditā construction, so called from the name conventionally applied to Livy's History.* — HENRICO IV : Quārtō.

4. PANNONIAM : *A Classicizing equivalent for 'Hungary'.*

5. STRIGONIVM : *The Latin toponym is* Strigōnium, -ī. — TVRCAR(um) : *The Latin name is* Tūrcae, -ārum.

6. RVTHENOS : *The Latin name is* Ruthēnī, -ōrum. — RO(mānae) EC(clēsiae) : *The* EL ecclēsia *transliterates Greek* ἐκκλησία (*'assembly', then* EG *'church'*).

7. MAXIMOR(um).

8. CHRISTIANAE REIP(ūblicae) : *The* EL *Adj.* Christiānus *transliterates* EG Χριστιανός (*'Christian', 'of Christ'), an odd Latinism that occurs thrice in the* NT (*Acts 11:26, Acts 26:28, I Pet. 4:16*).

9. FERRARIAM : *The Ital. toponym* Ferrara *appears in Latin as* Ferrāria. — CARD(inālis).

11. SANCTISSIMAQ(ue). — CONSTABILITAM : *The* CL cōnstabilīre *is* 'establish', 'set on a sound basis'.

12. PVB(licae).

13. SECVRITATISQ(ue). — REDVCTORI : *App. to* CLEMENTI (*line 1*).

Palazzo Senatorio: Façade above Main Portal

To Clement the Eighth,[a] Supreme Pontiff,
who by his eagerly anticipated return to the City[b]
restored the people's cheer and peace of mind
after the settlement of the realm of France
through the reconciliation of King Henry the Fourth,[c]
the preservation of Hungary by allied forces,
the liberation of Esztergom from the tyranny of the Turks,[d]
the restoration of the Ruthenians and Egyptians to the Roman church,[e]
the return of peace to Christendom
through the resolution of disagreements between mighty kings,[f]
the recovery of Ferrara without bloodshed[g]
under the captaincy of Cardinal Pietro Aldobrandini[h]
and its consolidation through his own most holy presence.

a. *Pope Clement VIII Aldobrandini (r. 1592–1605). The façade of Palazzo Senatorio was completed during his reign.*

b. *In 1598.*

c. *In 1595, Clement VIII absolved the freshly converted Henri IV of France from the excommunication imposed ten years earlier by Sixtus V (cf. 4.2L, note a). As part of the settlement, Clement was obliged to countenance the Edict of Nantes (1598), which guaranteed religious freedom and civil rights to the Protestant Huguenots.*

d. *In 1595, a Catholic army under the command of Karl von Mansfeld recovered Esztergom, Hungary's metropolis (see BISHOP).*

e. *By the Union of Brest-Litovsk (1596) the Metropolitan of Kiev, five bishops, and a majority of Ruthenians—an Orthodox Slavic community of the Grand Duchy of Lithuania—were united with Rome. In the following year, emissaries of Gabriel VIII, Coptic Patriarch of Alexandria, arrived in Rome to announce their master's repudiation of Monophysite Christology. Gabriel's conversion had no effect on the Coptic church at large.*

f. *Clement was the nominal architect of the Peace of Vervins (1598), by which an old territorial dispute between France and Spain was settled.*

g. *When Alfonso d'Este died without heir in 1597, Clement reasserted papal control of the duchy of Ferrara (see 11.5E, note a).*

h. *Together with his cousin, Cinzio, Pietro Aldobrandini conducted the affairs of the papacy during his uncle's reign.*

1.7B Tabularium: Dedication by Catulus

[q lu]TATIVS Q F Q [n catulus cos
de s]EN SENT FACIV[ndum coerauit]
EIDEMQVE [probauit]

1. [q(uīntus) lu]TATIVS : *The portions of the text enclosed in brackets represent tolerably reliable restorations (see 1.6B, line 1).* — Q(uīntī) F(īlius) Q(uīntī) [n(epōs). — co(n)s(ul).
2. s]EN(ātūs) SENT(entiā). — FACIV[ndum = faciendum : *The change of the* OL *gerund from* -und- *to* -end- *may reflect the influence of the present participle in* -ent- (facient- : faciend-). — coerauit = cūrāvit : *In* OL, *the diphthong* /oi/ *proceeded to* /oe/ *and then* /u:/; *as this process was complete by around 150 BC, the spelling in* -oe *represents a graphic archaism.*
3. EIDEMQVE = īdemque : EI *is found for long* I *in early inscriptions.*

1.8A Aracoeli Stair: Dedication

MAG̅R LAVRĒTI' SYMEONI'

ANDREOTII ANDREE KAROLI FA

BRICATOR DE ROMA DE RE

GIONE COLVPNE FV̅DAVIT

5   P'SECVT' Ē ET CO̅SVMAVIT

VT P¹NCIPAL' MAG̅R H OPVS

SCALARV̅ INCEPT' ANNO D¹ M⁰

CCC⁰ XL   VIII DIE

XXV OC   TOBRIS

1. MAG(iste)R : *In* ML, magister *is used of a master craftsman.* — LAVRE(n)TI(us). — SYMEONI(s) : *The Latin name is* Simeōn, -ōnis. *On the spelling, see 3.1, line 1.*
2. ANDREE = Andrēae : *See 11.5A, line 2.* — KAROLI = Carolī.
3–4. DE RE|GIONE COLVPNE = columnae : *The* P *is a hypercorrection (cf. 8.8A, line 2). The phrase represents the Ital.* di rione Colonna. — FV(n)DAVIT.
5. P(rō)SECVT(us) E(st). — CO(n)SVMAVIT = cōnsummāvit.
6. P(r)¹NCIPAL(is). — MAG(iste)R. — H(oc).
7. SCALARV(m). — INCEPT(um). — D(omin)¹. — M⁰ | CCC⁰ XL VIII : Mīllēsimō trecentēsimō quadrāgēsimō octāvō.
9. XXV : Vīcēsimō quīntō. — OCTOBRIS : *See 1.6G, line 11.*

Palazzo Senatorio: N Side, above Doorway at Street Level

Quintus Lutatius Catulus,[a] son of Quintus, grandson
of Quintus, Consul, in accordance with a vote of the Senate
undertook to have this built and himself approved it.[b]

a. *A partisan of Sulla, Catulus served as* Consul *in 78 BC.*

b. *Partly on the basis of an inscription transcribed in the Middle Ages but*
   subsequently lost, the structure on which the medieval Palazzo Senatorio
   rises is generally identified as the ancient Tabularium *(public archive).*
   Catulus' building formed part of his renovation of the Capitol after a fire
   in 83 BC and features the earliest surviving example of an applied architec-
   tural order: engaged columns frame superimposed arcades which, though
   devoid of structural function, impose visual order on the expanse of the
   building's façade.

S. Maria in Aracoeli: Façade, L of Main Portal

Master craftsman Lorenzo di Simone Andreozzi,
son of Andrea Carlo,
Roman builder,
of Rione Colonna,[a]
as chief craftsman initiated,
carried forward and completed
this flight of stairs,[b]
begun in the year of the Lord 1348,
on the twenty-fifth day of October.

a. *The* Rioni *are Rome's traditional administrative districts.*

b. *Consisting of 122 steps, the stair is said to have been constructed as a thank*
   offering to the BVM for salvation from the plague of 1348. With the excep-
   tion of the belfry of S. Maria Maggiore, it is the only notable public work
   undertaken in Rome during the Babylonian Captivity *(1309–1377).*
   The first to mount the stair was Cola di Rienzo, the self-styled 'Tribune'
   who undertook to right the depredations of the baronial nobility and the
   neglect of the absentee papal government. Cola's blend of megalomania
   and political naiveté exposed him to the machinations of the aggrieved
   barons, at whose instigation he was murdered on 8 October 1354 near
   the site where his statue now stands to the north side of Michelangelo's
   Cordonata.

1.8B   Commemoration of the Victory of Lepanto

IESV CHRISTO HVMANÆ SALVTIS AVCTORI
QVOD PIVS V PONT MAX ANIMI CELSITVDINE
CVM PHILIPPO II HISPANIAR REGE S Q VENETO
FOEDERE INITO SELYMVM TVRCARVM TYRANNVM
5   AD ECHINADAS INSVLAS NAVALI PRÆLIO POST
HOMINVM MEMORIAM MAXIMO DEVICERIT
S P Q R
M ANTONIO COLVMNA PONTIFICIÆ CLASSIS PRAEF
REDVCE OVANTEQVE OMNIVM ORDINVM
10   GRATVLATIONE RECEPTO ÆDEM HANC AVREO
LAQVEARI VEXILLISQVE HOSTIVM EXORNAVIT
ANNO SAL CXↃ D LXXXVI
(*Names of Magistrates*)

1. IESV CHRISTO : *Dat. (see 1.6A.ii, line 6).*

2–6. QVOD . . . DEVICERIT : *The Subj. in the causal clause signals 'virtual' indirect discourse (see 1.6B, lines 5–7).* — PIVS V : Quīntus. — PONT(ifex) MAX(imus). — CELSITVDINE : *The CL* celsitūdō *is 'height'.*

3. PHILIPPO II : Secundō. — HISPANIAR(um). — S(enātū) Q(ue).

5. ECHINADAS : *The name* Echīnadĕs *transliterates Greek* Ἐχινάδες. — PRÆLIO = proeliō : *Because in LL pronunciation the diphthong /ae/ was monophthongized to open /ɛ/ and the diphthong /oe/ to closed /e:/, the two are very often confused in spelling. Besides* praeliō *for* proeliō, *cf. such spellings as* moestus *for* maestus *and* foemina *for* fēmina (*the late spellings* coelum *and* coena *result instead from a spurious connection with* κοῖλον *and* κοινή).

7. S(enātus) P(opulus) Q(ue) R(ōmānus).

8–9. M(ārcō) ANTONIO COLVMNA . . . REDVCE : *Since there is no Pres.Part. to the verb* esse, *the Abl.Abs. may appear without a verbal element* ('Marcantonio Colonna [*being*] *safely returned*'). — PONTIFICIÆ : *In* EL, pontificius *is 'papal'.* — PRAEF(ectō).

10. ÆDEM : *In* EL, aedēs *is regularly 'church'.*

11. LAQVEARI : *In* CL, *normally Pl.* (laqueāria, -ium).

12. SAL(ūtis) CXↃ D LXXXVI : Mīllēsimō quīngentēsimō octōgēsimō sextō. *The notation* CXↃ *is a variation of* CIↃ (*see 1.3, line 6*).

S. Maria in Aracoeli: Entry Wall, above W Portal

On the occasion of the safe return of Marcantonio Colonna,[a]
captain of the papal fleet,
and his reception with the exultant thanksgiving of all orders,
in the year of Salvation 1586 the Senate and People of Rome
embellished this church with gilt coffering
and with the enemy's ensigns
for Jesus Christ, author of mankind's Salvation,
because Pius the Fifth,[b] Supreme Pontiff, in loftiness of spirit,
having entered into an alliance with Philip the Second, King of the Spains,[c]
and with the Senate of Venice,[d] in the greatest naval engagement
in human memory defeated Selim,[e] tyrant of the Turks,
at the Echinades Isles.[f]
(Names of Magistrates)

a. *Marcantonio Colonna (1535–1584) was commander of the papal fleet at the Battle of Lepanto. General command of the expedition was given to Don Juan of Austria, natural brother of Philip II.*

b. *Pope St. Pius V Ghislieri (r. 1566–1572). After the conquest of Cyprus in 1571 by the Ottoman sultan Selim II, Pius forged an anti-Turkish 'Holy League' comprising Spain, the Republic of Venice, and the Holy See. The League's forces defeated those of the Turks near the mouth of the Gulf of Corinth on 7 October 1571. The battle was the last major naval engagement involving fleets of galleys and the last Crusade.*

c. *Viz., the kingdoms of Aragón, Castile, and Léon. Son of the emperor Charles V, Philip II of Spain (r. 1556–1598) was likewise ruler of Portugal and of Naples and Sicily.*

d. *The Senate was the committee of the Venetian* Maggior Consiglio *('Greater Council') responsible for the formation of state policy.*

e. *Son of Süleyman I, Selim II (r. 1566–1574) has been characterized as the first Ottoman sultan entirely devoid of military virtue.*

f. *The battle is conventionally called that of 'Lepanto', Ital. name of the ancient Naupactus on the N coast of the Gulf of Corinth. Naupactus is in fact situated about sixty km E of the Echinades, a group of five small islands in the Ionian Sea at the mouth of the River Acheloüs, whose silt has since largely engulfed them.*

1.8C Inscription from the 'Imperial Bedchamber'

A CVBICVLO AVGVSTORVM

A CVBICVLO : *In* CL, *this phrase would signify 'attendant of the bedchamber', i.e., a chamberlain (see* 11.3G, *line* 5). *Here it literally indicates 'from the bedchamber'.*

1.8D Statue of Paul III: Dedication by Magistrates

PAVLO III PONT MAX

QVOD EIVS IVSSV AVSPICIIS ATQVE ÆRE CONLATO

VRBEM SITV ET DIVERTICVLIS VIARVM DEFORMEM

ET IMPERVIAM DISIECTIS MALEPOSITIS ÆDIFICIIS

5   IN MELIOREM FORMAM REDEGERINT

VIIS AREISQVE CVM VETERIBVS DIRECTIS ET AMPLIATIS

TVM NOVIS CONSTITVTIS AVXERINT ORNAVERIN̄QVE

(Names of Magistrates)

VRBE INSTAVRATA OFFICII ET MEMORIÆ ERGO

STATVAM IN CAPITOLIO OPT PONT POSVERVNT

10   ANNO CHRISTI M D XLIII

1. PAVLO III : Tertiō. — PONT(ificī) MAX(imō).
2–5. QVOD . . . REDEGERINT : *The Subj. in the causal clause signals 'virtual' indirect discourse (see* 1.6B, *lines* 5–7).
3. DIVERTICVLIS : *The* CL *word is* dēverticulum.
4. MALEPOSITIS = male positīs.
6–7. VIIS . . . CONSTITVTIS : *Abl.Absolute. Its Sub. is* VIIS AREISQVE, *which is subdivided by* CVM *and* TVM *into* VETERIBVS *and* NOVIS: *The* VE-TERIBVS *were both* DIRECTIS *and* AMPLIATIS, *while the* NOVIS *were simply* CONSTITVTIS. — ORNAVERIN(t)QVE.
8. OFFICII ET MEMORIÆ : *Best understood as hendiadys ('out of dutiful memory' rather than 'out of duty and memory'; see* 3.2B, *line* 6).
9. OPT(imī) PONT(ificis).
10. CHRISTI : *See* 1.6A.ii, *line* 6. — M D XLIII : Mīllēsimō quīngentēsimō quadrāgēsimō tertiō.

S. Maria in Aracoeli: Third Column L, High

From the bedchamber of the Caesars.[a]

> a. *According to the* GOLDEN LEGEND, *the emperor Augustus founded an al-tar at the spot in the Imperial bedchamber where he had beheld a vision of the BVM and Christ Child—a spot fancifully identified with the Chapel of St. Helen in the present church (see 1.8F, note b).*

S. Maria in Aracoeli: L Aisle, between First and Second Chapels

To Paul the Third,[a] *Supreme Pontiff, because at his bidding,*
on his authority and with funds collected by him,
(Names of Magistrates)
by demolishing inopportunely sited buildings
improved the set of the City, which had been disfigured
by neglect and made impassable by warrens of alleys,
and enriched and embellished it with streets and squares
both by straightening and widening existing ones and by tracing new ones.[b]
They placed on the Capitol this statue of a most excellent pontiff
in dutiful memory of the City's renewal
in the year of Christ 1543.

> a. *Pope Paul III Farnese (r. 1534–1549). Though Paul is remembered chiefly for the completion of Michelangelo's 'Last Judgment', for the renovation of Piazza del Campidoglio (see 1.5.ii, note a), and for Palazzo Farnese, here the magistrates in charge of public works commemorate the pontiff's exten-sive improvements to Rome's infrastructure.*
>
> b. *The occasion of Paul's most ambitious essay in urban planning was pre-sented by the triumphal entry of the emperor Charles V (r. 1519–1556) in 1536 after his victorious campaign in Tunisia. Paul laid a new, straight street (today's Via di S. Gregorio) from the Baths of Caracalla through the Arch of Constantine (2.11) to the Colosseum (2.12); in the Forum, more than 200 dwellings were cleared so that the route could continue through the Arch of Titus (2.9) and along the Sacra Via to the Arch of Septimius Severus (2.3). Paul also opened the Via Trinitatis (today's Via dei Con-dotti) and Via Paola, the latter connecting Ponte Sant'Angelo with Via Giulia.*

1.8E Epitaph of Felice Fredi

FELICI DE FREDIS QVI OB PROPRIAS
VIRTVTES ET REPERTVM
LACOOHONTIS DIVINVM QVOD IN
VATICANO CERNIS FERE
5   RESPIRAN SIMVLACR IMRTALITATEM
MERVIT FEDERICOQ PATERNAS
ET AVITAS ANIMI DOTES REFERENTI
INMATVRA NIMIS MORTE PRAEVETIS
HIERONIMA BRANCA VXOR ET
10   MATER IVLIAQ DE FREDIS DE MILITIB′
FILIA ET SOROR MŒSTISSIME P
ANN DII M D XXVIIII

1–5. OB . . . REPERTVM . . . SIMVLACR(um) : *On the construction, see 1.7A, lines 2–3.*

3. LACOOHONTIS : *Gen.Sg. of a presumptive* Lācoohōn, *an eccentric transliteration of the Greek* Λαοκόων (*in* CL Lāŏcōōn).

5. RESPIRAN(s) SIMVLACR(um). — IM(mo)RTALITATEM.

6. FEDERICOQ(ue).

8. INMATVRA = immātūrā. — PRAEVE(n)TIS : *Pf.Part.Pass. of* praevenīre (*i.e., 'forestalled by death'*).

9. HIERONIMA : *The Latin name is* Hierōnyma, *the feminine form of* Hierōnymus (*see 10.7, line 1*). *On the spelling, see 3.1, line 1.*

10. IVLIAQ(ue). — DE MILITIB(us).

11. MŒSTISSIME = maestissimē : *On the spelling, see 1.8B, line 5.* — P(osuērunt).

12. ANN(ō) D(om)I(n)I M D XXVIIII : Mīllēsimō quīngentēsimō vīcēsimō nōnō.

S. Maria in Aracoeli: Head of L Aisle, Low

Girolama Branca, wife and mother,[a]
and Giulia Fredi de' Cavalieri,[b] daughter and sister,
set this up in great sorrow
to Felice Fredi,
who earned immortality
both for his own merits and for the discovery of the divine,
well-nigh breathing effigy of Laocoön[c]
that you behold in the Vatican and to Federico—
both carried off by a death all too early—
who reproduced the intellectual gifts
of his father and grandfather,
in the year of the Lord 1529.

a. Girolama Branca was wife of Felice Fredi and mother of Federico and
Giulia.

b. Giulia Fredi's husband was a scion of the family of this name that resided
in the zone of today's Via Arenula; the Ital. name de' Cavalieri appears in
Latin as De Militibus. The best-known member of the clan is the handsome young Tommaso de' Cavalieri, to whom Michelangelo addressed his
love sonnets.

c. Made in Rhodes around 25 BC and brought to Rome, the Laocoön group
was unearthed in 1506 by Felice Fredi in his vineyard on the Esquiline Hill.
The location of the find was in the neighborhood of Nero's Golden House,
a part of which had been filled during the early second century to construct
foundations for the Baths of Trajan. Soon after its discovery, Pope Julius
II purchased the group and installed it in the Vatican's Belvedere Court,
where it has since remained.

1.8F Commemoration of Aracoeli's Founding

1 LVMINIS HANC ALMAM MATRIS QVI SCANDIS AD AVLAM ⌐
   CVNTARVM PRIMA QVE FVIT ORBE SITA
2 NOSCAS QVOD CESAR TVNC STRVXIT OCTAVIANVS ⌐
   HANC ARA CELI SACRA PROLES CVM PATET EI

> One ELEGIAC COUPLET and two HEXAMETERS (verses 1, 2, and 4 Leonine)

1. CVN(c)TARVM. — PRIMA : *Scans* primā *in ictus.* — QVE = quae : *On the spelling, see 1.8B, line 5.* — AVLAM : *See 2.14, line 1.*
2. QVOD . . . STRVXIT : *The* CL *construction would feature Acc. + Inf.* — CESAR = Caesar. — OCTAVIANVS : *Scans* Octăvianus. — ARA(m) CELI = caelī : *The juxtaposed but syntactically unrelated words* ARA(m) CELI *are likely the source of the church's name.* — PROLES : *Scans* prolĕs.

1.8G Statue of Leo X: Dedication by S.P.Q.R.

OPTIMO PRINCIPI LEONI X

MED IOAN PONT MAX

OB RESTITVTAM INSTAVRATAMQ

VRBEM AVCTA SACRA BONASQ

5   ARTES ADSCITOS PATRES

SVBLATVM VECTIGAL DATVMQ

CONGIARIVM

S P Q R P

1. LEONI X : Decimō.
2. MED(icī) : *The Ital. name* Medici *appears in Latin as* Medicēs, -is. — IOAN(nī) : *On the name, see 6.4.* — PONT(ificī) MAX(imō).
3. OB RESTITVTAM INSTAVRATAMQ(ue) | VRBEM : *On the construction, see 1.7A, lines 2–3.*
4. BONASQ(ue).
5. PATRES : *In* RL, *Classical diction is preferred to such* ML *formulations as* collēgium cardinālium (CL ascīscere in patrēs *is 'take into the senate').*
6. DATVMQ(ue).
8. s(enātus) P(opulus) Q(ue) R(ōmānus) P(osuit) : *In the reign of Leo X, the formula* SPQR *first makes its appearance in papal epigraphy to designate Rome's municipal administration (cf. 2.5, line 1).*

S. Maria in Aracoeli: Cappella di S. Elena, Altar

You who climb to this kindly church of the Mother of Light, [a]
   which was founded first of all in the world, [b]
know that at that time Caesar Octavian [c] *built this altar*
when the holy progeny of heaven appeared to him.

One ELEGIAC COUPLET and two HEXAMETERS (*verses 1, 2, and 4 Leonine*)

a. I.e., the BVM.
b. *According to legend, the altar was founded by the emperor Augustus on
   the day of Christ's birth and thus first of all Christian shrines (see 1.8C).*
c. *In his early career, Julius Caesar's grandnephew and heir Gaius Octavius
   never used the name 'Octavianus' on his coins or monuments, preferring
   instead the simple—and politically advantageous—'Gaius Julius Caesar'.*

S. Maria in Aracoeli: Left Transept, W Side

The Senate and People of Rome
placed this monument
to their most excellent prince Leo the Tenth, [a]
Giovanni de' Medici, Supreme Pontiff,
for restoring and renewing the City,
promoting religion and the fine arts, [b]
creating cardinals, [c] *abolishing the tax,*
and granting largesse.

a. *Pope Leo X de' Medici (r. 1513–1521). By a corrupt arrangement with the
   local archbishop, Leo sent the Dominican Johann Tetzel into the dioceses
   of Brandenburg and Mainz to preach indulgences. Tetzel's tactics roused
   the ire of the young Martin Luther, who in 1517 nailed his Ninety-Five
   Theses of protest to the church door at Wittenberg—four years before Leo
   conferred the title 'Defender of the Faith' on Henry VIII of England for his
   vigorous defense of the Seven Sacraments against Luther's attacks.*
b. *See 11.3F.i, note c.*
c. *Lit., 'recruiting senators'. Leo X raised money by the shabby expedient of
   elevating many of the city's churches to titles (see* TITULAR CHURCH*) and
   charging handsomely for their assignment.*

ARCH OF TITUS

In the beauty of its proportions, the clarity of its structure, and the restraint of its decoration, the Arch of Titus (r. 79–81) exemplifies the Classical ideal in architecture. It consists of a single barrel-vaulted archway framed by massive pylons. On each side of the archway, engaged columns of the Composite order rise on high pedestals to divide the façade into three bays, of which the middle is the largest; the entablature and central bay of the attic project so as to emphasize the opening. Although the monument was originally crowned by a colossal bronze statuary group of the emperor driving a quadriga *('four-horse chariot'), the careful design ensured that the inscription—originally set in letters of cast bronze—formed the focus of attention.*

II. The Forum & Environs

ARCHEOLOGY HAS ESTABLISHED that around 1000 BC villages sprang up throughout Latium on the spurs extending from the foothills of the Apennines to the coastal plain. The hills of Rome—particularly the Palatine, Esquiline, and Quirinal, with the Forum valley at their center— appear to have accommodated a number of such settlements. The site offered many advantages: easy access to the river, defensible heights with springs at their feet, and a hinterland suited to the requirements of a pastoral economy. Among the several hills, the Palatine was distinguished by its extensive surface and central situation. More important still was its proximity to the Tiber ford; there the salt route running inland from the mouth of the Tiber intersected the coastal road linking Etruria and southern Italy.

In the early centuries of the first millennium BC, the depression that would one day become the Roman Forum was too marshy for human use. Perennially irrigated by the watercourse that drained the Subura— the broad valley extending northeast between the Quirinal and the Oppian—the Forum of the earliest period may be imagined as a trackless swamp fringed by the cemeteries of the Iron Age villages that clustered on the surrounding hilltops. A clue to the original limits of usable terrain is furnished by the siting of the Forum's earliest monuments: at its western end, the Regia, the Shrine of Vesta, and the temples of Castor and Saturn all seem to shrink away from the valley's bottom to hug the slopes of the Palatine and Capitoline.

Reclamation of the marsh was a precondition of rendering the Forum valley usable. Towards the end of the seventh century, its ground level was artificially raised and the watercourse channeled. Only with this intervention was it possible to trace the first roadway of Rome's center: the Sacra Via. The fact that the Sacra Via required a bridge at the point where it crossed the watercourse is a matter of some interest. That bridge was likely the predecessor of the temple of Janus, which in marked contrast to the other archaic monuments of the Forum was situated squarely on the course of the stream. As Janus presided over boundaries, it has been speculated that the stream formed the northwest border of the earliest community on the Palatine. With the culverting of the watercourse in the Cloaca Maxima, the leading natural feature of the Forum valley was forever lost to sight.

For the Romans of later times, the Forum was hallowed by episodes of the city's earliest history. Here Romulus and his Latins defended the Palatine village against the Sabines of Titus Tatius; it was on the Comitium at the foot of the Capitoline Hill that the two kings made their peace. Here too, Mettius Curtius precipitated himself—fully armed and on horseback—into a chasm that had opened in the valley's floor. Later, through the golden centuries of the Middle Republic, the Forum flourished as the center of commerce, law, and government. At its western end, the ensemble of Curia, Rostra, and Comitium gave architectural expression to the concord of Senate, Magistrates, and People; the central piazza was framed by great basilicas that housed the courts of law.

It was the emperor Augustus (r. 27 BC–AD 14) who gave the Forum its definitive shape. As Caesar's heir, Augustus completed the Curia Julia and Basilica Julia. To delimit the eastern end of the piazza, he erected a temple on the site of his adoptive father's cremation, flanked by one or more triumphal arches commemorating his own achievements. The emperor's short-lived heirs were honored with the eponymous PORTICO OF LUCIUS AND GAIUS CAESAR. Members of the imperial family and others close to the regime rebuilt or restored such venerable monuments as the temples of Concord and Castor (the TEMPLE OF SATURN had already been restored in 42 BC by a partisan of Mark Antony's). Over the subsequent four centuries, this modest plot of land would acquire a crust of marble and bronze so dense that twelve centuries of earthquake, fire, spoliation, and neglect scarcely sufficed to unmake it.

The earliest major post-Augustan addition to the zone of the Forum was effected under the Flavian emperors—Vespasian (r. AD 69–79), Ti-

tus (r. 79–81), and Domitian (r. 81–96). Begun by Titus, the TEMPLE OF   2.4
VESPASIAN was completed in the 80s during the reign of his younger
brother, Domitian. Though the temple was long known as that of Jupiter
Tonans, its true identity is revealed by the eight characters still visible
on the frieze—ESTITVER—representing the abbreviated Latin word
RESTITVER(unt), 'they restored'. This fragment of text matches a copy
of the entire inscription made by a northern European pilgrim around
the year AD 800 when the temple (or at any rate its front) was still standing and the dedication to Vespasian complete. Known as the 'Einsiedeln
Catalogue', the pilgrim's collection of transcriptions is a mine of information on the topography of ancient Rome.

The Flavians are responsible for two other outstanding monuments in
the vicinity of the Forum. The ARCH OF TITUS, honoring his conquest   2.9
of Jerusalem in AD 70, was completed only after that emperor's death.
So much can be inferred from the dedicatory inscription alone, in which
Titus is designated *divus* ('divine'). Incorporated during the Middle
Ages into the fortress of the family Frangipane, the monument was isolated and restored in a campaign of works credited to Pope PIUS VII.   2.9A
More famous is the arena that Vespasian raised on the site of the Golden
House of Nero, his prodigal predecessor. 'Flavian Amphitheater' is the
proper name of Vespasian's monument; the moniker 'COLOSSEUM' first   2.12
appears in a prophecy attributed to the Venerable Bede. It alludes to the
Colossus, a bronze statue of Nero said to have exceeded 100 Roman feet
(29.5 meters) in height. Originally located in the forecourt of the Golden
House, it was rededicated to the Sun by Vespasian and transferred to the
side of the amphitheater at Hadrian's behest.

Memory of the fact that the vestibule of the Golden House stood at the
summit of the Sacra Via, near the present CHURCH OF SANTA FRAN-   2.13
CESCA ROMANA, is evidently preserved in the legend of Simon Magus.
Simon, a corrupt sorcerer who enjoyed the confidence of Nero, declared
his blasphemous intention of reenacting the Ascension of Christ. On
the appointed day, as Simon drifted skywards to the profound astonish-

ment of the emperor and his court, the Apostle Peter fell to his knees and, adjuring the angels of Satan to release their unholy burden, caused the charlatan to plummet to his death on the basalt flags of the street. Relics of the episode included two paving stones; one survives and purportedly bears the prints of the apostle's knees, and the other was shattered by the impact of Simon's body.

Nero's Colossus disappeared without a trace, no doubt broken up for its valuable metal, but the amphitheater itself survived earthquake and neglect to be incorporated during the Middle Ages into the fortresses of the Frangipane and Annibaldi and to serve as a quarry in the Renaissance. By a curious irony, though there is no evidence that Christians were ever martyred in the Colosseum, it is this belief that ultimately saved the structure from the pillaging that would have assured its an-

2.12A   nihilation: In 1749, Pope BENEDICT XIV (r. 1740–1758) consecrated the whole of the Colosseum to the passion of Christ and the martyrs. In the mid-nineteenth century the northeastern side, on the verge of collapse,

2.12B   was reinforced by Pope PIUS IX (r. 1846–1878).

The monuments of the great emperors of the second century—Trajan, Hadrian, Antoninus Pius, and Marcus Aurelius—are largely to be found in the Campus Martius. With the exception of Hadrian's Temple of

2.8   Venus and Rome, the TEMPLE OF ANTONINUS AND FAUSTINA is the only major building of this period in the old Forum. Despite its imposing proportions, the temple was so situated as to avoid impinging on the

2.3   venerable lines established by Augustus. It was the ARCH OF SEPTIMIUS SEVERUS, dating to the early years of the third century, that first disturbed the all but Euclidean regularity that had obtained since the days of the first emperor. Celebrating Severus' military campaigns against the Parthians, the arch was dedicated in his own name and that of his two sons. Apart from honorary columns, no major monument was erected in the Forum again before the triumph of Christianity.

2.11   The ARCH OF CONSTANTINE commemorates a watershed in the history of Rome, the victory of the first Christian emperor at the Battle

of the Milvian Bridge on 28 October 312. Constantine I (r. 306–337) legalized Christianity in 313. Over the subsequent eight decades, a series of imperial decrees abolished pagan sacrifice and closed the temples. A quixotic restoration of the traditional cult under Julian the Apostate was short lived; in 379 or thereabouts, the emperor Gratian restored the privileges of the Church and took the decisive step of rejecting the office of Pontifex Maximus, which from the time of Augustus without interruption had been held by the emperor.

Within less than a century after Constantine established his new capital on the Bosporus, a foreign army captured Rome for the first time since 390 BC. The sack of the year AD 410 is associated with the tragic figure of Stilicho, regent for Honorius (r. 395–423), ineffectual emperor of the West. Stilicho, having staved off the Visigoths in the opening years of the fifth century—an achievement commemorated on the base of a MONUMENT TO THE EASTERN AND WESTERN EMPERORS—fell vic- 2.2 tim in 408 to the intrigues of his enemies at court. In August of 410 the Goths, led by Alaric, captured and sacked Rome. The darkness of the times is suggested in the inscriptions on the bases of STATUES BY TI- 2.6 MARCHUS AND POLYCLITUS, removed to the shelter of the Basilica Julia for protection. By century's end, imperial rule in Italy had given way to the kingdom of the Ostrogoths.

Because its monuments enjoyed official protection, the Forum preserved its ancient aspect even as a new religion and a new regime transformed the larger city. Through the sixth century, secular buildings were converted into churches. The BASILICA OF SANTI COSMA E DAMI- 2.14 ANO, for example, a gift of the Ostrogothic king Theoderic (r. 493–526), was improvised in a hall of Vespasian's Temple of Peace. Only at the beginning of the seventh century did Pope St. Boniface IV (r. 608–615) initiate the practice of consecrating disused temples to Christian worship. Within a few years the Senate House—itself an inaugurated temple— had been converted by Pope Honorius I (r. 625–638) into the Church of St. Hadrian, a fitting epitaph for the Forum of Cato and Caesar.

After Italy had been recovered for the Empire by the valor of Belisarius and Narses, the charge of its imperial territories was entrusted to 'exarchs' (viceroys), whose seat was at Ravenna. In AD 608 the former

2.1   exarch Smaragdus dedicated the COLUMN OF PHOCAS. That this seemingly magnificent gesture consisted in setting a statue on an existing monument (itself recycled) and recutting the dedication is eloquent of the poverty of the age. Within a century and a half, the Lombards had eliminated the Byzantine presence in Italy. Thrown back on their own resources, the popes allied themselves with the Frankish kings of the north. The coronation of Charlemagne in AD 800 marked the birth of the Holy Roman Empire, an institution that would shape the city's destiny for more than half a millennium.

Within a few decades of Charlemagne's death in 814, many of Rome's ancient monuments at last succumbed to ruin. Those that remained owed their survival to their conversion to other uses—or they were too robust to be pulled down for their materials. Three centuries later, the wrecked and abandoned Forum had come to be called 'Campo Vaccino' ('Cows' Field'). By the fourteenth century, when Cola di Rienzo made a collection of ancient inscriptions, none of the dedications recorded by the pilgrim of Einsiedeln survived except those on the Arch of Severus and the temples of Saturn and of Antoninus and Faustina. Within a few years of Cola's death, the return of the papacy from the Babylonian Captivity at Avignon lent a savage impetus to the destruction of what yet remained.

There is a melancholy irony in the fact that the definitive annihilation of the Forum's monuments commenced in the decades that saw the first flowering of Renaissance humanism. As early as the 1430s, Poggio Bracciolini lamented that the *cella* ('sanctuary') of the Temple of Saturn—largely intact when he first came to Rome in 1402—had all but disappeared. During the reign of Pope Nicholas V, tons of stone were stripped from the Colosseum and the Senate House; the Temple of Venus and Rome was worked as a quarry for a period of four years. To minimize the inconvenience with which their marbles might be reduced to lime, the richest monuments were equipped with temporary kilns. The sober fact is that the temples and basilicas of the Caesars, imposing even in ruin at the dawn of the modern age, were more or less systematically pulverized between the fifteenth and seventeenth centuries.

In the seventeenth and eighteenth centuries, as the forces of nature and neglect conspired to close the wounds inflicted by the Renaissance, peace settled once more over the Forum. Between the Arches of Titus and Severus there extended a quiet promenade shaded by a double file of lofty elms; the ancient churches of the Sacra Via breathed an atmosphere of sylvan tranquility. So utterly had the link with the past been severed that by the eighteenth century the very identity of the place was disputed; for Goethe and his contemporaries, the Forum was the Campo Vaccino of medieval times. Beloved of artists, this consummately Romantic landscape would fall victim in the nineteenth century to the systematic archeological explorations that continue to the present day.

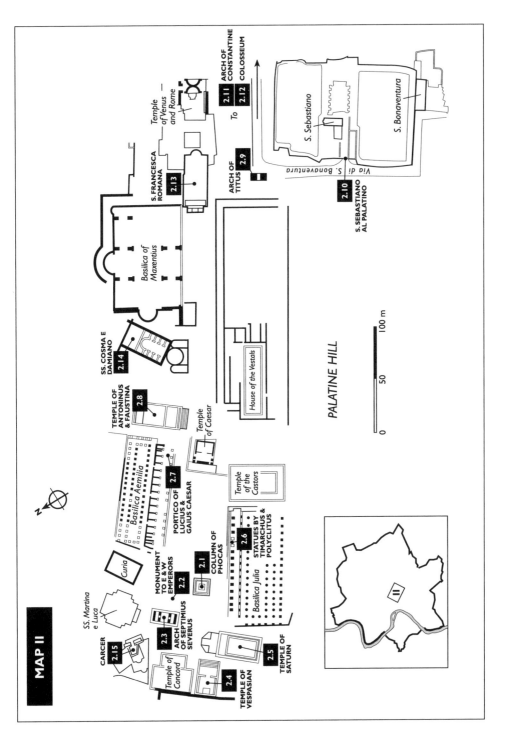

MAP II

SS. Martina e Luca

Temple of Concord

CARCER 2.15

ARCH OF SEPTIMIUS SEVERUS 2.3

TEMPLE OF VESPASIAN 2.4

TEMPLE OF SATURN 2.5

Curia

MONUMENT TO E & W EMPERORS 2.2

COLUMN OF PHOCAS 2.1

Basilica Aemilia

PORTICO OF LUCIUS & GAIUS CAESAR 2.7

Basilica Julia

Temple of Castors

STATUES BY TIMARCHUS & POLYCLITUS 2.6

TEMPLE OF ANTONINUS & FAUSTINA 2.8

Temple of Caesar

SS. COSMA E DAMIANO 2.14

Basilica of Maxentius

House of the Vestals

S. FRANCESCA ROMANA 2.13

Temple of Venus and Rome

ARCH OF TITUS 2.9

S. SEBASTIANO AL PALATINO 2.10

Via di S. Bonaventura

ARCH OF CONSTANTINE 2.11

To COLOSSEUM 2.12

S. Sebastiano

S. Bonaventura

PALATINE HILL

0   50   100 m

2.1 Column of Phocas: Dedication by Smaragdus

[opt]IMO CLEMENTISS[imo piissi]MOQVE
PRINCIPI DOMINO N [focae imp]ERA[to]RI
[p]ERPETVO A D̄Ō CORONATO [t]RIVMPHATORI
SEMPER AVGVSTO
5   SMARAGDVS EX PRAEPOS SACRI PALATII
AC PATRICIVS ET EXARCHVS
ITALIAE
DEVOTVS EIVS CLEMENTIAE
PRO INNVMERABILIBVS PI[e]TATIS EIVS
10   BENEFICIIS ET PRO Q[u]IETE
PROCVRATA ITAL AC CONSER[uat]A LIBERTATE
HANC ST[atuam maiestat]IS EIVS
AVRI SPLEND[ore fulgen]TEM HVIC
SVBLIMI COLV[mnae ad] PERENNEM
15   IPSIVS GLORIAM I[m]POSV[i]T AC DEDICAVIT
DIE PRIMA MENSIS AVGVSTI INDICT VND
P C PIETATIS EIVS ANNO QVINTO

1. [opt]IMO : *The bracketed letters are restored (cf. 1.6B, line 1).*
2. N(ostrō) [focae = Phōcae : *The name transliterates Greek* Φωκάς. *The passage of* /pʰ/ *to* /f/ *is attested in Pompeian inscriptions dating to the first century of the present era (e.g.,* DAFNE *for* DAPHNE = Δάφνη). *Cf. the traditional spelling of* TRIVMPHATORI *(line 3).*
3. [p]ERPETVO : *On the construction, see* VICE SACRA *(2.2, line 14).* — D(e)O.
5. SMARAGDVS : *Transliterates Greek* Σμαραγδός. — EX PRAEPOS(itō) SACRI PALATII : *Beginning in the early third century,* sacer *was used in a sense approximating 'imperial'.*
6. EXARCHVS : *The Latin* exarchus *transliterates Greek* ἔξαρχος *('chief').*
9–11. PRO . . . CONSER[uat]A LIBERTATE : *On the construction, see 1.7A, lines 2–3.* — ITAL(iae).
16. AVGVSTI : *See 1.6G, line 11.* — INDICT(iōne) : *Abl. of Time When. In* LL, indictiō *is used both of the declaration of a tax cycle and of the cycle itself.* — VND(ecimā) : *The numeral respects the year rather than the cycle.*
17. P(ost) C(ōnsulātum).

Base of Column, N Side

To the most excellent, gracious and merciful Prince
our Lord Emperor Phocas,[a]
crowned for eternity by God, Conqueror,
ever Augustus,
Smaragdus, former superintendent of the imperial palace,
likewise Patrician[b]
and Exarch of Italy,[c]
in devotion to his Grace,
in acknowledgment of the numberless blessings of his Mercy,
and of the peace secured for Italy
and the preservation of liberty,
placed atop this lofty column
this statue of his Majesty,[d]
to the everlasting glory of the same,
gleaming with the radiance of gold, and dedicated it
on the first day of the month of August in the eleventh indiction[e]
in the fifth year after the consulship of his Mercy.[f]

a. *Phocas (r. 602–610) began his career as a Cappadocian centurion; having gained the throne by assassinating the emperor Maurice and his five sons, he ended his reign himself deposed and executed. It was Phocas who ceded the Pantheon to Pope St. Boniface IV (see 11.3B.ii, note e).*

b. *Long after the ancient patriciate had died out, the emperor Constantine I (r. 306–337) revived 'Patrician' as an honorary title.*

c. *After its capture from the Goths under the emperor Justinian (r. 527–565), Byzantine Italy was governed by an Exarch (imperial governor) whose seat was at Ravenna (cf. 9.4, note a).*

d. *The column—or rather the lost statue set on it by Smaragdus—enjoys a certain distinction as the final monument to be dedicated in the Forum in Antiquity. The column itself had been salvaged and reerected at its present site in the fourth century. Smaragdus had only to recut the inscription and place the statue.*

e. *The* INDICTION *was a fifteen-year tax cycle dated from 312 and originally reckoned from 1 September. The year designated is 608.*

f. *Reckoned inclusively: Phocas was* CONSUL *in 604.*

2.2 Monument to E and W Emperors by S.P.Q.R.

FIDEI VIRTVTIQ DEVOTISSIMORVM

MILITVM DOMNORVM NOSTRORVM

ARCADI HONORI ET THEODOSI

PERENNIVM AVGVSTORVM

5   POST CONFECTVM GOTHICVM

BELLVM FELICITATE AETERNI

PRINCIPIS DOMNI NOSTRI HONORI

CONSILIIS ET FORTITVDINE

INLVSTRIS VIRI COMITIS ET

10   ⟦magistri utriusque militiae

praesentalis fl stilichonis⟧

S P Q R

CVRANTE PISIDIO ROMVLO V C

PRAEF VRBI VICE SACRA

15   ITERVM IVDICANTE

1. VIRTVTIQ(ue).
2. DOMNORVM = dominōrum : *This syncopated spelling of* dominus *is attested as early as the late second century* BC. *Its feminine counterpart* domna *is the source of Ital.* donna, *Span.* doña, *and Fr.* dame.
5. POST CONFECTVM GOTHICVM | BELLVM : *On the construction, see* 1.7A, *lines 2–3. The Adj.* Gothicus *answers to* Gotthī (*cf. 1.61, line 2*).
7. DOMNI = dominī.
9. *In* LL, comes *is 'count'.*
10. ⟦magistri utriusque militiae : *The words enclosed in double brackets were deliberately effaced and are conjecturally restored* (*cf. 1.6B, line 1*).
11. praesentalis fl(āvī) stilichonis⟧ : *The* LL *Adj.* praesentālis *is 'serving at court'. The Latin name is* Stilichō, -ōnis.
12. S(enātus) P(opulus) Q(ue) R(ōmānus).
13. V(irō) C(lārissimō).
14. PRAEF(ectō) VRBI : *The construction of* praeficere *is 'to place* x (*Acc.*) *over* Y (*Dat.*)'. *The substantive Pf.Part.* praefectus *continues the Dat. regimen of the verb* ('one placed over' + *Dat.*). — VICE SACRA : *The construction is Abl. of Manner with adverbial force* (*cf.* iūre, cōnsiliō, nocte). *On* sacer, *see 2.1, line 5.*

Rostra: NE End, N Side of Base

The Senate and People of Rome
to the fidelity and valor
of the most loyal troops
of our Lords Arcadius, Honorius, and Theodosius,[a]
imperishable Augusti,
on the conclusion of the Gothic War[b]
through the happy fortune
of the everlasting Prince, our Lord Honorius,
by the counsel and bravery
of his Eminence, the Count and
⟦Master of both Services,[c] *Flavius Stilicho,*[d]
in immediate attendance on the Emperor.⟧
Under the supervision of his Excellency Pisidius Romulus,[e]
City Prefect,[f] *in his second term*
as deputy judge for imperial appeals.

a. *Arcadius (r. 383–408) and Honorius (r. 395–423) were E and W emperors respectively; Theodosius II (E emperor, r. 408–450), was the son of Arcadius. Some such predicate as 'erected this monument' is implied.*

b. *I.e., the wars conducted in the opening years of the fifth century with Alaric's Visigoths and with the Goths led by Radagaisus.*

c. *Stilicho served as Master of the Foot and Master of the Horse.*

d. *By birth a Vandal, Stilicho was regent for Honorius and effectively the ruler of Italy from 395. Accused of collusion with the Visigoths, he was disgraced and executed in 408; his name was subsequently effaced from all public monuments—an act known as* damnatio memoriae *('condemnation of memory'). The text in brackets was deliberately effaced and is conjecturally restored. The more or less direct consequence of Stilicho's loss was the fall of Rome to Alaric on 24 August 410 (see 2.6B, note e). 'His Eminence' translates the title* Vir Illustris *(see* VIR CLARISSIMUS*).*

e. *'His Excellency' translates the title* VIR CLARISSIMUS *(Lit., 'Distinguished Gentleman'), used from the time of Constantine to designate the whole of the senatorial order.*

f. *The city* PREFECT *was the magistrate responsible for maintaining order within the city. Pisidius Romulus held the office in AD 405.*

2.3 Arch of Septimius Severus: Dedication by S.P.Q.R.

IMP CAES LVCIO SEPTIMIO M FIL SEVERO PIO PERTINACI AVG PATRI PATRIAE PARTHICO ARABICO ET

PARTHICO ADIABENICO PONTIFIC MAXIMO TRIBVNIC POTEST $\overline{XI}$ IMP $\overline{XI}$ COS $\overline{III}$ PROCOS ET

3 IMP CAES M AVRELIO L FIL ANTONINO AVG PIO FELICI TRIBVNIC POTEST $\overline{VI}$ COS PROCOS ⟨PP⟩

3a [[et]]

4 ⟨OPTIMIS FORTISSIMISQVE PRINCIPIBVS⟩

4a [[p septimio l fil getae nobiliss caes]]

5 OB REM PVBLICAM RESTITVTAM IMPERIVMQVE POPVLI ROMANI PROPAGATVM

INSIGNIBVS VIRTVTIBVS EORVM DOMI FORISQVE S P Q R

1. IMP(erātōrī) CAES(arī). — M(ārcī) FIL(iō). — AVG(ustō).

2. PONTIFIC(ī). — TRIBVNIC(iā) POTEST(āte) $\overline{XI}$: Ūndecimum. — IMP(erātōrī) $\overline{XI}$: Ūndecimum. — CO(n)s(ulī) $\overline{III}$: Tertium. — PROCO(n)s(ulī).

3. IMP(erātōrī) CAES(arī) M(ārcō). — L(ūcī) FIL(iō). — AVG(ustō). — TRIBVNIC(iā) POTEST(āte) $\overline{VI}$: Sextum. — CO(n)s(ulī) PROCO(n)s(ulī). — ⟨P(atrī) P(atriae)⟩ : See line 4a.

3a. [[et]] : See line 4a.

4a. [[p(ūbliō) septimio l(ūcī) fil(iō) getae nobiliss(imō) caes(arī)]] : The double brackets (lines 3a and 4a) indicate that these words were deliberately effaced and replaced by those between angle brackets (cf. 2.2, line 10). The text can be restored with a large measure of confidence from the pattern of holes for the dowels by which the bronze letters of the inscription were originally affixed to the marble.

5. OB REM PVBLICAM RESTITVTAM : On the construction, see 1.7A, lines 2–3. The wording recalls the line of the early Roman poet Ennius: Unus homo nobis cunctando restituit rem ('A single man, by delaying, restored the State to us', Enn.Ann. 370 V² = 363 Sk; see 13.5.iii).

6. s(enātus) p(opulus) q(ue) r(ōmānus).

Attic, E and W Sides

The Senate and People of Rome, to Imperator Caesar Lucius Septimius Severus, [a] *son of Marcus, Pius Pertinax Augustus, Father of his Country, Parthicus Arabicus and Parthicus Adiabenicus, Supreme Pontiff, vested with the Tribunician power for the eleventh time, acclaimed Imperator for the eleventh, Consul for the third, Proconsul, and to Imperator Caesar Marcus Aurelius Antoninus,* [b] *son of Lucius, Augustus Pius Felix, vested with the Tribunician power for the sixth time, Consul, Proconsul,* ⟨*Father of his Country*⟩ [c]   [[*and*]]*
⟨most excellent and valorous Princes⟩

[[*to Publius Septimius Geta,* [d] *son of Lucius, most noble Caesar*]]

for restoring the state and extending the empire of the Roman people by their signal virtues at home and abroad.

a. *Lucius Septimius Severus* (r. 193–211) *claimed the throne while serving as governor of Upper Pannonia. He took the titles Parthicus Arabicus and Parthicus Adiabenicus in 195; Pius was probably added in the same year. Severus assumed the* Tribunician Power *for the eleventh time on 10 December 202, was saluted as* Imperator *for the eleventh time probably in 198, and became* Consul *for the third time on 1 January 202. The title* Proconsul *was frequently used by Severus and his successors. Like all the successors of Augustus, he was granted the office of* Supreme Pontiff *on his accession. The title 'Father of his Country' was accepted by Augustus and nearly all succeeding emperors (see* Pater Patriae*).*

b. *Severus' elder son Septimius Bassianus* (r. 211–217) *is usually known by his nickname, 'Caracalla'; he was given the present name in 195. In 198, Severus made Caracalla joint emperor; the titles Pius and Felix were added in 200 and 'Father of his Country' in 205. Caracalla assumed the* Tribunician Power *for the sixth time on 10 December 202 and became* Consul *for the first time on 1 January 202.*

c. *The words enclosed in double brackets were replaced by those between angle brackets.*

d. *Lucius Septimius Geta, younger son of Severus, inherited the throne jointly with his brother on the death of their father at York in 211. The next year Caracalla arranged his brother's murder and imposed damnatio memoriae (see 2.2, note d): Geta's name and titulature were replaced by a formula of equal length that referred only to Severus and Caracalla.*

2.4 Temple of Vespasian: Dedication by S.P.Q.R.

[diuo uespasiano augusto s p q r

impp caess seuerus et antoninus pii felic augg r]ESTITVER

1–2. [diuo … r]ESTITVER(unt) : *The characters enclosed in brackets are restored from a transcription preserved in the Einsiedeln Catalogue.* — *diuo : Julius Caesar was the first Roman ruler posthumously deified. In the course of time, the honor was conferred on fifty-five emperors, including Constantine I.* — s(enātus) p(opulus) q(ue) r(ōmānus).

2. impp caess = imperātōrēs caesarēs : *In abbreviations, a doubled letter regularly indicates a plural; similarly* augg = augustī *(see 1.61, line 7).* — pii felic(ēs) : *The titles* pius *and* fēlīx *were first adopted by the Emperor Commodus in* AD *183 and 185, respectively.* — r]ESTITVER(unt).

2.5 Temple of Saturn: Dedication by S.P.Q.R.

SENATVS POPVLVSQVE ROMANVS

INCENDIO CONSVMPTVM RESTITVIT

1. SENATVS POPVLVSQVE ROMANVS : *From the Middle Ages, ingenious and fanciful interpretations were proposed for the ubiquitous abbreviation* SPQR. *These included* SAPIENS POPVLVS QVAERIT ROMAM *('A wise people seeks out Rome'),* SALVS PAPAE QVIES REGNI *('The health of the Pope is the peace of the realm'), and* SANCTVS PETRVS QVIESCIT ROMAE *('St. Peter reposes at Rome'). In the current vernacular:* SONO PAZZI QVESTI ROMANI *('They're mad, these Romans!'); a variant of the latter featuring* PORCI *instead of* PAZZI *is also attested.*

2.6A Statues by Timarchus and Polyclitus: Titles on Bases

i.   ii.

[opus] TIM[a]RCHI   [opus] POLYCLE[ti]

1. [opus] : *The portions of the text enclosed in brackets have been restored.* — TIM[a]RCHI : *The Latin* Timarchus *transliterates Greek* Τίμαρχος *('Chief in honor').* — POLYCLE[ti] : *The Latin* Polyclētus *(or Polycleitus or Polyclītus) transliterates Greek* Πολύκλειτος *('Far-famed').*

Frieze

The Senate and People of Rome, to the Divine Vespasian Augustus.[a]
The Emperors Caesars Severus and Antoninus Pius Felix Augustus restored it.[b]

a. On 1 July 69, Titus Flavius Vespasianus (r. 69–79) was proclaimed emperor by the legions of Egypt. The title 'Divine' (see DIVUS) was first conferred on Julius Caesar after his assassination (44 BC) and thereafter became a frequent posthumous honor of the emperors; by Vespasian's time it was sufficiently routine that on his deathbed, according to the imperial biographer Suetonius ('Life' of Vespasian, 23), he was able to quip, 'Vae, puto, deus fio' ('Mercy—I reckon I'm becoming a god!'). The present temple was begun by Titus (see 2.9B, note a) after the death of his father in 79 and completed by Domitian after the death of Titus two years later. The text in brackets is restored from the EINSIEDELN CATALOGUE.

b. For Severus and Antoninus ('Caracalla'), see 2.3.

Frieze

The Senate and People of Rome
restored this, destroyed in a fire.[a]

a. According to tradition, the temple of Saturn was founded in 498 BC. It housed the state treasury, famously looted by Julius Caesar in 49 BC. The present superstructure dates to a rebuilding in the fourth century. The columns are all salvaged from earlier buildings; the crudeness of the Ionic capitals—the only new elements—betrays the level to which the craft of stoneworking had sunk. Like many of the great buildings of the Forum, the temple was largely intact before the depredations of the Renaissance.

Basilica Julia: Bases of Statues, L and R

Left   Right
A work of Timarchus.[a]   *A work of Polyclitus.*[b]

a. Timarchus, son of Praxiteles (cf. 8.3A.ii, note a), was a Greek sculptor active in the late fourth and early third centuries BC.

b. Polyclitus was the leading Greek sculptor of the second half of the fifth century BC.

2.6B   Commemoration of Statues' Restoration

GABINIVS VETTIVS

PROBIANVS V C

PRAEF VRB

STATVAM FATALI

5   NECESSITATI CON

LABSAM CELEBERRI

MO VRBIS LOCO ADHI

BITA DILIGENTIA REPARAVIT

2. v(ir) c(lārissimus).

3. PRAEF(ectus) VRB(ī) : *On the construction, see 2.2, line 14.*

5. CON|LABSAM = collāpsam : *The spelling in* BS *is etymological* (< con +
lābī). *A similar orthography occurs in such words as* urbs *and* plēbs, *pro-*
nounced /urps/ *and* /ple:ps/, *but spelled with the* B *of their stems (see 13.1,*
line 9). The pronunciation /ps/ *resulted from the fact that before* /s/, *the*
voiced bilabial plosive /b/ *was reduced to its unvoiced counterpart* /p/ *to*
facilitate the transition to the unvoiced /s/. — CELEBERRI|MO.

7. ADHI|BITA DILIGENTIA : *I.e.,* cum dīligentiā. *In* LL, *Ablatives Absolute*
of this type are frequent.

2.7   Portico of Lucius and Gaius Caesar: Dedication by Senate

L CAESARI AV[gu]STI F DIVI N

PRINCIPI IVVENTV[ti]S COS DESIG

CVM [e]SSET ANN N[a]T XIIII AVG

SENATVS

1. L(ūciō). — AV[gu]STI : *The bracketed characters are easily restored from*
context. — F(īliō). — DIVI : *See 2.4, line 1.* — N(epōtī).

2. CO(n)S(ulī) DESIG(nātō).

3. CVM [e]SSET : *Temporal clauses with* cum *ordinarily use the Indic. when*
the clause merely specifies the time of an occurrence but the Subj. when the
the circumstances under which the occurrence takes place are the focus of
interest. — ANN(ōs) N[a]T(us) XIIII : Quattuordecim. *In* CL, *the nota-*
tions IIII, VIIII, *and* XIIII *are more common than* IV, IX, *and* XIV. *Latin*
expresses age using the Pf.Part.Dep. nātus (< nāscī, *'to be born') with the*
Acc. of Extent in Time (Lit., 'born for fourteen years'). — AVG(urī).

Basilica Julia: Bases of Statues, R

His Excellency [a]
Gabinius Vettius Probianus, [b]
City Prefect, [c]
carefully restored
this statue, [d] *located*
in the most famous spot in the City
and fallen
at a moment of fateful urgency. [e]

a. On the title, see 2.2, note e.
b. Gabinius Vettius Probianus likely served as city PREFECT in 416.
c. On the office, see 2.2, note f.
d. The bronze statues were evidently transferred from exposed locations into
the shelter of the BASILICA Julia. With small differences of lineation, the
present inscription duplicates that of the L statue's base.
e. An allusion to Alaric's sack of Rome in 410 (see 2.2, note d). Although it
was violent, the sack was brief: damage to the physical fabric of the city
was minimal. Christians themselves, the Visigoths made a point of sparing
churches (cf. 3.3A, note b).

Basilica Aemilia: SE Corner

The Senate
to Lucius Caesar, [a] *son of Augustus, grandson of the Divine,*
Prince of the Youth, [b] *Consul Designate* [c]
when he was fourteen years old, Augur. [d]

a. Lucius Caesar and his elder brother Gaius, sons of Marcus Vipsanius
Agrippa (see 11.3A, note a) and Julia, Augustus' daughter, were adopted by
the emperor (hence 'sons' of Augustus and 'grandsons' of the deified Julius
Caesar). Like Augustus' nephew Marcellus before them, the two died pre-
maturely—Lucius in AD 2 and Gaius in AD 4 (cf. 10.5, note a).
b. Gaius and Lucius were each styled PRINCE OF THE YOUTH at the age of
fourteen (in 5 and 2 BC respectively).
c. The consulship was early reduced to an honor conferred by the emperors.
d. The Augurs maintained the body of knowledge governing the auspices, by
which divine approval of a proposed course of action was determined.

2.8 Temple of Antoninus and Faustina: Dedication by Senate

DIVO ANTONINO ET

DIVAE FAVSTINAE EX S C

2. DIVAE : *The title* dīva *is the Fem. counterpart to* dīvus *('deified', 'divine'; see 2.4, line 1). In all, sixteen women of the several imperial dynasties were formally deified. The first was Livia Drusilla, widow of the Divine Augustus, who obtained the distinction during the reign of her grandson, Claudius I (r. 41–54). Her successors in the honor included Drusilla, sister of Gaius ('Caligula'); Poppaea, wife of Nero; Domitilla, wife of Vespasian; Marciana, sister of Trajan; Plotina, wife of Trajan; Matidia, niece of Trajan; Sabina, wife of Hadrian; Faustina, wife of Marcus Aurelius; and Julia, wife of Septimius Severus.* — EX S(enātūs) C(ōnsultō) : *As often,* ex *has the sense 'proceeding from', 'on the basis of' (cf. 1.1, line 3, where in a similar formula the simple Instrumental Abl. is used, and the more general expression* dē senātūs sententiā *at 1.7B, line 2).*

2.9A Arch of Titus: Dedication by Pius VII

INSIGNE RELIGIONIS ATQVE ARTIS MONVMENTVM

VETVSTATE FATISCENS

PIVS SEPTIMVS PONTIFEX MAX

NOVIS OPERIBVS PRISCVM EXEMPLAR IMITANTIBVS

5   FVLCIRI SERVARIQVE IVSSIT

ANNO SACRI PRINCIPATVS EIVS XXIIII

1. RELIGIONIS ATQVE ARTIS : *Both depend on* MONVMENTVM. *The ancients debated whether* religiō *derived from* religāre *('to bind'), with primary reference to the bond between gods and men, or from* relegĕre *('to reiterate'), with primary reference to the scrupulous performance of ritual. In usage,* religiō *signified both the communal relationship of gods and men and the system of obligations arising from it. Here it alludes to the sacred furniture of the Temple in Jerusalem depicted in the friezes.*

3. MAX(imus).

6. XXIIII : Vīcēsimō quārtō.

Frieze

To the Divine Antoninus^a and
to the Divine Faustina, in accordance with a decree of the Senate.

a. *Following his adoption by Hadrian on 25 February 138, Titus Aurelius*
Fulvus Boionius Arrius Antoninus became Imperator Titus Aelius Caesar
Antoninus. Best known as Antoninus Pius (r. 138–161), he succeeded on
Hadrian's death (10 July of the same year). On the title 'Divine', see 2.4,
note a. Antoninus had the present temple built for his wife Faustina on her
death in 141. When he himself died twenty years later, the temple was re-
dedicated and the frieze modified to accommodate his own (much larger)
inscription. The carcass of the Roman structure is occupied by the Church
of S. Lorenzo in Miranda, dating to 1600; its seventh-century predecessor
had been demolished in 1536 to expose the temple's portico on the occasion
of the triumphal entry of Charles V (see 1.8D, note b).

Attic, W Side

Pius the Seventh,^a Supreme Pontiff,
ordered that this outstanding monument of religion and art,^b
deteriorating with age,
should be stabilized and conserved
by new construction imitating the original pattern^c
in the twenty-fourth year of his sacred office.

a. *Pope Pius VII Chiaramonti (r. 1800–1823). The twenty-fourth year of his*
pontificate ran from 14 March 1823 through 20 August 1823 (the date of his
death).
b. *The friezes in the interior of the arch depict the triumph celebrated by Ti-*
tus and Vespasian for the capture of Jerusalem in 70. The cult objects taken
from the Second Temple are prominently displayed (cf. 2.14, note c).
c. *The restoration of the Arch of Titus was undertaken by the architect*
Giuseppe Valadier during the French occupation of Rome (1809–1814).
Here as elsewhere in the city, Pius VII appropriated credit for projects ini-
tiated by the French (see 3.2C, note b, 10.3.i, note b, and 11.2, note a).

2.9B   Arch of Titus: Dedication by S.P.Q.R.

SENATVS

POPVLVSQVE ROMANVS

DIVO TITO DIVI VESPASIANI F

VESPASIANO AVGVSTO

3. DIVO : *See 2.4, line 1.* — TITO . . . AVGVSTO : *In his own inscriptions, Titus is generally styled* Imperator Titus Caesar Vespasianus Augustus. *The Greek transliteration of such names as* Vespasiānus (Οὐεσπασιανός) *furnishes corroborative evidence that in* CL *consonantal* v *had the value* /w/. *Its passage to a fricative is attested by confusion with* B *as early as the first century (see 4.7B).* — F(īliō).

2.10   S. Sebastiano al Palatino: Dedication

SANCTO SEBASTIANO

CHRISTI MILITI ET MARTYRI

ECCLESIAE DEFENSORI

IN HIPPODROMO PALATII

5   FVSTIBVS AD NECEM VSQVE CÆSO

S

1. SEBASTIANO : *The name* Sebastiānus *is a derivative of Greek* σεβαστός *('reverend'), like* Christiānus < Χριστός *(cf. 1.7A, line 8).*
2. CHRISTI : *See 1.6A.ii, line 6.* — MARTYRI : *The* EL martyr *transliterates Greek* μάρτυς *('witness', then* EG *'martyr'). The Greek* Y *was first represented in Latin by* v; *as* Y *had a sound* /y/ *unknown in Latin (as in Fr.* lune), *in the first century* BC *the letter* Y *was introduced to distinguish it. In the common speech, this* /y/ *was assimiliated to the native* /i/.
3. ECCLESIAE : *See 1.7A, line 6.*
6. s(acrum).

Attic, E Side

The Senate
and People of Rome
to the Divine Titus Vespasian Augustus,[a]
son of the Divine Vespasian.

a. *Titus Flavius Vespasianus (r. 79–81) is conventionally styled 'Titus' to distinguish him from his homonymous father 'Vespasian' (see 2.4, note a). He conquered Jerusalem in 70 and celebrated a joint triumph with his father the following year. Titus was granted the* TRIBUNICIAN POWER *on 1 July 71 and succeeded his father on 24 June 79. The designation 'Divine' indicates that Titus was dead by the time the arch was dedicated (see* DIVUS*).*

Via di S. Bonaventura: Above Gate

Sacred
to Saint Sebastian,[a]
soldier and martyr of Christ,
defender of the Church,
beaten to death with cudgels
in the Palatine hippodrome.[b]

a. *St. Sebastian was martyred under Diocletian (r. 284–305) and buried near the site of the* BASILICA *on the Via Appia that bears his name (cf. 6.11). According to legend, he was a soldier whom Diocletian ordered shot for refusing to renounce his faith. He survived—to be beaten to death with clubs. The subject of his martyrdom was taken up with relish by artists of the Renaissance, to whom it furnished a pious pretext for depicting a comely and undraped youth transfixed by arrows.*

b. *The oval garden at the SE margin of the Palatine was called the 'hippodrome'.*

2.11A   Arch of Constantine: Dedication by S.P.Q.R.

i.

IMP CAES FL CONSTANTINO MAXIMO

P F AVGVSTO S P Q R

QVOD INSTINCTV DIVINITATIS MENTIS

MAGNITVDINE CVM EXERCITV SVO

5   TAM DE TYRANNO QVAM DE OMNI EIVS

FACTIONE VNO TEMPORE IVSTIS

REM PVBLICAM VLTVS EST ARMIS

ARCVM TRIVMPHIS INSIGNEM DICAVIT

1. IMP(erātōrī) CAES(arī) FL(āviō).
2. P(iō) F(ēlīcī). — S(enātus) P(opulus) Q(ue) R(ōmānus).
3–7. QVOD ... VLTVS EST : *Here, the 'virtual' indirect discourse is avoided* (*cf. 1.6B, lines 5–7*). — INSTINCTV DIVINITATIS MENTIS | MAGNI-TVDINE : *Note the word-order* (A-B-B-A). *Such a structure is called 'chiasmus'* (*Greek* χιασμός, *'figure in the form of the letter chi', i.e.,* x). — IVSTIS ... ARMIS : *The hyperbaton* (*see 9.9.i, line 2*) *lends special weight to the word* IVSTIS.

ii.

LIBERATORI VRBIS   FVNDATORI QVIETIS

iii.

VOTIS X   VOTIS XX

SIC X   SIC XX

1. VOTIS X : *decennālibus* (*sc.* solūtīs). — VOTIS XX : *vīcennālibus* (*sc.* susceptīs).
2. SIC X : *decennālibus* (*sc.* solūtīs). — SIC XX : *vīcennālibus* (*sc.* susceptīs).

Attic, Passageway and Frieze

Attic

The Senate and People of Rome
dedicated this arch, distinguished by his triumphs,
to Imperator Caesar Flavius Constantinus Maximus
Pius Felix Augustus,[a]
for having with his army, by divine prompting[b]
and greatness of mind,
avenged the state with righteous arms at once
against both the tyrant and his entire faction.[c]

a. *The emperor Constantine I (r. 306–337) assumed the title* Maximus Augustus *on 29 October 312, the day after he defeated his rival Maxentius at the Battle of the Milvian Bridge N of Rome.*

b. *This studiedly vague expression makes allusion to the intervention of the Christian god, supposed to have prompted Constantine to emblazon his soldiers' shields with the Cross (see 4.2L, note a).*

c. *The emperors and usurpers of the later Empire regularly branded their rivals 'tyrants'.*

Passageway

To the Liberator of the City.   To the Establisher of Peace.

Frieze, N and S

Vows for the tenth redeemed.[a]   Vows for the twentieth undertaken.
Thus for the tenth.   Thus for the twentieth.

a. *Constantine celebrated the* decennalia *('tenth anniversary') of his accession on 25 July 315. By inclusive reckoning, this was the tenth year since his acclamation as* Augustus *at York on the death of his father, Constantius Chlorus (25 July 306). Emperors made public vows in order to obtain divine favor. These were regularly undertaken and redeemed over a stipulated term (normally five or ten years). The redemption ordinarily involved a sacrifice to the deity or an offering at his or her temple. The ecclesiastical historian Eusebius notes with satisfaction that Constantine's* decennalia *were celebrated 'without fire and without smoke' (i.e., without the apparatus of pagan sacrifice).*

2.11B Arch of Constantine: Commemoration of Clement XII

CLEMENTI XII

PONT MAX

QVOD ARCVM

IMP CONSTANTINO MAGNO

5   ERECTVM

OB RELATAM SALVTARI

CRVCIS SIGNO

PRAECLARAM DE MAXENTIO

VICTORIAM

10   IAM TEMPORVM INIVRIA

FATISCENTEM

VETERIBVS REDDITIS

ORNAMENTIS RESTITVERIT

ANNO D MDCCXXXIII

15   PONT III

S P Q R

OPTIMO PRINCIPI

AC PRISTINAE MAIESTATIS

VRBIS ADSERTORI

20   POS

1. CLEMENTI XII : Duodecimō.
2. PONT(ificī) MAX(imō).
3–13. QVOD . . . RESTITVERIT : *On the construction, see 1.6B, lines 5–7.*
4. IMP(erātōrī).
6–9. OB RELATAM . . . VICTORIAM : *On the construction, see 1.7A, lines 2–3.*
— SALVTARI : *In* EL, salūtāris *is 'saving', 'salvific'.*
8. DE MAXENTIO : *On the use of the Prep., see 1.4, line 2.*
14. D(ominī) MDCCXXXIII : Mīllēsimō septingentēsimō trīcēsimō tertiō.
15. PONT(ificātūs) III : Tertiō.
16. S(enātūs) P(opulus) Q(ue) R(ōmānus).
20. POS(uit).

W Side

The Senate and People of Rome
set this up
to Clement the Twelfth,[a]
Supreme Pontiff,
most excellent Prince
and protector
of the City's ancient grandeur,
because
having returned
its ancient embellishments
he restored the arch[b]
erected to the emperor
Constantine the Great
for the famous victory
won over Maxentius[c]
through the saving emblem of the Cross,[d]
now deteriorating
under the assault of time,
in the year of the Lord 1733,
third of his office.

a. *Pope Clement XII Corsini (r. 1730–1740). The third year of his pontificate ran from 12 July 1732 through 11 July 1733.*

b. *The Arch of Constantine is the largest of the three such monuments that survive at Rome (cf. 2.3 and 2.9). It features a patchwork of elements pillaged from older structures. The columns of yellow Numidian marble date perhaps to the Flavian period; the panels in the interior of the passage likely came from a monument of either Domitian or Trajan; the eight roundels mounted in pairs on the N and S faces are from a monument of either Hadrian or Antoninus Pius; and the reliefs framing the inscription are assigned to the reign of Marcus Aurelius—the spoils of two centuries.*

c. *See 2.11A.i, note a.*

d. *See 4.2L, note a.*

2.12A   Colosseum: Dedication by Benedict XIV

AMPHITHEATRVM FLAVIVM

TRIVMPHIS SPECTACVLISQ INSIGNE

DIIS GENTIVM IMPIO CVLTV DICATVM

MARTYRVM CRVORE AB IMPVRA SVPERSTITIONE EXPIATVM

5   NE FORTITVDINIS EORVM EXCIDERET MEMORIA

MONVMENTVM

A CLEMENTE X P M

AN IVB MDCLXXV

PARIETINIS DEALBATIS DEPICTVM TEMPORVM INIVRIA DELETVM

10   BENEDICTVS XIV PONT M

MARMOREVM REDDI CVRAVIT

AN IVB MDCCL PONT X

2. SPECTACVLISQ(ue).

3. DIIS : *Like* quum (*see 2.12B, line 2*), *a late and artificial form. The regular* CL *declension of the Pl. of* deus *is* dī, deōrum, dīs, deōs, dīs. *The forms* deī *and* deīs, *for their part, first become common in the Augustan period.* — GENTIVM : *In* EL, *the* gentēs *are 'heathen' or 'pagans'.*

4. CRVORE : *Cf. 13.5.vii, line 3.* — SVPERSTITIONE : *In* EL, superstitiō *is used of all pre-Christian cult.*

7. CLEMENTE X : Decimō. — P(ontifice) M(aximō).

8. AN(nō) IVB(ilaeī) : *Deriving through* EG ἰωβηλαῖος *from Hebrew* yōbēl ('*ram's horn', the instrument employed to proclaim the festival of the Jubilee, Lev. 25:9*), *the* EL iōbēlēus *was assimilated to the unrelated Latin verb* iūbilāre ('*whoop', 'rejoice') to produce* iūbilaeus *and* iūbilaeum. — MDCLXXV : Mīllēsimō sescentēsimō septuāgēsimō quīntō.

10. BENEDICTVS XIV : Quārtus decimus. — PONT(ifex) M(aximus).

11. REDDI CVRAVIT : *With* cūrāre, *the gerundive construction is usual in* CL (*cf.* STATVENDA CVRAVERE, *1.4, line 6*).

12. AN(nō) IVB(ilaeī) MDCCL : Mīllēsimō septingentēsimō quīnquāgēsimō. — PONT(ificātūs) X : Decimō.

W Side, Upper

The Flavian Amphitheater,[a]
distinguished by triumphs and spectacles,
dedicated to the gods of the heathen in unholy reverence,
purified of unclean superstition by the blood of the martyrs.

In the year of the Jubilee 1750,[b] tenth of his office,
lest memory of their courage should lapse,
Benedict the Fourteenth,[c] Supreme Pontiff,
undertook to have rendered in marble
the memorial painted on the whitewashed tumbledown walls
in the year of the Jubilee 1675
by Clement the Tenth, Supreme Pontiff,[d]
and effaced under the assault of time.

a. *'Flavian Amphitheater' is the proper name of the Colosseum, begun under the emperor Vespasian (see 2.4, note a) and completed by his younger son, Domitian (r. 81–96). The building's exterior is organized in arcades framed by superimposed orders of engaged columns hierarchically arranged (Doric, Ionic, Composite; see 1.7B, note b), a motif destined for a long vogue in European architecture. The name 'Colosseum' is attested only after the year 1000; it alludes to the Colossus of Nero. A prophecy falsely attributed to the Venerable Bede (c. 673–735) has been erroneously thought to pertain to the amphitheater rather than the statue:* Quandiu stat Colysaeus, stat et Roma; quando cadet Colysaeus, cadet et Roma; quando cadet Roma, cadet et mundus. *Byron translates: 'While stands the Coliseum, Rome shall stand; | When falls the Coliseum, Rome shall fall; | And when Rome falls—the world'* (Childe Harold's Pilgrimage, *canto IV, stanza 145).*

b. *See 7.4H, note b.*

c. *Pope Benedict XIV Lambertini (r. 1740–1758). The tenth year of his pontificate ran from 17 August 1749 through 16 August 1750. In 1749 Benedict consecrated the Colosseum to the 'Passion of Christ and the Martyrs'. The erroneous belief that Christian martyrs had suffered there helped to put an end to the use of the building as a quarry.*

d. *Pope Clement X Altieri (r. 1670–1676).*

2.12B   Colosseum: Dedication by Pius IX

PIVS IX PONT MAX

QVVM PARTEM MEDIAM AD ESQVILIAS CONVERSAM

VETVSTATE FATISCENTEM

RESTITVENDAM ET MVNIENDAM CVRASSET

5   MEMORIAM RENOVAVIT

ANNO MDCCCLII PONT VII

1. PIVS IX : Nōnus. — PONT(ifex) MAX(imus).

2. QVVM = cum : *The late spelling* quum *constitutes an abortive essay in archaism. The* CL cum *represents an original* quom *(reconstructed* *kʷom*); as the* /o/ *before the final consonant proceeded to* /u/ *well after the labial element of the* /kʷ/ *had been lost, the* qu- *and* -um *belong to wholly separate phases of the word's phonological history.*

4. CVRASSET = cūrāvisset.

6. MDCCCLII : Mīllēsimō octingentēsimō quīnquāgēsimō secundō. — PONT(ificātūs) VII : Septimō.

2.13A   S. Francesca Romana: Dedication by Paul V

PAVLO V BVRGHESIO ROMANO P M

SEDENTE

OLIVETANA CONGREGATIO SVIS

ET MONASTERII SVMPTIBVS

5   TEMPLVM HOC IN HANC FORMAM

CONSTRVXIT ET ORNAVIT

ANNO DOMINI MDCXV

1. PAVLO V : Quīntō. — P(ontifice) M(aximō).

3. OLIVETANA CONGREGATIO : *In* EL, congregātiō *is a group of monasteries united under a superior but retaining individual autonomy. The* LL *epithet* olīvetānus *is Adj. to* olīvetum *('olive orchard'); in the Latin Gospels, the Mount of Olives is sometimes referred to as* mons qui vocatur oliveti *('the mount which is called that of the olive orchard').*

4. MONASTERII : *The* EL monastērium *transliterates* EG μοναστήριον *('monk's cell', then 'monastery'; cf. 5.5A, line 10).*

7. MDCXV : Mīllēsimō sescentēsimō quīntō decimō.

W Side, Lower

> *Pius the Ninth,[a] Supreme Pontiff,*
> *renovated the memorial[b]*
> *after undertaking to have the central portion facing the Esquiline,[c]*
> *which was deteriorating with age,*
> *restored and reinforced,*
> *in the year 1852, seventh of his office.*

a. Pope Pius IX Mastai-Ferretti (r. 1846–1878). The seventh year of his pontificate ran from 16 June 1852 through 15 June 1853 (cf. 15.4H, note a). Pius IX was the last Papa Re ('Sovereign Pontiff'). Having witnessed the absorption of the thousand-year-old papal state into the kingdom of Italy in 1870, he ended his days a self-styled prisoner in the Vatican (cf. 8.7B.ii, note b). His many monuments in the city of Rome include the Column of the Immaculate Conception (9.8).

b. See 2.12A.

c. I.e., the NE side of the ellipse described by the plan of the building.

Façade, above Portal

> *During the reign of Paul the Fifth Borghese[a]*
> *of Rome,*
> *the Congregation of the Olivetans[b]*
> *at their own expense and that of the monastery*
> *built and embellished this church[c]*
> *on the present lines*
> *in the year of the Lord 1615.*

a. Pope Paul V Borghese (r. 1605–1621).

b. The Olivetans are a CONGREGATION of Benedictine monks founded in 1319 by Bernardo Ptolomei at Monte Oliveto near Siena.

c. The church occupies the site of a shrine built on the site where St. Peter was believed to have knelt in prayer in order to bring down the diabolical Simon Magus (cf. Acts 8:9–24), who had employed his black arts to take flight. A paving stone from the Sacra Via bearing the prints of the apostle's knees is preserved in the right transept of the church, the structure of which dates to the reign of Pope St. Leo IV (r. 847–855). For a similar relic, see 6.8.

2.13B   S. Francesca Romana: Dedication

VIRG MARIAE AC S FRANCISCAE

VIRG(inī). — MARIAE : *On the name, see* 15.4G, *line 1.* — S(ānctae). — FRANCISCAE : *The Ital. name Francesca, here Latinized, is the feminine counterpart of Francesco, which owes its origin as a Christian name to St. Francis of Assisi (c. 1181–1226). Baptized Giovanni, he was nicknamed Francesco ('Frenchy') by his father, who had a French connection both through his wife (who was Provençal) and through the cloth trade.*

2.13C   Commemoration of Gregory XI

GREGORIO XI LEMOVICENSI
HVMANITATE DOCTRINA PIETATEQ ADMIRABILI
QVI VT ITALIAE SEDITIONIBVS LABORANT MEDERETVR
SEDEM PONTIFICIAM AVENIONI DIV TRANSLATAM
5   DIVINO AFFLATVS NVMINE HOMINVMQ MAXIMO PLAVSV
POST ANNOS SEPTVAGINTA ROMAM FELICITER REDVXIT
PONTIFICATVS SVI VII
S P Q R TANTAE RELIGIONIS ET BENEFICII NON IMMEMOR
GREGORIO XIII PONT OPT MAX COMPROBANTE
10   ANNO AB ORBE REDEMPTO CIƆ IƆ LXXXIIII POS
(*Names of Magistrates*)

1. GREGORIO XI : Ūndecimō. — LEMOVICENSI : *The* ML *Adj.* Lemo-vīcēnsis *answers to the toponym* Lemovīcum (*mod.* Limoges).
2. PIETATEQ(ue).
3. LABORANT(ī).
4. AVENIONI : *The* ML *toponym is* Aveniō (*mod.* Avignon).
5. DIVINO ... NVMINE HOMINVMQ(ue) ... PLAVSV : *A mild syllepsis. Syllepsis* (*Greek* ζεῦγμα, *'yoking'*) *is the association with one verb of two nouns in different constructions* (*Abl. of Instrument and Abl. of Manner*).
7. VII : Septimō.
8. S(enātus) P(opulus) Q(ue) R(ōmānus).
9. GREGORIO XIII : Tertiō decimō. — PONT(ifice) OPT(imō) MAX(imō).
10. CIƆ IƆ LXXXIIII : Mīllēsimō quīngentēsimō octōgēsimō quārtō. *On the notation, see* 1.3, *line 6.* — POS(uit).

Façade, above Portal

To the Virgin and Saint Frances.[a]

a. *Constrained at the age of twelve to marry Lorenzo de' Ponziani, Francesca Bussa de Leoni (1384–1440) pursued her religious vocation within the confines of matrimony. Daily bouts of demonic possession notwithstanding, 'Ceccolella' (as the Romans christened her) converted her home into a refuge for the aged, hungry, and infirm. Canonized in 1608, she is best known as 'Santa Francesca Romana'.*

S Transept, Rear Wall

In the year 1584 after the world's redemption, with the approval of Gregory the Thirteenth,[a] Supreme and most excellent Pontiff, the Senate and People of Rome, not unmindful of such great piety and so great a boon, set this up to Gregory the Eleventh of Limoges,[b] of marvelous learning and piety, who in the seventh year of his office, that he might bring healing to an Italy that was laboring under party strife,[c] by the influence of divine inspiration and with the emphatic approbation of men, auspiciously restored to Rome after a period of seventy years the papal see, long since transferred to Avignon.
(Names of Magistrates)

a. *Pope Gregory XIII Boncompagni (r. 1572–1585).*
b. *Pope Gregory XI de Beaufort (r. 1370–1378). Gregory is best remembered for ending the seventy-year* BABYLONIAN CAPTIVITY *of the Holy See at Avignon. He was the last French pope. Though resolved from the outset to go to Rome, Gregory had first to mediate the Hundred Years' War between France and England and to tame the Visconti of Milan. With the support of St. Catherine of Siena and others, in 1377 he transferred his court to Rome. The schism that erupted during the reign of his successor, Urban VI, which would culminate in a trio of claimants to the throne of St. Peter, was ended only in 1417 with the election of Pope Martin V (see 7.4G).*
c. *In addition to the threat posed by the aggressive Visconti, Gregory was faced with a revolt in the papal state provoked by Florence. At his death, the conflict remained unresolved.*

2.14 SS. Cosma e Damiano: Dedication by Felix IV

AVLA D̄Ī CLARIS RADIAT SPECIOSA METALLIS

IN QVA PLVS FIDEI LVX PRETIOSA MICAT

MARTYRIBVS MEDICIS POPVLO SPES CERTA SALVTIS

VENIT ET EX SACRO CREVIT HONORE LOCVS

5 OPTVLIT HOC DN̄O FELIX ANTISTITE DIGNVM

MVNVS VT AETHERIA VIVAT IN ARCE POLI

Three ELEGIAC COUPLETS

1. AVLA : *In* EL, aula (*'court', 'hall'*) *is regularly 'church'.* — D(e)I. —
   METALLIS : *In* LL metallum *is used of the colored* tesserae *of mosaic
   work (cf. 3.5A, line 1, 8.8B, line 1, and 13.13A, line 1).*
3. MARTYRIBVS : *See 2.10, line 2.*
5. OPTVLIT = obtulit : *The spelling is phonetic (see 2.6B, line 5).* —
   D(omi)NO. — ANTISTITE : *See 3.3C, line 13.*
6. AETHERIA : *The* CL aetherius *transliterates Greek* αἰθέριος (*'belonging
   to the upper air', 'celestial'*). *In early Greek cosmology,* aethēr (αἰθήρ) *was
   the bright upper air of the heavens as opposed to the gross and heavy* āēr
   (ἀήρ), *or terrestrial atmosphere.* — ARCE POLI : *The* CL polus *transliterates Greek* πόλος (*'end of an axis or pole'*); *it is used of the North Pole
   and, by synecdoche, of the celestial vault as a whole. Synecdoche (Greek*
   συνεκδοχή, *'understanding one thing by another') is the rhetorical use of
   a part to signify the whole.*

2.15 Carcer: Dedication by Rufinus and Nerva

C VIBIVS C F RVFINVS M COCCEIV[S] NERVA ¬

COS EX S C

1. C(āius) : *On the abbreviation, see 1.1, line 1.* — C(āiī) F(īlius). —
   M(ārcus). — CO(n)S(ulēs) : *The familiar abbreviation* COSS (*or* CONSS)
   for cōnsulēs *becomes current only in the fourth century.* — S(enātūs)
   C(ōnsultō) : *On the formula, see 2.8.*

Apse

The house of God shines in beauty with bright enamels [a]
in which gleams the light of faith, more precious still. From the
martyred physicians [b] *sure hope of salvation comes to the people,*
and it is out of their sacred honor that this place has waxed great.
Felix [c] *made this offering to the Lord, a gift worthy of the bishop,*
that he may gain life in the ethereal height of heaven.

> Three ELEGIAC COUPLETS

a. *The mosaic depicts Christ rising above the blood-red clouds of the dawn
of the Last Day. To his left, St. Peter presents St. Cosmas, with his martyr's crown, and St. Theodore; to his right, St. Paul presents the similarly
crowned St Damian and Pope Felix IV, who holds a model of the church.*
b. *According to legend, Cosmas and Damian were twin brothers renowned
for their surgical skill. Condemned under Diocletian for refusing to offer
sacrifice, they were beheaded.*
c. *Pope St. Felix IV (r. 526–530). From the Ostrogothic king Theoderic (r.
493–526) and his daughter Amalasuntha Felix received in gift a hall of
Vespasian's Temple of Peace. Dedicated in 75, Vespasian's complex had
housed the spoils of the Second Temple (cf. 2.9A, note b). The fact that
it accommodated a center of medical learning may have motivated the
dedication of the church to Cosmas and Damian, known in Greek as the
anargyroi, the physicians who accepted no payment.*

Carcer: Façade

Gaius Vibius Rufinus, son of Gaius, and Marcus Cocceius Nerva,
in accordance with a decree of the Senate. [a]

a. *The carcer ('prison') consists of two superimposed cells excavated into the
flank of the Capitoline Hill. In the lower cell, enemies of the state—including Jugurtha, Vercingetorix, and the Catilinarian conspirators—were
put to death. The present inscription records a restoration carried out by
Rufinus and Nerva, Suffect Consuls some time between AD 39 and 42 (see
CONSUL). In the Middle Ages, this was erroneously believed to have been
the place of St. Peter's imprisonment (see 3.4B, note b, and 6.8, note a).*

BASILICA DI SANTA PUDENZIANA

Its conventional appearance notwithstanding, the Basilica di Santa Pudenziana incorporates and preserves—substantially intact—the courtyard of an ancient insula ('apartment block'). Here a house of worship was improvised late in the fourth century. Some four hundred years thereafter, the building was given basilical form by replacing the pillars and arcades of the courtyard with columns. Santa Pudenziana is the only building in Rome which demonstrably was employed as a place of public Christian assembly before its architectural conversion into a church.

III. The Subura & Environs

IN ANTIQUITY, THE SUBURA, the valley that stretches to the northeast of the Forum, formed one of the most densely inhabited neighborhoods of the city. Unhealthy, overcrowded, and prone to fire, the Subura
of early imperial Rome is immortalized in the poems of Martial and Ju-
venal, who complain of its noise, dirt, and perilous multistoried *insulae*
('apartment blocks'). The Subura was adjacent to the Roman Forum.
Owing to insufficiency of space in that ancient and congested precinct,
the lower reaches of the Subura were gradually swallowed up by a series of new forum complexes extending from the Velia — the low hill that
bridged the gap between the Oppian and Palatine Hills — to the southeastern margin of the Campus Martius.

In order to accommodate the Forum of Trajan (r. AD 98–117), the low
saddle that united the Quirinal and Capitoline Hills was quarried away;
the conceit of the dedication of the COLUMN OF TRAJAN is that the
top of its shaft marks the elevation of the vanished ridge. Around 1540,
Pope Paul III (r. 1534–1549) isolated the column from surrounding structures; after a lapse of over 250 years, Paul's project was resumed by the
French authorities during the Napoleonic occupation of Rome (1809–
1814), to be completed under PIUS VII (r. 1800–1823). Today the column
is crowned by a STATUE OF ST. PETER: Pope Sixtus V (r. 1585–1590), famous for reerecting the Egyptian obelisks of ancient Rome, purged the
monument of its pagan associations by setting atop it an image of the
apostle.

The main thoroughfare of the ancient Subura was the Argiletum (today's Via della Madonna dei Monti); it provided communication between
the monumental center of Rome and the highlands to the northeast.
At the foot of the Cispian Hill, which projects deep into the valley between the Viminal and Oppian, the Argiletum was obliged to make a
fork; this feature of Rome's ancient street system was doubtless prefig-
ured in the footpaths trodden by Rome's Iron Age inhabitants. The Vicus

3.2B

3.2C
3.2A

Patricius (modern Via Urbana) branched to the north; in the Middle Ages, this route furnished the principal access to Santa Maria Maggiore and San Lorenzo beyond. To the east climbed the Clivus Suburanus (modern Via in Selci—Via di S. Martino ai Monti—Via di S. Vito). With the loss of the aqueducts in the Gothic wars of the sixth century, the highlands of Rome were gradually abandoned. By the eleventh century, the Subura itself had become largely deserted.

The hills that surround the Subura are distinguished by four *tituli* ('titular churches') of high antiquity. According to tradition Pope St. Cletus, Peter's successor as Bishop of Rome, had ordained presbyters for the city's twenty-five Christian congregations. These congregations came in time to be identified as the predecessors of the twenty-five ancient *tituli* that were eventually made the honorary charge of 'titular' cardinals. Now, it is virtually certain that Rome's earliest Christians met in *domus ecclesiae* ('houses of the church'). Near the end of his Epistle to the Romans, St. Paul sends greetings to Aquila and Prisca 'and the church that meets in their house' (καὶ τὴν κατ᾽ οἶκον αὐτῶν ἐκκλησίαν). It was consequently inferred that the *tituli* were originally domestic properties put at the disposal of the Christian community in the centuries before the church could hold legal title; the term *titulus* (Lit., 'title') will have referred to a plaque affixed to the house to identify the owner. When the *domus ecclesiae* began to be replaced by purpose-built churches in the age of Constantine, the memory of the original donors was preserved in their names: 'Titulus of Pudens', 'Titulus of Lucina', and so forth.

Most *tituli* did indeed replace domestic structures, but the idea that they are the direct descendants of Rome's earliest places of Christian worship rests on the assumption that the use of a given house by Christians in the first three centuries was necessarily followed by the foundation of a church there in the fourth. The difficulty lies in the fact that no structure surviving beneath a *titulus* has been identified, whether by graffiti or decoration, as a *domus ecclesiae*. Given the density of imperial Rome, virtually every *titulus* will have replaced some preexisting structure, yet there is no decisive archeological evidence that any of them represents the continuation of a house church. Not even the domestic oratory that survives beneath Santi Giovanni e Paolo can be shown to have served as a place of public Christian assembly before the establishment of a *titulus* on its site.

In all likelihood, most of the *tituli* originated as donations made no earlier than the era of Constantine. Indeed, the ecclesiastical entities to which the term *titulus* was applied in the mid-fourth century appear to have reproduced in miniature the essentials of the great Constantinian foundations—namely, a meeting hall, liturgical equipment, and a source of revenue to support clergy. Rather than the assembly place of a primitive congregation, the location of any given *titulus* most likely represents a site where some wealthy donor either happened to own a parcel of property or acquired land for the church at the request of ecclesiastical authorities. The many edifying foundation narratives of the *tituli*—the martyrdom of Pudentiana or Cecilia, of John and Paul or Callistus—must be consigned to the realm of pious imagination. In its zeal, the Roman hagiographical industry of the fifth and sixth centuries readily identified the site of the church where a saint was particularly venerated with the scene of his or her martyrdom.

At the head of the valley separating the Viminal and Cispian Hills stands the Basilica of Santa Pudenziana, long venerated as the most ancient *titulus* of the city—*omnium urbis ecclesiarum vetustissima*. Legend holds that soon after his arrival in the city in AD 42, the Apostle Peter baptized the senator Quintus Cornelius Pudens; the senator's children—Pudentiana, Praxedis, Timotheus, and Novatus—were converted as well. Entrusted after his death to a priest called 'Pastor', the house of Pudens became the city's first *titulus* and the seat of Peter's earliest successors. The church that replaced the *titulus* was founded in the second century by Pope St. Pius I (r. c. 142–c. 155). It was installed in a domestic bathhouse that had been constructed by Novatus on an adjacent property. At the request of Praxedis, the church was named after Pudentiana,

3.6A   who had devoted her short life to the pious labor of collecting the REL-
ICS OF MARTYRS.

So much for the legend. Archeology reveals that the church occupies
not a bath but the internal court of a second-century *insula*. The court
was supported on a vaulted substructure that accommodated streetfront
shops. Brick stamps of the second century bear the name 'Quintus Ser-
vilius Pudens'. It is plausible that a fourth-century scion of the family
who had inherited the property donated it to the church. Epigraphical
evidence indicates that by the 380s the site hosted a congregation and
clergy—sure sign that a *titulus* had been founded. Though remodeled as
a basilica in the eighth century, the hall that forms the church's core pre-
3.6B   serves the structure of the ancient *insula* intact; the MOSAIC of the apse
is the oldest figural representation in the medium to survive in a Roman
church. The legendary character of its earliest history notwithstanding,
the Basilica of Santa Pudenziana enjoys a distinction as the only surviving Christian structure at Rome shown to have been employed for
public worship before being architecturally converted into a church.

Rising upon the northern brow of the Oppian Hill, the Basilica of
San Pietro in Vincoli is a leading monument of the 'imperial' papacy
that emerged over the three-quarters century between Popes St. Damasus I (r. 366–384) and St. Leo I (r. 440–461). The great hilltop basilicas
of Santa Sabina and Santa Maria Maggiore belong to the same period.
Like the latter, San Pietro in Vincoli memorializes a victory of doctrine.
Philip, one of the church's presbyters, served as papal representative
at the Council of Ephesus (AD 431). Over the bitter opposition of Nestorius, Patriarch of Constantinople, the council vindicated the Virgin
Mary's title as *Theotókos* ('Mother of God'). On his return, Philip took
in hand the renovation of the church under the auspices of Pope St. Sixtus III (r. 432–440) and the empress Eudocia, who donated a chain by
which St. Peter himself was said to have been bound.

3.4D   The earliest literary evidence for the church is found in the DEDICA-
TORY INSCRIPTION OF SIXTUS III, the text of which is preserved in

medieval transcriptions. As for archeology, remains beneath the pavement show that the basilica was preceded by a *domus* that featured a modest apsidal hall; there is no evidence that this was used as a church. The present structure rises on the foundations of the *domus*, which had perhaps been ruined in the sack of Alaric (AD 410). Dedicated to Peter and Paul under the name *Basilica Apostolorum* ('Basilica of the Apostles'), it early acquired the popular name *ad vincula* attested in an inscription that commemorates the election of Pope JOHN II (r. 533–535). Other no- 3.4C
table monuments in San Pietro in Vincoli include the TOMBS OF NICH- 3.4A
OLAS OF CUSA and of the brothers POLLAIUOLO. 3.4B

Located on the eastern slope of the Quirinal Hill, the Basilica of Sant'Agata dei Goti constitutes a unique witness to the Gothic presence in the late fifth and early sixth centuries. The church was founded around AD 470 by Flavius Ricimer. Grandson of a Gothic king, Ricimer rose after the assassination of Valentinian III in 455 to become ruler of Italy and virtual kingmaker of the western Empire. The Goths had been converted by missionaries espousing an Arian Christology that rejected the orthodox doctrine of the coeternal Trinity. When they established kingdoms in the former territories of the western Empire in the course of the fourth and fifth centuries, they wore their heterodoxy as a badge of national honor. After their expulsion from Rome by Byzantine forces in 552, Sant'Agata dei Goti stood abandoned. Pope St. Gregory I (r. 590–604) rededicated it to ST. AGATHA, who had been credited 3.3A
with driving the Goths from her native Catania. The church houses the RELICS OF THE GREEK MARTYRS Hippolytus, Paulina, Hadrias, 3.3C
Maria, and Neon as well as the TOMB OF IANOS LASCARIS, a Greek 3.3B
humanist.

The Basilica of Santa Prassede stands on the ancient Clivus Suburanus, not far from Santa Maria Maggiore. This church is the most complete monument of the Carolingian Renaissance, when the papacy aspired to revive the glories of Constantine's Christian empire. Pope St. Paschal I (r. 817–824) sponsored a series of churches—including Santa

Maria in Domnica, Santa Cecilia, and this basilica—that looked to Constantinian precedents. Santa Prassede in fact replicates the plan of Old
St. Peter's, albeit on a much reduced scale. The MOSAIC of the apse depicts Christ at his second coming with Peter, Pudentiana, and Zeno to
his right and Paul and Prassede to his left, with Paschal. It is Paschal who
orchestrated the last great translation of the RELICS OF MARTYRS
from the extramural cemeteries.

3.5A

3.5B

In the early Middle Ages, the Cloaca Maxima, the sewer that drained
Rome's valleys, became obstructed. The lower Subura reverted to the
paludal conditions of prehistoric times. Passage through the zone—
called *dei Pantani* ('the Fens')—was eventually restricted to a circuitous
deviation that followed the high ground at the margins of the old imperial Fora. Because of its strategic location on the principal route between
the Vatican and the Lateran, by the thirteenth century the neighborhood bristled with fortified towers—so many indeed that it was known
as *Campo Torregiano* ('Field of Towers'). Of these, the most celebrated
is TOR DE' CONTI, so situated as to control traffic passing through the
valley between the Oppian Hill and Velia.

3.1

Though the upper reaches of the old Subura presented a rural aspect until the end of the nineteenth century, by the early Renaissance
the Pantani, like the quarters around Trevi and the Lateran, formed a
more or less isolated village within the city's walls. In the mid-sixteenth
century, Cardinal Michele Bonelli of Alessandria redeveloped the zone,
raising the ground level by about three meters and laying out Via Alessandrina, which extended from Palazzo Valentini to the foot of the Velia.
The roughly perpendicular Via Bonella opened a route from the Arch of
Septimius Severus to the Arco dei Pantani and the Subura beyond. The
quarter incorporated such venerable monuments as the Church of San
Basilio. With the addition of Renaissance palazzi and Baroque churches,
it constituted one of the city's most characteristic urban ensembles—
ancient, medieval, and modern interwoven in a dense fabric of eras and
styles.

In the nineteenth century, the isolation of the Column of Trajan and the opening of Via Cavour both inflicted damage on the Pantani, but it was the Fascist regime that effected the destruction not only of that quarter but of the entire zone between Piazza Venezia and the Colosseum. Demolition was initiated in 1930 and prosecuted with demonic fury, so that Via dei Monti (later Via dell'Impero, today's Via dei Fori Imperiali) might be inaugurated by Mussolini on 28 October 1932, the tenth anniversary of the Fascist March on Rome. The residents of the densely populated neighborhood were displaced to wretched *borgate*, hastily constructed settlements in the Campagna. The cost of the destruction is incalculable: apart from the eradication of an ancient and animated neighborhood—house and shop, street and piazza, palace and church—those monuments spared at its margins stand devoid of any physical or social context. Most melancholy of all, perhaps, are the ancient churches of the Sacra Via, which today turn their scarred and naked backs on an urban desert.

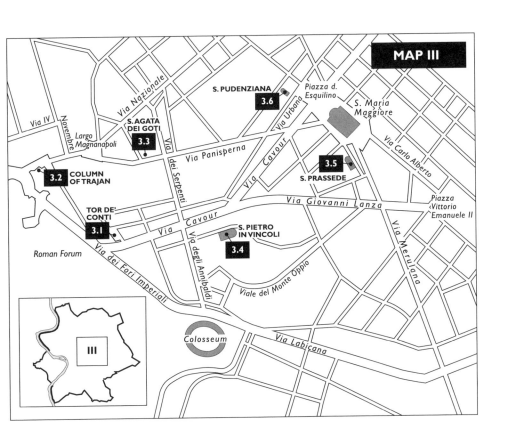

MAP III

S. PUDENZIANA

3.6

Piazza d.
Esquilino

S. Maria
Maggiore

Via Nazionale

Via IV

Novembre

Largo
Magnanapoli

S. AGATA
DEI GOTI

3.3

Via dei Serpenti

Via Panisperna

Via Urbano

Via Cavour

Via Carlo Alberto

COLUMN
OF TRAJAN

3.2

Via Cavour

S. PRASSEDE

3.5

Via Giovanni Lanza

Piazza
Vittorio
Emanuele II

TOR DE'
CONTI

3.1

Via Cavour

S. PIETRO
IN VINCOLI

3.4

Via degli Annibaldi

Via Merulana

Roman Forum

Via dei Fori Imperiali

Viale del Monte Oppio

III

Colosseum

Via Labicana

3.1 Tor de' Conti: Dedication by Pietro and Nicolò

HÆC DOM' Ē PETRI VALDE DEVOTA NYCOLE
STRENVV' ILLE FID' MILES FORTISSIM' ATQ'
CERNITE Q' VVLTIS SECV' HANC TRANSIRE Q'RITES
QVAM FORTI' INT' NIMIS COMPOSITA FORIS
5 EST VMQVĀ NVLLVS VOBIS Q' DICERE POSSIT

Five HEXAMETERS

1. DOM(us) : *In* ML, *the term* domus *('house') refers to a type of dwelling distinct from the* turris *('tower')*. — E(st). — NYCOLE = Nīcole : *Scans* Nīcōlae. *Because the sound of Greek* Υ *was assimiliated to that of Latin* I, *the two are frequently confused in spelling* (*see* 2.10, *line* 2). *On the* E, *see* 1.8B, *line* 5; *on the neglect of* H, *see* 8.8A, *line* 2.
2. STRENVV(s). — FID(us) : *Scans* fîdus. — FORTISSIM(us). — ATQ(ue) : *An indefensible emendation to* FID(ē) *and* AEQ(uē) *would improve both meter and sense* ('*A man steadfast in the faith, bravest of soldiers as well*').
3. Q(uī). — SECV(s) : *In* ML, secus *is used as a Prep. and Adv. with the sense 'beside', 'along'.* — Q(ui)RITES.
4. FORTI(s) : *Scans* fortīs. — INT(us). — NIMIS : *Scans* nīmis. — FORIS : *Scans* fōris.
5. VMQVA(m). — Q(uī).

3.2A Column of Trajan: Dedication by Sixtus V

SIXTVS V | B PETRO | APOST | PON A III

1. SIXTVS V : Quīntus.
2. B(eātō) PETRO : *The Latin* Petrus *transliterates the biblical* Πέτρος ('*rock*'), *a translation of the Aramaic name* Kêphā' *that appears in the New Testament as* Κηφᾶς. *Out of deference to St. Peter, the name has never been taken by a pope.*
3. APOST(olō) : *See* 1.61, *line* 7.
4. PON(tificātūs) A(nnō) III : Tertiō.

Tower, N Side

This is the house of Pietro, which is exceedingly loyal
to Nicolò, that mettlesome soldier, faithful and brave.[a]
Behold, citizens who wish to pass by: there is no one
who could ever tell you how extraordinarily strong it is
within, how very well constructed without.[b]

Five HEXAMETERS

a. *In an archival record of 1094 there appears one 'Nicolaus, filius Petri de*
Comite' (Nicolò, son of Pietro Conti). The plausibility of the identification
of this Pietro and Nicolò with those of the inscription is improved by the
date of the latter as suggested by analysis of the letter forms (late eleventh
or early twelfth century). If that is the case, the 'house' of the inscription is
assuredly not Tor de' Conti, constructed in 1203 by Pope Innocent III (Lo-
tario dei Conti di Segni). The most likely explanation is that the inscrip-
tion pertained to a preexisting unfortified dwelling (domus) of a type com-
mon in medieval Rome and was preserved when that house was replaced
by the tower.

b. *The tower excited the admiration of Petrarch, who mentions it in a letter*
penned not long after the earthquake of 1348 that caused the collapse of
its upper portion. Further collapses in the seventeenth century reduced the
structure to its present height of 29 meters.

Four Faces of Capital

Sixtus the Fifth,[a] to the Blessèd Apostle Peter,[b]
in the third year of his office.

a. *Pope Sixtus V Peretti (r. 1585–1590). The third year of his pontificate ran*
from 24 April 1587 through 23 April 1588.

b. *The bronze statue of St. Peter by Leonardo Sormani and Tommaso della*
Porta, set atop the column in 1587, occupies the same spot as an original
statue of Trajan (cf. 10.13.iv, note d). It seemed fitting that the image of
Trajan—Optimus Princeps (see 13.5.i, note a)—should be substituted by
that of the Prince of the Apostles.

3.2B   Column of Trajan: Dedication by S.P.Q.R.

SENATVS POPVLVSQVE ROMANVS

IMP CAESARI DIVI NERVAE F NERVAE

TRAIANO AVG GERM DACICO PONTIF

MAXIMO TRIB POT $\overline{\text{XVII}}$ IMP $\overline{\text{VI}}$ COS $\overline{\text{VI}}$ P P

5   AD DECLARANDVM QVANTAE ALTITVDINIS

MONS ET LOCVS TAN[tis oper]IBVS SIT EGESTVS

2. IMP(erātōrī). — DIVI : *See 2.4, line 1.* — F(īliō).

3. AVG(ustō). — GERM(ānicō). — PONTIF(icī).

4. TRIB(ūniciā) POT(estāte) $\overline{\text{XVII}}$: *Septimum decimum.* —
IMP(erātōrī) $\overline{\text{VI}}$: *Sextum.* — CO(n)S(ulī). — $\overline{\text{VI}}$: *Sextum.* — P(atrī)
P(atriae).

6. MONS ET LOCVS : *The complex idea 'elevated site' is expressed through a
pair of coordinated nouns ('hill and site'). This idiom is called 'hendiadys'
(Greek* ἓν διὰ δυοῖς: *'One [idea] through two [words]').* — TAN[tis oper]
IBVS : *The missing letters were damaged by grooves cut into the face of the
base to support the roof of the tiny Church of S. Nicola de Columna, for
which the column served as a ludicrously outsized belfry. They are restored
from the* EINSIEDELN CATALOGUE *(cf. 2.4, lines 1–2).*

3.2C   Forum of Trajan: Dedication by Pius VII

[p]IVS $\overline{\text{VII}}$ P M AN PONTIFICATVS SVI $\overline{\text{XV}}$

FORI TRAIANI AREAM

PRAECINCTIONIS OPERE ABSOLVTO

PODIO ET SCALIS EXSTRVCTIS

5   COLVMNARVM SCAPIS VETERI SEDE CONLOCATIS

IN HANC FORMAM REDIGI ORNARIQVE IVSSIT

1. [p]IVS $\overline{\text{VII}}$: *Septimus. The character in brackets is restored from context.*
— P(ontifex) M(aximus) AN(nō). — $\overline{\text{XV}}$: *Quīntō decimō.*

3. PRAECINCTIONIS : *The Roman architect Vitruvius uses the rare word
praecīnctiō for the walkway separating tiers of seats in a theater; here it
refers to the retaining wall that encloses the excavation.*

5. SCAPIS : *Among other things, the* CL *scapus denotes a variety of vertical
members in architecture, the shafts of columns included.*

Base, SE Side

The Senate and People of Rome
to Imperator Caesar Nerva Traianus Augustus Germanicus Dacicus,[a]
son of the Divine Nerva, Supreme Pontiff, vested with the Tribunician power
for the seventeenth time, acclaimed Imperator for the sixth, Consul for the sixth,
Father of his Country, in order to indicate how lofty was the hillside
removed through such mighty works.[b]

> a. *On his adoption by the emperor Nerva (r. 96–98), Marcus Ulpius*
> *Traianus (r. 98–117) was styled 'Imperator Caesar Nerva Traianus Augus-*
> *tus'. The title Germanicus was conferred jointly upon Nerva and Trajan*
> *in 97 for their victory over the Suebi in central Germany, while the title*
> *Dacicus was conferred on Trajan in 102 for his victory in Dacia. Like all*
> *the successors of Augustus, Trajan was granted the office of* SUPREME
> PONTIFF *on his accession. He assumed the* TRIBUNICIAN POWER *for the*
> *seventeenth time on 10 December 112, was saluted as* IMPERATOR *for the*
> *sixth time in 106 and became* CONSUL *for his sixth and final time on*
> *1 January 112. The title 'Father of his Country' was assumed by nearly all*
> *the emperors (see* PATER PATRIAE*).*
>
> b. *The column purports to indicate the original elevation of the site.*

Enclosure, SE Side

In the fifteenth year of his office Pius the Seventh,[a] *Supreme Pontiff,*
bade the zone of Trajan's Forum[b]
to be disposed and embellished on the present lines
by the completion of the enclosure,
the construction of the balustrade and steps,
and the setting of the shafts of the columns in their former place.

> a. *Pope Pius VII Chiaramonti (r. 1800–1823). The fifteenth year of his reign*
> *ran from 14 March 1814 through 13 March 1815.*
>
> b. *The excavations, carried out 1812–1814 by the French, uncovered a zone*
> *around the column amounting to roughly one-sixth of the Forum's total*
> *original area (cf. 2.9A, note c). The densely populated medieval quarter*
> *that surrounded the site was razed 1928–1934 for the construction of Via*
> *dei Monti (today's Via dei Fori Imperiali).*

3.3A S. Agata dei Goti: Dedication by Gregory XVI

D O M

TEMPLVM D AGATHÆ VIRG ET MART

EXPVLSIS PAGANIS DEITATIBVS

CONSTANTINI M IMP ÆVO DICATVM

5   A FL RICIMERO INSTAVRATVM OPERE MVSIVO

EXORNATVM ET GOTHICÆ IMPIETATI TRADITVM

GREGORIVS M AD VERVM CVLTVM

DEO CÆLESTIBVS PRODIGIIS ILLVSTRANTE

RESTITVIT A DXCI

10   IAMDIV INTER TITVLOS RECENSITVM

ASSIDVA CVRA A ROM PONTIFICIBVS

POTISSIMVM LEONE IX ET VRBANO VIII EXCVLTVM

GREGORIVS XVI PONTF MAX

COLLEGIO HIBERNENSIVM VRBANO

15   CVM ANNEXIS ÆDIBVS ET IVRIBVS CONCESSIT

A MDCCCXXXVI

1. D(eō) O(ptimō) M(aximō).

2. D(īvae) : *In* RL, dīvus *is used as an alternative to* sānctus *('saint')*; *similarly* templum *for* ecclēsia (*cf. 1.8G, line 5*). — VIRG(inis). — MART(yris) : *See 2.10, line 2.*

3. DEITATIBVS : *The* EL deitās *is 'deity', 'divinity'.*

4. M(agnī) IMP(erātōris).

5. FL(āviō). — MVSIVO : *The* LL mūsīvus *is 'of mosaic'.*

6. GOTHICÆ : *The Adj.* Gothicus *answers to* Gotthī (*cf. 1.61, line 2*).

7. M(agnus).

9. A(nnō) DXCI : Quīngentēsimō nōnāgēsimō prīmō.

10. TITVLOS : *See 3.6A, line 2.* — RECENSITVM = recēnsum : *In* LL, *certain verbs replaced the Part. in* -us *by one in* -ītus (*cf. Lat.* sēnsus > *Ital.* sentito).

11. ROM(ānīs).

12. LEONE IX : Nōnō. — VRBANO VIII : Octāvō.

13. GREGORIVS XVI : Sextus decimus. — PONT(i)F(ex) MAX(imus).

14. HIBERNENSIVM : *The* ML *Adj.* Hībernēnsis (*here used as a Subst.*) *answers to the toponym* Hībernia ('Ireland').

16. A(nnō) MDCCCXXXVI : Mīllēsimō octingentēsimō trīcēsimō sextō.

Portico, R of Entry

To God, best and greatest.
In the year 591,
as God lit the way with heavenly portents,
after the expulsion of the pagan divinities
Gregory the Great restored to the true cult
the Church of Saint Agatha, virgin and martyr,[a]
founded in the age of the emperor Constantine the Great,
restored, embellished with mosaic work,
and given over to the impiety of the Goths by Flavius Ricimer.[b]
Long enumerated among the Titles,[c]
refined by the unremitting pains of the Roman pontiffs—
particularly Leo the Ninth[d] and Urban the Eighth[e]—
in the year 1836
Gregory the Sixteenth,[f] Supreme Pontiff,
granted it along with its associated buildings and rights
to the Collegium Hibernensium Urbanum.[g]

a. *The date of St. Agatha's martyrdom is unknown. It involved the amputa-tion of her breasts, which in art frequently appear inverted on a platter:
By a natural if surprising misinterpretation of this iconographic attribute,
Agatha came to be venerated as the patron of bell founders.*

b. *The church was in fact founded around 470 by the Roman general Ricimer,
grandson of the Gothic king Vallia. After the expulsion of the Arian (or,
more correctly, 'homoean') Goths, who denied the consubstantiality of the
Son and the Father, Pope St. Gregory I (r. 590–604) reconsecrated it to
St. Agatha, who had been credited with driving the Goths from her native
Catania. On that occasion—according to a legend reminiscent of biblical
events at Gadara—the demons introduced by the practice of the heretical
cult issued from the church in the guise of a herd of swine (see Matt. 8:32).*

c. *See 3.6A, note a.*

d. *Pope St. Leo IX (r. 1049–1054).*

e. *Pope Urban VIII Barberini (r. 1621–1644).*

f. *Pope Gregory XVI Cappellari (r. 1831–1846).*

g. *The church remained in the charge of the Irish College at Rome until 1926.
It now belongs to the Padri Stimmatini (the 'Stigmatines').*

3.3B Epitaph of Ianos and Katerina Lascaris

ΛΑΣΚΑΡΙΣ ΑΛΛΟΔΑΠΗ ΓΑΙΗ ΕΝΙ ΚΑΤΘΕΤΟ ΓΑΙΗΝ

ΟΥ ΤΙ ΛΙΗΝ ΞΕΙΝΗΝ Ω ΞΕΝΕ ΜΕΜΦΟΜΕΝΟΣ

ΕΥΡΑΤΟ ΜΕΙΛΙΧΙΗΝ ΑΛΛ ΑΧΟΕΤΑΙ ΕΙΠΕΡ ΑΧΑΙΟΙΣ

ΟΥΔ ΕΤΙ ΧΟΥΝ ΧΕΥΕΙ ΠΑΤΡΙΣ ΕΛΕΥΘΕΡΙΟΝ

ΞΕΙΝΕ ΛΑΚΑΙΝ ΥΓ ΕΜΟΙ ΡΑΛΛΟΥ ΠΑΤΡΟΣ Η ΠΡΟΦΥΓΟΥΣΑ

6 ΔΟΥΛΟΣΥΝΑΝ ΠΑΤΡΑΣ ΗΛΘΕΝ ΕΣ ΙΤΑΛΙΗΝ

ΜΗΤΡΩ ΠΕΙΘΟΜΕΝΗ ΟΣ ΖΕΥΞΕ ΜΙΝ ΑΝΕΡΙ ΚΛΕΙΝΩ

ΤΟΙΣ ΚΑΙ ΚΟΣΜΟΣ ΕΗΝ ΤΑΙΣ ΙΔΙΑΙΣ ΑΡΕΤΑΙΣ

ΕΛΛΑΔΟΣ ΑΛΛ ΟΛΟΗ ΚΑΤΕΡΙΝΑΝ ΠΡΟΥΦΘΑΣΕ ΜΟΙΡΑ

10 ΤΗΛΕ ΠΕΡ ΟΥΔ ΩΚΤΕΙΡ ΕΓΚΥΟΝ ΟΥΤΕ ΝΕΗΝ

Five ELEGIAC COUPLETS

1. ΛΑΣΚΑΡΙΣ . . . ΝΕΗΝ : *Printed in accordance with modern typographical conventions—and with the correction of* ΑΧΟΕΤΑΙ *(line 3) and* ΥΓ *(line 5)—the text reads:* Λάσκαρις ἀλλοδαπῇ γαίῃ ἔνι κάτθετο, γαίην | οὔ τι λίην ξείνην, ὦ ξένε, μεμφόμενος. | Εὔρατο μειλιχίην ἀλλ᾽ ἄχθεται εἴπερ Ἀχαιοῖς | οὐδ᾽ ἔτι χοῦν χεύει πατρὶς ἐλευθέριον. | Ξεῖνε, Λάκαιν᾽ ὑπ᾽ ἐμοὶ Ῥάλλου πατρός, ἣ προφυγοῦσα | δουλοσύναν πάτρας ἦλθεν ἐς Ἰταλίην | μήτρῳ πειθομένη ὃς ζεῦξέ μιν ἀνέρι κλεινῷ. | Τοῖς καὶ κόσμος ἔην ταῖς ἰδίαις ἀρεταῖς, | Ἑλλάδος ἀλλ᾽ ὀλοὴ Κατερίναν προύφθασε μοῖρα | τῆλέ περ, οὐδ᾽ ᾤκτειρ᾽ ἔγκυον οὔτε νέην. — ΚΑΤΘΕΤΟ = κατέθετο.

3. ΑΧΟΕΤΑΙ : *Sic* (= ἄχθεται).

4. ΧΟΥΝ : *'Heaped earth', here in the sense 'tomb'.*

5. ΥΓ : *Sic* (= ὑπ᾽). — ΡΑΛΛΟΥ : *The Greek name is* Ῥάλλος, -ου.

7. ΜΙΝ = αὐτήν.

8. ΤΟΙΣ = αὐτοῖς.

S. Agata dei Goti: Entry Wall, L of Portal

Lascaris [a] was laid to rest in foreign soil,
in no way, stranger, faulting it as excessively strange:
he found it kind, but is grieved that his homeland
no longer raises a barrow in freedom for Greeks. [b]

Stranger, beneath me lies a woman of Laconia, daughter of Rhallos,
who came to Italy in flight from the enslavement of her country,
obedient to her grandfather, who married her to an illustrious man.
By reason of her own virtues she was indeed a credit to them,
but the evil fate of Hellas, albeit from afar, cut Katerina off,
pitying her neither for her being with child nor for her youth. [c]

Five ELEGIAC COUPLETS

a. *Ianos Lascaris (1445–1535) was son of the scholar Constantine Lascaris, who fled to Italy after the fall of Constantinople to the Turks in 1453 (see 7.1.i, note d). The younger Lascaris found refuge in Florence, where he was employed by Lorenzo de' Medici as an agent in the purchase of Greek manuscripts from the Ottoman sultan Bayezid II (cf. 15.4J.iii, note c). After the expulsion of the Medici in 1494, he was invited to Paris by Charles VIII, where he offered public instruction in Greek. In 1513, Pope Leo X called him to Rome to head a college for the teaching of Greek; the Collegio Greco del Quirinale was attached to the present church. After a further sojourn in France to assemble a library for François I at Fontainebleau, Lascaris returned to Rome, where he passed the remainder of his life.*

b. *Greece remained under Ottoman rule from the conquest of the mainland over the second half of the fifteenth century until the successful conclusion of the Greek war of independence in 1829.*

c. *The death of Katerina is imaginatively likened to that of 'free' (i.e., Byzantine) Greece.*

3.3C Dedication of Relics of Greek Martyrs

MARTYRVM GRAECORVM CORPORA

DIE DOMIN VI KAL DECEMB MDCCCCXXXIII

SOLLEMNI POMPA ET SVPPLICATIONE

PER VIAS CIRCA REGIONEM FORI ROMANI

5   DEDVCTA SVNT

ET PRID KAL DECEMB

MARTYRVM ARAE

A IOSEPHO ROSSINO ARCHIEP THESSALONICEN

DE MANDATO CARDINALIS TITVLARIS

10   CONSECRATAE

DEIN IN HOC TEMPLO

AD DEI LAVDEM SANCTORVMQVE HONOREM

PRAESVLES AMPLISSIMI

TVM LATINO TVM GRAECO RITV

15   MAGNIFICO APPARATV

SACRA FECERE

1. MARTYRVM : *See 2.10, line 2.*
2. DOMIN(icā) : *The* EL *dominicus is Adj. to* dominus *('Lord').*
— VI : *Sextō.* — KAL(endās) DECEMB(ris) : *See 1.6G, line 11.* —
MDCCCCXXXIII : *Mīllēsimō nōngentēsimō trīcēsimō tertiō.*
6. PRID(iē) KAL(endās) DECEMB(ris).
8. ARCHIEP(iscopō) THESSALONICEN(sī) : *The* EL archiepiscopus *transliterates* EG ἀρχιεπίσκοπος *('archbishop'); the Adj.* Thessalonicēnsis *answers to the toponym* Thessalonica (Θεσσαλονίκη, *mod.* Salonika). *In* EL, *the occupants of episcopal sees are regularly designated in this fashion.*
9. TITVLARIS : *The Adj.* titulāris *answers to* titulus *(see 3.6A, line 2); as a Subst., it denotes the ecclesiastical occupant of a* titulus.
13. PRAESVLES : *In* EL, praesul *is 'bishop'. From an early time, the Roman church employed such native terms as* praesul, antistes, sacerdōs, *and* pontifex *alongside the Greek* episcopus (ἐπίσκοπος; cf. 3.4B, line 2).
16. FECERE = fēcērunt : *The formulation* sacra facere *is a Classicizing alternative to* ML missam celebrāre (cf. 1.8G, line 5).

S. Agata dei Goti: Presbytery, L Wall

On Sunday 26 November 1933,[a]
the bodies of the Greek martyrs [b]
were conducted
in solemn procession and prayer
through the streets in the neighborhood
of the Roman Forum
and on 30 November [c]
consecrated at the altar of the martyrs
by Giuseppe Rossino,[d] Archbishop of Thessalonica,
in compliance with the charge of the titular cardinal.[e]
Thereupon in this church
eminent prelates
celebrated mass
with splendid pomp,
first according to the Latin rite, then according to the Greek,[f]
to the praise of God and honor of the saints.

a. Lit., 'on the sixth day before the Kalends of December'.

b. The Greek martyrs Hippolytus, his sister Paulina, her husband Hadrias and their children Maria and Neon are supposed to have suffered during the persecution of Valerian (r. 253–260); cf. 6.10, note d. Paulina is buried beneath the altar of St. Agatha and the others beneath the high altar. Their relics were transferred to the present church in the eleventh century.

c. Lit., 'on the day before the Kalends of December'. The Feast of the Greek Martyrs is 2 December.

d. Giuseppe Rossino served as titular Archbishop of Thessalonica 1931–1949.

e. A titular CARDINAL has the nominal charge of a TITULAR CHURCH.

f. The Latin (or Roman) rite is the liturgical usage of the Diocese of Rome; it remains that of the Roman Catholic Church at large. The Greek rite comprises a variety of usages cultivated by the Orthodox churches of the E—as well as those of the 'Uniat' churches, the latter in communion with Rome yet each retaining its characteristic language and rite. The leading Greek rites are the Byzantine, Alexandrian, Antiochene, and Chaldaean.

3.4A   Epitaph of the Brothers Pollaiuolo

ANTONIVS PVLLARIVS PATRIA FLORENTI
NVS FICTOR INSIGN QVI DVOR PONT
XYSTI ET INNOCENTI AEREA MONIMENT MIRO
OPIFIC EXPRESSIT REFAMIL COMPOSITA
5   EX TEST HIC SE CVM PETRO FRATRE CONDI
VOLVIT VIX ANN LXXII OBIT ANNO SAL M IID

1. PATRIA : *Abl. of Respect.* — FLORENTI|NVS.
2. INSIGN(is). — DVOR(um) PONT(ificum).
3. XYSTI : *On the spelling, see 3.4D, line 4.* — MONIMENT(a) = monumenta. *On the spelling, cf. 13.1, line 9.*
4. OPIFIC(iō) : *The* CL *opificium is 'work of construction'. In* LL *it has the sense 'craft'.* — REFAMIL(iārī) = rē familiārī.
5. TEST(āmentō).
6. VIX(it) ANN(ōs) LXXII : Septuāgintā duo. — SAL(ūtis) M IID : Mīllēsimō quadringentēsimō nōnāgēsimō octāvō (*on the notation* IID, *see 4.6B, line 2*).

3.4B   Epitaph of Nicholas of Cusa

1   NICOLAVS DE CVSA TREVERIN | SANCTI PETRI ADVINCLA ⌐
CARDINALIS BRIXINEN̄ EPV̄S TVDERTI OBIIT MCCCCLXIIII
3   XI AVGVSTI OB DEV̄CIONEM |CATHENARVM SANCTI PETRI ⌐
HIC SEPELIRI VOLVIT

5   DILEXIT DEVM TI
                            MVIT ET VENERA
                            TVS EST AC ILLI
                            SOLI SERVIVIT
                            PROMISSIO RETRI
10   BVCIONIS NON FE
                            FELLIT EVM

                        VIXIT ANNIS LXIII

S. Pietro in Vincoli: L of Portal, on Pier

Antonio Pollaiuolo,[a] Florentine by nationality,
distinguished sculptor, who by his marvelous craft
made the brazen monuments of the two pontiffs
Sixtus and Innocent,[b] his estate having been settled in accordance
with his will, desired to be buried here with his brother Pietro.
He lived seventy-two years. He died in the year of Salvation 1498.

> a. Antonio Pollaiuolo (Antonio di Jacopo d'Antonio Benci, c. 1432–1498)
> and his brother Pietro (c. 1441–c. 1496) worked as painters, sculptors, and
> goldsmiths in Florence. The greater artist of the two, Antonio made the fig-
> ures of Romulus and Remus beneath the Lupa Capitolina, long assigned
> to the fifth century BC but now dated to the age of Charlemagne (see 1.6G,
> note b).

> b. Antonio's greatest commissions were for the bronze tombs of Pope Sixtus
> IV della Rovere (r. 1471–1484) and Innocent VIII Cibò (r. 1484–1492),
> both in the Vatican. The latter features the first Renaissance tomb effigy to
> portray the deceased alive.

W End of Left Aisle, Tomb Slab

Nicholas of Cusa[a] in the Diocese of Trier, Cardinal
of San Pietro in Vincoli, Bishop of Brixen, died at Todi
in 1464 on 11 August. On account of his devotion
to the chains of St. Peter,[b] he desired to be buried here.

He loved God,
he feared and honored him
and him alone
did he serve:
the promise
of requital
did not deceive him.

He lived sixty-three years.

1. TREVERIN(ēnsis) : *The* ML *Adj.* Trēverinēnsis *answers to the* CL *toponym* Augusta Trēverōrum (*mod. Trier*).

2. ADVINCLA = ad vincula. — BRIXINEN(ēnsis) : *The* ML *Adj.* Brixinēnsis *answers to the toponym* Brixinium (*mod. Brixen or Bressanone*). — EP(iscop)VS : *The* EL episcopus *transliterates Greek* ἐπίσκοπος ('*overseer', then* EG '*bishop*'). — TVDERTI : Tudertum (*also* Tuder; *mod. Todi*). — MCCCCLXIIII : Mīllēsimō quadringentēsimō sexāgēsimō quārtō.

3. XI : Ūndecimō. — AVGVSTI : *See 1.6G, line 11.* — DEV(ō)CIONEM = dēvōtiōnem : *In* LL, T *and* C *were palatalized before front vowels to* /ts/ *and* /tʃ/ *and are frequently confused. In* EL, *dēvōtiō is 'obedience', 'piety'.*

4. CATHENARVM = catēnārum : *On the spelling, see 9.1A, line 2.*

5–7. TI|MVIT ET VENERA|TVS

9. RETRI|BVCIONIS = retribūtiōnis.

10. FE|FELLIT.

12. ANNIS LXIII : Sexāgintā sex. *The Abl. construction is common in* LL.

3.4C Commemoration of Election of Pope John II

SALBO PAPA N IOHANNE COGNOME

NTO MERCVRIO EX S̄C̄E EC̄C̄L R̄ŌM PRESBYTE

RIS ORDINATO EX TĪT S̄C̄I CLEMENTIS AD GLO

RIAM PONTIFICALEM PROMOTO BEATO PETRO

5   A̅P̅ PATRONO SVO A VINCVLIS EIVS SEVERVS PB OF̅R̅T

ET I̅T̅ P̅C̅ LAMPADI ET ORESTIS V̅V̅ C̅C̅ VRBI+CLVSCEDIRI·NVSEST

1. SALBO PAPA N(ostrō) IOHANNE : *On the construction, see 5.8B, line 1. On the spelling of* SALBO, *see 4.7B.* — COGNOME|NTO : *Abl. of Description.*

2. S(ān)C(t)E ECCL(ēsie) ROM(āne) : *On* ecclēsia, *see 1.7A, line 6. On* E *for* AE, *see 1.8B, line 5.* — PRESBYTE|RIS : *The* EL presbyter *transliterates Greek* πρεσβύτερος ('*elder', then* EG '*presbyter', 'priest*').

3. TIT(ulō) : *See 3.6A, line 2.* — S(ān)C(t)I. — GLO|RIAM.

4. PETRO : *On the name, see 3.2A, line 2.*

5. AP(ostolō) : *See 1.6I, line 7.* — P(res)B(yter). — OF(fe)RT.

6. IT(erum) P(ost) C(ōnsulātum): *The formula indicates the third year (inclusive) after the consulship.* — V̅V̅ C̅C̅ = virōrum clārissimōrum : *On the abbreviation, see 1.6I, line 7.* — VRBI+CLVSCEDIRI·NVSEST : *The interpretation is uncertain. The reference appears to concern some type of votive offering made of cedar wood.*

a. *Nicholas Krebs (1401–1464) was born at Kues on the Moselle, Latinized as Cusa. For his efforts on behalf of the papacy in its struggle with the Holy Roman Emperors, in 1448 he was created* CARDINAL *in the title of San Pietro in Vincoli by Pope Nicholas V. In 1450 he was appointed Bishop of Brixen (Bressanone) in the Tyrol and papal legate for the German-speaking countries. His most famous philosophical work is* De Docta Ignorantia *('On Learnèd Ignorance'), in which he argues that the search for truth must lead beyond reason in order to achieve the intuition of God. His scientific ideas influenced such varied thinkers as Nicolaus Copernicus, Galileo Galilei, Giordano Bruno, and Johannes Kepler.*

b. *According to legend, the chain of St. Peter was collected from the Mamertine Prison by St. Balbina, daughter of the jailer Quirinus (see 2.15, note a). When a second such chain, discovered in Jerusalem by the empress Eudocia (cf. 3.4D, note b), was sent to Rome and placed beside its fellow, the two are said to have spontaneously fused to produce the relic now venerated in the high altar of this church.*

S. Pietro in Vincoli: L Aisle, Head

During the lifetime of John, our pope, known as Mercurius [a]—
ordained from among the presbyters of the holy Roman church,
raised to the papal dignity from the Title of San Clemente [b]—
Severus, presbyter at his Chains, [c] *makes this offering*
to the blessèd Apostle Peter, his patron,
in the third year after the consulship of their Excellencies Lampadius and Orestes... [d]

a. *Mercurius, a presbyter of S. Clemente (6.1), was elected pope in this church on 31 December 532 and consecrated on 2 January 533. As his given name was that of a pagan god, he became the first pope to take a new name on election: John II (r. 533–535). The last pope to retain his Christian name was Marcellus II, baptized Marcello Cervini (r. 1555; cf. 12.5, note a).*

b. *See* TITULAR CHURCH.

c. *See 3.4B, note b.*

d. *Lampadius and Orestes were consuls in the year 530 (see* CONSUL*). The third year (inclusive) after their consulship was 532. Although the E emperor Justinian held his third consulship in that year, it was never officially proclaimed at Rome: the city was at that time ruled by Amalasuntha, daughter of the Ostrogothic king Theoderic (cf. 2.14, note c) and regent for her young brother Athalaric. On the title 'their Excellencies' see 2.2, note e. The concluding words of the line have hitherto defeated scholarly elucidation.*

3.4D San Pietro in Vincoli: Dedication by Sixtus III

[cede prius nomen nouitati cede uetustas
regia laetanter uota dicare libet
haec petri paulique simul nunc nomine signo
xystus apostolicae sedis honore fruens
5   unum quaeso pares unum duo sumite munus
unus honor celebret quos habet una fides
presbyteri tamen hic labor est et cura philippi
postquam ephesi x̄p̄s̄ uicit utrique polo
praemia discipulus meruit uincente magistro
10   hanc palmam fidei rettulit inde senex]

POSITA POST EPHESINAM SYNODVM IN OCCIDENTALI
PARTE ECCLESIAE S PETRI AD VINCVLA

Five ELEGIAC COUPLETS (*lines 1–10*)

1. [cede prius . . . senex] : *The text is restored from medieval copies.*

2. uota : *As often in Latin verse, the Neut.Pl. is used with no appreciable difference from the Sg. (cf.* praemia, *line 9).*

4. xystus : *The original form of the Greek name was* Ξυστός (*'smooth'*), *transliterated* Xystus. *Because Pope St. Xystus I (r. c. 116–125) was according to tradition the sixth successor of St. Peter, his name came to be understood as the Latin* Sixtus (*'sixth'*). — apostolicae : *The* EL apostolicus *transliterates Greek* ἀποστολικός, *the Adj. answering to* ἀπόστολος (*see 1.61, line 7*). — sedis : *In* EL, sēdēs *is 'see'.*

5. quaeso : *Scans* quaesō. *The license is frequent already in the poets of the Silver Age.*

7. presbyteri : *See 3.4C, line 2.*

8. ephesi. *Locative. In the original inscription, the name evidently appeared as* EFESI. *On the spelling, see 2.1, line 2.* — x̄p̄s̄ = Christus : *The abbreviation* XPS *combines the first two letters of Greek* ΧΡΙΣΤΟΣ *with the* S *of its Latin transliteration (see 1.6A ii, line 6).* — utrique polo : *Lit., 'for each pole', i.e., by synecdoche, 'for both E and W' (on synecdoche, see 2.14, line 6).*

11. EPHESINAM : *The Adj.* Ephesīnus *answers to the toponym* Ephesus (Ἔφεσος). — SYNODVM : *The* EL synodus *transliterates Greek* σύνοδος (*'assembly', then* EG *'synod'*).

12. ECCLESIAE : *See 1.7A, line 6.* — s(ānctī).

R Aisle at Seventh Intercolumniation

Yield, former name,[a] to one that is new; yield, what is past:
it is pleasing to dedicate a royal offering in joy.[b]
I, Sixtus,[c] who enjoy the honor of the Apostolic See,
now seal it in the name of Peter and Paul together.
As equals, I beg, do you both accept this single gift:
may a single honor celebrate those whom a single faith embraces.
This achievement and its custody nevertheless belong to the presbyter Philip,
after Christ triumphed for East and West at Ephesus.[d]
As a pupil, with his master's victory he deserved his reward:
an agèd man, he brought back thence this trophy of the Faith.

Placed following the Council of Ephesus at the west end
of the Church of S. Pietro in Vincoli.[e]

Five ELEGIAC COUPLETS (lines 1–10)

a. *The previous dedication is unknown: The earliest witnesses refer to the church as* Basilica Apostolorum *('Basilica of the Apostles'). The first mention of its dedication to the chains of St. Peter dates to 501–502.*

b. *The emperor Theodosius II (r. 408–450) and the empress Eudocia evidently promised to sponsor the rebuilding of the original church on the present site, which had perhaps suffered damage during the Gothic sack of AD 410 (see 2.2, note d). The promise was fulfilled by their daughter Eudoxia, wife of the W emperor Valentinian III; in consequence, it is also known as the* Titulus Eudoxiae *(see TITULAR CHURCH).*

c. *Pope St. Sixtus III (r. 432–440) dedicated the new basilica c. 440.*

d. *Philip was sent by Pope St. Celestine I (r. 422–432) to the Council of Ephesus in AD 431 (see THEOTÓKOS). Under Sixtus III, Celestine's successor, Philip supervised the reconstruction of the present church. The twenty fluted Doric columns, dating to the first century AD, are spolia. If the matronly Ionic order was deemed appropriate for the BASILICA of S. Maria Maggiore (see 4.2H, note d), St. Peter was here well served by the choice of the robust and manly Doric (cf. 14.4, note c).*

e. *The original inscription, the text of which is preserved in transcription, presumably resembled the contemporary specimen that survives at S. Sabina (5.4). The present copy was mounted in 1931 to commemorate the sesquimillenary of the Council of Ephesus.*

3.5A S. Prassede: Dedication by Paschal I

1   EMICAT AVLA PIAE VARIIS DECORATA METALLIS ⌐
    PRAXEDIS DN̄O SVPER AETHRA PLACENTIS HONORE
2   PONTIFICIS SVMMI STVDIO PASCHALIS ALVMNI ⌐
    SEDIS APOSTOLICAE PASSIM QVI CORPORA CONDENS
3   PLVRIMA SC̄ORVM SVBTER HAEC MOENIA PONIT ⌐
    FRETVS VT HIS LIMEN MEREATVR ADIRE POLORVM

   Six HEXAMETERS

   1. AVLA : *See 2.14, line 1.* — PIAE : *With* PRAXEDIS. — METALLIS : *See
   2.14, line 1.* — PRAXEDIS : *The Latin name is* Prāxēdis. — D(omi)NO.
   — AETHRA : *Syncopated form of* aethera (*cf. 2.14, line 6*). *Syncope
   (Greek* συγκοπή, *'cutting short') of unaccented syllables was pervasive
   in* LL, *whence the abbreviated structure of many Romance words, e.g.,*
   CL masculum > LL masclu(m) > *Ital.* maschio; CL viridem > LL
   virde(m) > *Ital.* verde; CL vetulum > LL veclu(m) > *Ital.* vecchio.
   2. APOSTOLICAE : *See 3.4D, line 4.*
   3. S(ān)C(t)ORVM. — SVBTER : *Scans* subtēr *in ictus.* — MOENIA : *Here
   used poetically of the structure of the church.* — HIS : *Refers to* CORPORA
   . . . PLVRIMA (*lines 2–3*). — LIMEN . . . POLORVM : *See 2.14, line 6.*

3.5B Commemoration of Martyrs' Burial

CONDITORIVM RELIQVIARVM SANCTORVM MARTYRVM ⌐
IN AEDIBVS SANCTAE PRAXEDIS ☧

   MARTYRVM : *See 2.10, line 2.*

Apse

Decorated with variegated enamels the hall glitters in honor of the godly Praxedis,[a] *pleasing to the Lord above the skies, through the zeal of Paschal,*[b] *Supreme Pontiff, nurseling of the Apostolic See who, laying to rest in all quarters the numerous bodies of saints,*[c] *plants them beneath these ramparts, that in reliance upon them he may deserve to approach the threshold of Heaven.*

Six HEXAMETERS

a. *Both the iconography of the mosaic and the language of the inscription take their inspiration from the mosaic of the* BASILICA *of SS. Cosmas and Damian (see 2.14). According to legend, St. Praxedis was daughter of St. Pudens and sister of St. Pudentiana (see 3.6A, note c). Praxedis is said to have donated property in Vicus Lateranus for the present church and to have been martyred during the reign of Antoninus Pius.*

b. *Pope St. Paschal I (r. 817–824) rebuilt the church* in toto *(cf. 6.3 and 13.13). Paschal himself appears to the left holding a model of the church; his square nimbus indicates that he was living at the time of the dedication.*

c. *According to a contemporary inscription preserved in the church, Paschal relocated the remains of more than 2,300 martyrs.*

Porphyry Slab near Portal

The vault of the relics of the holy martyrs[a]
in the house of St. Praxedis. ☧

a. *The slab ostensibly marks the place where Praxedis deposited the relics of martyrs (see 3.6A, note c). On the Chi-Rho emblem, see 4.2L.*

3.6A Commemoration of Martyrs' Burial

IN HAC SANCTA ANTIQVISSIMA ECCLESIA

TT S PASTORIS A S PIO PAPA DEDICATA

OLIM DOMO S PVDENTIS SENATORIS

ET HOSPITIO SANCTORVM APOSTOLORVM

5   TRIA MILLIA BEATORVM MARTYRVM

CORPORA REQVIESCVNT QVAE SANCTAE

CHRISTI VIRGINES PVDENTIANA ET

PRAXIDES SVIS MANIBVS SEPELIEBANT

1. ECCLESIA : *See 1.7A, line 6.*

2. T(i)T(ulō) : *App. to* ECCLESIA *(line 1). In* CL, titulus *is 'inscription' or 'notice'; in* EL, *it signifies one of a class of very ancient churches of the city. These were once supposed to have been identified by an inscription naming the owner of the property. The term may refer to the church itself or to its charge.* — s(ānctī). — s(ānctō). — PAPA : *The* EL papa *transliterates Greek* πάππας *('father', then* EG *'bishop'). From the sixth century the imperial chancery at Constantinople normally reserved the title for the Bishop of Rome, to whom in the W it has been applied exclusively since the eleventh century.*

3. s(ānctī).

4. APOSTOLORVM : *See 1.61, line 7.*

5. MILLIA = mīlia. — MARTYRVM : *See 2.10, line 2.*

7. CHRISTI : *See 1.6A.ii, line 6.*

8. PRAXIDES : *More usual is the spelling* Prāxēdis.

3.6B S. Pudenziana: Dedication of First Basilica

i.	*ii.*
DOMINVS	ECCLESIAE
CONSER	PVDENTI
VATOR	ANAE

*i.*2–3. CONSER|VATOR.

*ii.*2–3. PVDENTI|ANAE.

S. Pudenziana: Pavement near Portal

In this holy church of high antiquity,
dedicated by Pope Saint Pius as Title [a] of Saint Pastor,
formerly the home of Saint Pudens, the Senator,[b]
and lodging of the holy Apostles,
rest the bodies of three thousand blessèd martyrs
which Pudentiana and Praxedis,[c]
holy virgins of Christ,
buried with their own hands.

a. *The term 'Title' (titulus) is used both of a* TITULAR CHURCH *and of the honorary charge of such a church granted by the pope to a* CARDINAL. *S. Pudenziana was long believed to have been the first titular church.*

b. *According to legend, Quintus Cornelius Pudens—identified with the Pudens to whom St. Paul sends greetings at II Tim. 4:21—was converted by St. Peter, who resided AD 43–51 in his home in Vicus Patricius. Here Peter consecrated the first bishops (see* BISHOP), *including his successors Linus, Cletus, and Clement (see 6.1, note b). After the death of his wife, Pudens converted his home into a church for the (transparently fictitious) priest Pastor. Owing to the chronological discrepancy, this legend cannot be reconciled with the parallel tradition that the church was founded by Pope St. Pius I (r. c. 142–c. 155) at the request of Praxedis (see note c).*

c. *SS. Pudentiana and Praxedis, daughters of Pudens, busied themselves with collecting the bones of martyrs. Praxedis founded a second church on a nearby parcel of family property (see 3.5A, note a).*

Apse

Left	Right
The Lord	*of the Church*
is the	*of*
Preserver	*Pudens.[a]*

a. *The saint called 'Pudentiana' is quite likely an artifact of the present inscription: the phrase* ECCLESIAE PVDENTIANAE *('Church of Pudens', Lit., 'Pudentian Church') was misinterpreted as 'Church of Pudentiana'. This is the earliest figural mosaic to survive in a Roman church and was probably among the first to be produced.*

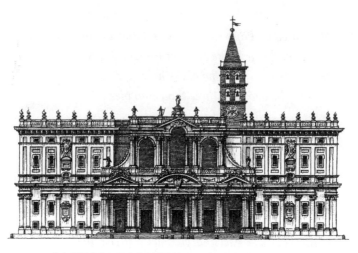

BASILICA DI SANTA MARIA MAGGIORE

The Basilica of Santa Maria Maggiore has been memorably character-
ized as a 'symphony of centuries'. The apse is preceded by an Egyptian
obelisk, the façade by the only surviving column from the Basilica of
Constantine in the Forum. Inside, two magnificent files of antique col-
umns line the nave; the mosaics and the belfry constitute signal monu-
ments of medieval art. The Pauline and Sistine Chapels for their part
recall the pomp of the Counter Reformation, while the façade is a mon-
ument of the late Baroque. The church is a virtual précis of Rome's ar-
tistic history.

IV. The Esquiline Hill

CALLED BY THE ROMANS 'ESQUILIAE' OR 'MONS ESQUILINUS', the Esquiline Hill is said to have been incorporated into the city in the sixth century BC by Servius Tullius, Rome's penultimate king. Whatever the historical worth of that tradition, the hill was almost certainly inhabited from a much earlier time. The probable derivation of the toponym *Esquiliae*—and of the corresponding adjective *Esquilīnus*—is **eks* ('out') + **kʷel* ('cultivate'). If this etymology is sound, the epithet *esquilīnus* (**eks-kʷel-īno-*) possesses the sense 'out-dwelling' and is the formal antonym of *inquilīnus* (**en-kʷel-īno-*), literally 'inhabiting'. The name will have referred to the primitive status of the hill as a suburb to the village on the neighboring Palatine.

According to tradition, it is Servius Tullius who caused the first walls of Rome to be built, in the sixth century BC. The walls that are today called 'Servian', however, date to the fourth. Constructed in the wake of the Gallic sack of 390, they extended eleven kilometers to enclose the Quirinal, Viminal, Esquiline, Caelian, and Aventine hills. On the Esquiline, the zone outside the walls was given over to a vast public necropolis. Pit graves indiscriminately accommodated the corpses of slaves and the poor; picked clean by bird and beast, the bones lay exposed to bleach in the sun. Judicial executions were conducted just outside the Porta Esquilina, later rededicated as the ARCH OF GALLIENUS. In the first 4.4
century BC, the whole of the foul place was reclaimed by Gaius Cilnius Maecenas, Augustus' unofficial minister of culture, who covered it over with luxurious gardens. It is from a tower in the gardens of Maecenas that Nero is said to have recited the epic poem *Iliupersis* ('Sack of Troy') as Rome burned below.

By Augustus' time, the 'Servian' walls had long since become superfluous and had indeed largely disappeared; today, the only considerable section to be seen is on the grounds of Stazione Termini. The imposing walls that survive to gird the historic center of modern Rome were begun by the emperor Aurelian (r. AD 270–275), when the city once more required military defense. In their haste, the architects of Aurelian's wall incorporated numerous existing buildings into the fabric: as much as one-sixth of the total length consists of structures—including the Pyramid of Cestius, an amphitheater, and long tracts of aqueduct—that were pressed into unforeseen military service. It was at this stage that PORTA TIBURTINA and Porta Maggiore became gates; originally they were the arcades of aqueducts monumentalized at points where they passed over major roads in the open countryside. At the beginning of the fifth century the walls of Aurelian were restored by Arcadius and Honorius in the vain hope of staving off the Visigoths of Alaric.

4.6

With Trastevere and the Subura, the Esquiline Hill was the most populous zone of ancient Rome. It lodged numerous ancient shrines, including those of Tellus (Mother Earth) and of Juno Lucina, patron of mothers in childbirth. In the early Christian centuries, the ranks of shrines were swelled by a number of *tituli*—and eventually by the CHURCH OF SANTA MARIA MAGGIORE, one of the city's four great patriarchal basilicas. The church that we see today was founded by Pope St. Sixtus III (r. 432–440) to commemorate the decree of the Council of Ephesus (AD 431) by which the use of the title *Theotókos* ('Mother of God') was approved. The fact that Sixtus built his basilica near the temple of Juno Lucina can hardly be due to coincidence: it doubtless seemed fitting that the cult of the patron of childbirth should be superseded by that of the mother of the world's savior.

4.2

The Basilica of Santa Maria Maggiore was the first large church to be planned and financed by the papacy. Though today the structure is sheathed in an elaborate baroque envelope, the Classicizing proportions of the interior exhale the noble restraint of Antiquity. The basilica has been felicitously characterized as a 'manifesto' of Classical majesty reborn in a Christian context. The same spirit pervades on a lesser scale the basilicas of San Pietro in Vincoli on the Oppian, Santa Sabina on the Aventine, and Santo Stefano on the Caelian—each a product of the fertile hybrid of Classical and Christian in Roman ecclesiastical architecture of the fifth century. The triumphal arch still bears the original dedicatory inscription of Pope St. SIXTUS III, his name spelled 'Xystus' in the Greek fashion. The numerous pontiffs whose manifold improvements to the basilica are commemorated include SIXTUS V (r. 1585–1590) in the sixteenth century, PAUL V (r. 1605–1621) and CLEMENT X (r. 1670–1676) in the seventeenth, BENEDICT XIV (r. 1740–1758) in the eighteenth, and, in the early twenty-first, JOHN PAUL II (r. 1978–2005). Among the many funerary monuments is that of the sculptor and architect GIANLORENZO BERNINI.

4.2I

4.2A

4.2C&B

4.2F–H

4.2M

4.2K

Before the façade of Santa Maria Maggiore rises the COLONNA DELLA PACE ('Column of Peace'), erected by Pope Paul V between 1613 and 1615. The symbolism of the monument takes its point of departure from a topographical error of long standing. The 14.3-meter column was removed from the Basilica of Constantine on the Forum, which for centuries was wrongly identified as Vespasian's nearby Temple of Peace. This misapprehension permitted Paul V the conceit of rededicating an ostensible monument of Vespasian's false peace to the one vouchsafed by the Mother of God—PAX VNDE VERA EST ('of true peace the source'). The notorious immodesty of Paul's dedicatory inscription on the façade of St. Peter's Basilica pales beside that of the present column's: TE PAVLE NVLLIS OBTICEBO SAECVLIS (roughly, 'Paul, I shall sing your praises unto the end of time').

4.3

More venerable even than Santa Maria Maggiore is the Basilica of San Lorenzo fuori le Mura, which rises over the tomb of St. Lawrence on the Via Tiburtina. Though reputedly of Spanish origin, St. Lawrence came to be the most beloved post-apostolic martyr of the city of Rome. He was a deacon of Pope St. Sixtus II (r. 257–258). After the summary execution of Sixtus and four of his seven deacons, Lawrence was arrested and required to surrender the wealth of the Church to the imperial authorities. When he refused, he was condemned to die; according to a late tradition he was scourged and then roasted on a gridiron, his attribute in art. In the course of his martyrdom Lawrence is supposed to have quipped to his executioners, 'This side is done; turn me over and tuck in!' (*Assasti unam partem, gira et aliam et manduce*). When his tomb was opened in the seventh century to receive the relics of St. Stephen, Lawrence's body is said to have shifted to accommodate his fellow martyr, whence his sobriquet 'the courteous Spaniard'.

Lawrence's tomb was located in the cemetery of Cyriaca, which consisted of galleries and chambers cut into the hillside along the road. (Though all such subterranean graveyards are loosely known as 'catacombs', this name belongs properly to the cemetery on the Via Appia called *ad catacumbas*—'at the hollows'.) Like those of St. Sebastian and St. Agnes, the tomb of Lawrence was equipped by the emperor Constantine I with a large 'cemetery basilica' on a neighboring plot of land that enabled the faithful to be buried near the saint. By the sixth and seventh century, when pilgrimage to the tombs of Rome's martyrs reached its zenith, closer contact with the relics was desired: the cemetery basilicas were abandoned and smaller churches constructed directly over the tombs. In the case of San Lorenzo, the cliff face in which the tomb was located was quarried away to expose the tomb on all sides, and a small basilica was erected to enclose it. This operation, carried out under Pope Pelagius II (r. 579–590), is commemorated in the inscription on the TRI-UMPHAL ARCH.

4.7B

The basilica of San Lorenzo houses a remarkable relic of Rome's *secolo di ferro*—the Iron Century, tenth of the Christian era. As the empire established by Charlemagne disintegrated, the government of Rome fell into the hands of powerful local families. The most durable of these was the house of Theophylact, which dominated the city for the greater part of the tenth century. With the rise of the Saxon dynasty, which set about to revive the power and prestige of Charlemagne's empire, the Romans resorted with mounting frequency to armed rebellion against their Teutonic overlords. The most famous rebels of Theophylact's lineage were his grandson Crescenzio and his great-grandson of the same name. A less

4.7C conspicuous representative of the family was the hapless LANDOLFO, slain at a tender age in 963. With authentically Virgilian pathos, his epitaph records the boy's youth, his beauty, and the fact that he perished VVLNERE FOSSVS ('pierced by a wound').

At the end of Antiquity, the natural weakness of the Esquiline had been underscored in the assault of the Ostrogoth Totila (AD 546). Besides its military vulnerability, the zone possessed no natural supply of water. With the failure of the aqueducts, residents of the townhouses and villas of Rome's *monti* ('hills') retreated to the plain of the Tiber bend. Indeed, until the late Renaissance the city's *abitato*—the inhabited zone—was effectively restricted to the Campus Martius and the Capitoline Hill; the bulk of the area within the walls was desolate except for the sporadic monasteries and other religious establishments that punctuated the vastness of the *disabitato*—the deserted zone. The reclamation of the *monti* dates to the sixteenth century: Pope Gregory XIII (r. 1572–1585) opened Strada Gregoriana (the modern Via Merulana), while his immediate successor, Sixtus V, constructed an aqueduct and a network of streets centered on Santa Maria Maggiore.

Pope Sixtus V is conventionally lionized as the first urban planner of modern Rome. As declared in a bull of 1586, the pope's pious intention was to unite the city's great corona of pilgrimage churches by a system of roads to facilitate the progress of pilgrims; the hub of the network was to be Santa Maria Maggiore, center of Marian devotion and Sixtus' chosen burial site. To this end, Sixtus strengthened the laws governing expropriation and committed the execution of the project to his architect, the indefatigable Domenico Fontana. The pope's preoccupation with the city's neglected southeastern quarter abruptly reversed the northward trend of expansion that had been fostered by his predecessors in the early sixteenth century.

Because the scheme was organized around the holy places at their termini, Sixtus' broad arteries struck out across the vast wilderness of the *disabitato*; perfectly rectilinear, they took no heed of the deep folds in the landscape. The spine of the system was Strada Felice, which ran from Trinità dei Monti to Santa Croce in Gerusalemme—a distance of 3.3 kilometers. A ramification of Strada Felice led in the direction of the Basilica of San Lorenzo fuori le Mura to the southeast, while Via Merulana was mirrored by Via Panisperna, which led towards Piazza Venezia and the center of the city. Had Sixtus realized his purported ambition of incorporating San Paolo into the plan, he would have succeeded in linking nearly all of the seven pilgrimage churches—San Pietro, San Giovanni, San Paolo, Santa Maria Maggiore, Santa Croce, Santa Maria del Popolo (which Sixtus had substituted for the remote San Sebastiano), and San Lorenzo fuori le Mura.

Strangely, Sixtus pursued his project for less than three years; only a fragment of the original scheme was ever brought to completion. The reason appears to be that the urban plan as announced in 1586 was executed only to the extent that it coincided with improvement of the pontiff's extensive villa on the Esquiline. What excited Sixtus' liveliest interest was the portion of the road system that defined the boundaries of his estate. Indeed, he caused high walls to be erected along the length of those roads long before he had succeeded in acquiring all the property they enclosed. Beyond this, only those thoroughfares were completed that served to improve communications between Villa Montalto and various important zones of the city. Like the ACQUA FELICE, the pope's roads appear to have been primarily adapted to enhancing the value of his property. All of this was baptized in Sistine propaganda as 'urban planning' and long furnished the theme of an uncritical and ill-deserved hagiography.

Unlike his namesake Sixtus IV a century before, Sixtus V was at bottom uninterested in the real city and its problems. His predominant concern was to ensure that his villa was adequately equipped to become the seat of an enduring dynasty. The sheer opportunism that underlay his urban initiatives is perhaps seen to best advantage in a brief issued in March of 1589 in which he exempted Villa Montalto from all taxes and tariffs in perpetuity. As for Santa Maria Maggiore, far from being the raison d'être and fulcrum of the scheme, it effectively plays the same role to the pope's villa as San Marco to Palazzo Venezia, Santi Dodici Apostoli to Palazzo Colonna, and San Lorenzo in Damaso to the Cancelleria—namely, that of a grandiose palatine chapel. Finally, the OBELISCO ESQUILINO—ostensibly erected in honor of the relic of Christ's manger preserved in the basilica—is situated to the church's rear. As this was the location of the principal entrance of Villa Montalto, it would appear that the obelisk's principal function was rather to aggrandize the residence of a megalomaniacal pontiff whose legacy as an urban planner is today regarded with skeptical ambivalence.

4.1

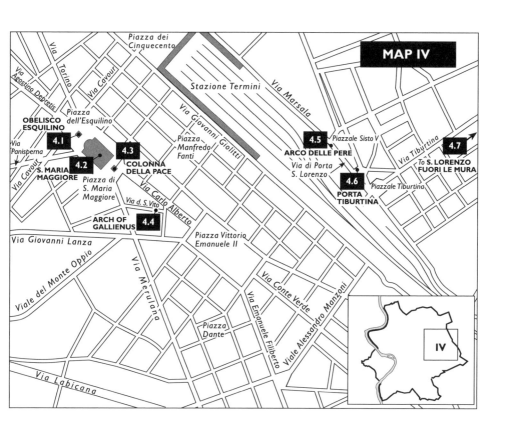

MAP IV

Piazza dei Cinquecento

Stazione Termini

Via Marsala

Via Torino

Via Cavour

Via Giovanni Giolitti

Via Agostino DePretis

Piazza dell'Esquilino

OBELISCO ESQUILINO

Piazza Manfredo Fanti

Via Panisperna

4.1

S. MARIA MAGGIORE

4.2

4.3

COLONNA DELLA PACE

Via Cavour

Piazza di S. Maria Maggiore

Via Carlo Alberto

Via d. S. Vito

ARCH OF GALLIENUS

4.4

Piazza Vittorio Emanuele II

Via Giovanni Lanza

Viale del Monte Oppio

Via Merulana

Piazza Dante

Via Conte Verde

Via Emanuele Filiberto

Viale Alessandro Manzoni

Via Labicana

4.5

Piazzale Sisto V

ARCO DELLE PERE

Via di Porta S. Lorenzo

Via Tiburtina

To S. LORENZO

4.7

S. LORENZO FUORI LE MURA

4.6

PORTA TIBURTINA

Piazzale Tiburtina

IV

4.1   Obelisco Esquilino: Dedication by Sixtus V

i.

SIXTVS V PONT MAX

OBELISCVM

AEGYPTO ADVECTVM

AVGVSTO

5   IN EIVS MAVSOLEO

DICATVM

EVERSVM DEINDE ET

IN PLVRES CONFRACTVM

PARTES

10   IN VIA AD SANCTVM

ROCHVM IACENTEM

IN PRISTINAM FACIEM

RESTITVTVM

SALVTIFERAE CRVCI

15   FELICIVS

HIC ERIGI IVSSIT AN D

M D LXXXVII PONT III

EQVES DOMINICVS FONTANA ARCHITECTVS EREXIT

1. SIXTVS V : Quīntus. *The name* Sixtus *appears in inscriptions variously as* SIXTVS, XYSTVS, *and* SYXTVS. *See 3.4D, line 4.* — PONT(ifex) MAX(imus).

3. AEGYPTO : *In CL prose, this Abl. of Place Whence would regularly be accompanied by the Prep.* ab *or* ex.

8–9. IN PLVRES . . . PARTES : *The hyperbaton (see 9.9.i, line 2) lends emphasis to* PLVRES.

11. ROCHVM : *The Ital. saint's name* Rocco *(Fr.* Roch*) appears in Latin as* Rochus.

14. SALVTIFERAE : *In EL,* salūtifer *is 'salvation-bringing' (EL* salūs *= 'salvation'; cf.* SALVTARI, *2.11B, line 6).*

16. AN(nō) D(ominī).

17. M D LXXXVII : Mīllēsimō quīngentēsimō octōgēsimō septimō. — PONT(ificātūs) III : Tertiō.

Piazza dell'Esquilino: Base of Obelisk

SW

> Sixtus the Fifth,[a] Supreme Pontiff,
> bade the obelisk
> lying in the street
> by San Rocco[b] —
> which had been transported from Egypt,
> dedicated
> to Augustus
> at his mausoleum,[c]
> then overturned
> and broken up into numerous pieces—
> to be restored
> to its original appearance
> and erected here
> in more auspicious wise
> to the Cross which brings salvation,[d]
> in the year of the Lord 1587,
> third of his office.

Cavaliere Domenico Fontana, Architect, erected this.[e]

a. *Pope Sixtus V Peretti (r. 1585–1590). The third year of his pontificate ran from 24 April 1587 through 23 April 1588.*

b. *The obelisk was found in 1519 beside the Church of S. Rocco, to the S of the Mausoleum of Augustus. It remained there in four pieces until 1586, when it was removed to the Esquiline to be raised at its present site. It is the twin of the Obelisco Quirinale (cf. 8.4C, note d). Damage observed at the time of its relocation indicates that the obelisk was deliberately toppled (see 7.1.iv, note b).*

c. *See 10.5.*

d. *Located as it is directly before the entrance of the pope's Villa Montalto, the obelisk would appear to have been erected primarily to aggrandize the suburban estate begun some years before his election.*

e. *See 7.1.ii, note c.*

ii.

CHRISTVS

PER INVICTAM

CRVCEM

POPVLO PACEM

5   PRAEBEAT

QVI

AVGVSTI PACE

IN PRAESEPE NASCI

VOLVIT

1. CHRISTVS : *See 1.6A.ii, line 6.*

7. PACE : *Abl. of Time When. The notion of a span of time is implicit in the sense of the word.*

8. PRAESEPE = praesaepe : *On the spelling, see 1.8B, line 5.*

iii.

CHRISTI DEI

IN AETERNVM VIVENTIS

CVNABVLA

LAETISSIME COLO

5   QVI MORTVI

SEPVLCRO AVGVSTI

TRISTIS

SERVIEBAM

1. CHRISTI : *See 1.6A.ii, line 6.*

2. IN AETERNVM : *The* CL *Neut.Subst.* aeternum *(from* aeternus, -a, -um*) is 'perpetuity' (cf. 11.5B, line 2).*

3. CVNABVLA : *The* CL cūnābula, -ōrum *('cradle') is Pl. only (like* castra, -ōrum*).*

SE

> *May Christ,*
> *who during the peace*
> *of Augustus*[a]
> *consented to be born*
> *in a manger,*
> *grant peace*
> *to his people*
> *through the Cross*
> *invincible.*

a. *In his own lifetime, Augustus (r. 27 BC–AD 14) was revered for having put an end to Rome's endemic civil wars and having restored peace to the Roman world. Here the false peace of the pagans is contrasted with the true peace of Christ (cf. 4.3.i, note d, and 13.5.viii, note a).*

NE

> *I who in sadness*[a]
> *formerly served*
> *the tomb*
> *of the dead*
> *Augustus*
> *with greatest joy*
> *revere the cradle of Christ,*[b]
> *the everliving God.*

a. *The obelisk speaks in propria persona (cf. 8.4A.iii, 8.4B, 10.4B.ii and 10.13.v). The Latin text is neatly constructed around four pairs of opposing terms:* IN AETERNVM VIVENTIS : MORTVI *('everliving' : 'dead');* CVNABVLA : SEPVLCRO *('cradle' : 'tomb');* LAETISSIME : TRISTIS *('most joyfully' : 'sad');* COLO : SERVIEBAM *('I revere' : 'I served'). Like all the texts of 4.1, it was dictated by Cardinal Silvio Antoniano (see 7.1.i, note a).*

b. *See 4.2A, note b.*

iv.

CHRISTVM DOMINVM

QVEM AVGVSTVS

DE VIRGINE

NASCITVRVM

5   VIVENS ADORAVIT

SEQ DEINCEPS

DOMINVM

DICI VETVIT

ADORO

1. CHRISTVM : *See 1.6A.ii, line 6.*

6. SEQ(ue) : *The* QVE *connects* ADORAVIT *(line 5) and* VETVIT *(line 8).*

4.2A Cappella Sistina: Dedication by Sixtus V

SANCTISS PRAESEPI

DOMINI NOSTRI

IESV CHRISTI

SIXTVS PAPA V

5   DEVOTVS

SACELLVM

EXTRVXIT

AN SAL MDLXXXVII

PONTIFICATVS

10   TERTIO

1. SANCTISS(imō) PRAESEPI = praesaepī : *On the spelling, see 1.8B, line 5. The Dat. case follows* DEVOTVS *(line 5).*

3. IESV CHRISTI : *See 1.6A.ii, line 6.*

4. SIXTVS PAPA V : Quīntus. *On* PAPA, *see 3.6A, line 2.*

7. EXTRVXIT = exstrūxit : *As the digraph* x = /ks/, *the etymological spelling in* EXS- *is strictly redundant.*

8. AN(nō) SAL(ūtis) MDLXXXVII : Mīllēsimō quīngentēsimō octōgēsimō septimō.

NW

I worship Christ as Lord,
whom Augustus
in his own lifetime worshipped
on the eve of his birth
from a Virgin
and subsequently
forbade himself
to be called
Lord.[a]

a. *The text alludes to the legend according to which Augustus beheld a vision of the BVM and Christ Child (see 1.8c).*

S. Maria Maggiore: External Façade of Choir, L

Pope Sixtus the Fifth,[a]
in devotion
to the most holy manger
of our Lord
Jesus Christ,
erected
this chapel[b]
in the year of Salvation 1587,
third
of his office.

a. *See 4.1.i, note a.*

b. *The inscription is mounted on the exterior of the Cappella Sistina ('Chapel of Sixtus'). The chapel was constructed by Domenico Fontana onto the right aisle of the* Basilica *to house an elaborate artificial grotto containing the relics of the Holy Manger, which Sixtus wished to move inside the church. Despite Fontana's best efforts, the ensemble—with its irreplaceable medieval statuary—did not survive the transfer intact.*

4.2B S. Maria Maggiore: Dedication of N Façade

CLEMENS X PONT MAX

LIBERIANAE BASILICAE

SEPTENTRIONALEM

FRONTEM SVA

5   IN VIRGINEM MAGNAM

PIETATE

MAGNIFICENTIVS

EXTRVXIT

ET EXORNAVIT

10   AN SAL MDCLXXIII

PONTIFICATVS IV

1. CLEMENS X : Decimus. — PONT(ifex) MAX(imus).
2. LIBERIANAE : *The* EL *Adj.* Līberiānus *answers to the name* Līberius.
8. EXTRVXIT = exstrūxit : *On the spelling, see 4.2A, line 7.*
10. AN(nō) SAL(ūtis) MDCLXXIII : Mīllēsimō sescentēsimō
    septuāgēsimō tertiō.
11. IV : Quārtō.

4.2C Cappella Paolina: Dedication by Paul V

SANCTAE VIRGINI

DEI GENITRICI

MARIAE

PAVLVS PAPA V

5   HVMILIS SERVVS

SACELLVM

OBTVLIT

AN SAL MDCXI

PONTIFICATVS

10   SEXTO

2. DEI GENITRICI = genetrīcī : *See 4.2D, line 3.*
4. PAVLVS PAPA V : Quīntus. *On* PAPA, *see 3.6A, line 2.*
8. AN(nō) SAL(ūtis) MDCXI : Mīllēsimō sescentēsimō ūndecimō.

External Façade of Choir, Center

Clement the Tenth,[a] Supreme Pontiff,
out of his devotion
to the mighty Virgin
erected
and embellished
in grander fashion
the north
façade
of the Liberian basilica [b]
in the year of Salvation 1673,
fourth of his office.

a. Pope Clement X Altieri (r. 1670–1676). *The fourth year of his pontificate ran from 29 April 1673 through 28 April 1674.*

b. See 4.2G, note c. *The façade and stair of the apse were built by Carlo Rainaldi.*

External Façade of Choir, R

Pope Paul the Fifth,[a]
her humble servant,
offered
to the Holy Virgin
Mary,
Mother of God,
this chapel [b]
in the year of Salvation 1611,
sixth
of his office.

a. Pope Paul V Borghese (r. 1605–1621). *The sixth year of his pontificate ran from 16 May 1610 through 15 May 1611.*

b. *The inscription is mounted on the exterior of the Cappella Paolina.*

4.2D Commemoration of Transfer of Icon of the BVM

PAVLVS V PONT MAX

CELEBERRIMAM

DEI GENITRICIS

IMAGINEM

5   EX MEDIA BASILICA

IN SPLENDIDIOREM

SEDEM

A FVNDAMENTIS

EXTRVCTAM

10   TRANSTVLIT

A PONTIFICATVS VI

1. PAVLVS V : Quīntus. — PONT(ifex) MAX(imus).
3. DEI GENITRICIS = genetrīcis : *The* EL Deī genitrīx *represents* EG Θεοτόκος (*'She who gave birth to God'; see 9.3, line 7*).
9. EXTRVCTAM = exstrūctam : *On the spelling, see 4.2A, line 7.*
11. A(nnō). — VI : Sextō.

4.2E S. Maria Maggiore: Dedication of Baptistery and Sacristy

PAVLVS V PONT MAX

PONTIF SVI

AN I SAL M DCV

1. PAVLVS V : Quīntus. — PONT(ifex) MAX(imus).
2. PONTIF(icātus).
3. AN(nō) I : Prīmō. — SAL(ūtis) M DCV : Mīllēsimō sescentēsimō quīntō.

4.2F S. Maria Maggiore: Dedication of Portico

i.

BENEDICTUS XIV P M A FUNDAMENT EREX

BENEDICTUS XIV : Quārtus decimus. — P(ontifex) M(aximus). — FUNDAMENT(īs) EREX(it).

S. Maria Maggiore: Exterior of Cappella Paolina

Paul the Fifth,[a] Supreme Pontiff,
transferred
the renowned
image
of the Mother of God[b]
from the midst of the basilica
to a more distinguished
place,
erected
from its foundations
in the sixth year of his office.

a. See 4.2C, note a.

b. *The ardently venerated image of the BVM known as the* Salus Populi Romani *('Salvation of the Roman People') was thought to have been painted by the hand of St. Luke (see 9.3, note d). It in fact dates from the seventh or eighth century and is first attested in Rome c.* AD 1000.

Façade, R

Paul the Fifth,[a] Supreme Pontiff,
in the first year of his office,
1605 of Salvation.

a. *Pope Paul V Borghese (r. 1605–1621). The first year of his pontificate ran from 16 May 1605 through 15 May 1606. In 1605, Paul had the baptistery and sacristy built onto the NE side of the basilica by Flaminio Ponzio. It forms a pendant to the Cappella Sistina (see 4.2A, note b).*

Loggia

Frieze

Benedict the Fourteenth,[a] Supreme Pontiff, built this from its foundations.

a. *Pope Benedict XIV Lambertini (r. 1740–1758). Benedict engaged Ferdinando Fuga to construct the portico and Benediction Loggia.*

ii.

BENEDICTUS XIV P M

PONTIF SUI AN III

SAL MDCCXLIII

1. BENEDICTUS XIV : Quārtus decimus. — P(ontifex) M(aximus).
2. PONTIF(icātūs). — AN(nō) III : Tertiō.
3. SAL(ūtis) MDCCXLIII : Mīllēsimō septingentēsimō quadrāgēsimō tertiō.

4.2G S. Maria Maggiore: Commemoration of Benedict XIV

BENEDICTO XIV PONT MAX

QUOD LIBERALITATE OPTIMI PRINCIPIS

LIBERIANAE BASILICAE FRONTEM

A FUNDAMENTIS EREXERIT

5   IMPOSITIS SIGNIS ORNAVERIT

LABENTEM PORTICUM RESTITUERIT

COMMUNES CANONICORUM AEDES

A SOLO EXTRUXERIT

EXTERIORES GRADUS

10   AD AVERSAM ABSIDIS PARTEM REPARAVERIT

TECTUM VETUSTATE CORRUPTUM REFECERIT

CAPITULUM ET CANONICI MUNIFICENTISS PONT

PP

1. BENEDICTO XIV : Quārtō decimō. — PONT(ificī) MAX(imō).
2–11. QUOD . . . REFECERIT : *On the construction, see 1.6B, lines 5–7.*
3. LIBERIANAE : *See 4.2B, line 2.*
7. CANONICORUM : *The* EL *canonicus (Greek* κανονικός) *denotes a member of a body of clerics assigned to a church.*
8. EXTRUXERIT = exstrūxerit : *On the spelling, see 4.2A, line 7.*
10. ABSIDIS : *The* CL *apsis (transliterating Greek* ἅψις) *refers to an arc or a segment of a circle; it is used in describing the shape of a semicircular niche, the sense in which it entered* EL. *On the neglect of* H, *see 8.8A, line 2.*
12. CAPITULUM : *The* CL *capitulum is a diminutive of* caput *('head'; cf. 4.2H, line 5); in* EL, *it is 'chapter'.* — MUNIFICENTISS(imō) PONT(ificī).
13. PP = posuērunt : *On the abbreviation, see 1.61, line 7.*

Façade, L

Benedict the Fourteenth,[a] Supreme Pontiff,

in the third year of his office,

1743 of Salvation.

a. *Pope Benedict XIV Lambertini (r. 1740–1758). The third year of his pon-*
   tificate ran from 17 August 1742 through 16 August 1743 (the inscription
   pertains to Ferdinando Fuga's portico and Benediction Loggia; see 4.2F.i,
   note a).

Portico, above R Portal

The chapter and canons[a]

set this up

for Benedict the Fourteenth, Supreme Pontiff,[b]

a pontiff most generous,

inasmuch as with the liberality of a most excellent Prince

he erected the façade of the Liberian Basilica[c]

from its foundations,

embellished it by decking it with statues,

restored the portico, which was collapsing,

built from the ground up

the common quarters of the canons,

restored the exterior steps to the rear of the apse,

and rebuilt the roof, which was spoiled by age.

a. *Canons are clergy attached to a cathedral or collegiate church (see*
   Canon).

b. *See 4.2F.ii, note a.*

c. *The Basilica of S. Maria Maggiore is called also* Sancta Maria ad Nives
   ('Our Lady of the Snows') and Basilica Liberiana. *According to legend,*
   on the night of 4–5 August 352 (or 363), the BVM appeared simultaneously
   in a dream to Pope St. Liberius and to the patrician Ioannes; indicating the
   Cispian Hill, she instructed that a church be built there. In the morning, a
   miraculous fall of snow had traced the plan of a basilica on the hill's summit.
   The pope proceeded to found the church, to the construction of which Ioannes
   devoted his fortune. The present church is not that of Liberius, but one later
   erected near the same site by Pope St. Sixtus III (r. 432–440; see 4.2I, note a).

4.2H   Commemoration of Benedict XIV

BENEDICTO XIV PONT MAX

QUOD LIBERIANAE BASILICAE LACUNAR REPARAVERIT

DE INTEGRO PAVIMENTUM REFECERIT

COLUMNIS AD VERAM FORMAM REDACTIS ET EXPOLITIS

5   NOVA CAPITULA IMPOSUERIT NOVAS BASES SUBIECERIT

PLASTICUM OPUS OMNE INAURAVERIT

PICTURIS DETERSO SITU VENUSTATEM RESTITUERIT

ABSIDEM EXORNAVERIT

CHORUM NOVIS SUBSELLIIS INSTRUXERIT

10   ARAM MAXIMAM EXCITAVERIT

SACRAM DENIQUE AEDEM ANTEA INCONDITAM

AD ELEGANTIAM PARTIUMQUE CONSENSUM REVOCAVERIT

CAPITULUM ET CANONICI BENEFICENTISSIMO PRINCIPI

ANNO IUBILAEI MDCCL PP

1. BENEDICTO XIV : Quārtō decimō. — PONT(ificī) MAX(imō).

2. LIBERIANAE : *See 4.2B, line 2.* — QUOD . . . REVOCAVERIT : *On the construction, see 1.6B, lines 5–7.*

5. CAPITULA : *Among its many senses, the* CL *capitulum* (*diminutive of* caput, *'head'*) *denotes the capital of a column* (*cf. 4.2G, line 12*).

6. PLASTICUM : *The* CL *plasticus transliterates Greek* πλαστικός (*'pertaining to the art of modeling'*). *Here, used as a Subst., it refers to stucco work.*

8. ABSIDEM : *See 4.2G, line 10.*

9. CHORUM : *The* EL *chorus transliterates Greek* χόρος (*'choral dance'*); *as a liturgical and architectural term in* EL, *it is 'choir'.*

11. AEDEM : *See 1.8B, line 10.*

13. CAPITULUM : *See 4.2G, line 12.* — CANONICI : *See 4.2G, line 7.*

14. IUBILAEI : *See 2.12A, line 8.* — MDCCL : Mīllēsimō septingentēsimō quīnquāgēsimō. — PP = posuērunt : *On the abbreviation, see 1.6I, line 7.*

S. Maria Maggiore: Entry Wall, above Central Portal

The Chapter and Canons [a] set this up

to Benedict the Fourteenth,[b] Supreme Pontiff, their most obliging Prince,

for having repaired the ceiling of the Liberian Basilica,[c]

for having entirely remade the pavement,

for having installed new capitals and bases on the columns

once these had been polished up and restored to their proper aspect,[d]

for having gilded all the stucco-work,

for having restored grace to the mosaics by removing grime,

for having embellished the apse,

for having equipped the choir with new stalls,

for having built the high altar—

in sum, for having reduced this holy church, formerly uncouth,

to refinement and harmony of its parts,[e]

in the year of the Jubilee 1750.[f]

a. See 4.2G, note a.

b. See 4.2F.ii, note a.

c. For the epithet 'Liberian', see 4.2G, note c.

d. *The nave is divided by twin colonnades, each comprising nineteen magnificent unfluted Ionic columns of Hymettan marble. The Christian basilicas of the fourth and fifth centuries were ordinarily made as splendid as possible by the use of fluted columns of the Corinthian and Composite orders, coveted for their florid capitals. Under these circumstances, the choice of the plainer Ionic appears eccentric. It has been proposed that in building this colossal church to the BVM, Sixtus III and his advisers not only avoided surpassing the dimensions of those of the Apostles Peter and Paul but also selected the Ionic—according to the Roman architect Vitruvius, a 'feminine' order—for its matronly modesty (cf. 3.4D, note d).*

e. *In his restoration of 1746–1750, Ferdinando Fuga expertly improved the uniformity of the basilica's interior by making subtle adjustments to the colonnades.*

f. See 7.4H, note b.

4.2I S. Maria Maggiore : Dedication by Sixtus III

XYSTVS EPISCOPVS PLEBI DEI

XYSTVS : *On the spelling, see 3.4D, line 4.* — EPISCOPVS : *See 3.4B, line 2.*
— PLEBI : *Besides its familiar sociopolitical application,* plēbs *is used even in* CL *to denote a 'folk' bound together by some common tie.*

4.2J Dedication of Mosaic

1   MARIA VIRGO ASSV̄PTA Ē AD ETHEREV̄ THALAMV̄ ⌐
     IN QVO REX REGV̄ STELLATO SEDET SOLIO

2   EXALTATA EST SANCTA DEI GENITRIX SVPER CHOROS ⌐
     ANGELORVM AD CELESTIA REGNA

1. MARIA : *On the name, see 15.4G, line 1.* — ASSV(m)PTA E(st). —
ETHEREV(m) : *See 2.14, line 6; on the spelling, see 1.8B, line 5.* —
THALAMV(m). — REGV(m).
2. DEI GENITRIX = genetrīx : *See 4.2D, line 3.* — CHOROS : *I.e., 'choir'*
(cf. 4.2H, line 9). — ANGELORVM : *The* EL angelus *transliterates Greek*
ἄγγελος *('messenger', then* EG *'angel').* — CELESTIA = caelestia.

4.2K Epitaph of Gianlorenzo Bernini

IOANNES LAVRENTIVS BERNINI
DECVS ARTIVM ET VRBIS
HIC HVMILITER QVIESCIT

1. IOANNES LAVRENTIVS BERNINI : *As often, the Christian name (here*
Gianlorenzo, *i.e.,* Giovanni Lorenzo) *is Latinized while the surname retains its Ital. form (cf. 12.3B, line 8).*

Triumphal Arch

Sixtus,[a] their Bishop, for the People of God.

a. Pope St. Sixtus III (r. 432–440). Sixtus had the BASILICA constructed to celebrate the decision of the Council of Ephesus (AD 431) permitting the title THEOTÓKOS ('Mother of God') to be used of the BVM.

Apse

The Virgin Mary has been taken up to the heavenly bridal chamber in which the King of Kings is seated upon a starry throne.
The holy Mother of God has been raised up above the choirs of angels to the Kingdom of Heaven.[a]

a. The magnificent mosaic of 1295, signed by Jacopo Torriti, depicts Christ enthroned with the BVM, upon whose head he places a crown. The text of the inscription is drawn from the liturgy for the Assumption of the BVM. The doctrine that Mary was assumed into heaven was defined in 1950 in the Apostolic Constitution Munificentissimus Deus of Pope Pius XII (r. 1939–1958).

R Aisle, on Step of the Choir

Giovanni Lorenzo Bernini,[a]
glory of the arts and of the City,
humbly reposes here.

a. Gianlorenzo Bernini (1598–1680) was the leading architect and sculptor of the Italian Baroque. Among his most famous works in Rome are the Fontana dei Quattro Fiumi (12.4) and the elephant of Piazza della Minerva (11.4).

4.2L Commemoration of the Conversion of Henri IV

IN HOC SIGNO VINCES

HOC SIGNO : *I.e., the* labarum, *or Chi-Rho emblem. To judge by the opaque description that the ecclesiastical historian Eusebius of Caesarea furnishes, in its original form the* labarum *consisted simply of an elongated* rho *with a single transverse stroke below the bowl. It would in that case have resembled the specimen found in the dedicatory inscription of Pope St. Siricius at S. Paolo fuori le Mura but without the* A *and* Ω *(see 5.8A). According to Eusebius, the words accompanying Constantine's vision of the* labarum *were:* ΤΟΥΤΩ ΝΙΚΑ *('Conquer by this').*

4.2M Museo Liberiano: Dedication by John Paul II

IOANNES PAVLVS II PONTIFEX MAXIMVS

MVSEVM LIBERIANVM

A CAROLO CARD FVRNO

ARCHIPRESBYTERO HVIVS BASILICÆ

5   VNA CVM CAPITVLO ET CANONICIS

INCHOATVM ABSOLVTVMQVE

DEDICAVIT

VI IDVS DECEMBRES A MMI PONTIFICATVS XXIV

FESTO IMMACVLATI CONCEPTVS

10   MAGNÆ DEI PARENTIS

1. IOANNES PAVLVS II : Secundus.
2. MVSEVM : *The* CL mūsēum *transliterates Greek* μουσεῖον *('shrine of the Muses'). —* LIBERIANVM : *See 4.2B, line 2.*
3. CARD(ināli).
4. ARCHIPRESBYTERO : *The* EL archipresbyter *transliterates* EG ἀρχιπρεσβύτερος *('archpriest').*
5. CAPITVLO : *See 4.2G, line 12. —* CANONICIS : *See 4.2G, line 7.*
6. INCHOATAM = incohātam : *On the spelling, see 8.8A, line 2.*
8. VI : Sextō. — DECEMBRES : *Here the* CL *usage is observed (see 1.6G, line 11). —* A(nnō) MMI : Bis mīllēsimō prīmō. — XXIV : Vīcēsimō quārtō.
9. IMMACVLATI : *The* CL immaculātus *is 'unstained'.*
10. DEI PARENTIS : *Cf. 4.2D, line 3.*

S. Maria Maggiore: Court, on Barrel of Cannon

By this sign will you conquer.[a]

a. *These words accompanied the vision of the Holy Cross vouchsafed to Constantine on the eve of the battle of the Milvian Bridge (cf. 2.11A.i, note a). Having grasped the drift of the portent, Constantine caused his soldiers' shields to be emblazoned with the* labarum, *or Chi-Rho emblem:* ☧. *The cannon formed part of a monument erected near the basilica to celebrate the conversion of Henri IV of France (see 1.7A, note c). As its martial character was generally taken for a tasteless allusion to the St. Bartholomew's Day Massacre (24 August 1572), the monument was eventually dismantled.*

Above Entrance to Sacristy

John Paul the Second, Supreme Pontiff,[a]
dedicated
the Liberian Museum,
begun and completed
by Cardinal Carlo Furno,[b]
Archpriest of this Basilica,
together with the Chapter and Canons,[c]
on 8 December 2001,[d]
the Feast of the Immaculate Conception
of the mighty Mother of God.[e]

a. *Pope John Paul II Wojtyła (r. 1978–2005). John Paul placed special emphasis on Marian devotion. His papal arms bore the letter* M *and the motto* Totus Tuus *('Wholly Thine').*

b. *Carlo Furno was named* ARCHPRIEST *of S. Maria Maggiore in 1998.*

c. *See 4.2G, note a.*

d. *Lit., 'on the sixth day before the Ides of December'.*

e. *The doctrine of the Immaculate Conception of the Blessèd Virgin Mary holds that of all Eve's progeny, the BVM alone was without stain of original sin from the moment of her conception. In the thirteenth century, the doctrine was developed on scholastic lines by Duns Scotus. In 1854 it was defined as a dogma by Pope Pius IX (see 9.8.ii, note c). It has remained controversial.*

4.3 Colonna della Pace: Dedication by Paul V

i.

PAVLVS V PONT MAX

COLVMNAM

VETERIS MAGNIFICENTIAE

MONVMENTVM

5   INFORMI SITV OBDVCTAM

NEGLECTAMQVE

EX IMMANIBVS TEMPLI RVINIS

QVOD VESPASIANVS AVGVSTVS

ACTO DE IVDAEIS TRIVMPHO

10   ET REI PVB STATV CONFIRMATO

PACI DICAVERAT

IN HANC SPLENDIDISSIMAM SEDEM

AD BASILICAE LIBERIANAE

DECOREM AVGENDVM

15   SVO IVSSV EXPORTATAM

ET PRISTINO NITORI RESTITVTAM

BEATISSIMAE VIRGINI

EX CVIVS VISCERIBVS

PRINCEPS VERAE PACIS GENITVS EST

20   DONVM DEDIT

AENEAMQVE EIVSDEM VIRGINIS

STATVAM FASTIGIO IMPOSVIT

ANNO SAL MDCXIIII PONTIF IX

1. PAVLVS V : Quīntus. — PONT(ifex) MAX(imus).

3. VETERIS MAGNIFICENTIAE : *Gen. of Description.*

9. DE IVDAEIS : *On the use of the Prep., see* DE TEVTONIS, *1.4, line 2.*

10. PVB(licae).

13–14. AD . . . DECOREM AVGENDVM : *On the construction, see 1.6H, lines 11–12.* — LIBERIANAE : *See 4.2B, line 2.*

21. AENEAMQVE : ăēnčăm (*cf. 11.3B.i, line 2*).

23. SAL(ūtis) MDCXIIII : Mīllēsimō sescentēsimō quārtō decimō. — PONTIF(icātūs) IX : Nōnō.

Piazza di S. Maria Maggiore: Base of Column

NW

Paul the Fifth, Supreme Pontiff,[a]
gave as a gift
this column—
a monument
of ancient grandeur,
covered with foul grime
and neglected,
brought at his bidding
from the vast ruins of the temple
which Vespasian Augustus
had dedicated to Peace [b]
on the celebration of his triumph over the Jews
and the consolidation of the Republic,
to this eminently distinguished site
before the Liberian Basilica [c]
and restored to its former splendor—
to the most blessèd Virgin,
from whose womb was born
the Prince of true Peace,[d]
and set on its height
a bronze statue of the selfsame Virgin
in the year of Salvation 1614,
ninth of his office.

a. *Pope Paul V Borghese (r. 1605–1621). The ninth year of his pontificate ran from 16 May 1613 through 15 May 1614.*

b. *The 14.3-meter monolith in fact belonged to the BASILICA of Constantine, long misidentified as Vespasian's Temple of Peace (see 2.14, note c). It was transferred by Carlo Maderno (see 12.11), who had collaborated with Domenico Fontana in erecting obelisks for Sixtus V (see 7.1.ii, note c).*

c. *See 4.2G, note c. The statue of the BVM is by Guillaume Berthélot.*

d. *The reference to Christ as the 'Prince of true Peace' obliquely censures the false peace commemorated in Vespasian's temple.*

ii.

VASTA COLVMNAM MOLE

QVAE STETIT DIV

PACIS PROFANA IN AEDE

PAVLVS TRANSTVLIT

5   IN EXQVILINVM QVINTVS

ET SANCTISSIMAE

PAX VNDE VERA EST

CONSECRAVIT VIRGINI

Four Iambic Senarii

1. VASTA . . . MOLE : *Abl. of Description.*
4–5. PAVLVS . . . QVINTVS : *I.e., Paul V.* — EXQVILINVM = Esquilīnum (*sc.* mōntem).

iii.

IGNIS COLVMNA

PRAETVLIT LVMEN PIIS

DESERTA NOCTV

VT PERMEARENT INVIA

5   SECVRI AD ARCES

HAEC RECLVDIT IGNEAS

MONSTRANTE AB ALTA SEDE

CALLEM VIRGINE

Four Iambic Senarii

2. PIIS : *Dat. case follows* PRAETVLIT. *The construction is similar to that of* praeficere (*see 2.2, line 14*).
5–6. ARCES . . . IGNEAS : *In a Christian context, the phrase denotes the 'heights of heaven' (see 2.14, line 6).*
7–8. MONSTRANTE . . . VIRGINE : *Abl. Absolute.*

SE

Paul the Fifth[a]
transported to the Esquiline

the column of vast bulk
which long stood

in the unholy Temple of Peace[b]
and consecrated it

to the most holy Virgin,
of true peace the source.[c]

Four Iambic Senarii

a. *See 4.3.i, note a.*
b. *See 4.3.i, note b.*
c. *See 4.3.i, note d.*

NE

A column of fire
shed a guiding light for the faithful,[a]

that by night
they might fearlessly traverse

the trackless wastes: as the Virgin
from her lofty station points the way,

the present column discloses the path
to the ethereal heights.

Four Iambic Senarii

a. *'And the* LORD *went before them by day in a pillar of cloud, to lead them the way; and by night in a pillar of fire, to give them light; to go by day and night: He took not away the pillar of cloud by day, nor the pillar of fire by night, from before the people' (Exod. 13:21–22).*

iv.

IMPVRA FALSI TEMPLA

QVONDAM NVMINIS

IVBENTE MOESTA

SVSTINEBAM CAESARE

5   NVNC LAETA VERI

PERFERENS MATREM DEI

TE PAVLE NVLLIS

OBTICEBO SAECVLIS

Four IAMBIC SENARII

3–4. IVBENTE . . . CAESARE : *Abl.Absolute.* — MOESTA = maesta : *On the spelling, see 1.8B, line 5.*

4.4 Arch of Gallienus: Dedication by Aurelius Victor

1   GALLIENO CLEMENTISSIMO PRINCIPI CVIVS INVICTA VIRTVS ⌐

SOLA PIETATE SVPERATA EST ET SALONINAE SANCTISSIMAE

2   AVG AVRELIVS VICTOR V E DICATISSIMVS NVMINI ⌐

MAIESTATIQVE EORVM

1. GALLIENO CLEMENTISSIMO : *The present inscription, which occupies the narrow moulding of the architrave, replaces an original dedication of Augustus. The fact that the entire surface of the attic was cleared of the Augustan dedication yet left uninscribed has suggested that it was meant to receive a celebratory dedication to Gallienus' father, Valerian, on his triumphant return from a military expedition in Parthia. When Valerian's Parthian campaign ended in his defeat, capture, and execution, this pious intention was naturally left unfulfilled.* — SVPERATA EST : *In LL, the Pf.Part.Pass. is regularly felt as a tenseless Adj., lending the phrase the value of* CL superātur (*see 1.6G, line 7*).

2. AVG(ustae). — V(ir) E(grēgius).

SW

At Caesar's bidding
I in sadness once upheld

the unclean temple
of a false divinity.

Now, bearing joyfully
the mother of the true God,

in your regard, O Paul,
shall I observe silence in no age.[a]

Four IAMBIC SENARII

a. For the conceit that the column serves its new mistress with joy, see 4.1.iii.
The formulation is so vainglorious that Pope Alexander VII (r. 1655–1667)
explored the possibility of having the inscription recut.

Via di S. Vito: E and W Sides

His Eminence Aurelius Victor [a] to Gallienus,[b] most merciful prince,
whose invincible valor is surpassed by his goodness alone, and to
Salonina,[c] most blameless Augusta, in greatest dedication to their
authority and majesty.

a. Marcus Aurelius Victor (not to be confused with the historian Sextus Aurelius Victor) rededicated the present arch, of Augustan date, to Gallienus.
It is in fact the Porta Esquilina of the city's republican wall. The phrase 'his
Eminence' translates the Latin Vir Egregius ('Eminent Gentleman'; cf.
2.2, note e).

b. Publius Licinius Egnatius Gallienus (r. 253–268) was son and colleague
of the emperor Valerian (r. 253–260). He was murdered in a plot involving
two future emperors, Claudius II and Aurelian.

c. Cornelia Salonina, raised to the rank of AUGUSTA on the appointment of
her husband as AUGUSTUS in 253, was a great patron of letters and learning. She was murdered at the same time as Gallienus.

4.5 Arco delle Pere: Dedication by Sixtus V

i.

SIXTVS V PONT MAX

DVCTVM AQVAE FELICIS

RIVO SVBTERRANEO

MILL PASS XIII

5   SVBSTRVCTIONE ARCVATA VII

SVO SVMPTV EXTRVXIT

ANNO DOMINI M D LXXXV PONTIFICATVS I

1. SIXTVS V : Quīntus. — PONT(ifex) MAX(imus).
2. AQVAE FELICIS : *The name* Fēlīx *is used as an Adj. with* aqua (*in this context, 'aqueduct'*).
4. MILL(e) PASS(ūs) XIII : Tredecim.
5. ARCVATA : *The CL* arcuātus *is 'arched'.* — VII : Septem.
6. EXTRVXIT = exstrūxit : *On the spelling, see 4.2A, line 7.*
7. M D LXXXV : Mīllēsimō quīngentēsimō octōgēsimō quīntō. — I : Prīmō.

ii.

SIXTVS V PONT MAX

VIAS VTRASQ ET AD S MARIAM

MAIOREM ET AD S MARIAM

ANGELORVM AD POPVLI

5   COMMODITATEM ET DEVOTIONEM

LONGAS LATASQ

SVA IMPENSA STRAVIT

1. SIXTVS V : Quīntus. — PONT(ifex) MAX(imus).
2. VTRASQ(ue). — S(ānctam) MARIAM | MAIOREM : *I.e., the Basilica of S. Maria Maggiore.*
3. S(ānctam) MARIAM | ANGELORVM : *I.e., the Basilica of S. Maria degli Angeli. On* ANGELORVM, *see 4.2J, line 2.*
6. LATASQ(ue).

Piazzale Sisto Quinto: Attic of Arch

East

> *Sixtus the Fifth,[a] Supreme Pontiff,*
> *built at his own expense[b]*
> *the conduit of the Acqua Felice,*
> *thirteen miles*
> *in an underground channel,*
> *seven on a supporting arcade,[c]*
> *in the year of the Lord 1585, first of his office.*

a. *Pope Sixtus V Peretti (r. 1585–1590). The first year of his pontificate ran from 24 April 1585 through 23 April 1586.*

b. *The expense of the project was in fact largely borne by the Commune (see* CONSERVATORS*).*

c. *The arch is a relic of the intramural tract of the arcade, demolished 1869– 1874 for the construction of Stazione Centrale di Termini. On account of the pears that figure prominently in the papal arms, the arch is known in Ital. as* Arco delle Pere *('Arch of the Pears').*

West

> *For the convenience and piety*
> *of the people,*
> *Sixtus the Fifth,[a] Supreme Pontiff,*
> *paved at his own cost*
> *the length and breadth of the two roads,[b]*
> *both to Santa Maria Maggiore*
> *and to Santa Maria degli Angeli.*

a. *See 4.5.i, note a.*

b. *The first of these roads, Via di Porta San Lorenzo, was eliminated after 1870 for the development of the present residential quarter and railway station (see 4.5.i, note c); the second corresponds to the present Via Marsala, traced under Sixtus' detested predecessor, Gregory XIII. The true function of the thoroughfares was rather to define the limits of the pope's estate than to facilitate the circulation of pilgrims (see 4.1.i, note d).*

4.6A Porta Tiburtina: Dedication by Augustus

IMP CAESAR DIVI IVLI F AVGVSTVS

PONTIFEX MAXIMVS COS $\overline{\text{XII}}$

TRIBVNIC POTESTAT $\overline{\text{XIX}}$ IMP $\overline{\text{XIIII}}$

RIVOS AQV[a]RVM OMNIVM REFECIT

1. IMP(erātor). — DIVI : *On dīvus, see 2.4, line 1.* — F(īlius).
2. CO(n)S(ul) $\overline{\text{XII}}$: Duodecimum.
3. TRIBVNIC(iā) POTESTAT(e) $\overline{\text{XIX}}$: Ūndēvīcēsimum. — IMP(erātor) $\overline{\text{XIIII}}$: Quārtum decimum.
4. RIVOS : *The word* rīvus *is used of both natural and artificial water-courses.* — AQV[a]RVM : *The character enclosed in brackets is restored from context. In this usage,* aqua *is 'aqueduct'.*

4.6B Porta Tiburtina: Dedication by Vespasian

IMP TITVS CAESAR DIVI F VESPASIANVS AVG PONTIF MAX

TRIBVNICIAE POTESTAT $\overline{\text{IX}}$ IMP $\overline{\text{XV}}$ CENS COS $\overline{\text{VII}}$ DESIG $\overline{\text{IIX}}$ P P

RIVOM AQ[uae marci]AE VETVSTATE DILAPSVM REFECIT

ET AQVAM QVAE IN VSV ESSE DESIERAT R[e]DVXIT

1. IMP(erātor). — F(īlius). — AVG(ustus). — PONTIF(ex) MAX(imus).
2. TRIBVNICIAE POTESTAT(is) : *Gen. of Description (the Abl. is more usual in this formula).* — $\overline{\text{IX}}$: Nōnum. — IMP(erātor) $\overline{\text{XV}}$: Quīntum decimum. — CENS(or). — CO(n)S(ul) $\overline{\text{VII}}$: Septimum. — DESIG(nātus) $\overline{\text{IIX}}$: Octāvum. *The subtractive style of notation ordinarily extends to just a single place (whereas* IX *is usual for* novem, *octō is typically represented by the additive* VIII *rather than by* IIX).
3. RIVOM = rīvum : *In speech, the passage of short /o/ > /u/ before final consonants was complete by about the middle of the first century* BC (*cf.* 2.12B, *line 2). Around* AD *95, the grammarian Quintilian reported that his own teachers had nevertheless favored such spellings as* SERVOS (= servus), *a graphic archaism of which the spelling* RIVOM *is likewise an example.* — AQ[uae marci]AE : *The name of the aqueduct derives from the name* Mārcius (*it was built by Quintus Marcius Rex; cf.* 4.5.i, *line 2). The portions enclosed in brackets are restored from context.* — VETV-STATE DILAPSVM : *On this formula, cf.* 13.12, *line 4.*

Piazzale di Porta S. Lorenzo: Attic of Arch, Top Register

Imperator Caesar Augustus,[a] son of the Divine Julius,
Supreme Pontiff, Consul for the twelfth time,
vested with the Tribunician power for the nineteenth,
acclaimed Imperator for the fourteenth,
rebuilt the channels of all the aqueducts.

a. On 16 January 27 BC Caesar's heir formally took the name IMPERATOR CAESAR AUGUSTUS. He was granted the office of SUPREME PONTIFF in 12 BC, became CONSUL for the twelfth time on 1 January 5 BC, assumed the TRIBUNICIAN POWER for the nineteenth on 1 July 5 BC and was saluted as IMPERATOR for the fourteenth on 1 January 8 BC. Before the construction of the wall of Aurelian, the function of the arch was to permit the passage of the aqueducts over the Via Tiburtina (cf. 7.5D, note c).

Central Register

Imperator Titus Caesar Vespasian Augustus,[a] son of the Divine,[b]
Supreme Pontiff, vested with the Tribunician power for the ninth time,
acclaimed Imperator for the fifteenth, Censor, Consul for the seventh,
Consul Designate for the eighth, Father of his Country,
rebuilt the channel of the Aqua Marcia,[c] dilapidated with age,
and reintroduced a water supply that had fallen into disuse.

a. Titus Flavius Vespasianus (r. 79–81), conventionally styled 'Titus' to distinguish him from his homonymous father ('Vespasian'), assumed the TRIBUNICIAN POWER on 1 July 71; he assumed the power for the ninth time on 1 July 79. Titus became CONSUL for the seventh time on 1 January of the same year, in which he was also saluted as IMPERATOR for the fifteenth time; he became CENSOR for the first time in April of 73. Like all the successors of Augustus, he was granted the office of SUPREME PONTIFF on his accession. The title 'Father of his Country' was conferred on Augustus in 2 BC and assumed by nearly all the emperors (see PATER PATRIAE).

b. On the designation 'Divine', see 2.4, note a.

c. The Aqua Marcia was built 144–140 BC by Quintus Marcius Rex. Because of its coldness and purity, the water of the Marcia was always considered the city's best.

4.6C Porta Tiburtina: Dedication by Caracalla

IMP CAES M AVRELLIVS ANTONINVS PIVS FELIX AVG PARTH MAXIM

BRIT MAXIMVS PONTI[f]EX MAXIMVS

[aqua]M MARCIAM VARIS KASIBVS IMPEDITAM PVRGATO FONTE EXCISIS ET PERFORATIS

MONTIBVS RESTITVTA F[o]RMA ADQVISITO ET[ia]M FONTE NOV[o] ANTONINIANO

5   IN SACRAM VRBEM SVAM PERDVCEND[am] CVRAVIT

1. IMP(erātor) CAES(ar) M(ārcus) AVRELLIVS : *The spelling with doubled* L *is not uncommon in the inscriptions of Caracalla.* — AVG(ustus). — PARTH(icus) MAXIM(us).

2. BRIT(tannicus) : *The spelling with doubled* T *is usual in the inscriptions of the Severans.* — PONTI[f]EX : *The characters enclosed in brackets are restored from context.*

3. [aqua]M MARCIAM : *See* 4.6B, *line* 3. — VARIS = variis. — KASIBVS = cāsibus : *The character* K *early fell into desuetude except in a few old abbreviations, e.g.,* KAL(endae) *and* K(aesō). *In Quintilian's time and later, however, certain grammarians prescribed the use of* K *always before* A.

4. FORMA : *Among its many senses,* CL fōrma *is used of the conduit of an aqueduct.* — ANTONINIANO : *The Adj.* Antōniniānus *answers to the name* Antōninus (*line* 1).

5. SACRAM : *In* LL, *the Adj.* sacer *is virtually 'imperial'* (cf. 2.1, *line* 5).

A fourth inscription, of Arcadius and Honorius, duplicates the text of 7.5D.

Lower Register

Imperator Caesar Marcus Aurelius Antoninus Pius Felix Augustus Parthicus Maximus Britannicus Maximus,[a] Supreme Pontiff, by clearing the source, excavating and tunneling through hills, restoring the conduit and also adding the new Antonine source,[b] undertook to have the Aqua Marcia,[c] obstructed through sundry calamities, brought into his imperial City.

a. *Septimius Bassianus (r. 211–217), eldest son of the emperor Septimius Severus (see 2.3, note a), is better known by his nickname 'Caracalla'. In 198, he was made co-ruler under the name 'Imperator Caesar Marcus Aurelius Antoninus Augustus' (see 2.3, note b). The title Parthicus Maximus was added in 199, Pius and Felix in 200 and Britannicus in 210, the year before Caracalla and his hapless brother Geta (see 2.3, note d) succeeded their father. Like all the successors of Augustus, Caracalla was granted the office of SU-PREME PONTIFF on his accession.*

b. *Caracalla built the Aqua Antoniniana, a branch of the Aqua Marcia, to supply his baths.*

c. *See 4.6B, note c.*

A fourth inscription, of Arcadius and Honorius, duplicates the text of 7.5D.

4.7A San Lorenzo fuori le Mura: Commemoration of Repairs

AEDES

LAVRENTI

BELLO DISIECTA

XIV KAL AVG A MCMXLIII

5   DEO ADIVVANTE

FELICITER

REFECTA

1. AEDES : *See 1.8B, line 10.*
4. XIV : Quārtō decimō. — KAL(endās) AVG(ustās) : *This completion assumes* CL *usage* (*vs.* ML Augustī; *see 1.6G, line 11, and cf. 4.2M, line 8*). — A(nnō) MCMXLIII : Mīllēsimō nōngentēsimō quadrāgēsimō tertiō.

4.7B San Lorenzo fuori le Mura: Dedication to Lawrence

MARTYRIVM FLAMMIS OLIM LEVVITA SVBISTI ¬

IVRE TVIS TEMPLIS LVX BENERANDA REDIT

One Elegiac Couplet

MARTYRIVM : *The* EL martyrium *transliterates Greek* μαρτύριον (*'testimony', then* EG *'martyrdom'). It forms the abstract noun to* martyr (*see 2.10, line 2*). — LEVVITA = levīta : *Transliterates* EG λευείτης (*'Levite', then 'deacon'*). — TVIS TEMPLIS : *Especially in Neut. nouns, the use of the Pl. without difference in sense from the Sg. is usual in Latin verse* (*cf. 3.4D, line 2*). *The Dat. case following* REDIT (*where in prose the Acc. of Place Whither would be usual*) *is likewise a feature of poetic idiom.*

— BENERANDA = veneranda : *By the early imperial period, intervocalic* /b/ *and the semiconsonant* /w/ *had merged in the bilabial fricative* /β/ (*pronounced as in Span.* lavar), *which in turn proceeded to the labiodental fricative* /v/. *The results of this phonological trend are seen in the parallel development of Latin* movēre *to Ital.* muovere = /'muɔ:vere/ *and Latin* habēre *to Ital.* avere = /a've:re/. *In orthography, a confusion between* B *and* V *is evident as early as the first century.*

Pavement, Center of Nave

*The fane
of Lawrence,
shattered by war
on 19 July in the year 1943,[a]
has with God's help
been auspiciously
rebuilt.*

a. Lit., 'on the fourteenth day before the Kalends of August'. Alone among the
   city's churches to suffer serious damage during the Second World War,
   S. Lorenzo was struck by an errant Allied aerial bomb that destroyed
   much of the façade and S wall. Some 1,500 Romans perished in the attack,
   which devastated the entire quarter.

Triumphal Arch, Inner Face

*Once upon a time, as deacon, you suffered martyrdom in the flames.[a]
Justly does noble light return to your shrine.[b]*

One ELEGIAC COUPLET

a. St. Lawrence was ordained DEACON by Pope St. Sixtus II (r. 257–258).
   After the summary execution of Sixtus and four of his deacons on 6 August
   258 (see 6.10, note a) Lawrence was arrested and ordered to surrender
   the Church's wealth. According to legend, he was martyred on 10 August,
   roasted on a gridiron (his attribute in art).
b. The original church on the site was a large cemetery BASILICA (see 8.8A,
   note a) erected by Constantine. The emperor's vanished foundation stood
   to the W of the present building, which itself incorporates two structures.
   The first was built by Pope Pelagius II (r. 579–590). In order to furnish
   direct access to the martyr's relics, the hillside in which they were located
   was excavated and the church constructed so as to enclose the tomb. This
   type of basilica ad corpus ('in the presence of the body') is seen also at the
   shrines of SS. Nereus and Achilleus (6.9) and of St. Agnes (8.8). At the end
   of the twelfth century the apse of the Pelagian church was demolished and
   replaced by a second, much larger, basilical nave contiguous with the first.
   This modification reversed the liturgical orientation of the original church,
   which henceforth served as a presbytery.

4.7C   Epitaph of Landolfo

[pr]ECLV[is] HIC RECVBAT L[andolfus uulnere f]OSSVS
   QVEM FLE[ui]T NIMIVM CON . . .
CARA SEN[at]RICIS THEODO[rae atque ioha]NNIS
   CONSV[lis] ATQVE DVCIS [inclyta progenies]
5 CVM FLOR[e]RET ENIM PRIME[uo flore iu]VENTE
   EFFVDIT VITAM SANG[uine purpu]REO
[moribus] ENITVIT CV[mulato] ET D[ig]NIOR AEVO
          . . . [p]EREM[it] EVM
HVNC SIBI FECIT ADOPTIV[um m]AROZA SENATRIX
10   AC NVTRIVIT EVM DELIC[iis] VARIIS
CVI TVMVLVM LVGENS MA[te]R CONSTRVXIT AB IMO
   IN QVO MEMBRA SVA PVLC[hr]A NIMIS POSVIT
MARTYRIS AD TEMPLVM PROP[er]ANTES DICITE CIVES
   LANDOLFO IVVENI PARCE [b]ENIGNE DEVS
15 D̄EP XV K̄L̄ AVḠ TĒMP [do]M IOHI XII P̄P̄ INDĪC VI
ANNO DN̄ICE INCARNATIONIS DN̄I DCCCC LXIII

Seven *ELEGIAC COUPLETS* (lines 1–14)

1. [pr]ECLV[is] = praecluis : *On the spelling, see 1.8B, line 5. The* LL *Adj.*
   praecluis *is 'illustrious', 'renowned'. The portions of the text enclosed in*
   brackets have been restored from context as well as by clever if perhaps
   incautious conjecture (cf. 1.6B, line 1).
2. CON . . . : *Lines 2 and 8 are too fragmentary to permit restoration.*
3. THEODO[rae atque : *Elision is neglected.*
4. inclyta = incluta : *On the spelling, see 8.8A, line 10.*
5. PRIME[uo = prīmaevō.
9. m]AROZA : *A variant of* Marotia *or* Marozia.
12. SVA : *I.e.,* ēius (*Landolfo's limbs, not her own*). *It scans* suā.
15. DEP(ositus). — XV : Quīntō decimō. — K(a)L(endās). — AVG(ustī). —
    TEMP(ore). — [do]M(inī) IOH(ann)I(s) XII : Duodecimī. — P(a)P(a) :
    See 3.6A, line 2. — INDIC(tiōne) : *See 2.1, line 16.* — VI : Sextā.
16. D(omi)NICE : *See 3.3C, line 2.* — INCARNATIONIS : *The* EL incarnātiō
    represents Greek σάρκωσις (*'enfleshing'*). — D(omi)NI : *Redundant with*
    D(omi)NICE *above.* — DCCCC LXIII : Nōngentēsimō sexāgēsimō
    tertiō.

S. Lorenzo fuori le Mura: Lower Church, R Wall

Here reposes the illustrious Landolfo,[a] pierced by a wound,
who was deeply mourned by . . .[b]
the dear offspring, and renowned, of Theodora, Senatrix,
and of Giovanni, Consul and Captain.[c] For as he flourished
in the first flower of youth, he poured forth his life in red blood,
He was outstanding for his qualities of character
and worthier as his age advanced.

. . . slew him.

Marozia,[d] Senatrix, made him her adoptive son
and fostered him with multifarious delights.
For him his mother in grief raised a tomb from its foundations
in which she, exceedingly fair, laid his limbs.
O citizens, as you hasten to the martyr's shrine, offer a prayer:
'God, in your kindness spare the young Landolfo'.
Buried on 18 July[e] in the time of Pope John XII,[f] in the sixth
indiction,[g] in the year of the Lord's Incarnation of the Lord[h] 963.

Seven ELEGIAC COUPLETS (lines 1–14)

a. Great-grandson of Theophylact, whose family controlled Rome for much of the tenth century, Landolfo died amid the endemic factional fighting that followed the coronation of the Saxon emperor Otto I in February of 962. Owing in part to clerical disapproval of the prominent role played in ecclesiastical affairs by Theophylact's wife, Theodora, and daughters, Theodora and Marozia, the period from the accession of Pope Sergius III (AD 904) to the death of Pope John XII (964) has been stigmatized as the 'pornocracy' of the Holy See. The ladies are taxed in particular with imposing a succession of their paramours and bastards on the throne of St. Peter.

b. The second and eighth lines are too fragmentary to permit restoration.

c. Landolfo's mother was Theodora, granddaughter of Theophylact. Crescenzio 'de Theodora' (see 5.5) was his uncle.

d. Not the infamous Marozia, Theodora's daughter, but her niece of the same name.

e. Lit., 'on the fifteenth day before the Kalends of August'.

f. Pope John XII (r. 955–964) was grandson of the infamous Marozia.

g. The INDICTION was a fifteen-year tax cycle; see 2.1, note e.

h. The redundancy appears to be unintentional.

PYRAMID OF GAIUS CESTIUS

Like the insubstantial Caecilia Metella whose mausoleum dominates the Campagna, Gaius Cestius would be lost to history but for the magnificence of his tomb. His pyramid is 100 Roman feet square at the base and 125 Roman feet in height—sufficiently imposing to merit inclusion in the wall of Aurelian in the late third century. The fact that pyramidal funerary monuments were found with particular frequency in Nubia (Sudan) has fostered speculation that Cestius perhaps served in that province, annexed in 24 BC. A similar monument near Castel Sant'Angelo was demolished at the end of the fifteenth century to make way for the Borgo Nuovo of Pope Alexander VI.

V. From the Forum Boarium to San Paolo fuori le Mura

THE WATERCOURSE THAT IN PREHISTORIC TIMES flooded the Forum fell away to the Tiber through the little valley of the Velabrum. In remote Antiquity, the marshy plain at its mouth played host to Rome's earliest port. Located just below the Tiber Island, this propitious plot of ground was quite literally the crossroads of Iron Age Italy. Here the ancient coastal road linking Etruria to the north with Latium and Campania to the south intersected the salt route that followed the river valley from the sea to the Sabine hinterland. The presence of this crossroads, determined by the location of the ford at Tiber Island, furnished Rome's initial raison d'être.

Ancient tradition unanimously attested a strong eastern or Greek influence in the neighborhood. In the pages of Livy and Virgil we read of a community of Arcadian refugees domiciled on the Palatine in the misty heroic age that preceded the foundation of Rome. The Greek hero Hercules is supposed to have slain the monster Cacus in his lair on the slopes of the neighboring Aventine. Most famously, the Trojan Aeneas was said to have visited the site during the same period, long before the traditional date of the founding of the city. Unsurprisingly, no epigraphic evidence of these legendary events survives, though they figure in a charming if awkward poem commemorating the improvements of Pope CALLIS- 5.6 TUS III (r. 1455–1458) to the Church of Santa Prisca.

After the canalization of the Velabrum watercourse in the seventh century BC, the zone between the Tiber and the Forum developed with increasing intensity. The commercial district that grew up by the riverside was known as the Forum Boarium ('Cattle Market'). In addition to the market and a burgeoning residential quarter, a major sanctuary of Hercules—the Ara Maxima—was established at an early date. The presence of the cult of Heracles, together with the abundance of Greek ceramics found here, has encouraged speculation that this emporium found special favor with Greek merchants. Throughout Antiquity the Forum Boarium conserved a popular and mercantile character.

At the end of the ancient period, in the centuries following Constantine's transfer of the imperial capital to the shores of the Bosporus (AD 330), Rome dwindled to little more than a village. By the year 600, the bulk of the city's population occupied a narrow zone delimited by Trastevere to the southwest and the foot of the Capitoline Hill to the northeast—a zone whose geographical center coincided with the ancient Forum Boarium. Perhaps as early as the second half of the sixth century, Christian *diaconiae* ('deaconries') began to be established in this area. These were charitable foundations instituted for the purpose of providing material assistance to the impoverished populace. The earliest appear to have been situated by preference in the vicinity of the old Tiber docks or near grain magazines.

Though as a rule they were equipped with an oratory or chapel, deaconries were not in origin proper churches. The officials who administered them were civil functionaries whose activity continued a traditional service of the old Roman government. Indeed, the fact that many deaconries were founded by officers of Rome's Byzantine garrison explains the frequency of dedications to such eastern soldier-saints as George and Theodore. Deaconries proliferated with the increasing popularity of Rome as a destination for pilgrims; by AD 800 there were at least twenty-four. In the course of time, all were transformed into regular churches; much as Rome's ancient titular foundations were assigned to cardinal priests, the deaconries were made the honorary charge of cardinal deacons.

One of the oldest of the deaconries is the Church of San Teodoro: though first attested in the eighth century, it likely dates to the period following the city's recapture from the Goths in AD 552. The church stands at the foot of the western slope of the Palatine Hill, near the site where the ancients imagined that Romulus and Remus had been suckled by the she-wolf; indeed, in later centuries it was erroneously believed to have been a pagan temple converted for Christian use. Restorations were carried out in the mid-fifteenth century by Pope Nicholas V (r. 1447–1455) and in the early eighteenth by Pope Clement XI (r. 1700–1721). In 2004, San Teodoro was reconsecrated by papal concession as a Greek Orthodox church.

The Basilica of San Giorgio in Velabro is of comparable antiquity. Perhaps in the sixth century, structures on its site were adapted as a deaconry. The improvisatory character of the initial conversion has left traces in the asymmetry of the existing basilica, built probably in the late sixth or early seventh century. The association with St. George is not original; the church was first dedicated to St. Sebastian, whose corpse was said to have been thrust into the Cloaca Maxima near this place. The present dedication was made in the eighth century, when the skull of St. George was deposited in the church by Pope St. Zacharias (r. 741–752). A belfry was added in the twelfth century and the portico, bearing the inscription of one STEFANO DELLA STELLA, dates to the early thirteenth.   5.2

The Basilica of Santa Maria in Cosmedin, too, is built into an ancient structure: the original deaconry was improvised in a freestanding portico, the back of which abutted a large ancient platform constructed in tufa, a local vocanic stone. When the deaconry was enlarged by Pope Hadrian I (r. 772–795), considerable effort was expended in demolishing this structure. Although scholarly consensus has yet to be reached on its identity, the preponderance of opinion runs in favor of the Ara Maxima of Hercules. Further improvements were made three centuries later by the papal chamberlain ALFANO. These included the installation 5.3A of a lovely pavement, choir stalls, and an episcopal throne. All but annihilated in the sixteenth century to accommodate the requirements of Counter Reformation liturgy, the sumptuous medieval stonework was recreated in a restoration of the nineteenth.

In the sixth century, the presence of the Byzantine administration on the Palatine Hill had renewed the ancient Greek associations of the Velabrum and Forum Boarium. Over the course of the seventh, Rome saw a more or less continuous influx of 'Greeks'—not only native Hellenes but also Syrians, Palestinians, and Africans of Greek speech. Though most were refugees from the conquests of the Arabs, others had been driven west by the Iconoclastic persecutions. Under pressure from Islam, the Byzantine emperors not infrequently espoused doctrines of dubious orthodoxy in their effort to retain the loyalty of the largely Monophysite populations of Syria and Egypt; unencumbered by the subtleties of Trinitarian theology, the religion of Muhammad was perilously congenial to their strict if heterodox monotheism. An indirect result of the emperors' zealotry was the emergence of a thriving Greek quarter at Rome. In the Middle Ages, the zone of the old Forum Boarium was known as the 'Ripa Greca' ('Greek Bank') and its community as the 'Schola Greca' ('Greek Colony').

Having been inhabited continuously since Antiquity, the zone extending from the Forum Boarium to the foot of the Capitoline Hill presented a characteristically labyrinthine fabric of churches, palaces, streets, and piazzas. Though it escaped the upheavals that beset large sections of intramural Rome after Italy's unification in 1870, the quarter was destined to fall victim in its entirety to the urban improvements of Mussolini. Between 1926 and 1932, the corridor centering on the ancient Via Tor de' Specchi was razed to accommodate Via del Mare (today's Via del Teatro di Marcello). The Theater of Marcellus was liberated of encroaching construction; Piazza Montanara was erased. Demolitions carried out for the construction of the national registry offices brought the path of destruction as far as the Forum Boarium itself. Apart from a few isolated monuments, by 1941 the whole of the medieval quarter between Piazza Venezia and Santa Maria in Cosmedin had been replaced by a modern thoroughfare lined by nondescript government buildings.

5.1   One of the few structures to be spared was the 'CASA DEI CRESCENZI'. This ramshackle construction is the surviving fragment of a fortified dwelling built in the mid-eleventh century to control Ponte Santa Maria, today's Ponte Rotto. The dedicatory inscription identifies the builder as Nicolaus, son of Crescentius and Theodora. Because of the father's name, the house has been conventionally associated with the so-called 'Crescenzi', but the name 'Crescenzio' (in Latin, *Crescentius*) was not yet that of a family. The name belonged to several individuals, particularly a father and son who played a prominent role in Rome of the late tenth century. The use of their name to designate a clan is a convenience of historians; no connection by blood or marriage with the Crescentius who built the 'Casa dei Crescenzi' has been established.

The elder and younger Crescenzio were scions of the house of Theophylact, a strongman of the tenth century who had succeeded in erecting a dynasty on the ruins of Carolingian authority at Rome. Their kin included such infamous figures as Theophylact's wife Theodora and daughter Marozia, protagonists of a 'pornocracy' that appears to have owed its most lurid episodes to the overheated imagination of censorious clerics. The younger Crescenzio—distinguished by historians as Crescenzio II or Crescenzio 'Nomentano'—seized control of Castel Sant'Angelo in 998. Though he held it for some weeks against the Saxon emperor Otto III, he was defeated and captured after a bitter siege and then decapitated on the battlements.

The memory of the father—Crescenzio I—is preserved in the remarkable EPITAPH OF CRESCENZIO 'DE THEODORA' that survives 5.5 in the former monastery of Sant'Alessio on the Aventine Hill. A grandson of Theophylact, Crescenzio the elder was the father of Crescenzio II and the uncle of the Landolfo whose tomb is found at San Lorenzo fuori le Mura. In 974, Crescenzio instigated a rebellion in which the proimperial Pope Benedict VI was deposed by the deacon Franco; the latter assumed the throne of St. Peter as 'Boniface VII'. When word arrived that the emperor Otto II had determined to intervene, Franco ordered Benedict VI strangled in his cell at Castel Sant'Angelo. Though Franco was eventually forced to flee for his life, Crescenzio emerged from the turmoil unscathed to pass his declining years as a monk at Sant'Alessio.

Like the other *monti* ('hills'), the Aventine wore a rural look through-

out the Middle Ages and well into the modern era. In late Antiquity, the hill had been covered with opulent townhouses. Perhaps as a consequence, it is the quarter that suffered most during the sack of Alaric in AD 410. Indeed, no ancient dwelling excavated on the hill lacks signs of damage by fire. It is likely that the ancient temple of Juno Regina was damaged or destroyed on the same occasion, liberating its site
5.4   for the construction of the BASILICA OF SANTA SABINA. Following the Gothic wars of the mid-sixth century, the Aventine Hill was more
5.7   or less abandoned; beyond its southern slopes, the PYRAMID OF CESTIUS rose in isolation on the open Campagna beside Porta San Paolo, the gate of St. Paul.

According to the closing chapters of the Acts of the Apostles, St. Paul was taken before the Roman governor Festus at Caesarea; there he exercised his right of appeal to Caesar. Tradition holds that Paul was brought to Rome and martyred during the reign of Nero (r. AD 54–68). He is supposed to have been buried at the site of the basilica that bears his name. Despite his prominence in the New Testament, St. Paul suffered neglect in Rome by comparison with St. Peter: whereas the latter was honored by Constantine with an imposing basilica, Paul had only a modest *memoria*, a monument marking the site of his burial. With the efforts of the fourth-century papacy to court the city's educated elite, there arose a new interest in the intellectual achievement of St. Paul, the *Doctor Gentium* ('Teacher of the Nations'). Paul's growing prestige is seen in the replacement of Constantine's modest shrine at the site of
5.8   his tomb by a monumental basilica—SAN PAOLO FUORI LE MURA—consecrated in 390 by Pope St. Siricius (r. 384–399). It is telling that the initiative for the basilica dates to the reign of the great 'Romanizer', Pope St. Damasus I (r. 366–384).

After standing for fourteen centuries, on the night of 14 July 1823 San Paolo was gutted by an accidental fire. The ruins of the nave were demolished and replaced with a soulless neoclassical structure of the same dimensions. Of the original architecture, only the triumphal arch, transepts, apse, and cloister were preserved. Despite this catastrophe, sundry relics of the old basilica survive. These include the Epitaph of St. Paul inscribed on the lid of a sarcophagus concealed beneath the high altar, the dedications of HONORIUS and GALLA PLACIDIA, and the elabo- 5.8E&F rate bronze doors donated in 1070 by the Amalfitan merchant PANTA- 5.8D LEONE.

The epigraphical collection in the cloister includes a stone purporting to commemorate a concluding episode in the life of the emperor NERO. 5.8G

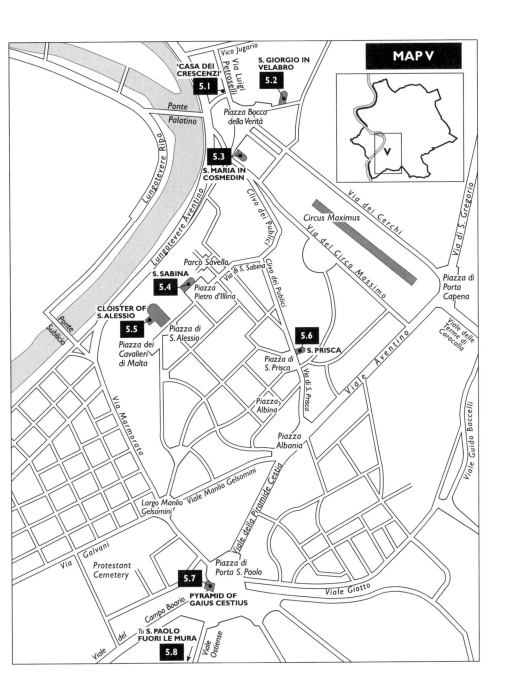

MAP V

'CASA DEI CRESCENZI' 5.1

S. GIORGIO IN VELABRO 5.2

Vico Jugario

Via Luigi Petroselli

Ponte Palatino

Piazza Bocca della Verità

5.3 S. MARIA IN COSMEDIN

Lungotevere Ripa

Lungotevere Aventino

Clivo dei Publici

Via dei Cerchi

Circus Maximus

Via del Circo Massimo

Via di S. Gregorio

Parco Savello

Via di S. Sabina

Clivo dei Publici

S. SABINA 5.4

Piazza Pietro d'Illiria

CLOISTER OF S. ALESSIO 5.5

Piazza di S. Alessio

Piazza dei Cavalieri di Malta

5.6 S. PRISCA

Piazza di S. Prisca

Via di S. Prisca

Piazza Albina

Piazza Albania

Viale Aventino

Piazza di Porta Capena

Viale delle Terme di Caracalla

Viale Guido Baccelli

Ponte Sublicio

Via Marmorata

Viale Manlio Gelsomini

Largo Manlio Gelsomini

Viale della Piramide Cestia

Via Galvani

Protestant Cemetery

Piazza di Porta S. Paolo

5.7 PYRAMID OF GAIUS CESTIUS

Viale Giotto

Campo Boario

To S. PAOLO FUORI LE MURA 5.8

Viale del

Viale

Viale Ostiense

5.1 Casa dei Crescenzi: Dedication by Nicolò

1   NON FVIT IGNARVS CVIVS DOMVS HEC NICOLAVS ¬
    QVOD NIL MOMENTI SIBI MVNDI GLORIA SENTIT

2   VERVM QVOD FECIT HANC NON TAM VANA COEGIT ¬
    GLORIA QVAM ROME VETEREM RENOVARE DECOREM

3   IN DOMIBVS PVLCRIS MEMORES ESTOTE SEPVLCRIS
    CONFISIQVE TIV NON IBI STARE DIV ¬

4   MORS VEHIT PENNIS | NVLLI SVA VITA PHENNIS ¬
    MANSIO NRA BREVIS CVRSV ET IPSE LEVIS ¬
    SI FVGIAS VENTV SI CLAVDAS OSTIA C

5   LISGOR MILLE IVBES N [S]INE MORTE CVBES ¬
    SI MANEAS CASTRIS EFM VICIN[um et] ASTRIS ¬

6   OCIVS INDE SOLET TOLLE|RE QOSQE VO[l]LET ¬
    SVRGIT IN ASTRA DOMVS SVBLIMIS [c]VLMINA CVIVS ¬
    PRIM DE [p]RIM[i]S MAGNVS NICHOLAVS AB IMIS

7   EREXIT PATV DECVS OB RENOVARE [s]VORV ¬
    STAT PATRIS CRESCENS MATRISQ THEODORA NOM

8   HOC CVLMEN CLARV CARO P' PIGNERE GESTV ¬
    DAVIDI TRIBVIT QVI PATER EXHIBVIT

Eight HEXAMETERS (*verses 1–2, 6–7*), *Five* ELEGIAC COUPLETS (*verses 3–6, 8*)

1. HEC = haec : *On the spelling, see 1.8B, line 5.*
2. FECIT : *Scans* fecīt. — ROME = Romae.
3. PVLCRIS = pulchrīs : *On the spelling, see 8.8A, line 2.* — TIV : *A pronunciation spelling of Greek* θεῷ. — VEHIT(ur).
4. P(er)HENNIS : *The* H *is spurious* (*cf. 11.3B.i, line 2*). — MANSIO : *Scans* mansiŏ. — N(ost)RA. — CVRSV(s) : *Scans* cursŭs. — VENTV(m). — C(entum).
5. LISGOR : *Probably 'sentinel'.* — N(ōn). — EFM = fermē. — VICIN[um et] : *Elision is neglected.* — TOLLE|RE.
6. Q(u)OSQ(u)E. — VO[l]LET = volet : *Scans* vŏllet. — PRIM(us).
7. PAT(r)V(m). — OB RENOVARE : *In* CL, ut renovāret. — [s]VORV(m). — MATRISQ(ue). — CRESCENS . . . THEODORA : *The syntax calls for Gen. not Nom.* — THEODORA : *Scans* Theōdŏra. — NOM(en).
8. CLARV(m). — P(rō). — GESTV(m). — DAVIDI : *Scans* Dāvidi.

Via Luigi Petroselli 54: Façade, above Portal

Nicolò,[a] proprietor of this house,[b] was not unaware
that the glory of the world was of no consequence to him:
in truth, what drove him to build this was not vainglory
but the desire to renew the ancient splendor of Rome.
Within your beautiful houses, remember the tomb and,
having put your faith in God, that you will not abide here long.
Death wings its way; no one's life lasts forever. Our sojourn
is brief and its course fleeting. If you should escape the wind,
should close your doors a hundredfold, if you command
a thousand guards, you will not retire to rest without death.
If you should dwell in a fortress all but as high as the stars,
the more swiftly is death accustomed to snatch away whomsoever
it will. The lofty house rises to the stars, whose towers the great
Nicolò, first among the first, built from their foundations
to renew the splendor of his ancestors. Here stands the name
of his father Crescenzio and his mother Theodora:
the father who flaunted this illustrious house,
built for his dear child, gave it to David.[c]

Eight Hexameters *(verses 1–2, 6–7), Five* Elegiac Couplets *(verses 3–6, 8)*

a. *This Nicolò is not otherwise known. He should perhaps be associated with the family of Crescenzio 'de Theodora', grandson of Theophylact (see 5.5). Though the names 'Giovanni' and 'Benedetto' are equally frequent in that family, the prominence of Crescenzio 'de Theodora' and his son Crescenzio 'Nomentano' has led to the anachronistic use of 'Crescenzio' as if it were a surname.*

b. *So situated as to dominate the E bridgehead of what is today Ponte Rotto (see 13.12), the twelfth-century house is a ramshackle construction incorporating odd fragments of ancient architectural ornament in its crude brickwork. The tower with which it was formerly crowned is believed to have fallen victim to disturbances consequent on the coronation of the emperor Henry VII in 1312. In the nineteenth century, as a result of attempts to associate cryptic abbreviations in the building's inscriptions with Cola di Rienzo, it was popularly known as the 'House of Rienzi' (cf. 1.8A, note b).*

c. *David was Nicolò's son.*

5.2 S. Giorgio in Velabro: Dedication of Portico

STEFANVS EX STELLA CVPIĒS CAPTARE SVP'NA ⌐
ELOQ'O RARVS VIRTVTV̄ LVMINE CLARVS ⌐
EXPENDENS AVRV̄ STVDVIT RENOVARE P'AVLV̄ ⌐
SV̄PTIBVS EX P'PRIIS TI FECIT SC̄E GEORGI ⌐
CL'IC' HIC CVI' PIOR ECCL'IE FVIT HVI' ⌐
HIC LOC' AD VELV̄ P'NOĪE DICITVR AVRI

Six HEXAMETERS (verses 1, 3, and 5 Leonine)

STEFANVS : On the spelling, see 2.1, line 2. It scans Stĕphanus and features F for PH (see 2.1, line 2). The Latin EX STELLA may represent Ital. de(lla) Stella or de(lle) Stelle. — CVPIE(n)s. — SVP(er)NA. — ELOQ(ui)O. — VIRTVTV(m). — AVRV(m). — P(ro)AVLV(m) : The usual Latin form is proaulium, transliterating Greek προαύλιον ('vestibule'). — SV(m)PTIBVS. — P(ro)PRIIS. — T(ib)I. — S(an)C(t)E GEORGI : The Latin Geōrgius transliterates Greek Γεώργιος. — CL(ēr)IC(us) : The EL clericus transliterates Greek κληρικός ('cleric'; cf. 15.4H, line 5). — CVI(us). — P(r)IOR ECCL(ēs)IE : See 1.7A, line 6; on the spelling, see 1.8B, line 5. Scans ecclĕsiae. — HVI(us). — LOC(us). — VELV(m) . . . AVRI : In the Middle Ages, the Latin toponym Velabrum was corrupted to Velum Aureum or Velum Auri. — P(rae)NO(m)I(n)E.

5.3A Epitaph of Alfano

VIR P'BVS ALFANVS CERNENS Q'A CVNCTA PERIRENT ⌐
HOC SIBI SARCOFAGVM STATVIT NE TOTVS OBIRET ⌐
FABRICA DELECTAT POLLET QVIA PENITVS EXTRA ⌐
SED MONET INTERIVS QVIA POST HÆC TRISTIA RESTANT

Four HEXAMETERS

P(ro)BVS. — Q(ui)A . . . PERIRENT : The CL construction would feature Acc. + Inf. (cf. 1.8F, line 2). — SARCOFAGVM = sarcophagum : On the spelling, see 2.1, line 2. — PENITVS : Scans pĕnitus.

Portico, Frieze

> *Stefano della Stella, a man of rare eloquence and famed*
> *for the brilliance of his virtues, in his desire to gain the heights*
> *was zealous by the expenditure of gold to restore this portico.*[a]
> *He built it for you, Saint George,*[b] *at his own cost.*
> *He was a cleric of this church, of which he was prior.*
> *This place is called by the name 'At the Golden Sail'.*[c]

> Six HEXAMETERS (*verses 1, 3, and 5 Leonine*)

a. On the basis of the Gothic majuscules of the inscription, the portico may be dated to the early decades of the thirteenth century.

b. St. George was a soldier-saint of the E supposed to have suffered martyrdom in the early fourth century. In the eighth century, when his cult was gaining currency in Italy, George's skull was deposited in this church by Pope St. Zacharias (r. 741–752). The DEACONRY, already characterized as 'venerable' in Zacharias' day, may date as early as the end of the sixth century. Here, on 14 February 1347, Cola di Rienzo heralded his revolution by posting a manifesto that called for an uprising of the populace (see 1.8A, note b).

c. The medieval toponym Velum Aureum *is a corruption of* CL Velabrum, *the name of the little valley in which the church stands.*

S. Maria in Cosmedin: Portico, Sarcophagus of Alfano

> *Alfano,*[a] *an upright man, seeing that all things perish,*
> *set up this tomb for himself lest he should pass away altogether.*
> *The work itself delights, for on the outside it is thoroughly*
> *prepossessing, yet within it warns that hereafter waits gloom.*

> Four HEXAMETERS

a. Alfano was chamberlain to Pope Callistus II (r. 1119–1124). He donated much of the decorative furniture of the present church, including the altar enclosure and episcopal throne. The church replaces a DEACONRY improvised in a Roman structure. Its name is first attested in the time of Pope Hadrian I (r. 772–795), who is said to have rendered the church vere cosmedin ('an ornament forsooth').

5.3B S. Maria in Cosmedin: Commemoration of Restoration

INSTAVRATIS PLVTEIS AC SVBSELLIIS

MAGNAM PARTEM EXCISIS ET EVERSIS

VETVS SCHOLA CANTORVM

AD PRISTINVM DECVS REVOCATA EST

5   ANNO DOMINI MDCCCXCVIII

2. MAGNAM PARTEM : *The Acc. indicates extent (cf. 1.6A.i, line 4). In* CL, *the phrase* magnā ex parte *is also common in this sense.*

3. SCHOLA CANTORVM : *Lit., 'singers' school', and by extension the enclosure for the choir.*

5. MDCCCXCVIII : *Mīllēsimō nōngentēsimō nōnāgēsimō octāvō.*

5.4 S. Sabina: Dedication by Peter of Illyria

CVLMEN APOSTOLICVM CVM CAELESTINVS HABERET

PRIMVS ET IN TOTO FVLGERET EPISCOPVS ORBE

HAEC QVAE MIRARIS FVNDAVIT PRESBYTER VRBIS

ILLYRICA DE GENTE PETRVS VIR NOMINE TANTO

5   DIGNVS AB EXORTV CRHISTI NVTRITVS IN AVLA

PAVPERIBVS LOCVPLES SIBI PAVPER QVI BONA VITAE

PRAESENTIS FVGIENS MERVIT SPERARE FVTVRAM

Seven HEXAMETERS

1. CVLMEN APOSTOLICVM : *In the fifth century, this was almost a technical term for the Petrine supremacy. On* APOSTOLICVM, *see* 3.4D, *line 4.*

2. EPISCOPVS : *See* 3.4B, *line 2.*

3. PRESBYTER : *See* 3.4C, *line 2.*

5. CRHISTI : *Sic* (= Christī). *On the name, see* 1.6A.ii, *line 6. On the spelling, see* 8.8A, *line 2.* — AVLA : *See* 2.14, *line 1.*

5.5 Epitaph of Crescenzio 'de Theodora'

CORPORE HIC RECVBAT CRESCENTIVS INCLI

TVS ECCE: EXIMIVS CIVIS ROMANVS

DVX QVOQ' MAGNVS: EX MAGNIS MAGNA

PLES GENERATVR ET ALTA: IOH PATRE

Schola Cantorum, Inside R

The ancient choir enclosure[a]
was restored to its former grace
with the setting up of the balustrades and benches,
for the most part torn out and toppled,[b]
in the year of the Lord 1898.

a. *The practice of employing a body of trained singers in Christian worship is said to have begun with Pope St. Gregory I (r. 590–604).*

b. *The choir enclosure and pergola donated by Alfano (see 5.3A) were demolished 1573–1577. In the 1890s, the church was restored insofar as possible to its appearance in Alfano's day.*

S. Sabina: Entry Wall, Center

When Celestine[a] possessed the Apostolic preeminence
and shone forth as first bishop in all the world,[b]
this at which you marvel was founded by a presbyter of the City
of Illyrian family—Peter,[c] a man worthy of so great a name—
raised from birth in Christ's Church, rich towards the poor,
poor towards himself, who shunning the good things
of the present life deserved to hope for that yet to be.

Seven HEXAMETERS

a. *Pope St. Celestine I (r. 422–432).*

b. *Probably a reference to the Council of Ephesus (AD 431), at which Celestine was represented by a delegation of legates that included Philip, presbyter of S. Pietro in Vincoli (see 3.4D, note d).*

c. *Peter of Illyria is known only from the present inscription and from a reference in the* LIBER PONTIFICALIS, *where he figures as a bishop.*

Piazza Cavalieri di Malta 2: S. Alessio: Cloister, NE Wall

Behold, here reposes in body the renowned Crescenzio,[a]
outstanding citizen of Rome, also a great captain.
He was born the high and mighty scion of mighty sires,
illustrious for his father Giovanni and his mother Theodora.

5 THEODORA MATRE NITESCENS:

QVEM XP̄S ANIMAR AMANS MEDICVSQ' PERITVS:

CORRIPVIT LANGORE PIO LONGEVO VT AB OM̄I:

SPE MVNDI LAPSVS PROSTRATVS LIMINI SC̄I:

MARTIRIS INV[i]CTI BONIFATII AMPLEXVS ET

10 ILLIC: SE DN̄O TRADIDIT HABITV̄ MONACHO

RVM ADEPTVS: QVOD TEMPLVM DONIS

[amplis di]T[a]VIT ET AGRIS

[hic omnis quicumque legis cogitare memento

ut tandem scelerum ueniam mereatur habere

15 et obiit die vii mens iul ann dnice incarna

dcccclxxxiiii c r m]

Twelve HEXAMETERS *(lines 1–14)*

1–2. INCLI|TVS = inclitus : *On the spelling, see 8.8A, line 10.* — ECCE : *The colon indicates the end of a verse.*

3. QVOQ(ue).

4. P(rō)LES. — IOH(anne) : *Scans* Iohannē. *The same irregularity is seen in* PATRE *(scans* patrē).

6. XP̄S = Christus : *See 1.6A.ii, line 6; on the abbreviation, see 3.4D, line 8.* — ANIMAR(um). — AMANS : *Scans* āmans. — MEDICVSQ(ue).

7. LANGORE : *Sic* (= languōre). *In* LL, languor *can have the sense 'illness'.* — LONGEVO = longaevō : *On the spelling, see 1.8B, line 5.* — OM(n)I.

8. S(ān)C(t)I.

9. MARTIRIS = martyris : *See 2.10, line 2; on the spelling, see 3.1, line 1.* — BONIFATII : *Both the fourth and fifth syllables appear to be lost to elision.* — AMPLEXVS : *Sc.* sit.

10. D(omi)NO. — TRADIDIT : *Scans* tradidīt. — HABITV(m). — MONACHO|RVM : *The* EL monachus *transliterates Greek* μοναχός *('unique', 'solitary', then* EG *Subst.* 'monk').

12. [amplis di]T[a]VIT : *The missing portions of the text are restored from a transcription made in the sixteenth century by Cesare Baronio.*

15. vii : Septimō. — mens(is) iul(iī) : *See 1.6G, line 11.* — ann(ō) d(omi)nice = dominicae : *See 3.3C, line 2.* — incarna(tiōnis) : *See 4.7C, line 16.*

16. dcccclxxxiiii : Nōngentēsimō octōgēsimō quārtō. — c(ūius) r(equiēscant) m(embra).

Christ, lover of souls and skilled physician,
seized him with a godly illness of long duration,[b]
so that having withdrawn from every worldly ambition,
laid low, he embraced the portal of St. Boniface,[c]
invincible martyr, and there gave himself
over to the Lord, taking up the habit of a monk.[d]
Because he enriched the church with gifts and lands,
you, whoever read this, remember to give thought
that at last he may deserve to obtain forgiveness for his crimes.[e]
And he died on the seventh day of the month of July,
in the year of the Lord's incarnation 984.
May his limbs find rest.

   Twelve HEXAMETERS (lines 1–14)

a. *In former times, the present Crescenzio was fancifully identified as the fruit of an illicit union between Theodora, wife of Theophylact, and Pope John X, Theodora's protégé (see 4.7C, note a). It is altogether more probable that Crescenzio was born of Theodora, daughter of Theodora and Theophylact, and a man called Iohannes (i.e., Giovanni) 'de Episcopo'.*

b. *I.e., a physical malady that proved the source of spiritual healing. St. Augustine likened Christ's ordeal to the act of a devoted physician who reassures his patient by tasting unpleasant medicine first.*

c. *Pope Benedict VII (r. 974–983) ceded the present monastery to Sergius, Metropolitan of Damascus (see BISHOP), who transformed it into a headquarters for the mission to the Slavic peoples. It is from here that St. Adalbert of Prague—the Bohemian Vojtĕch—departed on his ill-fated mission to the Prussians, by whom he was martyred in 997.*

d. *Crescenzio retired to the present monastery to pass the concluding years of his life in saintly seclusion. His son, likewise called Crescenzio, was the bête-noire of the Saxon emperor Otto III.*

e. *Displeased with Pope Benedict VI (r. 973–974), elected against his wishes by elements favorable to the emperor Otto I, Crescenzio in June of 974 led an insurrection in which Benedict was deposed and imprisoned; Crescenzio's man, the DEACON Franco di Ferrucio, was crowned as 'Boniface VII'. Otto II (who had succeeded his father the previous year) sent forces to Rome to liberate the imprisoned Benedict, whereupon Franco ordered him strangled.*

5.6 S. Prisca: Commemoration of Callistus III

PRIMA VBI AB EVĀDRO SACRATA Ē HERCVLIS ARA
VRBIS ROMANAE PRIMA SVPERSTITIO
POST VBI STRVCTĀ AEDES LŌGE CELEBRATA DIANAE
STRVCTĀQVE TOT VET[e]RVM TĒPLA PVDĒDA DEV̄
5 MONTIS AVĒTINI NV̄C FACTĀ Ē GLORIA MAIOR
VNIVS VERI RELLIGIONE DEI
PRAECIPVE OB PRISCAE QVOD CERNIS NOBILE TĒPLV̄
QVOD PRISCV̄ MERITO PAR SIBI NOMEN HABET
NĀ PETRVS ID COLVIT POPVLVM DV̄ SAEPE DOCRET
10 DV̄ FACERET MAGNO SACRAQVE SAEPE DEO
DVM QVOS FAVNORV FONTIS DECEPERAT ERROR
HIC MELIVS SACRA PVRIFICARET AQVA
QVOD DEMV̄ MVLTIS SE SE VOLVETIBVS AN̄IS
CORRVIT HAVD VLLA SVBVENIĒTE MANV
15 SV̄MVS AT ANTISTES CALSTVS TERTIVS IPSV̄
EXTVLIT OMNE EIVS RESTITVIT QVE DECVS
CVI SIMVL AETERNAE TRIBVIT DONA AMPLA SAIVTIS
IPSVIS NE QVA PARTE OARERET OPE

Nine ELEGIAC COUPLETS

1. EVA(n)DRO. — E(st).
3. STRVCTĀ : *The mark of contraction* (T̄) *is superfluous.* — LO(n)GE.
4. STRVCTĀQVE : *See* STRVCTĀ *above* (*line 3*). — TE(m)PLA
   PVDE(n)DA. — DEV(m) : *On the desinence* -um, *see* 15.3A, *line 3a.*
5. AVE(n)TINI. — NV(n)C. — FACTĀ : *See* STRVCTĀ *above* (*line 3*). —
   E(st).
6. RELLIGIONE = rēligiōne : *The spelling with doubled* L *is frequent after
   the Augustan period, when the initial syllable commonly scanned* rē-.
7. TE(m)PLV(m).
8. PRISCV(m).
9. NA(m). — DV(m). — DOCRET : *Sic* (= docēret).
10. DV(m). — SACRAQVE : *The* QVE *connects the present clause with the
    preceding. Such postponement of* -que *is not infrequent in post-Classical
    verse. On the phrase* sacra facere, *see* 3.3C, *line 16.*

Choir, L Wall

Where the first altar of Hercules was dedicated by Evander,[a]
first superstition of the City of Rome, where afterwards
was built the shrine of Diana,[b] renowned far and wide,
and were built so many shameful temples of the old gods,
now has the glory of the Aventine Hill been made greater
by the worship of the one true God, chiefly on account
of the celebrated Church of Prisca[c] which you behold,
which deservedly possesses an ancient renown that is equal to it.[d]
For Peter frequented it as he often taught the people,[e]
as he often celebrated mass for mighty God,
as here in better wise he purified with sacred water
those whom the error of the fount of the Fauns had deceived.[f]
At last, as many years rolled by,
it fell into ruin, with scarce a hand to help.
But the Supreme Bishop Callistus the Third
raised up the church itself and restored all its splendor,[g]
to which at the same time he granted the generous gift
of eternal salvation, lest in any respect it should lack his succor.

Nine ELEGIAC COUPLETS

a. I.e., the Great Altar ('Ara Maxima') of Hercules. According to legend, it
   was founded by Evander, the Arcadian king who established the earliest
   settlement on the site of Rome. The massive tufa podium into which the
   crypt of S. Maria in Cosmedin is excavated is likely that of the altar.
b. The Temple of Diana, which crowned the Aventine Hill, was attributed by
   the Romans to Servius Tullius, semilegendary sixth king of Rome (traditionally r. 578–535 BC).
c. The Church of S. Prisca is identified in tradition with the home of Prisca and
   Aquila, friends of St. Paul and prominent members of the Christian community (Rom. 16:3–5). According to Acts 18:2, the two were forced to leave
   Rome in AD 52 by the decree of the emperor Claudius expelling the Jews. The
   imperial biographer Suetonius reports that the Jews of Rome were causing
   disturbances at the instigation of one 'Chrestus' ('Life' of Claudius, 25).
d. Lit., 'ancient name'. The Latin text exploits the fact that the name Prisca is
   a form of the Adj. priscus ('ancient', 'pristine', 'venerable').

11. FAVNORV(m) : *Reversing the error of* STRVCTA *(line 3), the ordinary mark of contraction (i.e.,* FAVNORV̄) *is here neglected.*

13. DEMV(m). — VOLVETIBVS = volventibus : *See* FAVNORV(m) *above (line 11).* — AN(n)IS.

14. SVBVENIE(n)TE.

15. SV(m)MVS. — ANTISTES : *See 3.3C, line 13.* — CALSTVS : *Sic* (= Calistus; *the spelling with a single* L *is not uncommon).* — IPSV(m).

17. SAIVTIS : *Sic* (= salūtis).

18. IPSVIS *Sic* (= ipsīus). — OARERET : *Sic* (= carēret).

5.7A Epitaph of Gaius Cestius

i.

C CESTIVS L F POB EPVLO PR TR PL

VII VIR EPVLONVM

1. C(āius) : *On the abbreviation, see 1.1, line 1.* — L(ūcī) F(īlius) POB(liliā) : *Abl. of Description; the word* tribū *('tribe') is implied.* — PR(aetor). — TR(ibūnus) PL(ēbis).

2. VII VIR = Septemvir : *The membership of the* septemvirī epulōnēs *numbered first three, then seven. The designation* septemvirī *remained unchanged even after the membership was further raised to ten.*

ii.

OPVS APSOLVTVM EX TESTAM[e]NTO DIEBVS CC[cx]XX

ARBITRATV

PONTI P F CLA MELAE HEREDIS ET POTHI L

1. APSOLVTVM = absolūtum : *The spelling in* P *is phonetic (see 2.6B, line 5).* — CC[cx]XX : Trecentīs trīgintā. *The characters enclosed in brackets are restored from context.*

3. P(ūbliī) F(īliī). — CLA(udiā) : *Cf.* POB(lilia) *above, 5.7A.i, line 1.* — L(ībertī).

5.7B Pyramid of Cestius: Commemoration of Restoration

INSTAVRATVM AN DOM MDCLXIII

INSTAVRATVM : *The primary sense of the verb is to repeat a religious rite that has been interrupted or wrongly performed. Its extended senses include resuming an activity or restoring a thing.* — AN(nō) DOM(inī) MDCLXIII : Mīllēsimō sescentēsimō sexāgēsimō tertiō.

e. St. Peter is thought to have spent twenty-five years in Rome (see 15.4H).

f. 'Fount of the Fauns' is a spurious toponym inferred from Ovid, Fasti 3.297–299. Fauns were sylvan deities whose activities included the production of mysterious noises in the woods and the inspiration of poets.

g. Pope Callistus III de Borja y Borja (r. 1455–1458). Callistus undertook a major restoration of the church 1455–1456. Although the TITULAR CHURCH of Prisca is attested in synodal acts of 499 and 595, the oldest physical evidence of Christian cult at the site dates to the twelfth century.

Pyramid of Cestius: E and W Sides

Above

Gaius Cestius Epulo,[a] son of Lucius, of the tribe Poblilia,[b] Praetor, Tribune of the Plebs, member of the Board of Seven of the Epulones.[c]

a. This Cestius may be the builder of Pons Cestius (cf. 13.11A, note b).

b. For the purpose of voting, every Roman citizen was enrolled in one of thirty-five 'tribes', the origins of which remain obscure.

c. The Praetors handled various aspects of civil jurisdiction. On the office of tribune, see TRIBUNICIAN POWER. The primary duty of the septemviri epulones was to organize the epulum Iovis ('Feast of Jove').

Below

The work was completed in accordance with the will in 330 days[a]
at the discretion of Pontius Mela,
son of Publius, of the tribe Claudia, his heir, and of the freedman Pothos.

a. The pyramid is based on Egyptian exemplars, but of Hellenistic rather than pharaonic vintage. It may be dated to between 18 and 12 BC (the latter a firm terminus ante quem as Marcus Agrippa, son-in-law of Augustus and one of Cestius' heirs, died in that year; cf. 11.3A).

E and W Sides, Below

Restored in the year of the Lord 1663.[a]

a. Like other outlying constructions, the pyramid was incorporated into the wall of Aurelian (see 4.6A, note a, and 7.5D, note c). Pope Alexander VII Chigi (r. 1655–1667) disencumbered the monument of accumulated debris and reerected two of the columns that had formerly stood at its corners.

5.8A S. Paolo fuori le Mura: Dedication by Siricius

SIRICIVS EPISCOPVS ☧ TOTA MENTE DEVOTVS

☧ : *The monogram combines the original form of the Chi-Rho emblem (cf. 4.2L) with the letters alpha and omega, which together symbolize Christ as the beginning and end of all things (Rev. 1:8).*

5.8B S. Paolo fuori le Mura: History of the Basilica and Its Rebuilding

BASILICAM PAVLI APOSTOLI IMP VALENTINIANO THEODOSIO HONORIO
DENVO EXTRVCTAM NOCTV ANTE IDVS IVLIAS AN MDCCCXXIII COMBVSTAM
LEO XII IN PRISTINAM FORMAM REFICIENDAM SVSCEPIT
PIVS VIII EST PROSEQVVTVS GREGORIVS XVI VLTERIVS PROVEXIT
5   PIVS IX AN MDCCCLIV AD FINEM PROPE PERDVXIT ET ABSOLVENDAM DECREVIT

1. APOSTOLI : *See 1.6I, line 7.* — IMP (erantibus) : *The participle here forms a temporal Abl.Absolute construction with the names of the three emperors ('during the reigns of').*

2. EXTRVCTAM = exstrūctum : *On the spelling, see 4.2A, line 7.* — IDVS IVLIAS : *Here the* CL *usage is observed (cf. 1.6G, line 11).* — AN(nō) MDCCCXXIII : *Millēsimō octingentēsimō vīcēsimō tertiō.*

3. LEO XII : *Duodecimus.*

4. PIVS VIII : *Octāvus.* — PROSEQVVTVS = prōsecūtus : *A spurious archaism modeled on* sequuntur *which, though almost certainly pronounced* /se'kuntur/, *is authentic (<* sequontur; *on the O, cf. 4.6B, line 3). The* CL *Part.* secūtus *was made on the analogy of such forms as* volūtus *and* solūtus; *the original form* *sectus *is implied by the frequentative* sectāre *(cf.* dictus > dictāre*). The form* ×sequūtus *is thus the stillborn fruit of philological fancy (cf.* quum, *2.12B, line 2).* — GREGORIVS XVI : *Sextus decimus.*

5. PIVS IX : *Nōnus.* — AN(nō) MDCCCLIV : *Millēsimō octingentēsimō quīnquāgēsimō quārtō.*

N Portico, Inner Filade, First Shaft from R, Top

Siricius,[a] Bishop, in whole-hearted devotion.

a. *The original basilica was dedicated in AD 390 by Pope St. Siricius (r. 384–399). Construction was not completed until 395.*

Entry Wall, above R Portal

Leo the Twelfth[a] undertook to have the Basilica of Paul the Apostle— constructed afresh under the Emperors Valentinian, Theodosius, and Honorius[b] and burned the night of 14 July in the year 1823—rebuilt in its original form.[c] Pius the Eighth[d] continued it, Gregory the Sixteenth carried it further forward,[e] Pius the Ninth[f] brought it virtually to a conclusion in the year 1854, and decreed that it be finished.

a. *Pope Leo XII della Genga (r. 1823–1829). Elected two months after the fire that gutted the BASILICA, he formed a commission that recommended rebuilding to the plan and dimensions of the original structure (see note c below).*

b. *Consecrated by Pope St. Siricius in 390 (see 5.8A, note a), the basilica replaced a shrine built by Constantine at the traditional site of St. Paul's tomb. Valentinian II (r. 375–392) was nominal ruler of the W Empire under Theodosius I (r. 379–395), who married Valentinian's sister, Galla. Honorius (r. 395–423), son of Theodosius by a previous marriage, ruled the W after his father's death.*

c. *Only the transept and apse of the original structure were preserved in rebuilding after the catastrophic fire of 1823, caused by a lamp left burning on the roof by a repair crew.*

d. *Pope Pius VIII Castiglione (r. 1829–1830). Pius continued the contracting for the new construction.*

e. *Pope Gregory XVI Cappellari (r. 1831–1846). Gregory consecrated the transept in 1840.*

f. *Pope Pius IX Mastai-Ferretti (r. 1846–1878). Pius consecrated the whole of the basilica in 1854, when the restoration was nearly complete.*

5.8c S. Paolo fuori le Mura: Commemoration of Dedication of New Basilica

HANC PAVLI DOCTORIS GENTIVM BASILICAM AB INCENDIO RESTITVTAM
PIVS $\overline{IX}$ PONTIFEX MAXIMVS CHRISTIANI ORBIS EPISCOPIS STIPATVS
BIDVO POST QVAM MARIAM SINE LABE CONCEPTAM
ECCLESIAE VNIVERSAE CATHOLICA FIDE CREDENDAM EDIXIT
5   IV ID DEC AN REPARATAE SALVTIS $\overline{MDCCCLIV}$ SOLEMNI RITV CONSECRAVIT

2. PIVS $\overline{IX}$: Nōnus. — CHRISTIANI : *See 1.7A, line 8.* — EPISCOPIS : *See 3.4B, line 2.*
4. ECCLESIAE : *See 1.7A, line 6.* — CATHOLICA : *See 1.6I, line 6.*
5. IV : Quārtō. — ID(ūs) DEC(embrēs) : *See* IDVS IVLIAS, *5.8B, line 2. The usage in the two contemporary inscriptions may be assumed to be parallel.* — AN(nō) REPARATAE SALVTIS : *On the construction, see 1.7A, lines 2–3.* — MDCCCLIV : Millēsimō octingentēsimō quīnquāgēsimō quārtō.

Entry Wall, above L Portal

On the second day after he decreed that the Church Universal should believe by the Catholic faith
that Mary was conceived without stain,[a] Pius the Ninth, Supreme Pontiff,[b]
thronged by the bishops of the Christian world, consecrated in solemn rite this Basilica of Paul,
teacher of the nations,[c] which was restored after the fire,
on 10 December[d] in the year of renewed Salvation 1854.

a. The dogma of the Immaculate Conception of the BVM was proclaimed on 8 December 1854 (see 9.8.ii, note c).
b. Pope Pius IX Mastai-Ferretti (r. 1846–1878).
c. St. Paul cast himself as 'Apostle of the Gentiles' (Gal. 1:15–16).
d. Lit., 'on the sixth day before the Ides of December'.

5.8D Commemoration of Repair to Doors of Pantaleone

HVIVS IANVAE VALVAE QVAS CONSTANTINOPOLI CONFLATAS

ATQVE A PANTALEONE CONSVLE AMALPHIGENO

ANNO $\overline{\text{MLXX}}$ APOSTOLO PAVLO DONO DATAS

DIRO INCENDIO ANNO $\overline{\text{MDCCCXXIII}}$ CORRVPTAS

5   IOANNES XXIII CVM CONCILIVM VATICANVM $\overline{\text{II}}$ A D $\overline{\text{VIII}}$ KAL FEBR A $\overline{\text{MCMLIX}}$

CELEBRANDVM NVNTIARET REFICIENDAS DECREVIT

MVNIFICENTIA PAVLI $\overline{\text{VI}}$ PONTIFICIS MAXIMI

AD PRISTINAE FORMAE DECVS RESTITVTAE SVNT ANNO $\overline{\text{MCMLXVII}}$

1. CONSTANTINOPOLI : *Locative.*
2. PANTALEONE : *The Latin name is* Pantaleō, -ōnis. — AMALPHIGENO : *A Hellenizing variant on the* ML Amalfitānus, *as if from Greek* Ἀμαλφἴγενος (*cf. 9.1A, line 2*). *The Adj. answers to the toponym* Amalfi, -is (*Acc.* -im). — CONSVLE : *Pantaleone's title at the court of Constantinople was* ἀνθὔπατος (*in Greek writers of the imperial period, this term ordinarily represents the Latin* prō cōnsule).
3. $\overline{\text{MLXX}}$: Millēsimō septuāgēsimō. — APOSTOLO : *See 1.61, line 7.* — DONO : *Dat. of Purpose.*
4. $\overline{\text{MDCCCXXIII}}$: Millēsimō octingentēsimō vīcēsimō tertiō.
5. IOANNES XXIII : Vīcēsimus tertius. — $\overline{\text{II}}$: Secundum. — A(nte) D(iem) $\overline{\text{VIII}}$: Octāvum. — KAL(endās) FEB(ruāriī) *or* FEB(ruāriās) : *See 1.6G, line 11.* — A(nnō) $\overline{\text{MCMLIX}}$: Millēsimō nōngentēsimō quīnquāgēsimō nōnō.
7. PAVLI $\overline{\text{VI}}$: Sextī.
8. $\overline{\text{MCMLXVII}}$: Millēsimō nōngentēsimō sexāgēsimō septimō.

Entry Wall, above Porta Santa

The leaves of this door,[a] which were forged in Constantinople
and given by Pantaleone, Amalfitan consul,[b]
as a gift to the Apostle Paul in the year 1070,
damaged in the fearful conflagration in the year 1823,[c]
and which John the Twenty-Third[d] declared should be remade
when he announced on 25 January[e] 1959 that the Second Vatican Council was to be celebrated,
were restored to the splendor of their original beauty
through the generosity of Paul the Sixth,[f] Supreme Pontiff in the year 1967.

a. The leaves are each divided into twenty-seven panels decorated in silver, enamel, and niello inlay. They illus-
trate scenes from the Old and New Testaments.

b. Amalfitan merchants traded throughout the E Mediterranean, where their activities extended as far as Constantinople, Antioch, and Jerusalem. The high status of Pantaleone may be gauged by his title of 'consul' and
by the fact that he was in a position to order commissions from the imperial workshops.

c. See 5.8B, notes a and c.

d. Pope John XXIII Roncalli (r. 1958–1963).

e. Lit., 'on the eighth day before the Kalends of February'.

f. Pope Paul VI Montini (r. 1963–1978). Paul was the last pope to be crowned with the triple tiara, which he later
sold to Cardinal Francis Spellman of New York; the proceeds were distributed to the poor.

5.8E S. Paolo fuori le Mura: Dedication by Honorius

TEODOSIVS CEPIT PERFECIT ONORIVS AVLAM ⌐
DOCTORIS MVNDI SACRATAM CORPORE PAVLI

Two HEXAMETERS

TEODOSIVS = *Theodosius : By synizesis, the first two vowels scan as a single syllable. Synizesis (Greek* συνίζησις, *'collapse') is the merging into a single syllable of two vowels that do not ordinarily form a diphthong. On the spelling, see 8.8A, line 2.* — CEPIT = *coepit : On the spelling, see 1.8B, line 5.* — ONORIVS = *Honōrius.* — AVLAM : *See 2.14, line 1.*

5.8F S. Paolo fuori le Mura: Dedication by Galla Placidia

PLACIDIAE PIA MENS OPERIS DECVS HOMNE PATERNI ⌐
GAVDET PONTIFICIS STVDIO SPLENDERE LEONIS

Two HEXAMETERS

PLACIDIAE : *Scans* Plācidiae. — HOMNE = *omne : On the spelling, see 8.8A, line 2.* — PONTIFICIS : *On the title, see 3.3C, line 13.*

5.8G Commemoration of Nero's Hiding Place

HOC SPECVS EXCEPIT
POST AVREA TECTA NERONEM
NAM VIVVM INFERIVS
SE SEPELIRE TIMET

One ELEGIAC COUPLET

2. NERONEM : *Along with the famous* Qualis artifex pereo (*'What an artist dies in me!'), the imperial biographer Suetonius (Ner. 49) preserves a collection of the emperor's latest eloquence in both Latin and Greek:* Vivo deformiter, turpiter (*'I live in ugliness and disgrace!'*); Οὐ πρέπει Νέρωνι, οὐ πρέπει (*'It is unbefitting Nero, unbefitting!'*); Νήφειν δεῖ ἐν τοῖς τοιούτοις (*'One must be level-headed in such circumstances!'*); Ἄγε, ἔγειρε σεαυτόν (*'Come, rouse yourself!'*); *and, as the hoofbeats of his approaching captors were heard, a fanciful quotation from Homer:* Ἵππων μ᾿ ὠκυπόδων ἀμφὶ κτύπος οὔατα βάλλει (*'The thud of swift-footed horses beats about my ears!', Hom.Il. 10.535).*

Triumphal Arch, Top

> *Theodosius began and Honorius completed this church,[a]*
> *sanctified by the body of Paul, teacher of the world.[b]*

TWO HEXAMETERS

a. *According to tradition, St. Paul was tried and executed at the site of the abbey of the Tre Fontane near Rome. Paul had appealed to Caesar before Festus at Caesarea (Acts 25:11).*
b. *The title* Doctor Mundi *('Teacher of the World') is a variation of* Doctor Gentium *('Teacher of the Nations'; cf. 5.8C, note c).*

Triumphal Arch, Span

> *The pious heart of Placidia[a] rejoices that all the splendor of her*
> *father's undertaking shines bright through the zeal of the Pontiff Leo.[b]*

TWO HEXAMETERS

a. *Galla Placidia (c. 388–450) was daughter of the emperor Theodosius I and half-sister of Honorius (see 5.8B, note b).*
b. *Pope St. Leo I (r. 440–461). Leo carried out repairs to the basilica in 441.*

Cloister W Wall

> *This cavity received Nero*
> *after the Golden House,*
> *for he feared to bury himself lower*
> *while yet alive.[a]*

ONE ELEGIAC COUPLET

a. *According to Suetonius ('Life' of Nero 49), when Nero fled Rome at the advance of the rebel Vindex, his freedman Phaon urged him to conceal himself in a pit on the grounds of his villa. Nero refused, saying that he would not go under the earth before his death. The stone—a forgery from the seventeenth century—purports to commemorate the site of an alternative place of hiding. The following account of the stone's history is appended on a stone below the first: 'Discovered near the Anio between the Via Salaria and Via Nomentana in the suburban villa of the freedman Phaon, today "La Serpentara", taken thence to Nazzano about 100 years ago and then to Rome in the month of October 1756'.*

PORTA SAN SEBASTIANO

Like Porta San Paolo and Porta San Lorenzo, Porta San Sebastiano takes its name from the extramural shrine of a saint. Though the gate was built contemporaneously with the wall of Aurelian in the late third century, the present structure dates to a rebuilding carried out AD 401–403 under the emperor Honorius. The square bastions and curtain wall between are faced with blocks of marble stripped from tombs along the Via Appia. The defenses of which Porta San Sebastiano forms a part served as Rome's bulwark from its initial construction in the 270s until its final breach on 20 September 1870 by Italian national forces, sent to incorporate the city into the kingdom of Italy.

VI. From San Clemente to the Via Appia

THE GEOGRAPHY OF CHRISTIAN ROME was shaped by three principal elements, each emerging from a characteristic historical and topographical matrix. The first comprised the ancient *tituli* and deaconries, predecessors of the city's parish churches; these foundations are predictably concentrated in the densely populated residential zones of late Antique Rome. The second element was the great basilicas erected in the first half of the fourth century by the emperor Constantine I and his family; most were situated on outlying imperial estates near the tombs of martyrs. (Of these, the most important were San Giovanni in Laterano, which was the seat of Rome's bishop, and San Pietro in Vaticano; together with San Paolo fuori le Mura and Santa Maria Maggiore, they rank as Rome's 'patriarchal' basilicas.) Finally there were the catacombs. Clustering around the great consular highways that radiated from the city, this network of subterranean cemeteries encircled Rome with a more or less continuous belt of Christian burial sites.

Extramural disposal of the dead was hardly a Christian innovation. By a provision of the Twelve Tables—ancient Rome's earliest codified law—no burial was permitted within the confines of the *pomerium*. Throughout Antiquity, as a consequence, the traveler approaching Rome had first to pass through a city of the dead before entering the gates of the living. Of the tombs that fringed the suburban tracts, few were grander than that of CAECILIA METELLA—a masonry drum 100 Roman feet *6.12* in diameter. Owing to the characteristic *bucrania* ('ox skulls') with which its frieze is decorated, the vicinity of the tomb was known in the Middle Ages as *Capo di Bove* ('Ox Head'). In the eleventh century the Counts of Tusculum incorporated the structure into a fortress. Having passed to the family Caetani during the reign of Pope Boniface VIII, this was dismantled in the late sixteenth century. Little survives today besides the ruined Church of San Nicola and the battlements with which the drum of the tomb is crowned.

The subterranean cemeteries of the early Christians are traditionally known as 'catacombs'; in point of fact, 'cemetery' is the proper generic term. The Latin *coemētērium* transliterates Greek *koimētēríon* (κοιμητη-ρίον, 'dormitory'). For the early church, the choice of this term reflected a critical distinction between the resting places of the faithful—'asleep' in Christ—and those of the pagans, whose ashes reposed in *nekropóleis* (νεκροπόλεις, 'cities of the dead'). The term 'catacombs' derives from the

6.11 name of the most venerable of the Christian cemeteries—that of San Sebastiano on the Via Appia, which was designated by the phrase *ad catacumbas* ('at the hollows'), in allusion to the sunken terrain of the zone, part of which occupied the site of an ancient quarry. As a verbal formula, *ad catacumbas* is strictly redundant: the Latin *catacumbās* transliterates the Greek phrase *katà kúmbās* (κατὰ κύμβας), itself signifying 'at the hollows'.

The Basilica of San Sebastiano was originally known as the Basilica Apostolorum ('Basilica of the Apostles'). According to a tradition at least as old as the mid-fourth century, Pope St. Cornelius (r. 251–253) transferred the relics of the Apostles Peter and Paul from their gravesites to the cemetery *ad catacumbas*. We know in addition that on 29 June of each year the Apostles were venerated both at their *memoriae* on the Via Cornelia and Via Ostiensis and at the Basilica Apostolorum on the Appia. Today it is generally assumed that the relics were moved during the persecutions of Decius (249–251) or Valerian (257–260) to protect them. As Christian cemeteries remained inviolate even during periods of persecution and no trace of an apostolic tomb has been uncovered at the site, it is nevertheless more likely that the basilica was built to provide a place to commemorate the apostles during the period when assemblies in the cemeteries were forbidden.

Near to San Sebastiano in both situation and dignity are the cem-
6.10 eteries of San Callisto, housing the celebrated Crypt of the Popes,
6.9 and that of Santa Domitilla, notable for its subterranean basilica.

Enclosing the tomb of Saints Nereus and Achilleus, the latter was served
by the clergy of the nearby Titulus Fasciolae—better known, in consequence, as the Church of SANTI NEREO E ACHILLEO.   6.6

Popular opinion notwithstanding, the Christian cemeteries were
never used as places of refuge. That stubborn error likely arose as a dis-
torted memory of the spectacular martyrdom of Pope St. Sixtus II. Indeed, the utilization of the catacombs reached its zenith not in the age
of persecutions but after the Peace of the Church introduced by Constantine in AD 313. Decisive impetus to their development was furnished
late in the fourth century by Pope St. Damasus I (r. 366–384), zealous
for Rome's standing at a time when her spiritual hegemony was at risk of
passing to the new imperial capital of Constantinople. Though marginal-
ized in the official arena, Rome possessed the tombs of the Apostles Peter and Paul. A master of ecclesiastical politics, Damasus enhanced the
city's unique penumbra of sanctity with small but sumptuous shrines
situated at the tombs of these and several dozen other martyrs of lesser
eminence. A verse *elogium* composed by Damasus himself formed the
centerpiece of each.

Through the sixth and seventh centuries, the cemeteries and their associated basilicas attracted increasing devotion throughout the Christian West; indeed, with the fall of Jerusalem to the Arabs in 640, Rome
found herself the sole 'holy city' accessible to European pilgrims. At
the same time, the popularity of burial in the Constantinian basilicas
conspired with the breakdown of the ancient taboo against intramural
sepulture to bring about a marked decline in the use of subterranean
cemeteries. The fate of the latter was effectively sealed in the Gothic
Wars of the sixth century, when they were ransacked by the army of Vitiges in the 530s and by that of Totila in the following decade. Though
restored after the expulsion of the Goths in 552, they fell into irreversible
decay. By the middle of the seventh century the relics of the martyrs had
in large part been transferred to intramural churches. With the advent

of seafaring Saracen marauders in the ninth century, the Campagna reverted to wilderness. The abandoned cemeteries reposed in the silence of virtual oblivion for a thousand years.

Situated at the center of a field of tension generated by pope, emperor, and local nobility, medieval Rome was the object of repeated military assaults. Between the ninth and the nineteenth centuries, her walls served to deter (albeit with mixed success) not only Saracens but also Normans, imperial forces, and a bewildering miscellany of Italians from other regions of the peninsula. An invasion of the last sort is recalled
6.7 in a remarkable inscription surviving at PORTA SAN SEBASTIANO. It preserves the memory of a skirmish that took place before the gate on 29 September 1327, feast day of the Archangel Michael. The text declares with pride that foreign invaders were repelled by the militia of Rione Sant'Angelo under the command of one Giacomo de' Ponziani. These 'foreigners' were the troops of Robert d'Anjou, king of Naples, fighting in alliance with the Guelf (pro-papal) Orsini.

The zone to the north of Porta San Sebastiano is distinguished by a constellation of ancient churches that cluster on and about the slopes of the Caelian Hill. Of these, none is more venerable than the Basilica of San Clemente, whose architectural history of two millennia is laid bare in excavations that reach ten vertical meters beneath the modern street level. Today's twelfth-century church rises on the site of a fourth-century predecessor, itself occupying the site of structures that date to the first century BC. The basilica of the fourth century was destroyed in 1084 on the occasion of Rome's violent liberation by Robert Guiscard, Norman duke of Apulia, who had been summoned by Pope St. Gregory VII (r. 1073–1085) to champion the Holy See in its contest with Henry IV of Germany. The structure raised on its ruins by Pope Paschal II (r. 1099–1118) remained substantially unaltered until the eigh-
6.1 teenth century. It was restored by Pope CLEMENT XI (r. 1700–1721), elected on the saint's feast day. One may well regret that calendrical coincidence: To modern taste, the profusion of gilt-stucco *putti* and fo-

liage that festoons the basilica's austere marbles tends only to diminish its impact on the historical imagination.

From remote times the basilica has been associated with the memory of Pope St. Clement, reckoned by tradition the third successor of St. Peter. Clement—in Latin, *Clemens*—was early identified with Titus Flavius Clemens, consul in AD 95. Clemens, a cousin of the emperor Domitian, is said to have been put to death for 'atheism' and 'Jewish practices'—which is as much as to say that he was a Christian. The identification of the bishop and consul is complicated by the evidently Jewish background of the author of the First Epistle of Clement to the Corinthians, the only constituent of the 'Clementine' literature generally accepted as authentic. These disparate facts are supposedly reconciled by the theory—more ingenious than persuasive—that the bishop Clemens was a Jewish freedman of the consul Clemens and that the consul's *domus* ('townhouse') is to be identified in one of the first-century buildings over which the church is built. Explained at a stroke are the Jewish education of the author of the epistle, his name (an emancipated slave ordinarily assumed the name of his former master), the association of the bishop with the consul, and the site of the church. Aside from archeological evidence that neither of the structures beneath the church was a house, this speculative tour de force founders on the fact that a freedman assumed not his master's *cognomen* (viz., Clemens) but his *nomen* and *praenomen* (Titus Flavius).

Of comparable archeological interest is the Basilica of Santi Giovanni e Paolo, situated on the western slope of the Caelian Hill. The preexisting structures on the site include an *insula* that featured characteristic shop fronts at street level; in time, a room at the rear of one of the shops was adapted as a private oratory. The oratory was eventually enlarged by the incorporation of a neighboring *domus*. In the mid-fourth century, a *titulus* was founded and a *confessio* added—the latter an enclosure marking the location of the tomb of Saints John and Paul, held to have been martyred on this site during the fourth century. Finally, at the dawn of the fifth century, the *titulus* was replaced: the upper floors of the complex were razed and the lower filled with rubble; the basilica that stands today was erected on the resulting platform. The sole element of the *titulus* preserved was the *confessio*, kept accessible through a vertical shaft. The shaft was closed when the basilica was restored in the twelfth century by GIOVANNI DEI CONTI DI SEGNI.

6.4

Called the 'Sphinx of the Caelian' for its baffling architectural form, Santo Stefano Rotondo dates to the latter decades of the fifth century; it was probably conceived as a liturgical surrogate for the distant cathedral at the Lateran. Its original plan consisted of a Greek cross inscribed within circular walls that formed concentric ambulatories. So novel was this design that in the Middle Ages the church was generally thought to have been an ancient structure adapted for Christian use. In the 1450s it was heavily restored under Pope NICHOLAS V (r. 1447–1455); in the course of the work, the ruinous outer ambulatory was demolished and the building reduced to its present plan. Nicholas assigned the church to the Hermits of St. Paul of Hungary, a nation with long-standing ties to the papacy. The Magyar prince Vajk, who in AD 1001 was acknowledged by Pope Silvester II (r. 999–1003) as king of Hungary, had taken the baptismal name 'István' (i.e., Stephen). Santo Stefano has since formed the focus of Hungarian piety at Rome and furnished the burial place of such expatriates as JÁNOS LÁSZAI, a canon of the cathedral of Gyulafehérvár in Transylvania. After the Church of Santo Stefano degli Ungheresi was pulled down in 1778 to make way for a new sacristy at St. Peter's Basilica, Pope Pius VI had a Hungarian chapel constructed in Santo Stefano Rotondo as a replacement.

6.2A

6.2B

A near neighbor of Santo Stefano and Santi Giovanni e Paolo, the CHURCH OF SAN GREGORIO MAGNO constitutes an uninterrupted historical link with the age of Pope St. Gregory I (r. 590–610). The scion of a distinguished senatorial family, Gregory in 573 obtained the post of city prefect, highest in the civil hierarchy. He withdrew from public life soon thereafter to enter the monastery that he had founded on the site

6.5B

of his ancestral home, the site occupied by the present church. Gregory came to the throne of St. Peter at a moment of crisis. While the Byzantine authorities were preoccupied with defending the Exarchate of Ravenna from Lombard invaders, it was left to Rome's bishop to organize her defenses, provide for the grain supply, and see to the repair of failed aqueducts. Though it would be simplistic to regard Gregory's pontificate as marking the inauguration of the popes' temporal power, his reign nevertheless represents a milestone in the development of the papacy. Gregory is emblematic of the transition from Antiquity to the Middle Ages; imbued on the one hand with the ancient Roman genius for civil administration, on the other he is the subject of characteristically medieval legends involving apparitions and angels.

Notable among the monuments of the forecourt is that of the Welshman Sir EDWARD CARNE, who argued the case for the divorce of King   6.5A
Henry VIII at Rome.

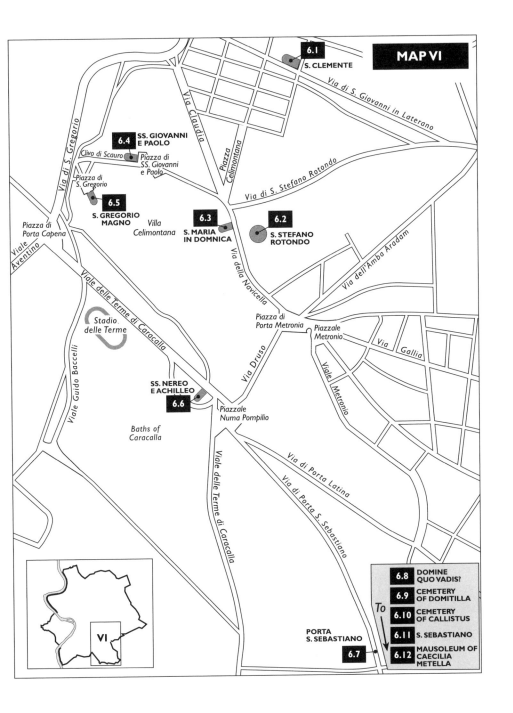

MAP VI

6.1 S. CLEMENTE

Via di S. Giovanni in Laterano

Via Claudia

Piazza Celimontana

6.4 SS. GIOVANNI E PAOLO

Via di S. Gregorio

Clivo di Scauro

Piazza di SS. Giovanni e Paolo

Via di S. Stefano Rotondo

Piazza di S. Gregorio

6.5 S. GREGORIO MAGNO

Villa Celimontana

6.3 S. MARIA IN DOMNICA

6.2 S. STEFANO ROTONDO

Via dell'Amba Aradam

Piazza di Porta Capena

Viale Aventino

Via della Navicella

Viale delle Terme di Caracalla

Stadio delle Terme

Piazza di Porta Metronia

Piazzale Metronio

Via Gallia

Viale Guido Baccelli

Via Druso

Viale Metronio

6.6 SS. NEREO E ACHILLEO

Piazzale Numa Pompilio

Baths of Caracalla

Via di Porta Latina

Viale delle Terme di Caracalla

Via di Porta S. Sebastiano

VI

To →

6.8 DOMINE QUO VADIS?

6.9 CEMETERY OF DOMITILLA

6.10 CEMETERY OF CALLISTUS

6.11 S. SEBASTIANO

6.12 MAUSOLEUM OF CAECILIA METELLA

PORTA S. SEBASTIANO

6.7

6.1   S. Clemente: Dedication by Clement XI

ANTIQVISSIMAM HANC ECCLESIAM

QVÆ PENE SOLA ÆVI DAMNIS INVICTA

PRISCARVM VRBIS BASILICARVM

FORMAM ADHVC SERVAT

5   EO IPSO IN LOCO ÆDIFICATAM

AC IN TITVLVM S R E PRESBYTERI CARDINALIS ERECTAM

VBI S CLEMENTIS PAPÆ ET MART PATERNA DOMVS

FVISSE CREDITVR

A S GREGORIO MAGNO

10   GEMINIS HIC HABITIS HOMILYS

ET SACRA QVADRAGESIMALI STATIONE

CONDECORATAM

CLEMENS XI PONT MAX

IPSO ANNIVERSARIÆ CELEBRITATIS EIVSDEM S CLEMENTIS DIE

15   AD CATHOLICÆ ECCLESIÆ REGIMEN ASSVMPTVS

IN ARGVMENTVM PRÆCIPVI SVI IN EVM CVLTVS

INSTAVRAVIT ORNAVITQVE

ANNO SAL MDCCXV PONTIF XV

1. ECCLESIAM : *See 1.7A, line 6.*

2. PENE = paene : *On the spelling, see 1.8B, line 5.*

6. TITVLVM : *See 3.6A, line 2.* — S(ānctae) R(ōmānae) E(cclēsiae). — PRESBYTERI : *See 3.4C, line 2.*

7. S(āncti). — PAPÆ : *See 3.6A, line 2.* — MART(yris) : *See 2.10, line 2.*

9. S(ānctō).

10. HOMILYS = homiliīs : *The* EL *homilia transliterates Greek* ὁμιλία, *('conversation', then* EG *'sermon'). The* Y *is a species of ligature.*

11. QVADRAGESIMALI STATIONE : *In* EL, *Quadrāgēsima ('fortieth') is 'Lent'; the corresponding Adj. is quadrāgēsimālis. In* EL, *statiō refers to a papal mass celebrated on special days at certain churches.*

13. CLEMENS XI : Ūndecimus. — PONT(ifex) MAX(imus).

14. S(āncti).

15. CATHOLICÆ : *See 1.61, line 6.*

18. SAL(ūtis) MDCCXV : Mīllēsimō septingentēsimō quīntō decimō. — PONTIF(icātūs) XV : Quīntō decimō.

Entry Wall

Clement the Eleventh,[a] Supreme Pontiff,
raised to the governance of the Catholic Church
on the very day of the annual solemnity of the same Saint Clement,[b]
as proof of his especial veneration towards him
restored and embellished
this church of high antiquity which,
nearly alone unvanquished by the injuries of time,
preserves to this day the aspect
of the City's primitive basilicas,[c]
built in the very place, and erected as the Title
of a Cardinal Priest of the Holy Roman Church,[d]
where the ancestral house of Saint Clement, Pope and Martyr,
is believed to have stood,
ennobled
by Saint Gregory the Great,[e]
who delivered here two homilies,
and by its holy Lenten station,[f]
in the year of Salvation 1715, fifteenth of his office.

a. *Pope Clement XI Albani (r. 1700–1721). The fifteenth year of his pontificate ran from 23 November 1714 through 22 November 1715.*

b. *St. Clement is reckoned the third Bishop of Rome after St. Peter. Tradition identified him with Titus Flavius Clemens, a cousin of the emperor Domitian executed for atheism and 'Jewish practices'. Clemens' wife, Flavia Domitilla (niece of the same emperor) was exiled to the rocky islet of Pandateria. The bishop's memory attached itself to the complex of buildings on the present site, which early became a center of Christian worship. Like that of S. Pudenziana (3.6), the titulus of S. Clemente was founded in the fourth century.*

c. *The eighteenth century was unaware that the BASILICA rises on the ruins of its paleo-Christian predecessor, replaced after grave damage in 1084 during the sack of Robert Guiscard.*

d. *See 3.6A, note a.*

e. *Pope St. Gregory I (r. 590–604).*

f. *The STATION of S. Clemente is Monday of the second week of Lent.*

6.2A   S. Stefano Rotondo: Dedication by Nicholas V

ECCLESIAM HANC PROTOMARTYRIS STEPHANI DIV ANTE COLLAPSAM
NICOLAVS V PONT MAX EXINTEGRO INSTAVRAVIT M CCCC LIII

1. ECCLESIAM : *See 1.7A, line 6.* — PROTOMARTYRIS : *The* EL
   prōtomartyr *transliterates* EG πρωτομάρτυς *(see 2.10, line 2).*
2. NICOLAVS V : Quīntus. — PONT(ifex) MAX(imus). —
   EXINTEGRO = ex integrō. — M CCCC LIII : Mīllēsimō
   quadringentēsimō quīnquāgēsimō tertiō.

6.2B   Epitaph of János Lászai

IO LAZO ARCH

IDI TRANSSIL PANNO PENIT AP DVM

ANN AGERET

LXXV OBIIT XVII AVG M D XXIII

5   NATVM Q' GELIDVM VIDES AD ISTRV̄

ROMANA TEGIER VIATOR VRNA

NON MIRABERE SI EXTIMABIS ILLVD

Q' ROMA EST PATRIA OMNIVM FVIT Q'

Four HENDECASYLLABLES *(lines 5–8)*

1. IO(annēs). — ARCH|IDI(āconus) : *The* EL archidiāconus *transliterates*
   EG ἀρχιδιάκονος *('archdeacon').*
2. TRANSSIL(vānus) : *The* ML *Adj.* Trānssilvānus *answers to the toponym*
   Trānssilvānia. — PANNO(niae) : *See 1.7A, line 4.* — PENIT(entiārius) =
   paenitentiārius : *The* EL *Subst.* paenitentiārius *is 'penitentiary'. On the*
   spelling, see 1.8B, line 5. — AP(ostolicus) : *See 3.4D, line 4.*
3. ANN(um).
4. LXXV : Septuāgēsimum quīntum. — XVII : Septimō decimō. —
   AVG(ustī) : *See 1.6G, line 11.* — M D XXIII : Mīllēsimō quīngentēsimō
   vīcēsimō tertiō.
5. Q(uem). — ISTRV(m) = Histrum : *On the spelling, see 8.8A, line 2.*
6. TEGIER = tegī : *The linguistic history of the Inf.Pass. in -ier is unclear.*
7. EXTIMABIS = existimābis : *In* LL, *both* existimāre *and* aestimāre *ap-*
   pear in the form extimāre *(see 1.8B, line 5, and cf.* sancxerunt, *7.4B).* —
   MIRABERE = mīrāberis.
8. Q(uod). — FVIT Q(ue).

Over Portal of Ambulatory

Nicholas the Fifth,[a] Supreme Pontiff,[b] restored in its entirety
this Church of St. Stephen, Protomartyr, long since dilapidated, in 1453.[c]

a. *Pope Nicholas V Parentucelli (r. 1447–1455).*
b. *The present is one of the earliest surviving datable inscriptions in which the*
   title SUPREME PONTIFF *is used of the pope.*
c. *Nicholas entrusted the Florentine architect Bernardo Rossellino with a*
   major restoration of the fifth-century church (1452–1454).

Left of High Altar

János Lászai,[a] Archdeacon,[b]
native of Transylvania in Hungary,[c] Apostolic Penitentiary,[d]
died on 17 August 1523,
while he was in his seventy-fifth year.

Wayfarer, if you consider this,
that Rome is and ever was the homeland of all, you will not marvel
that one whom you behold enclosed in a tomb[e] at Rome
was born on the banks of the icy Danube.

Four HENDECASYLLABLES *(lines 5–8)*

a. *János Lászai was a* CANON *of the Cathedral of Gyulafehérvár (the an-*
   cient Alba Julia) in Transylvania. In 1512 he had its N porch converted into
   a chapel whose decorative reliefs include the figure of Lászai himself kneel-
   ing before the BVM.
b. *An archdeacon (see* DEACON*) is a cleric to whom a* BISHOP *has delegated*
   a defined administrative authority within his diocese.
c. *In* AD 1001 *Stephen of Hungary had established ten bishoprics as well as*
   the archbishopric of Esztergom (cf. 1.7A, note d). Known in Hungarian as
   Szent István király ('St. Stephen king'), Stephen was granted the crown
   of Hungary by Pope Silvester II after defeating his uncle, the pagan prince
   Koppány.
d. *A penitentiary is a priest authorized to grant absolution for sins the*
   remission of which is ordinarily reserved to the bishop. Lászai served as
   Hungarian penitentiary at St. Peter's.
e. *Lit., 'urn'. As Christians traditionally practice inhumation, the Latin word*
   urna ('cinerary vase') is here used figuratively.

6.3 S. Maria in Domnica: Dedication by Paschal I

1 ISTA DOMVS PRIDEM FVERAT CONFRACTA RVINIS ⌐
 NVNC RVTILAT IVGITER VARIIS DECORATA METALLIS
2 ET DECVS ECCE SVVS SPLENDET CEV PHOEBVS IN ORBE ⌐
 QVI POST FVRVA FVGANS TETRAE VELAMINA NOCTIS
3 VIRGO MARIA TIBI PASCHALIS PRAESVL HONESTVS ⌐
 CONDIDIT HANC AVLAM LAETVS PER SAECLA MANENDAM

   Six HEXAMETERS

1. FVERAT CONFRACTA : *On the tense, see 1.6G, line 7.* — IVGITER : *Scans* iŭgiter. — METALLIS : *In* LL metallum *is used of the colored* tesserae *of mosaic work (see 2.14, line 1).*
2. DECVS ... SVVS : *In* CL, decus *is Neut.* — TETRAE = taetrae : *In* CL, *both* taeter *and* tēter *are attested; but on the spelling, see 1.8B, line 5.* — QVI ... NOCTIS : *The syntax can be saved only at the cost of an indefensible emendation of* FVGANS *to* FVGAT. — POST FVRVA : *Evidently with* VELAMINA *('dusky robes'). Some such sense as 'after the darkness' may also be possible.*
3. VIRGO : *Scans* virgŏ. — MARIA : *On the name, see 15.4G, line 1.*

6.4 SS. Giovanni e Paolo: Dedication by Cardinal Giovanni

PRESBITER ECCLESIE ROMANE RITE IOHANNES ⌐
HEC ANIMI VOTO DONA VOVENDA DEDIT ⌐
MARTYRIBVS CRISTI PAVLO PARITERQVE IOHANI ⌐
PASSIO QVOS EADEM CONTVLIT ESSE PARES

Two ELEGIAC COUPLETS

PRESBITER = presbyter : *See 3.4C, line 2; on the spelling, see 3.1, line 1.* — ECCLESIE ROMANE = ecclēsiae Rōmānae : *On* ecclēsia, *see 1.7A, line 6. The word* ecclēsia *here scans* ecclĕsia. *On the spelling, see 1.8B, line 5.* — HEC = haec. — MARTYRIBVS : *See 2.10, line 2.* — CRISTI = Christī : *See 1.6A.ii, line 6. On the spelling, see 8.8A, line 2.* — IOHANI : *The Latin* Ioannēs *(Greek* Ἰωάννης*) frequently appears with inauthentic* H *in the hiatus. Despite the spelling of the Greek original, the name regularly scans* Iŏannēs. — PASSIO : *Scans* passiŏ. *In* EL, passiŏ *is 'passion', 'suffering' (especially of Christ and the martyrs).*

Apse

This house had long since been broken down in ruins: Now,
embellished with variegated enamels, it gleams ruddy throughout,
and lo! its beauty shines like Phoebus[a] in the firmament
who afterwards, putting to flight the dusky robes of hateful night . . .[b]
O Virgin Mary, Paschal,[c] a goodly bishop, founded this church
for you in joy, destined to stand through the centuries.

Six HEXAMETERS

a. I.e., the sun. By this learned reference the author evidently intended to
   flaunt his erudition (cf. 13.13A, note b).
b. The syntax of the line is incomplete.
c. Pope St. Paschal I (r. 817–824). Paschal entirely rebuilt a number of ancient
   churches (cf. 3.5 and 13.13). He appears in this mosaic with the square nimbus of the living (see 3.7A, note b). The earliest appearance of the church's
   name is in the EINSIEDELN CATALOGUE, where the church is called Santa
   Maria Domnica; the most satisfactory explanation is that it arose from
   the phrase in dominica praedia ('on imperial property'; ML praedia = CL
   praedium).

Frieze of Portico

Giovanni, presbyter of the Roman Church, duly gave
this gift,[a] vowed in accordance with his heartfelt prayer,
to Paul and equally to John, martyrs of Christ,[b]
whom a shared fate made equal.

Two ELEGIAC COUPLETS

a. Badly damaged in the sack of Robert Guiscard in 1084, the church was
   restored 1154–1159 by Cardinal Giovanni de' Conti di Segni.
b. According to their late 'Acts', the brothers John and Paul were Christian
   soldiers condemned to death under Julian the Apostate (r. 361–363) and
   executed in their house on the Caelian Hill. Excavations beneath the BA-
   SILICA, constructed in the fifth century, have uncovered remains of both a
   domus ('townhouse') and an insula ('apartment block'). The first Christian cult place on the site was a private oratory installed at the rear of a
   shop on the ground floor.

6.5A Epitaph of Sir Edward Carne

D O M

EDOVARDO CARNO BRITANNO EQVITI AVRATO IV

RISCONSVLTO ORATORI SVMMIS DE REBVS BRITA

NNIÆ REGVM AD IMPERATOREM AD REGES BISQ

5   AD ROMANAM ET APOSTOLICAM SEDEM QVARVM

IN ALTERA LEGATIONE A PHILIPPO MARIAQ PIIS

REGIBVS MISSVS OBORTO DEINDE POST MORTEM

MARIÆ IN BRITANNIA SCHISMATE SPONTE PATRIA

CARENS OB CATHOLICAM FIDEM C̄V MAGNA INTE

10   GRITATIS VERÆQ PIETATIS EXISTIMATIONE DECE

SSIT HOC MONVMENTVM GALFRIDVS VACHANVS

ET THOMAS FREMANNVS AMICI EX TESTAMENTO POS

OBIIT ANN SALVTIS M D LXI XIIII CAL FEBR

1. D(eō) O(ptimō) M(aximō).
2. EDOVARDO : *The name ordinarily appears as* Eduardus. —
   IV|RISCONSVLTO.
3. BRITA|NNIÆ.
4. BISQ(ue).
5. APOSTOLICAM SEDEM : *See 3.4D, line 4. The* EL apostolica sēdēs *('Apostolic See') is a frequent periphrasis for the papal government.*
6. MARIAQ(ue) : *On the name, see 15.4G, line 1.*
7–8. OBORTO . . . SCHISMATE : *Abl.Absolute. The* EL schisma *transliterates
   Greek* σχίσμα *('cleft', then 'division of opinion').* — PATRIA : *Abl. with*
   CARENS.
9–11. CATHOLICAM : *See 1.61, line 6.* — CV(m) : *Governs* MAGNA . . .
   EXISTIMATIONE. — INTE|GRITATIS.
10. VERÆQ(ue). — DECE|SSIT.
12. THOMAS : *The Latin name is* Thōmās, -ae. — POS(uērunt).
13. ANN(ō). — M D LXI : Mīllēsimō quīngentēsimō sexāgēsimō prīmō.
    — XIIII : Quārtō decimō. — CAL(endīs) = Kalendīs : *On the spelling,
    see 4.6C, line 3.* — FEBR(uāriī) : *See 1.6G, line 11.*

S. Gregorio Magno: Forecourt, NW Corner

To God, Best and Greatest.
To Edward Carne,[a] Briton, Knight of the Golden Spur,[b]
advocate, on matters of the greatest moment
ambassador of the sovereigns of Britain to the emperor,
to kings, and twice to the Roman and Apostolic See:[c]
dispatched on the second of these missions by the godly monarchs
Philip and Mary,[d] and subsequently—with the onset of schism in Britain after the
death of Mary—in voluntary exile from his country
on account of his Catholic faith,[e]
he died in high repute for his uprightness and true godliness.
His friends Geoffrey Vaughan and Thomas Freeman
set up this monument in accordance with his will.
He died on 19 January in the year of Salvation 1561.[f]

a. *Sir Edward Carne was the last ambassador of the sovereigns of England to the Holy See before the break with Rome.*

b. *In 1538, King Henry VIII (r. 1509–1547) appointed Carne ambassador to the emperor Charles V, who created him a Knight of the Golden Spur (a purely honorific title).*

c. *In 1531 Carne was sent to Rome as* Excusator *('advocate') for Henry VIII, to obtain the consent of Pope Clement VII for the annulment of the king's marriage to Catherine of Aragon, widow of Henry's elder brother. The following year, Pope Clement VII pronounced against the English king's case. In January of 1533, Henry was married to Anne Boleyn in Westminster Abbey; Anne was crowned queen on Whitsunday (June 1 that year).*

d. *In 1554 the future King Philip II of Spain (see 1.8B, note b) entered a marriage arranged by his father, Charles V, with the Catholic Mary I of England, who had succeeded Henry VIII in 1547. Philip and Mary charged Carne with the task of effecting the submission of England to Pope Julius III.*

e. *The text alludes circumspectly to a third embassy, undertaken on behalf of Elizabeth I to seek recognition from Pope Paul IV. After failing in this object, Carne was recalled to England but declined to return, preferring instead to pass the evening of his days in Rome.*

f. *Lit., 'on the fourteenth day before the Kalends of February'.*

6.5B   S. Gregorio Magno: History

ADSTA HOSPES

ET LEGE

HIC OLIM FVIT M GREGORI DOMVS

IPSE IN MONASTERIVM CONVERTIT

5   VBI MONASTICEN PROFESSVS EST

ET DIV ABBAS PRAEFVIT

MONACHI PRIMVM BENEDICTINI

MOX GRAECI TENVERE

DEIN BENEDICTINI ITERVM

10   POST VARIOS CASVS

QVVM IAMDIV

ESSET COMMENDATVM

ET POENE DESERTVM

ANNO MDLXXIII

15   CAMALDVLENSES INDVCTI

QVI ET INDVSTRIA SVA

ET OPE PLVRIVM

R E CARDINALIVM

QVORVM HIC MONVMENTA EXSTANT

20   FAVENTE ETIAM CLEMENTE XI P M

TEMPLVM ET ADIACENTES AEDES

IN HANC QVAM CERNIS FORMAM

RESTITVERVNT

3. M(agnī).

4. MONASTERIVM : *See 2.13A, line 4.*

5. MONASTICEN : *The* EL *monasticē transliterates the* EG μοναστική (*'religious life'*). *The desinence is a Greek Acc.Sg.*

6. ABBAS : *The* EL *abbās transliterates* EG ἀββᾶς (*'abbot'*).

7. MONACHI : *See 5.5, line 10.*

8. TENVERE = tenuērunt.

11. QVVM = cum : *A spurious archaism (see 2.12B, line 2).*

12. COMMENDATVM : *In* EL, commendāre (*or* dare in commendā) *signifies the transfer of the control of church property to a secular authority.*

Forecourt, First Pillar R, N Face

Stay, stranger,
and read.

Here once stood the house of Gregory the Great.[a]
He himself converted it into a monastery
where he took his religious vows
and long presided as abbot.
Benedictine monks first possessed it,
subsequently Greeks,
then Benedictines a second time.[b]
Following sundry calamities,
when it had long
been transferred to secular control
and all but abandoned,
in the year 1573
the Camaldolese were installed,[c]
who both by their own hard work
and the aid of many cardinals
of the Roman Church[d]
whose monuments are here to be seen,
and also with the support of Clement XI,[e] *Supreme Pontiff,*
restored
the church and associated structures
to the aspect which you behold.

a. *Around AD 580, after the death of his father, the future Pope St. Gregory I (r. 590–604) converted his ancestral mansion on the Caelian Hill into a Benedictine monastery dedicated to St. Andrew. Here he deposited that apostle's relics, which had been brought from Constantinople. The monastery became a thriving center of religious life. Because it is from here that St. Augustine of Canterbury departed for Kent in AD 596, the church has always had a special significance for the English.*
b. *Around 750, the monastery passed under the control of Greek monks. It was restored to the Benedictines in the tenth century.*

13. POENE = paene : *On the spelling, see 1.8B, line 5.*
14. MDLXXIII : Mīllēsimō quīngentēsimō septuāgēsimō tertiō.
15. CAMALDVLENSES : *The Adj.* Camaldulēnsis *answers to the Ital. top-onym* Camaldoli (*from Latin* Campus Maldulī); *as a Subst. it furnishes the name of the Camaldolese order.*
18. R(ōmānae) E(cclēsiae): *On* ecclēsia, *see 1.7A, line 6.*
20. CLEMENTE XI : Ūndecimō. — P(ontifice) M(aximō).

6.6 SS. Nereo e Achilleo: Dedication of Cardinal Baronio

SS NEREI ET ACHILLEI FRATRVM

FORTISSIMOR CHRISTI MARTYRVM

QVI A S PETRO BAPTIZATI SVNT

TITVLVM HVNC AB ANTIQVIS TEMPORIBVS

5 IN EORVM HONOREM ERECTVM VBI ET

S GREGORIVS MAGNVS PP CONCIONEM HABVIT

A S LEONE PP III INSTAVRATVM

ET AB ALIIS ROMANIS PONTIFICIB ORNATVM

CVM VETVSTATE PENITVS COLLAPSVS ESSET

10 CAESAR BARONIVS SORANVS

EIVSDEM TIT PRESB CARD ET BIBLIOTHEC AP

IN HANC FORMAM RESTITVIT

SACRAQ ILLOR CORPORA VNA CVM CORPORE

S FLAVIAE DOMITILLAE VIRG ET MART

15 CVIVS AMBO EVNVCHI LONGVM CVM EA

PRO CHRISTO EXILIVM IN INSVLA PONTIA

DVXERVNT

EX DIACONIA S HADRIANI ACCEPTA

IN HVNC EVNDEM TIT VBI OLIM CONDITA FVERANT

20 RITV PROCESSIONIS SOLEMNI REDVXIT

ALIASQ COMPLVRES SS RELIQVIAS ADDIDIT

CVNCTA BENIGNE DECRETIS SVIS CONCEDENTE

CLEMENTE VIII PONT MAX

QVI HVNC ITEM ECCLESIAE IVS PERPETVVM

    c. *The Camaldolese Order was founded by St. Romuald (c. 950–1027), a nobleman of Ravenna who withdrew to the neighboring marshes to practice a rigid asceticism. The monastery he founded at Camaldoli became the order's center.*

    d. *Numbering among the illustrious patrons of the church are Cesare Baronio and Scipione Caffarelli-Borghese.*

    e. *The Baroque transformation of the monastery and church was initiated during the reign of Pope Clement XI (r. 1700–1721).*

Apse, R of Bishop's Throne

When on account of age it had all but collapsed,
through the kind dispensation
of Clement the Eighth,[a] Supreme Pontiff—
who on 12 May[b] in the year of Salvation 1596, sixth of his office,
likewise by his own decree assigned to this church the perpetual right
of a Station with sacred indulgences[c]—
Cesare Baronio of Sora,
Cardinal Priest of the same Title and Apostolic Librarian,[d]
restored on the present lines
this Title of the brothers Saints Nereus and Achilleus,[e]
valiant martyrs of Christ
baptized by Saint Peter—
which had been erected in their honor,
where also Pope Saint Gregory the Great delivered an oration,[f]
which had been restored by Pope Saint Leo the Third[g]
and embellished by other Roman pontiffs—
and in a solemn ceremony of procession
returned to this same Title,
where they once had been buried,
their sacred bodies received from the Deaconry of Sant'Adriano,[h]
together with the body
of Saint Flavia Domitilla, Virgin and Martyr,
in whose service as eunuchs
both endured a long exile for the sake of Christ

25   STATIONIS CVM SACRIS INDVLGENTIIS ATTRIBVIT

AN SAL M D XCVI IIII ID MAII PONTIF VI

PRESBYTER CARD SVCCESSOR QVISQVIS FVERIS

ROGO TE PER GLORIAM DEI ET

PER MERITA HORVM MARTYRVM

30   NIHIL DEMITO NIHIL MINVITO NEC MVTATO

RESTITVTAM ANTIQVITATEM PIE SERVATO

SIC TE DEVS MARTYRVM SVORVM PRECIBVS

SEMPER ADIVVET

1. SS = sānctōrum : *On the abbreviation, see 1.61, line 7.*

2. FORTISSIMOR(um). — CHRISTI : *See 1.6A.ii, line 6.* —
MARTYRVM : *See 2.10, line 2.*

3. S(ānctō) PETRO : *See 3.2A, line 2.* — BAPTIZATI SVNT : *The EL*
baptizāre *represents Greek* βαπτίζειν *('immerse', then EG 'baptize').*

4. TITVLVM : *See 3.6A, line 2.*

6. S(ānctus). — P(a)P(a) : *See 3.6A, line 2.* — CONCIONEM =
contiōnem : *On the spelling, see 3.4B, line 3.*

7. S(ānctō) LEONE P(a)P(ā) III : *Tertiō.*

8. PONTIFICIB(us).

10. SORANVS : *The Adj.* Sōrānus *corresponds to the toponym* Sōra.

11. TIT(ulī). — PRESB(yter) : *See 3.4C, line 2.* — CARD(inālis).
— BIBLIOTHEC(ārius) : *The LL* bibliothēcārius *is 'librarian'.* —
AP(ostolicus) : *See 3.4D, line 4.*

13. SACRAQ(ue) ILLOR(um).

14. S(ānctae). — VIRG(inis). — MART(yris).

16. CHRISTO : *See 1.6A.ii, line 6.* — EXILIVM = exsilium : *See 4.2A, line 7.*

18. DIACONIA : *The EL* diāconia *transliterates Greek* διακονία *('deaconry').*
— S(ānctī).

19. TIT(ulum). — CONDITA FVERANT : *On the tense, see 1.6G, line 7.*

21. ALIASQ(ue). — SS = sānctissimās : *See 1.61, line 7.*

23. CLEMENTE VIII : *Octāvō.* — PONT(ifice) MAX(imō).

24. ECCLESIAE : *See 1.7A, line 6.*

25. STATIONIS : *See 6.1, line 11.* — INDVLGENTIIS : *In EL,* indulgentia *is
remission of punishment of sin granted under prescribed conditions.*

26. AN(nō) SAL(ūtis) M D XCVI : *Mīllēsimō quīngentēsimō nōnāgēsimō
sextō.* — IIII : *Quārtō.* — ID(ibus) MAII : *See 1.6G, line 11.* —
PONTIF(icātūs) VI : *Sextō.*

27. PRESBYTER : *See 3.4C, line 2.* — CARD(inālis).

on the isle of Pontia[i] —
and he added numerous other relics of saints.
Succeeding Cardinal Priest, be you who you may,
I adjure you by the glory of God
and by the merits of these martyrs:
remove nothing, diminish nothing, nor make alteration;
reverently preserve the antiquity that has been restored.
So help you God for aye by the prayers
of his martyrs.

a. Pope Clement VIII Aldobrandini (r. 1592–1605). The date indicated in fact fell in Clement's fifth year (30 January 1596 to 29 January 1597).

b. Lit., 'on the fourth day before the Ides of May'.

c. In the Middle Ages, the city's STATION churches were the scene of annual observances involving a procession and papal mass.

d. Cesare Baronio (1538–1607) served as cardinal priest of SS. Nereo and Achilleo from 1596 until his death and as librarian of the Holy Roman Church from 1597. He obtained the use of the present church for the Congregation of the Oratory, a community of priests headed by Filippo Neri.

e. Nereus and Achilleus were second-century martyrs; their cult is ancient and well attested. According to their late 'Acts', the two were eunuchs of Flavia Domitilla (see 6.1, note b) and were martyred under Trajan.

f. The twenty-eighth homily of Pope St. Gregory I was in fact delivered at the saints' BASILICA in the Cemetery of Domitilla (see 6.9).

g. Pope St. Leo III (r. 795–816). The church is first attested in AD 377 under the name Titulus Fasciolae ('Title of the Bandage'; see TITULAR CHURCH). According to legend, as St. Peter was fleeing from prison in Rome, the bandage with which he had bound an injury caused by his fetters fell from his ankle at this spot (see 2.15, note a; 3.4B, note b; and 6.9, note a). The silence of the sources after the sixth century suggests that it was absorbed by a new titulus of SS. Nereus and Achilleus, first attested about the same time. The present structure, dating to the time of Leo III, was evidently built at a short distance from the original site to avoid marshy ground. The relics of the martyrs were brought in from the extramural Cemetery of Domitilla, by then exposed to the incursions of Saracen raiders.

h. Dismantled in 1937, S. Adriano occupied the former Senate House in the Forum (see DEACONRY).

i. Though the isle of Pontia (mod. Ponza) was indeed used as a place of exile, it is Pandateria to which Domitilla was sent.

6.7 Commemoration of Victory of 1327

ANNO DN̄I M CC°C

XXVII INDICTIONE

XI MENSE SEPTEM

BRIS DIE PENVLTIM

5   A INFESTO SC̄I MICHA

ELIS INTRAVIT GENS

FORESTERIA IN VRB

E ET FVIT DEBELLA

TA A POPVLO ROMA

10   NO EXISTENTE IA

COBO DE PONTIA

NIS CAPITE REGIO

NIS

1. D(omi)NI. — M CC°C|XXVII : Mīllēsimō trecentēsimō vīcēsimō
septimō.

2. INDICTIONE : *See 2.1, line 16.*

3. XI : Ūndecimā. — SEPTEM|BRIS.

4. PENVLTIM|A.

5. INFESTO = in fēstō. — S(ān)C(t)I. — MICHA|ELIS.

7. FORESTERIA : *The* ML *foresterius is* 'foreign'. — VRB|E.

8. FVIT DEBELLA|TA : *On the tense, see 1.6G, line 7.*

9. ROMA|NO.

10–13. EXISTENTE IA|COBO DE PONTIA|NIS CAPITE REGIO|NIS : *Abl.*
Absolute (cf. 1.8B, lines 8–9). The Latin caput rēgiōnis *represents the Ital.*
caporione *('chief of the* rione'; *cf. 1.8A, line 3).*

6.8 Impression of the Feet of Christ

[steterunt pedes eius]

steterunt : *Like the Eng.* stand, *with which it is cognate, Lat.* stāre *can
signify both rising up and coming to a halt.* — eius : *I.e., Christ's. The relic
in the present church is a cast of the original, preserved in the Basilica of S.
Sebastiano (cf. 6.11).*

Porta S. Sebastiano: Passageway, W Face

In the year of the Lord 1327,
in the eleventh indiction,[a]
on the last day but one
of the month of September,
on the feast of Saint Michael,[b]
a foreign race
entered within the city
and was defeated
by the
Roman people,[c]
Iacopo de' Ponziani
being
Caporione.[d]

a. *The* INDICTION *was a fifteen-year tax cycle (see 2.1, note e). Whether on the Greek, Roman, or Bedan system (see 12.10, note b), 29 September 1327 fell in the tenth year of the indiction.*

b. *The inscription is accompanied by a magnificent if crude graffito of the Archangel Michael serenely impaling a dragon at his feet.*

c. *The inscription records a Ghibelline victory over the forces of Robert D'Anjou, king of Naples. The main conflict took place around the* Civitas Leonina *(see 15.5C.i, note a). At Porta S. Sebastiano the militia of Rione Sant'Angelo repelled the 'foreign' troops.*

d. *Each of the fourteen* rioni *('quarters') of papal Rome was headed by a* caporione; *the* caporione *of Rione dei Monti, known as the* priore, *served as chief of the* caporioni *(see* CONSERVATORS*).*

Domine, Quo Vadis?: Slab at Center of Nave

His feet stood fast.[a]

a. *As St. Peter fled the persecution of Nero, he is said to have been confronted at this place by Christ, to whom he addressed the question:* Domine, quo vadis? *('Lord, whither goest thou?'). Christ replied:* Romam eo iterum crucifigi *('I go to Rome to be crucified anew'). Stung by this oblique censure, Peter returned to the city to face martyrdom (cf. 14.4, note b).*

6.9 Damasian Elogium of SS. Nereus and Achilleus

[nereus et achilleus martyres
militiae nomen dederant saeuumq gerebant
officium pariter spectantes iuss]A TY[ranni
praeceptis pulsante metu serui]RE PAR[ati]
5 M[ira fides rerum subito posue]RE FVRORE
CON[uersi fugiunt ducis inpia castr]A RELINQVVNT
PROI[ciunt clipeos faleras tel]AQ CRVENTA
CONFES[si gaudent christi portar]E TRIVMFOS
CREDITE P[er damasum possit quid] GLORIA CHRISTI

Eight HEXAMETERS *(lines 2–9)*

1. nereus : *Only small fragments of the original inscription survive. The portions enclosed in brackets have been restored from copies made in the early Middle Ages.* — martyres : *See 2.10, line 2.*
2. saeuumq(ue).
3. spectantes iuss]A : *I.e., they complied with their orders.* — TY[ranni : *Damasus regularly uses* tyrannus *with reference to persecuting officials.*
5. posue]RE = posuērunt. — FVRORE(m).
6. CON[uersi : *In* EL, *convertī is 'turn to God'.* — ducis : *If Nereus and Achilleus were soldiers, the* dux *of the present reference may have been the* praefectus praetōriō *(prefect of the Praetorian Guard). Alternatively, it may refer to the emperor.*
7. faleras = phalerās : *On the spelling, see 2.1, line 2.* — tel]AQ(ue) : *Scans* telāque *(among his many metrical licenses, Damasus permits the lengthening of a short grammatical desinence in ictus preceding the enclitic -que).* — CRVENTA : *Either Lit., 'bloody' or Fig., 'cruel'.*
8. TRIVMFOS = triumphōs.
9. CHRISTI : *See 1.6A.ii, line 6.*

Cemetery of S. Domitilla: Basilica di SS. Nereo e Achilleo

Nereus and Achilleus, Martyrs.[a]
They had given their allegiance to military service and were performing
their savage duty with equal zeal, heedful of the tyrant's orders,
ready under the hand of fear to obey his instructions. Wondrous
is the truth of the tale: Of a sudden, they put off their madness,
with a change of heart they flee, they abandon the unholy barracks
of their commander. They cast away their shields, decorations,
and bloody arms. Confessing Christ, they rejoice to bear his triumphs.[b]
Believe on the authority of Damasus[c] *what the glory of Christ can effect.*

Eight HEXAMETERS (lines 2–9)

a. Regarded by Damasus as soldiers, the pair were likely victims of Diocletian's persecution, which in its initial phase (AD 295–298) concentrated
on the military. According to their late and legendary 'Acts', Nereus and
Achilleus were eunuchs in the service of Flavia Domitilla (see 6.1, note b).
At the end of the fourth century, the galleries surrounding the saints' tomb
were excavated on all sides to form a subterranean BASILICA ad corpus
(see 4.7B, note b). Along with many of the extramural shrines, the Cemetery of St. Domitilla was abandoned in the wake of the Saracen invasions
of the ninth century. The complex was rediscovered only in 1874.

b. I.e., to suffer martyrdom.

c. Pope St. Damasus I (r. 366–384). Damasus embellished the shrines of
the Roman martyrs with large marble slabs bearing epigrams of his own
composition; the distinctive alphabet was designed by Furius Dionysius
Filocalus, the leading calligrapher of the day. At a period when the stone-
cutter's art had lapsed into general decadence, Filocalus' altogether original letter forms represent a revival of the best traditions of the monumental
Roman capital.

6.10 Damasian Elogium of the Popes

HIC CONGESTA IACET QVAERIS SI TVRBA PIORVM

CORPORA SANCTORVM RETINENT VENERANDA SEPVLCRA

SVBLIMES ANIMAS RAPVIT SIBI REGIA CAELI

HIC COMITES XYSTI POR[t]ANT QVI EX HOSTE TROPAEA

5   HIC NVMERVS PROCERV[m s]ERVAT QVI ALTARIA X̄P̄Ī

HIC POSITVS LONGA VIXIT QVI IN PACE SAC[e]RDOS

HIC CONFESSORES SANCTI QVOS GRA[ecia] MISIT

HIC IVVENES PVERIQ SENES CA[stiq nep]OTES

QVIS MAGE VIRGINEVM PLACVIT R[etinere pud]OREM

10 HIC FATEOR DAMASVS VOLVI M[ea condere m]EMBRA

SED CINERES TIMVI SANCTOS V[exare pi]ORVM

      Eleven HEXAMETERS

1. HIC : *Viz., in the Cemetery of Callistus. The 126 fragments of the inscription were discovered in 1854 amid the earth and rubble that had filled the Crypt of the Popes. The portions enclosed in brackets are restored from medieval transcriptions.* — QVAERIS SI : *I.e., sī quaeris. The clause is rather in the nature of a parenthesis than a true protasis.* — TVRBA : *In* EL, *'throng' or 'multitude' and not necessarily 'mob'.* — PIORVM : *Damasus uses the Subst.Adj.* pius *with reference to the 'blessed' or 'saints'.*

2. SANCTORVM : *Damasus uses the Subst.Adj.* sānctus *for martyrs only, not all the faithful.*

4. XYSTI : *On the spelling, see 3.4D, line 4.*

5. X̄P̄Ī = Christī : *See 1.6A.ii, line 6. The abbreviation combines the first two letters of the Greek* ΧΡΙΣΤΟΣ *with the Gen.Sg. inflection of its Latin transliteration; see 3.4D, line 8.*

7. CONFESSORES : *The* EL *cōnfessor is 'one who confesses Christianity', ordinarily with the implication of subsequent martyrdom.*

8. PVERIQ(ue). — CA[stiq(ue) nep]OTES : *The layout of the lines on the reconstituted slab suggests the abbreviation of* -que *printed here.*

9. MAGE = magis. — VIRGINEVM : *The sense is 'chaste'. In early Christian epitaphs, for example, young married couples are not infrequently characterized as* virginēs.

10. FATEOR : *Parenthetical; the main verb is* VOLVI (vŏlŭī).

11. CINERES : *As the Christians practiced inhumation rather than cremation, the word is not to be understood literally.*

Cemetery of S. Callisto: Crypt of the Popes, before Altar

Here, in case you ask, lies gathered together a throng of godly men:
venerable tombs imprison the bodies of the martyrs, but the royal
palace of heaven has caught up their souls on high unto itself. Here
are the companions of Sixtus,[a] who bear off trophies from the enemy;
here the complement of captains[b] that serves the altar of Christ;
here is laid the priest[c] who lived during a long peace;
here the holy confessors whom Greece dispatched;[d]
here young men and boys, elders and chaste grandsons
who preferred to preserve a maidenly modesty.
Here I, Damasus, confess that I wished my limbs to be laid,
but I feared to disturb the holy remains[e] of these godly souls.[f]

> Eleven HEXAMETERS

a. *On 6 August 258 Pope St. Sixtus II (r. 257–258) was presiding over an illegal assembly at the Cemetery of Praetextatus on the Via Appia. According to a letter of St. Cyprian, Sixtus and four of his deacons (see DEACON) were arrested and summarily executed. These deacons—Stephanus, Januarius, Magnus, and Vincentius—are the 'companions' of the present inscription. According to tradition, two other deacons were arrested and executed later the same day, while Lawrence, who had charge of the Church's meager wealth, suffered martyrdom four days later (see 4.7B, note a).*

b. *Viz., the popes buried in the present crypt. The epitaphs of five of them are preserved in situ. The Cemetery of Callistus is named after Pope St. Callistus I (r. 217–222), a slave who rose to be appointed deacon under Pope St. Zephyrinus. In this capacity, Callistus superintended this cemetery.*

c. *Opinion has varied as to whether this expression refers to a particular pope or represents a collective expression for all those bishops of Rome whose reigns were undisturbed by persecutions. For example, though it ended violently, the fourteen-year reign of Pope St. Fabian was largely tranquil.*

d. *The 'Greek Martyrs' are Hippolytus, Paulina, Hadrias, Maria, and Neon (see 3.3C, note b).*

e. *Lit., 'ashes' (see 6.2B, note e).*

f. *See 6.9, note c. Damasus here alludes censoriously to the practice of paying for burial near the tombs of martyrs.*

6.11 Damasian Elogium of SS. Peter and Paul

[hic habitasse prius sanctos cognoscere debes
nomina quisque petri pariter paulique requiris
discipulos oriens misit quod sponte fatemur
sanguinis ob meritum christumque per astra secuti
5 aetherios petiere sinus regnaque piorum
roma suos potius meruit defendere ciues
haec damasus uestras referat noua sidera laudes]

Seven HEXAMETERS

1. hic : *The text of the inscription is preserved in transcription.* — habitasse
= habitāvisse. — prius : *I.e.,* ōlim. — sanctos : *See 6.10, line 2.*

2. nomina : *I.e., the martyrs' relics.*

4–5. christumque . . . piorum : *The clause constitutes a parenthetical elaboration of* sanguinis ob meritum. *On* christum, *see 1.6A.ii, line 6.* —
petiere = petīvērunt. — regnaque : *Scans* regnăque (*see 6.9, line 7*). —
piorum : *See 6.10, line 1.*

6. defendere : *The* CL dēfendere *can have the sense 'to claim possession of'.*

7. uestras . . . laudes : *App. to* haec.

6.12 Epitaph of Caecilia Metella

CAECILIAE

Q CRETICI F

METELLAE CRASSI

2. Q(uīntī). — F(īliae) : *In the republican period, a woman's name ordinarily comprised the feminine form of her father's* nōmen gentīle *together
with his* praenōmen *in the Gen. and the word* fīlia: *The daughter of Marcus Tullius Cicero was thus* Tullia Marci filia (*abbreviated* TVLLIA M F).
*In the present case, the daughter of Quintus Caecilius Metellus Creticus
is styled* Caecilia Quinti Cretici filia Metella Crassi, *with the inclusion
of the father's* agnōmen (Creticus), *the feminine form of his* cognōmen
(Metellus) *and the Gen.Sg. of her husband's gentile name* (Crassus).

Basilica di S. Sebastiano: Above Second Chapel R

You who seek the names of Peter and likewise Paul
must recognize that the martyrs formerly dwelt in this place.[a]
The East sent the apostles: This we freely acknowledge. But in virtue
of their martyrdom—for, following Christ through the stars,
they sought the heavenly regions and the kingdom of the saints—
Rome has deserved to claim them rather as her own citizens.[b]
Let Damasus relate these things to your praise, ye new luminaries.

Seven HEXAMETERS

a. *Originally known as the* Basilica Apostolorum *('Basilica of the
Apostles'), S. Sebastiano was founded by Constantine I or one of his sons.
The language employed by Damasus in the present text does not clarify
whether he regarded the shrine as the apostles' temporary burial site or as
a place where they were believed to have resided. In any case, the cult of the
apostles eventually reverted to their major basilicas. In the eighth century,
the church was rededicated to St. Sebastian (see 2.10, note a).*

b. *The co-opting of the apostles is to be understood in the context of
Damasus' deliberate Romanizing of the Church.*

Mausoleum of Caecilia Metella: Façade, W Side

To Caecilia Metella,
daughter of Quintus Creticus,
wife of Crassus.[a]

a. *For all the magnificence of her tomb, the lady is known to history only as
the daughter of her father and wife of her husband. The former was Quintus Caecilius Metellus 'Creticus', CONSUL in 69 BC; for his conquest of
Crete, he was awarded a triumph and assumed the traditional sobriquet
taken by Roman conquerors (Creticus signifies 'Conqueror of Crete'). The
latter was a Crassus—probably the grandson of Marcus Licinius Crassus
Dives ('the Rich'), colleague of Caesar and Pompey in the 'First Triumvirate', who met his end in 53 BC on the far side of the Euphrates near Car-
rhae (the biblical Haran) at the head of an ill-conceived expedition against
the Parthians.*

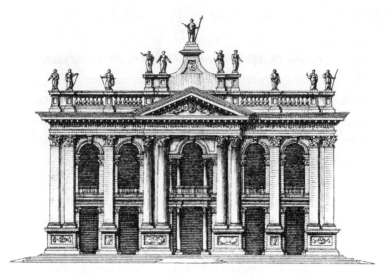

BASILICA DI SAN GIOVANNI IN LATERANO

The Baroque style in architecture may be imagined as a tempestuous marriage of Classical order and Romantic anarchy. At the height of the Barocchetto (the so-called 'Roman Rococo'), when romantic riot was in the ascendant, the sobriety of Alessandro Galilei's Lateran façade marked a swing towards Classical composure. The façade consists of two stories articulated on five axes by a colossal order of pilasters and crowned by a continuous entablature; the central axis is defined by a monumental aedicule consisting of paired half-columns and a Classicizing pediment. The Baroque affinities of the design are nonetheless evident in the dramatic chiaroscuro effect produced by the extensive voids as well as in the exuberant sculptural decoration.

VII. The Lateran & Environs

As the city's aqueducts fell victim to the violence and neglect of the early Middle Ages, her highlands were gradually abandoned in favor of the low-lying plain of the Campus Martius. The Campagna—Rome's desolate hinterland—invaded the walls to produce a landscape of unprecedented novelty: from the Pincio to the Aventine there stretched a vast and undulating plain littered with the Brobdingnagian carcasses of aqueducts and baths. Sporadic monasteries, their vineyards and orchards lending grace to the ruins, were linked by the herdsmen's tracks to which the thoroughfares of the ancient city had been reduced. The considerable area that had reverted to wilderness was called in Italian *disabitato*—the deserted zone; its churches were *chiese della campagna*—countryside churches. With the frenetic speculation in land that followed on the unification of Italy in 1870, this collaborative masterpiece of nature and civilization was swiftly crushed beneath the juggernaut of urban growth. Fugitive shreds of its magic cling to odd corners of the remnant preserved between Porta San Paolo and Porta Metronia.

Among the salient features of the *disabitato* was Porta Maggiore. The monument probably owes its name to the fact that in the Middle Ages it furnished direct access to the Basilica of Santa Maria Maggiore from the southeast. Dual inscriptions on the east and west faces record its original construction by the emperor Claudius I (r. AD 41–54) as well as restorations carried out under Vespasian (r. 69–79), Titus (r. 79–81), and Honorius (r. 395–423). Like the Porta Tiburtina, Porta Maggiore was originally a section of aqueduct monumentalized where it passed over a major road in the open country. Here the course of the Aqua Claudia coincided with the junction of two consular highways, the Via Praenestina and the Via Labicana; a tomb of the first century BC was situated in the triangular plot where the roads converged. The architects of the aqueduct devised a double arch that would accommodate the roads while respecting the integrity of the Sepulcher of Marcus Vergilius Eurysaces. When the wall of Aurelian was built and the twin archway

7.5A
7.5B&C
7.5D

7.6

217

fortified as a gate in the late third century, the tomb was incorporated into a tower; it came to light fifteen centuries later, when Pope Gregory XVI (r. 1823–1846) had Porta Maggiore liberated of its fortifications and restored.

The Basilica of San Giovanni in Laterano was a fortuitous beneficiary of the development stimulated by Italy's unification: orphaned for centuries in the vastness of the *disabitato*, the seat of Rome's bishop was at last reunited with the city. No ancient authority corroborates the story that the Lateran takes its name from Plautius Lateranus, condemned by Nero for his role in the Pisonian conspiracy of AD 65. The toponym likely dates instead to the early third century, when Septimius Severus presented a townhouse on the Caelian to one Titus Sextus Lateranus. After the property had passed into the imperial possession, part of it was occupied by the barracks of the *Equites Singulares*, an elite cavalry corps. Constantine I (r. 306–337) disbanded the corps for having supported Maxentius, his rival, and granted the site of its barracks to Pope St. Miltiades (r. 311–314) for the construction of a basilica, a bishop's residence, 7.2 and a BAPTISTERY. Helen, the emperor's mother, was given a villa near Porta Maggiore, and a large hall on that property was converted into the Basilica of Santa Croce in Gerusalemme to house the fragment of the True Cross that the dowager empress was believed to have obtained in Jerusalem.

The remote location of the Lateran complex, situated squarely within the imperial demesne, has long been interpreted as a token of prudent deference on the part of Constantine towards the pagan element in the aristocracy. The large but unprepossessing Christian basilica was ostensibly relegated to the obscurity of the outskirts, whereas in the monumental center the emperor pursued such unexceptionably traditional projects as a bath complex on the Quirinal and a triumphal arch near the Colosseum. The reality appears to be more complicated. Most tellingly, the imperial quarter on the Caelian was prestigious and wealthy; its choice as a site for the seat of the Christian bishop was a mark of conspicuous honor. As for Constantine's monuments in the center, rather than an effort to conciliate the aristocracy by a show of traditionalism, they more likely betoken the ambition of a parvenu to outdo his defeated predecessor in the customary idiom of public architecture.

Diminished by its squalid modern surroundings, the Lateran of today reflects little of the prestige that it enjoyed for a thousand years as the nerve center of western Christendom. Over the millennium that elapsed between its foundation and the departure of the papacy for Avignon in 1308, the Lateran was the 'capitol' of the Latin Church, citadel of the Holy City that had superseded the Rome of the Caesars. Commanding a legion of deacons, notaries, and scribes, the Vicar of Christ stood at the head of an ecclesiastical bureaucracy whose influence penetrated every corner of medieval Europe. Little is known of the earliest episcopal residence, which probably rose somewhere behind the apse of the basilica; only in the mid-eighth century did the Patriarchium—the great palace of the popes—begin to take shape. Modeled on the seat of the Byzantine emperors at Constantinople, the Patriarchium gave unambiguous architectural expression to the imperial pretensions of the papacy. By the mid-ninth century, it boasted three large halls: the Triclinium of Leo III, in which Charlemagne was entertained on 30 November 800, the Triclinium of Gregory IV, and the Hall of Council.

The Benediction Loggia at the Hall of Council was scene of the inauguration of the first Jubilee in 1300 by Pope BONIFACE VIII (r. 1294– *7.4H* 1303). For Dante, who visited Rome in that year, the Lateran was a marvel that surpassed all things mortal—*a le cose mortali andò di sopra* (*Paradiso* XXXI. 36). The privilege conferred by its august origins would nevertheless prove insufficient over time to sustain the Lateran's primacy. Unlike St. Peter's at the Vatican, the Lateran had never been the focus of popular devotion; and with the relentless drift of the population towards the river, it was increasingly isolated. The inevitable decline provoked by the departure of the Curia for Avignon was exacerbated by a fire, the outbreak of plague at Rome in 1348, an earthquake in 1349, and a second fire in 1361. By the time the papacy was definitively restored to Rome in 1420, the Lateran's day was done. Within a few decades, a new citadel was rising on the far side of the Tiber, in the shadow of Castel Sant'Angelo. In 7.4G   a sense, the era of the Lateran has its epitaph in the tomb of Pope MAR-TIN V (r. 1417–1431)—equally the last pope of the Middle Ages and the first of the Renaissance.

After nearly three centuries of neglect, the Lateran was renovated under Pope Sixtus V (r. 1585–1590). The improvements called for the wholesale demolition of the venerable Patriarchium. Even in ruin, the Patriarchium as it yet stood in 1585 has been memorably characterized as the most marvelous museum of medieval art that ever existed—a fantastic agglomeration of courts and chapels, towers and loggias, private apartments and rooms of state. Sharing the indifference of his contemporaries to the 'Gothic' Middle Ages, Sixtus V acted without compunction. In the span of a few months, the halls that had hosted Charlemagne, with their irreplaceable stonework, inscriptions, and mosaics, fell to rubble under the pickaxes of the wrecking crews; the only elements preserved were the mutilated apse mosaic of the Triclinium of Leo III and the Chapel of San Lorenzo (the *Sancta Sanctorum*, now incorporated into 7.3   the Church of SS. SALVATORE DELLA SCALA SANTA). The wantonness of the destruction is underscored by the superfluity of Domenico Fontana's Palazzo Lateranense, employed variously as an orphanage, a spillover for the Vatican collections, and an ethnological museum.

The impetus for this orgy of destruction was furnished by the pontiff's desire to erect an obelisk in Piazza San Giovanni so that it should rise at the ideal point of conjunction of his Strada Felice and Stradone di San 7.1   Giovanni. Cut in the fifteenth century BC, the OBELISCO LATERAN-ENSE is thirty-two meters in height and weighs some 522 tons. It is the world's largest obelisk and the oldest at Rome. The monolith had been removed from Thebes by Constantine for his circus at Constantinople; at the emperor's death it still lay on the quay at Alexandria. Constantius II,

Constantine's son, had the obelisk transported to Rome and set up on the *spina* ('central partition') of the Circus Maximus in AD 357. In erecting it, Constantius concluded with a flourish the emperors' three-and-a-half-century habit of decorating their city with the purloined monuments of the pharaohs. It stood for less than two hundred years; like the Obelisco Flaminio and the Obelisco Campense, the Lateranense appears to have been deliberately toppled during the Ostrogothic occupation of 547.

The obelisk of Constantius II was deemed suitable for the Lateran both because it was the city's largest and because of its association with Constantine. It was the first of the Sistine obelisks conceived as the focal point of a long street; the effect commended itself and was reprised in the siting of both the Obelisco Flaminio and the Obelisco Esquilino. The text of Constantius' original dedication survives; like the dedication of the arch of Constantine, it makes no overt mention of religion. It was copied at the time of the excavation by Michele Mercati, author of *Degli Obelischi di Roma* ('On the Obelisks of Rome'). The granite base had evidently been shattered when the obelisk was pulled down; after the dedication was transcribed, the fragments were broken up and used to repair the obelisk. The inscription of Sixtus V that replaced it was dictated by Cardinal Silvio Antoniano and executed by Matteo Castello da Melide to designs of the writing master Luca Orfei.

Though the Lateran basilica itself escaped the fate of the Patriarchium, its history is a litany of travails; it has been rebuilt so frequently that nothing of the original structure remains visible. Constantine's building was of generous size; though it followed the plan of Trajan's five-aisled Basilica Ulpia rather than that of the vaulted Basilica of Maxentius in the Forum, it was fully as large as the latter. Decorated with precious materials and lined with thirty columns of yellow Numidian marble, it was known as the *Basilica Aurea* ('Golden Basilica'). Having survived the sack of Alaric in 410 and of Genseric in 455, the basilica was badly damaged by earthquake in 896 and largely reconstructed under Pope

Sergius III. After fires in 1308 and 1361, the basilica and the Patriarchium were both in a ruinous state. Petrarch laments the Lateran's condition in a letter: *Lateranum humi iacet, et ecclesiarum mater omnium, tecto carens, et ventis patet ac pluviis* ('the Lateran lies prostrate and the Mother of all Churches, roofless, lies exposed to the wind and rain').

Following a second reconstruction carried out in the late fourteenth century under Popes Urban V and Urban VI, the basilica was damaged in 1413 during the sack of Ladislaus of Naples. With the return of the papacy in the person of Martin V, the Lateran was restored and decorated with frescoes by Gentile da Fabriano and Antonio Pisanello. At the end of the sixteenth century, the transept was renovated by Giacomo della Porta under the supervision of Cesare Baronio, who ensured that its medieval marble furniture was saved and installed in the Church of San

7.4D Cesareo. Borromini undertook a third major reconstruction for INNO-CENT X (r. 1644–1655) in advance of the Jubilee of 1650. Charged with rebuilding the basilica, the architect's brief was 'to maintain it insofar as possible in its ancient shape and to beautify it' ('*per mantenerla quanto sarà possible nella sua primitiva forma e abbellirla*'). As a result, considerable remains of the Constantinian and medieval basilicas survive entombed beneath their seventeenth-century mantle of stucco and marble.

7.4F Works undertaken in the eighteenth century by CLEMENT XI (r. 1700–
7.4E 1721) and BENEDICT XIII (r. 1724–1730) are likewise recorded.

The last appreciable relic of the old basilica was eliminated in 1884,
7.4K when Pope LEO XIII (r. 1878–1903) had the apse demolished and reconstructed so as to enlarge the presbytery. Jacopo Torriti's great mosaic,
7.4J executed at the end of the thirteenth century under Pope NICHOLAS IV (r. 1288–1292), was broken up and reassembled; the work that we see today must consequently be considered a copy rather than an original work of art. Numerous monuments of ages past have nonetheless been preserved in the Lateran basilica. Signal among them is the epitaph of
7.4I Pope SILVESTER II (r. 999–1003), rumored to have been an adept of necromancy. When a pope was nearing death, the bones of Silvester

were said to rattle. This legend arose from a misunderstanding of his epitaph, which refers to the coming of Christ at the last trumpet. According to the popular understanding, the words VENTVRO DOMINO ('coming Lord') indicated the succeeding pontiff; the phrase AD SONITVM ('at the sound') was held to signify an ominous clatter issuing from within the sarcophagus.

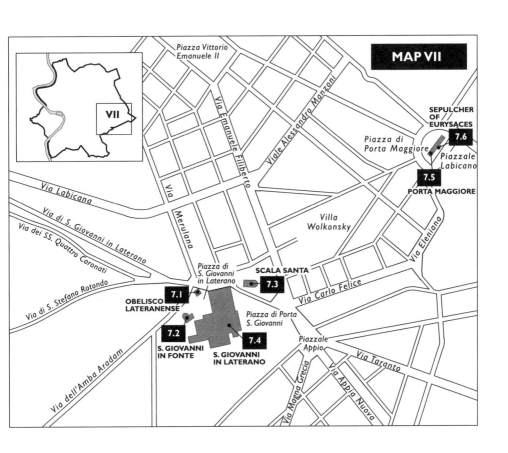

7.1 Obelisco Lateranense: Dedication by Sixtus V

i.

FL CONSTANTINVS

MAXIMVS AVG

CHRISTIANAE FIDEI

VINDEX ET ASSERTOR

5   OBELISCVM

AB AEGYPTIO REGE

IMPVRO VOTO

SOLI DEDICATVM

SEDIB AVVLSVM SVIS

10   PER NILVM TRANSFERRI

ALEXANDRIAM IVSSIT

VT NOVAM ROMAM

AB SE TVNC CONDITAM

EO DECORARET

15   MONVMENTO

1. FL(āvius) CONSTANTINVS | MAXIMVS AVG(ustus).

3. CHRISTIANAE : *See 1.7A, line 8.*

9. SEDIB(us). *When the obelisk was recovered in the sixteenth century, the text of Constantius' dedication in twenty-four hexameter verses was transcribed from the fragments of the original base, now lost. The central lines read:* [at dominus mundi constantius omnia fretus | cedere uirtuti terris incedere iussit | haut partem exiguam montis pontoque tumenti || credidit et placido uexerunt aequora fluctu | litus ad hesperium tiberi mirante carinam ... nunc ueluti rursus rufis auulsa metallis | emicuit pulsatque polos haec gloria dudum] (*'But Constantius, Lord of the world, confident that all things yield to valor, bade this not inconsiderable portion of a mountain to march over the earth, and committed it to the swelling main; and as the Tiber marveled at the vessel, the seas bore it on gentle billow to the shore of Hesperia ... Now, as though wrenched anew from the ruddy quarry, this glory has leapt up and long smitten the heavens'*).

Piazza di S. Giovanni in Laterano: Base of Obelisk

West

> *Flavius Constantinus*
> *Maximus Augustus,*[a]
> *champion and protector*
> *of the Christian faith,*[b]
> *bade this obelisk,*
> *dedicated to the sun*
> *in unclean offering*
> *by the king of Egypt,*[c]
> *to be wrenched from its foundations*
> *and transported down the Nile*
> *to Alexandria,*
> *that with such a monument*
> *he might adorn*
> *the new Rome*[d]
> *founded by him at that time.*

a. *Constantine I (r. 306–337) assumed the title* Maximus Augustus *on 29 October 312 (see 2.11A.i, note a). The text was dictated by Cardinal Silvio Antoniano (1540–1603), who supervised the drafting of epigraphical texts for the monuments of Pope Sixtus V.*

b. *Following the lead of his predecessor and rival Maxentius, Constantine guaranteed universal freedom of worship in the W. By the terms of an agreement reached at Milan, Constantine's colleague Licinius extended the same concessions in AD 313 to the provinces of the E in a circular letter misleadingly called the 'Edict of Milan'.*

c. *The obelisk was taken to Karnak by Thutmosis III early in the fifteenth century BC and was set up before the Temple of Amun some decades later by Thutmosis IV. Constantine, who intended the monument for Constantinople, had it removed to Alexandria; there it lay on the quay until Constantius II took it to Rome (see 7.1.ii, note b).*

d. *On 11 May 330 Constantine inaugurated Constantinople as his new capital. The 'Latin' parenthesis of 1204–1261 apart, that city remained the capital of E Christendom until 29 May 1453, when it was captured by the forces of the Ottoman sultan Mehmet II.*

ii.

FL CONSTANTIVS AVG

CONSTANTINI AVG F

OBELISCVM A PATRE

LOCO SVO MOTVM

5   DIVQ ALEXANDRIAE

IACENTEM

TRECENTORVM REMIGVM

IMPOSITVM NAVI

MIRANDAE VASTITATIS

10   PER MARE TIBERIMQ

MAGNIS MOLIBVS

ROMAM CONVECTVM

IN CIRCO MAX

PONENDVM

15   S P Q R D D

EQVES DOMENCVS FONTANA

ARCHITECT EREXIT

1. FL(āvius). — AVG(ustus).
2. AVG(ustī) F(īlius).
5. DIVQ(ue). — ALEXANDRIAE : *Locative.*
6. IACENTEM : *The* CL *verb* iacēre *often connotes idleness or neglect.*
7. TRECENTORVM REMIGVM : *Gen. of Description. The noun is* rēmex, rēmigis.
10. TIBERIMQ(ue) : *The proper noun* Tiberis *is an* I-stem (Tiberis, -is, -ī, -im, -ī).
13. MAX(imō).
15. S(enātuī) P(opulō) Q(ue) R(ōmānō) D(ōnum) D(edit).
16. DOMEN(i)CVS.
17. ARCHITECT(us).

East

Flavius Constantius Augustus,[a]
son of Flavius Constantine,
gave to the Senate and People of Rome
as a gift to be placed
in the Circus Maximus
the obelisk moved from its site
by his father
and long neglected
at Alexandria,
set aboard
a 300-oared ship
of astonishing size,
by mighty labors
conveyed across the sea
and up the Tiber to Rome.[b]

Cavaliere Domenico Fontana,[c]
Architect, erected this.

a. *Constantius II (r. 337–361).*

b. *The obelisk was transported to Rome and erected in the Circus Maximus on the occasion of an imperial visit in 357. The oldest and loftiest of its kind at Rome, the Obelisco Lateranense was the third such monument relocated for Sixtus V by Domenico Fontana. The others were the Vaticano (15.3), the Esquilino (4.1), and the Flaminio (10.4).*

c. *A native of Canton Ticino, Domenico Fontana (1543–1607) began his career as architect to Cardinal Felice Peretti, known from the place of his education as 'Cardinal Montalto'. Fontana laid out Peretti's opulent villa on the Esquiline; it was erased after 1870 to accommodate a new residential quarter (cf. 4.1.i, note d). After Peretti was elected pope in 1585 as Sixtus V, he engaged Fontana to relocate obelisks.*

iii.

CONSTANTINVS
PER CRVCEM
VICTOR
A S SILVESTRO HIC
5   BAPTIZATVS
CRVCIS GLORIAM
PROPAGAVIT

4. s(ānctō).
5. BAPTIZATVS : *See 6.6, line 3.*

iv.

SIXTVS V PONT MAX
OBELISCVM HVNC
SPECIE EXIMIA
TEMPORVM CALAMITATE
5   FRACTVM CIRCI MAX
RVINIS HVMO LIMOQ
ALTE DEMERSVM MVLTA
IMPENSA EXTRAXIT
HVNC IN LOCVM MAGNO
10   LABORE TRANSTVLIT
FORMAEQ PRISTINAE
ACCVRATE RESTITVTVM
CRVCI INVICTISSIMAE
DICAVIT
15   A M D LXXXVIII PONT IIII

1. SIXTVS V : Quīntus. — PONT(ifex) MAX(imus).
2. OBELISCVM HVNC : *The postpositioning of* HVNC *lends flair.*
5. MAX(imī).
6. LIMOQ(ue).
11. FORMAEQ(ue).
15. A(nnō) M D LXXXVIII : Mīllēsimō quīngentēsimō octōgēsimō octāvō.
— PONT(ificātūs) IIII : Quārtō.

South

Constantine,

through the Cross

victorious,

baptized in this place

by Saint Silvester,[a]

furthered

the Cross's glory.

a. Pious legend notwithstanding, Constantine was baptized on his deathbed at Nicomedia (mod. Izmit) by Eusebius, the local bishop.

North

Sixtus the Fifth,[a] Supreme Pontiff,

at great expense

withdrew from the ruins

of the Circus Maximus

this obelisk

of exceptional beauty,

shattered in the calamity of the ages,[b]

sunk deep in earth and mire,

by a mighty labor

transported it to this place and,

once it had been carefully restored

to its former beauty,

dedicated it

to the Cross most invincible

in the year 1588, fourth of his office.

a. Pope Sixtus V Peretti (r. 1585–1590). The fourth year of his pontificate ran from 24 April 1588 through 23 April 1589.

b. Like the Flaminio (10.4) and the Campense (10.11), the Obelisco Lateranense bears the scars of its deliberate overthrow by the application of fire and iron. The author of the obelisks' ruin was most probaby Totila, king of the Ostrogoths, whose army occupied Rome in the winter and spring of AD 546–547.

7.2 S. Giovanni in Fonte: Dedication by Sixtus III

1 GENS SACRANDA POLIS HIC SEMINE NASCITVR ALMO ⌐
   QVAM FECVNDATIS SPIRITVS EDIT AQVIS
2 MERGERE PECCATOR SACRO PVRGANDE FLVENTO ⌐
   QVEM VETEREM ACCIPIET PROFERET VNDA NOVVM

3 NVLLA RENASCENTVM EST DISTANTIA QVOS FACIT VNVM ⌐
   VNVS FONS VNVS SPIRITVS VNA FIDES
4 VIRGINEO FETV GENETRIX ECCLESIA NATOS ⌐
   QVOS SPIRANTE DEO CONCIPIT AMNE PARIT

5 INSONS ESSE VOLENS ISTO MVNDARE LAVACRO ⌐
   SEV PATRIO PREMERIS CRIMINE SEV PROPRIO
6 FONS HIC EST VITAE QVI TOTVM DILVIT ORBEM ⌐
   SVMENS DE CHRISTI VVLNERE PRINCIPIVM

7 CAELORVM REGNVM SPERATE HOC FONTE RENATI ⌐
   NON RECIPIT FELIX VITA SEMEL GENITOS
8 NEC NVMERVS QVEMQVAM SCELERVM NEC FORMA SVORVM ⌐
   TERREAT HOC NATVS FLVMINE SANCTVS ERIT

Eight ELEGIAC COUPLETS

1. POLIS : *See 2.14, line 6.*
2. MERGERE : *The form is Pres.Sg.Imp.Pass (see 1.6D, line 6).*
4. ECCLESIA : *See 1.7A, line 6.*
5. MVNDARE : *The LL* mundāre *is 'blot out', 'purify'. On the form, see*
   MERGERE *above, line 2.* — LAVACRO : *The CL* lavācrum *is 'bath'.*
6. CHRISTI : *See 1.6A.ii, line 6.*

7.3 SS. Salvatore della Scala Santa: Dedication by Sixtus V

SIXTVS V FECIT SANCTIORQ LOCO SCALAM SANCTAM ⌐
POSVIT A MDLXXXIX P IV

SIXTVS V : Quīntus. — SANCTIORQ(ue). — A(nnō) MDLXXXIX :
Mīllēsimō quīngentēsimō octōgēsimō nōnō. — P(ontificātūs) IV :
Quārtō.

Octagonal Architrave, Inner Frieze

N   *Here from a fostering seed is born to be consecrated to Heaven*
     a people which the Spirit brings forth from the fructified waters.
     Immerse yourself, O sinner who require to be cleansed in the
     sacred stream: whom the flood receives old it shall bring forth new.

E   *There is no distinction among those reborn,*
     whom one fount, one Spirit, one faith make one.
     By a virgin birth, Mother Church brings forth in the river
     the children whom she conceives by the breath of God.

S   *If you wish to be guiltless, be cleansed in this bath,*
     whether you are burdened by hereditary guilt or your own.
     This is the fount of life that bathes the whole world,
     taking its source from the wound of Christ.

W   *Reborn in this fount, set your hopes on the kingdom of Heaven:*
     the life of the blessèd will not receive those born but once.
     Let no one be dismayed whether by the number or the nature
     of his transgressions: born in this water, he shall be made holy.[a]

        Eight Elegiac Couplets

   a. *The disposition of the architectural orders in the present building, adapted*
      from the arrangement of spolia *in the Constantinian basilica of St. Peter,*
      is deliberate. The axis of the entry is built in Ionic, the E side in Corinthian,
      and the W in Composite (cf. 4.2H, note d). This arrangement—as well as
      the order of the verses—implies that the catechumen entered from the S,
      faced N, then turned to face E, S, and W in the course of the rite.

Façade: Frieze

Sixtus the Fifth built this and placed the Holy Steps in a holier place
in the year 1589, fourth of his office.

   a. *Pope Sixtus V Peretti (r. 1585–1590). The fourth year of his pontificate ran*
      from 24 April 1588 through 23 April 1589. The steps, which had formed part
      of the demolished Lateran palace, were supposed to have come from the
      house of Pontius Pilate and to have been trodden there by Christ himself.

7.4A S. Giovanni in Laterano: Title

SACROS LATERAN ECCLES

OMNIVM VRBIS ET ORBIS

ECCLESIARVM MATER

ET CAPVT

1. SACROS(āncta) LATERAN(ēnsis) : *The Adj.* Laterānēnsis *answers to the name* Laterānus, *cognōmen of the property's owner in the early third century.* — ECCLES(ia) : *See 1.7A, line 6.*

7.4B S. Giovanni in Laterano: Dedication of Medieval Basilica

[dogmate papali datur ac simul imperiali ¬

quod sim cunctarum mater caput ecclesiar ¬

hinc saluatoris cœlestia regna datoris ¬

nomina sancxerunt cum cuncta peracta fuerunt ¬

sic nos ex toto conuersi supplice uoto ¬

nostra quod hec ædes tibi x͞p͞e sit inclita sedes]

Six Leonine HEXAMETERS

dogmate : *The Latin* dogma *transliterates Greek* δόγμα *('decree', 'resolution,' then* EG *'dogma'). The inscription on the façade (built 1733–1735 by Alessandro Galilei) reproduces the text of that which appeared on the portico added c. 1170 to the E front of the church by Nicolò di Angelo. The surviving fragments of the twelfth-century inscription are mounted on the S wall of the cloister.* — papali : *The* EL *Adj.* papālis *answers to* papa *(see 3.6A, line 2). Here it scans* pāpali. — imperiali : *The* CL imperiālis *is Adj. to* imperium *('empire'), and thus 'of the emperor', 'imperial'.* — quod sim : *The* CL *construction would feature a Substantive Clause of Result introduced by* ut *(cf. 1.8F, line 2).* — ecclesiar(um) : *See 1.7A, line 6.* — saluatoris : *The* EL salvātor *represents Greek* σωτήρ *('savior').* — cœlestia = caelestia : *On the spelling, see 1.8B, line 5.* — sancxerunt = sānxērunt : *In the* ML *of Italy, the pronunciation of* x *was indistinguishable from that of doubled* s *(cf. Latin* dīxī > *Ital.* dissi). *The* c *here serves to enforce the complete pronunciation of the cluster* /ks/. — ædes : *See 1.8B, line 10.* — quod . . . sit : *See* quod sim *above.* — hec = haec. — x͞p͞e = Christe : *See 1.6A.ii, line 6; on the abbreviation, see 3.4D, line 8.* — inclita = incluta: *On the spelling, see 8.8A, line 10.*

Both Sides of Central Portal

The sacrosanct Lateran Church,
Mother and Head
of all churches
of the City and the World.[a]

a. *As seat of the* Bishop *of Rome,* Patriarch *of the West, the* Basilica *of
St. John Lateran enjoys a dignity superior to that of all other churches in
Roman Catholic Christendom.*

Frieze over Portico

It is granted by decree of pope and emperor alike
that I should be Mother and Head of all churches;[a]
from here they solemnly ordained it in the name of the Savior,
bestower of the heavenly kingdom, when all had been completed.
So we pray, imploring with our whole and humble prayer,
that this our church may be your renowned seat, O Christ.

Six Leonine Hexameters

a. *The present text was inscribed on the portico of the medieval* Basilica;
*fragments of the original inscription are displayed in the epigraphical col-
lection of the cloister. The text refers to the basilica's founding by Constantine I. The emperor's support of the Christian church was influenced by his
eagerness to find a basis of ideological unity for the whole of the Empire. In
keeping with this aim, Constantine sponsored the construction of monumental churches throughout the Roman world, of which the Lateran basilica was the first. As an architectural form, the basilica furnished an ideal
pattern for the emperor's Christian assembly halls: it could accommodate
large crowds; the clerestory above the nave admitted ample light; and the
timber roof, though less grand than stone vaulting, could be adapted to a
wide spectrum of scales and budgets. The chief modification of the traditional design consisted in the addition of an apse to establish a liturgical
focus. The adaptation of the basilical form as a house of worship represents
a momentous novelty: with the exception of the Pantheon (never a temple
in the technical or the ordinary sense), the Lateran basilica is the first
building in which the formal language of imperial Roman architecture was
employed to articulate monumental interior space in a sacred structure.*

7.4C S. Giovanni in Laterano: Dedication by Clement XII

CLEMENS XII PONT MAX ANNO V CHRISTO SALVATORI ⌐
IN HON SS IOAN BAPT ET EVANG

CLEMENS XII : Duodecimus. — PONT(ifex) MAX(imus). —
ANNO V : Quīntō. — CHRISTO : *See 1.6A.ii, line 6.* — SALVATORI : *See*
7.4B. — HON(ōrem). — SS = sānctōrum : *See 1.61, line 7.* — IOAN(nis)
BAPT(tistae) : *The* EL baptista *transliterates* EG βαπτιστής *('baptist').*
— EVANG(elistae) : *The* EL evangelista *transliterates* EG εὐαγγελιστής
('evangelist'). Though ordinarily reserved for the authors of the Gospels,
the word is used in a more general sense in the Vulgate, Is. 41:27.

7.4D S. Giovanni in Laterano: Dedication by Innocent X

INNOCENTIVS X

PONT MAX

LATERANENSEM BASILICAM

CONSTANTINI MAGNI IMPERATORIS

5   RELIGIONE AC MVNIFICENTIA EXTRVCTAM

SVMMORVMQVE PONTIFICVM PIETATE

SAEPIVS INSTAVRATAM

VETVSTATE IAM FATISCENTEM

NOVA MOLITIONE AD VETEREM

10   EX PARTE ADHVC STANTEM CONFORMATA

ORNATV SPLENDIDIORE RESTITVIT

ANNO IVBILAEI MDCL PONT VI

1. INNOCENTIVS X : Decimus.
2. PONT(ifex) MAX(imus).
3. LATERANENSEM : *See 7.4A, line 1.*
5. EXTRVCTAM = exstrūctam : *On the spelling, see 4.2A, line 7.*
12. IVBILAEI : *See. 2.12A, line 8.* — MDCL : Mīllēsimō sescentēsimō
quīnquāgēsimō. — PONT(ificātūs) VI : Sextō.

Frieze

*Clement the Twelfth,[a] Supreme Pontiff, in his fifth year, to Christ
the Savior in honor of Saints John the Baptist and Evangelist.[b]*

> a. *Pope Clement XII Corsini (r. 1730–1740). Clement engaged Alessandro
> Galilei to design the façade. The fifth year of his pontificate ran from 12 July
> 1734 through 11 July 1735.*
> b. *Constantine's church was dedicated to the Savior. As the neighboring bap-
> tistery was dedicated to SS. John the Baptist and John the Evangelist, from
> the time of Pope St. Gregory I (r. 590–604) the dedication of the* BASILICA
> *itself had a tendency to oscillate between the Savior and the two Johns.*

Entry Wall, Center

Innocent the Tenth,[a]
Supreme Pontiff,
by new construction harmonious with the old
that in part still stood,
restored with finer embellishment
the Lateran Basilica,
built through the piety and largesse
of the emperor Constantine the Great
and oft renewed
through the devotion of the Supreme Pontiffs,
and by now deteriorating with age,[b]
in the year of the Jubilee 1650,[c] sixth of his office.

> a. *Pope Innocent X Pamphilj (r. 1644–1655). The sixth year of his pontificate
> ran from 15 September 1649 through 14 September 1650.*
> b. *The remodeling of the interior was undertaken 1646–1649 by Borromini,
> who was instructed to alter the existing structure as little as possible.*
> c. *See 7.4H, note b.*

7.4E S. Giovanni in Laterano: Dedication by Benedict XIII

PRINCIPEM HANC ECCLESIAM

INCENDIIS VASTATIONIBUS

TERRÆ INSUPER MOTIBUS

DISIECTAM EVERSAMQUE

5   AC SÆPIUS A SUMMIS PONT REPARATAM

POSTMODUM AB INNOCENTIO X

NOVA MOLITIONE RESTITUTAM

BENEDICTUS XIII P M ORD PRÆD

SOLENNI RITU CONSECRAVIT

10   DIE XXVIII APRILIS MDCCXXVI

EIUSQUE CELEBRITATIS MEMORIAM

QUOTANNIS RECOLENDAM DECREVIT

IX DIE NOVEMB QUA PRIMVM A B SILVESTRO

BASILICA DEO ADDICTA EST AC DICATA

1. ECCLESIAM : *See 1.7A, line 6.*

5. PONT(ificibus).

6. INNOCENTIO X : Decimō.

8. BENEDICTUS XIII : Tertius decimus. — P(ontifex) M(aximus).
— ORD(inis) PRÆD(icātōrum) : *In* EL, ōrdō *is 'religious order' and* praedicātor *'preacher'. The* CL praedicāre *('proclaim') is the source both of Eng.* 'preach' *(through the ancestor of modern Fr.* prêcher) *and of Ger.* predigen.

9. SOLENNI = sollemnī.

10. XXVIII : Vīcēsimō octāvō. — APRILIS : *See 1.6G, line 11.* —
MDCCXXVI : Mīllēsimō septingentēsimō vīcēsimō sextō.

13. IX : Nōnō. — NOVEMB(ris) : *See* APRILIS *above (line 10).* — PRIMVM :
Sic (all other instances of vocalic V *in the present inscription appear as* U).
— B(eātō).

Entry Wall, L

Benedict the Thirteenth,[a] Supreme Pontiff,
of the Order of Preachers,[b]
in a solemn ceremony consecrated this foremost church—
shattered and thrown down
by fires, depredations,
and earthquakes besides,[c]
and oft repaired by the Supreme Pontiffs,
presently restored with new construction
by Innocent the Tenth [d]—
and decreed that the memory of that celebration
should be observed anew each year
on the ninth day of November, on which the Basilica
was first dedicated and consecrated to God by the blessèd Silvester,[e]
on the twenty-eighth day of April, 1726.

a. *Pope Benedict XIII Orsini (r. 1724–1730).*
b. *'Order of Preachers' is the proper name of the Dominican Order.*
c. *The Lateran would appear to have been singularly prone to disasters both natural and of human provocation. The tale of her woes includes the sack of Alaric and his Visigoths in 410 (cf. 2.2, note d), the sack of Genseric and his Vandals in 455, an earthquake in 896, damage by lightning in 1115, fire in 1308, earthquake in 1349, fire in 1361, the sack of Ladislaus of Naples in 1413, and lightning again in 1493. Its elevated situation, on the other hand, exempted the Lateran from the floods that repeatedly devastated the lower city (cf. 10.1D, note c).*
d. *Pope Innocent X Pamphilj (r. 1644–1655); cf. 7.4D.*
e. *Pope St. Silvester I (r. 314–335). According to traditional but unreliable inferences from ancient sources, the original* BASILICA *had been dedicated on 9 November 318.*

7.4F   Commemoration of Clement XI

CLEMENTI XI PONT MAX
QVOD BASILICAM
OMNIVM MATREM ET CAPVT ECCLESIARVM
DVPLICI APOSTOLORVM ET PROPHETARVM CORONA
5   EXORNANDO
RELIGIONI ET MAIESTATI PROSPEXERIT
BENEDICTVS S R E CARD PAMPHILIVS
ARCHIPRESBYTER ET CANONICI
MONVMENTVM POSVERE
10   ANNO DOMINI MDCCXXIX

1. CLEMENTI XI : Ūndecimō. — PONT(ificī) MAX(imō).
2–6. QVOD . . . PROSPEXERIT : On the construction, see 1.6B, lines 5–7. —
   BASILICAM . . . EXORNANDO : Here the Acc. Dir.Ob. is retained (see
   1.6H, lines 11–12).
3. ECCLESIARVM : See 1.7A, line 6.
4. APOSTOLORVM : See 1.6I, line 7. — PROPHETARVM : The EL prophēta
   transliterates Greek προφήτης ('seer', then EG 'prophet').
7. S(ānctae) R(ōmānae) E(cclēsiae) CARD(inālis).
8. ARCHIPRESBYTER : See 4.2M, line 4. — CANONICI : See 4.2G, line 7.
9. POSVERE = posuērunt.
10. MDCCXXIX : Mīllēsimō septingentēsimō vīcēsimō nōnō.

7.4G   Epitaph of Martin V

MARTINVS P̄P̄ V SEDIT ANNOS XIII
MENS̄ III DIES XII OBIIT AN
M CCCC XXXI DIES XX FEBRVARII
TEMPORVM SVORVM FILICITAS

1. P(a)P(a) : See 3.6A, line 2. — V : Quīntus. — XIII : Tredecim.
2. MENS(ēs) III : Trēs. — DIES XII : Duodecim. — AN(nō).
3. M CCCC XXXI : Mīllēsimō quadringentēsimō trīcēsimō prīmō. —
   DIES : Sic (= diē). — XX : Vīcēsimō. — FEBRVARII : See 1.6G, line 11.
4. FILICITAS : Sic (= fēlīcitās).

S. Giovanni in Laterano: Entry Wall, R

Benedetto Pamphilj,[a] Cardinal of the Holy Roman Church,
Archpriest, and the canons[b]
set up this monument
to Clement the Eleventh,[c] Supreme Pontiff,
because by embellishing
this Basilica,
Mother and Head of all churches,
with a double file of Apostles and Prophets[d]
he took care for its sanctity and grandeur
in the year of the Lord 1729.

a. *A grandnephew of Pope Innocent X, Benedetto Pamphilj (1653–1730)*
was named ARCHPRIEST *of the Lateran basilica in 1699. A patron of the*
arts and a man of letters in his own right, Pamphilj penned librettos for
the cantatas of (among others) George Frideric Handel and Alessandro
Scarlatti, whose compositions were performed at Palazzo Pamphilj under
the direction of the violinist and composer Arcangelo Corelli (see 11.3D).
Corelli's own Concerti Grossi, Opus 6, were premiered at Palazzo
Pamphilj.

b. *See 4.2G, note a.*

c. *Pope Clement XI Albani (r. 1700–1721).*

d. *The statues lining the nave were executed 1703–1719 by various hands.*

In Confessio before High Altar

Pope Martin the Fifth[a] reigned thirteen years,
three months, twelve days.
He died in the year 1431, on 20 February.
Happiness in his times.

a. *Pope Martin V Colonna (r. 1417–1431). Elected under the auspices of the*
Council of Constance, Martin was the first pope to make Rome his perma-
nent residence following the BABYLONIAN CAPTIVITY *of the papacy, at*
the conclusion of which there were three claimants for the throne of
St. Peter (cf. 2.13C, note b). On his arrival in 1420, Martin took in hand
the repair of the city's dilapidated infrastructure (see 11.5A, note b).

7.4H S. Giovanni in Laterano: Fragment of Giotto's Fresco

IMAGO ICONICA BONIFACI $\overline{\text{VIII}}$ PONT MAX

IOBELAEVM PRIMVM IN ANNVM $\overline{\text{M}}$ $\overline{\text{CCC}}$ INDICENTIS

PICTVRA GIOTTI AEQVALIS EORVM TEMPORVM

QVAM E VETERI PODIO IN CLAVSTRA INDE IN TEMPLVM TRANSLATAM

GENS CAIETANA NE AVITVM MONVMENTVM VETVSTATE DELERETVR

6   ANNO $\overline{\text{M}}$ $\overline{\text{DCC}}$ $\overline{\text{LXXXVI}}$ CRYSTALLO OBTEGENDAM CVRAVIT

1. ICONICA : *The* CL *īconicus transliterates Greek* εἰκονικός *('giving an exact likeness', used of a work of art).* — BONIFACI = Bonifátiī : *On the spelling, see 3.4B, line 3.* — $\overline{\text{VIII}}$: Octāvī. — PONT(ificis) MAX(imī).

2. IOBELAEVM = iūbilaeum : *See 2.12A, line 8. Whether by accident or by design, the present transliteration reflects the Greek* ἰωβηλαῖος *more accurately than the usual* iūbilaeum. — $\overline{\text{M}}$ $\overline{\text{CCC}}$: Mīllēsimum trecentēsimum.

3. GIOTTI : *The Ital. name* Giotto *is Latinized as* Giottus (*cf. 12.3B, line 8*).

4. CLAVSTRA : *In* EL, claustrum *is 'cloister' or 'monastery'.*

5. CAIETANA : *The Adj.* Cāiētānus *answers to the name* Caetani.

6. ANNO $\overline{\text{M}}$ $\overline{\text{DCC}}$ $\overline{\text{LXXXVI}}$: Mīllēsimō septingentēsimō octōgēsimō sextō.

7.4I Epitaph of Silvester II

1   ISTE LOCVS MVNDI SILVESTRI MEMBRA SEPVLTI ⌐
     VENTVRO DOMINO CONFERET AD SONITVM

2   QVEM DEDERAT MVNDO CELEBRE DOCTISSIMA VIRGO ⌐
     ATQ CAPVT MVNDI CVLMINA ROMVLEA

3   PRIMVM GERBERTVS MERVIT FRANCIGENA SEDE ⌐
     REMENSIS POPVLI METROPOLIM PATRIAE

4   INDE RAVENNATIS MERVIT CONSCENDERE SVMMVM ⌐
     ÆCCLESIÆ REGIMEN NOBILE SITQ POTENS

5   POST ANNVM ROMAM MVTATO NOMINE SVMPSIT ⌐
     VT TOTO PASTOR FIERET ORBE NOVVS

6   CVI NIMIVM PLACVIT SOCIALI MENTE FIDELIS ⌐
     OBTVLIT HOC CESAR TERTIVS OTTO SIBI

7   TEMPVS VTERQ COMIT CLARA VIRTVTE SOPHIAE ⌐
     GAVDET ET OMNE SECLVM FRANGITVR OM$\overline{\text{E}}$ REV$\overline{\text{}}$

Inner Nave R, First Pier L

A faithful portrait of Boniface the Eighth,[a] Supreme Pontiff,
declaring the first Jubilee for the year 1300,[b]
a painting by Giotto,[c] his contemporary, which the family Caetani,
lest this ancestral monument should be effaced by age,
moved from its former mounting into the cloisters and thence into the church,
and undertook to have it covered with glass in the year 1786.

- a. *Pope Boniface VIII Caetani (r. 1294–1303). During his reign, the Caetani acquired enormous power and influence at the expense of their rivals, the Colonna. Having nevertheless failed to revive the imperial papacy of Innocent III a century before, Boniface died after a brief captivity at the hands of soldiers in the service of Philip IV the Fair of France.*
- b. *The original scheme called for the* JUBILEE, *or Holy Year, to recur every 100 years. The interval was reduced to fifty years, then to thirty-three, and is currently twenty-five years.*
- c. *The fragment pertains to a large fresco attributed to the Tuscan painter Giotto di Bondone (1266–1336); it adorned the old Loggia of Benediction, barbarously demolished under Pope Sixtus V.*

Inner Nave R, Second Pier Left

At the trumpet's sound, this neighborhood of the world
shall convey the limbs of the buried Silvester[a] to the Lord
at his coming—Silvester the renowned, whom the learned maiden[b]
and the heights of Romulus, capital of the world, on the world
bestowed. A son of France, he first merited the see
of the people of Reims, metropolis of his country,
then merited to rise to the supreme governance
of the church of Ravenna, and to wax powerful.[c]
After a year, with a change of name he took up Rome
that he might be the new pastor over all the world.
The emperor Otto the Third bestowed this dignity on him:
faithful partner of his counsels, he enjoyed his especial favor.[d]
Each adorns the times with the brilliant virtue of his wisdom:
the whole age rejoices; every crime is vanquished.

8   CLAVIGERI INSTAR ERAT CÆLORVM SEDE POTITVS ⌐
    TERNA SVFFECTVS CVI VICE PASTOR ERAT
9   ISTE VICEM PETRI POSTQVAM SVSCEPIT ABEGIT ⌐
    LVSTRALIS SPATIO SECVLA MORTE SVI
10 OBRIGVIT MVNDVS DISCVSSA PACE TRIVMPHVS ⌐
    ÆCCLESIÆ NVTANS DEDIDICIT REQVIEM
11 SERGIVS HVNC LOCVLVM MITI PIETATE SACERDOS ⌐
    SVCCESSORQ SVVS COMPSIT AMORE SVI
12 QVISQVIS AD HVNC TVMVLVM DEVEXA LVMINA VERTIS ⌐
    OMNIPOTENS DOMINE DIC MISERERE SVI
13 OBIIT ANNO DOMINICE INCARNATIONIS M̄ III ⌐
    INDĪC I M M̄ĀI D̄ XII

Twelve ELEGIAC COUPLETS *(lines 1–12)*

2. CELEBRE(m). — ATQ(ue).
3. FRANCIGENA : *The* ML Francīgena *is* '*Frenchman*'.
   — SEDE(m) : *See 3.4D, line 4.* — REMENSIS : *The* ML *toponym is*
   Rēmēnsis. — METROPOLIM : *The* EL mētropolis *transliterates Greek*
   μητρόπολις (*'mother city', then* EG *'archiepiscopal see'*).
4. RAVENNATIS : *The* ML *Adj.* ravennās, -ātis *answers to the toponym*
   Ravenna. — ÆCCLESIÆ = ecclēsiae : *The initial* Æ *represents a hyper-*
   correction (see 1.8B, line 5). — SITQ(ue).
6. CESAR = Caesar. — OTTO : *The Latin name is* Ottō, Ottōnis.
7. VTERQ(ue). — SECLVM = saeculum. — OM(n)E REV(m) : *Neut. Sub-*
   stantive.
8. CLAVIGERI : *In* ML, clāviger (*'key bearer'*) *is a common title of St. Peter.*
   — TERNA . . . VICE : *'In third turn', i.e., 'third in turn'.*
9. LVSTRALIS : *Here used as a substantive (Gen.Sg.).*
10. ÆCCLESIÆ = ecclēsiae. — REQVIEM = requiētem : *The abbreviated*
    form is not uncommon even in CL.
11. SVCCESSORQ(ue).
12. SVI = ēius : *The confusion is not infrequent in* ML (*cf. 4.7C, line 12*).
13. DOMINICE = dominicae : *See 3.3C, line 2.* — INCARNATIONIS : *See*
    4.7C, line 16. — M̄ III : Mīllēsimō tertiō. — INDIC(tiōne) : *See 2.1,*
    line 16. — I : Prīmā. — M(ēnse) MAI(ī) : *See 1.6G, line 11.* — D(iē)
    XII : Duodecimō.

The very image of the keeper of the keys, whom he succeeded
third in turn as pastor,[e] had gained his heavenly home.
After taking up the succession of Peter, within five years
he banished the things of the world in death.
Peace shattered, the world froze with horror;
the wavering triumph of the church forgot repose.[f]
Out of love for him, Sergius,[g] priest and his successor,
in kind devotion adorned this grave.
Whoever you are who lower your gaze to this tomb,
pray, 'O Lord almighty, have mercy on him!'
He died in the year of the Lord's incarnation 1003, in the
first indiction,[h] on the twelfth day of the month of May.

Twelve ELEGIAC COUPLETS (lines 1–12)

a. *Pope Silvester II (r. 999–1003). Born Gerbert d'Aurillac, Silvester was the first French pope. A misunderstanding of the opening couplet of the epitaph gave rise to the legend that the impending death of a pope could be predicted by an ominous rattle issuing from Silvester's tomb.*

b. *I.e., the Benedictine abbey of Santa Maria de Ripoll in Catalonia, where Gerbert acquired wide learning in science, music, and mathematics.*

c. *Gerbert became Archbishop of Reims in 991 and of Ravenna in 998.*

d. *In 999 Gerbert was appointed pope by the emperor Otto III of the Saxon dynasty (r. 996–1002). On the eve of the millennium, the pair set out to establish a renewed Christian Roman Empire. The ideological cast of the program is seen in Gerbert's choice of the name 'Silvester', calculated to evoke the partnership of Pope St. Silvester I and the emperor Constantine I.*

e. *Viz., Gregory V (r. 996–999), appointed pope by his cousin, Otto III. Gregory was succeeded by 'John XVI' (r. 997–998), installed without imperial consent by Crescenzio II 'Nomentano', son of Crescenzio I 'de Theodora' (see 5.5). For his impertinence, John was deposed, defrocked, imprisoned, blinded, mutilated, and branded an antipope.*

f. *Silvester died in 1003. With Otto's death the year before, the grandiose 'Renewal' had come to nought. Its only durable achievement was the conversion of Hungary (see 6.2B, note c).*

g. *Pope Sergius IV (r. 1009–1012).*

h. *The* INDICTION *was a fifteen-year tax cycle (see 2.1, note e).*

7.4J S. Giovanni in Laterano: Dedication by Nicholas IV

POSTERIOREM ET ANTERIOREM RVINOSAS HVIVS SANCTI ¬

TEMPLI A FVNDAMENTIS R̄EEDIFICARI FECIT ET ORNARI OPE ¬

MOSYACO NICOLAVS P P IIII FILIVS BEATI FRANCISCI ET ¬

SACR̄V VVLT̄V SALVATORIS N̄TEḠV REPONI FECIT IN LOCO ¬

VBI PRIMO MIRACVLOSE POPVLO ROMANO APPARVIT QVĀDO ¬

FVIT ISTA ECCL'IA C̄OSECRATA ANNO D̄NI M CC NONAGES II

> REEDIFICARI = reaedificārī : *The* ML *reaedificāre is 'rebuild' (on the
> spelling, see 1.8B, line 5).* — MOSYACO = mosaicō : *The* LL *mosaicum is a
> variant of* mūsīvum *(see 3.3A, line 5). On the* Y, *see 3.1, line 1.* — P(a)P(a) :
> *See 3.6A, line 2.* — IIII : Quārtus. — SACRV(m) VVLTV(m). — SALVA-
> TORIS : *See 7.4B.* — (i)NTEG(r)V(m). — MIRACVLOSE : *The* LL *Adj.*
> mīrāculōsus *and its Adv. answer to* mīraculum *('wonder', 'marvel').* —
> QVA(n)DO. — FVIT . . . CO(n)SECRATA : *On the tense, see 1.6G, line 7.*
> — ECCL(ēs)IA : *See 1.7A, line 6.* — D(omi)NI. — M CC : Mīllēsimō
> ducentēsimō. — NONAGES(imō) II : Secundō.

7.4K S. Giovanni in Laterano: Dedication by Leo XIII

1 LEO XIII CELLAM MAXIMAM VETVSTATE FATISCENTEM ¬

INGENTI MOLITIONE PRODVCENDAM LAXANDAMQVE CVRAVIT

2 VETVS MVSIVVM MVLTIS IAM ANTEA PARTIBVS ¬

INSTAVRATVM AD ANTIQVVM EXEMPLAR RESTITVI

3 ET IN NOVAM ABSIDEM OPERE CVLTVQVE MAGNIFICO ¬

EXORNATAM TRANSFERRI AVLAM TRANSVERSAM

4 LAQVEARI ET CONTIGNATIONE REFECTIS EXPOLIRI IVSSIT ¬

ANNO CHR M̄D̄C̄C̄C̄L̄X̄X̄X̄ĪV̄ SACRI PRINC V̄ĪĪ

> 1. LEO XIII : Tertius decimus. — CELLAM : *In* CL, cella *is used of the
> niche in a temple where the cult image stands. Here, it designates the choir
> and apse of the basilica.*
> 4. LAQVEARI : *See 1.8B, line 11.* — CHR(istī) : *See 1.6A.ii, line 6.* —
> M̄D̄C̄C̄C̄L̄X̄X̄X̄ĪV̄ : Mīllēsimō octingentēsimō octōgēsimō quārtō. —
> PRINC(ipātūs) V̄ĪĪ : Septimō.

Choir, Foot of Apse Mosaic

Pope Nicholas the Fourth,[a] a son of the blessèd Francis, caused the
ruined rear and front of this holy church to be rebuilt from its foundations
and to be embellished with mosaic work, and caused the holy face
of the Savior to be replaced intact in the spot where it first appeared
miraculously to the people of Rome when this church was consecrated,
in the year of the Lord 1292.[b]

> a. *Pope Nicholas IV Masci (r. 1288–1292). Nicholas was the first pope pro-*
> *duced by the Franciscan order. He devoted enormous energy to the embel-*
> *lishment of Rome's churches, employing the services of such artists as Ar-*
> *nolfo di Cambio, Pietro Cavallini, and Giacomo Torriti; the last was the*
> *author of the present mosaic (or rather its original; see 7.4K). The transept*
> *was added during Nicholas' works at the Lateran.*
>
> b. *According to medieval legend, the face of Christ appeared on the occasion*
> *of the basilica's consecration by Pope St. Silvester I. Its representation in*
> *mosaic is the sole element of the preexisting apse decoration that was incor-*
> *porated into Torriti's work.*

Choir, Apse Wall

Leo the Thirteenth,[a] in a mighty undertaking,
caused the vast choir, which was deteriorating with age,
to be extended and widened, ordered the ancient mosaic,
already restored in many places in times past, to be reset
to the original pattern and transferred to the new apse,[b]
adorned with magnificent construction and ornament, and the
transept to be refined by the replacement of the coffering and ceiling,
in the year of Christ 1884, seventh of his sacred office.

> a. *Pope Leo XIII Pecci (r. 1878–1903). The seventh year of his pontificate ran*
> *from 20 February 1884 through 19 February 1885.*
>
> b. *As the apse was the only element of the Constantinian structure that had*
> *remained substantially intact, Leo's intervention amounted to a colossal*
> *act of organized vandalism.*

7.5A Porta Maggiore: Dedication by Claudius

TI CLAVDIVS DRVSI F CAISAR AVGVSTVS GERMANICVS PONTIF MAXIM
TRIBVNICIA POTESTATE $\overline{\text{XII}}$ COS $\overline{\text{V}}$ IMPERATOR $\overline{\text{XXVII}}$ PATER PATRIAE
AQVAM CLAVDIAM EX FONTIBVS QVI VOCABANTVR CAERVLEVS ET CVRTIVS A MILLIARIO XXXXV
ITEM ANIENEM NOVAM A MILLIARIO LXII SVA IMPENSA IN VRBEM PERDVCENDAS CVRAVIT

1. TI(berius). — F(ilius). — CAISAR = Caesar : *On the spelling, see 1.6B, line 1.* — PONTIF(ex) MAXIM(us).
2. $\overline{\text{XII}}$: Duodecimum. — CO(n)s(ul) $\overline{\text{V}}$: Quintum. — $\overline{\text{XXVII}}$: Vicēsimum septimum.
3. XXXXV : Quadrāgēsimō quintō. *On the absence of the supralinear bar, see 1.6B, line 3.*
4. LXII : Sexāgēsimō secundō. *It has been proposed that the original figure was LVIIII or LIX (quīnquāgēsimō nōnō) but was altered after Trajan tapped a new source for the Anio Novus several miles upland from the town of Sublaqueum (mod. Subiaco). The text of 7.5A–C is duplicated on the opposite side of the arch.*

7.5B Porta Maggiore: Dedication by Vespasian

1 IM[P C]AESAR VESPASIANVS AVGVST PONTIF MAX TRIB POT $\overline{\text{II}}$ ⌐
  IMP $\overline{\text{VI}}$ COS $\overline{\text{III}}$ DESIG $\overline{\text{IIII}}$ P P
2 AQVAS CVRTIAM ET CAERVLEAM PERDVCTAS A DIVO CLAVDIO ET ⌐
  POSTEA INTERMISSAS DILAPSASQVE PER ANNOS NOVEM SVA ⌐
  IMPENSA VRBI RESTITVIT

Piazza di Porta Maggiore: Attic of Arch, N & S Sides, Top Register

Tiberius Claudius Caesar Augustus Germanicus,[a] son of Drusus, Supreme Pontiff, vested with the Tribunician power for the twelfth time, Consul for the fifth, acclaimed Imperator for the twenty-seventh, Father of his Country, at his own expense undertook to have the Aqua Claudia[b] brought into the City from the forty-fifth milestone, and likewise the Anio Novus from the sixty-second milestone, from the sources called 'Caeruleus' and 'Curtius'.

a. Tiberius Claudius Nero Germanicus (r. 41–54) was proclaimed emperor by the Praetorian Guard on 25 January 41. He assumed the TRIBUNICIAN POWER for the twelfth time on that date in 52, became CONSUL for the fifth on 1 January 51 and was saluted as IMPERATOR for the twenty-seventh in 52. Like all the successors of Augustus, he was granted the office of SUPREME PONTIFF on his accession. The title 'Father of his Country' was accepted by Augustus in 2 BC and assumed by nearly all succeeding emperors (see PATER PATRIAE).

b. Greatest of the Roman aqueducts, the Aqua Claudia was begun by Gaius ('Caligula') in AD 38 and dedicated by Claudius on 1 August 52, the emperor's sixtieth birthday. Its terminal tract was demolished for the construction of Acqua Felice (see 4.5).

Central Register

Imperator Caesar Vespasian Augustus,[a] Supreme Pontiff, vested with the Tribunician power for the second time, acclaimed Imperator for the sixth, Consul for the third, Consul Designate for the fourth, Father of his Country, restored to the City at his own expense the Aqua Curtia and Aqua Caerulea, brought in by the Divine Claudius[b] and subsequently disrupted and fallen into disrepair for a period of nine years.[c]

1. IM[p(erātor) c]AESAR : *The characters enclosed in brackets are restored from context.* — AVGVST(us). — PONTIF(ex) MAX(imus). — TRIB(ūniciā) POT(estāte) $\overline{\text{II}}$: Iterum. *When ordinal adverbs signify 'for the Nth time' (rather than 'N times'), the verbal equivalents of* I, II, *and* III *are* prīmum, iterum, *and* tertium (*cf.* 11.3A). — IMP(erātor) $\overline{\text{VI}}$: Sextum. — CO(n)s(ul) $\overline{\text{III}}$: Tertium. — DESIG(nātus) $\overline{\text{IIII}}$: Quārtum. — P(ater) P(atriae).

2. DIVO : *See* 2.4, *line* 1.

7.5C   Porta Maggiore: Dedication by Titus

IMP T CAESAR DIVI F VESPASIANVS AVGVSTVS PONTIFEX MAXIMVS TRIBVNIC
POTESTATE $\overline{\text{X}}$ IMPERATOR $\overline{\text{XVII}}$ PATER PATRIAE CENSOR COS $\overline{\text{VIII}}$
AQVAS CVRTIAM ET CAERVLEAM PERDVCTAS A DIVO CLAVDIO ET POSTEA
A DIVO VESPASIANO PATRE SVO VRBI RESTITVTAS CVM A CAPITE AQVARVM ⌐
4 A SOLO VETVSTATE DILAPSAE ESSENT NOVA FORMA REDVCENDAS SVA IMPENSA CVRAVIT

1. IMP(erātor) T(itus). — F(īlius). — TRIBVNIC(iā).
2. $\overline{\text{X}}$: Decimum. — $\overline{\text{XVII}}$: Septimum decimum. — CO(n)s(ul) $\overline{\text{VIII}}$: Octāvum.
3. DIVO : *See* 2.4, *line* 1.
4. FORMA : *See* 4.6C, *line* 4.

a. Titus Flavius Vespasianus was proclaimed emperor by his troops on 1 July 69. He assumed the TRIBUNICIAN POWER for the second time on that date in 70, was saluted as IMPERATOR for the sixth time in 71, and became CONSUL for the third time—and Consul Designate for the fourth—in 71. On the office of SUPREME PONTIFF and the title 'Father of his Country', cf. 7.5A, note a.

b. See 7.5A, note b.

c. By this account, the Aqua Claudia failed ten years after its inauguration and remained out of service for nine.

Piazza di Porta Maggiore: Attic of Arch, N & S Sides, Lower Register

Imperator Titus Caesar Vespasian Augustus,[a] son of the Divine Vespasian,[b] Supreme Pontiff, vested with the Tribunician power for the tenth time, acclaimed Imperator for the seventeenth, Father of his Country, Censor, Consul for the eighth time, at his own expense undertook to have the Aqua Curtia and Aqua Caerulea, introduced by the Divine Claudius and afterwards restored to the City by the Divine Vespasian, his father, reintroduced in a new channel since from their sources they had fallen into disrepair from their foundations.

a. Titus Flavius Vespasianus (r. 79–81), conventionally styled 'Titus' to distinguish him from his homonymous father, assumed the TRIBUNICIAN POWER for the first time on 1 July 71; he assumed it for the tenth time in 80. He became CONSUL for the eighth time on 1 January of the same year, in which he was likewise saluted as IMPERATOR for the seventeenth time. Titus became CENSOR for the first time in April of 73. On the office of SUPREME PONTIFF and the title 'Father of his Country', see 7.5A, note a.

b. Titus Flavius Vespasianus père (r. 69–79); see 7.5B, note a.

7.5D Porta Maggiore: Dedication by S.P.Q.R.

1　　　　　　S P Q R

2　IMPP CAESS D̄D̄ N̄N̄ IN[uic]TISSIMIS PRINCIPIB ARCADIO ET HONORIO ⌐

　　VICTOR[ib ac tri]VMFATORIB s[emper au]ḠḠ

3　OB INSTAVRATOS VRBI AETERNAE MVROS PORTAS AC TVRRES EGESTIS ⌐

　　INMENSIS RVDERIB EX SVG[g]ESTIONE V̄ C̄

4　[e]T INLVSTRIS COM̄ ET MAḠ VTR[ius]Q MILITIAE STILICHONIS AD ⌐

　　PERPETVITATEM NOMIN[i]S EORV[m]

5　SIMVLACRA CONSTITVIT

6　CVRANTE FL MACROBIO LONGINIANO V̄ C̄ P[raef urb d n m q eorum]

1. s(enātus) P(opulus) Q(ue) R(ōmānus).

2. IMPP CAESS D̄D̄ N̄N̄ = imperātōribus Caesaribus dominis nostrīs : *On the abbreviations, see 1.61, line 7.*
— PRINCIPIB(us). — VICTOR[ib(us) ac tri]VMFATORIB(us) : *The lost portions of the text are restored from a duplicate inscription at Porta Tiburtina (4.6). On the spelling of* TRIVMFATORIBVS, *see 2.1, line 2.* — au]ḠḠ = Augustīs.

3. OB INSTAVRATOS . . . MVROS : *On the construction, see 1.7A, lines 2–3.* — v(irī) c(lārissimī).

4. COM(itis) : *See 2.2, line 9.* — MAG(istrī). — VTR[ius]Q(ue).

6. FL(āviō). — v(irō) c(lārissimō). — P[raef(ectō) urb(ī) : *On the construction, see 2.2, line 14.* — d(ēvōtus) n(ūminī) m(āiestātī) q(ue) eorum] : *The formula is common in dedications of the period.*

Piazzale Labicano: Outside Porta Maggiore, to S

The Senate and People of Rome,

under the supervision of his Excellency Flavius Macrobius Longinianus,[a] City Prefect,
in devotion to their authority and majesty, set up effigies to the Emperors Caesars our Lords
the two invincible princes Arcadius and Honorius,[b] victors and conquerors, ever Augusti,
for restoring the walls, gates, and towers of the Eternal City,[c] with the removal of a vast amount
of rubble, in accordance with the prompting of his Excellency Flavius Stilicho,[d] distinguished
Count and master of both services,[e] to the lasting memory of their name.

a. *Longinianus was slain at the same time as Stilicho (cf. note d below). On the title 'his Excellency', cf. 2.2, note e.*

b. *Arcadius (r. 383–408) and Honorius (r. 395–423) were E and W emperors respectively.*

c. *The double arch, which carried the Aqua Claudia across the Via Praenestina and Via Labicana at this point, had been incorporated into the wall of Aurelian in the 270s. The fragments of masonry on which the present text is inscribed have been reassembled outside the gate.*

d. *Cf. 2.2, note d.*

e. *Cf. 2.2, note c.*

7.6 Epitaph of Marcus Vergilius Eurysaces

1 [est hoc monimentu]M MARCEI VERGILEI EVRYSACIS ¬
  PISTORIS REDEMPTORIS APPARET

2 EST HOC MONIMENTVM MARGEI VERGILEI EVRYSACI[S] ¬
  PISTORIS REDEMPTORIS APPARET

3 EST HOC MONIMENTVM MARCI VERGILI EVRYSAC[is]

> 1. monimentu]M = monumentum : *On the spelling, see 13.1, line 9.* —
> MARCEI VERGILEI = Mārcī Vergilī : *The spelling in -ei reflects an or-*
> *thographical confusion that arose after the pronunciation of the diphthong*
> */ei/ had fallen together with that of /i:/ (see 1.6c, line 6).* — EVRYSACIS :
> *The Latin* Eurysacēs *transliterates Greek* Εὐρυσάκης.
>
> 2. MARGEI : *On the hesitation between* C *and* G, *cf. 1.1, line 1.*

Piazzale Labicano: Frieze of Sepulcher

N *This monument belongs to Marcus Vergilius Eurysaces,[a] baker and contractor. He attends...[b]*

W *This monument belongs to Marcus Vergilius Eurysaces, baker and contractor. He attends...*

S *This monument belongs to Marcus Vergilius Eurysaces.*

a. *Eurysaces evidently made his fortune fulfilling public contracts for bread in the first century BC. The form of the tomb, comprising a complex arrangement of large cylinders, has thus far eluded explanation. The monument was eventually incorporated into the fortifications of the walls of Aurelian (cf. 5.7B, note a).*

b. *The inscription breaks off where the monument is mutilated.*

MOSTRA DELL'ACQUA FELICE

Like the aqueducts of the ancient city, those of papal Rome terminated at monumental fountains. The Italian name for such a fountain
is mostra ('display'). As the provision of water was an act of munif-
icence for which a pope could expect to be remembered with lasting
gratitude, the heirs of Peter spared no expense in erecting mostre of
suitable splendor. Domenico Fontana's design for the mostra of the Acqua Felice adopts the motif of the triumphal arch: three niches divided
by engaged columns support an entablature and large attic which is
covered with a monumental dedicatory inscription. The attic is in turn
surmounted by obelisks and a curvilinear pediment that encloses the
arms of Pope Sixtus V.

VIII. The Quirinal Hill

THREE SALIENT TOPOGRAPHICAL FEATURES condition the site of Rome. First is the Tiber River, which separates Trastevere and the Vatican from the rest of the city and lends the Campus Martius its characteristic profile; then the steep hills—the Palatine at the center, with the Capitoline, Quirinal, Viminal, Esquiline, Caelian, and Aventine forming a semicircle around it; and finally the low-lying areas between, the largest of which are the Forum valley and the Campus Martius. Over the first several centuries of Rome's history, a more or less consistent pattern of development emerged. The open areas of the Forum and the Campus Martius became monumental centers; the hilltops—with the exception of the Capitoline, a sacred citadel—became fashionable residential quarters; and the unhealthy valley floors and the comparatively remote quarter across the Tiber were inhabited by the masses. Because of erosion and the gradual filling of the valleys with debris, Rome's terrain has tended to become more regular with each century of human occupation. At points, the ancient street level lies more than twenty meters beneath the modern.

In Antiquity, the dramatic irregularity of the city's landforms was especially pronounced at the southeastern margins of the Campus Martius. Here the Quirinal Hill presented a veritable cliff face to the plain below. At its foot, the street corresponding to VIA DELLA DATARIA *8.1* and SALITA DI MONTECAVALLO was obliged to climb some twenty- *8.2* five meters. The heights of the ancient Quirinal were dominated by three monumental public buildings. In a porticoed precinct on the summit rose the Temple of Quirinus, splendidly reconstructed by Augustus with a dipteral colonnade of seventy-six Doric columns. This was joined early in the third century of the Christian era by Caracalla's mighty Temple of Serapis on the hill's northwestern slope; the Colonna gardens are littered with fragments of its massive entablature. A century later, Constantine erected his baths close by.

257

The hill's spine was traversed from southwest to northeast by a long, straight street, the *Alta Semita* ('High Way', today's Via Venti Settembre). This ancient right-of-way formed part of the prehistoric salt route that followed the right bank of the Tiber inland from the salt pans at its mouth. Between the sea and Rome, this route was known as the *Via Campana* (from *campus salinarum*, 'salt field'). At the Tiber ford, it crossed to the left bank, changing its name to *Via Salaria* (i.e., 'Salt Road') and continuing up the river valley into the Sabine hinterland. In imperial times, the Via Salaria passed out of the city by the Porta Salaria of the walls of Aurelian, demolished in 1871 to facilitate the circulation of traffic.

The Quirinal Hill is comparatively poor in Christian antiquities: its only church of remote origins is the former Titulus of Gaius—today's Santa Susanna. Beyond the walls, however, on the Via Nomentana, rises one of the most venerable shrines of Christian Rome, the basilica of Sant'Agnese fuori le Mura. Agnes, virgin and martyr, is supposed to have suffered under Diocletian in the persecution of AD 305. Her 'Acts', written in the fifth century, portray a girl of thirteen who preferred death to the compromise of her chastity. The site of her tomb—a subterranean cemetery, or catacombs, excavated in a tufa hillside along the Via Nomentana—early became the focus of pious veneration and in the fourth
8.8A century was embellished with a shrine by Pope St. DAMASUS I (r. 366–384).

As at San Lorenzo fuori le Mura, the first church on the site was a basilica of the fourth century constructed near the entrance to the cemetery. When the galleries of the cemetery were cut away and a basilica *ad corpus* constructed around the martyr's tomb to improve its accessibility to pilgrims, the earlier building was abandoned and allowed to fall into
8.8B ruin. The basilica that survives today was constructed by Pope HONORIUS I (r. 625–638), whose dedication forms part of the apse mosaic. Memorializing a young girl murdered for her profession of faith, this strange, half-buried church is one of the city's most evocative monuments. By a custom arising from the similarity of 'Agnes' to Latin *agnus* ('lamb'), on

20 January of each year—the Feast of St. Agnes—two lambs are blessed at the altar of her church; they furnish the wool used to weave the *pallia* of archbishops consecrated in the coming year (a *pallium* is a band of wool that forms part of the papal and archiepiscopal vestments).

The Quirinal Hill was largely deserted after the Gothic wars of the mid-sixth century. Forming part of the vast and desolate *disabitato*, it wore a rustic look for the subsequent millennium. The reclamation of the zone was fostered by the popes of the Counter Reformation, who found its airy heights a healthful alternative to the malarial miasma that enveloped the Vatican in summertime. It is noteworthy that the popes now felt themselves at liberty to range at will beyond the neighborhood of their stronghold at Castel Sant'Angelo; a century and a half after the return from Avignon, their domination of the city was secure.

In the 1560s, Pope Pius IV (r. 1559–1565) gave initial impetus to the revitalization of the Quirinal by having the Alta Semita leveled and widened. His newly christened 'Via Pia' (named for himself, as was customary) extended some 1,600 meters from Piazza del Quirinale to the wall of Aurelian. The ancient Porta Nomentana was replaced by Michelangelo's PORTA PIA, which serves as a monumental focus at the eastern end of the street. The curious medallions on its façade are said to represent basins with towel and soap: Pius IV hailed from a long line of Milanese barbers.

8.7

Porta Pia was the scene of a climactic episode in the Risorgimento ('unification of Italy'). In March of 1861, Victor Emanuel II of Savoy was named king by the first Italian parliament. Over the succeeding decade, as the kingdom took shape, the ancient Papal State shrank to the dimensions of the city of Rome; by 1870, the only question was whether Pope Pius IX (r. 1846–1878) would permit Victor Emanuel to enter Rome peacefully. The pontiff refused. On the morning of 20 September 1870, after an artillery bombardment of four hours, Italian forces breached the wall of Aurelian to the north of Porta Pia. The *bersaglieri* ('light rifle') quickly overcame perfunctory resistance on the part of papal troops and took possession of the city. As for Pius IX, he spent the remaining eight years of his life a self-styled prisoner in the Vatican. The odium that he incurred by his intransigence pursued him beyond the grave: in 1881, as his mortal remains were conveyed by night to their permanent resting place in the Basilica of San Lorenzo fuori le Mura, a mob attempted to fling them into the Tiber.

In the early decades of the sixteenth century, the dissolution of the pope's temporal power still belonged to the distant future; wealthy cardinals laid out sumptuous villas on either side of the Alta Semita. One such estate, built by Ippolito d'Este on the Quirinal's northwestern brow, became a favorite resort of the popes. Gregory XIII (r. 1572–1585) determined to transform Villa d'Este into a papal palace. Free of tombs, shrines, and other sacred alluvia, the Quirinal was the ideal site for a secular pendant to the Vatican. The reclamation of the Quirinal—and of the *monti* ('hills') in general—could nevertheless commence in earnest only with the provision of water. Gregory turned his attention to the matter of an aqueduct. The ancient Aqua Virgo, which terminated at Fontana di Trevi, had been reactivated in 1570; its many subsidiary fountains furnished the greater part of the Campus Martius with a copious supply of fresh water. Gregory's new aqueduct would serve the southeastern quarters that the Aqua Virgo could not reach. A project to tap the sources of the ancient Aqua Alexandrina was approved, but the pope died in April of 1585 before construction could be undertaken.

The task of building—and the privilege of naming—the new aqueduct fell to Gregory's successor, Sixtus V (r. 1585–1590), the former Cardinal Felice Peretti. While still 'Cardinal Montalto', Peretti had acquired a villa on the Esquiline Hill; it lay between the present Stazione Termini and the Basilica of Santa Maria Maggiore. This circumstance perhaps illuminates the alacrity with which the new pope took up his detested predecessor's plans to bring water to the *monti*. Entering the city at Arco delle Pere, the projected aqueduct would flank the northeastern confine of Villa Montalto, permitting the installation of fountains in its gardens and elevating its value considerably. Work commenced within a few days of Sixtus' election. Despite flaws in the original design that resulted in a considerable loss of time and money, the pope's engineers succeeded in completing the project within two years. This formidable pace was facilitated by the proximity of the Aqua Marcia and the Aqua Claudia, whose ancient arcades were ruthlessly cannibalized for their cut stone.

Previous pontiffs had christened their projects using an adjectival form of their papal name: Pope Sixtus IV built the 'Cappella Sistina'; the streets opened by Julius II, Leo X, and Clement VII were called, respectively, 'Via Julia', 'Via Leonina', and 'Via Clementina'. Choosing instead his Christian name, Sixtus V named his aqueduct 'ACQUA FE- 8.6 LICE'; as the Italian adjective *felice* connotes prosperity and good fortune, the choice was a happy one.

At the aqueduct's terminus stands an impressive fountain. Beneath the great inscription commemorating the pope's achievement, columns separate three high niches. The central niche is occupied by a powerful if ungainly figure of Moses in the act of smiting the rock at Rephidim to bring forth water for the Children of Israel. Legend has it that its sculptor, Prospero da Brescia, perished in grief over the derision provoked by the sculpture. In fact, Prospero was only an assistant: Moses' true author was the same Leonardo Sormani who collaborated with Tommaso della Porta to fashion the colossal figures of St. Peter for the Column of Trajan and of St. Paul for that of Marcus Aurelius.

Over the forty years that elapsed between the pontificates of Sixtus V and Paul V (r. 1605–1621), Palazzo del Quirinale became the effective seat of the church's temporal power; another forty were required to bring the enormous fabric, with its gardens and dependencies, to a final state of completion. The elaboration of Piazza del Quirinale followed naturally on the emergence of this new fulcrum of power. Since the Middle Ages, the part of the Quirinal Hill in which the papal compound took shape had been known as Montecavallo ('Horse Mountain'); the toponym derives from a pair of colossal STATUES OF CASTOR AND POLLUX 8.3

that formed part of the decoration of the Baths of Constantine and were never entirely lost to view. With a superb disdain for chronology, these Roman copies of Greek originals were identified in the Middle Ages as Alexander and Bucephalus and ultimately attributed to Phidias and Praxiteles. The erroneous attribution is perpetuated in the inscriptions on the bases. Sixtus V restored the ruinous figures and—in order to exploit the long perspective of Via Pia—had them transferred to the center of the piazza in line with the axis of the street; the Acqua Felice fed a fountain at their base.

The final ornament of the ensemble—the Obelisco Quirinale—was added after a lapse of two centuries. Pope Sixtus V enjoys the unique distinction of having erected four obelisks in five years: the Vaticano (1586), the Esquilino (1587), the Lateranense (1588), and the Flaminio (1589). His only rival in this department is Pius VI (r. 1775–1799), who in the space of seven years erected a further three: the Quirinale (1786), the Sallustiano (1789), and the Campense (1792). The Obelisco Quirinale is the twin of the Esquilino at Santa Maria Maggiore. Both originated at the Mausoleum of Augustus; each lacks the usual *pyramidion* ('cusp') at its apex. After being buried for centuries, the obelisk was uncovered in 1549, but subsequently reburied and forgotten. It was rediscovered in 1781; five years later, Pope Pius VI engaged Giovanni Antinori to mount it between the statues of the Dioscuri in Piazza del Quirinale. It was Antinori who proposed that the statues be skewed, in order to avoid *una certa uniformità poco plausibile* ('a certain scarcely admirable regularity'). The final addition was the fountain that Raffaele Stern added in 1818 at the bidding of Pius VII (r. 1800–1823).

8.4

With the unification of Italy came inevitable change. Palazzo del Quirinale was taken over by the House of Savoy; today it is the official residence of the presidents of the Italian Republic. As for Via Pia, it was renamed Via Venti Settembre in honor of the victory of the Bersaglieri in 1870. Because of its length, its state of relative underdevelopment, and its convenience to Palazzo del Quirinale and the new railway station,

Via Venti Settembre was designated a government quarter. The tale of its transformation furnishes one more variation on a familiar theme: on the Quirinal the fathers of modern Italy, elated by their newfound autonomy, swept aside an ancient and lovely tissue of churches, convents, gardens, and villas to make way for monotonous ranks of ugly, outsized ministries that might as well have been located a kilometer beyond the walls.

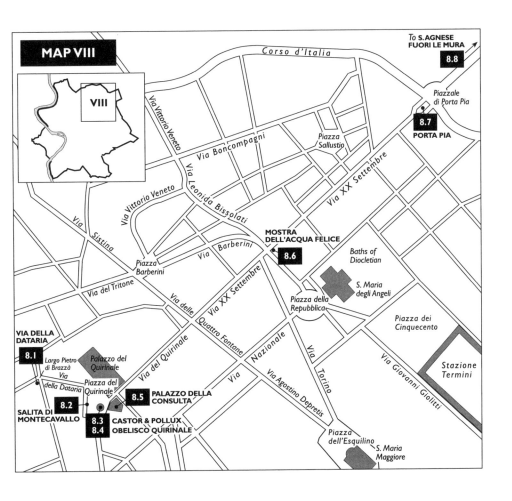

MAP VIII

VIII

To S. AGNESE
FUORI LE MURA
8.8

Corso d'Italia

Via Vittorio Veneto

Via Boncompagni

Piazza
Sallustio

Piazzale
di Porta Pia

8.7
PORTA PIA

Via Leonida Bissolati

Via XX Settembre

Via Vittorio Veneto

Via Sistina

MOSTRA
DELL'ACQUA FELICE

8.6

Baths of
Diocletian

Via Barberini

Piazza
Barberini

Via del Tritone

Via delle Quattro Fontane

Via XX Settembre

S. Maria
degli Angeli

Piazza della
Repubblica

Piazza dei
Cinquecento

VIA DELLA
DATARIA

8.1

Largo Pietro
di Brazzà
Via
della Dataria

Palazzo del
Quirinale

Piazza del
Quirinale

Via del Quirinale

Via Nazionale

Via Torino

Via Giovanni Giolitti

Stazione
Termini

SALITA DI
MONTECAVALLO

8.2

8.5

PALAZZO DELLA
CONSULTA

Via

Via Agostino Depretis

8.3
8.4

CASTOR & POLLUX
OBELISCO QUIRINALE

Piazza
dell'Esquilino

S. Maria
Maggiore

8.1 Via della Dataria: Dedication by Paul V

PAVLVS V PONT MAX

AD QVIRINALE A SE AVCTVM

ORNATVMQVE

VIAM MOLLITO CLIVO

5   DILATAVIT ATQVE DIREXIT

ANNO SAL MDCXI PONTIF VII

1. PAVLVS V : Quīntus. — PONT(ifex) MAX(imus).
2. QVIRINALE : Sc. palātium.
5. DIREXIT : *The* CL *word is* dērigere.
6. SAL(ūtis) MDCXI : Mīllēsimō sescentēsimō ūndecimō. —
PONTIF(icātūs) VII : Septimō.

8.2 Salita di Montecavallo: Dedication by S.P.Q.R.

PIO IX̄ PONTIFICE MAXIMO

S P Q R

VT ADITVS AD COLLEM QVIRINALEM

COMMODIOR PATEFIERET

5   ANTIQVIS SVBSTRVCTIONIBVS EGESTIS

AQVARIIS FISTVLIS CVNICVLO COLLECTIS

CLIVO SVBACTO ADSTRVCTOQVE AGGERE

VIAM NOBILIOREM APERVIT STRAVIT

ANNO MD̄C̄C̄C̄L̄X̄V̄Ī SACRI PRINC X̄X̄

(Names of Magistrates)

1. PIO IX̄ : Nōnō.
2. S(enātus) P(opulus) Q(ue) R(ōmānus).
4. PATEFIERET : *The functional Pass. of* patefacere ('*lay open*') *is* patefierī.
7. ADSTRVCTOQVE : *In* CL, astrūctō. *In pronunciation, the assimilation of* ad- *to* as- *was simplified before a stop preceded by* s (*so* ad + struō > astruō *but* ad + sequor > assequor, *etc.; cf.* 4.2A, *line* 7).
9. MD̄C̄C̄C̄L̄X̄V̄Ī : Mīllēsimō octingentēsimō sexāgēsimō sextō. —
PRINC(ipātūs) X̄X̄ : Vīcēsimō.

Largo Pietro di Brazzà 24: Corner, High

Paul the Fifth, Supreme Pontiff,[a]
having eased its grade,
widened and straightened
the street leading to Palazzo del Quirinale,[b]
which he had enlarged and embellished,
in the year of Salvation 1611, seventh of his office.

a. Pope Paul V Borghese (r. 1605–1621). *The seventh year of his pontificate ran from 16 May 1611 through 15 May 1612.*

b. *Known in the Middle Ages as 'Salita di Montecavallo', Via della Dataria replaces the ancient Clivus Salutis (see 8.2, note b). Paul V completed the Quirinal Palace.*

E Side, on Retaining Wall

During the Supreme Pontificate of Pius the Ninth,[a]
that the approach to the Quirinal Hill
might be made more conveniently accessible,[b]
by removing ancient foundations,
by gathering the water pipes into a subterranean conduit
and by banking the slope and building a retaining wall against it
the Senate and People of Rome
opened and paved a nobler street
in the year 1866, twentieth of his sacred office.
(Names of Magistrates)

a. Pope Pius IX Mastai-Ferretti (r. 1846–1878). *The twentieth year of his pontificate ran from 16 June 1865 through 15 June 1866.*

b. *Given the constant attrition of Rome's hills and concomitant filling of her valleys, it is difficult to appreciate the fact that in ancient times the NW slope of the Quirinal Hill formed a lofty escarpment that isolated it from the Campus Martius below. Although the level of the Campus has risen by some fifteen meters over the intervening centuries, the grade of Via della Dataria and Salita di Montecavallo is nonetheless still quite steep.*

8.3A Statues of Castor and Pollux: Titles

i.	*ii.*
OPVS PHIDIAE	OPVS PRAXITELIS

i. PHIDIAE : *The Latin* Phīdiās *transliterates Greek* Φειδίας.

ii. PRAXITELIS : *The Latin* Prāxitelēs *transliterates Greek* Πραξιτέλης.

8.3B Statues of Castor and Pollux: Dedication by Sixtus V

XYSTVS V PONT MAX

COLOSSEA HAEC SIGNA TEMPORIS VI DEFORMATA

RESTITVIT

VETERIBVSQVE REPOSITIS INSCRIPTIONIBVS

5   E PROXIMIS CONSTANTINIANIS THERMIS

IN QVIRINALEM AREAM TRANSTVLIT

ANNO SALVTIS MDLXXXIX

PONTIFICATVS QVARTO

EQVES DOMINICVS

10   FONTANA ARCHITECT

INSTAVRABAT

1. XYSTVS V : Quīntus. *The name* Sixtus *appears in inscriptions variously as* SIXTVS, XYSTVS *and* SYXTVS (*see* 3.4D, *line 4*). — PONT(ifex) MAX(imus).

2. COLOSSEA : *The* CL colossēus *is 'colossal'.*

5. CONSTANTINIANIS : *The Adj.* Cōnstantīniānus *answers to the name* Cōnstantīnus.

6. QVIRINALEM AREAM : *The Ital.* piazza *is frequently represented in* RL *by* ārea *or* forum.

7. MDLXXXIX : Mīllēsimō quīngentēsimō octōgēsimō nōnō.

10. ARCHITECT(us).

Piazza del Quirinale: Base of Statues

Left	*Right*
A work of Phidias.[a]	*A work of Praxiteles.*[b]

a. *Phidias was the leading Greek sculptor of the mid-fifth century* BC.

b. *The Athenian sculptor Praxiteles was active in the mid-fourth century* BC.

Base of Statues L, on Side

Sixtus the Fifth,[a] *Supreme Pontiff,*

repaired

these colossal statues,[b] *disfigured by the violence of time,*

and, their ancient inscriptions restored,[c]

transported them from the nearby Baths of Constantine[d]

to Piazza del Quirinale,

in the year of Salvation 1589,

fourth of his office.

Cavaliere Domenico
Fontana, Architect,
restored this.[e]

a. *Pope Sixtus V Peretti (r. 1585–1590). The fourth year of his pontificate ran from 24 April 1588 through 23 April 1589.*

b. *The figures, Roman copies of Greek originals, represent the divine horsemen Castor and Pollux (the Dioscuri; see 1.3, note a). Never entirely lost to view, the statues are responsible for the medieval name of the Quirinal Hill: Montecavallo ('Mount of the Horses').*

c. *I.e., the erroneous attribution to Phidias and Praxiteles.*

d. *The last of the great baths of Rome, Constantine's complex was early damaged by fire and earthquake then restored in the fifth century; it is uncertain whether the present statues originally pertained to the Baths of Constantine or to the adjacent Temple of Serapis.*

e. *See 7.1.ii, note c.*

8.4A Obelisco Quirinale: Dedication by Pius VI

i.	*ii.*
XII KAL OCT	ANNO XII
ANNO	SACRI PRINCIPATVS
MDCCLXXXVI	EIVS

*i.*1. XII : Duodecimō. — KAL(endās) OCT(ōbris) : *See 1.6G, line 11.*

2. MDCCLXXXVI : Mīllēsimō septingentēsimō octōgēsimō sextō.

*ii.*1. XII : Duodecimō.

iii.

SALVE

OPTIME PRINCEPS

SALVE

PARENS POPVLI ROMANI

5   VOTISQVE VIVE NOSTRIS

VIVE VRBI TVAE

VIVE

ORBI CHRISTIANO

CVI TE DEVS

10   MAXIMVM RECTOREM

DEDIT

8. CHRISTIANO : *See 1.7A, line 8.*

Base of Obelisk

West	*East*
20 September[a]	*in the twelfth year*
in the year	*of his sacred*
1786,	*office.*[b]

a. Lit., 'on the twelfth day before the Kalends of October'.

b. *The twelfth year of the pontificate of Pius VI Braschi (r. 1775–1799) ran from 15 February 1786 through 14 February 1787.*

South

Hail,[a]
best of princes,
hail,
Father of the Roman People,
and live in our prayers:
live for your City,
live
for Christendom,
on which God
has bestowed you
as its supreme ruler.

a. *The obelisk speaks* in propria persona *(see 4.1.iii, note a). Items 8.4A–C were composed by Stefano Antonio Morcelli (1737–1822), an erudite Jesuit who made a special study of ancient Latin inscriptions.*

8.4B Obelisco Quirinale: The Obelisk's History

ME QVONDAM AEGYPTI DESECTVM E CAVTIBVS VNDAS
VIS QVEM PER MEDIAS ROMVLA TRANSTVLERAT
VT STAREM AVGVSTI MOLES MIRANDA SEPVLCRI
CAESAREVM TIBERIS QVA NEMVS ADLVERET
5   IAM FRVSTRA EVERSVM FRACTVMQVE INFESTA VETVSTAS
NISA EST AGGESTIS CONDERE RVDERIBVS
NAM PIVS IN LVCEM REVOCAT SARTVMQVE QVIRINI
SVBLIMEM IN COLLIS VERTICE STARE IVBET
INTER ALEXANDRI MEDIVS QVI MAXIMA SIGNA
10   TESTABOR ⟨SEXTI GRANDIA FACTA PII⟩
10a   ⟦quanto sit minor ille pio⟧

Five Elegiac Couplets

1. ME : *Dir.Ob. of* CONDERE (*line 6*). — VNDAS : *Follows* PER (*line 2*).
2. VIS . . . ROMVLA : *The name* Rōmulus *forms the Adj.* Rōmuleus *or simply* Rōmulus.
3. MOLES : *App. to the unexpressed Sub. of* STAREM.
7–8. REVOCAT : *Sc.* mē. — QVIRINI . . . COLLIS : *I.e., the Quirinal Hill.* — SVBLIMEM : *Pred.Acc. to the implicit* mē.
9. MEDIVS : *Pred.Nom. to* QVI.
10a. ⟦quanto sit minor ille pio⟧ : *The double brackets indicate that these words were deliberately effaced and replaced by those between angle brackets. The alteration left its mark in the presence of the tail of the* Q *of* QVANTO, *plainly visible on the stone beneath the* S *of* SEXTI.

Foundation of the Obelisk, SE Side

Now in vain has hostile time striven to bury me,[a]
overturned and shattered, in heaps of rubble—
me, once hewn from the cliffs of Egypt and borne
through the midst of the sea by the strength of Romulus
that I might rise, mighty marvel of Augustus' tomb[b]
where the Tiber lapped at the grove of the Caesars—
for Pius[c] recalls me to the light and bids me, remade,
to stand tall on the summit of the Hill of Quirinus,[d]
where between the mighty figures of Alexander[e]
I shall attest ⟨to the great works of Pius the Sixth.⟩[f]
            ⟦*how far inferior is the latter to Pius*⟧

    Five ELEGIAC COUPLETS

a. The obelisk speaks in propria persona (see 4.1.iii, note a).
b. See 10.5.
c. Pope Pius VI Braschi (r. 1775–1799).
d. The Quirinal Hill took its name from the ancient Italic deity Quirinus,
   whom the Romans identified with the deified Romulus.
e. The twin horsemen (see 8.3B, note b) were long supposed to represent the
   young Alexander taming Bucephalus.
f. Following the exile of Pius VI and his death in France in 1799, the comparison with Alexander the Great appeared more grotesque than fatuous
   and the last line of the inscription was recut. The words enclosed in double
   brackets were replaced by the more modest formulation that appears in
   angle brackets.

8.4C   Obelisco Quirinale: Dedication of Fountain

PIVS $\overline{\text{VI}}$ PONT MAX

SIGNIS ET BASIBVS

QVAE XYSTVS $\overline{\text{V}}$ AEQVATA IN FRONTEM

CONSTITVERAT

5 FAVSTA MOLITIONE

ET OPERE INTACTO IN LATERA AVERSIS

OBELISCVM C CAESARIS AVGVSTI

GEMINVM EIVS QVI IN EXQVILIIS STAT

E MAVSOLEI RVDERIBVS TRANSLATVM

10 AREAE QVIRINALI EXORNANDAE

INTERMEDIVM STATVI

LACVM ET SALIENTES RESTITVI IVSSIT

1. PIVS $\overline{\text{VI}}$: Sextus. — PONT(ifex) MAX(imus).

3. XYSTVS $\overline{\text{V}}$: Quīntus. *On the form* XYSTVS, *see* 3.4D, *line 4.*

7. C(āiī) : *On the abbreviation, see* 1.1, *line 1.*

8. EXQVILIIS = Esquiliīs.

10. AREAE QVIRINALI EXORNANDAE : *On* AREAE, *see* 8.3B, *line 6. The construction is Dat. of Purpose (on the construction with the gerundive, see* 1.6H, *lines 11–12).*

11. INTERMEDIVM : *The* LL *intermedius is 'in the midst'. A second inscription recording the works appears on the obverse of twelve medallions minted for the occasion and enclosed in a stone casket in the foundation of the present monument:* OBELISCVM | RVINIS MAVSOLEI AVGVSTALIS A TOT SAECVLIS | OBRVTVM INSTAVRARI ORNARI ET EQVIS AD LAXANDVM FRON|TIS SPATIVM IN OBLIQVVM VERSIS ERIGI IVSSIT | ANNO MDCCLXXXVI | PONTIF IX (*'He bade the obelisk, buried by so many centuries in the ruins of the Mausoleum of Augustus, to be restored and embellished and to be erected once the horses had been skewed to the sides to enlarge the area in front, in the year 1786, ninth of his office'*). — STATVI . . . RESTITVI : *Note the asyndeton (cf.* 1.2.i, *line 4).*

Base of Obelisk, N

> *Pius the Sixth,[a] Supreme Pontiff,*
> *having in an auspicious endeavor,*
> *and without damage to the work,*
> *skewed to their sides the statues and bases*
> *which Sixtus the Fifth[b] had set up*
> *aligned at the front,[c]*
> *ordered the obelisk of Gaius Caesar Augustus,*
> *twin of that which stands on the Esquiline,[d]*
> *to be conveyed from the ruins of his mausoleum*
> *and set up between them*
> *for the embellishment of Piazza del Quirinale,*
> *and the basin and fountains to be restored.[e]*

a. *Pope Pius VI Braschi (r. 1775–1799).*

b. *See 8.3B, note a.*

c. *The new arrangement was not universally admired. After the statues had been shifted, in a labored* PASQUINADE *a waggish contemporary altered the inscription* OPVS PHIDIAE *('A work of Phidias', see 8.3A.i) so that it read* OPVS perPHIDIAE pii sexti *('a work of the per-Phidias-ness of Pius VI'). Pius likewise erected the Obelisco Sallustiano at SS. Trinità dei Monti (9.11) and the Obelisco Campense at Piazza di Montecitorio (10.11).*

d. *The present obelisk is indeed the twin of the Obelisco Esquilino (see 4.1.i, note b), which likewise stood before the Mausoleum of Augustus. The pair is first mentioned in the fourth century by the historian Ammianus Marcellinus. The fact that they were overlooked in the first century by Strabo and the elder Pliny, both of whom catalogued the city's obelisks, has suggested—probably wrongly—that they represent a late addition to the mausoleum. They are the only two among the city's obelisks to lack a pyramidion ('cusp').*

e. *See 8.4D.*

8.4D Obelisco Quirinale: Dedication of Fountain

PIVS VII PONT MAX

QVOD ABSOLVENDVM SVPERERAT

ADDITO CRATERE EXCITATO SALIENTE

SYMPLEGMA CONSVMMAVIT

5   A D MDCCCXVIII PONTIF XIX

1. PIVS VII : Septimus. — PONT(ifex) MAX(imus).

3. CRATERE : *The* CL crātēr *transliterates Greek* κρατήρ *('mixing bowl'); the word is used by ancient writers for 'basin of a fountain'.*

4. SYMPLEGMA : *The* CL symplegma *transliterates Greek* σύμπλεγμα *('intertwining'); it ordinarily denotes sculptural representations of wrestlers or of couples engaged in sexual intercourse.*

5. A(nnō) D(ominī) MDCCCXVIII : Mīllēsimō octingentēsimō duodēvīcēsimō. — PONTIF(icātūs) XIX : Ūndēvīcēsimō.

8.5 Palazzo della Consulta: Dedication by Clement XII

CLEMENS XII PONT MAX

ADMINISTRIS

PONTIFICIAE DITIONIS NEGOCIIS CONSVLTANDIS

ATQVE A BREVIORIBVS EPISTVLIS

5   LEVIS ARMATVRAE ET THORACATORVM EQVITVM TVRMIS

A FVNDAMENTIS EXSTRVXIT

ANNO SAL MDCCXXXIV PONT V

1. CLEMENS XII : Duodecimus. — PONT(ifex) MAX(imus).

2. ADMINISTRIS ... CONSVLTANDIS : *The Dat. case of* ADMINISTRIS *is Ind.Obj. following* EXSTRVXIT *(line 6);* NEGOCIIS CONSVLTANDIS *is Dat. of Purpose. On the gerundive construction, see 1.6H, lines 11–12.*

3. PONTIFICIAE : *See 1.8B, line 8.* — DITIONIS = diciōnis : *On the spelling, see 3.4B, line 3.* — NEGOCIIS = negōtiīs.

4. A BREVIORIBVS EPISTVLIS : *On the use of the Prep. to designate an office, see 1.8C. The phrase is parallel to* ADMINISTRIS *(line 2).*

5. THORACATORVM EQVITVM : *The* CL thōrācātus *is 'equipped with a* thōrāx' *(Greek* θώραξ, *'cuirass').*

7. ANNO SAL(utis) MDCCXXXIV : Mīllēsimō septingentēsimō trīcēsimō quārtō. — PONT(ificātūs) V : Quīntō.

Foundation of Obelisk

Pius the Seventh,[a] Supreme Pontiff,
by adding the basin and erecting the fountain,[b]
brought to completion the ensemble,
which remained to be finished,
in the year 1818, nineteenth of his office.

a. Pope Pius VII Chiaramonti (r. 1800–1823). The nineteenth year of his pontificate ran from 14 March 1818 through 13 March 1819.

b. The fountain, designed by Raffaelo Stern (1774–1820), is constructed around a massive granite basin removed from the Forum, where it had served as a watering trough for livestock. Stern is best known for the Braccio Nuovo ('New Wing') of the Vatican museum, which completed the mutilation of Bramante's great Cortile del Belvedere. The latter had originally extended uninterrupted from the Vatican palaces to the Belvedere.

Piazza del Quirinale 41: Above Portal

In the year of Salvation 1734, fifth of his office,
Clement the Twelfth,[a] Supreme Pontiff,
erected this from its foundations
for the Sacra Congregazione
della Consulta,[b]
for the Segnatura dei Brevi,[c]
for the Corazze[d] and for the Cavalleggeri.[e]

a. Pope Clement XII Corsini (r. 1730–1740). The fifth year of his pontificate ran from 12 July 1734 through 11 July 1735.

b. Lit., 'for the officials who conduct the legal business of the papal jurisdiction'. The Sacra Congregazione della Consulta was an ecclesiastical tribunal with both civil and criminal jurisdiction in the Papal State. The author has gone to heroic lengths to devise Classical equivalents for the names of the several entities that figure in the present text.

c. Lit., 'those who handle the briefer correspondence'. The Segnatura dei Brevi drafted letters ('briefs') concerning indulgences and dispensations.

d. Lit., 'corps of light infantry'. The Corazze were the foot guard that escorted the papal carriage.

e. Lit., 'armored cavalry'. The Cavalleggeri were the papal horse guard.

8.6 Fontana del Mosè: Dedication by Sixtus V

SIXTVS V PONT MAX PICENVS

AQVAM EX AGRO COLVMNAE

VIA PRAENEST SINISTRORSVM

MVLTAR COLLECTIONE VENARVM

5   DVCTV SINVOSO A RECEPTACVLO

MIL XX A CAPITE XXII ADDVXIT

FELICEMQ DE NOMINE ANTE PONT DIXIT

COEPIT PONT AN I ABSOLVIT III MDLXXXVII

LVCAS FANEN

1. SIXTVS V : Quīntus. — PONT(ifex) MAX(imus). — PICENVS : *The Adj.* Pīcēnus *answers to the toponym* Pīcēnum (*mod. Ascoli Piceno*).

2. COLVMNAE : *The Ital. name* Colonna *appears in Latin as* Columna (*cf. 1.8A, line 3*).

3. PRAENEST(īnā) : *The Adj.* Praenestīnus *answers to the toponym* Praeneste (*mod. Palestrina*). *The Abl. follows the Adv.* sinistrōrsum, *used quasiprepositionally.*

4. MVLTAR(um).

6. MIL(ia passuum) XX : Vīgintī. — XXII : Vīgintī duo.

7. FELICEMQ(ue) : *See 4.5.i, line 2.* — PONT(ificātum).

8. PONT(ificātūs) AN(nō) I : Prīmō. — III : Tertiō. — MDLXXXVII : Mīllēsimō quīngentēsimō octōgēsimō septimō.

9. LVCAS FANEN(sis) : *The Latin name is* Lūcās, -ae. *The Adj.* Fānēnsis *answers to the toponym* Fānum (*mod. Fano*).

Piazza di S. Bernardo: Attic & Frieze of Fountain

Sixtus the Fifth,[a] Supreme Pontiff, native of Ascoli Piceno,[b]
by the gathering of many rivulets
brought water by a winding channel
from the Colonna territory
to the left of the Via Praenestina,[c]
twenty miles from the reservoir, twenty-two from its source,
and called it Felice from his name before his office.[d]

He began it in the first year of his office and completed it in the third, 1587.

Luca of Fano.[e]

a. *Pope Sixtus V Peretti (r. 1585–1590). The third year of his pontificate ran from 24 April 1587 through 23 April 1588.*

b. *Sixtus was born at Grottammare in the region of Ascoli Piceno.*

c. *The Colonna territory lay to the S of the Via Praenestina. Considered from the direction of the water's flow, this is the left side.*

d. *The aqueduct was planned and begun under Sixtus' immediate predecessor Gregory XIII to complement the Acqua Vergine (see 9.5D, note b). Its course as realized appears calculated to favor Sixtus' estate, through which it passed (see 4.1.i, note d), as well as the papal summer residence, near which it terminated.*

e. *The writing master Luca Orfei, a native of Fano, was engaged by Sixtus V to letter about fifty inscriptions for his public works, many of which remain in situ. Among these number the inscriptions of the Obelisco Lateranense (7.1), Esquilino (4.1), Flaminino (10.4), and Vaticano (15.3), and those of Arco delle Pere (4.5).*

8.7A Porta Pia: Dedication by Pius IV

PIVS IIII PONT MAX

PORTAM PIAM

SVBLATA NOMENTANA EXSTRVXIT

VIAM PIAM

5   AEQVATA ALTA SEMITA DVXIT

1. PIVS IIII : Quārtus. — PONT(ifex) MAX(imus).

2. PORTAM PIAM : *The name is like* Aqua Fēlīx (*see 4.5.i, line 2*).

3. SVBLATA NOMENTANA : *Abl.Abs. The Adj.* Nōmentānus *answers to the toponym* Nōmentum (*mod. La Mentana*), *destination of the Via Nomentana. The great consular highways of ancient Rome took their names variously from a destination* (Via Nomentana, Via Tiburtina), *a builder* (Via Appia, Via Flaminia), *or a function* (Via Salaria, Via Portuensis).

4. VIAM PIAM : *See line 2 above.*

5. AEQVATA ALTA SEMITA : *Abl.Abs.* — DVXIT : *In asyndeton with* EXSTRVXIT (*cf. 1.2.i, line 4*).

8.7B Porta Pia: Dedication by Pius IX

i.

PIVS $\overline{\text{IX}}$ PONTIFEX MAXIMVS

TVRRIM DIV IMPERFECTAM FVLMINE TACTAM

REPARAVIT ABSOLVIT AN $\overline{\text{M}}$ $\overline{\text{DCCC}}$ $\overline{\text{LIII}}$

1. PIVS $\overline{\text{IX}}$: Nōnus.

3. REPARAVIT ABSOLVIT : *Note the asyndeton* (*1.2.i, line 4*). — AN(nō) $\overline{\text{M}}$ $\overline{\text{DCCC}}$ $\overline{\text{LIII}}$: Mīllēsimō octingentēsimō quīnquāgēsimō tertiō.

Internal Façade above Gate

Pius the Fourth,[a] Supreme Pontiff,
having done away with Porta Nomentana
built Porta Pia
and traced Via Pia
by leveling the Alta Semita.[b]

a. *Pope Pius IV de' Medici (r. 1559–1565).*

b. *The Alta Semita was the ancient street that ran along the crest of the Quirinal, which by the 1550s had become the neighborhood of choice for the villas of wealthy cardinals. Pius rebuilt the 1600-meter stretch between Piazza del Quirinale and the wall of Aurelian, rechristened it 'Via Pia', and engaged Michelangelo to design Porta Pia as a replacement for Porta Nomentana. Via Pia was Rome's first thoroughfare with a monumental focus at each end: Porta Pia and the Obelisco Quirinale (8.4). On the modern name of the street ('Via XX Settembre'), see 8.7B.ii, note b. The English version cannot rival the lapidary neatness of the Latin, with its paired predicates consisting of Dir.Obj., Abl.Abs., and verb.*

Tower

Internal Façade

Pius the Ninth,[a] Supreme Pontiff, repaired the tower,
long unfinished, which had been struck by lightning,
and completed it in the year 1853.[b]

a. *Pope Pius IX Mastai-Ferretti (r. 1846–1878).*

b. *The incomplete upper portion of Porta Pia can be seen in early illustrations.*

ii.

HIEROMARTYRIBVS MAGNIS ALEXANDRO PONT MAX AGNETI VIRG
QVORVM TROPAEIS VIA NOMENTANA NOBILITATVR
PIVS IX PONTIFEX MAXIMVS ANNO SACRI PRINC XXIII
PORTAM PIAM NOVIS OPERIBVS COMMVNITAM EXORNATAM
5   DEDICAVIT
DECESSORI INVICTO   SOSPITATRICI SVAE
(Name of Magistrate)

1. HIEROMARTYRIBVS : *The* EL *hieromartyr transliterates* EG ἱερομάρτυς *('holy martyr'; cf. 2.10, line 2).* — PONT(ificī) MAX(imō). — AGNETI : *The Latin name is* Agnēs, Agnētis *(see 8.8A, line 2).* — VIRG(inī).
2. TROPAEIS : *A martyr's 'victory monument' is his or her tomb.* — VIA NOMENTANA : *See 8.7A, line 3.*
3. PIVS IX : Nōnus. — PRINC(ipātūs) XXIII : Vīcēsimō tertiō.
4. PORTAM PIAM : *See 8.7A, line 2.*
6. SOSPITATRICI : *The* CL *sōspitātrix is the Fem. counterpart to* sōspitātor *('savior'). The epithet evokes the cult name* Sōspita, *under which the goddess Juno was worshiped at the ancient Latin town of Lanuvium. Although the Romans assimilated the name to the Latin* sōspes *('safe'), its original form was* sispes *or* seispes.

iii.

ORNAT ET FOVET   REGIT ET TVETVR

External Façade, Attic

In the twenty-third year of his sacred office, Pius the Ninth,[a] Supreme Pontiff,
dedicated Porta Pia,
fortified with new works and embellished,[b]
to the great martyrs for the faith Alexander,[c] Supreme Pontiff,
his invincible predecessor, and the virgin Agnes,[d] his preserver,
by whose victory memorials Via Nomentana[e] is ennobled.

(Name of Magistrate)

a. See 8.7B.i, note a. The twenty-third year of Pius' pontificate ran from 16 June 1868 through 15 June 1869.
b. The Neoclassical external façade of Porta Pia was designed by Virginio Vespignani. On 20 September 1870, a year after the improvements of Pius IX had been completed, the bersaglieri ('sharpshooters') of the Italian army entered Rome through a breach in the wall of Aurelian, bringing to an end the temporal sovereignty of the popes.
c. Pope St. Alexander I (r. c. 109–c. 116) is reckoned as the fifth successor of St. Peter. He was early confused with the martyr of the same name whose tomb was uncovered on the Via Nomentana in 1855.
d. According to legend, St. Agnes was a martyr of the third or early fourth century (see 8.8A, note a).
e. The ancient Via Nomentana led from Rome to Nomentum.

Over Statues of Agnes and Alexander

She beautifies and cherishes.   He guides and guards.

8.8A   Damasian Elogium of St. Agnes

[fam]A REFERT SANCTOS DVDVM RETVLISSE PARENTES
[ag]NEN CVM LVGVBRES CANTVS TVBA CONCREPVISSET
[n]VTRICIS GREMIVM SVBITO LIQVISSE PVELLAM
SPONTE TRVCIS CALCASSE MINAS RABIEMQ TYRANNI
5   VRERE CVM FLAMMIS VOLVISSET NOBILE CORPVS
VIRIB INMENSVM PARVIS SVPERASSE TIMOREM
NVDAQVE PROFVSVM CRINEM PER MEMBRA DEDISSE
NE DOMINI TEMPLVM FACIES PERITVRA VIDERET
O VENERANDA MIHI SANCTVM DECVS ALMA PVDORIS
10   VT DAMASI PRECIB FAVEAS PRECOR INCLYTA MARTYR

Ten HEXAMETERS

1. [fam]A : *The characters enclosed in brackets are restored from context. This is the only Damasian inscription that survives virtually intact.*

2. [ag]NEN : *The Latin name* Agnēs *represents the Greek name* Ἀγνή *('Holy'). It appears in variant forms:* Hagnē, -ēs *(transliterating* Ἀγνή, -ῆς*);* Hagna, -ae; Hagnēs, -ētis. *Already by the first century* BC, *the aspirate represented by* H *had so far disappeared from Latin that knowledge of where to pronounce it was restricted to a cultured elite. Cicero reports that he avoided current but unetymological pronunciations such as* pulcher *and* sepulchrum. *In the second century, Aulus Gellius wrote that the pronunciation of medial* H *in such words as* vehemēns *and* incohāre *was archaic. The disappearance of the aspirate in pronunciation led to widespread orthographical uncertainty: words such as* ūmor *and* umerus *were hypercorrected to* hūmor *and* humerus, *while in others, such as* harēna, H *was mistakenly neglected.* — LVGVBRES : *Scans* lūgubres.

4. CALCASSE = calcāvisse. — RABIEMQ(ue). — TYRANNI : *See 6.9, line 3.*

6. VIRIB(us). — SVPERASSE = superāvisse.

7. PROFVSVM : *Scans* prōfusum.

8. PERITVRA : *I.e., 'human'.*

9. ALMA : *Voc. Substantive.*

10. PRECIB(us). — INCLYTA = incluta : *In* LL, *the Adj.* inclutus *is falsely assimilated to its Greek cognate* κλυτός *(the spelling* inclitus *represents a variant of the same error).*

S. Agnese fuori le Mura: Foot of the Entry Stair

The story has it that of old her holy parents related that,
when the trumpet had sounded its mournful tones,[a]
the young Agnes suddenly quitted the lap of her nurse
and of her own accord scorned the threats and rage of the tyrant;[b]
that when he had decreed the burning of her noble body with fire,
with her paltry strength she overcame the mighty terror
and in her nakedness covered her limbs with her hair
lest mortal countenance should behold the temple of the Lord.
Kindly one, deserving of my worship, holy glory of chastity, I pray,
renowned martyr, that you hear with favor the prayers of Damasus.[c]

> Ten HEXAMETERS

a. *I.e., to herald an edict of persecution. The martyrdom of Agnes is assigned to the persecution of Valerian (258–259) or of Diocletian (304). Her cult is attested as early as the mid-fourth century; around that time, Constantina (also called 'Constantia')—daughter of Constantine—built a cemetery BASILICA near the site of her tomb; its ruins still stand to the NW of the present church. Such 'memorial churches' were constructed near the shrines (memoriae) of martyrs; their floors were carpeted with the tomb slabs of the faithful who wished to be buried near their spiritual heroes. The earliest of the type was the Basilica of SS. Peter and Marcellinus on the Via Labicana; others included that of St. Lawrence on the Via Tiburtina (4.7) and, most famously, that of St. Peter on the Via Cornelia (15.4). With the exception of the last, these basilicas were not constructed directly over the martyrs' tombs.*

b. *In the version of her story elaborated in her late 'Acts', Agnes was a girl of twelve or thirteen denounced as a Christian by the son of the PREFECT of Rome, whose advances she had resisted. Stripped and exposed in a brothel built into the vaulting of Domitian's stadium, Agnes succeeded in preserving her modesty by a miraculous growth of hair that covered her nakedness. After she survived an attempt to burn her, her throat was cut.*

c. *Pope St. Damasus I (r. 366–384; see 6.9, note c). The present stone was recovered in 1728 from the floor of the church, where it had been used to repair the pavement (for similar finds, cf. 9.1A, note a, and 15.5A.ii, note b).*

8.8B S. Agnese fuori le Mura: Dedication by Honorius I

AVREA CONCISIS SVRGIT PICTVRA METALLIS

ET COMPLEXA SIMVL CLAVDITVR IPSA DIES

FONTIBVS E NIBEIS CREDAS AVRORA SVBIRE

CORREPTAS NVBES RVRIBVS ARVA RIGANS

5   VEL QVALEM INTER SIDERA LVCEM PROFERET IRIM

PVRPVREVSQVE PAVO IPSE COLORE NITENS

QVI POTVIT NOCTIS VEL LVCIS REDDERE FINEM

MARTYRVM E BVSTIS HINC REPPVLIT ILLE CHAOS

EVRSVM VERSA NVTV QVOD CVNCTIS CERNITVR VNO

10 PRAESVL HONORIVS HAEC VOTA DICATA DEDIT

VESTIBVS ET FACTIS SIGNANTVR ILLIVS ORA

AECETET ASPECTV LVCIDA CORDA GERENS

Six ELEGIAC COUPLETS

1. METALLIS : *See 2.14, line 1.*

3. NIBEIS = niveīs : *On the spelling, see 4.7B.* — CREDAS AVRORA SVB-IRE : *In CL,* AVRORA *would be the Acc. Sub. of the Inf.*

4. RIGANS : *With* AVRORA.

5–6. QVALEM . . . NITENS : *The syntax is so irregular as to render the language scarcely intelligible.* — PAVO : *Scans* păvo.

8. MARTYRVM : *See 2.10, line 2. Scans* martyrum. — HINC : *This word obtrudes an unmetrical syllable on the line.* — CHAOS : *The EL* chaos *transliterates Greek* χάος *('primordial void'); it is sometimes used of the nether world.*

9. EVRSVM : *Sic* (= sūrsum). *Here and in line 12 the authentic reading is restored from transcriptions made in the Middle Ages.* — VERSA : *Appears to reinforce* SVRSVM, *but without clear syntax.* — NVTV : *Scans* nūtu. — CVNCTIS : *The Pass.* CERNITVR *notwithstanding, best understood as Dat. of Reference.*

10. PRAESVL : *See 3.3C, line 13.* — HAEC . . . VOTA : *On the Pl., cf. 3.4D, line 2.*

11. ILLIVS : *The scansion* illĭus *is frequent even in CL verse (the short quantity is an archaism).*

12. AECETET : *Sic* (= lūcet et). *See* EVRSVM *above (line 9).*

Apse

The golden painting rises forth on the cut enamels
and daylight at once embraces it and is itself confined.[a]
You might suppose that Aurora[b] was rising from snowy founts
above the gathered vapors, watering the fields in the countryside,
or such light as the rainbow produces in the heavens
or the bright peacock, gleaming with his own color.
He who had the power to set a limit on night or day
has driven back darkness hence from the martyrs' tombs.
What is evident to all in a single upward glance,
the bishop Honorius has made this dedicated offering.[c]
His likeness is marked by his raiment and his gift:
Wearing a radiant heart, he shines in aspect as well.

SIX ELEGIAC COUPLETS

a. The mosaic represents St. Agnes standing on an ignited pyre and flanked
by Popes St. Symmachus (r. 498–514) and Honorius I (r. 625–638), the latter holding a model of the church (cf. 3.5A, note b). As in other inscriptions
of the type, the text dilates on the splendor of the decoration (cf. 2.14, 3.5A,
6.3, 9.1B, and 13.13A). The source of the motif is the dedication of SS. Cosmas and Damian (2.14), earliest of the genre.

b. I.e., dawn personified. The exuberance of the imagery is seconded by the
obscurity of the syntax.

c. I.e., the church. The cemetery dates to the second century; the complex
where Agnes is buried was added at a later time. Around AD 400, a small
chapel situated above the tomb itself was converted into a basilica ad
corpus (see 4.7B, note b). It is this basilica that Honorius I replaced with
the present structure. Like that of S. Lorenzo fuori le Mura, the Church of
Sant'Agnese was constructed by excavating the hillside that enclosed the
martyr's tomb; here as there, the language of the inscription alludes to the
dispelling of darkness from the holy place.

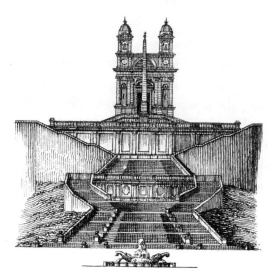

SCALINATA DELLA SANTISSIMA TRINITÀ DEI MONTI

In a fashion all but unique among the architectural productions of its day, the Scalinata della Santissima Trinità dei Monti conveys a quintessentially Roman monumentality in the delicate idiom of the Barocchetto (the so-called 'Roman Rococo'). Though the stair takes its cue from the dramatic and anarchical topography of the site, the grand sweep of the ramps is disciplined and controlled by a complex pattern of interlocking geometrical forms. The monument was expressly intended to serve as a place of leisure. The gentle contours, low parapets, and broad landings invite the spontaneous lounging that the stair has inspired since its inauguration.

IX. From San Marco to Piazza di Spagna

FROM THE TIME OF CAESAR AND POMPEY, the expanse of the central Campus Martius served as a canvas for the grandiose self-representation of dynasts and emperors. As a consequence, the military exercise grounds to which the plain owed its name were displaced farther and farther northwards. This explains why the toponym 'Campus Martius' came to be restricted to the tract beyond the 'Via Recta' (the name 'Via Recta' is nowhere attested in ancient sources) and accounts for the location of the medieval Rione di Campo Marzio which lies much farther north than its name would suggest. Between the sixth and twelfth centuries, the monumental zone of the Campus underwent a profound metamorphosis as the population of Rome gravitated to the lowlands to seek water at the Tiber. This demographic trend was fostered as well by a progressive disequilibrium between Rome's twin centers of ecclesiastical power: with the passage of centuries, the Vatican waxed in prestige as the distant Lateran waned. Owing to its situation, the Campus Martius was a natural beneficiary of that process.

The ancient Campus was traversed from south to north by the Via Flaminia, named for the Gaius Flaminius who ordered its construction in 220 BC to link Rome with Rimini. The modern Via del Corso, which runs from the northern foot of the Capitoline Hill to Porta del Popolo, corresponds to the road's urban tract. In Antiquity, the 450-meter section of the Via Flaminia between the Sepulcher of Bibulus and the Arch of Claudius was largely urbanized; it was called the 'Via Lata' ('Broad Way'). The Arch of Claudius was one of three such monuments with which the Corso was punctuated, and of which nothing today remains *in situ*. The southernmost arch, dating to the reign of Diocletian, was demolished in 1491 for the reconstruction of Santa Maria in Via Lata. The Arch of Claudius stood some 175 meters farther north, near the intersection of the modern Via Caravita. A third structure, located adjacent to Palazzo Fiano, was called 'ARCO DI PORTOGALLO'. It was demolished in 1662. *9.7*

By the middle of the eighth century, the Via Lata had become the neighborhood of choice for the urban aristocracy that emerged from the city's territorialized Byzantine militia to dominate the papacy for three centuries. The family of Pope Paul I (r. 757–767) possessed an estate to the north and east of the street. Paul converted this property into a monastery endowed with an extensive territory; the Church of San Silvestro in Capite is the surviving relic of that once-great foundation. At the southern end of the Via Lata, near San Marco, stood the house of Pope Hadrian I (r. 772 –795), nephew of the influential Byzantine official Theodotus, who had founded the Deaconry of Sant'Angelo in Pescheria. In the tenth century, Alberic, son of the infamous Marozia and cousin of Crescenzio 'de Theodora', likewise had his palace in this quarter. For the greater part of the Middle Ages, however, the Via Flaminia lay at the farthest margins of the *abitato*; to its east, all was wilderness except a small enclave around Trevi and Santi Dodici Apostoli, sustained by the diminished waters of the Aqua Virgo.

With the ecclesiastical reforms of the eleventh century, the Roman nobility lost its monopoly of the papacy. Towers and fortified dwellings began to spring up in the robust ruins of ancient buildings. In the course of time, the Colonna family built fortresses at the Mausoleum of Augustus and Montecitorio, while the Orsini—their great rivals—possessed the Theater of Pompey (called the *Arpacata*) and Monte Giordano, as well as a tower on the banks of the Tiber. By the fourteenth century, the partition of the Campus Martius between these two great clans had assumed definite outlines: the Colonna dominated the northeast from the Tiber to the Quirinal, with strongholds at the Mausoleum of Augustus, Montecitorio, and Santi Dodici Apostoli; the Orsini controlled the southwest from the Borgo to the Capitol, with strongholds at Castel Sant'Angelo, Monte Giordano, and the Theater of Pompey. Around the fortified compounds of the barons, the masses—now serving as foot soldiers in the quarrels of the aristocracy, now rebelling against their cruelty and caprice—were crowded into the dark and narrow streets.

From about 1350, the bulk of Rome's urban development took place in the zone under Colonna influence, which included the entire urban tract of the Via Flaminia. In the mid-fifteenth century, Cardinal Pietro Barbo, the future Pope Paul II (r. 1464–1471), transformed the muddy and irregular area at the street's southern terminus into a piazza—Piazza Venezia; at its western margin he constructed a large palace—Palazzo di Venezia. Before it was eliminated in the late nineteenth and early twentieth centuries, Piazza Venezia formed one of most spectacular urban assemblages in papal Rome. To the west bulked the imposing mass of Palazzo di Venezia; on the opposite side of the piazza rose Palazzo Bolognetti-Torlonia. The southern end was delimited by Palazzetto Venezia, behind which towered the ancient convent of Santa Maria in Aracoeli and the Belvedere of Paul III on the Capitol. The decision in 1882 to erect the monument to Victor Emanuel II as a backdrop to Via del Corso spelled doom for this uniquely Roman ensemble: Palazzo di Venezia alone survives—and in a void.

By comparison with the city's southeastern hills, the Campus Martius is poor in early titular churches. Apart from San Lorenzo in Damaso and San Lorenzo in Lucina, the ancient churches of the Campus are all concentrated at its southeastern margins. The most venerable is that of San Marco, the first place of public Christian worship to be located in Rome's monumental center. The earliest basilica on the site was built over a structure of the fourth century; destroyed in the upheavals of the fifth or sixth century, it was reconstructed at more than a meter above the level of its predecessor. In the ninth century, Pope GREGORY IV (r. 827–844), titular cardinal of San Marco when elected to the papacy, replaced this second basilica with the structure that would be incorporated six hundred years later into the fabric of Palazzo di Venezia. Despite extensive alterations of the Renaissance and Baroque periods, the apse mosaic and dedicatory inscription of Gregory's building survive intact. One of the church's most remarkable monuments is the battered tombstone of VANNOZZA CATTANEI, who bore four children to the

9.1B

9.1A

Spanish Cardinal Rodrigo Borgia in the years before his election as Pope Alexander VI (r. 1492–1503).

Like the ancient churches of the Forum Boarium, Santa Maria in Via Lata is an early deaconry. The original facility was improvised in a first-century portico that had been adapted as a granary. The legendary history of the church is genuinely august. While under house arrest at this site, St. Paul is said to have penned his epistles to the churches at Ephesus, Colossae, and Philippi, and that to Philemon, master of the runaway slave Onesimus (along with St. Luke, Onesimus was the supposed companion of St. Paul during his sojourn at the present site). Paul is further reported to have received St. Peter and St. John as visitors in the course of his detention and to have baptized the centurion Martialis, his jailer. Members of this *dramatis personae* receive mention in an inscription of

9.3   Pope ALEXANDER VII (r. 1655–1667).

Originally dedicated to Saints Philip and James, the great basilica of Santi Dodici Apostoli was in origin neither a *titulus* nor a deaconry; it functioned instead as a meeting hall for the congregations of the several *tituli* near by. As a pendant to San Marco, it served as well to impose a monumental Christian presence at the head of the Via Lata. The basilica that stood on the site for twelve centuries was constructed under Popes Pelagius I (r. 556–561) and John III (r. 561–573). Particularly in view of its dedication to Philip and James—saints with strong eastern ties—the church may well have been founded to celebrate the recovery of Rome from the Goths by the Byzantine general Narses in AD 552. In the Middle Ages, Santi Dodici Apostoli became a dependency of the neighboring Colonna stronghold. When it was rebuilt in the eighteenth century, the basilica was absorbed into the structure of that family's palace. Notable among the monuments of the cloister is the spurious tomb

9.2B   of MICHELANGELO.

9.4   The much smaller Church of SANTA MARIA IN TRIVIO likewise recalls the period of the Gothic Wars. The original foundation on the site was a *xenodochium* ('guesthouse') sponsored by Belisarius, who had been sent by the eastern emperor Justinian to recover Italy from the Ostrogoths. The *xenodochia* were devised to meet the needs of pilgrims, whose sojourns at times lasted for weeks; that of Belisarius was unusual in not being closer to the Vatican. Its foundation was an act of penance. In 537 Belisarius had forced Pope St. Silverius (r. 536–537) to abdicate in favor of the deacon Vigilius, a tool of Justinian's wife Theodora: the empress desired the assistance of Rome in rehabilitating the Patriarch of Constantinople, a Monophysite who had been deposed by Silverius' predecessor. Belisarius is said to have founded the *xenodochium* in expiation of his role in this affair. The dedicatory inscription that commemorates its foundation pertains to a reconstruction carried out at some time between the eleventh and thirteenth centuries.

The name of the Church of Santa Maria in Trivio enshrines a toponym most familiar in its Italian form: 'Trevi'. The celebrated FON- 9.5 TANA DI TREVI forms the medieval and modern terminus of the Aqua Virgo, introduced in 19 BC by Marcus Agrippa to supply his baths near the Pantheon. Emerging from the slopes of the Pincio, the aqueduct crossed the eastern Campus on a lofty stone arcade; the demolition of the arcade by Caligula and its reconstruction under CLAUDIUS I are 9.6 commemorated in an inscription from AD 45. Though the demolition has been credited to the emperor's notorious madness, it is likely that it was implemented preparatory to a reconstruction. Like the Aqua Claudia, the reconstructed Virgo was completed and dedicated in the name of Caligula's successor.

Except during the siege of Vitiges (AD 537), when Belisarius obstructed the channel to prevent the Goths from using it as a means of entering the city, the Aqua Virgo has functioned uninterruptedly. By the end of the Gothic Wars, nevertheless, the arcades had fallen so far into disrepair that water was carried no farther than Trevi. Indeed, only the fact that the Aqua Virgo ran underground for much of its course ensured that it continued in service after the failure of its more exposed fellows on the eastern highlands.

With the considerable growth of Rome's population in the second quarter of the sixteenth century, the Virgo proved insufficient to meet demand inasmuch as the water was now collected from sources that were less copious than the original had been. Although a reconstruction was proposed under Pope Paul III (r. 1534–1549), several decades elapsed before the project was brought to completion. Not the least cause of the delay was a fierce rivalry among the architects contending for this important commission, each of whom exerted himself to discredit the proposals of his competitors. Only in 1570 was the Aqua Virgo finally reactivated under the name 'Acqua di Salone'. There followed the construction of a network of subterranean ducts that permitted the water to be distributed over the entire northwestern quarter of the city.

The zone between Trevi and the Pincio was the last portion of the Campus Martius to be urbanized. King Charles VIII of France, who occupied the city in January of 1495, took the opportunity of acquiring 9.10 land on the Pincio for the royal church and convent of SANTISSIMA TRINITÀ DEI MONTI and for a villa—the future Villa Medici. The presence of the French stimulated the interest of their perennial rivals the Spanish: Piazza di Spagna, at the foot of the Pincio, was long known as 'Piazza di Francia e Spagna'.

The steep slope intervening between piazza and church presented an inconvenience obviated only in part by the opening of Via Gregoriana in the 1580s; a monumental stair was long felt to be a desideratum and 9.9 many models were proposed. Finally dedicated in 1725, the SCALINATA DELLA SANTISSIMA TRINITÀ DEI MONTI (known in English as the 'Spanish Steps') was madly popular from the beginning; until comparatively recent times, the monument was frequented particularly by flower vendors and artists' models. Piazza di Spagna is home to one of the last 9.8 monuments of papal Rome: the COLONNA DELL'IMMACOLATA, dedicated in 1854 to celebrate the definition of the dogma of the Immaculate Conception of the Virgin Mary.

9.11   The OBELISCO SALLUSTIANO, which stands before Trinità dei

Monti, originated in the gardens of Gaius Sallustius Crispus (the historian Sallust). The gardens eventually passed to Tiberius, thereby becoming part of the imperial demesne. The obelisk was probably installed at the center of a hippodrome by the emperor Aurelian in the late third century. Like its fellows, it was almost certainly toppled during the occupation of Totila (AD 547). The gardens, having belonged to the Orsini, were acquired in 1621 by Cardinal Ludovico Ludovisi; in the following century, Ippolita Ludovisi gave the obelisk to Pope Clement XII (r. 1730–1740), who had it transported to the Lateran to be set up before the basilica. After Clement's death, the project was abandoned and the obelisk lay neglected for nearly forty years. By setting it up at Trinità dei Monti in 1789, Pope Pius VI (r. 1775–1799) created a spectacular vista at the intersection of Via dei Quattro Fontane and Via Venti Settembre, where one has a simultaneous view of Porta Pia and of three obelisks: the Sallustiano, the Esquilino, and the Quirinale.

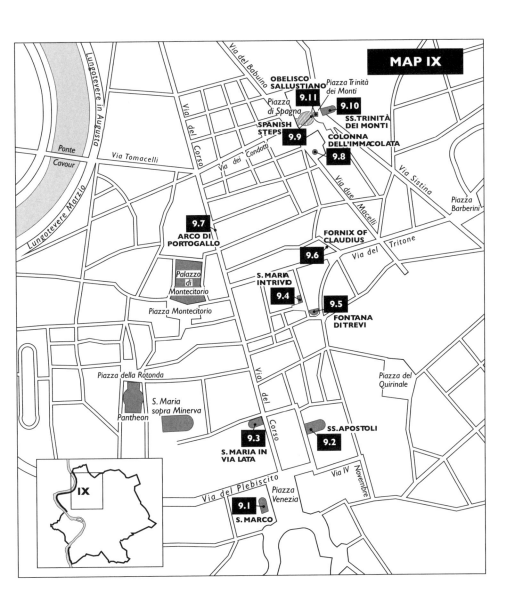

9.1A   Epitaph of Vannozza Cattanei

D O M

VANNOTIAE CATHANEAE CAESARE VALENTIAE

IOANNE GANDIA[e] IAFREDO SCYLLATII ET

LVCRETIA FERRARIAE DVCIBVS FILIIS NOBILI

5   PROBITATE INSI[g]NI RELLIGIONE EXIMIA

PARI ET AETATE ET PRVDENTIA OPTIME

DE XENODOCHI[o] LATERANEN MERITAE

HYERONIMVS PIC[u]S FIDEICŌMISS PROCVR̄

[ex tes]TO POS

10   VIX ANN LXXVI MEN IIII D[i]ES XIII

OBIIT ANNO [m] D XVIII X[x]VI NO

1. D(eō) O(ptimō) M(aximō).

2. CATHANEAE : *Represents the Ital. name* Cattanei. *Note the inauthentic* H. *Aspirated consonants* (p^h, t^h, k^h) *are a feature of Greek; already in Antiquity, the Latin poets had employed them in fanciful Hellenizing coinages (e.g.,* Thybris *as if from* Θύβρις; *cf. 11.5D, line 2). In LL, inauthentic* H *found its way into many Latin words (cf. 8.8A, line 2); in* RL *it is employed once more as a Hellenizing affectation.* — CAESARE . . . DVCIBVS : *Abl.Abs.;* DVCIBVS *is in App. to each of the names.*

3. GANDIA[e] : *The characters enclosed in brackets are restored from context.* — SCYLLATII : *The present transliteration reflects Greek* Σκυλλήτιον *more faithfully than the conventional* CL Scylacēum.

4. FERRARIAE : *See 1.7A, line 9.* — FILIIS : *In App. to* CAESARE . . . DVCIBVS (*lines 2–4*).

5. RELLIGIONE = rēligiōne : *The spelling with doubled* L *is frequent after the Augustan period, when the initial syllable commonly scanned* rē-.

7. XENODOCHI[o] : *The* LL xenodochīum *transliterates Greek* ξενοδοχεῖον ('*hospice*'). — LATERANEN(sī) : *See 7.4A, line 1.*

8. HYERONIMVS = Hierōnymus : *On the name, see 10.7, line 1. In* LL, I *and* Y *are frequently confused (see 3.1, line 1).* — FIDEICOM(m)ISS(ī) : *The* CL fideīcommissum *is 'will'.* — PROCVR(ātor).

9. tes]T(āment)O. — POS(uit).

10. VIX(it) ANN(ōs) LXXVI : Septuāgintā sex. — MEN(sēs) IIII : Quattuor. — D[i]ES XIII : Tredecim.

11. [m] D XVIII : Mīllēsimō quīngentēsimō duodēvīcēsimō. — X[x]VI : Vīcēsimō sextō. — NO(vembris) : *See 1.6G, line 11.*

S. Marco: Portico, R Wall

To God, Best and Greatest.
To Vannozza Cattanei,[a] noble in her children—
the dukes Cesare of Valentinois,[b] Giovanni of Gandía,[c]
Goffredo of Squillace,[d] and the duchess Lucrezia of Ferrara[e]—
a woman of outstanding uprightness, exceptional piety,
of a discretion equal to her age,
well deserving of the Lateran Hospice.[f]
Girolamo Pico, executor, placed this
in accordance with her will.
She lived seventy-six years, four months, and thirteen days.
She died in the year 1518, on 26 November.

a. *Mistress of the Spanish cardinal Rodrigo de Borja y Borja—elected pope as Alexander VI in 1492—Vannozza Cattanei (c. 1442–1518) bore four children out of wedlock. She was buried in S. Maria del Popolo beside her eldest son Giovanni Borgia (see note c below; the Spanish name 'Borja' appears in Ital. as 'Borgia'). After the Borgia monuments were dismantled under Alexander VII in the seventeenth century, the present stone found its way into the pavement of S. Marco. Here it was rediscovered—face down—during excavations of 1947–1949.*

b. *While serving as papal legate to France, Cesare Borgia (César Borja, 1475–1507) was created duke of Valentinois by Louis XII. Cesare was much admired by Nicolò Machiavelli, for whom he exemplified the ideal prince—cruel, intelligent, and ruthlessly opportunistic.*

c. *Named duke of Gandía in 1488, Giovanni Borgia (Juan Borja, 1474–1497) died under obscure circumstances, probably at the hands of his brother Cesare.*

d. *Through his marriage with Sancia of Aragón, Goffredo Borgia (Jofré Borja, c. 1481–c. 1516) became prince of Squillace.*

e. *At the age of thirteen, Lucrezia Borgia (Lucrecia Borja, 1480–1519) entered the first of three marriages arranged for political motives by her father. After the annulment of the first—and the murder, by Cesare, of both her lover, Pedro Calderón, and of her second husband—she was married to Alfonso d'Este, duke of Ferrara.*

f. *The hospices (xenodochia) were guesthouses established by the papacy to provide lodging for foreigners and pilgrims.*

9.1B   S. Marco: Dedication by Gregory IV

1   VASTA THOLI PRIMO SISTVNT FVNDAMINE FVLCHRA ⌐

   QVAE SALOMONIACO FVLGENT SVB SIDERE RITV ⌐

   HAEC TIBI PROQVE TVO PERFECIT PRAESVL HONORE

2   GREGORIVS MARCE EXIMIO CVI NOMINE QVARTVS ⌐

   TV QVOQVE POSCE DEVM VIVENDI TEMPORA LONGA ⌐

   DONET ET AD CAELI POST FVNVS SYDERA DVCAT

   Six HEXAMETERS

   1. SISTVNT : *Intrans.* — FVNDAMINE : *In* EL, fundāmen *can refer to the spiritual foundations of the Church.* — FVLCHRA = fulcra : *In* LL, *fulcrum is used of any support, Lit. or Fig. On the spelling, see 8.8A, line 2.* — SALOMONIACO : *The* EL *Adj.* Salomōniacus *corresponds to the biblical name* Salomōn (Σαλωμών *or* Σολομών). — PRAESVL : *See 3.3C, line 13.*
   2. GREGORIVS . . . QVARTVS : *I.e., Gregory IV. The name* Grēgorius *is formed from* γρηγορώς, *Pf.Part.Act. of* ἐγείρω ('wake') *and hence signifies 'wakeful', 'vigilant'.* — POSCE . . . DONET : *In* CL *prose, the Inf. is usual with* poscere. *In verse of the Augustan period, it is construed with* nē + *Subj.* — SYDERA = sīdera : *On the spelling, see 3.1, line 1.*

9.2A   SS. Dodici Apostoli: Dedication of Roman Eagle

   TOT RVINIS SERVATAM IVL CAR SIXTI IIII PONT ⌐

   NEPOS HIC STATVIT

   RVINIS : *The* CL ruīna *is 'downfall' or 'collapse' but is used by extension of destruction in general and, by a further extension, of the resulting debris. Such 'concretizing' of verbal and abstract nouns is pervasive in Latin. The abstract noun* cīvitās, *properly 'citizenship', assumes the progressively concrete senses of 'citizenry', 'state', and 'city' (the last being the sense continued in Fr.* cité, *Sp.* ciudad *and Ital.* città). *Similarly* frūctus (*properly 'enjoyment'*), legiō ('levy'), vestis ('act of dressing'), *and countless others.* — SERVATAM : *The fem. gender is due to an implicit noun* aquilam. — IVL(iānus). — CAR(dinālis). — SIXTI IIII : Quārtī. — PONT(ificis).

Apse

The mighty footings of the vault rise upon their prime foundation
and gleam in Solomonic wise beneath the heavens.[a]
It is for thee, Mark,[b] and in thy honor that the bishop Gregory[c]—
fourth of that distinguished name—brought this to completion.
Do thou in turn beseech God that he may grant him a long life
and conduct him after his death to the stars of heaven.

> Six HEXAMETERS

a. In medieval Christian thought, the Temple of Solomon (1 Kgs 6:1 – 7:51)
   represented the typological exemplar of ecclesiastical architecture.
b. The mosaic depicts Christ flanked by saints including Pope St. Mark
   (r. 336), eponymous founder of the church. Pope Gregory IV appears with
   the square nimbus of the living (see note c below, and cf. 3.5A, note b).
c. Pope Gregory IV (r. 827–844). Titular CARDINAL of S. Marco when
   elected (see TITULAR CHURCH), Gregory had the church entirely rebuilt.
   The pavement of the present church, though lying at more than 2.5 m above
   the level of the fourth-century basilica, nevertheless lies 1.5 m below the
   present street level—which has, we can therefore surmise, risen by four
   meters since late Antiquity.

Portico, R End

The Cardinal Giuliano,[a] nephew of Pope Sixtus the Fourth,[b]
set this here, preserved from so many calamities.[c]

a. Giuliano della Rovere (1443–1513), the future Pope Julius II, served 1474–
   1503 as cardinal priest in the title of SS. Dodici Apostoli (see TITULAR
   CHURCH).
b. Pope Sixtus IV della Rovere (r. 1471–1484).
c. The inscription accompanies an ancient relief depicting an eagle surrounded by a garland, probably taken from the Forum of Trajan or the Baths
   of Constantine to adorn the original basilica of the sixth century. In the
   restoration carried out by della Rovere, the eagle was mounted above the
   main portal of the basilica.

9.2B Pretended Epitaph of Michelangelo

MICHEL ANGELVS

BONARROTIVS

SCVLPTOR PICTOR ARCHITECTVS

MAXIMA ARTIFICVM FREQVENTIA

5   IN HAC BASILICA SS XII APOST F M C

XI KAL MART A MDLXIV ELATVS EST

CLAM INDE FLORENTIAM TRANSLATVS

ET IN TEMPLO S CRVCIS EORVMD F

V ID MART EIVSD A CONDITVS

10   TANTO NOMINI

NVLLVM PAR ELOGIVM

2. BONARROTIVS : *On the Latinization, cf. 12.3B, line 8.*

4. MAXIMA . . . FREQVENTIA : *Abl. of Attendant Circumstance.*

5. SS = sānctōrum : *On the abbreviation, see 1.61, line 7.* — XII : Duodecim. — APOST(olōrum) : *See 1.61, line 7.* — F(rātrum) M(inōrum)
C(onventuālium) : *Members of the Order of St. Francis are officially*
Frātrēs Minōrēs (*'Lesser Brothers'*); *the* EL conventuālis *is 'conventual'*
(*i.e., belonging to a convent or monastery*).

6. XI : Ūndecimō. — KAL(endās) MART(iī) : *See 1.6G, line 11.* — A(nnō)
MDLXIV : Mīllēsimō quīngentēsimō sexāgēsimō quārtō. — ELATVS
EST : *The* CL efferre *frequently has the sense 'bear to the grave', 'bury'.*

7. FLORENTIAM : *Acc. of Place to Which.*

8. TEMPLO S(ānctae) CRVCIS : *I.e. the Franciscan Church of S. Croce in*
Florence. On the Classicizing templum (*vs.* ecclēsia), *cf. 1.8G, line 5.* —
EORVMD(em) : *Sic* (= eōrundem). *In* CL *pronunciation, the bilabial*
nasal /m/ *was assimilated as an alveolar nasal* /n/ *to a following alveolar*
plosive /d/. *Though the assimilated pronunciation of such combinations as*
eundem (< eumdem) *and* quendam (*i.e.,* quem + dam) *is convention-*
ally written ND *only within words, it is probable that even in* CL *it was*
so pronounced in virtual compounds as well (*e.g., that the phrase* tam
dūrum *was pronounced as a single word* /tan'du:rum/). — F(rātrum).

9. V : Quīntō. — ID(ūs) MART(iī) : *See line 6 above.* — EIVSD(em)
A(nnī).

SS. Dodici Apostoli: Cloister, S Wall

Michelangelo
Buonarroti,[a]
Sculptor, Painter, Architect,
was buried[b] on 20 February[c] in the year 1564 in this Basilica
of the Twelve Holy Apostles of the Friars Minor Conventual[d]
with a very numerous assembly of artists,
thence transported in secret to Florence
and on 11 March[e] of the same year
buried in the Church of Santa Croce of the same Friars.
No praise is equal
to so great a name.

a. *Michelangelo Buonarroti (1475–1564) died in Rome.*

b. *Although funeral services were held for him here, Michelangelo was never laid to rest at SS. Dodici Apostoli. The identification of the present tomb with that of Michelangelo was first proposed by the French painter Jean-Baptiste Wicar (1762–1834), who based his notion on a fancied resemblance between the features of the unknown subject of the present funerary portrait (possibly the philosopher Ferdinando Eustachi) and those of the great Florentine.*

c. *Lit., 'on the eleventh day before the Kalends of March'. Under the Julian calendar, the additional day required for leap year was made up by intercalating a second instance of the sixth day (inclusive) before the Kalends of March: this day was designated* bis vi Kalendas Martias *('twice sixth before the Kalends of March'), whence the term* annus bissextilis *('bissextile year'). As 1564 was a bissextile year, the eleventh day before the Kalends of March fell on the twentieth—rather than the nineteenth—of February.*

d. *Early in its history, the Franciscan order suffered a rift between those (the 'Spiritual' Franciscans) who insisted on strict adherence to the Rule of St. Francis—which obliges the friars to live by the labor of their hands and by begging—and those (the 'Conventuals') who advocated the adaptation of the Rule to circumstances and countenanced the accumulation of property. Though settled in favor of the latter, the dispute was renewed in 1363 with the rise of the 'Observant' Franciscans, who in 1517 were formally separated from the Conventuals and recognized as the true Order of St. Francis.*

e. *Lit., 'on the fifth day before the Ides of March'.*

9.3 S. Maria in Via Lata: Dedication by Alexander VII

ALEXANDRO VII PONT MAXIMO

LOCVS ANTIQVA VENERATIONE SACER ET NOBILIS

IN QVO S PAVLVM APOSTOLVM DIV MORATVM

NON SEMEL VNA CVM IPSO ECCLESIAE CAPITE S PETRO

5   DE REBVS CHRISTIANAE FIDEI DELIBERASSE

VBI S LVCAM EVANGELISTAM ET SCRIPSISSE

ET DEIPARAE VIRGINIS IMAGINES DEPINXISSE

IAM INDE A PRIMIS TEMPORIBVS TRADITVM

CONGESTV TERRAE OLIM DEPRESSVS ATQ INACCESSVS

10   FACILI SCALARVM DESCENSV

IMMISSOQVE FENESTRIS LVMINE

PERVIVS FACTVS

PERPVRGATVS EXORNATVSQVE

PIO FIDELIVM CVLTVI RESTITVTVS EST

15   ANNO SAL M DC LXI

1. ALEXANDRO VII : Septimō. — PONT(ifice) MAXIMO : *On the construction, see 5.8B, line 1.*

3. S(ānctum). — APOSTOLVM : *See 1.61, line 7.*

4. ECCLESIAE : *See 1.7A, line 6.* — s(ānctō).

5. CHRISTIANAE : *See 1.7A, line 8.* — DELIBERASSE − dēlīberāvisse.

6. s(ānctum) LVCAM : *On the name, see 8.6, line 9.* — EVANGELISTAM : *See 7.4C.*

7. DEIPARAE : *The EL Subst.* deipara *(Fem. only) represents* EG Θεοτόκος *('Mother of God'; cf. 4.2D, line 3). The position of the accent in the Greek word indicates that the verbal element of the compound has an active sense ('She who bore God'). In compound nouns featuring a verbal root, Greek uses accent to make a systematic differentiation between those in which the verbal element has active force (e.g.,* πατροκτόνος, *'parricide') and those in which it has passive force (*πατρόκτονος, *'slain by one's father').*

9. ATQ(ue).

15. SAL(ūtis) M DC LXI : Mīllēsimō sescentēsimō sexāgēsimō prīmō.

Portico, R Wall

During the Supreme Pontificate of Alexander the Seventh,[a] this place—
sacred with ancient reverence and renowned,[b]
in which from the earliest times tradition has held
that Saint Paul the Apostle long tarried,[c] on more
than one occasion consulted about matters of the Christian faith
with Saint Peter himself, the Church's head,
where Saint Luke the Evangelist both wrote
and painted icons of the Virgin, Mother of God,[d]—
formerly sunk in an accumulation of earth and inaccessible,
once thoroughly cleaned and embellished,
was restored to the godly worship of the faithful,
rendered practicable
by stairs to furnish a convenient way down[e]
and with light let in through windows,
in the year of Salvation 1661.

a. *Pope Alexander VII Chigi (r. 1655–1667).*

b. *Although it does not date to apostolic times, the Church of S. Maria in Via Lata is very ancient indeed. It was probably founded in the seventh century as a* DEACONRY. *For the construction of the present building in 1491, the Arcus Novus of Diocletian—one of three such monuments that stood on the Via Lata—was demolished (cf. 9.7, note c).*

c. *According to a legend probably no older than the eleventh century, St. Paul resided in a building on the present site for two years, either in prison or under house arrest. As the structure in which the deaconry was improvised was a monumental hall of Claudian date, it is most unlikely that it ever served as a place of detention.*

d. *St. Luke is credited with painting the icon venerated at S. Maria Maggiore as the Salus Populi Romani (see 4.2D, note b).*

e. *Lit., 'by an easy descent [consisting] of stairs'. In the course of the construction of the present façade, the subterranean 'oratorio' was equipped with a double flight of stairs.*

9.4 S. Maria in Trivio: Commemoration of Belisarius

1 HANC VIR PATRICIVS VILISARIVS VRBIS AMICVS OB ⌐
   CVLPE VENIĀ CONDIDIT ECCLE

2 SIAM HANC HIC CIRCO PEDEM SACRAM QVI PONIS IN ⌐
   EDEM VT MISERETVR EVM

3 SEPE PRECARE D̄M IANVA HEC EST TEMPLI D̄N̄O ⌐
   DEFENSA POTENTI

> *Two Leonine* ELEGIAC COUPLETS *followed by one Leonine* HEXAMETER

1. VILISARIVS = Belisārius (*Greek* Βελισάριος) : *On the spelling in* V, *see 4.7B.* — CVLPE = culpae. — VENIA(m). — ECCLE|SIAM : *See 1.7A, line 6.*

2. CIRCO . . . IN : *The Leonine hexameter permits instances of tmesis the boldness of which recalls Ennius'* saxo cere comminuit brum *('with a stone, he dashed his brains'). Here the adverb* incircum, *governing the Acc., is split and its components reversed* (circo = circum). — EDEM = aedem : *See 1.8B, line 10. On the spelling, see 1.8B, line 5.*

3. SEPE = saepe. — PRECARE : *On the form, see 1.6D, line 6.* — D(eu)M. — HEC = haec : *Scans* hĕc. — EST . . . DEFENSA : *On the tense, see 1.6G, line 7.* — D(omi)NO : *Dat. of Agent.*

9.5A Fontana di Trevi: Dedication by Clement XII

CLEMENS XII PONT MAX

AQVAM VIRGINEM

COPIA ET SALVBRITATE COMMENDATAM

CVLTV MAGNIFICO ORNAVIT

5   ANNO DOMINI MDCCXXXV PONTIF VI

1. CLEMENS XII : Duodecimus. — PONT(ifex) MAX(imus).

2. AQVAM VIRGINEM : *Used thus,* aqua *is 'aqueduct'. Here* VIRGINEM *is App. to* AQVAM (*cf. 4.5.i, line 2*).

5. MDCCXXXV : Mīllēsimō septingentēsimō trīcēsimō quīntō. — PONTIF(icātūs) VI : Sextō.

9.5B Fontana di Trevi: Dedication by Benedict XIV

PERFECIT BENEDICTVS XIV PON MAX

BENEDICTVS XIV : Quārtus decimus. — PON(tifex) MAX(imus).

R Exterior Wall

The Patrician Belisarius,[a] friend of the City,
founded this church to obtain forgiveness of his guilt.[b]
You who set foot here about this sacred shrine,
oft beseech God that he may have mercy on him.
This is the door of the church, defended by the mighty Lord.

Two Leonine ELEGIAC COUPLETS *followed by one Leonine* HEXAMETER

a. *In 535 Belisarius was charged by the E emperor Justinian with the task of recovering Italy from the Ostrogoths; by 540 he had captured Naples, Rome, and Ravenna, the Ostrogothic capital (cf. 2.1, note c).*

b. *During the Gothic siege of Rome (537), Belisarius engineered the deposition of Pope St. Silverius, because of the latter's refusal to abdicate in favor of the deacon Vigilius, protégé of the Monophysite empress Theodora. In expiation of his role in this affair, it is said, Belisarius founded two* xenodochia *(see 9.1A, note f). The inscription, which dates to between the eleventh and thirteenth centuries, was presumably mounted over the portal of the church that replaced the hospice.*

Attic

Clement the Twelfth,[a] Supreme Pontiff,
embellished with splendid refinement
the Aqua Virgo,[b]
esteemed for its abundance and wholesomeness,
in the year of the Lord 1735, sixth of his office.

a. *Pope Clement XII Corsini (r. 1730–1740). The sixth year of his pontificate ran from 12 July 1735 through 11 July 1736.*

b. *The Aqua Virgo was so called from the tale that the soldiers who had been dispatched to seek a source of water for the aqueduct were assisted in their search by a maiden who indicated its head.*

Upper Frieze

Benedict the Fourteenth,[a] Supreme Pontiff, brought it to completion.

a. *Pope Benedict XIV Lambertini (r. 1740–1758).*

9.5C Fontana di Trevi: Dedication by Clement XIII

POSITIS SIGNIS ET ANAGLYPHIS TABVLIS IVSSV ⌐

CLEMENTIS XIII PONT MAX OPVS CVM OMNI CVLTV ⌐

ABSOLVTVM A DOM MDCCLXII

ANAGLYPHIS : *The* CL anaglyphus *transliterates Greek* ἀνάγλυφος, *'wrought in bas-relief'.* — CLEMENTIS XIII : Tertiī decimī. — PONT(ificis) MAX(imī). — A(nnō) DOM(inī) MDCCLXII : Mīllēsimō septingentēsimō sexāgēsimō secundō.

9.5D Commemoration of Repairs by Benedict XIV

BENEDICTVS XIV P O M

[r]IVOS AQVÆ VIRGINIS COMPLVRIBVS LOCIS MANANTES

QVIQVE IN VSV ESSE DESIERANT

IN VRBEM REDVXIT

5   AQVÆDVCTVS VETVSTATE COLLAPSOS

RESTAVRAVIT

FISTVLAS TVBVLOS CASTELLA LACVS

PVRGATO FONTE RESTITVTA FORMA

INGENTI LIBERALITATE

10   IN AMPLIOREM FORMAM REDEGIT

AN SAL MDCCXLIV PONT IV

1. BENEDICTVS XIV : Quārtus decimus. — P(ontifex) O(ptimus) M(aximus).

2. AQVÆ VIRGINIS : *See 9.5A, line 2.*

3–4. IN VSV ESSE DESIERANT ... REDVXIT : *The phrasing is adapted from the dedication of Titus on the Porta Tiburtina (see 4.6B). The asyndeton of* REDVXIT ... RESTAVRAVIT ... REDEGIT *lends a note of pomp (cf. 1.2.i, line 4).*

5. AQVÆDVCTVS = aquae ductūs.

7. TVBVLOS : *The* CL tubulus *is 'small pipe'.* — CASTELLA : *'Cisterns' (see 1.4, line 4).*

8. FORMA: *See 4.6C, line 4.*

11. AN(nō) SAL(ūtis) MDCCXLIV : Mīllēsimō septingentēsimō quadrāgēsimō quārtō. — PONT(ificātūs) IV : Quārtō.

Lower Frieze

> *With the mounting of the statues and relief panels [a] by order of Clement the Thirteenth,[b] Supreme Pontiff, the work was finished with every refinement in the year of the Lord 1762.*

a. *The panels depict the maiden indicating the source of the Aqua Virgo to the soldiers (see 9.5A, note b) and Agrippa approving the design of the aqueduct.*

b. *Pope Clement XIII Rezzonico (r. 1758–1769).*

Via della Stamperia 1: Above Door

> *Benedict the Fourteenth,[a] Supreme and most excellent Pontiff, reintroduced into the City the channels of the Aqua Virgo,[b] which were leaking in many places and which had fallen into disuse, restored the aqueducts, ruined with age, and, its source dredged and its conduit restored, with immense generosity reduced the pipes, ducts, cisterns, and basins to a more dignified aspect in the year of Salvation 1744, fourth of his office.*

a. *Pope Benedict XIV Lambertini (r. 1740–1758). The fourth year of his pontificate ran from 17 August 1743 through 16 August 1744.*

b. *The Aqua Virgo was constructed in 19 BC to supply the baths of Agrippa on the Campus Martius, located just to the S of his Pantheon (see 11.3A). Fed from sources at the eighth milestone of the Via Collatina, the aqueduct ran in a subterranean channel for most of its twenty-kilometer course, emerging from the slopes of the Pincio to traverse the NE Campus on an arcade (cf. 9.6, note b). Because it ran in large part below ground, the Virgo continued in service long after more exposed aqueducts had failed. The modern Acqua Vergine dates to 1453, when the ancient aqueduct was replaced at the order of Pope Nicholas V. After further works under Popes Pius IV and St. Pius V, it entered continuous service in 1570 under the name 'Acqua di Salone' (the new sources were at Salone).*

9.6 Fornix of Aqua Claudia: Dedication by Claudius

TI CLAVDIVS DRVSI F CAESAR AVGVSTVS GERMANICVS

PONTIFEX MAXIM TRIB POTEST V̄ IMP X̄Ī P P COS DESIGN ĪĪĪĪ

ARCVS DVCTVS AQVAE VIRGINIS DISTVRBATOS PER C CAESAREM

A FVNDAMENTIS NOVOS FECIT AC RESTIVIT

1. TI(berius). — F(īlius). — CAESAR : *In Claudian inscriptions, the spelling* CAISAR *is also found (cf. 1.6B, line 1). The best view of the inscription is to be had in the neighboring Caffè Accademia, from the window at the landing of the stair leading to the* WC.

2. MAXIM(us). — TRIB(ūniciā) POTEST(āte) V̄ : Quīntum. — IMP(erātor) X̄Ī : Ūndecimum. — P(ater) P(atriae) CO(n)S(ul) DESIGN(ātus) ĪĪĪĪ : Quārtum.

3. ARCVS : *Acc.Pl.* — DVCTVS : *Gen.Sg.* — AQVAE VIRGINIS : *See 9.5A, line 2.* — C(āium) : *On the abbreviation* C *for Gāius, see 1.1, line 1.*

4. NOVOS : *Predicate Acc. with* ARCVS *(line 3).*

9.7 Commemoration of Alexander VII's Works on the Corso

ALEXANDER VII PONTIF MAX

VIAM LATAM FERIATAE VRBIS HIPPODROMVM

QVA INTERIECTIS AEDIFICIIS IMPEDITAM

QVA PROCVRRENTIBVS DEFORMATAM

5   LIBERAM RECTAMQVE REDDIDIT

PVBLICAE COMMODITATI ET ORNAMENTO

ANNO SAL MDCLXV

1. ALEXANDER VII : Septimus. — PONTIF(ex) MAX(imus).

3–5. QVA . . . QVA . . . LIBERAM RECTAMQVE : *The language exhibits the same refinement as the pope's other epigraphic texts (see 11.4). Elaborating* VIAM LATAM, *the clauses* QVA . . . IMPEDITAM *and* QVA . . . DEFORMATAM—*the first featuring a Part.Pass. (*INTERIECTIS*) and the second a Part.Act. (*PROCVRRENTIBVS*)—find a neat and definitive closure in the collocation* LIBERAM RECTAMQVE.

7. SAL(ūtis) MDCLXV : Mīllēsimō sescentēsimō sexāgēsimō quīntō.

Via del Nazareno 14: Attic of Arch

*Tiberius Claudius Caesar Augustus Germanicus,[a] son of Drusus,
Supreme Pontiff, vested with the Tribunician power for the fifth time,
acclaimed Imperator for the eleventh, Father of his Country, Consul Designate
for the fourth, built anew from their foundations the arches of the channels
of the Aqua Virgo, demolished by Gaius Caesar, and restored them.[b]*

    a. *Claudius I (r. 41–54) was proclaimed emperor by the Praetorian Guard
on 25 January 41. He assumed the* TRIBUNICIAN POWER *for the fifth
time on that date in 45, was saluted as* IMPERATOR *for the eleventh in the
same year, and became* CONSUL DESIGNATE *for the fourth in 46. Like all
the successors of Augustus, Claudius was granted the office of* SUPREME
PONTIFF *on his accession. The title 'Father of his Country' was assumed
by nearly all the emperors (see* PATER PATRIAE*).*

    b. *See 1.6B, note b. The arcade of the Aqua Virgo had likely been demolished for
a reconstruction that remained incomplete at the death of Gaius ('Caligula',
r. 37–41).*

Via del Corso 167: Façade

*Alexander the Seventh, Supreme Pontiff,[a]
for the general convenience and embellishment,
caused Via Lata, racecourse of the City during Carnival,[b]
to be disencumbered where obstructed by buildings in its path[c]
and to be straightened where diverted
by those that projected,
in the year of Salvation 1665.*

    a. *Pope Alexander VII Chigi (r. 1655–1667). He dictated the present text.*

    b. *Lit., 'on holiday' (see 1.6H, note d).*

    c. *Together with the Arch of Claudius (see 1.6B, note b) and the Arcus Novus
(see 9.3, note b), the arch that stood on the present site succumbed to the
exigencies of traffic on the Corso. Known as 'Arco di Portogallo' and demolished in 1662, the arch was evidently a late-Antique pastiche of earlier
monuments, incorporating among other things the relief panels of Hadrian
now mounted in Palazzo dei Conservatori (see 1.6H).*

9.8 Colonna dell'Immacolata: Dedication by Pius IX

i.

AVE

GRATIA PLENA

DOMINVS TECVM

BENEDICTA TV

5   IN MVLIERIBVS

LVC I 28

2. GRATIA : *Abl. following* PLENA.

6. LVC(ae) I 28 : Prīmō (*sc.* capitulō) vīcēsimō octāvō (*sc.* versū).

ii.

MARIAE VIRGINI

GENITRICI DEI

IPSA ORIGINE

AB OMNI LABE IMMVNI

5   PIVS V̅I̅I̅I̅I̅ P M

INSIGNIS PRAECONII

FIDE CONFIRMATA

DECRETO Q D E VI EID DEC

A M̅D̅C̅C̅C̅L̅I̅I̅I̅I̅

10   PONENDAM CVRAVIT

AERE CATH ORB CONLATO

AN SAC PRINCIP X̅I̅I̅

1. MARIAE : *On the name, see 15.4G, line 1.*

2. GENITRICI = genetrīcī : *See 4.2D, line 3.*

5. PIVS V̅I̅I̅I̅I̅ : Nōnus. — P(ontifex) M(aximus).

8. Q(uod) D(atum) E(st) VI : Sextō. — EID(ūs) = Īdūs : *On the spelling, see 1.61, line 16.* — DEC(embris) : *See 1.6G, line 11.*

9. A(nnō) M̅D̅C̅C̅C̅L̅I̅I̅I̅I̅ : Mīllēsimō octingentēsimō quīnquāgēsimō quārtō.

11. CATH(olicī) : *See 1.61, line 6.* — ORB(is).

12. AN(nō) SAC(rī) PRINCIP(ātūs) X̅I̅I̅ : Duodecimō.

Piazza di Spagna: Base of Column

North

> *Hail,*
> *full of grace,*
> *the Lord is with thee.*
> *Blessèd art thou*
> *among women.*[a]
> Luke 1:28

a. *The words 'blessèd art thou among women' are not found in the Greek text of the Gospel.*

South

> *Pius the Ninth,*[a] *Supreme Pontiff,*
> *with funds gathered from the Catholic world*
> *undertook to have this column*[b] *set up*
> *to the Virgin Mary,*
> *Mother of God,*
> *from her very conception*
> *free of all stain,*[c]
> *after the reliability of this illustrious proclamation*
> *had been confirmed by the decree*
> *which was issued on 8 December*[d]
> *of the year 1854,*
> *in the twelfth year of his sacred office.*

a. *Pope Pius IX Mastai-Ferretti (r. 1846–1878). The twelfth year of his pontificate ran from 16 June 1857 through 15 June 1858.*

b. *The fine Corinthian column of* cipollino *marble had been found in 1777 in the Campus Martius.*

c. *After centuries-long disputation, the dogma of the Immaculate Conception of the BVM was defined in the bull* Ineffabilis Deus *of Pius IX (see 4.2M, note e). Because Spain had made special exertions on behalf of the definition, it was proclaimed in Piazza di Spagna before the residence of the Spanish ambassador to the Holy See.*

d. *Lit., 'on the sixth day before the Ides of December'.*

iii.

a.   INIMICITIAS PONAM

INTER TE

ET MVLIEREM

GEN III 15

4. GEN(esis) III 15 : Tertiō (*sc.* capitulō) quīntō decimō (*sc.* versū).

b.   PORTA HAEC

CLAVSA ERIT

EZECH XLIV 2

3. EZECH(iēlis) XLIV 2 : Quadrāgēsimō quārtō (*sc.* capitulō) secundō (*sc.* versū).

c.   ECCE VIRGO

CONCIPIET

IS VII 14

3. IS(aiae) VII 14 : Septimō (*sc.* capitulō) quārtō decimō (*sc.* versū).

d.   SANCTIFICAVIT

TABERNACVLVM

SVVM ALTISSIMVS

PS XLV 4

1. SANCTIFICAVIT : *The* EL sānctificāre *represents Greek* ἁγνίζω (*'hallow'*).

4. PS(altērii) XLV 4 : Quadrāgēsimō quīntō (*sc.* capitulō) quārtō (*sc.* versū).

9.9 Scalinata della SS. Trinità dei Monti: Dedication

i.

DOM

MAGNIFICAM HANC SPECTATOR QVAM MIRARIS SCALAM

VT COMMODVM AC ORNAMENTVM NON EXIGVVM

4   REGIO COENOBIO IPSIQ VRBI ALLATVRAM

Corners

NE   *I shall set enmity*
between thee
and woman.[a]
Genesis 3:15

a. *The text forms part of the curse of the Lord on the Serpent.*

SE   *This gate*
shall be closed.[a]
Ezekiel 44:2

a. *The text, from Ezekiel's prophecy of the Temple, was understood typologi-*
cally as a reference to the perpetual virginity of the BVM.

SW   *Behold, a virgin*
shall conceive.[a]
Isaiah 7:14

a. *The text forms part of Isaiah's prophecy to Ahaz, king of Judah.*

NW   *The Most High*
hath sanctified
his tabernacle.[a]
Psalm 45:4

a. *The Vulgate version of the verse, which appears on the monument, trans-*
lates the Greek Septuagint. The New Jerusalem Bible renders the Hebrew
thus: 'There is a river whose streams bring joy to God's city, it sanctifies the
dwelling of the Most High'.

Spanish Steps: Lower & Upper Landings

Lower Landing

To God, Best and Greatest.
Étienne Gueffier,[a] *a noble son of France,*
who passed to his reward at Rome on 30 June 1661
after long and distinguished employment in the royal service

ANIMO CONCEPIT LEGATAQ SVPREMIS IN TABVLIS PECVNIA

VNDE SVMPTVS SVPPEDITARENTVR CONSTRVI MANDAVIT

NOBILIS GALLVS STEPHANVS GVEFFIER

QVI REGIO IN MINISTERIO DIV PLVRES APVD PONTIFICES

ALIOSQVE SVBLIMES PRINCIPES EGREGIE VERSATVS

10   ROMAE VIVERE DESIIT XXX IVNII MDCLXI

OPVS AVTEM VARIO RERVM INTERVENTV

PRIMVM SVB CLEMENTE XI

CVM MVLTI PROPONERENTVR MODVLI ET FORMAE

IN DELIBERATIONE POSITVM

15   DEINDE SVB INNOCENTIO XIII STABILITVM

ET R P BERTRANDI MONSINAT TOLOSATIS

ORD MINIMORVM S FRANCISCI DE PAVLA CORRECTORIS GENLIS

FIDEI CVRAEQ COMMISSVM AC INCHOATVM

TANDEM BENEDICTO XIII FELICITER SEDENTE

20   CONFECTVM ABSOLVTVMQVE EST

ANNO IVBILEI M DCC XXV

1. D(eō) O(ptimō) M(aximō).

2. MAGNIFICAM HANC . . . SCALAM : *The postpositioning of* HANC *and the hyperbaton lend flair. Hyperbaton (Greek* ὑπερβατόν) *is the separation for rhetorical effect of words grammatically related.*

4. COENOBIO : *The* EL coenobium *transliterates* EG κοινόβιον *('monastery'); the diphthong* OE *is authentic (cf. 1.8B, line 5).* — IPSIQ(ue).

5. LEGATAQ(ue).

7. GALLVS : *In* LL, Gallus *is 'French'.*

10. XXX : Trīcēsimō. — IVNII : *See 1.6G, line 11.* — MDCLXI : Mīllēsimō sescentēsimō sexāgēsimō prīmō.

12. CLEMENTE XI : Ūndecimō.

15. INNOCENTIO XIII : Tertiō decimō.

16. R(everendī) P(atris). — TOLOSATIS : *The* ML *Adj.* Tolōsātis *answers to the toponym* Tolōsa *(mod. Toulouse).*

17. ORD(inis) : *See 7.4E, line 8.* — S(ānctī). — GEN(erā)LIS.

18. CVRAEQ(ue). — INCHOATAM = incohātam : *See 8.8A, line 2.*

19. BENEDICTO XIII : Tertiō decimō.

21. IVBILEI = iūbilaeī : *See 2.12A, line 8; on the spelling, see 1.8B, line 5.* — M DCC XXV : Mīllēsimō septingentēsimō vīcēsimō quīntō.

at the court of many pontiffs and other lofty princes,
conceived in his mind, onlooker, this grand stair at which you marvel,[b]
as a thing destined to lend no small convenience and embellishment
to the royal cloister and the City itself,[c]
and with a bequest of money in his last will
whereby the cost should be defrayed, instructed that it be built.
Owing to sundry interruptions, moreover, the work—
first mooted
under Clement the Eleventh,[d]
when many scales and plans were proposed,
then decided under Innocent the Thirteenth[e]
and entrusted to the good faith and care
of the Reverend Father Bertrand Monsinat of Toulouse,
Corrector General of the Friars Minim of San Francesco di Paola,[f]
and finally begun during the happy reign of Benedict the Thirteenth[g]*—*
was completed and finished
in the year of the Jubilee 1725.[h]

a. Étienne Gueffier (who in fact died in 1660) served as French chargé d'affaires at Rome.
b. The consummate monument of the Barocchetto (or 'Roman Rococo'), the Spanish Steps were designed by Francesco de Sanctis (1693–1740). De Sanctis' design was influenced by that of his rival, Alessandro Specchi (1668–1729), which—like de Sanctis' own—depended on an idea of Bernini's.
c. The cloister is that of the Friars Minim (see note f below), founded by Charles VIII of France (r. 1483–1498).
d. Pope Clement XI Albani (r. 1700–1721).
e. Pope Innocent XIII dei Conti (r. 1721–1724).
f. Revered as a miracle worker, Francesco di Paola (1416–1507) served as spiritual adviser to Louis XI, Charles VIII, and Louis XII of France. He was canonized in 1519. His Order of Friars Minim, founded around 1435, was granted the privileges of a mendicant order in 1474 by Pope Sixtus IV; its rule was confirmed by Alexander VI. Having found inspiration among the Franciscans (Fratres Minores, 'lesser brothers'), the saint went them one better by calling his friars Fratres Minimi ('least brothers').
g. Pope Benedict XIII Orsini (r. 1724–1730).
h. See 7.4H, note b.

ii.

D O M

SEDENTE BENEDICTO XIII

PONT MAX

LUDOVICO XV

5   IN GALLIS REGNANTE

EIUSQ APUD SANCTAM SEDEM

NEGOTIIS PRÆPOSITO

MELCHIORE S R ECCLESIÆ

CARDINALI DE POLIGNAC

10   ARCHIEPISCOPO AUSCITANO

AD SACRÆ ÆDIS ALMÆQUE URBIS

ORNAMENTUM

AC CIVIUM COMMODUM

MARMOREA SCALA

15   DIGNO TANTIS AUSPICIIS OPERE

ABSOLUTA

ANNO DOMINI MDCCXXV

1. D(eō) O(ptimō) M(aximō).
2. SEDENTE BENEDICTO XIII : Tertiō decimō. *On the construction, see* 5.7B, *line 1.*
3. PONT(ifice) MAX(imō).
4. LUDOVICO XV : Quīntō decimō.
5. GALLIS : *See* 9.9.i, *line 7.*
6. EIUSQ(ue). — SEDEM : *See* 3.4C, *line 4.*
8. MELCHIORE : *The Latin name is* Melchior, -ōris. — S(ānctae) R(ōmānae) ECCLESIÆ : *See* 1.7A, *line 6.*
10. ARCHIEPISCOPO : *See* 3.3C, *line 8.* — AUSCITANO : *The ML Adj.* Auscitānus *corresponds to the toponym* Augusta Ausciōrum (*mod.* Auch).
11. ÆDIS : *See* 1.8B, *line 10.*
17. MDCCXXV : Mīllēsimō septingentēsimō vīcēsimō quīntō.

Upper Landing

To God, Best and Greatest.
During the incumbency of Benedict the Thirteenth,[a]
Supreme Pontiff,
and the reign of Louis the Fifteenth[b]
among the French,
and while Melchior de Polignac,[c]
Archbishop of Auch,
Cardinal of the Holy Roman Church,
was in charge of the affairs of the latter
at the Holy See,
the marble stair
was completed,
for the embellishment of the sacred church
and of the kindly City
and for the convenience of the citizens,
with workmanship worthy of such great patronage,
in the year of the Lord 1725.

a. *Pope Benedict XIII Orsini (r. 1724–1730).*
b. *King Louis XV of France (r. 1715–1774).*
c. *Melchior de Polignac (1661–1741) was created cardinal* in pectore (*i.e., secretly*) *by Pope Clement XI. Named Archbishop of Auch in 1726, he served as ambassador of France to the Holy See 1724–1732. His tenure was troubled by the repercussions of Clement's bull* Unigenitus Dei Filius, *a condemnation of 101 propositions of the French Jansenist Pasquier Quesnel. De Polignac's nine-book* Anti-Lucretius, *a refutation of the Epicurean poet's materialist doctrine, is a marvel of Neo-Latin verse: Voltaire quipped that de Polignac was* aussi bon poète qu'on peut l'être dans une langue morte (*'as good a poet as one can be in a dead language'*).

9.10A SS. Trinità dei Monti: Dedication by Friars Minim

S TRINITATI REGVM GALLIÆ MVNIFICENTIA ET PIOR' ⌐
ELEMOSYNIS ADIVTA MINIMOR' SODALITAS STRVXIT ⌐
AC D D ANNO D MDLXX

> s(ānctae) TRINITATI : *The* EL *trīnitās represents Greek* τριάς (*'tri-ad', then* EG *'Trinity'*). — PIOR(um). — ELEMOSYNIS : *The* EL *eleēmosyna transliterates Greek* ἐλεημοσύνη (*'mercy', then* EG *'alms'*). — MINIMOR(um). — D(ōnum) D(edit). — D(ominī) MDLXX : *Mīllēsimō quīngentēsimō septuāgēsimō.*

9.10B SS. Trinità dei Monti: Dedication by Louis XVIII

LVDOVICVS XVIII EXOPTATVS GALL REX

TEMPLVM SS TRINITATIS IN PINCIO

RESTITVIT

CVRAM AGENTE COMITE BLACAS DE ALPIBVS

REGIS LEGATO

AD

PIVM VII PONTIFICEM MAXIMVM

ANN SAL MDCCCXVI

5

> 1. LVDOVICVS XVIII : *Duodēvīcēsimus.* — EXOPTATVS : *The Latin exoptātus represents Fr. le Désiré* (*'the Longed-for'*). — GALL(ōrum) : *See 9.9.i, line 7.*
> 2. TEMPLVM : *On the Classicizing diction, cf. 1.8G, line 5.* — SS = *sānctissimae : On the abbreviation, see 1.61, line 7.* — TRINITATIS : *See 9.10A.* — PINCIO : *The Latin name is Pincius* (*the Ital. Pincio derives from the late toponym Mōns Pincius; cf. 9.11.iii, line 6*).
> 4. COMITE : *See 2.2, line 9.* — DE ALPIBVS : *The toponym Aulps appears in* ML *as Alpēs.*
> 7. PIVM VII : *Septimum.*
> 8. ANN(ō) SAL(ūtis) MDCCCXVI : *Mīllēsimō octingentēsimō sextō decimō.*

Façade

Assisted by the generosity of the kings of France[a] and the alms of the godly, the brotherhood of the Friars Minim[b] built this and gave it as a gift to the Holy Trinity in the year of the Lord 1570.

> a. *The church was begun in 1502 under the patronage of Louis XII (1498–1515) for the French members of the Order of S. Francis da Paola but was interrupted following the sack of Rome in 1527. Constructed in stone imported from Narbonne, the church was finally consecrated in 1585.*
> b. *See 9.9.i, note f.*

Podium of Stair

Louis the Eighteenth 'le Désiré',[a] King of France,
restored the Church of Santa Trinità[b]
on the Pincio[c]
through the agency
of Comte de Blacas d'Aulps,[d]
the king's envoy
to Pius the Seventh,[e] Supreme Pontiff,
in the year of Salvation 1816.

> a. *Louis XVIII of France (r. 1814–1824) was brother to Louis XVI and Charles X. In exile from 1791, he took the royal title on the death of his ten-year-old nephew Louis XVII in 1795 and in 1814 entered Paris as king.*
> b. *The church had been founded by Charles VIII (see 9.9.i, note c).*
> c. *Long under control of the friars of Sant'Agostino, the hill was expropriated by Napoleon for a park to be called 'Jardin du Grand César'; though that name was never adopted, the park was laid out 1811–1814 by Giuseppe Valadier.*
> d. *On the restoration of the French monarchy in 1814, Pierre-Louis-Jean-Casimir, Compte de Blacas d'Aulps (1771–1839), entered the royal service; in 1830 he followed Charles X into exile, ending his days at Prague.*
> e. *Pope Pius VII Chiaramonti (r. 1800–1823).*

9.11 Obelisco Sallustiano: Dedication by Pius VI

i.	*ii.*
III EIDVS	SACRI
APRIL	PRINCIPATVS
ANNO M̄ D̄C̄C̄	EIVS
L̄X̄X̄X̄V̄ĪĪĪĪ	ANNO X̄V̄

*i.*1. III : Tertiō. — EIDVS = Īdūs : *On the spelling, see 1.61, line 16.*

2. APRIL(is) : *See 1.6G, line 11.*

3. M̄ D̄C̄C̄ | L̄X̄X̄X̄V̄ĪĪĪĪ : Mīllēsimō septingentēsimō octōgēsimō nōnō.

*ii.*4. X̄V̄ : Quīntō decimō.

iii.

PIVS V̄Ī PONT MAX

OBELISCVM SALLVSTIANVM

QVEM PROLAPSIONE DIFFRACTVM

SVPERIOR AETAS

5   IACENTEM RELIQVERAT

COLLI HORTVLORVM

IN SVBSIDENTIVM VIARVM

PROSPECTV IMPOSITVM

TROPAEO

10   CRVCIS PRAEFIXO

TRINITATI AVGVSTAE

DEDICAVIT

1. PIVS V̄Ī : Sextus. — PONT(ifex) MAX(imus).

6. COLLI HORTVLORVM : *The Pincio was anciently called 'Hill of the Gardens'.*

7. SVBSIDENTIVM : *The verb is* subsidēre *('to underlie').*

9. TROPAEO : *Cf. 1.4, line 2.*

11. TRINITATI : *See 9.10A.*

Base of Obelisk

<table>
<tr><td align="center">North</td><td align="center">South</td></tr>
<tr><td align="center">11 April[a]</td><td align="center">fifteenth year</td></tr>
<tr><td align="center">in</td><td align="center">of</td></tr>
<tr><td align="center">the year</td><td align="center">his sacred</td></tr>
<tr><td align="center">1789,</td><td align="center">office.[b]</td></tr>
</table>

a. Lit., 'on the third day before the Ides of April'.

b. The fifteenth year of the pontificate of Pope Pius VI Braschi (r. 1775–1799) ran from 15 February 1789 through 14 February 1790.

West

Pius the Sixth,[a] Supreme Pontiff,
dedicated
to the august Trinity
the obelisk of Sallust[b]—
which, shattered in its fall,
a former age
had abandoned prostrate—
set atop the Hill of the Gardens
in view
of the streets below
and surmounted by the victory monument
of the Cross.

a. Pope Pius VI Braschi (r. 1775–1799).

b. Manufactured at Rome, the obelisk is inscribed with hieroglyphs imitating those of the Obelisco Flaminio (10.4)—so ineptly, however, that some of the glyphs are reversed. The monument owes its name to the fact that it was found on the site of the gardens of Gaius Sallustius Crispus (86–35 BC), partisan of Caesar and historian. It was likely erected by Aurelian (r. 270–275) in a circus on the E side of the gardens. It lay at the Lateran for many years before being set up at the present site in 1789. The text was composed by Stefano Antonio Morcelli (see 8.4A.iii, note a).

COLUMN OF MARCUS AURELIUS

Reprising the Column of Trajan in both design and dimensions, the Column of Marcus Aurelius was originally associated with a temple dedicated to the deified emperor. In the Middle Ages, the monument rose at the eastern limit of the abitato, *the inhabited area. With the expansion of the city during the Renaissance, the column came to form the centerpiece of a square, Piazza Colonna. The impressive effect of the square commanded by a commemorative column was imitated in Napoleon's Colonne de la Grande Armée in Place Vendôme and in the palace square at St. Petersburg.*

X. From Piazza del Popolo to Piazza Colonna

IN THE FIRST CENTURY OF THE CHRISTIAN ERA the Campus Martius still lay outside the city. For the traveler approaching from the north on the Via Flaminia, vineyard and pasture yielded but gradually to the military exercise grounds that evoked Mars, god of war and eponymous patron of the Campus from remote times. On the uplands to the east of the road, the pavilions of sumptuous villas gave notice that Rome was near; so too did the sepulchers that crowded the suburban tracts of all the great consular highways. Of these, the greatest by far was the massive Mausoleum of Augustus, situated between the Via Flaminia and the Tiber River in a precinct laid out with formal gardens. To the south of the mausoleum, an obelisk erected by the same emperor towered in isolation above the travertine flagstones of a vast solar calendar. A kilometer beyond, the Theater of Pompey bulked like a mountain amid the parks and porticoes of the central Campus.

As the traveler proceeded citywards, the view to the east of the Via Flaminia was dominated by the beetling cliff face of the Quirinal Hill, its long brow fringed by the ramparts of the Servian wall and its eminence crowned by the mighty Temple of Quirinus. Before the hill's foot marched the arcade of the Aqua Virgo, traversing the Campus to pass over the Via Flaminia at the Arch of Claudius; the arch served also as gateway to the monumentalized zone that lay beyond. In the distance, on the summit of the Capitoline Hill, the gilt-bronze roof tiles of the temple of Jupiter glittered in the sun. The splendor of the Augustan Campus excited the liveliest admiration of contemporaries: set against a scene of temple-crowned hills, its verdant parks and gleaming colonnades presented a spectacle from which the geographer Strabo confessed that he found it difficult to tear his gaze.

Over the course of the first and second centuries, the monumental zone of the Campus expanded to the north and west. Nero contributed baths, Domitian a stadium and recital hall, Hadrian—with a great-

ness of soul that has been characterized as *sui generis*—a temple to his
mother-in-law. The filial devotion of Antoninus Pius found expression
10.13 in a temple to Hadrian; that of Commodus in the COLUMN OF MAR-
CUS AURELIUS (r. 161–180). In design and dimensions alike, the latter
monument reprised the Column of Trajan. Erroneously identified in the
Middle Ages as the Column of Antoninus Pius (r. 138–161), it was in the
keeping of the monks of San Silvestro, who charged a fee for the privilege of climbing the narrow spiral stair to enjoy the panorama. Like the
Column of Trajan, that of Marcus was rededicated in the sixteenth century by Pope Sixtus V (r. 1585–1590); the inscriptions on its pedestal exhale the fire of that pontiff's quixotic vendetta against paganism.

Immediately to the west of Piazza Colonna, Piazza di Montecitorio
10.11 lodges the OBELISCO CAMPENSE, in Antiquity the gnomon of the solar calendar of Augustus (r. 27 BC–AD 14). The calendar took the form of
a circular pavement of travertine inlaid with bronze markers; at its center
rose the obelisk, topped by a gilt-bronze globe. The apparatus was more
than a simple sundial; it included indications of the day of the month, the
seasons of the year, and the constellations of the zodiac. The Obelisco
Campense is one of two that the emperor had brought to Rome from
Heliopolis in 10 BC in celebration of the twentieth anniversary of his an-
nexation of Egypt. The second is the Obelisco Flaminio, originally set
up in the Circus Maximus. Identical Augustan dedicatory inscriptions
survive on the bases of both. The Obelisco Campense was excavated in
10.9 1748 at the order of Pope BENEDICT XIV (r. 1740–1758), who mounted
an inscription to commemorate the site of the discovery. In 1792 it was
10.11 repaired and erected in the present location under PIUS VI (r. 1775–
B&C 1799).

Like the Obelisco Flaminio and the Obelisco Lateranense, the Campense bears in its mutilated shaft the evidence of its deliberate ruin. This
circumstance has nourished a controversy of long standing: Who can
have possessed the leisure, the resources, and the concentrated malice
to perpetrate so cyclopean an act of vandalism? Suspicion has naturally

gathered around the Christians, who are known to have demolished pagan shrines and who could well have sought more prominent targets for their terrorism. This hypothesis is, however, controverted by the fact that at least through the seventh century, the domestic pillaging of Rome's monuments remained the exclusive privilege of the emperors. As late as AD 608 Pope St. Boniface IV required imperial consent to transform the Pantheon into a Christian church.

As for barbarians, the incursions of the Visigoth Alaric (AD 410) and the Vandal Genseric (455) were each of two weeks' duration or less; the Ostrogoth Vitiges departed unsuccessful after a siege lasting an entire year (537). It was only in 547 that the city was subjected to an occupation of sufficient length for so arduous a task as the toppling of obelisks: The Ostrogoth Totila entered Rome on 17 December 546 and remained there into the spring of the following year. Having failed to obtain the recognition of the emperor Justinian, Totila vowed to destroy the city. Procopius reports that the walls of Aurelian were demolished in a third of their circuit and that on Totila's departure Rome stood empty for forty days. Though the historian surely exaggerates, it is reasonable to suppose that the obelisks were the first and most prominent victims of the vengeful king's fury. Like their Visigothic brethren, the Ostrogoths were Arian Christians. It would appear that the blame for the overthrow of the obelisks may be assigned indifferently to Christian barbarians or to barbarous Christians.

Immediately to the east of the solar calendar stood the *Ara Pacis Augustae* ('Altar of the Peace of Augustus'). Uncovered in various locations through the centuries, its surviving fragments were reassembled during the Fascist period beside the emperor's mausoleum, some 450 meters to the northwest of their original site; the dedication took place on 23 September 1938, the two thousandth anniversary of the imperial birth. The podium of the structure built to house the monument is inscribed with the text of the RES GESTAE, an autobiographical conspectus of Augus-   *10.6* tus' political and military achievements originally displayed on brazen tablets near the entrance to the mausoleum. Though the tablets were early broken up for their metal, the text survived in copies made for the Temple of Rome and Augustus at Ankara. An ungainly modern pavilion opened to the public in 2006 incorporates the podium and inscription of its Fascist predecessor.

The post-Classical fortunes of the Mausoleum of Augustus form a characteristic episode in the urban history of Rome. Situated well north of the medieval *abitato,* the massive ruin was adapted as a fortress in the twelfth century by the family Colonna; it was known by the name 'Agosta', which eventually encompassed the whole of the surrounding quarter. After the fortress was dismantled at papal order, the site was eagerly quarried for its abundant deposits of travertine. In 1354 it was used to cremate the mutilated corpse of the megalomaniacal revolutionary Cola di Rienzo. Three hundred years later the family Soderini cleared the structure to form an arena for fireworks and bullfights. Ultimately, at the beginning of the twentieth century, it was furnished with a roof and converted into an acoustically outstanding concert hall dubbed the 'Augusteo'. This was the monument's final role. Its long series of creative adaptations was brought to a brutal and definitive conclusion by the decision of the Fascist regime to eviscerate, isolate, and seclude it as an archaeological site.

Because the northern Campus was largely unencumbered by the ruins of ancient buildings, in the Middle Ages it came to be dominated by large ecclesiastical foundations interspersed with infrequent dwellings. The great landholders of the area were the monastery of San Silvestro in Capite, founded in the eighth century, and the Ospedale di San Giacomo in Agosta, founded in the fourteenth. Large parts of the zone were eventually assigned to various national communities. Following the Ottoman victory of Kosovo Polje (Blackbird Field, 28 June 1389), large numbers of South Slavs migrated to the west; with the fall of Constantinople (29 May 1453), the exodus was swelled by Greeks. Pope Nicholas V (r. 1447–1455) granted the Slavs the right to build a church and hospice for their

compatriots; the ILLYRIAN COLLEGE followed three centuries later.   *10.7*
The Greek refugees were settled nearby, to the east of Via del Corso;
their community was centered on the Church of Sant'Atanasio. Another
'foreign' nation—the Lombards—built their own hospice in the same
zone; this was later incorporated into the complex of Sant'Ambrogio e
Carlo.

Pope Sixtus IV (r. 1471–1484) reconstructed Santa Maria del Popolo
and its Augustinian convent at Porta del Popolo. Over the succeeding
decades, the western corridor of the northern Campus—as yet largely
rural—was incorporated into the city. The parceling of the vast property of Ospedale di San Giacomo in 1509 lent considerable impetus to
the process of urbanization. The old Roman street leading from the 'Via
Recta' to Porta del Popolo (today's Via della Scrofa to Via di Ripetta) was
ideally situated to serve as the chief artery of the new quarter. Between
1517 and 1519, Pope Leo X (r. 1513–1521) undertook the straightening and
paving of the street. In addition to completing the link between Porta del
Popolo and Ponte Sant'Angelo, the new Via Leonina furnished a grand
approach to the Medici palace at Piazza Navona.

One of the outstanding monuments of the Agosta quarter was the
delightful Porto di Ripetta, which accommodated a brisk commercial
traffic in timber and wine from the Sabine hinterland. Constructed in
1704 by Alessandro Specchi, this jewel of the Barocchetto—the 'Roman
Rococo'—presented an exuberant cascade of ramped terraces whose
grace and vivacity are echoed in the design of the Spanish Steps. The
port and surrounding neighborhood were eliminated in two campaigns.
The building of the massive Tiber embankments between 1876 and 1926
entailed the demolition of all riverside construction, including Porto di
Ripetta. Grave as this loss was, it is dwarfed by the wound inflicted for
the 'liberation' of the Mausoleum of Augustus (1937–1940), commemorated in the dedicatory inscription of PIAZZA DI AUGUSTO IMPERA-   *10.5*
TORE. The whole of the Renaissance quarter between Via Tomacelli and
Via della Frezza was razed to reveal the miserable brick core of the mon-

ument, whose precinct long served as a rubbish pit and public convenience. A competition for projects to redevelop the zone was announced in 2006.

Within a few decades, the Via Leonina found its counterpart in the Via Clementina (today's Via del Babuino) of Clement VII (r. 1523–1534). With Via del Corso between, these symmetrically disposed streets converged on Piazza del Popolo to form what was felicitously dubbed the 'Tridente Romano', the Trident of Rome. The importance of Piazza del Popolo in the northward growth of the city received de facto recognition in 1572, when Pope Gregory XIII (r. 1572–1585) located the first of his public fountains at its center. It remained for Gregory's successor, Sixtus V (r. 1585–1590), to exploit the scenographic potential of the site by erecting the OBELISCO FLAMINIO at the vertex of the Tridente. The current form was given to the piazza under PIUS VII (r. 1800–1823), who—as he did elsewhere in the city—here completed projects initiated during the French regime of 1809–1814. It was in this final phase that the roughly trapezoidal plan of the old piazza was replaced by its characteristic hemicycles (the semicircular niches that close the north and south sides).

By a fortunate coincidence, in the mid-ninth century the land route from transalpine Europe through central Italy had been liberated from the Lombard threat just as the Saracens interdicted the sea route from Marseilles to Centumcellae (modern Civitavecchia), Rome's seaport. The Via Flaminia and Porta del Popolo emerged as the principal approach to Rome for pilgrims arriving from the north. In the Middle Ages, Porta del Popolo was called Porta San Valentino after the ancient basilica that stood near the first milestone of the Via Flaminia; it later took the name of its close neighbor, the Church of Santa Maria del Popolo. Pope Pius IV (r. 1559–1565) erected the external façade of PORTA DEL POPOLO. For the triumphal entry of CHRISTINA OF SWEDEN in 1655, Alexander VII (r. 1655–1667) had the internal façade reworked by Gianlorenzo Bernini and approved the construction of the twin churches that mark the start of the Corso at the southern end of the piazza. The lateral passages were opened in 1878, with the demolition of the two original flanking towers. Contrary to the usage prevalent after 1870, the DEDICATION of the passages appears in Latin rather than Italian; in the freshly minted kingdom of Italy, Latin was avoided in public inscriptions as an unwelcome reminder of papal rule.   *10.1B*

Two of the Tiber's most disastrous inundations, those of 1530 and 1598, are commemorated in FLOOD TABLETS affixed to the gate's internal façade where it joins Caserma Giacomo Acqua.   *10.1 D&E*

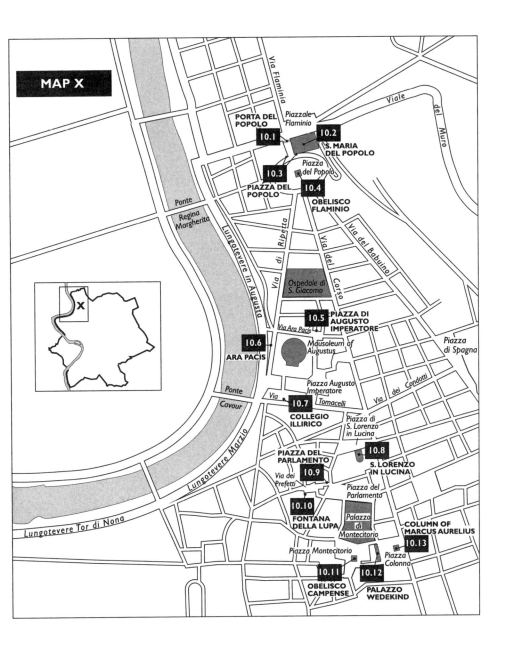

MAP X

PORTA DEL POPOLO
Piazzale Flaminio

10.1   10.2
S. MARIA DEL POPOLO

Via Flaminia

Viale del Muro

10.3   Piazza del Popolo

PIAZZA DEL POPOLO   10.4
OBELISCO FLAMINIO

Ponte Regina Margherita

Lungotevere in Augusta

Via di Ripetta

Via del Corso

Via del Babuino

Ospedale di S. Giacomo

10.5   PIAZZA DI AUGUSTO IMPERATORE

Via Ara Pacis

10.6   Mausoleum of Augustus

ARA PACIS

Piazza di Spagna

Piazza Augusto Imperatore

Via dei Condotti

Ponte Cavour

Via Tomacelli

10.7
COLLEGIO ILLIRICO

Piazza di S. Lorenzo in Lucina

PIAZZA DEL PARLAMENTO   10.8
S. LORENZO IN LUCINA

Via dei Prefetti   10.9

Piazza del Parlamento

Lungotevere Marzio

10.10
FONTANA DELLA LUPA

Palazzo di Montecitorio

COLUMN OF MARCUS AURELIUS

10.13

Lungotevere Tor di Nona

Piazza Montecitorio

Piazza Colonna

10.11   10.12
OBELISCO CAMPENSE   PALAZZO WEDEKIND

10.1A Porta del Popolo: Dedication by Pius IV

> PIVS IIII PONT MAX
> PORTAM IN HANC AMPLI
> TVDINEM EXTVLIT
> VIAM FLAMINIAM
> 5 STRAVIT ANNO III

1. PIVS IIII : Quārtus. — PONT(ifex) MAX(imus).
2. AMPLI|TVDINEM.
3–5. EXTVLIT ... STRAVIT : *The asyndeton lends a note of pomp (cf. 1.2.i, line 4).* — III : Tertiō.

10.1B Porta del Popolo: Dedication by S.P.Q.R.

i.

> ANNO MDCCCLXXIX
> RESTITVTAE LIBERTATIS X
> TVRRIBVS VTRINQVE DELETIS
> FRONS PRODVCTA INSTAVRATA

1. ANNO MDCCCLXXIX : Mīllēsimō octingentēsimō septuāgēsimō nōnō.
2. RESTITVTAE LIBERTATIS X : Decimō. *On the construction, see 1.7A, lines 2–3.*
3. VTRINQVE = utrimque : *On the spelling, cf. 9.2B, line 8.*
4. PRODVCTA INSTAVRATA : Sc. est. *Note the asyndeton (cf. 1.2.i, line 4).*

ii.

> S P Q R
> VRBE ITALIAE VINDICATA
> INCOLIS FELICITER AVCTIS
> GEMINOS FORNICES CONDIDIT

1. S(enātus) P(opulus) Q(ue) R(ōmānus).

Porta del Popolo: Outer Attic, Center

Pius the Fourth,[a] Supreme Pontiff,
elevated the gate to its present grandeur
and paved
the Via Flaminia[b]
in his third year.

a. *Pope Pius IV de' Medici (r. 1559–1565). The third year of his pontificate ran from 25 December 1561 through 24 December 1562.*

b. *Opened in 223 BC by Gaius Flaminius, the Via Flaminia continued the Via Lata (mod. Via del Corso) to Ariminum (mod. Rimini).*

Outer Attic, L and R

Left

In the year 1879,
tenth of the restoration of liberty,[a]
with the demolition of the tower on each side[b]
the façade was extended and restored.

a. *The 'era' of the restoration of liberty is reckoned from 20 September 1870, the date on which Italian forces entered Rome and put an end to the temporal sovereignty of the popes (see 8.7B.ii, note b).*

b. *The bastions had been constructed in the fifteenth century under Pope Sixtus IV, who rebuilt the neighboring Church of S. Maria del Popolo (see 10.2, note a).*

Right

In view of the City's appropriation for Italy
and the auspicious increase of its population,
the Senate and People of Rome
built twin arches.[a]

a. *I.e., the arches flanking the central passage.*

10.1C   Porta del Popolo: Dedication by Alexander VII

FELICI FAVSTOQ INGRESSVI

ANNO DOM MDCLV

1. FAVSTOQ(ue). — INGRESSVI : *Dat. of Purpose.*
2. DOM(inī) MDCLV : Mīllēsimō sescentēsimō quīnquāgēsimō quīntō.

10.1D   Porta del Popolo: Flood Tablet of 1530

SEPTIMVS AVRATV̄ CLEMENS GESTABAT HETRVSCVS

SORTE PEDVM HVC SALIIT QVOM VAGVS VSQ TYBER

QVIPPE MEMOR CĀPI QVĒ NŌ [c]OLVERE PRIORES

AMNIBVS EPOTIS IN NOVA TECTA RVIT

5   VT[q] FORET SPACII IMPLACABILIS VLTOR ADĒPTI

ET CEREREM BACCHVM SVSTVLIT ATQ LARES

RESTAGNAVIT VIII ID OCTOB AN

M D XXX

Three ELEGIAC COUPLETS (*lines 1–6*)

1. SEPTIMVS . . . CLEMENS : *I.e., Pope Clement VII.* — AVRATV(m). — HETRVSCVS = Etruscus : *Fanciful Hellenizing forms featuring spurious aspirates are common in* RL (*see 9.1A, line 2*).
2. PEDVM : *In* EL, *pedum is 'bishop's crozier'.* — QVOM = cum : *A genuinely archaic form* (*see 2.12B, line 2*). — VSQ(ue). — TYBER = Tiber : *On the spelling, see 9.1A, line 2, and 3.1, line 1.*
3. CA(m)PI : *I.e., the Campus Martius.* — QVE(m) NO(n). — [c]OLVERE = coluērunt : *The few characters enclosed in brackets are restored from context.*
5. VT[q(ue)]. — SPACII = spatiī : *On the spelling, see 3.4B, line 3.* — ADE(m)PTI.
6. CEREREM BACCHVM . . . LARES : *As often in* CL *verse, the names of gods are employed by metonymy. Metonymy* (*Greek* μετωνυμία) *is the use of a term to convey a distinct but related notion.* — ATQ(ue).
7. VIII : Octāvō. — ID(ūs) OCTOB(ris) : *See 1.6G, line 11.* — AN(nō).
8. M D XXX : Mīllēsimō quīngentēsimō trīcēsimō.

Inner Attic

To a happy and auspicious entrance.[a]
In the year of the Lord 1655.

a. *For the triumphal entry of Queen Christina of Sweden into Rome (see 1.61, note a), Pope Alexander VII (r. 1655–1667) engaged Gianlorenzo Bernini to remodel the interior of Porta del Popolo.*

Corner of Gate and Caserma Giacomo Acqua

Clement the Seventh, a son of Etruria,[a] *chanced to bear
the gilded crozier when Tiber in his spread rose to this point.
Indeed, mindful of the Campus, which the ancients did not inhabit,*[b]
*having swallowed up his tributaries he rushed upon the new buildings
and, that in avenging the land taken away from him he might prove
implacable, he destroyed field, vine, and dwelling.*[c]

He overflowed his banks on 8 October [d]

1530.

Three ELEGIAC COUPLETS (lines 1–6)

a. *Pope Clement VII de' Medici (r. 1523–1534). Clement was a scion of the Florentine Medici; as modern Tuscany is more or less coextensive with ancient Etruria, the Latin epithet* Etruscus *furnishes a suitable Latin equivalent for 'Tuscan'.*

b. *In Antiquity, the Campus Martius, a natural flood plain, lay outside the city proper (see 1.1, note b). Its northern reaches remained largely unoccupied until the early sixteenth century. It was Clement's cousin and predecessor at one remove, Leo X (r. 1513–1521), who had developed the riverside corridor between Palazzo Madama—his cardinalitial palace—and Piazza del Popolo.*

c. *Lit., 'Ceres, Bacchus, and Lares'. The names of the gods stand by metonymy for their spheres of competency. In the sixteenth century alone, there were six grave floods. Three of these (in 1530, 1557, and 1598) were catastrophic, causing thousands of deaths as well as the destruction of houses, crops, and bridges (see 11.5C–E and 13.12, note b).*

d. *Lit., 'on the eighth day before the Ides of October'.*

10.1E   Porta del Popolo: Flood Tablet of 1598

SVBIECTVM VT AVDAX INDICEM FLVVIVS SVI

TETIGIT SIBI ÆQVVS PROXIMO AT DEPRESSIOR

FONTE IMVS INQVIT ALTIVS VINCI HAVD DECET

FAMAM AVCVPABOR OMNIVM CÆLO FRVAR

5   PROPINQVIORE ET SECVLO TRADAR NOVO

MEMINISSE QVĀTVM VIETA NŌ ÆTAS POTEST

NOTAS QVIRINE HIC IMPRIME HIC TYBRIS FVI

EX IX KAL IANVAR CIƆ IƆ XCVIIII

CLEMENTIS VIII P M ANNO VII

Seven IAMBIC SENARII (lines 1–7)

1. svi : *Obj.Gen. depending on* INDICEM.
4. cælo : *The Abl. complement with deponent verbs is usually instrumental; with* fruī *and* fungī, *however, it is probably Abl. of Separation ('reap profit from' and 'free oneself of').*
5. secvlo = saeculō : *On the spelling, see 1.8B, line 5.*
6. qva(n)tvm. — vieta : *Scans* vjēta *(two syllables).* — no(n).
7. tybris = Tiberis : *On the spelling, see 9.1A, line 2, and 3.1, line 1.*
8. ex(undāvit) ix : Nōnō. — kal(endās) ianvar(iī) : *See 1.6G, line 11.*
   — ciƆ iƆ xcviiii : Mīllēsimō quīngentēsimō nōnāgēsimō nōnō; *on the notation, see 1.3, line 6.*
9. clementis viii : Octāvī. — p(ontificis) m(aximī). — vii : Septimō.

10.2   Epitaph of Cardinals della Rovere

CONCORDES ANIMOS PIASQ MENTES

VT DICAS LICET VNICAM FVISSE

COMMISTI CINERES SEQVENTVR ET SE

CREDI CORPORIS VNIVS IVVABIT

Four HENDECASYLLABLES

1. piasq(ue).
3. commisti = commīxtī : *The spelling reflects an Italianate pronunciation; cf. Ital.* misto < mīxtu(m). *For a similar case, see* INSINGNES (1.6G, line 3).
4. vnivs : *Scans* unĭus *(see 8.8B, line 11).*

Corner of Gate and Caserma Giacomo Acqua

As the river in his boldness touched his marker mounted below[a]—
thereby matching himself yet falling short of the nearby fountain[b]—
'We shall rise higher,' he said: 'It is scarcely fitting
that I should be bested; I shall seize fame in the eyes of all;
I shall reap the enjoyment of a nearer sky and in the new century
shall have a report greater than withered old age can recall.
Make your marks here, Quirinus:[c] Here was I—Tiber.'
He overflowed his banks on 24 December 1599,[d]
in the seventh year of Clement the Eighth,[e] Supreme Pontiff.

Seven IAMBIC SENARII (lines 1–7)

a. See 10.1D.
b. In 1572, Rome's first public fountain had been installed in Piazza del Popolo by Giacomo della Porta (cf. 9.5D, note b). Displaced by the obelisk, it ultimately found a home on Piazza Nicosia in Via della Scrofa.
c. I.e., 'Rome' (see 10.1D, note c).
d. Lit., 'on the ninth day before the Kalends of January'. As the inundation in fact took place in 1598 (see 11.5E), the subsequent year was evidently substituted for the current in order to substantiate the reference to the 'new century' (line 5).
e. Pope Clement VIII Aldobrandini (r. 1592–1605). The seventh year of his pontificate ran from 30 January 1598 through 29 January 1599.

S. Maria del Popolo: First Chapel R, L Wall

Just as you might say that our harmonious hearts
and godly minds were one, so shall our mingled ashes
follow suit, and it will please us that they be thought
those of a single body.[a]

Four HENDECASYLLABLES

a. The tomb is that of Cristoforo della Rovere and his brother Domenico della Rovere, both created cardinal by Pope Sixtus IV della Rovere (r. 1471–1484). The church stands on the site of an oratorio built under Pope Paschal II (r. 1099–1118) to exorcise the unhappy ghost of Nero. It was rebuilt under Sixtus IV as a species of pantheon for the della Rovere dynasty.

10.3   Piazza del Popolo: Dedication by Pius VII

i.

PIVS VII PONT MAX

FORI AREAM

PER HEMYCICLOS PORREXIT

ET GEMINO FONTE EXORNAVIT

5   VT ÆDIFICIIS BINIS VTRIMQVE

VNA PARITER EXSTRVCTIS

PRINCIPEM VRBIS ADITVM

NOVO CVLTV NOBILITARET

PONT ANNO XXIV

1. PIVS VII : Septimus. — PONT(ifex) MAX(imus).
2. AREAM : *See 8.3B, line 6.*
3. HEMYCICLOS : *Sic* (= hēmicyclos). *On the spelling, see 2.10, line 2, and 3.1, line 1. The Latin* hēmicyclus *transliterates Greek* ἡμικύκλος *('semicircle').*
9. PONT(ificātūs). — XXIV : Vīcēsimō quārtō.

ii.

PIVS VII PONT MAX

AEDEM HANC

QVAE IN FORI PROSPECTVM

EXCITATA EST

5   ARTIFICVM OPERIBVS

PVBLICE SPECTANDIS DESTINAVIT

ATQVE OMNI CVLTV INSTRVI IVSSIT

PONT ANNO XXIV

1. PIVS VII : Septimus. — PONT(ifex) MAX(imus).
2. AEDEM : *In* RL, aedēs *often represents Ital.* palazzo (*though more usually in* Pl.; *see 1.6H, line 12*).
3. FORI : *See 8.3B, line 6.*
5–6. OPERIBVS . . . SPECTANDIS : *Dat. of Purpose. On the construction, see 1.6H, lines 11–12.*
8. PONT(ificātūs). — XXIV : Vīcēsimō quārtō.

To R and L of Porta del Popolo

East

> *Pius the Seventh,[a] Supreme Pontiff,*
> *extended the confines of the square*
> *with hemicycles*
> *and embellished it with twin fountains,*
> *in order that by the two buildings*
> *constructed uniformly on each side*
> *he might ennoble with new refinement*
> *the City's chief approach [b]*
> *in the twenty-fourth year of his office.*

a. *Pope Pius VII Chiaramonti (r. 1800–1823). The twenty-fourth year of his pontificate ran from 14 March 1823 through 20 August 1823.*

b. *The improvement of the piazza, hitherto roughly trapezoidal in outline, was undertaken by Camille de Tournon, prefect of Rome during the French occupation (1809–1814), and carried out 1816–1824 by Giuseppe Valadier (cf. 2.9A, note c).*

West

> *Pius the Seventh,[a] Supreme Pontiff,*
> *appointed this building,*
> *constructed*
> *in clear view of the piazza,*
> *for the public display of artists' works,*
> *and ordered that it should be furnished*
> *with every refinement [b]*
> *in the twenty-fourth year of his office.*

a. *See 10.3.i, note a.*

b. *Eventually converted into a barracks for the papal gendarmes, the building was renamed for Giacomo Acqua, commander of the* carabinieri *('mounted rifle') of the kingdom of Italy who had participated in the assault on Porta Pia (see 8.7B.ii, note b). Today it is headquarters of the Lazio contingent of the modern* carabinieri, *who serve as the civil, military, and judicial police of the Italian state.*

10.4A   Obelisco Flaminio: Dedication by Augustus

IMP CAESAR DIVI [f]

AVGVSTVS

PONTIFEX MAXIMVS

IMP $\overline{\text{XII}}$ COS $\overline{\text{XI}}$ TRIB POT $\overline{\text{XIV}}$

5   AEGVPTO IN POTESTATEM

POPVLI ROMANI REDACT[a]

SOLI DONVM DEDIT

1. IMP(erātor) CAESAR DIVI [f(īlius)] | AVGVSTVS : *This was the full formal style of the emperor Augustus from January of 27 BC. The inscription has minor damage to its right side; the identical inscription on the N face has minor damage to its left side.*

4. IMP(erātor) $\overline{\text{XII}}$: Duodecimum. — CO(n)S(ul) $\overline{\text{XI}}$: Ūndecimum. — TRIB(ūniciā) POT(estāte) $\overline{\text{XIV}}$: Quārtum decimum.

5. AEGVPTO = Aegyptō : *From Greek* Αἴγυπτος. *In early borrowings, the pronunciation of* Υ *was assimilated to Latin vocalic* V (*see 2.10, line 2, and 3.1, line 1*).

10.4B   Obelisco Flaminio: Dedication by Sixtus V

i.

SIXTVS V PONT MAX

OBELISCVM HVNC

A CAES AVG SOLI

IN CIRCO MAX RITV

5   DICATVM IMPIO

MISERANDA RVINA

FRACTVM OBRVTVMQ

ERVI TRANSFERRI

[f]ORMAE SVAE REDDI

10   [c]RVCIQ INVICTISS

[d]EDICARI IVSSIT

[a m] D LXXXIX PONT I[v]

Piazza del Popolo: Base of Obelisk, S Face

Imperator Caesar Augustus,[a]
son of the Divine, Supreme Pontiff,
acclaimed Imperator for the twelfth time,
Consul for the eleventh,
vested with the Tribunician power for the fourteenth,
upon the subjection of Egypt to the authority of the Roman People
gave this as a gift to the sun.[b]

> a. *On 16 January 27 BC, Caesar's heir (born Gaius Octavius; see 1.8F, note c) formally took the name* IMPERATOR CAESAR AUGUSTUS. *He was granted the office of* SUPREME PONTIFF *in 12 BC, was saluted as* IMPERATOR *for the twelfth time in 11 BC, became* CONSUL *for the eleventh time on 1 January 23 BC and assumed the* TRIBUNICIAN POWER *for the fourteenth time on 1 July 10 BC.*

> b. *The obelisk is one of two removed from the temple at Heliopolis and erected at Rome in 10 BC, twentieth anniversary of the annexation of Egypt. The other is the Obelisco Campense (10.11).*

Base of Obelisk, W and E Faces

West

Sixtus the Fifth,[a] Supreme Pontiff,
bade this obelisk—
consecrated in the Circus Maximus[b]
by Caesar Augustus
in unholy rite to the sun,
broken and buried
in pitiable ruin—
to be dug out, moved
and restored to its beauty,
and dedicated
to the Cross most invincible
in the year 1589, fourth of his office.

1. SIXTVS V : Quīntus. *The name 'Sixtus' appears in various forms (see 3.4D, line 4).* — PONT(ifex) MAX(imus).
2. OBELISCVM HVNC : *The postpositioning of* HVNC *lends flair.*
3. CAES(are) AVG(ustō).
4. MAX(imō).
7. OBRVTVMQ(ue).
10. [c]RVCIQ(ue) INVICTISS(imae) : *On the restorations of lost text, see 10.4B.ii, line 2.*
12. [a(nnō) m] D LXXXIX : Mīllēsimō quīngentēsimō octōgēsimō nōnō. — PONT(ificātūs) I[V] : Quārtō.

ii.

ANTE SACRAM
ILLIVS A[e]DEM
AV[gu]s[t]IOR
LAETIORQ SVRGO
5   CV[i]VS EX VTERO
[ui]RGINA[li]
AV[g i]MPERA[n]TE
SO[l i]VSTITIAE
EXO[rt]VS E[s]T

10   [eques dominicus fontana]
ARCHITECT EREXIT

2. A[e]DEM : *See 1.8B, line 10. The characters enclosed in brackets are restored from transcriptions made before 13 August 1983, when the obelisk was badly damaged by a bolt of lightning.*
4. LAETIORQ(ue).
7. AV[g(ustō) i]MPERA[n]TE : *On the construction, see 5.8B, line 1.*
11. ARCHITECT(us).

a. Pope Sixtus V Peretti (r. 1585–1590). *The fourth year of his pontificate ran from 24 April 1588 through 23 April 1589.*

b. *Originally erected in the thirteenth century* BC *by Seti I and bearing also the hieroglyphs of his son Ramesses II, the obelisk was brought by Augustus from Heliopolis—as its Greek name suggests, a center of solar worship—at the same time as the Obelisco Campense (see 10.11A) and set on the* spina *of the Circus Maximus. Discovered in three fragments in 1587 (see 7.1.iv, note b), it was erected at the ideal point of convergence of Via di Ripetta, Via del Corso and Via del Babuino.*

East

More august

I rise,

and more joyous,[a]

before the sacred shrine of her

from whose

virgin womb

during the reign of Augustus

arose

the Sun of Righteousness.[b]

Cavaliere Domenico Fontana,[c]
Architect, erected this.

a. *The obelisk speaks* in propria persona *(see 4.1.iii, note a). The epithet 'august' alludes to the name of the emperor (see 10.4A, note a).*

b. *The obelisk stands before the Church of S. Maria del Popolo (10.2). The reference to the 'Sun of Righteousness' (Mal. 4:2) implicitly corrects the obelisk's original dedication (cf. 4.3.i, note d, and 10.13.v, note b). The text was dictated by Cardinal Silvio Antoniano (cf. 7.1.i, note a).*

c. *See 7.1.ii, note c.*

10.5 Piazza di Augusto Imperatore: Dedication by Mussolini

HVNC LOCVM VBI AVGVSTI MANES VOLITANT PER AVRAS

POSTQVAM IMPERATORIS MAVSOLEVM EX SAECVLORVM TENEBRIS

EST EXTRACTVM ARAEQVE PACIS DISIECTA MEMBRA REFECTA

MVSSOLINI DVX VETERIBVS ANGVSTIIS DELETIS SPLENDIDIORIBVS

5 VIIS AEDIFICIIS AEDIBVS AD HVMANITATIS MORES APTIS

ORNANDVM CENSVIT ANNO MDCCCCXL A F R XVIII

3. DISIECTA MEMBRA : *A reminiscence of Horace's reference to the fragments of Ennius as* disiecti membra poetae *(Sat. 1.4.62).*

4. MVSSOLINI : *The surname is not Latinized (cf. 12.3B, line 8).*

6. MDCCCCXL : Mīllēsimō nōngentēsimō quadrāgēsimō. — A F(ascibus) R(enovātīs) XVIII : Duodēvīcēsimō. *On the construction, see 1.7A, lines 2–3. The* fascēs *were bundles of wooden rods enclosing an axe and bound by red thongs. They were carried by lictors, official attendants of the Roman magistrates. The number of lictors—and hence of* fascēs—*was strictly correlated with rank: The dictator was assigned twenty-four, the consul twelve and the praetor six. In 19 BC, Augustus was granted the right of twelve* fascēs *in perpetuity. Mussolini called his political movement* Fasci di combattimento: *Derived from* fascēs, *the Ital.* fascio *('band') had been used in preceeding decades of agricultural and labor organizations. The choice of the* fascēs *as a symbol thus enabled Mussolini both to evoke Rome's imperial past and to draw a parallel between fascism and progressive movements of the recent past.*

10.6 Quotation from *Res Gestae* of Augustus

RES GESTAE DIVI AVGVSTI QVIBVS ORBEM TERRARVM ⌐

IMPERIO POPVLI ROMANI SVBIECIT ET INPENSAE QVAS ⌐

IN REM PVBLICAM POPVLVMQVE ROMANVM FECIT

RES GESTAE : *In CL, this expression is frequent in the sense 'military exploits' (cf. 13.5.iii, line 6). —* ORBEM TERRARVM : *The phrase* orbis terrārum *(Lit., 'circle of the lands') is the usual CL expression for the known world as a whole. The reference is to the continents of Europe, Asia, and Africa, conceived as lobes of a central land mass embraced by the circumfluent stream of Ocean.*

Piazza di Augusto Imperatore: N Side

The emperor's mausoleum[a] having been withdrawn from the darkness of centuries and the scattered fragments of the Ara Pacis reassembled,[b] Mussolini, 'Il Duce',[c] decreed that the ancient warren of alleys should be erased and that this place, where the shade of Augustus flits in the breezes, should be embellished with finer streets, houses, and buildings suited to the manners of human beings,[d] in the year 1940, eighteenth after the revival of the fasces.[e]

> a. *The first member of the family of Augustus to be interred in the mausoleum was his nephew Gaius Claudius Marcellus, who died in 23 BC at the age of nineteen (cf. 2.7, note a).*
>
> b. *Originally located immediately to the E of Augustus' solar calendar (see 10.9, note d), the Ara Pacis ('Altar of Peace') was dedicated in 9 BC to celebrate the Pax Augusta (see 13.5.viii, note a).*
>
> c. *The fascist dictator Benito Amilcare Andrea Mussolini (1883–1945) headed the government of Italy from 29 October 1922 through 25 July 1943 and again—under the Repubblica Sociale Italiana—from 1 December 1943 until his arrest and summary execution on 28 April 1945.*
>
> d. *To liberate the mausoleum, the Renaissance quarter that surrounded it was razed and replaced by the present dismal arrangements.*
>
> e. *The fasces were the emblem of the authority of ancient Roman magistrates. The Fascist era is reckoned from 28 October 1922, date of Mussolini's triumphant march on Rome.*

Piazza di Augusto Imperatore: W Side

The exploits of the Divine Augustus,[a] through which he subjugated the world to the authority of the Roman people, and the expenditures that he made on the commonwealth and people of Rome.

> a. *The text is adapted from the preamble to the Res Gestae Divi Augusti ('Achievements of the Divine Augustus'), an autobiographical catalogue of the deeds of the emperor (r. 27 BC–AD 14) inscribed on bronze tablets and set up before his mausoleum. A copy of the entire text appears on the foundation of the present structure, which houses the fragments of the Ara Pacis (see 10.5, note b).*

10.7 Collegio Illirico: Dedication

> COLLEGIUM A S HIERONYMO ILLYRICORUM
> VETERE DIRUTO AEDIFICIO
> AD NOVUM URBIS ORNAMENTUM
> ET CROATICAE GENTIS DECUS
> 5   RELIGIONISQUE CATHOLICAE INCREMENTUM
> MAGNIFICENTIUS RESTITUTUM
> ANNO DOMINI M DCCCCXXXVIII

1. COLLEGIUM A S(ānctō) HIERONYMO : *In* EL, collēgium *is an ecclesiastical college or association. The Latin* Hierōnymus *transliterates Greek* Ἱερώνυμος. *On the use of the Prep., see 11.3C, line 11a.*

4. CROATICAE : *The* ML *Adj.* Croāticus *corresponds to the toponym* Croātia.

7. M DCCCCXXXVIII : Mīllēsimō nōngentēsimō trīcēsimō octāvō. *As at 12.3B, also a religious building, reference to the Fascist era is tactfully omitted (cf. 10.5 and 12.1).*

10.8 Epitaph of Nicholas Poussin

> PARCE PIIS LACRYMIS VIVIT PUSSINUS IN URNA
> VIVERE QUI DEDERAT NESCIUS IPSE MORI
> HIC TAMEN IPSE SILET SI VIS AUDIRE LOQUENTEM
> MIRUM EST IN TABULIS VIVIT ET ELOQUITUR
>
> *Two* ELEGIAC COUPLETS

1. LACRYMIS = lacrimīs : *On the spelling, see 3.1, line 1.* — PUSSINUS : *On the Latinization, cf. 12.3B, line 8.*

2. NESCIUS . . . MORI : *The Inf. dependent on an Adj. in imitation of the Greek is typical of verse (and post-Augustan prose).*

4. MIRUM EST : *The clause forms a syntactical parenthesis without effect on the construction of the subsequent verbs.*

Via Tomacelli 132: Above Portal

Its former seat demolished,
the Collegio di San Girolamo degli Illirici [a]
was rebuilt in grander fashion
to the new embellishment of the City
and the glory of the nation of Croatia
and the increase of the Catholic religion
in the year of the Lord 1938.

a. *The Collegio Illirico (Illyrian College) was founded in 1790 by Pope Pius VI Braschi (r. 1775–1799) and in 1902 renamed* Collegium Sancti Hieronymi Illyricorum *('College of St. Jerome of the Illyrians'). St. Jerome was a native of Dalmatia. In the course of demolitions carried out 1937–1940 for the liberation of the Mausoleum of Augustus (see 10.5, note d), the college's former seat was eliminated to make way for the existing structure, which forms the S limit of Piazza di Augusto Imperatore.*

S. Lorenzo in Lucina: R Aisle, Second Pilaster

Spare your kind tears: Poussin [a] lives on in this tomb,[b]
himself incapable of death who had given the gift of life.
Yet here he is himself silent. If you wish to hear him speak,
in wondrous wise he lives and is eloquent in his paintings.

Two ELEGIAC COUPLETS

a. *The French painter Nicholas Poussin (1594–1665) arrived in Rome in 1624. Influenced by the masters from Raphael (see 11.3F) to the Carracci (see 11.3H), he elaborated an idiom as rational as it is monumental. Poussin's system became the basis of the Classicism perpetuated by the academies. The tomb was sponsored by François-René, vicomte de Chateaubriand (1768–1848).*
b. *Lit., 'urn.' (cf. 6.2B, note e).*

10.9 Commemoration of Excavation of Obelisco Campense

BENEDICTUS XIV PONT MAX

OBELISCUM HIEROGLYPHICIS NOTIS ELEGANTER INSCULPTUM

ÆGYPTO IN POTESTATEM POPULI ROMANI REDACTA

AB IMP CÆSARE AUGUSTO ROMAM ADVECTUM

5   ET STRATO LAPIDE REGULISQUE EX ÆRE INCLUSIS

AD DEPREHENDENDAS SOLIS UMBRAS

DIERUMQUE AC NOCTIUM MAGNITUDINEM

IN CAMPO MARTIO ERECTUM ET SOLI DICATUM

TEMPORIS ET BARBAROR INJURIA CONFRACTŪ JACENTEMQ

10   TERRA AC ÆDIFICIIS OBRUTUM

MAGNA IMPENSA ATQUE ARTIFICIO ERUIT

PUBLICOQ REI LITERARIÆ BONO PROPINQVŪ IN LOCŪ TRANSTULIT

ET NE ANTIQUÆ SEDIS OBELISCI MEMORIA

VETUSTATE EXOLESCERET

15   MONUMENTUM PONI JUSSIT

ANNO REP SAL MDCCXLVIII PONTIF IX

1. BENEDICTUS XIV : Quārtus decimus. — PONT(ifex) MAX(imus).

2. HIEROGLYPHICIS : *The Latin* hieroglyphicus *transliterates Greek* ἱερογλυφικός (*'pertaining to sacred glyphs'*).

3. ÆGYPTO . . . REDACTA : *The text quotes that of 10.11A, lines 5–6.*

4. IMP(erātōre).

9. BARBAROR(um). — CONFRACTU(m) JACENTEMQ(ue).

11. MAGNA IMPENSA ATQUE ARTIFICIO : *A mild syllepsis (see 2.13C, line 5). Here Abl. of Price and Abl. of Manner are both construed with* ERUIT.

12. PUBLICOQ(ue). — REI LITERARIÆ = litterāriae : *The phrase* rēs litterāria *connotes humanistic pursuits in the widest sense.* — PROPINQVU(m) : *The* V, *otherwise absent from the present inscription, introduces a graphic distinction between the labial element in the cluster* QV (= /kʷ/) *and the vocalic* /u/ *that immediately follows, ensuring that* -QVUM *is read as a single syllable.* — LOCU(m).

16. REP(arātae) SAL(ūtis) : *On the construction, see 1.7A, lines 2–3.* — MDCCXLVIII : Mīllēsimō septingentēsimō quadrāgēsimō octāvō. — PONTIF(icātūs) IX : Nōnō.

Piazza del Parlamento 3: Above Portal

Benedict the Fourteenth,[a] Supreme Pontiff,
at great expense and with great ingenuity excavated the obelisk[b]—
elegantly engraved with hieroglyphic signs,
brought to Rome by Imperator Caesar Augustus
upon the subjection of Egypt to the authority of the Roman People,[c]
set up in the Campus Martius and dedicated to the sun
on a stone pavement set with brazen rules
for observing the sun's shadows
and the length of the nights and days,[d]
broken up under the assault of the ages and of the barbarians[e]
and lying buried by earth and buildings[f]—
and for the general benefit of learning
transported it to a nearby place and, lest with the passage of time
the memory of the obelisk's ancient site should fade,
he ordered this memorial to be set up
in the year 1748 of the renewal of Salvation, ninth of his office.

a. *Pope Benedict XIV Lambertini (r. 1740–1758). The ninth year of his pontificate ran from 17 August 1748 through 16 August 1749.*

b. *I.e., the Obelisco Campense (10.11).*

c. *A direct quotation of the Augustan dedication (see 10.11A).*

d. *The obelisk formed the gnomon of the great solar calendar laid out in the Campus Martius by Augustus. Much of the language of the present text derives from the elder Pliny's description. The text was dictated by Rudolfino Venuti (1705–1763), founder of the Etruscan Academy of Cortona.*

e. *See 7.1.iv, note b. Despite the fact that the obelisk is mentioned in the itinerary appended to the* EINSIEDELN CATALOGUE, *it is unlikely that it still stood in the ninth century; its fallen fragments must nevertheless have remained visible. There is no evidence that it was toppled in 1084 by the Normans and Saracens of Robert Guiscard.*

f. *First uncovered in the early sixteenth century, the fragments of the obelisk remained in situ until the excavation commemorated in the present inscription. The monument was repaired with material taken from the Column of Antoninus Pius (see 10.13.ii, note b).*

10.10 Fontana della Lupa: Dedication

LAC PVERIS LVPA DVLCE DEDIT NON SAEVA GEMELLIS

SIC VICINE LVPVS DAT TIBI MITIS AQVAM

QVAE FLVIT ASSIDVE QVAE LACTE EST DVLCIOR IPSO

PVRIOR ELECTRO FRIGIDIORQVE NIVE

5 HINC IGITVR LYMPHAS BENE TERSA SEDVLVS VRNA

ET PVER ET IVVENIS PORTET ANVSQVE DOMVM

FONTICVLO PROHIBENTVR EQVI PROHIBENTVR ASELLI

NEC CANIS HINC FOEDO NEC CAPER ORE BIBIT

M D LXXVIII

Four ELEGIAC COUPLETS (lines 1–8)

1–2. LAC . . . DEDIT . . . DAT . . . AQVAM : *The chiastic structure (see 2.11A.i,
lines 3–4) and the variation of* LVPA-LVPVS *lend the couplet an untranslatable neatness and point.* — NON SAEVA : *By litotes, 'gentle'. Litotes
(Greek* λιτότης, *'simplicity') is assertion by means of understatement.*
7. PROHIBENTVR . . . PROHIBENTVR : *Asyndeton (see* 1.2.i, *line 4).*
9. M D LXXVIII : Mīllēsimō quīngentēsimō septuāgēsimō octāvō.

10.11A Obelisco Campense: Dedication by Augustus

[imp caesar diui f

augustus

pont]IFEX MAXIMVS

[imp] $\overline{\text{XII}}$ COS $\overline{\text{XI}}$ TRIB POT $\overline{\text{XIV}}$

5 [a]EGVPTO IN POTESTATEM

[po]PVLI ROMANI REDACTA

SOLI DONVM DEDIT

1. [imp(erātor)] caesar diui f(īlius) : *The missing portions are restored on
the basis of the identical text in 10.4A. The inscription on the N side is even
more fragmentary.*
4. [imp(erātor)] $\overline{\text{XII}}$: Duodecimum. — co(n)s(ul) $\overline{\text{XI}}$: Ūndecimum. —
TRIB(ūniciā) POT(estāte) $\overline{\text{XIV}}$: Quārtum decimum.

Via dei Prefetti 17: Atrium, R Wall

The she-wolf gently proffered sweet milk to the twin boys.[a]
Thus to you, neighbor, does the wolf mildly proffer water
that flows without ceasing, that is sweeter than very milk,
purer than amber, and colder than snow.
From here, therefore, let boy and youth
and aged dame diligently bear the waters home in a well-scoured jug.
Horses and likewise asses are forbidden the fount,
neither does dog or goat take drink hence with its foul maw.[b]

1578

FOUR ELEGIAC COUPLETS (*lines 1–8*)

a. I.e., *Romulus and Remus*.

b. *Formerly in Via della Lupa, the fountain to which the present inscription pertained was the twin of one still extant in Piazza di S. Salvatore in Lauro, and whose inscription makes allusion to it (see 12.7). Both figure among the public fountains made possible by the reactivation of the Acqua Vergine in 1570 (see 9.5D, note b).*

Piazza di Montecitorio: Base of Obelisk, S & N Faces

Imperator Caesar Augustus,
son of the Divine, Supreme Pontiff,
acclaimed Imperator for the twelfth time,
Consul for the eleventh,
vested with the Tribunician power for the fourteenth,
upon the subjection of Egypt to the authority of the Roman People
gave this as a gift to the sun.[a]

a. *The text repeats that of 10.4A, which is substantially complete. The missing portions were reproduced and patched in when the obelisk was erected in 1792 (see 10.11B). A casual inspection of the monument's shaft and base reveals how heavily it has been restored (see 10.9, note f).*

10.11B Obelisco Campense: Dedication by Pius VI

i.

PIVS V̄Ī PONT MAX

OBELISCVM

REGIS SESOSTRIDIS

A C CAESARE AVGVSTO

5   HORARVM INDICEM

IN CAMPO STATVTVM

QVEM IGNIS VI

ET TEMPORVM VETVSTATE

CORRVPTVM

10   BENEDICTVS X̄ĪĪĪĪ P M

EX AGGESTA HVMO AMOLITVS

RELIQVERAT

SQVALORE DETERSO

CVLTVQVE ADDITO

15   VRBI CAELOQVE RESTITVIT

ANNO M̄ D̄C̄C̄ X̄C̄ĪĪ

SACRI PRINCIPATVS EIVS X̄V̄ĪĪĪ

1. PIVS V̄Ī : Sextus. — PONT(ifex) MAX(imus).
4. C(āiō) : *On the abbreviation, see 1.1, line 1.*
10. BENEDICTVS X̄ĪĪĪĪ : Quārtus decimus. — P(ontifex) M(aximus).
16. M̄ D̄C̄C̄ X̄C̄ĪĪ : Mīllēsimō septingentēsimō nōnāgēsimō secundō.
17. X̄V̄ĪĪĪ : Duodēvīcēsimō.

ii.

QVAE CELERES OLIM SIGNABAT PYRAMIS HORAS

FRACTA DEHINC LAPSV SPRETA IACEBAT HVMO

ANTIQVVM RENOVATA DECVS NVNC FRONTE SVPERBA

DINVMERAT SEXTI TEMPORA FAVSTA PII

Two Elegiac Couplets

1. PYRAMIS : *The word* pȳramis *(Greek* πυραμίς, *'pyramid') is regularly used of obelisks in medieval topographical writings.*
4. SEXTI . . . PII : *I.e., Pius VI.*

Piazza di Montecitorio: Base of Obelisk

West

Pius the Sixth,[a] Supreme Pontiff,
after the removal of grime
and the addition of ornament
restored to the City and to Heaven
the obelisk
of King Sesostris,[b]
set up in the Campus
by Gaius Caesar Augustus
as a marker of the hours
and which,
damaged by the violence of fire[c]
and long flight of the ages,
Benedict the Fourteenth,[d] Supreme Pontiff,
having wrested it from the accumulated earth,
had abandoned,
in the year 1792,
eighteenth of his sacred office.

a. Pope Pius VI Braschi (r. 1775–1799). The eighteenth year of his pontificate ran from 15 February 1792 through 14 February 1793.
b. It dates in fact to the reign of Psammetichus II (r. 594–589 BC).
c. See 7.1.iv, note b.
d. Pope Benedict XIV Lambertini (r. 1740–1758); see. 10.9, note a.

East

The pyramid[a] that once marked the swift hours[b]
thereafter lay spurned on the ground, broken in its fall:
Its former beauty renewed, now with proud mien
it counts off the happy hours of Pius the Sixth.[c]

Two ELEGIAC COUPLETS

a. I.e., the obelisk, which has a tapering shaft and pyramidal apex.
b. See 10.9, note d.
c. See 10.11B.i, note a; on the felicity of Pius' reign, see 8.4B, note f.

10.12 Palazzo Wedekind: Dedication of Portico

GREGORIVS XVI PONTIF MAXIM ANNO M DCCCXXXVIII ⌐
FRONTEM AEDIFICII EXORNANDAM PORTICVM VEIORVM ⌐
COLVMNIS INSIGNEM ADSTRVENDAM CVRAVIT

GREGORIVS XVI : Sextus decimus. — PONTIF(ex) MAXIM(us). —
M DCCCXXXVIII : Mīllēsimō octingentēsimō trīcēsimō octāvō. —
FRONTEM . . . EXORNANDAM . . . PORTICVM . . . ADSTRVENDAM :
Note the asyndeton (cf. 1.2.i, line 4). — VEIORVM : On the Pl., cf.
Volsiniī, Δελφοί. — ADSTRVENDAM : On the spelling, see 8.2, line 7.

10.13 Column of Marcus Aurelius: Dedication by Sixtus V

i.

SIXTVS V | S PAVLO | APOST | PONT A IIII

1. SIXTVS V : Quīntus.
2. S(ānctō).
3. APOST(olō) : See 1.61, line 7.
4. PONT(ificātūs) A(nnō) IIII : Quārtō.

ii.

M AVRELIVS IMP

ARMENIS PARTHIS

GERMANISQ BELLO

MAXIMO DEVICTIS

5   TRIVMPHALEM HANC

COLVMNAM REBVS

GESTIS INSIGNEM

IMP ANTONINO PIO

PATRI DEDICAVIT

1. M(ārcus). — IMP(erātor).
2. ARMENIS = Armeniīs.
3. GERMANISQ(ue).
8. IMP(erātōrī).

Piazza Colonna 366: Frieze

In the year 1838 Gregory the Sixteenth,[a] Supreme Pontiff, undertook to have the façade of the building embellished and the portico, distinguished by its columns from Veii,[b] to be added.

a. *Pope Gregory XVI Cappellari (r. 1831–1846).*

b. *The portico of Palazzo Wedekind incorporates eleven fluted Ionic columns excavated 1812–1817 at the site of ancient Veii, the Etruscan city conquered by Marcus Furius Camillus in 396 BC. Palazzo Wedekind houses the offices of the daily newspaper Il Tempo.*

Piazza Colonna: Capital and Base of Column

Capital

Sixtus the Fifth,[a] to Saint Paul the Apostle, in the fourth year of his office.

a. *Pope Sixtus V Peretti (r. 1585–1590). The fourth year of his pontificate ran from 24 April 1588 through 23 April 1589. As the Column of Trajan was dedicated to the Prince of the Apostles, that of Marcus was dedicated to the first philosopher of the faith (cf. 3.2A, note b).*

West

*Upon the defeat
of the Armenians, Parthians,
and Germans
in a mighty war,
the emperor Marcus Aurelius[a]
dedicated to his father,
the emperor Antoninus Pius,[b]
this triumphal column,
distinguished by his exploits.*

a. *Adopted in 138 by his uncle, Antoninus Pius, Marcus Aurelius (r. 161–180) spent much of his reign engaged in wars.*

b. *The column was in fact erected to Marcus Aurelius after his death. The confusion was sorted out only in 1704 with the identification of the shattered Column of Antoninus Pius; the fragments of its shaft of red Egyptian granite were used to repair the Obelisco Campense (see 10.9, note f).*

iii.

SIXTVS V PONT MAX

COLVMNAM HANC

COCHLIDEM IMP

ANTONINO DICATAM

5   MISERE LACERAM

RVINOSAMQ PRIMAE

FORMAE RESTITVIT

A M D LXXXIX PONT IV

1. SIXTVS V : Quīntus. — PONT(ifex) MAX(imus).
2. COLVMNAM HANC : *The postpositioning of* HANC *lends flair.*
3. COCHLIDEM : *The Latin* cochlis *transliterates Greek* κοχλίς
   ('spiral shell', 'conch'); here it is used as an Adj. — IMP(erātōrī).
6. RVINOSAMQ(ue).
8. A(nnō) M D LXXXIX : Mīllēsimō quīngentēsimō octōgēsimō nōnō. —
   PONT(ificātūs) IV : Quārtō.

iv.

SIXTVS V PONT MAX

COLVMNAM HANC

AB OMNI IMPIETATE

EXPVRGATAM

5   S PAVLO APOSTOLO

AENEA EIVS STATVA

INAVRATA IN SVMMO

VERTICE POSITA D D

A M D LXXXIX PONT IV

1. SIXTVS V : Quīntus. — PONT(ifex) MAX(imus).
2. COLVMNAM HANC: *See 10.13.iii, line 2.*
5. S(ānctō). — APOSTOLO : *See 1.61, line 7.*
6. AENEA : ăēnĕā (*cf. 11.3B.i, line 2*).
8. D(ōnum) D(edit).
9. A(nnō) M D LXXXIX : Mīllēsimō quīngentēsimō octōgēsimō nōnō. —
   PONT(ificātūs) IV : Quārtō.

South

> *Sixtus the Fifth,^a Supreme Pontiff,*
> *restored to its original beauty*
> *this spiral column,^b*
> *dedicated*
> *to the emperor Antoninus,^c*
> *pitiably mutilated*
> *and threatening to collapse,*
> *in the year 1589, fourth of his office.*

a. See 10.13.i, note a.

b. The spiral reliefs of the column document Marcus' campaigns in Germania (172–173) and Sarmatia (174–175). The imposing height of the original base (10.5 m), still intact beneath Piazza Colonna, preserved the shaft itself from partial interment with the rise in the ground level of the Campus Martius.

c. See 10.15.ii, note b.

East

> *Sixtus the Fifth,^a Supreme Pontiff,*
> *gave as a gift this column,^b*
> *cleansed*
> *of all wickedness,^c*
> *to Saint Paul, Apostle,*
> *setting on its topmost height*
> *his statue*
> *in gilt bronze^d*
> *in the year 1589, fourth of his office.*

a. See 10.13.i, note a.

b. In 949, Pope Agapitus II had assigned the column to the monastery of S. Silvestro. The monks collected a fee for the privilege of climbing the column's internal stair of some 200 steps to enjoy the view.

c. The column was exorcised at its inauguration (cf. 15.3B.iii, note a).

d. The bronze statue of St. Paul is by Leonardo Sormani and Tommaso della Porta (cf. 3.2A, note b).

v.

TRIVMPHALIS

ET SACRA NVNC SVM

CHRISTI VERE PIVM

DISCIPVLVM FERENS

5   QVI PER CRVCIS

PRAEDICATIONEM

DE ROMANIS

BARBARISQ

TRIVMPHAVIT

3. CHRISTI : *See 1.6A.ii, line 6.*

4. DISCIPVLVM : *In* EL, discipulus *is 'follower of Christ', frequently with reference to one or another of the Apostles.*

6. PRAEDICATIONEM : *In* EL, praedicātiō *is 'preaching' (cf. 7.4E, line 8).*

7. DE ROMANIS | BARBARISQ(ue) : *On the use of the Prep., see 1.4, line 2.*

North

Triumphant

and sacred now am I[a]

inasmuch as I bear the Disciple of Christ,

pious forsooth,[b]

who by preaching

the Cross

triumphed

over Romans

and barbarians alike.

a. *The column proclaims* in propria persona *the triumph of Christianity that supersedes the victories catalogued at 10.13.ii (see 4.1.iii, note a). The texts were dictated by Silvio Antoniano (see 7.1.i, note a); the letters and layout were drafted by Luca Orfei (see 8.6, note e).*

b. *The use of the epithet 'pious' lends point to the contrast between the genuine piety of St. Paul and that of Antoninus 'Pius'—probably so called for his insistence on the deification of Hadrian, his predecessor and adoptive father.*

THE PANTHEON

The marriage of the Greek colonnade and the Roman vault is consummated in the Pantheon, whose columned portico both lends the building's exterior the appearance of a traditional temple front and establishes an axis for its circular cella. Strangely, the pediment of the portico fails to rise to the full height of the block that forms the transition to the rotunda. It appears that the plan called for columns with shafts of sixty Roman feet in height, whereas columns of only forty-eight feet were available at the time of construction. The projected height of the portico can be gauged by the curious second pediment that rises above and behind the first.

XI. *The Pantheon & Environs*

ROME IS THE CITY OF PIAZZAS PAR EXCELLENCE—Piazza Navona, Piazza di Spagna, Piazza del Popolo; a list of the major representatives alone would run to at least a dozen. Yet, in the period following the unification of Italy in 1870, a great many of these urban oases fell victim to the builders of the 'Third Rome', successor to the capitals of Caesar and of Christ. Emblematic of the earliest losses is Piazza di Ponte Sant'Angelo, interred beneath the Tiber embankments. In the 1880s, Corso Vittorio Emanuele II swallowed up Piazza di Sant'Andrea della Valle, while Piazza Venezia was dealt a fatal blow by the imposition of the Victor Emanuel monument. The rhythm of destruction was accelerated with the advent of the Fascist regime in the second decade of the twentieth century: Piazza Venezia was finished off as a vast traffic circle; Piazza d'Aracoeli, vestibule to Michelangelo's Campidoglio, succumbed to the construction of Via di Teatro di Marcello; Piazza Montanara and Piazza Bocca della Verità were swept away in the same campaign. The vanished squares have all but passed from living memory—though some preserve a ghostly afterlife in names that cling to urban spaces now mutilated beyond recognition.

It is sobering to contemplate how closely Piazza della Rotonda came to sharing a similar fate. The isolation of the Pantheon was first proposed under the French administration of 1809–1814: decrees signed by Napoleon in the summer of 1811 called for the demolition of the structures surrounding its *cella* and of those intervening between Piazza della Rotonda and Piazza della Maddalena. The resultant void—large, perfectly rectangular, and dead—would no doubt have borne the name of its obliterated predecessor. Owing to the brevity of the French regime, the project remained on paper; it nevertheless survived to reappear in the urban plan of 1873, which provided in addition for broad boulevards that should converge on the enlarged piazza from the direction of Piazza Borghese and Largo Magnanapoli. One may be grateful that the proposed interventions were realized only in small part: in the early nineteenth century, structures at the north end of the piazza were removed

11.2   in works credited to Pope PIUS VII (r. 1800–1823); a few decades later,

11.3C   PIUS IX (r. 1846–1878) demolished those constructed against the side of the Pantheon itself. Piazza della Rotonda remains substantially intact.

The southern end of the square is occupied by the Pantheon, not only the best preserved ancient structure in Rome but also the largest domed building of Antiquity. Owing to the continuous rise in the surrounding ground level, the huge edifice now appears to sink into the pavement under its own weight. In Antiquity, by contrast, it towered high on a podium and was approached by a stair. Today the focus of the piazza is furnished by Giacomo della Porta's fountain of 1575. It is surmounted

11.1   by the OBELISCO MACUTÈO, placed early in the eighteenth century by order of Pope Clement XI (r. 1700–1721). Like those in the nearby Piazza Navona and Piazza della Minerva, the obelisk pertained to the *Iseum Campense*, a shrine of the Egyptian goddess Isis situated to the southeast of the Pantheon. It owes its modern name to the fact that in the fifteenth century it was reassembled and erected before the nearby Church of San Macuto.

The Pantheon was constructed in its original form between 27 and 25 BC by Marcus Vipsanius Agrippa, lieutenant and son-in-law of Augustus. Agrippa's structure appears to have been a rectangular temple coinciding with the portico of the present building. The area now occupied by the rotunda was an open piazza, perhaps surrounded by a circular ambulatory. Twice destroyed by fire, Agrippa's Pantheon was reconstructed by the emperor Hadrian (r. 117–138), who may himself have been the architect. As he had done with other monuments that he restored, Hadrian ordered the Pantheon to be dedicated in the name of its original

11.3A   founder: M AGRIPPA L F COS TERTIVM FECIT.

From a technical point of view, the Pantheon constitutes a 'summa' of the classical architectural tradition. It fuses the conservative post-and-lintel temple architecture of the Greeks with the Roman vault, leitmotif of the great imperial baths and basilicas that so enthralled the architects of the Renaissance. The sophisticated geometry of the structure instantiates Archimedes' demonstration of the relationship of a cylinder and a sphere that share a diameter. The original function of the Pantheon is not entirely clear. The Latin *pantheum* transliterates πάνθειον—literally 'shrine of all gods'—yet no cult of the twelve Olympians is known to have existed at Rome. Hadrian, for his part, appears to have employed the rotunda primarily as an audience hall. The fact that the structure aligns axially with the mausoleum of Augustus, which stands three-quarters of a kilometer to the north, and that its principal niche housed a statue of the deified Julius Caesar, accords with the dynastic tenor of the Augustan building program.

After the closure of the temples, the Pantheon stood abandoned for nearly two and a half centuries. It was the first Roman shrine to be converted into a Christian church. In 608 or 609, the Byzantine emperor Phocas presented the Pantheon to Pope St. Boniface IV (r. 608–615), who rededicated it in the name of Mary the Virgin and All Saints. At the ceremony of consecration, Boniface is said to have caused the relics of numerous martyrs to be interred beneath the pavement; as the practice of disturbing the gravesites of martyrs was not common in the West before the mid-eighth century, this report is unlikely to be true. Be that as it may, the conversion of a shrine of all gods into a church of all saints eloquently instances the canniness with which Christianity absorbed and transfigured the legacy of the pagan past. It will hardly have been fortuitous that the ceremony took place on 13 May, the culminating day of the *Lemuria*—the pagan festival of the dead. Two centuries later, Pope Gregory IV (r. 827–844) transferred the Feast of All Saints to 1 November. This is the date of Samhain, the great Celtic harvest festival; the Roman *Lemuria* having been effectively neutralized, the Feast of All Saints was available to be deployed further afield.

Despite its status as a church, called *Sancta Maria ad Martyres* ('Saint Mary by the Martyrs'), the Pantheon suffered depredation at the hands of the Eastern Roman emperors. In AD 663, on the last occasion of an imperial visit to the city, Constans II ordered the structure's gilt-bronze roof tiles removed to be transported to Constantinople; the shipment was intercepted by Saracens before reaching its destination. The survival of the building to modern times is due to the leaden roof installed in the eighth century by order of Pope St. Gregory III (r. 731–741).

11.3B During the Middle Ages, the portico of the Pantheon sustained extensive damage; old illustrations show the corner column and left end of the pediment entirely collapsed. In 1626, Pope URBAN VIII Barberini (r. 1623–1644) had the missing column replaced by one brought from Castel Gandolfo; the two behind it were replaced in the 1660s under Pope Alexander VII (r. 1665–1667). The damage notwithstanding, the portico's massive brazen beams had survived intact from Antiquity. It was Urban VIII who ordered them removed. The metal was used to cast eighty cannon for Castel Sant'Angelo—the papal fortress—as well as for Gianlorenzo Bernini's baldacchino above the high altar in the Basilica of St. Peter. For his vandalism, the pope earned a famous pasquinade: *Quod non fecerunt barbari fecerunt Barberini* ('What the barbarians started, the Barberini finished'). (In this connection, it is worth remembering that while Rome has been sacked by Visigoths [AD 410], Vandals [455], Ostrogoths [547], Saracens [847], Normans [1084], and Lutherans [1527], the damage inflicted on her monuments by 'barbarians' is minimal by comparison with the systematic and unremitting destruction wrought over the centuries by the Romans themselves.) Perhaps as a gesture of expiation, Urban commissioned Gianlorenzo Bernini to ornament the building with two bell-towers to replace the medieval belfry; these were demolished only in 1883.

Since the early sixteenth century, the Pantheon has housed the tombs of leading Italian artists; the word 'Pantheon' has come to be used by metonymy of any monument in which the illustrious dead of a nation

11.3F are interred or memorialized. The precedent was set by RAPHAEL, buried in the Pantheon at his own request; other artistic luminaries reposing here include TADDEO ZUCCARO, ANNIBALE CARRACCI, and BALDASSARE PERUZZI; likewise the composer ARCANGELO CORELLI. In the course of time, the rotunda became so crowded with the busts of distinguished persons that Pope Pius VII (r. 1800–1823) caused them to be transferred en masse to the Capitoline Museums, incidentally thus founding the Capitoline *Protomoteca* ('gallery of busts'). By a natural transition, in the late nineteenth century the Pantheon became a species of mausoleum for the Italian royal family. For the generation that followed the unification of Italy, the monument took on the character of a patriotic shrine. In order to foster an atmosphere of quiet reverence by muting the noise of the street, Piazza della Rotonda was paved with tropical hardwood donated by the Italian community of Argentina. *11.3E&H* *11.3I&D*

To the southeast of the Pantheon, on Piazza della Minerva, rises the Basilica of Santa Maria sopra Minerva. The church is so named because it was thought to have replaced a temple to Minerva Chalcidica now known to have stood some 200 meters to the east. The origins of the earliest Christian foundation on the site are obscure. Pope St. Zacharias (r. 741–752) is said to have assigned a church here to a community of Basilian nuns fleeing the Iconoclastic persecutions. Whether or not that is the case, there is no doubt that a church was present by the time the Einsiedeln Itinerary was compiled around the beginning of the ninth century. Having passed in due course to the Dominicans, Santa Maria sopra Minerva was rebuilt in the early fourteenth century. It is Rome's only major Gothic edifice: reproducing the design of the great Dominican foundation of Santa Maria Novella in Florence, the church seems to fling a challenge at the rival Franciscans' Santa Maria in Aracoeli on the Capitoline Hill. The façade and the vaulting of the nave were not completed until 1453.

Piazza della Minerva is home to one of Rome's strangest monuments. Designed by Bernini, it is an ensemble consisting of a diminutive and oddly porcine Elephant bearing on its back an Egyptian Obelisk—the OBELISCO MINERVEO. The genesis of the monument was the dis- *11.4* covery in 1665 of the obelisk in the garden of the Dominican convent. Formerly part of the decoration of the *Iseum* (a shrine of Isis that had stood on the site), it dates from the reign of Apries (the biblical Hophra) in the early sixth century BC; the hieroglyphs celebrate the recently elevated pharaoh. The fact that the obelisk came from a site associated successively with Isis, Minerva, and the Virgin Mary furnished Pope Alexander VII, the monument's sponsor, with the opportunity to execute an intellectual pirouette of authentically baroque sophistication: the conceit of the texts inscribed on the base of the monument is that the worship of Isis and Minerva, paragons of pagan wisdom, had now given way to the cult of the Mother of God, vessel of the wisdom of the true God. The pope himself dictated the texts.

Although the elephant-cum-obelisk is one of his most famous creations, Bernini appears to have disowned it. It is omitted from the list of works that the artist drew up at the close of his career. The fact is that Bernini proposed a freestanding elephant but was required by his official Dominican collaborator to design the figure in such a way that the sculptured drapery formed a solid extension of the base. The reason for the friar's insistence on this point is evidently to be sought in the *Hypnerotomachia Poliphili*, a philosophical-architectural romance of prodigious opacity composed in the sixteenth century by Francesco Colonna, himself a Dominican. In the course of his fantasy, Colonna found occasion to describe an imaginary monument much on the lines of Bernini's elephant. Colonna expressly condemned the superposition of a perpendicular load on a void. The whimsical genius of Bernini did not flourish under theoretical proscriptions. The 'floating' obelisk of the Fontana dei Quattro Fiumi in Piazza Navona, designed over a decade before, demonstrates the extent to which the design of the Minerva monument represents a step backwards.

Before the construction of San Giovanni dei Fiorentini in the sixteenth century, Santa Maria sopra Minerva was the Florentine 'national' church, for which reason it houses the tombs—uninscribed—of the

Medici popes Leo X (r. 1513–1521) and Clement VII (r. 1523–1534). The
most illustrious tenant of the church, however, is the painter FRA AN-   *11.5F*
GELICO, who died in Rome while decorating the apartments of Pope
Nicholas V (r. 1447–1455) in the Vatican. His epitaph is attributed to the
humanist scholar Lorenzo Valla.

Because Santa Maria sopra Minerva occupies the lowest point of the
Campus Martius, before the canalization of the Tiber in the late nineteenth century it suffered the worst flooding in the city. As a consequence, its façade hosts a large number of FLOOD TABLETS recording   *11.5A–E*
the level reached by the waters of the Tiber in various inundations of the
fifteenth and sixteenth centuries. As these have been rearranged over
the intervening centuries, their indications are no longer reliable.

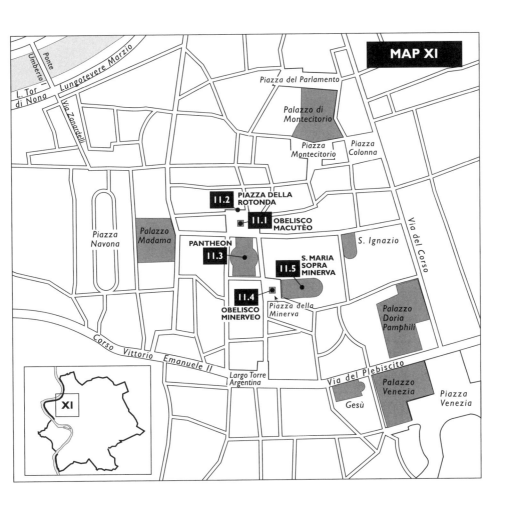

MAP XI

Umberto I

Ponte

L. Tor di Nona

Lungotevere Marzio

Via Zanardelli

Piazza del Parlamento

Palazzo di Montecitorio

Piazza Montecitorio

Piazza Colonna

Piazza Navona

Palazzo Madama

11.2 PIAZZA DELLA ROTONDA

11.1 OBELISCO MACUTÈO

PANTHEON **11.3**

S. Ignazio

S. MARIA SOPRA MINERVA **11.5**

Via del Corso

11.4 OBELISCO MINERVEO

Piazza della Minerva

Palazzo Doria Pamphilj

Corso Vittorio Emanuele II

Largo Torre Argentina

Via del Plebiscito

Gesù

Palazzo Venezia

Piazza Venezia

XI

11.1 Obelisco Macutèo: Dedication by Clement XI

CLEMENS XI

PONT MAX

FONTIS ET FORI

ORNAMENTO

5   ANNO SAL

MDCCXI

PONTIF XI

1. CLEMENS XI : Ūndecimus.
2. PONT(ifex) MAX(imus).
3. FORI : See 8.3B, line 6.
4. ORNAMENTO : Dat. of Purpose.
5. SAL(ūtis).
6. MDCCXI : Mīllēsimō septingentēsimō ūndecimō.
7. PONTIF(icātūs) XI : Ūndecimō.

11.2 Commemoration of Works of Pius VII

PIVS VII P M AN PONTIFICATVS SVI XXIII

AREAM ANTE PANTHEON M AGRIPPAE

IGNOBILIBVS TABERNIS OCCVPATAM

DEMOLITIONE PROVIDENTISSIMA

5   AB INVISA DEFORMITATE VINDICAVIT

ET IN LIBERVM LOCI PROSPECTVM PATERE IVSSIT

1. PIVS VII : Septimus. — P(ontifex) M(aximus) AN(nō). — XXIII : Vīcēsimō tertiō.

2. AREAM : See 8.3B, line 6. — PANTHEON : The Latin panthēon transliterates Greek πάνθειον ('Shrine of All Gods'), ordinarily Latinized as panthēum. The Ital. pronunciation /'panteon/ indicates that, despite its long penultima, the Latin panthēum retained the accent of its Greek original. The same phenomenon is seen in ἀκαδήμεια > Latin acadēmīa > Ital. accademia = /akka'dε:mia/ and its converse in φιλοσοφία > Latin philosophĭa > Ital. filosofia = /filozo'fi:a/. — M(ārcī).

Piazza della Rotonda: Base of Obelisk, E & W Sides

Clement the Eleventh,[a]
Supreme Pontiff,
for the embellishment
of the fountain and square,[b]
in the year of Salvation
1711,
eleventh of his office.

a. *Pope Clement XI Albani (r. 1700–1721). The eleventh year of his pontificate ran from 23 November 1710 through 22 November 1711.*
b. *The fountain was built by Giacomo della Porta in 1578. Like that of Piazza della Minerva (see 11.4.i, note b), the obelisk added by Clement XI came from the shrine of Isis on the Campus Martius; it dates to the reign of Ramesses II (thirteenth century BC) and originally stood before the temple of Ra at Heliopolis (cf. 10.4B.i, note b).*

Piazza della Rotonda 14: Façade

In the twenty-third year of his office Pius the Seventh,[a]
Supreme Pontiff, in an eminently wise act of demolition
freed from its hateful disfigurement
the square before Marcus Agrippa's Pantheon,
which was encumbered by tawdry shops,[b]
and bade it to command a clear view.

a. *Pope Pius VII Chiaramonti (r. 1800–1823). The twenty-third year of his pontificate ran from 14 March 1822 through 13 March 1823. The text alludes to the demolition under the French regime (1809–1814) of structures at the N end of the piazza (see 2.9A, note c).*
b. *In a view of Piranesi's dating to the second half of the eighteenth century, the N end of the piazza is still encumbered by a disorderly cluster of utilitarian structures. It may yet require to be purged of 'tawdry shops': in an amusing irony, at the present writing (AD 2009) the building on which the inscription is mounted is tenanted by a MacDonald's restaurant.*

11.3A Pantheon: Dedication by Agrippa

[m agrippa l f cos tertium fecit]

[m(ārcus). — l(ūcī) f(īlius) co(n)s(ul). — *tertium* : *According to the antiquarian Aulus Gellius, when Pompey the Great was planning the inscription for his amphitheater, he inquired of Rome's most erudite men whether* CONSVL TERTIVM *or* CONSVL TERTIO *was the preferable formula. On receiving divergent recommendations, Pompey applied to Cicero for a definitive ruling. Fearing that he might give offense if he rendered judgment, the latter prudently advocated the use of the abbreviation* TERT.

11.3B Pantheon: Dedication by Urban VIII

i.

VRBANVS VIII PONT MAX

VETVSTAS AHENEI LACVNARIS

RELIQVIAS

IN VATICANAS COLVMNAS

5   ET BELLICA TORMENTA CONFLAVIT

VT DECORA INVTILIA

ET IPSI PROPE FAMAE IGNOTA

FIERENT

IN VATICANO TEMPLO

10   APOSTOLICI SEPVLCHRI ORNAMENTA

IN HADRIANA ARCE

INSTRVMENTA PVBLICAE SECVRITATIS

ANNO DOMINI MDCXXXII PONTIF IX

1. VRBANVS VIII : Octāvus. — PONT(ifex) MAX(imus).

2. AHENEI = ăēnĕī : *On the spelling, see 8.8A, line 2.*

5. BELLICA TORMENTA : *As* CL *tormentum* ('*windlass*') *is used of catapults and ballistas, it furnishes an apt Classical equivalent for* '*cannon*'.

9. VATICANO TEMPLO : *On* templum, *cf. 1.8G, line 5.*

10. APOSTOLICI : *See 3.4D, line 4.* — SEPVLCHRI = sepulcrī : *On the spelling, see 8.8A, line 2.*

11. HADRIANA ARCE : *As often, the Latin* arx *represents Ital.* castello.

13. MDCXXXII : Mīllēsimō sescentēsimō trīcēsimō secundō. — PONTIF(icātūs) IX : Nōnō.

Frieze

Marcus Agrippa,[a] son of Lucius, built this in his third consulship.[b]

> a. *Marcus Vipsanius Agrippa (c. 63–12 BC) was the son-in-law and presumptive successor of the emperor Augustus (cf. 2.7, note a).*
>
> b. *Agrippa served as* CONSUL *in the years 37, 28, and 27 BC. Completed around 25 BC, his Pantheon was rebuilt in its present form under Hadrian (r. 117–138). The bronze letters on the frieze, mounted at the end of the nineteenth century, restore Hadrian's inscription, which itself reproduced that of Agrippa.*

Portico, above

Left

Urban the Eighth,[a] Supreme Pontiff,
forged the ancient remnants
of bronze coffering[b]
into columns for the Vatican
and into engines of war,[c]
in order that these idle
and well-nigh forgotten baubles
might be made
ornaments of the Apostle's tomb
in the Vatican basilica
and implements of the public safety
in Castel Sant'Angelo,[d]
in the year of the Lord 1632, ninth of his office.

> a. *Pope Urban VIII Barberini (r. 1623–1644). The ninth year of his pontificate ran from 6 August 1631 through 5 August 1632.*
>
> b. *The bronze coffering of the portico had survived from Antiquity (see 11.3B.ii, note c). For his act of vandalism, Urban earned a famous* PASQUINADE: Quod non fecerunt barbari, fecerunt Barberini *('What the barbarians started, the Barberini finished').*
>
> c. *The bronze was used to cast the columns of Bernini's vast baldacchino in the Basilica of St. Peter and eighty cannon for Castel Sant'Angelo.*
>
> d. *Lit., 'Citadel of Hadrian', that emperor's massive mausoleum, situated near the Vatican and long used as a papal fortress (see 15.2).*

ii.

PANTHEON

ÆDIFICIVM TOTO TERRARVM ORBE

CELEBERRIMVM

AB AGRIPPA AVGVSTI GENERO

5   IMPIE IOVI CETERISQ MENDACIBVS DIIS

A BONIFACIO IIII PONTIFICE

DEIPARAE ET SS CHRISTI MARTYRIBVS PIE

DICATVM

VRBANVS VIII PONT MAX

10   BINIS AD CAMPANI AERIS VSVM

TVRRIBVS EXORNAVIT

ET NOVA CONTIGNATIONE MVNIVIT

ANNO DOMINI MDCXXXII PONTIF IX

1. PANTHEON : *See 11.2, line 2.*
4–8. AB AGRIPPA . . . IMPIE . . . A BONIFACIO . . . PIE : *Both phrases are to be construed with* DICATVM *(line 8).*
5. CETERISQ(ue). — DIIS : *Not a* CL *form (see 2.12A, line 3).*
6. BONIFACIO IIII : Quārtō. *The authentic spelling of the name is* Bonifātius *(see 3.4B, line 3).*
7. DEIPARAE : *See 9.3, line 7.* — SS = sānctīs : *On the abbreviation, see 1.61, line 7.* — CHRISTI : *See 1.6A.ii, line 6.* — MARTYRIBVS : *See 2.10, line 2.*
9. VRBANVS VIII : Octāvus. — PONT(ifex) MAX(imus).
10. CAMPANI AERIS : *Although the* LL *noun* campāna *was in use by the early Middle Ages in the sense 'church bell', the connection with the toponym* Campānia *is unclear.*
13. MDCXXXII : Mīllēsimō sescentēsimō trīcēsimō secundō. — PONTIF(icātūs) IX : Nōnō.

Right

> Urban the Eighth,[a] Supreme Pontiff,
> embellished
> with twin towers for the use of bells[b]
> and equipped with a new ceiling[c]
> the Pantheon,
> the world's most renowned building,
> once dedicated
> in wickedness by Agrippa,[d]
> son-in-law of Augustus,
> to Jupiter and the other false gods,
> then in righteousness by Pope Boniface the Fourth[e]
> to the Mother of God and the holy martyrs of Christ,
> in the year of the Lord 1632, ninth of his office.

a. See 11.3B.i, note a.

b. Lit., 'for the use of Campanian bronze'. The belfries in question were designed by Bernini; long derided as orecchie d'asino ('donkey's ears'), at the end of the nineteenth century they were finally pulled down.

c. The wooden beams with which Urban VIII replaced the ancient bronzework had little to commend them but their novelty (see 11.3B.i, note b).

d. See 11.3A, note a.

e. Pope St Boniface IV (r. 608–615) received the Pantheon in gift from the Emperor Phocas (cf. 2.1, note a) and dedicated it to the BVM and all the saints; its Latin name is Sancta Maria ad Martyres ('Saint Mary by the Martyrs'). Legend notwithstanding, it is most unlikely that Boniface ordered the transfer of relics into the church. This Eastern practice was introduced over the century between Pope St. Theodore (r. 642–649) and Pope St. Zacharias (r. 741–752), when the papacy was dominated by Greeks and Hellenophone Syrians, Palestinians, and North Africans.

11.3C Pantheon: Dedication by Pius IX

PIO IX PONT MAX

OPTIMO ET MVNIFICENTISSIMO PRINCIPI

3a   FAVTORI BONARVM ARTIVM

3b   VINDICI ANTIQVITATIS

QVOD DOMIBVS LOCATITIIS

5   CELLAM AREAMQ PANTHEI

SINISTRORSVM OCCVPANTIBVS

PER CAMILLVM IACOBINVM PRAEF OPER PVBL

REDEMPTIS AC SOLO AEQVATIS

TEMPLI HVIVS DECORI

10   VRBIS ORNAMENTO PROSPEXERIT

11a   COLLEGIVM ARTIFICVM A DIVO LVCA

11b   COLLEGIVM ARCHEOLOGORVM

$\overline{\text{MDCCCLIII}}$

1. PIO IX : Nōnō. — PONT(ificī) MAX(imō).

3a&b. *The text appears in two slightly different versions on stones set on each side of the portal. Lines 3b and 11b show the text that appears on the right panel.*

4–10. QVOD . . . PROSPEXERIT : *On the construction, see 1.6B, lines 5–7.* — LOCATITIIS = locātīciīs : *The* LL locātīcius *is 'for let' (on the spelling, see 3.4B, line 3).*

5. AREAMQ(ue) : *See 8.3B, line 6.* — PANTHEI : *On the spelling, see 11.2, line 2.*

6. SINISTRORSVM = sinistrōrsus.

7. PRAEF(ectum) OPER(ibus) PVBL(icīs) : *Like the verb* praeficere *from which it derives, the Part.* praefectus *governs the Dat. case even when it is used as a Subst. (cf. 2.2, line 14).*

11a. A DIVO LVCA : *The Prep.* ab *is used in* CL *in the sense 'of' or 'from the side of' the person or department in question. On the Classicizing* DIVO, *see 3.3A, line 2. On* LVCA, *see 8.6, line 9.*

11b. ARCHEOLOGORVM = archaeologōrum : *The* NL archaeologus *('archeologist') is a derivative of* NL archaeologia, *which transliterates Greek* ἀρχαιολογία *('antiquarian lore').*

12. $\overline{\text{MDCCCLIII}}$: Mīllēsimō octingentēsimō quīnquāgēsimō tertiō.

Portico, L and R, below

Left: The Accademia degli Artisti di San Luca[a]

Right: The Accademia Romana di Archeologia[b]

to Pius the Ninth,[c] Supreme Pontiff,

most excellent and generous Prince,

Left: patron of the arts,

Right: champion of Antiquity,

because he, by purchasing through the agency

of Camillo Giacobini, superintendent of public works,

the tenements that encumbered the fabric

and precinct of the Pantheon on the left side,[d]

and by leveling them to the ground,

took care for the beauty of this church,

an ornament to the City.

1853.

a. The Accademia di San Luca, an artists' guild, received official recognition in 1577 under Pope Gregory XIII; in 1588 Sixtus V assigned it headquarters at the Church of SS. Luca e Martina (it had formerly been housed at the Church of S. Luca in Piazza dell'Esquilino, eliminated to accommodate the Obelisco Esquilino; cf. 4.1.i, note d). With the demolition of SS. Luca e Martina for the construction of Via dei Monti (cf. 3.2c, note b), in 1934 the Academy was transferred to Palazzo Carpegna.

b. Founded in 1810 under the auspices of the French government at Rome, the Libera Accademia Romana di Archeologia (Free Roman Academy of Archeology) was suppressed on the restoration of Pope Pius VII in 1814. Revived in 1816—but without the epithet Libera—its brief is to promote research in archeology and in the history of art.

c. Pope Pius IX Mastai-Ferretti (r. 1846–1878).

d. In old illustrations these structures can be seen crowding the N side of the Pantheon, the left side for one facing the building.

11.3D   Epitaph of Arcangelo Corelli

D O M

ARCANGELO CORELLIO E FVSIGNANO

PHILIPPI WILLELMI COMITIS PALATINI RHENI

S R I PRINCIPIS AC ELECTORIS

5   BENEFICENTIA

MARCHIONI DE LADENSBOVRG

QVOD EXIMIIS ANIMI DOTIBVS

ET INCOMPARABILI IN MVSICIS MODVLIS PERITIA

SVMMIS PONTIFICIBVS APPRIME CARVS

ITALIÆ ATQVE EXTERIS NATIONIBVS ADMIRATIONI FVERIT

11   INDVLGENTE CLEMENTE XI P O M

PETRVS CARDINALIS OTTHOBONVS S R E VIC CAN

ET GALLIARVM PROTECTOR

LIIRISTI CELEBERRIMO

15   INTER FAMILIARES SVOS IAM DIV ADSCITO

EIVS NOMEN IMMORTALITATI COMMENDATVRVS

M P C

VIXIT ANNOS LIX MENS X DIES XX

OBIIT VI ID IANVARII ANNOS SAL MDCCXIII

1. D(eō) O(ptimō) M(aximō).
3. COMITIS : *See 2.2, line 9.*
4. S(acrī) R(ōmānī) I(mperiī).
6. MARCHIONI : *The* ML *marchiō is* 'marquis'.
7–10. QVOD . . . FVERIT : *On the construction, see 1.6B, lines 5–7.*
11. CLEMENTE XI : Ūndecimō. — P(ontifice) O(ptimō) M(aximō).
12. OTTHOBONVS : *For the inauthentic* H, *see 9.1A, line 2.* — S(ānctae)
    R(ōmānae) E(cclēsiae) : *See 1.7A, line 6.* — VIC(e) CAN(cellārius).
14. LIIRISTI : *Sic* (= lyristī). *The form implies a noun* lyristēs.
17. M(onumentum) P(ōnendum) C(ūrāvit).
18. LIX : Quīnquāgintā novem. — MENS(ēs) X : Decem. — XX : Vīgintī.
19. OBIIT VI : Sextō. — ID(ūs) IANVARII : *See 1.6G, line 11.* — ANNOS :
    Sic (= annō). *The* S *owes its presence to the initial character of* SAL. —
    SAL(ūtis) MDCCXIII : Mīllēsimō septingentēsimō tertiō decimō.

First Chapel L, First Stone to L of Altar

To God, Best and Greatest.
To Arcangelo Corelli^a of Fusignano,
Marquis of Ladensburg
by favor
of Philipp Wilhelm,^b Count Palatine of the Rhine,
Prince and Elector of the Holy Roman Empire,
because by his outstanding gifts of intellect
and unequaled skill in musical measures
he was exceedingly dear to Supreme Pontiffs
and an object of wonder to Italy and foreign nations,
by leave of Clement the Eleventh,^c Supreme and most excellent Pontiff,
Cardinal Pietro Ottoboni, Vice Chancellor of the Holy Roman Church
and Protector of France,^d
for the purpose of committing his name to immortality
undertook to have this monument set up
for a violinist of high renown
who had long numbered among his intimate friends.
He lived fifty-nine years, ten months, twenty days.
He died on 8 January^e in the year of Salvation 1713.

a. *In Rome, the violinist and composer Arcangelo Corelli (1653–1713) served in turn at the courts of Queen Christina of Sweden (see 1.61, note a), Cardinal Benedetto Pamphilj (see 7.4F, note a), and Cardinal Pietro Ottoboni (see note d below).*

b. *Corelli received the honorary title of Marquis von Ladensburg after his sojourn in Düsseldorf at the court of Philipp Wilhelm, Elector Palatine.*

c. *Pope Clement XI Albani (r. 1700–1721).*

d. *Pietro Ottoboni (1667–1740) was nephew to Pope Alexander VIII (see 14.5B, note a). He composed librettos for leading Roman musicians, whose works were performed at Palazzo della Cancelleria, his residence as vice chancellor (see 13.3). As Protector of France, Ottoboni was empowered to block the election of any papal candidate unacceptable to the French crown; as vice chancellor, he headed the papal chancery.*

e. *Lit., 'on the sixth day before the Ides of January'.*

11.3E Epitaph of Taddeo Zuccaro

D O M

TADÆO ZVCCARO IN OPPIDO DIVI ANGELI

AD RIPAS METAVRI NATO

PICTORI EXIMIO

5   VT PATRIA MORIBVS PICTVRA RAPHAELI

VRBINATI SIMILLIMO ET VTILLE NATALI

DIE ET POST ANNVM SEPTIMVM ET TRIGE

SIMVM VITA FVNCTO ITA TVMVLVM

EIDEM PROXIMVM

10   FOEDERICVS FRATRI SVAVISS MOERENS

POS ANNO CHRISTIANÆ SAL

M D L XVI

MAGNA QVOD IN MAGNO TIMVIT RAPHAELE PERÆQVE

TADÆO IN MAGNO PERTIMVIT GENETRIX

One ELEGIAC COUPLET (lines 13–14)

1. D(eō) O(ptimō) M(aximō).

2. TADÆO ZVCCARO : *Ind.Ob. of* POS(uit), *line 11; the intervening datives are all App. to* TADÆO. — DIVI : *See 3.3A, line 2.* — ANGELI : *See 4.2J, line 2.*

5. RAPHAELI | VRBINATI : *See 11.3F.i, line 1.*

6. VTILLE : *Sic* (= ut ille).

7–8. TRIGE|SIMVM : *Sic* (= trīcēsimum). — VITA : *On the construction, see 10.1E, line 4.*

10. FOEDERICVS . . . MOERENS = Fēderīcus . . . maerēns : *On the spellings, see 1.8B, line 5.* — SVAVISS(imō).

11. POS(uit). — CHRISTIANÆ : *See 1.7A, line 8.* — SAL(ūtis).

12. M D L XVI : Mīllēsimō quīngentēsimō sexāgēsimō sextō.

First Chapel L, R of Altar

> *To God, Best and Greatest.*
> *For Taddeo Zuccaro,[a] outstanding painter,*
> *born in the town of Sant'Angelo [b]*
> *on the banks of the Metauro.*
> *As he was a man most like Raphael of Urbino*
> *with respect to his homeland, character, and art,*
> *and like him took departure of life*
> *on the birthday that concluded his thirty-seventh year,[c]*
> *so Federico,[d] in grief for a beloved brother,*
> *set a tomb near his [e]*
> *in the year of Christian Salvation*
> *1566.*

> *That which the great Mother feared in the case of great Raphael,*
> *she dreaded equally in that of great Taddeo.[f]*

One ELEGIAC COUPLET (lines 13–14)

a. *Taddeo Zuccaro or Zuccari (1529–1566) was third regent of the Compagnia dei Virtuosi del Pantheon, founded in 1543 by Pope Paul III. His most famous work is the cycle of frescoes that he painted for the Farnese in their palace at Caprarola.*

b. *Zuccaro was born at Sant'Angelo in Vado, not far from Urbino.*

c. *See 11.3F.i, note e.*

d. *Federico Zuccaro (c. 1540–1609) was the first president of the Accademia di San Luca (see 11.3C, note a).*

e. *I.e., Raphael's. The monuments are located in neighboring chapels.*

f. *The couplet follows in the tradition of that for the tomb of Raphael (11.3F).*

11.3F   Epitaph of Raphael

i.

RAPHAELI SANCTIO IOANN F VRBINATI

PICTORI EMINENTISS VETERVMQ ÆMVLO

CVIVS SPIRANTEIS PROPE IMAGINES SI

CONTEMPLERE NATVRÆ ATQVE ARTIS FOEDVS

5   FACILE INSPEXERIS

IVLII ĪĪ ET LEONIS X PONTT MAXX PICTVRÆ

ET ARCHITECT OPERIBVS GLORIAM AVXIT

V A X̄X̄X̄V̄I̅I̅ INTEGER INTEGROS

QVO DIE NATVS EST EO ESSE DESIIT

10   V̄I̅I̅I̅ ID APRIL M̄D̄ XX

ILLE HIC EST RAPHAEL TIMVIT QVO SOSPITE VINCI

RERVM MAGNA PARENS ET MORIENTE MORI

One ELEGIAC COUPLET *(lines 11 and 12)*

1. RAPHAELI : *The Latin name is* Raphaël, -ēlis. — SANCTIO : *The Ital. name* Sanzio *appears in Latin as* Sānctius. — IOANN(is) F(īlio). — VRBINATI : *The* ML *Adj.* Urbīnās, -ātis, *corresponds to the toponym* Urbīnum *(mod. Urbino).*

2. EMINENTISS(imō) VETERVMQ(ue).

3. SPIRANTEIS = spīrantēs : *A spurious archaism. Though the Pl. desinence* -eis (< IE *-eyes) *is indeed found alongside* -īs *in* OL *texts, it is Nom.Pl., not Acc.Pl.* (CL *Acc.Pl.* -ēs < *Italic* *-ens < IE *-m̥s).

4. CONTEMPLERE = contemplēris : *The form of the condition* sī contemplēris . . . inspexeris *is unusual (one might expect* sī contemplātus eris . . . īnspiciēs).

6. IVLII ĪĪ : Secundī. — LEONIS X : Decimī. — PONTT MAXX = pontificum maximōrum : *On the abbreviation, see 1.61, line 7.*

7. ARCHITECT(ūrae).

8. V(īxit) A(nnōs) X̄X̄X̄V̄I̅I̅ : Trīgintā septem.

10. V̄I̅I̅I̅ : Octāvō. — ID(ūs) APRIL(is) : *See 1.6G, line 11.* — M̄D̄ XX : Mīllēsimō quīngentēsimō vīcēsimō.

11. QVO SOSPITE : *Abl.Abs.* ('who [being] safe', i.e., 'while he was living'; *cf. 1.8B, lines 8–9).*

Second Chapel L

Wall

To Raphael Sanzio [a] *of Urbino, son of Giovanni,*
most preeminent painter and rival of the ancients.
If you examine his well-nigh breathing images,
you will easily observe the bond
between art and nature.
With his works of painting and architecture, he magnified the glory
of the Supreme Pontiffs Julius the Second [b] *and Leo the Tenth.* [c]
He lived hale for thirty-seven whole years. [d]
He died on the same day as he was born, [e]
6 April 1520. [f]

Living, great Nature feared he might outvie
Her works and, dying, fears herself may die. [g]

One ELEGIAC COUPLET *(lines 11 and 12)*

a. *In his frescoes for the Vatican's Stanza della Segnatura, Raffaello Sanzio (1483–1520) brought the ideals of the High Renaissance to their most complete expression. He was interred in the Pantheon at his own request.*

b. *Unable to bear the 'Borgia' apartments decorated for his detested predecessor, Alexander VI, Pope Julius II della Rovere (r. 1503–1513) entrusted to Raphael the decoration of a new suite of rooms—the celebrated* stanze *(see note a above).*

c. *Pope Leo X de' Medici (r. 1513–1521) continued Raphael's employment on the Vatican Stanze and commissioned the frescoes of the Sala di Costantino.*

d. *A play on the Latin word* integer *('whole', 'sound').*

e. *According to Giorgio Vasari's* Lives of the Most Excellent Painters . . . , *Raphael was born on Good Friday (28 March) in 1483; as 6 April was Good Friday in 1520, after a manner of speaking he died on the same day as he was born.*

f. *Lit., 'on the eighth day before the Ides of April'.*

g. *The couplet was composed for Raphael's tomb by the eminent humanist scholar Cardinal Pietro Bembo (1470–1547); the translation is Alexander Pope's.*

ii.

OSSA ET CINERES RAPH SANCTII VRBIN

RAPH(aēlis) SANCTII VRBIN(ātis) : *See 11.3F.i, line 1.*

GREGORIVS XVI P M ANNO III INDICT VI ARCAM ⌐

ANTIQVI OPERIS CONCESSIT

GREGORIVS XVI : Sextus decimus. — P(ontifex) M(aximus). — III :
Tertiō. — INDICT(iōne) : *See 2.1, line 16.* — VI : Sextā. — ANTIQVI
OPERIS : *Gen. of Description.*

11.3G Epitaph of Maria Bibiena

MARIAE ANTONII F BIBIENAE SPONSAE EIVS

QVAE LAETOS HYMENAEOS MORTE PRÆVERTIT

ET ANTE NVPTIALES FACES VIRGO EST ELATA

BALTASSAR TVRINVS PISCIEN LEONI X DATAR

5   ET IO BAPT BRANCONIVS AQVILAN A CVBIC

B M EX TESTAMENTO POSVERVNT

CVRANTE HIERONIMO VAGNINO VRBINATI

RAPHAELI PROPINQVO

QVI DOTEM QVOQVE HVIVS SACELLI

10   SVA PECVNIA AVXIT

1. F(īliae).

4. PISCIEN(sis) : *The* ML *Adj.* Pisciēnsis *corresponds to the toponym* Piscia
(*mod. Pescia*). — LEONI X : Decimō. — DATAR(ius) : *The* EL datārius
is 'President of the Datary'.

5. IO(annēs) BAPT(ista) : *On the name, see 7.4C.* — AQVILAN(us). — A
CVBIC(ulō) : *See 1.8C. Here a characteristically Classical formulation is
preferred to* cubiculārius (*cf. 1.8G, line 5*).

6. B(ene) M(erentī).

7. HIERONIMO = Hierōnymō : *On the name, see 10.7, line 1; on the spelling,
see 3.1, line 1. The Latin* Hierōnymus Vagnīnus *represents Ital.* Girolamo
Vagnino (*cf. 12.3B, line 8*). — VRBINATI : *See 11.3F.i, line 1.*

8. RAPHAELI : *See 11.3F.i, line 1.*

Sarcophagus

The bones and ashes of Raphael Sanzio of Urbino.[a]

a. See 11.3F.i, note a.

In the third year of his office, in the sixth indiction,[a] Gregory the Sixteenth,[b] Supreme Pontiff, donated the sarcophagus, crafted in Antiquity.

a. In the 1830s, dating by INDICTION was a medievalizing conceit.
b. Pope Gregory XVI Cappellari (r. 1831–1846). The third year of his pontificate ran from 2 February 1833 through 1 February 1834. The remains of Raphael were reinterred in 1833.

Second Chapel L, to R of Altar, above

For Maria Bibiena,[a] daughter of Antonio, his betrothed, who by death forestalled her joyous nuptials and was carried off as a maiden before her wedding.[b]

In accordance with her deserts and by provision of her will, Baldassare Turini of Pescia, President of the Datary to Leo X,[c] and Giovanni Battista Branconio dell'Aquila,[d] Chamberlain, under the supervision of Girolamo Vagnini of Urbino— a kinsman of Raphael's, who also increased the endowment for this shrine with his own money— placed this monument.

a. Maria, niece of Cardinal Bernardo Dovizi (called 'il Bibiena' from his place of birth) and Raphael's betrothed, died shortly before Raphael.
b. Lit., 'before the wedding torches'. As ancient Roman weddings traditionally featured a procession by torch light, the expression is used by metonymy for 'marriage ceremony' (cf. 10.1D, note c).
c. Pope Leo X de' Medici (r. 1513–1521). The Apostolic Datary is an office of the CURIA by which certain types of dispensations and appointments are issued.
d. In another epitaph—that of Annone ('Hanno'), pet elephant of Leo X— Giovanni Battista Branconio dell'Aquila (1473–1522) was styled 'Chamberlain and Superintendent of the Care of the Elephant'. Hanno's (lost) funerary portrait was painted by Raphael.

11.3H Epitaph of Annibale Carracci

D O M

HANNIBAL CARACCIVS BONONIENSIS

HIC EST

RAPHAELI SANCTIO VRBINATI

5   VT ARTE INGENIO FAMA SIC TVMVLO PROXIMVS

PAR VTRIQVE FVNVS ET GLORIA

DISPAR FORTVNA

AEQVAM VIRTVTI RAPHAEL TVLIT

HANNIBAL INIQVAM

10   DECESSIT DIE XV IVLII AN MDCIX AET XXXXIX

CAROLVS MARATTVS SVMMI PICTORIS

NOMEN ET STVDIA COLENS P AN MDCLXXIV

ARTE MEA VIVIT NATVRA ET VIVIT IN ARTE

MENS DECVS ET NOMEN COETERA MORTIS ERANT

One ELEGIAC COUPLET (lines 13 and 14)

1. D(eō) O(ptimō) M(aximō).
2. CARACCIVS : *On the Latinization, cf. 12.3B, line 8.*
4. RAPHAELI SANCTIO VRBINATI : *See 11.3F.i, line 1.*
8–9. AEQVAM . . . RAPHAEL . . . HANNIBAL INIQVAM : *The chiastic arrangement* (A-B-B-A) *lends rhetorical flair (cf. 2.11A.i, lines 3–4).*
10. XV : Quīntō decimō. — IVLII : *See 1.6G, line 11.* — AN(nō) MDCIX : Mīllēsimō sescentēsimō nōnō. — AET(ātis) XXXXIX : Quadrāgēsimō nōnō.
11. MARATTVS : *See* CARACCIVS *above, line 2.*
12. P(osuit). — AN(nō) MDCLXXIV : Mīllēsimō sescentēsimō septuāgēsimō quārtō.
14. COETERA = cētera : *On the spelling, see 1.8B, line 5.*

Second Chapel L, to R of Altar, below

> *To God, Best and Greatest.*
> *Annibale Carracci[a]*
> *of Bologna lies here,*
> *neighbor to Raphael Sanzio of Urbino*
> *in his tomb as in his art, talent, and fame.*
> *Like was the burial and reputation of each*
> *yet unlike the fortune:*
> *Raphael enjoyed a fortune equal to his excellence,*
> *Annibale an unequal.[b]*
> *He died on the fifteenth day of July in the year 1609, in his forty-ninth year.*
> *Carlo Maratti,[c] revering the fame and ambitions*
> *of a superlative painter, set this up in the year 1674.*
>
> *Through my art, Nature lives, and in my art lives my wit,*
> *glory, and fame. The rest belonged to Death.[d]*

One ELEGIAC COUPLET (*lines 13 and 14*)

a. *Born into a family of painters in Bologna, Annibale Carracci (1560–1609) set up a studio there with his brother, Agostino, and cousin Ludovico. In 1595, Annibale was engaged by Cardinal Odoardo Farnese to decorate the gallery of Palazzo Farnese in Rome: his fresco cycle treating the Loves of the Gods was long reckoned a masterpiece fit to stand comparison with Raphael's stanze (see 11.3F.i, note b) and Michelangelo's Sistine ceiling.*

b. *This complaint notwithstanding, Carracci enjoyed great posthumous fame, garnering the praise of artists as varied as Bernini, Poussin and Rubens.*

c. *Carlo Maratti or Maratta (1625–1713) was the leading painter in Rome in the latter half of the seventeenth century.*

d. *The couplet follows in the tradition of those for the tombs of Raphael (11.3F) and Zuccaro (11.3E).*

11.31 Epitaph of Baldassare Peruzzi

[balthasari perutio senensi uiro et pictura
et architectura altisque ingeniorum artibus
adeo excellenti ut si priscorm occubuisset
temporibus nostra illum felicius legerent
5   uix ann lv mens xi dies xx
lucretia et jo salustius optimo conjugi et
parenti non sine lachrymis simonis honorii
claudii æmiliae ac sulpitiae minorum filiorum
dolentes posuerunt
10   die iiii januarii mdxxxvi]

RESTITVITA ALL'ONORE DEL PANTHEON
A CVRA DEI SENESI MCMXXI

1. [balthasari . . . mdxxxvi] : *The text of the epitaph is preserved in the* Lives
of the Most Excellent Painters *. . . by Giorgio Vasari (with minor orthographical variations in the oldest editions). On the Latinization of the
name, cf. 12.3B, line 8.* — senensi : *The Adj.* Sēnēnsis *corresponds to the
toponym* Sēna Iūlia (*mod.* Siena), *to be distinguished from* Sēna *on the
Adriatic* (*mod.* Sinigaglia, *i.e.,* Sēna Gallica).

2. ingeniorum : *In* LL, ingenium *is used in the sense 'contrivance', with particular reference to siege fortifications* (*cf. Fr.* ingénieur, *Ital.* ingegnere).

3. priscorm : *Sic* (= prīscōrum)

5. uix(it) ann(ōs) lv : Quīnquāgintā quīnque. — mens(ēs) xi : Ūndecim.
— xx : Vīgintī.

6. jo(annēs) : *On the name, see 6.4.*

7. lachrymis = lacrimīs : *Already by the end of the second century* BC, *unetymological aspirates were appearing in native Latin words such as* lacrima
(*cf. Greek* δάκρυα); *so also* pulcer, sepulcrum, *etc.* (*see 8.8A, line 2*). *The
use of* Y *for* I *represents a much later development* (*see 3.1, line 1*).

8. sulpitiae = Sulpiciae : *On the spelling, see 3.4B, line 3.*

10. iiii : Quārtō. — januarii : *See 1.6G, line 11.* — mdxxxvi : Mīllēsimō
quīngentēsimō trīcēsimō sextō.

11. MCMXXI : Millenovecentoventuno.

L of Second Aedicula

To Baldassare Peruzzi,[a] native of Siena,
and so distinguished in painting, architecture, and the rarefied arts
of engineering that, had he died in the times of the Ancients,
our own would have received him more favorably.[b]
He lived fifty-five years, eleven months, twenty days.
Lucrezia and Giovanni Sallustio[c] in grief placed
to their most excellent spouse and father,
not without the tears of Simone, Onorio,
Claudio, Emilia, and Sulpizia, the younger children,
on the fourth day of January 1536.

Restored to the dignity of the Pantheon
under the auspices of the people of Siena, 1921.[d]

a. *Baldassare Tommaso Peruzzi (1481–1536), architect and painter, came to Rome from Siena in 1503. His masterpiece is Villa Farnesina, built for the Sienese banker Agostino Chigi and decorated in collaboration with Raphael. He also designed Palazzo Massimo alle Colonne and the Ponzetti chapel in S. Maria della Pace (12.6). Having worked at St. Peter's under Bramante, Peruzzi succeeded Raphael as its architect after the latter's death in 1520. With Bramante and Raphael, Peruzzi made a triumvirate of High Renaissance architects to be matched a century later by the Baroque trio of Bernini, Borromini, and Pietro da Cortona.*

b. *I.e., the quality of Peruzzi's work is such that, had it been the product of Antiquity, it would have enjoyed greater favor. In his* Lives of the Most Excellent Painters . . . , *Giorgio Vasari remarks that Peruzzi's retiring nature resulted in his being undercompensated for his work.*

c. *Giovanni Sallustio Peruzzi, himself an architect, died in 1573.*

d. *Though the original stone had been lost, the text of the epitaph was transmitted by Vasari—as was a false date for Peruzzi's death, which in fact occurred on 6 January (the numeral* vi *might be misread as* iv, *whence perhaps a further corruption to* iiii).

11.4   Obelisco Minerveo: Dedication by Alexander VII

i.

VETEREM OBELISCVM

PALLADIS ÆGYPTIÆ MONVMENTVM

E TELLVRE ERVTVM

ET IN MINERVAE OLIM

5   NVNC DEIPARAE GENITRICIS

FORO ERECTVM

DIVINAE SAPIENTIAE

ALEXANDER VII DEDICAVIT

ANNO SAL MDCLXVII

4. MINERVAE OLIM | NVNC DEIPARAE GENITRICIS : *The chiastic arrangement of the elements* (A-B-B-A; *cf. 2.11A.i, lines 3–4) reinforces the contrast between the square's former and present patrons.* — DEIPARAE GENITRICIS : *The conflation of the titles* DEIPARA (*see 9.3, line 7) and* DEI GENITRIX (*see 4.2D, line 3) is singular.*

6. FORO : *See 8.3B, line 6.*

8. ALEXANDER VII : Septimus.

9. SAL(ūtis) MDCLXVII : Mīllēsimō sescentēsimō sexāgēsimō septimō.

ii.

SAPIENTIS AEGYPTI

INSCVLPTAS OBELISCO FIGVRAS

AB ELEPHANTO

BELLVARVM FORTISSIMA

5   GESTARI QVISQVIS HIC VIDES

DOCVMENTVM INTELLIGE

ROBVSTAE MENTIS ESSE

SOLIDAM SAPIENTIAM SVSTINERE

4. BELLVARVM = bēluārum.

7. ROBVSTAE MENTIS : *The etymological sense of* rōbustus *is 'oaken', here in allusion to the oak in the arms of the family Chigi.*

8. SVSTINERE : *Sub. of* ESSE *in the Ind. Statement introduced by* DOCVMENTVM INTELLIGE (*line 6*).

Piazza della Minerva: Base of Obelisk

West

Alexander the Seventh[a] dedicated
to the divine wisdom
this ancient obelisk,
a monument of the Egyptian Athena,[b]
unearthed from the ground
and set up in the square
once Minerva's,[c]
now belonging to the Mother of God,[d]
in the year of Salvation 1667.

a. *Pope Alexander VII Chigi (r. 1655–1667) dictated the present texts.*
b. *The 'Egyptian Athena' is Isis. The obelisk was found in 1665 in the garden of the Dominican convent of S. Maria sopra Minerva, which occupies the site of an ancient shrine of Isis (see 11.1, note b).*
c. *The conceit of the present inscription is that the BVM, as true representative of the divine wisdom, is legitimate heir not only to Athena and Minerva, classical goddesses of wisdom, but also to Isis.*
d. *See 4.21, note a.*

East

You, whoever you are, who see
that the figures of wise Egypt
engraved on the obelisk[a]
are borne by the elephant,[b]
strongest of beasts,
understand it as proof
that to uphold sound wisdom
is the part of the sturdy mind.

a. *I.e., the hieroglyphs. For the Renaissance as for Classical Antiquity, Egypt was the archetypal repository of wisdom (cf. 12.4.iii).*
b. *The elephant that bears the obelisk was executed in 1667 by Ercole Ferrata to a design of Bernini's.*

11.5A   Flood Tablet of 1422

$\overline{\text{A}}$NO D^{I} M^{O} CCCC^{O} XXII° INDIE S$\overline{\text{C}}$I

ANDREE CREVIT AQVA TIBERIS VSQVE

AD SVMITAT$\overline{\text{E}}$ ISTI' LAPIDIS T$\overline{\text{P}}$RE D$\overline{\text{N}}$I

MARTINI PP^{E} V^{I} A^{O} VI°

1. A(n)NO D(omin)^{I}. — M^{O} CCCC^{O} XXII° : Mīllēsimō quadringentēsimō vīcēsimō secundō. — INDIE = in diē. — S($\overline{\text{a}}$n)C(t)I.
2. ANDREE = andrēae : *The Latin name is* Andrēās, -ae, *transliterating Greek* Ἀνδρέας. *On the spelling, see 1.8B, line 5.*
3. SVM(m)ITATE(m). — ISTI(us). — T(em)P(o)RE D(omi)NI.
4. P(a)P^{E} = papae : *See 3.6A, line 2.* — V^{I} : Quīntī. — A(nn)^{O} VI° : Sextō.

11.5B   Flood Tablet of 1495

ANN CHR MVD NON DECEMB

AVCTVS IN IMMENSVM TIBERIS DVM

PROFLVIT ALVEO

EXTVLIT HVC TVMIDAS TVRBIDVS

5   AMNIS AQVAS

One ELEGIAC COUPLET *(lines 2–5)*

1. ANN(ō) CHR(istī) : *See 1.6A.ii, line 6.* — MVD : Mīllēsimō quadringentēsimō nōnāgēsimō quīntō. — NON(īs) DECEMB(ris) : *See 1.6G, line 11.*
2. IN IMMENSVM : *Latin verse makes free use of Neut. Substantives with the force of abstract nouns; here, 'to* [the point of] *immeasurability', i.e., 'to an immense degree'.*
3. ALVEO : *The* E *and* O *are scanned as a single syllable by synizesis (see 5.8E).*

S. Maria sopra Minerva: Façade

In the year of the Lord 1422, on Saint Andrew's Day,[a]
the water of the Tiber rose
to the level of this stone, in the time of the Lord
Pope Martin the Fifth,[b] in his sixth year.

a. I.e., 30 November.

b. *Pope Martin V Colonna (r. 1417–1431). The sixth year of Martin's pontificate ran from 11 November 1422 through 10 November 1423 (see 7.4G). When he entered Rome in 1420, the city had suffered neglect for more than seventy years (see 2.13C, note b). One of his most provident measures was to revive the office of the* MAGISTRI VIARUM *('Superintendents of Streets').*

Façade

In the year of Christ 1495, on the fifth of December,[a]
as the Tiber, enormously swollen,
overflowed its bed,
the churning stream raised its waters
to this level.[b]

One ELEGIAC COUPLET (lines 2–5)

a. *Lit., 'on the Nones of December'. In March, May, July, and October the Nones fall on the seventh, in the other months on the fifth.*

b. *The flood of 1495 is recorded also at the neighboring Church of Sant'Eustachio.*

11.5C Flood Tablet of 1530

ANNO DN̄I M D XXX

OCTAVO IDVS OCTOBRIS PONT

VERO SANCTISSIMI DN̄I

CLEMEN PAPE VII ANNO VII

5   HVC TIBER ASCENDIT IAMQ

OBRVTA TOTA FVISSET

ROMA NISI HVIC CELEREM

VIRGO TVLISSET OPEM

One ELEGIAC COUPLET *(lines 5–8)*

1. ANNO D(omi)NI M D XXX : Mīllēsimō quīngentēsimō trīcēsimō.
2. OCTOBRIS : *See 1.6G, line 11.* — PONT(ificātūs).
3. D(omi)NI.
4. CLEMEN(tis) PAPE = papae : *See 3.6A, line 2; on the spelling, see 1.8B, line 5.* — VII : Septimī. — VII : Septimō.
5. IAMQ(ue).
6. OBRVTA . . . FVISSET : *On the tense, see 1.6G, line 7.*
8. VIRGO : *Scans* virgŏ *(cf. 3.4D, line 5).*

11.5D Flood Tablet of 1557

M D LVII DIE XV SEPTEMBRIS

HVC THYBER ADVENIT PAVLVS DVM

QVARTVS IN ANNO

TERNO EIVS RECTOR MAXIMVS

5   ORBIS ERAT

One ELEGIAC COUPLET *(lines 2–5)*

1. M D LVII : Mīllēsimō quīngentēsimō quīnquāgēsimō septimō. — XV : Quīntō decimō. — SEPTEMBRIS : *See 1.6G, line 11.*
2. THYBER : *A Hellenizing variant of* Tiber *(as if transliterating* Θύβρις; *the ordinary Greek form is* Θύμβρις). *The form* Thybris *is found in* CL *verse (see 9.1A, line 2).*
3–4. ANNO | TERNO : *In* CL *verse, a distributive numeral is sometimes used in place of a cardinal but not, as here, of an ordinal (i.e.,* tertiō; *cf. 1.6C, line 2).*

S. Maria sopra Minerva: Façade

In the year of the Lord 1530,
on 8 October,[a]
but in the seventh year
of the Lord Pope Clement the Seventh,[b]
the Tiber rose to this point
and now all Rome would have been overwhelmed
had not the Virgin
proffered swift aid.[c]

One ELEGIAC COUPLET (lines 5–8)

a. Lit., 'on the eighth day before the Ides of October'.
b. Pope Clement VII de' Medici (r. 1523–1534). The seventh year of his pontificate ran from 19 November 1529 through 18 November 1530. Clement is best known to history for his refusal to sanction the divorce of Henry VIII of England from Catherine of Aragon and his subsequent marriage to Anne Boleyn (cf. 6.5A, note c). The disastrous sack of Rome by imperial forces took place during Clement's reign (cf. 15.2B, note a).
c. The flood of 1530 is recorded also at 10.1D.

Façade

In 1557, on the fifteenth day of September:
the Tiber reached this point,
while Paul the Fourth[a]
was in his third year
as supreme ruler of the world.

One ELEGIAC COUPLET (lines 2–5)

a. Pope Paul IV Carafa (r. 1555–1559). The third year of his pontificate ran from 23 May 1557 through 22 May 1558. A leading spirit of the Roman Inquisition, Paul was a fanatical reformer who ordered the Jews of Rome confined to a ghetto (see 13.7.i, note b) and who published the first edition of the Index Librorum Prohibitorum ('Catalogue of Forbidden Books'). On Paul's death, the seat of the Inquisition was burned and his statue on the Capitoline broken up.

11.5E Flood Tablet of 1598

REDVX RECEPTA PON

TIFEX FERRARIA

NON ANTE TAM SVPERBI

HVCVSQVE TYBRIDIS

5   INSANIENTES EXECRA

TVR VORTICES

ANNO DN̄I M D XCVIII

VIIII KAL IANVARII

Three IAMBIC SENARII *(lines 1–6)*

1–2. PON|TIFEX. — FERRARIA : *See 1.7A, line 9.*

4. HVCVSQVE = hūc usque. — TYBRIDIS : *A Hellenizing variant of*
Tiberis *(see 11.5D, line 2).*

5–6. EXECRA|TVR = exsecrātur : *On the spelling, see 4.2A, line 7.* — VOR-
TICES = verticēs.

7. D(omi)NI. — M D XCVIII : Millēsimō quīngentēsimō nōnāgēsimō
octāvō.

8. VIIII : Nōnō. — KAL(endās) IANVARII : *See 1.6G, line 11.*

11.5F Elogium of Beato Angelico

NON MIHI SIT LAVDI QVOD ERAM VELVT ALTER APELLES   M^{O}

SED QVOD LVCRA TVIS OMNIA CHRISTE DABAM   CCCC

ALTERA NAM TERRIS OPERA EXTANT ALTERA CÆLO   L

VRBS ME IOANNEM FLOS TVLIT ETRVRIÆ   V

Two ELEGIAC COUPLETS

1. MIHI . . . LAVDI : *A Dat. of the Person in tandem with a Dat. of Purpose*
('Double Dative'). — SIT : *Jussive Subj.* — APELLES : *The Latin* Apellēs
transliterates Greek Ἀπέλλης.

1–4. M^{O} | CCCC | L | V : Millēsimō quadringentēsimō quīnquāgēsimō
quīntō.

2. CHRISTE : *See 1.6A.ii, line 6.*

3. EXTANT = exstant : *On the spelling, see 4.2A, line 7.*

4. IOANNEM : *Scans* Iōannem *(see 6.4).*

S. Maria sopra Minerva: Façade

Returned from the capture
of Ferrara, the Pontiff[a]
pronounced a curse upon
the waters of the Tiber,
never before so haughty,
which were raging as far as this
in the year of the Lord 1598,
on 24 December.[b]

Three IAMBIC SENARII (lines 1–6)

a. *Pope Clement VIII Aldobrandini (r. 1592–1605). In 1598, Clement traveled to Ferrara to reassert papal suzerainty over its duchy. Ferrara had been a fief of the Holy See since the time of Matilda of Tuscany (see 15.4E) but was under the de facto rule of the d'Este dynasty. With the support of Henri IV of France (see 1.7A, note c), Clement was able to make good his claim after the death of Alfonso II d'Este.*

b. *Lit., 'on the ninth day before the Kalends of January'. On the date of the flood, see 10.1E, note d.*

S. Maria sopra Minerva: Cappella Frangipane, above Altar

Let it not stand to my credit that I was as a second Apelles,[a]	1
but rather that I gave all gain for yours, O Christ;	4
for some of my works have their place on Earth, others in Heaven.	5
The city that is Tuscany's flower[b] *gave me birth.*	5

Two ELEGIAC COUPLETS

a. *Called 'Fra Giovanni' after entering the Dominican order, Guido di Pietro (c. 1400–1455) was known for his piety as 'Beato Angelico'. Apelles, active in the second half of the fourth century BC, was regarded in Antiquity as the greatest of Greek painters. None of his work survives.*

b. *Viz., Florence. The present epitaph is attributed to the humanist scholar Lorenzo Valla, famed for his philological attack on the authenticity of the 'Donation of Constantine'.*

PALAZZO DEL BANCO DI SANTO SPIRITO

The Palazzo del Banco di Santo Spirito of the younger Antonio da San-
gallo was built in the second decade of the sixteenth century to house
the papal mint. Projecting an image of conscious strength, the heavily
rusticated basement responds confidently to the weight of the super-
structure. The latter comprises a colossal order of pilasters uniting the
piano nobile and upper story to frame a triumphal arch at the center.
The carrying of an order over two stories was a novelty in palace archi-
tecture. Combined with the breaking of the cornice and the base course
by the pilasters and their pedestals, it anticipates by half a century the
innovations of the Baroque.

XII. From Corso del Rinascimento to Via Giulia

AT THE DAWN OF THE MODERN ERA, Rome presented a peculiarly awkward urban profile. In most cities of Italy—in Florence, for example—the major church stood at the epicenter, not infrequently occupying the site of the old Roman forum. In such cases, the growth of the medieval town can be charted as a series of roughly concentric circles, proceeding in successive phases of expansion to fill the area enclosed by the Roman walls and eventually spilling over into the countryside beyond. At Rome, by contrast, there were two churches of first importance: San Giovanni in Laterano—founded by Constantine as Rome's cathedral but from late Antiquity isolated on the waterless hills to the east of the city; and San Pietro in Vaticano—repository of the bones of St. Peter and hence the millennial cynosure of popular devotion.

The prodigious scale of Rome as capital of an erstwhile empire introduced a further complication. Because the medieval city had resulted from the contraction of its much larger ancient predecessor, a handful of more or less isolated villages existed within the walls, most notably at the foot of the Capitoline Hill, in the Trevi quarter, and on the site of the ancient imperial fora (the Pantani, or 'Fens'). Other such aggregations were to be found around the major basilicas and monasteries of the *disabitato*. The challenge presented by the urban revival of Rome over the century and a half between Pope Nicholas V and Pope Sixtus V was to stimulate development across the Campus Martius to the eastern highlands so as to absorb the intervening villages and neutralize the ancient polarity of Lateran and Vatican.

By establishing the Vatican as the seat of the papacy, Nicholas V (r. 1447–1455) fixed the trajectory of Rome's future growth: development would proceed south and east on the axis of Ponte Sant'Angelo, an indispensable link between the Vatican and the city. Within three decades, Sixtus IV had urbanized the central Campus and secured its continuity with the zone of the Campidoglio. By the beginning of the sixteenth century, the *abitato* more or less filled the area between the Tiber bend and the Corso. Over the succeeding fifty years, Leo X, Clement VII, and Paul III extended the *abitato* north and east to the slopes of the Pincio; and by century's end, Pius IV, Gregory XIII, and Sixtus V had incorporated the *monti* to the east. The problems that remained for succeeding urbanists were essentially local and cosmetic; their solutions did not require coordinated planning on any considerable scale.

The pattern of development initiated by Nicholas V in the fifteenth century assured a central role for the three ancient streets that radiated from Ponte Sant'Angelo across the Campus Martius: the 'Via Recta', leading due east past Piazza Navona to the Colonna territory east of the Via Lata; the Via Papalis, leading through the central Campus to the Capitoline Hill and thence to the Lateran; and the Via Peregrinorum, leading by way of Campo de' Fiori to Rione Sant'Angelo—site of the future Ghetto—and to Trastevere. The 'Via Recta' (Via dei Coronari —Via di S. Salvatore delle Coppelle) established a link between Ponte Sant'Angelo and the Via Lata, the principal route for pilgrims arriving from the transalpine north. The Via Papalis (Via dei Banchi Nuovi—Via del Governo Vecchio—Via di San Pantaleo—Via di Torre Argentina) formed the initial tract of the papal processional route between the Vatican and Lateran, while the Via Peregrinorum (Via dei Banchi Vecchi— Via del Pellegrino—Campo de' Fiori—Via dei Giubbonari—Via del Portico di Ottavia) formed the initial tract of the major artery between the Vatican and San Paolo fuori le Mura.

Before the mid-fifteenth century, the limits of the *abitato* had been effectively coextensive with the ancient *rioni* of the southern Campus. With the new growth of the Vatican and the Borgo, Rione Ponte at the head of the Tiber bend increasingly prospered. The development of the contiguous but sparsely populated central Campus was initiated by Sixtus IV (r. 1471–1484). The 'Via Recta', Via Papalis, and Via Peregrinorum were widened and paved. To the north of the 'Via Recta', Via Sistina (Via di Tor di Nona—Via di Monte Brianzo) facilitated the approach to the Vatican from Porta del Popolo. Other streets were straightened and disencumbered of the many balconies that impeded traffic. Street-front porticoes, a typical feature of the city's medieval urban fortresses, were walled up. In addition to improving the security of pedestrians, this measure served to assert papal authority over the local aristocracy.

Half a kilometer to the southeast of Ponte Sant'Angelo lay Piazza Navona, an open area occupying the site of the Stadium of Domitian. In the eighth century, an oratory dedicated to St. Agnes had been founded in the ruinous arcades of its western flank; by the thirteenth, a miscellany of houses and towers had sprung up on the robust foundations of the structure's perimeter. Around 1450, the Spanish built a hospice and church at the southeastern end, a precedent soon to be followed by other national communities. Sixtus IV recognized the potential of the site as a commercial focus for the central Campus. In 1478 he set up a new market at Piazza Navona to replace the medieval market at the foot of the Capitoline Hill. In concert with the newly rehabilitated Campo de' Fiori, the market stimulated the emergence of an animated commercial and residential quarter. Notable among its national churches is the Germans' Santa Maria dell'Anima, which houses the monument of Pope HADRIAN VI. 12.5

The renovation of the Vatican undertaken by Pope Julius II (r. 1503–1513) in the first decade of the sixteenth century lent further impetus to the development of the zone at the head of Ponte Sant'Angelo. Here, at the doorstep of St. Peter, major banking houses began to establish offices. To accommodate these, the pope restructured the city-side approach to the bridge under the new name of Via dei Banchi. A commemorative stone to JULIUS II is located where Via dei Banchi bifurcated to form 12.9 the Via Papalis (Via dei Banchi Nuovi) and the Via Peregrinorum (Via dei Banchi Vecchi), the point of convergence for traffic arriving from the central and southern Campus. This prominent intersection was chosen as the site of PALAZZO DEL BANCO DI SANTO SPIRITO, intended 12.8 for the new papal mint (when the building was assigned to the Banco di Santo Spirito, founded in 1605, Julius' Via dei Banchi became known as 'Via del Banco di Santo Spirito'). On the street's south side, Arco dei

12.10   Banchi shelters a FLOOD PLAQUE recording an inundation in 1277. It is the city's earliest surviving memorial of its type.

In 1505, Cardinal Giovanni de' Medici acquired a palace to the east of Piazza Navona. On his election as Pope Leo X (r. 1513–1521), this scion of the great Florentine dynasty undertook a campaign of improvements in the quarter; the centerpiece was to be a vast palace replacing one that he had occupied as cardinal. Although the extravagant new structure was never built, the existing palace—today's Palazzo Madama—served as the point of departure for the pope's major urban project, the renovation of the ancient street connecting Porta del Popolo with the 'Via Recta'. Baptized 'Via Leonina' (modern Via della Scrofa—Via di Ripetta), the thoroughfare furnished a stately approach both to Palazzo Madama and to the Church of San Luigi dei Francesi, whose site was granted to the French crown in 1517.

Located adjacent to Palazzo Madama, the seat of the University of Rome—La Sapienza—was a further beneficiary of the pope's neighborly solicitude. Founded in 1303 by Boniface VIII, the university was reorganized in the 1430s after the long decadence of the Babylonian Captivity. Leo X enlarged the complex, adding new structures, including a chapel. After numerous interventions over the course of the sixteenth century, the complex was given definitive shape by Giacomo della Porta under Gregory XIII (r. 1572–1585). As in other cases, Gregory's work

12.2   was completed under SIXTUS V (r. 1585–1590), whose inscription stands above the main entrance. Having occupied its historic seat for five centuries, in 1935 the University of Rome was removed to a functional and cheerless Città Universitaria outside the walls and the buildings of the Sapienza were employed to house the Italian state archives.

In the seventeenth century, Pope Urban VIII (r. 1623–1644) engaged Borromini to replace Leo's chapel with a structure of a scale and dignity to suit the importance of Rome's university. Sant'Ivo alla Sapienza remains one of the most celebrated monuments of the Roman Baroque. The Advocates of the Sacred Consistory—the curial lawyers—sponsored the construction of the church and are responsible for its dedication to St. Ivo of Brittany, patron saint of lawyers and judges. The church is framed by the twin wings of the Biblioteca Alessandrina, constructed by Pope ALEXANDER VII (r. 1655–1667), during whose reign the church was finally completed. Closed after the unification of Italy in 1870, Sant'Ivo was restored in 1926 under the auspices of King VICTOR EMANUEL III. 12.3A
12.3B

Over the course of the sixteenth century, Piazza Navona became a center of popular life, the scene of jousts and tourneys—and of armed skirmishes among members of the numerous foreign colonies that possessed national churches in the neighborhood. The piazza was given its modern form in the mid-seventeenth century by Pope Innocent X Pamphilj (r. 1644–1655). Palazzo Pamphilj, the pontiff's residence, swallowed up the bulk of its western side; the adjacent Church of Sant'Agnese was rebuilt as a glorified palatine chapel. The market was banished and the piazza used more or less as an open-air Pamphilj salon. In 1652, Innocent inaugurated the Lago di Piazza Navona. On Saturday and Sunday evenings in August, the piazza was artificially flooded so that representatives of noble families might parade through the water in ornate carriages to the accompaniment of music performed on the steps of Sant'Agnese. The custom was abandoned in the late seventeenth century, revived in 1703, and then continued until 1866. As for the market, it was eventually transferred to Campo de' Fiori, where it remains to the present day.

Piazza Navona is dominated by Bernini's celebrated Fountain of the Four Rivers, which forms an elaborate pedestal for the OBELISCO AGONALE. The obelisk's hieroglyphs bear the name of the emperor Domitian (r. AD 81–96), invoked as 'King of Upper and Lower Egypt, Lord of the Two Lands'. It is owing to the hieroglyphs' inscrutability that the obelisk survived the zealous obliteration of the emperor's name that followed his assassination. The obelisk originally stood in the Iseum Campense, a 12.4

shrine to Isis founded by Domitian. Removed by Maxentius in the early fourth century to his villa on the Via Appia, it is likely the first of Rome's obelisks to have been toppled. The Ostrogoth Vitiges, who besieged Rome in AD 537, encamped near the emperor's villa. Eleven centuries after it had been removed from Domitian's Iseum to the Via Appia, the obelisk's migrations ended with its transportation to the site of Domitian's stadium, just half a kilometer from its original location.

The obelisk is surmounted by the figure of a dove that is rich in symbolism. As an emblem of the Holy Spirit, it evokes the status of Pope Innocent X as Christ's divinely ordained vicar on earth; inasmuch as the dove figures prominently in the Pamphilj family arms, it also alludes to the temporal power of the pope's family. Finally, the dove is an ancient symbol of peace. In the present case, however, that symbol is charged with defiance. The fountain was completed in 1651, three years after the Treaty of Westphalia had formalized the Catholic Church's loss of northern Europe to Protestantism. The monument thus constitutes an obstinate gesture of Catholic triumphalism. With its colossal figures representing the rivers of the four corners of the world, the fountain expresses the limitless pretensions of the late Counter Reformation papacy.

The Campus Martius was largely spared the wholesale demolitions effected in Rome's historic center in the decades following the unification of Italy and in the Fascist period. The urban freeway known as Corso Vittorio Emanuele II, begun in 1883, represents a conspicuous and lamentable exception. Intended as a continuation of Via Nazionale, the new thoroughfare cut through the heart of papal Rome to link Piazza Venezia with the Borgo and Vatican. Aside from the many buildings that were annihilated outright, Corso Vittorio effectively destroyed the context of such monuments as Sant'Andrea della Valle, the Chiesa Nuova and the Cancelleria, all of which formerly rose on modest piazzas of which they formed the focus. At the same time, the street ruptured the continuity of the western Campus by interposing a formidable barrier between its twin poles at Piazza Navona and Campo de' Fiori.

In the Fascist era, the opening of Corso del Rinascimento (1936–1938) further mutilated the precious quarter around Piazza Navona. Its construction entailed the demolition of ancient blocks of buildings between Piazza delle Cinque Lune and Piazza Madama. It also displaced Palazzetto delle Cinque Lune and truncated other buildings so that their façades might be set back to accommodate the street. These accomplishments are aired in a verse DEDICATION mounted on the façade of the *12.1* Palazzo dell'Istituto Nazionale delle Assicurazioni (INA). The intervention elicited a mordant epigram from the poet 'Trilussa' (Carlo Alberto Salustri, 1871–1950): *Se questo è il corso del Rinascimento ogni aborto sarebbe un lieto evento* ('If this is the thoroughfare of the Renaissance [Lit., 'rebirth'], every miscarriage would be a blessèd event').

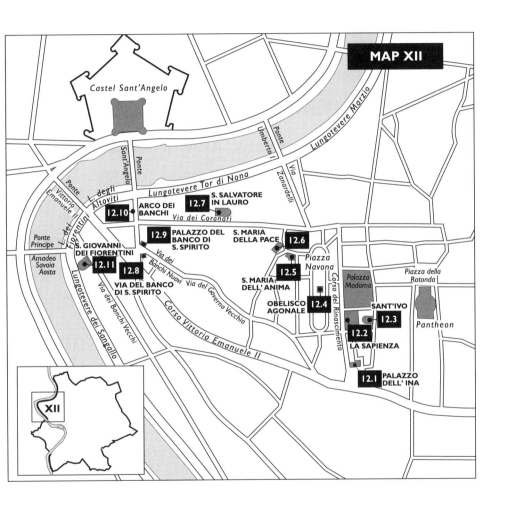

MAP XII

Castel Sant'Angelo

Lungotevere Marzio

Ponte Umberto I

Via Zanardelli

Lungotevere Tor di Nona

Via dei Coronari

12.7 S. SALVATORE IN LAURO

12.10 ARCO DEI BANCHI

12.9 PALAZZO DEL BANCO DI S. SPIRITO

S. MARIA DELLA PACE **12.6**

12.5

Piazza Navona

S. MARIA DELL'ANIMA

OBELISCO AGONALE **12.4**

Corso del Rinascimento

Palazzo Madama

Piazza della Rotonda

SANT'IVO **12.3**

Pantheon

12.2
LA SAPIENZA

12.1 PALAZZO DELL'INA

S. GIOVANNI DEI FIORENTINI

12.11

12.8

VIA DEL BANCO DI S. SPIRITO

Via dei Banchi Nuovi

Via del Governo Vecchio

Corso Vittorio Emanuele II

Lungotevere dei Sangallo

Via dei Banchi Vecchi

Ponte Sant'Angelo

L. degli Altoviti

L. dei Fiorentini

Ponte Vittorio Emanuele II

Ponte Principe Amadeo Savoia Aosta

XII

12.1 Corso del Rinascimento: Dedication

ITALIAE FINES PROMOVIT BELLICA VIRTVS

ET NOVVS IN NOSTRA FVNDITVR VRBE DECOR

ANNO DOMINI MCMXXXVII IMPERII PRIMO

One ELEGIAC COUPLET (lines 1–2)

1. ITALIAE : *In* CL *verse, the quantity of the initial vowel of the word may be treated as either long or short.*
3. MCMXXXVII : Mīllēsimō nōngentēsimō trīcēsimō septimō. *The Christian and Fascist eras are cited in tandem (cf. 10.7, line 7).*

12.2 Palazzo della Sapienza: Dedication by Sixtus V

INITIVM

SAPIENTIAE

TIMOR DOMINI

XYSTVS V PONT MAX A II

1–3. INITIVM ... DOMINI : *The text is quoted from the Vulgate, Ps. 110:10.*
4. XYSTVS V : Quīntus. *The name Sixtus appears in inscriptions variously as* SIXTVS, XYSTVS, *and* SYXTVS. *See 3.4D, line 4.* — PONT(ifex) MAX(imus) A(nnō) II : Secundō.

12.3A Biblioteca Alessandrina: Dedication to Alexander VII

ALEXANDRO VII PONT MAX

OB AEDEM SAPIENTIAE

TOTO AMBITV PERFECTAM

ET BIBLIOTHECA

5 HORTOQVE MEDICO INSTRVCTAM

SACRI CONSISTORII ADVOCATI

POSS MDCLX

1. ALEXANDRO VII : Septimō. — PONT(ificī) MAX(imō).
2–3. OB AEDEM ... PERFECTAM : *On the construction, see 1.7A, lines 2–3.*
6. SACRI CONSISTORII : *I.e., 'College of Cardinals'.*
7. POSS = posuērunt : *On the abbreviation, see 1.61, line 7.* — MDCLX : Mīllēsimō sescentēsimō sexāgēsimō.

Piazza di S. Andrea della Valle 6: Above Portal

Martial valor has advanced the borders of Italy,
and a new beauty is shed in our City.[a]
In the year of the Lord 1937, first of the Empire.[b]

One ELEGIAC COUPLET (*lines 1–2*)

a. *The inscription commemorates the inauguration of Corso del Rinascimento, opened at the cost of massive demolitions around Piazza Navona.*

b. *The Fascist era was reckoned from 1922 (see 10.5, note e). The era of the Fascist 'empire' was introduced in 1936 with the conquest of Ethiopia.*

Corso del Rinascimento 40: Above Portal

The fear of the Lord
is the beginning
of wisdom.[a]

Sixtus the Fifth, Supreme Pontiff,[b] *in his second year.*

a. *The text is quoted from the Vulgate, Ps. 110:10. The word 'wisdom' (Latin* sapientia) *gave its name to the university* (La Sapienza).

b. *Pope Sixtus V Peretti (r. 1585–1590). The second year of his pontificate ran from 24 April 1586 through 23 April 1587.*

S. Ivo: Façade, above Portal

The advocates of the Sacred Consistory[a]
set this up to Alexander the Seventh,[b] *Supreme Pontiff,*
for having brought Palazzo della Sapienza
to completion in its entire extent
and for having equipped it
with a library and medicinal garden,
in 1660.

a. *I.e, the* CURIA. *The consistorial advocates were generally laymen.*

b. *Pope Alexander VII Chigi (r. 1655–1667). Alexander founded the Biblioteca Alessandrina, library of the university. The University of Rome had its origin in the Studium Urbis instituted by Pope Boniface VIII in 1303. It was effectively refounded by Eugenius IV (r. 1431–1447).*

12.3B S. Ivo: Dedication by Victor Emanuel III

AEDES PVLCHERRIMA
SANCTORVM IVONIS LEONIS
PANTALEONIS LVCAE CATHARINAE
DIV NEGLECTA
5   AVSPICIO REGIS VICTORII EMMANVELIS III
HOMINVM PIETATI ATQVE ADMIRATIONI
RESTITVTA EST
BENITO MVSSOLINI
REM PVBLICAM MODERANTE
PETRO FEDELE ADMINISTRO STVDIIS REGENDIS PROVEHENDIS
11   GEORGIO DEL VECCHIO RECTORE MAGNIFICO
MENSE MARTIO AN MCMXXVI

1. AEDES : *See 1.8B, line 10.*
2. IVONIS : *The Latin name is* Ivō, -ōnis.
3. PANTALEONIS : *On the name, see 5.8D, line 2.* — LVCAE : *On the name, see 8.6, line 9.*
5. EMMANVELIS : *The Latin name is* Emmanuel, -ēlis. — III : *Tertiī.*
8. BENITO MVSSOLINI : *As often in modern inscriptions, whereas the surname is not Latinized, the Christian name is artfully placed in a Dat. or Abl. phrase so as to coincide with its Italian form. Given the Latinized* PETRO *(line 10) and* GEORGIO *(line 11), the reader is left to doubt whether* BENITO *may not be meant as the Abl. of a Latinized* Benītus.
9. REM PVBLICAM MODERANTE : *More usual in* CL *than* moderārī *in this context are such verbs as* gerere, administrāre, regere, tractāre, *and* gubernāre *(cf. also the phrase* summī moderātōrēs, *1.6F, line 7). On the construction, see 5.8B, line 1.*
10. ADMINISTRO STVDIIS REGENDIS PROVEHENDIS : *The phrase represents Ital.* Ministro della Pubblica Istruzione *('Minister of Public Instruction'). On the construction, see 1.6H, lines 11–12.*
11. RECTORE MAGNIFICO : *The phrase represents Ital.* Magnifico Rettore *('Grand Rector'), formal title of university chancellors in Italy.*
12. AN(nō) MCMXXVI : *Mīllēsimō nōngentēsimō vīcēsimō sextō. The year of the Fascist era is not cited (cf. 10.7, line 7).*

Sacristy, N Wall

At the initiative of King Victor Emanuel the Third [a]
this outstandingly beautiful church [b]
of Saints Ivo, [c] Leo, [d]
Pantaleon, [e] Luke, [f] and Catherine, [g]
long neglected,
was restored
to men's piety and wonder
while Benito Mussolini [h] was head of state,
and during the tenure
of Pietro Fedele as Minister of Public Instruction
and Giorgio del Vecchio as Chancellor, [i]
in the month of March, 1926.

a. Son of Umberto I and Queen Margherita, Vittorio Emanuele III (r. 1900–1946) permitted himself to be made the tool of Mussolini's regime. After the Second World War he went into exile in Egypt, where he died in 1947.

b. Designed by Borromini, the church was commissioned under Urban VIII and completed under Alexander VII. It had been deconsecrated in 1870 and used as a depository for the Biblioteca Alessandrina.

c. After finishing his studies in canon law at Paris, St. Ivo of Brittany (c. 1235–1303) won a reputation for impartiality as a judge in ecclesiastical courts. He is patron saint of lawyers and judges.

d. Pope St. Leo I the Great (r. 440–461) authored the celebrated Tome, a dogmatic statement of the perfect union of divine and human natures in the person of Christ. It was read out at the Council of Chalcedon in 451.

e. St. Pantaleon was a physician of Nicomedia martyred c. 305.

f. The Apostle (cf. 9.3, note d).

g. According to her legend, St. Catherine (fourth century?) confuted fifty pagan philosophers who had been summoned to persuade her of the error of Christianity. After being broken on the 'Catherine Wheel' she was beheaded. She is the patron of students and of philosophers and apologists.

h. See 10.5, note c.

i. Pietro Fedele and Giorgio del Vecchio assisted at the restoration of S. Ivo to Christian cult on 21 March 1926.

12.4 Obelisco Agonale: Dedication by Innocent X

i.

OBELISCVM

AB IMP ANT CARACALLA ROMAM ADVECTVM

CVM INTER CIRCI CASTRENSIS RVDERA

CONFRACTVS DIV IACVISSET

5   INNOCENTIVS DECIMVS PONT OPT MAX

AD FONTIS FORIQ ORNATVM

TRANSTVLIT INSTAVRAVIT EREXIT

ANNO SAL MDCLI PONTIF VII

2. IMP(erātōre) ANT(ōnīnō) CARACALLA : *Originally called* Septimius Bassianus, *in 195 the elder son of Septimius Severus was renamed* Imperator Caesar Marcus Aurelius Antoninus Augustus (*in the same year, his father had proclaimed himself son of the deified Marcus Aurelius*). *The nickname* Caracalla *is due to the hooded Gallic cloak that he favored.*

5. PONT(ifex) OPT(imus) MAX(imus) : *See 14.1.ii, line 3.*

6. FORIQ(ue) : *See 8.3B, line 6.*

7. TRANSTVLIT INSTAVRAVIT EREXIT : *The asyndeton lends solemnity* (*cf. 1.2.i, line 4*).

8. SAL(ūtis) MDCLI : Mīllēsimō sescentēsimō quīnquāgēsimō prīmō. — PONTIF(icātūs) VII : Septimō.

ii.

NOXIA AEGYPTIORVM MONSTRA

INNOCENS PREMIT COLVMBA

QVAE PACIS OLEAM GESTANS

ET VIRTVTVM LILIIS REDIMITA

5   OBELISCVM PRO TROPHEO SIBI STATVENS

ROMAE TRIVMPHAT

4. VIRTVTVM LILIIS : *The phrase is borrowed from the hymn* Salve, mater misericordiae.

5. TROPHEO = tropaeō : *Cf. 1.4, line 2. The form shows both inauthentic* H (*see 8.8A, line 2*) *and* E *for* AE (*see 1.8B, line 5*).

Piazza Navona: Base of Obelisk

North

For the embellishment of the fountain and the square,
Innocent the Tenth,[a] Supreme Pontiff,
transported, restored, and erected
the obelisk
brought to Rome by Imperator Antoninus Caracalla[b]
after it had long lain in fragments
amid the ruins of the Circus Castrensis,[c]
in the year of Salvation 1651, seventh of his office.

a. *Pope Innocent X Pamphilj (r. 1644–1655). The seventh year of his pontificate ran from 15 September 1650 through 14 September 1651.*

b. *Septimius Bassianus, nicknamed 'Caracalla', was formally 'Marcus Aurelius Antoninus' (see 2.3, note b). Though it has been associated with the name of Caracalla since the Middle Ages, the Obelisco Agonale—like the Minerveo and Macutèo—in fact probably came from the shrine of Isis on the Campus Martius. It is of Roman manufacture. The inexpertly cut hieroglyphs record a hymn in honor of Domitian and the Flavian dynasty.*

c. *I.e., the villa of the emperor Maxentius on the Via Appia, where the obelisk was taken in the fourth century. When Innocent X saw it there in 1647, it lay broken in five pieces (cf. 7.1.iv, note b).*

East

The innocent dove
subdues the guilty beasts of Egypt:
bearing the olive of peace
and crowned with the lilies of virtue,
in setting up the obelisk as a trophy to herself
she triumphs at Rome.[a]

a. *The obelisk is surmounted by the dove of the Pamphilj arms. In this case there is no pretence that the monument is dedicated either to the Cross (see 15.3B.v) or to the BVM (cf. 4.3.i).*

iii.

INNOCENTIVS DECIMVS PONT MAX

NILOTICIS AENIGMATIBVS EXARATVM LAPIDEM

AMNIBVS SVBTER LABENTIBVS IMPOSVIT

VT SALVBREM

5 SPATIANTIBVS AMOENITATEM

SITIENTIBVS POTVM

MEDITANTIBVS ESCAM

MAGNIFICE LARGIRETVR

1. PONT(ifex) MAX(imus).
2. AENIGMATIBVS : *Borrowed in* CL *to refer to any obscure utterance, the Greek* αἴνιγμα *was originally used of the riddles proposed by the participants of Athenian symposia.*
5–7. SPATIANTIBVS . . . SITIENTIBVS . . . MEDITANTIBVS : *Once again, the asyndeton confers an elevated tone (see 12.4.i, line 7).*

iv.

INNOCENTIVS DECIMVS PONT MAX

NATALI DOMO PAMPHILIA

OPERE CVLTVQ AMPLIFICATA

LIBERATAQ INOPPORTVNIS AEDIFICIIS

5 AGONALI AREA

FORVM VRBIS CELEBERRIMVM

MVLTIPLICI MAIESTATIS INCREMENTO

NOBILITAVIT

1. PONT(ifex) MAX(imus).
3. CVLTVQ(ue).
4. LIBERATAQ(ue). — INOPPORTVNIS : *The* CL *inopportūnus is* 'inappropriate', 'unseasonable'.
5. AGONALI AREA : *As the Ital. toponym Navona ultimately derives from agōn (transliterating Greek* ἀγών, 'contest'*), the phrase* agōnālis ārea *furnishes a hyper-Classicizing equivalent for* 'Piazza Navona' *(cf. 8.3B, line 6).*

South

Innocent the Tenth,[a] Pontiff,

set this stone, graven with the riddles of the Nile,[b]

atop the streams that glide below,[c]

that in grand style he might furnish

wholesome

delight for those who stroll,

drink for those who thirst,

sustenance for those who reflect.

a. See 12.4.i, note a.

b. Only in 1822 did Jean-François Champollion decipher the Rosetta Stone.

c. The obelisk forms the centerpiece of Bernini's Fontana dei Quattro Fiumi
(Fountain of the Four Rivers). The four colossal figures represent the Nile,
Ganges, Danube, and Rio de la Plata (separating Argentina and Uruguay),
in allusion to the triumph of the Gospel in the four corners of the world.

West

Innocent the Tenth,[a] Supreme Pontiff,

on the occasion of improvements both structural and cosmetic

to his ancestral Pamphilj home[b]

and the clearing of Piazza Navona

of unsuitable constructions,[c]

by a manifold increase

of its grandeur

ennobled the city's most frequented square.

a. See 12.4.i, note a.

b. Palazzo Pamphilj incorporates an agglomeration of preexisting houses,
one of them owned by the Pamphilj family since the fifteenth century.

c. The market that had been moved from the foot of the Campidoglio to
Piazza Navona in the fifteenth century was banished during the reign of
Innocent X. The piazza occupies the site of the Stadium of Domitian, the
plan of which is preserved in the modern structures that define its limits.

12.5 Epitaph of Pope Hadrian VI

ADRIANVS

VI PP

PROH DOLOR QVANTVM REFERT IN QVAE TEMPORA ⌐

VEL OPTIMI CVIVSQVE VIRTVS INCIDAT

1. ADRIANVS | VI : *Sextus. On the spelling of the name, see 8.8A, line 2.* —
P(a)P(a) : *See 3.6A, line 2.*

3. PROH = prō : *In CL, the interjection* prō *is used with the Nom., the Voc. or the Acc. of Exclamation. The phrase* prō dolor *in particular is typical of the poets of the Silver Age and later (Statius, Claudian, Ausonius).* —
QVANTVM . . . INCIDAT : *The text is adapted from Plin.HN 7.106:* Etenim plurimum refert, in quae cuiusque virtus tempora inciderit. *The sentence takes the form of an exclamation introduced by* QVANTVM *and incorporating an indirect question* (IN QVAE TEMPORA . . . INCIDERIT) *depending on* REFERT.

12.6 Epitaph of Beatrice and Lavinia Ponzetti

D O M

BEATRICI ET LAVINIAE PONZETTIS

INDOLIS FESTIVITATISQ

ADMIRANDAE QVAS NEAPOLIS

5   TVLIT ROMA A QVAE DESIISSE

FEREBATVR VNA DIE ABSVMPSIT

VIXER HAEC VI ILLA ANN VIII

FERNANDVS PATRVVS APOSTOLICI

10   FISCI VII VIR DECANVS MAGNO

SOLATIO SPEQ ORBATVS

DELITIIS ANIMVLISQVE

SVIS MOERENS POSVIT

V KL DECEMBR M^O D^O V^O

S. Maria dell'Anima: Presbytery

Pope Hadrian
the Sixth.[a]
Alas, of what great moment are the times
in which the virtue of even the best of men finds itself.[b]

a. *Pope Hadrian VI Florensz Dedal (r. 1522–1523). A stern reformer, Hadrian was loathed by the Romans. He was the last* pontefice barbaro *('foreign pope') before Benedict XVI (r. 2005–) and the only pontiff of modern times besides Marcellus II to retain his baptismal name (cf. 3.4C, note a).*
b. *The text is adapted from the Elder Pliny's* Naturalis Historia *7.106: 'In fact, it is of great moment in what times each man's virtue has found itself'—that is, even the best of men may be born in times unsuited to their virtues. Hadrian's cerebral and ascetic character was decidedly unsuited to an age in which western Europe was dominated by the personalities of Henry VIII, François I, and Charles V and eastern Europe by the Turkish threat.*

S. Maria della Pace: R of Ponzetti Chapel (First Chapel L)

To God, Best and Greatest.
To Beatrice and Lavinia Ponzetti,
wonderfully talented and cheerful,
whom Naples brought to birth,
Rome fitly reared,
and the plague, rumored to have ceased,
carried off in the course of a single day.
The latter lived six years, the former eight.

Their uncle Ferdinando,[a]
Dean of the Board of Seven of the Apostolic Purse,[b]
bereft of his great comfort and hope,
in grief set this up
to his dear little souls
on 27 November 1505.[c]

1. D(eō) O(ptimō) M(aximō).
2. PONZETTIS : On the Latinization, cf. 12.3B, line 8.
3. INDOLIS FESTIVITATISQ(ue) | ADMIRANDAE : Gen. of Character-
   istic.
8. VIXER(unt). — VI : Sex. — ANN(ōs) VIII : Octō.
9. APOSTOLICI : See 3.4D, line 4.
10. VII VIR = septemvir(ōrum) : See 1.61, line 13. — DECANVS : The EL
    decānus is 'dean' (etymologically, 'overseer of ten men').
11. SOLATIO = sōlāciō : On the spelling, see 3.4B, line 3. — SPEQ(ue).
12. DELITIIS = dēliciīs : The phrase DELITIIS ANIMVLISQVE is best taken
    as an instance of hendiadys (see 3.2B, line 6).
13. MOERENS = maerēns : On the spelling, see 1.8B, line 5.
14. V : Quīntō. — K(a)L(endās) DECEMBR(is) : See 1.6G, line 11. —
    Mᵒ Dᵒ Vᵒ : Mīllēsimō quīngentēsimō quīntō.

12.7　Fountain of S. Salvatore in Lauro: Dedication

VT LVPVS IN MARTIS CAMPO MANSVETIOR AGNO

VIRGINEAS POPVLO FAVCE MINISTRAT AQVAS

SIC QVOQVE PERSPICVAM CVI VIRGO PRAESIDET VNDAM

MITIOR HIS HOEDO FVNDIT AB ORE LEO

5　NEC MIRVM DRACO QVI TOTI PIVS IMPERAT ORBI

EXEMPLO PLACIDOS REDDIT VTROSQVE SVO

M D LXXVIIII

Three ELEGIAC COUPLETS (lines 1–6)

3. CVI : Dat. with PRAESIDET. Its antecedent is VNDAM.
4. HIS : I.e., the multitude of individuals implicit in the collective POPVLVS
   (line 2). — HOEDO = haedō : On the spelling, see 1.8B, line 5.
7. M D LXXVIIII : Mīllēsimō quīngentēsimō septuāgēsimō nōnō. The
   notation VIIII (vs. IX) is more typical of ancient inscriptions than modern.

a. *When the present chapel was founded (1516), Ferdinando Ponzetti (1444–1527) was dean of the papal treasury and Archdeacon of Sorrento (see* DEACON*). The following year, while* BISHOP*-elect of the titular see of Melitene, Ponzetti was created* CARDINAL *by Leo X in the title of S. Pancrazio (cf. 1.8G, note c). The chapel is by Baldassare Peruzzi (see 11.31).*

b. *Before the abolition of the papacy's temporal power in 1870 (see 8.7B.ii, note b), the Reverenda Camera Apostolica ('Apostolic Chamber') was the central board of finance of the papal administration, headed by the Cardinal Camerlengo. The membership of the board was fixed at seven by Eugenius IV (r. 1431–1447) and raised to twelve by Sixtus V (r. 1585–1590). Since 1870, the administrative functions of the Chamber have gradually been taken over by various departments of the Vatican bureaucracy. Today the chief duty of the Cardinal Camerlengo is to act as head of state during vacancies of the Holy See.*

c. *Lit., 'on the fifth day before the Kalends of December'.*

Piazza di S. Salvatore in Lauro: L of Portal of Church

As in the Field of Mars the wolf, milder than a lamb,
dispenses the Virgin's waters to the people from its throat,[a]
so also from its mouth does the lion,[b] milder than a kid,
pour forth for them the flood over which the Virgin presides.[c]
Nor any wonder: by his example, the dragon that in godliness
rules over the whole world renders them both peaceable.[d]

1579

Three ELEGIAC COUPLETS (lines 1–6)

a. *I.e., the Fontana della Lupa in Via dei Prefetti (see 10.10).*
b. *The spout of the fountain is made in the form of a lion's head.*
c. *I.e., the Acqua Vergine (see 9.5D, note b).*
d. *The dragon referred to here is that which figures prominently in the arms of Pope Gregory XIII Boncompagni (r. 1572–1585).*

12.8 Palazzo del Banco di S. Spirito: Dedication by Clement IX

MENSAM

NVMMVLARIAM

S SPIRITVS

A SEMP MEM PAVLO V ERECTAM

5   HAS IN AEDES

A CLEM VII MEDICE CVDENDIS NVMMIS DESTINATAS

AB ALEXANDRO VII NOVA STRVCTIONE MVNITAS

CLEMENS IX PONT MAX

FELICIBVS AVSPICIIS

10   TRANSTVLIT STABILIVIT

ANNO DOMINI M DC LXVII

2. NVMMVLARIAM : *The* CL nummulārius *is 'pertaining to coinage' (most frequently as a Masc.Subst., 'money-changer').*

3. S(ānctī) SPIRITVS : *The Latin* sānctus spīritus *represents Greek* ἅγιον πνεῦμα *('holy spirit').*

4. SEMP(iternae) MEM(oriae) PAVLO V : *Quīntō.*

6. CLEM(ente) VII : *Septimō.* — MEDICE : *See 1.8G, line 2.* — CVDENDIS NVMMIS : *On the construction, see 1.6H, lines 11–12.*

7. ALEXANDRO VII : *Septimō.*

8. CLEMENS IX : *Nōnus.* — PONT(ifex) MAX(imus).

11. M DC LXVII : *Mīllēsimō sescentēsimō sexāgēsimō septimō.*

12.9 Via del Banco di S. Spirito: Dedication to Julius II

IVLIO II PONT OPT MAX QVOD FINIB

DITIONIS S R E PROLATIS ITALIAQ

LIBERATA VRBEM ROMAM OCCVPATE

SIMILIOREM QVAM DIVISE PATEFACTIS

5   DIMENSISQ VIIS PRO MAIESTATE

IMPERII ORNAVIT

(Names of Magistrates)   AEDILES F C MDXII

Via dei Banchi Nuovi 31: Façade

In the year of the Lord 1667
Clement the Ninth, Supreme Pontiff,[a]
under a happy star
transferred and set up
in this edifice—
intended by Clement the Seventh de' Medici [b]
for the coining of money
and augmented by Alexander the Seventh [c]
with new construction—
the Bank of the Holy Spirit,[d]
founded by Paul the Fifth [e] of everlasting memory.

a. *Pope Clement IX Rospigliosi (r. 1667–1669).*
b. *Pope Clement VII de' Medici (r. 1523–1534).*
c. *Pope Alexander VII Chigi (r. 1655–1667).*
d. *Planned by Julius II (r. 1503–1513), the papal mint was transferred to new quarters in 1541 and the Banco di Santo Spirito installed in the present building in 1605. Before the violent disruption of the neighborhood occasioned by the opening of Corso Vittorio Emanuele II in the 1880s, the structure lent a monumental prominence to the junction of the Via Papalis and the Via Peregrinorum.*
e. *Pope Paul V Borghese (r. 1605–1621).*

Via del Banco di S. Spirito 29: Façade, High

To Julius the Second,[a] Supreme and most excellent Pontiff,
because after extending the territory under the jurisdiction
of the Holy Roman Church and liberating Italy,
in accordance with the majesty of her empire
he embellished with broad, surveyed streets the City of Rome,
which was more like a city settled piecemeal than one well ordered.[b]
(Names of Magistrates) Superintendents of Streets,
undertook to have this mounted in 1512.

1. IVLIO II : Secundō. — PONT(ificī) OPT(imō) MAX(imō) : *See 14.1.ii, lines 3–4.* — FINIB(us).

2. DITIONIS = diciōnis : *On the spelling, see 3.4B, line 3.* — S(āncte) R(ōmāne) E(cclēsie) : *On ecclēsia, see 1.7A, line 6. On the spelling, see 1.8B, line 5.* — ITALIAQ(ue).

3–4. OCCVPATE . . . DIVISE : *The wording echoes Livy 5.55.5 and Suet.Aug. 28.*

5. DIMENSISQ(ue).

7. AEDILES : *A Classicizing substitute for* magistrī viārum (*itself representing Ital.* maestri di strada); *cf. 13.4, line 8.* — F(aciendum) C(ūrāvērunt) MDXII : Mīllēsimō quīngentēsimō duodecimō.

12.10   Commemoration of 1277 Flood

HVC TIBER

ACCESSIT

SET TVRBI

DVS HINC

5 CITO CESSIT

ANNO DOMINI

MCC LXXVI

IND VI M NO

VEMB DIE VII

10 ECCL'A VAC

ANTE

One HEXAMETER (*lines 1–5*)

3. SET = sed : *In LL pronunciation, proclitic words such as* haud, sed, *and* ad *tended to lose their voicing before a surd, becoming* /haut/, /sɛt/, *and* /at/. *This resulted in orthographical confusion in such pairs as* atque *and* adque (*i.e.,* ad + que). — TVRBI|DVS.

7. MCC LXXVI : Mīllēsimō ducentēsimō septuāgēsimō sextō.

8. IND(ictiōne) : *See 2.1, line 16.* — VI : Sextā. — M(ēnsis) NO|VEMB(ris) : *See 1.6G, line 11.*

9. VII : Septimō.

10. ECCL(ēsi)A : *See 1.7A, line 6.* — VAC|ANTE : *The conventional expression for a papal interregnum is* apostolicā sēde vacante *or simply* sēde vacante (*Abl.Abs.*).

a. *Pope Julius II della Rovere (r. 1503–1513). Called by contemporaries* Il Terribile, *the pontiff incarnated the imperial aspirations of his namesake, Julius Caesar. Though he is responsible for organizing the papal state on the lines that it would maintain for more than three centuries, Julius is best known for his decision to replace the Constantinian basilica of St. Peter.*

b. *The stone commemorates the widening of Via del Banco di Santo Spirito to accommodate banking houses that clustered in the early sixteenth century at the head of Ponte Sant'Angelo. The language echoes Livy's characterization of the city, rebuilt haphazardly after the Gallic sack of 390 BC, and Suetonius' account of the improvements made by the emperor Augustus.*

Via dell'Arco dei Banchi: L Wall

The Tiber rose

to this point[a]

but

in its churning

quickly receded

in the year of the Lord

1276,

in the sixth indiction,

in the month of November, on the seventh day,

the church

being vacant.[b]

One HEXAMETER (lines 1–5)

a. *The stone was formerly mounted on the nearby Church of SS. Celso e Giuliano, rebuilt in 1733; it is the oldest of its kind extant.*

b. *As the Holy See was vacant between the death of John XXI (20 May 1277) and the election of Nicholas III (25 November 1277) but not in November of 1276, the date* MCC LXXVI *must be an error for* MCC LXXVII. *On the assumption that the year in question was 1277, the* INDICTION *cited is either the Greek (reckoned from 1 September and in regular use at the papal chancery 584–1187) or the Bedan (reckoned from 24 September and in use from 1147). The year 1277 was the fifth of the Roman indiction (reckoned from 25 December or, more frequently, from 1 January, in which case it is concurrent with the civil year).*

12.11 Epitaph of Carlo Maderno

D O M
CAROLVS MADERNVS
EQVES NOVOCOMENSIS
EQVITIS DOMENICI FONTANAE
5   SIXTI V ARCHITECTI NEPOS
EIVSDEMQVE IN EXCITANDIS
OBELISCIS ADIVTOR
CVM PAVLI V IVSSV ANTIQVAM
VATICANI TEMPLI PARTEM
10   CVM PORTICV DELINEASSET
COLVMNAMQVE EX DELVBRO PACIS
AMOTAM
ANTE LIBERII BASILICAM
IN EXQVILIIS IMPOSITO SIGNO
15   DEIPARE VIRGINIS EREXISSET
V[rb]ANO VIII PONT MAX
CVIVS ARCHITECTVS ERAT
SEPVLCRVM SIBI SVISQVE
VIVENS POSVIT

1. D(eō) O(ptimō) M(aximō).
2. CAROLVS MADERNVS : *On the Latinization, cf. 12.3B, line 8.*
3. NOVOCOMENSIS : *The Adj.* Novocōmēnsis *answers to the toponym* Novum Cōmum *or* Cōmum (*mod. Como*).
5. SIXTI V : Quīntī.
6. IN EXCITANDIS | OBELISCIS : *On the construction, see 1.6H, lines 11–12.*
8. PAVLI V : Quīntī.
10. DELINEASSET = dēlineāvisset : *The CL* dēlineāre *is 'to trace the outline' of a thing.*
13. LIBERII : *On the name, see 4.2B, line 2.*
14. EXQVILIIS = Esquiliīs.
15. DEIPARE = deiparae : *See 9.3, line 7; on the spelling, see 1.8B, line 5.*
16. V[rb]ANO VIII : Octāvō. *The characters enclosed in brackets are restored from context.* — PONT(ifice) MAX(imō) : *See 5.8B, line 1.*
18. SEPVLCRVM : *On the spelling, see 8.8A, line 2.*

S. Giovanni dei Fiorentini: Pavement L of High Altar

To God, Best and Greatest.
Carlo Maderno,
Cavaliere of Como,[a]
nephew of Cavaliere Domenico Fontana,[b]
architect of Sixtus the Fifth,[c]
and assistant to the same
in raising obelisks,
after at the bidding of Paul the Fifth [d]
he had made designs for the old portion
of the Vatican basilica with its portico
and had erected the column
from the Shrine of Peace
before the Basilica of Liberius[e]
and placed atop it
an image of the Mother of God,[f]
during the reign of Urban the Eighth,[g] Supreme Pontiff,
whom he served as architect,
in his own lifetime set up this tomb
for himself and his descendants.

a. *Born at Capolago on Lake Lugano in Canton Ticino, Carlo Maderno (1556–1629) completed the dome of S. Giovanni dei Fiorentini in 1620. He is likewise responsible for the dome of Sant'Andrea della Valle, the largest on the Roman skyline after that of St. Peter's. Until 1889, much of Canton Ticino formed part of the Diocese of Como.*

b. *The fame of Domenico Fontana rests largely on the prodigies of engineering that he performed for Pope Sixtus V (see 7.1.ii, note c).*

c. *Pope Sixtus V Peretti (r. 1585–1590).*

d. *Pope Paul V Borghese (r. 1605–1621). Paul appointed Maderno architect of St. Peter's (cf. 15.4B, note d).*

e. *I.e., S. Maria Maggiore. On the name, see 4.2G, note c.*

f. *See 4.3.i, note b.*

g. *Pope Urban VIII Barberini (r. 1623–1644). Maderno conceived Palazzo Barberini, which at various stages benefited also by the contributions of Bernini and Borromini.*

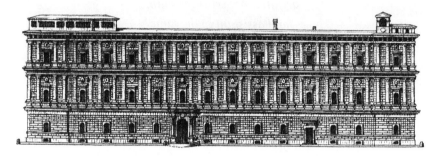

PALAZZO DELLA CANCELLERIA

The Cancelleria follows the pattern established by Bernardo Rossellini's Palazzo Rucellai in Florence, where the Classical pattern of superimposed orders employed in the Colosseum was adapted to palace architecture for the first time. At the Cancelleria, the massive and all but featureless basement supports two upper stories articulated by pilasters paired so as to produce a rhythmic alternation of wide and narrow bays, the former occupied by windows. At both ends of the façade a risalto ('projection') imposes a vertical element to countervail the diffuseness of the design's horizontal bias.

XIII. From Via del Pellegrino to Santa Cecilia

FOR ALL THE GRANDEUR OF HER ANCIENT RUINS, Rome of the early fifteenth century was a small, poor medieval town. Fragmented into territories controlled by baronial families, her *abitato* lacked any semblance of physical cohesion. There were probably no more than 20,000 residents. Malaria was rampant. The violence of war and earthquake had reduced bridges, churches, and dwellings to ruins and had rendered the streets impassable; reconstruction was the task at hand. The stage for Rome's rebirth was set by Pope Martin V (r. 1417–1431), the first pontiff to make the city his permanent home after the Babylonian Captivity. To supervise the reclamation of the streets, Martin reinstituted the office of the Magistri Viarum ('Superintendents of Streets'). He restored the Lateran as well as his own ancestral palace and its associated basilica, SS. Dodici Apostoli, and invited his cardinals to perform the same service for their respective titular churches.

The city's renewal commenced in earnest with Nicholas V (r. 1447–1455). In his reign, the Magistri Viarum were made papal appointees. Their office, the prime instrument of Rome's urban development over the subsequent two centuries, was henceforth to remain under the direct control of the papacy. Statutes of 1452 provided for the improvement of the principal arteries radiating from Ponte Sant'Angelo—the 'Via Recta', the Via Papalis, and the Via Peregrinorum. A refurbished Campo de' Fiori fostered commercial activity in the central Campus Martius, the development of which would be promoted in the subsequent generation by the institution of a new market at Piazza Navona. Although Nicholas's ambitious plans for the Vatican and Borgo went largely unrealized, they determined the Classicizing tenor of future urban projects.

As the Lateran remained the pope's seat in his capacity as Bishop of Rome, Nicholas' removal of the papal court to the Vatican necessitated frequent processions between the city's two great ecclesiastical poles—hence the special prominence of the Via Papalis in early modern Rome.

From its head at Ponte Sant'Angelo, the processional route traversed the central Campus in a southeasterly direction to arrive at the Capitol, passing thence around the Pantani and across the *disabitato* to the Lateran. The most spectacular papal procession was that of the *presa di possesso*, the ceremonial claiming of the Lateran basilica by the new pope after his coronation. Accompanied by a large and splendidly attired entourage, the pontiff advanced through the territories of the local aristocracy; the narrow and sinuous streets were decorated with flowers, banners, and ersatz triumphal arches erected for the occasion. At certain points established by tradition, he paused to receive the homage of the communal officials and to reject a Torah ceremonially proffered by the city's rabbis. Coins were scattered to alleviate the inevitable blockages caused by crowding; riots and stoning were more or less de rigueur.

It was Pope Sixtus IV (r. 1471–1484) who first put forth a plan calculated to address the full gamut of the city's infrastructural needs. Preparatory to Holy Year 1475 Sixtus rebuilt the ancient Pons Valentiniani as Ponte Sisto, Rome's first new bridge since Antiquity. In addition to providing an alternative to Ponte Sant'Angelo for pilgrims approaching the Vatican from the southern Campus, Ponte Sisto facilitated communications between Trastevere and the emerging commercial district centered on Piazza Navona and Campo de' Fiori. After the end of the Holy Year, Sixtus undertook a comprehensive rehabilitation of the central Campus. The 'Via Recta', Via Papalis, and Via Peregrinorum were 13.4   paved; in 1483, VIA FLOREA—the stretch of the Via Peregrinorum centered on Campo de' Fiori—was rebuilt. Parodying the famous boast of the emperor Augustus that he had found Rome brick and left it marble, a wit of the day quipped that Sixtus IV had found Rome mud and left it brick.

The pilgrim who came to Rome for the Holy Year of 1500 and climbed the tower of Palazzo Senatorio for a view would have encountered an unforgettable scene. At his feet, about the black foundations of the fortified palace, goats clambered over the steep crags of the Capitol. On the hill's southern height, shanties and gardens nestled amid colossal white fragments of column and entablature—the relics of Jupiter's great temple. In the valley to the east lay the Forum; reduced to a confusion of crumbling temples, battered arches, and dilapidated churches, the showplace of the Caesars was a pasture for cattle. At its eastern extremity, begirt by rubble, the Colosseum bulked like a shattered ziggurat. To the south, the ruinous and ivy-clad walls of the imperial palaces towered on the silent Palatine; to the north, Torre delle Milizie and Tor de' Conti impended over the *Pantani* like giants frozen in midstride.

In the middle distance, the hilltops were conspicuous with ruins and basilicas. The Oppian was crowned by San Pietro in Vincoli and the lofty wreck of the Baths of Trajan, and the Caelian by Santo Stefano Rotondo, Santi Giovanni e Paolo, and the arcade of the Aqua Claudia. On the western brink of the Aventine, the somber ramparts of Santa Sabina gripped the yellow cliff face above the Tiber with millennial pertinacity. Beyond the Pyramid of Cestius, the Basilica of San Paolo dominated the vastness of the Campagna. In a broad arc from north to south, the distant highlands were strewn with the cyclopean relics of imperial baths and aqueducts. Amid the huge and shapeless masses of ancient masonry, the belfry of Santa Maria Maggiore and the fortified towers of the Lateran made prominent landmarks. Here and there a wisp of smoke arose from the isolated hamlets that clustered around the larger churches and monasteries.

In the opposite direction, to the west, lay the *abitato*. Immediately across the river, Trastevere bristled with fortified towers; on the slopes of the Janiculum, the travertine façade of San Pietro in Montorio shone white against the verdure. Mantled with villas and gardens, the hill's long height stretched northwards to terminate at a thicket of battlements and belfries. Fluttering pennants and the glint of arms gave notice that this was a sacred citadel, the seat of Christ's Vicar. Rising behind the crenellated towers of the Leonine walls, the massive fabric of St. Peter's Basilica commanded the Vatican plain with its glittering façade; the great forecourt would have been black with a surging tide of pilgrims. On the basilica's southern flank, the granite shaft of the Obelisco Vaticano glowed ruddy against muted tones of brick and tufa; to the north, the hillside was concealed beneath the sprawling ramifications of the Apostolic Palace. On the summit beyond, the Belvedere villa rose in isolation. Towards the river stretched the Borgo with the brooding form of Castel Sant'Angelo at its eastern limit.

On the near side of the Tiber, the Campus Martius presented a chaotic agglomeration of rude dwellings and labyrinthine streets everywhere bristling with a growth of belfries and fortified towers. Opposite Castel Sant'Angelo, the uncouth pile of the Orsini fortress at Monte Giordano dominated the city-side approach to the bridge. Closer at hand, 13.3 the CANCELLERIA (the papal chancery) and Palazzo Venezia—both of recent vintage—stood out for the geometrical regularity of their imposing volumes. Along the northern margins of the *abitato*, the shallow convexity of the Pantheon was conspicuous both for its size and its shape; so, too, the elongated void of Piazza Navona. The density diminished in the direction of the Via Lata. Long and perfectly rectilinear, the roadway was flanked by a scattering of houses and churches; of its three triumphal arches, only Arco di Portogallo yet stood. Beyond the Via Lata to the east and the 'Via Recta' to the north, the *abitato* gave way to the vast holdings of Ospedale San Giacomo and the monastery of San Silvestro. Vineyards and gardens extended as far as Porta del Popolo and the slopes of the Quirinal. On the brow of the Pincio, Trinità dei Monti had just begun to rise.

The panorama terminated at the western foot of the Capitoline. Here the narrow plain between the slopes of the hill and the Tiber was crowded with the ramshackle houses and winding alleyways of Rione Sant'Angelo, the heart of medieval Rome. With the founding of the Roman Commune in 1143 and the establishment of a municipal administration on the Capitoline Hill, commercial activity gravitated to the neighborhood, which emerged as the hub of civic life; by the fourteenth century it had become the city's busiest quarter. During the Babylonian Captivity, Rione Sant'Angelo was the epicenter of Cola di Rienzo's attempt to establish an independent government at Rome. Returned from Avignon, the popes shrewdly assessed the political challenge presented by this prosperous and independent quarter. Having established their autonomy in the shadow of Castel Sant'Angelo, they employed every means at their disposal to draw the center of civic life away from the Capitol and in the direction of the Vatican. With the gradual consolidation of papal power during the fifteenth and early sixteenth centuries, Rione Sant'Angelo and the neighboring quarters lapsed into poverty and decadence.

Rione Sant'Angelo is also the historic center of Rome's Jewish community. Here, at the crossroads of the Via Peregrinorum and the route from the port at Civitavecchia into the city, the ebb and flow of pilgrims ensured a consistent business in moneychanging and the few other trades that were open to Jews. As home to the city's Jewish population, Rione Sant'Angelo was also the site of the Roman Ghetto. The formal institution of the Ghetto dates to 1555, when Pope Paul IV (r. 1555–1559) decreed the erection of a walled compound on the site of the Circus Flaminius. Gentile residents of the zone were obliged to relinquish their homes; a few small churches were deconsecrated and eventually demolished. The gates of the compound were locked from dusk till dawn. Among the indignities to which its residents were subjected was compulsory attendance at sermons delivered at nearby Christian churches including SAN 13.9 GREGORIO DELLA DIVINA PIETÀ. Overcrowded and disastrously unsanitary, the Ghetto was first liberated in 1799 under the Jacobin Republic. After papal rule was reestablished in 1815, the Ghetto was revived and was definitively abolished only in 1848 when its walls were pulled down. The quarter was entirely rebuilt in 1888. Notable among the monuments at the margins of the old Ghetto is the Casa di Lorenzo Manlio, a fifteenth-century house featuring a DEDICATORY INSCRIPTION in 13.7 splendid Classicizing capitals.

13.12   With the loss of the PONS SENATORIUS (thereafter known as Ponte
13.10&11 Rotto) to a flood in 1598, the PONS FABRICIUS and PONS CESTIUS
bore the brunt of traffic between Rione Sant'Angelo and Trastevere. Issuing at the southern corner of the Ghetto, the Pons Fabricius was long
known as the Pons Iudaeorum ('Jews' Bridge'). It bears the inscriptions
of its original builder, Gaius Fabricius, as well as those of the consuls
of 23 BC, under whom it was restored after a violent flood. It was under
the spell of the view from the Pons Fabricius that the young Ferdinand
Gregorovius conceived the idea of writing his monumental *Geschichte
der Stadt Rom im Mittelalter* ('History of the City of Rome in the Middle
Ages'). When the Tiber embankments were erected in the late nineteenth century, the bridge narrowly escaped destruction: a proposal was
put forth that the Tiber Island should be united with the left bank by
filling the smaller branch of the river. On the Trastevere side, the Pons
Cestius was demolished and reconstructed; the central arch is the only
portion of the ancient structure that was preserved.

Before the flood of 1598, the route across the Pons Senatorius de-
bouched on the Trastevere side at the conjunction of two important
roads. To the right, the Via Aurelia led across the Janiculum to the port
of Civitavecchia; to the left, the Via Campana-Portuensis led along the
right bank of the Tiber to its mouth at Ostia. In the early Christian
centuries, at points equidistant from the bridge, each of the two roads
13.13   was distinguished by a major church: that of SANTA CECILIA on the
Campana-Portuensis and, on the Aurelia, that of San Crisogono. The
symmetry of their sites is unlikely to be due to chance and indeed reflects
a pattern seen in other parts of the city: At the northern foot of the Capitoline Hill, the basilicas of San Marco and of Santi Dodici Apostoli were
located so as to flank the head of the Via Lata, midway between the Vatican and the Lateran; not far from San Crisogono, the Julian Basilica—
Santa Maria in Trastevere—rose at the intersection of the Via Aurelia
and the Via Septimiana. Like prominent hilltops, major thoroughfares

were evidently deemed desirable sites for churches in the fourth and fifth centuries.

While on any reckoning St. Chrysogonus must count as a minor figure in the celestial caucus, St. Cecilia ranks with St. Agnes as the city's most fervently venerated virgin martyr. According to her legend, Cecilia had vowed her chastity to Christ at an early age; espoused to a young pagan named Valerian, she converted him to Christianity and—marvelous to relate—persuaded him to respect her vow. After Valerian and his brother Tiburtius were martyred, Cecilia buried them and was condemned to be suffocated in the bath of her *domus* in Trastevere (here as elsewhere, hagiographical enthusiasm readily identified the principal church dedicated to the saint with her house). Having survived the ordeal, Cecilia was beheaded—so inexpertly, however, that she lived on for three days. She was buried in the Cemetery of Callistus; her incorrupt body was transferred to the basilica that bears her name when it was restored by Pope St. Paschal I (r. 817–824). Although the preexisting *titulus* has not been identified, it is reasonable to suppose that its site was used for the present basilica.

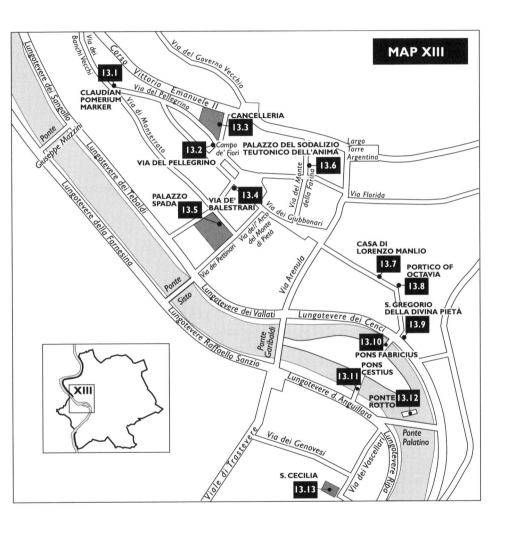

MAP XIII

Via del Governo Vecchio

Via dei Banchi Vecchi

Via dei Pellegrino

Corso Vittorio Emanuele II

Lungotevere del Sangallo

Ponte Giuseppe Mazzini

Via di Monserrato

13.1

CLAUDIAN POMERIUM MARKER

CANCELLERIA

13.3

Campo de' Fiori

13.2

VIA DEL PELLEGRINO

PALAZZO DEL SODALIZIO TEUTONICO DELL'ANIMA

Via del Monte della Farina

13.6

Largo Torre Argentina

Via Florida

Lungotevere dei Tebaldi

Lungotevere della Farnesina

PALAZZO SPADA

13.5

VIA DE' BALESTRARI

13.4

Via dei Giubbonari

Via dei Pettinari

Via dell' Arco del Monte di Pietà

Via Arenula

CASA DI LORENZO MANLIO

13.7

PORTICO OF OCTAVIA

13.8

Ponte Sisto

Lungotevere dei Vallati

Lungotevere Raffaello Sanzio

Ponte Garibaldi

Lungotevere dei Cenci

S. GREGORIO DELLA DIVINA PIETÀ

13.9

13.10

PONS FABRICIUS

PONS CESTIUS

13.11

PONTE ROTTO

13.12

Lungotevere d. Anguillara

Ponte Palatino

XIII

Via dei Genovesi

Viale di Trastevere

Via dei Vascellari

Lungotevere Ripa

S. CECILIA

13.13

13.1 Pomerium: Dedication by Claudius

[t]ı CLAVDIVS

[d]RVSI FILIVS CAISAR

[a]VG GERMANICVS

[po]NT MAX TRIB POT

5 [v̄]ĪĪĪĪ IMP X̄V̄Ī COS ĪĪĪĪ

CENSOR P P

[au]CTIS POPVLI ROMANI

[fi]NIBVS POMERIVM

[a]MPLIAꓒIT TERMINAꓒITQ

1. [t]ı(berius) : *The left side of the stone has been damaged. The portions of the text enclosed in brackets are restored from surviving exemplars of the same dedication.*

2. CAISAR : *On the spelling, see 1.6B, line 1.*

3. [a]VG(ustus).

4. [po]NT(ifex) MAX(imus) TRIB(ūniciā) POT(estāte).

5. [v̄]ĪĪĪĪ : Nōnum. — IMP(erātor) X̄V̄Ī : Sextum decimum. — CO(n)s(ul) ĪĪĪĪ : Quārtum.

6. P(ater) P(atriae).

9. [a]MPLIAꓒIT TERMINAꓒITQ(ue) = ampliāvit termināvitque : *According to the imperial biographer Suetonius and the historian Tacitus, the emperor Claudius I introduced three new characters into the Latin alphabet. These were an inverted digamma (ꓒ) to represent consonantal v (as in the present inscription); a reversed lunate sigma, or* antisigma (Ɔ), *to represent the combinations* BS *and* PS; *and the Greek sign for the* spiritus asper, *or 'rough breathing' (Ⱶ) to represent the Latin vowel intermediate between /u/ and /i/. The ꓒ clarified the distinction between such words as* voluit *and* volvit, *both* VOLVIT *in conventional orthography but* ꓒOLVIT *and* ꓒOLꓒIT *(respectively) in the Claudian. The Ɔ eliminated inconsistency in such spellings as* CAELEBS *and* AVCEPS, *in which the* BS *and* PS *were both pronounced /ps/ (Claudian* CAELEƆ *and* AVCEƆ; *see 2.6B, line 5). The Ⱶ resolved the orthographical confusion that ensued when the vowel /u/ or /i/ preceded a medially situated labial consonant (P, B, F, M)— e.g.,* MONIMENTVM *and* MONVMENTVM *(Claudian* MONⱵMENTVM*). The first and last of these characters are found with some frequency in inscriptions of Claudian date; thereafter, all three fell into complete and permanent disuse.*

Via del Pellegrino 145: Façade

Tiberius Claudius Caesar
Augustus Germanicus, son of Drusus,[a]
Supreme Pontiff, vested
with the Tribunician power for the ninth time,
acclaimed Imperator for the sixteenth,
Consul for the fourth, Censor, Father of his Country,
on the enlargement of the territory
of the Roman people
increased and delimited the Pomerium.[b]

a. *Claudius I (r. 41–54) was proclaimed emperor on 25 January 41. He as-sumed the* TRIBUNICIAN POWER *for the ninth time on that date in 49, was saluted as* IMPERATOR *for the sixteenth time and was made* CEN-SOR *in the year 48, and became* CONSUL *for the fourth time on 1 January 47. Like all the successors of Augustus, Claudius was granted the office of* SUPREME PONTIFF *on his accession. The title 'Father of his Country' was assumed by almost all the emperors (see* PATER PATRIAE*).*

b. *The* pomerium, *a narrow strip of land encircling the city, delimited the civil zone from that which lay without and which was consequently subject to a different religio-juridical regime. Such distinctions as that between town and territory (*urbs *and* ager*) and the peacetime and wartime activi-ties of the citizen (*domi *and* militiae*) were articulated by the* pomerium. *Neither commanders with* imperium *nor soldiers under arms were permit-ted within it except in the context of a triumphal celebration. By a similar logic, the authority of a Tribune (see* TRIBUNICIAN POWER*) was effective only within the* pomerium, *that of a* PROCONSUL *only without. Accord-ing to tradition, the* pomerium *had been established by Romulus and extended by Servius Tullius; a further extension did not take place until the dictatorship of Lucius Cornelius Sulla (81–79 BC). Sulla, in his (lost) autobiography, evidently furnished no explanation for this curious revival; it has been surmised that he wished to bathe himself in the glamour of a new founder. However that may be, Marcus Valerius Messala 'Rufus', appointed augur under Sulla, wrote a treatise De auspiciis in which he assigned the right of extending the* pomerium *to those who had increased Roman terri-tory at enemies' expense. This is the rationale adopted by the emperors. The increase of territory in virtue of which Claudius undertook to extend the* pomerium *consisted in the conquest of Britain (see 1.6B, note b).*

13.2   Commemoration of Works of Alexander VI

ALEX VI PONT MAX

POST INSTAVRATAM ADRIA

NI MOLEM ANGVSTAS VRBIS

VIAS AMPLIARI IVSSIT

5   MCCCC LXXXXVII

1. ALEX(ander) VI : Sextus. — PONT(ifex) MAX(imus).

2. POST INSTAVRATAM ADRIA|NI MOLEM : *On the construction, see 1.7A,
lines 2–3. On the spelling* ADRIANI (= Hadriānī), *see 8.8A, line 2.*

5. MCCCC LXXXXVII : Mīllēsimō quadringentēsimō nōnāgēsimō
septimō.

13.3   Palazzo della Cancelleria: Dedication by Raffaele Riario

RAPHAEL RIARIVS SAVONENSIS SANCTI GEORGII ¬

DIACONVS CARDINALIS SANCTAE ROMANAE ECCLESIAE ¬

CAMERARIVS A SYXTO IIII PONTIFICE MAXIMO HONORIBVS¬

AC FORTVNIS HONESTATVS TEMPLVM DIVO LAVRENTIO ¬

MARTYRI DICATVM ET AEDIS A FVNDAMENTIS SVA ¬

IMPENSA FECIT MCCCCLXXXXV ALEXANDRO VI P M

RAPHAEL : *On the name, see 11.3F.i, line 1.* — RIARIVS : *The Ital. name
Riario is Latinized as* Riārius (*cf. 12.3B, line 8*). — SAVONENSIS : *The
ML Adj.* Savōnēnsis *corresponds to the toponym* Savōna (*in* CL, Savō). —
GEORGII : *On the name, see 5.2.* — DIACONVS : *The* EL diāconus *trans-
literates Greek* διάκονος ('*servant*', *then* EG '*deacon*'). — ECCLESIAE :
See 1.7A, line 6. — CAMERARIVS : *The* ML camerārius *is* '*chamberlain*'.
— SYXTO IIII : Quārtō. *The name* Sixtus *appears variously in inscrip-
tions as* SIXTVS, XYSTVS, *and* SYXTVS (*see 3.4D, line 4*). — TEMPLVM :
On the Classicizing diction, cf. 1.8G, line 5. — DIVO : *See 3.3A, line 2.* —
MARTYRI : *See 2.10, line 2.* — AEDIS : *Acc.Pl.* — MCCCCLXXXXV :
Mīllēsimō quadringentēsimō nōnāgēsimō quīntō. — ALEXANDRO
VI : Sextō. — P(ontifice) M(aximō) : *The Abl.Abs. has temporal force
(see 5.8B, line 1).*

Via del Pellegrino 10: Corner, High

Alexander the Sixth,[a] Supreme Pontiff,
after restoring the Mausoleum of Hadrian[b]
ordered the City's narrow streets
to be widened[c]
in 1497.

a. *Pope Alexander VI de Borja y Borja (r. 1492–1503); cf. 9.1A, note a.*
b. *See 15.2A.*
c. *With the 'Via Recta' and the Via Papalis, the Via Peregrinorum was the major route by which the Campus Martius communicated with Ponte Sant'Angelo and the Vatican (cf. 13.4, note c).*

Frieze

Raffaele Riario of Savona,[a] Cardinal Deacon of San Giorgio,[b]
Camerlengo of the Holy Roman Church,[c] distinguished
with offices and riches by Sixtus the Fourth,[d] Supreme Pontiff,
at his own expense erected from their foundations the basilica
dedicated to Saint Lawrence and the palace, during
the reign of Alexander the Sixth,[e] Supreme Pontiff, in 1495.

a. *Raffaele Riario (1461–1521), a great-nephew of Pope Sixtus IV, as titular* CARDINAL *of the* BASILICA *of S. Lorenzo in Damaso rebuilt both the church and its adjacent cardinal's palace (see* TITULAR CHURCH*). The original basilica, one of the few early Christian foundations in the central Campus Martius, was built by Pope St. Damasus I (r. 366–383). Its large size notwithstanding, the basilica was wholly incorporated into the fabric of the palace, reducing it to a species of outgrown court chapel.*
b. *Riario served as Cardinal Deacon of S. Giorgio in Velabro 1477–1480 and of S. Lorenzo in Damaso 1480–1503.*
c. *On the office, see 12.6, note b.*
d. *Pope Sixtus IV della Rovere (r. 1471–1484); see 1.6G, note a.*
e. *See 13.2, note a.*

13.4 Via Florea: Commemoration of Sixtus IV

QVAE MODO PVTRIS ERAS ET OLENTI SORDIDA COENO

PLENAQVE DEFORMI MARTIA TERRA SITV

EXVIS HANC TVRPEM XYSTO SVB PRINCIPE FORMAM

OMNIA SVNT NITIDIS CONSPICIENDA LOCIS

5 DIGNA SALVTIFERO DEBENTVR PREMIA XYSTO

O QVANTVM EST SVMMO DEBITA ROMA DVCI

VIA FLOREA

(*Names of Magistrates*)   CVRATORES VIAR   ANNO SALVTIS MCCCCLXXXIII

Three ELEGIAC COUPLETS (*lines 1–6*)

1. COENO = caenō : *On the spelling, see 1.8B, line 5.*
3. XYSTO : *On the spelling, see 3.4D, line 4.*
5. SALVTIFERO : *Cf. 4.1.i, line 14.* — PREMIA = praemia : *On the Neut.Pl., see 3.4D, line 2.*
6. QVANTVM EST . . . DEBITA ROMA : *The* CL *construction would be* quantum dēbet Rōma.
9. CVRATORES VIAR(um) : *The medieval title* magistrī viārum (*Ital.* maestri di strada) *is substituted by a* CL *formulation* (*cf. 1.8G, line 5*).
10. MCCCCLXXXIII : Mīllēsimō quadringentēsimō octōgēsimō tertiō.

13.5 Elogia of Roman Heroes

i. Elogium of Trajan

INVICTAE

VIRTVTIS

IMPERATOR

OPTIMI

5 COGNOMEN

PROMERVIT

TRAIANVS

1. INVICTAE | VIRTVTIS : *Gen. of Description.*
7. TRAIANVS : *Each inscription appears on a panel mounted above a statue, on the pedestal of which is inscribed the hero's name.*

Via de' Balestrari at Corner of Via dei Giubbonari

Field of Mars,[a] you who were lately rotten
and filthy with noisome muck, and full of hideous decay,
with Sixtus[b] as your prince you lay aside this foul aspect.
Everything is resplendent with spruce spaces.
A fitting reward is due to the salutiferous Sixtus.
How indebted is Rome to her supreme ruler!

VIA FLOREA[c]

(Names of Magistrates)	*Superintendents of Streets*	*in the year of Salvation 1483*

Three ELEGIAC COUPLETS (lines 1–6)

a. I.e., the Campus Martius (Ital. Campo Marzio).

b. Among the improvements to Rome's urban infrastructure made by Pope Sixtus IV della Rovere (r. 1471–1484) were the rectification and paving of numerous streets including the Via Peregrinorum (mod. Via dei Banchi Vecchi—Via del Pellegrino—Campo de' Fiori—Via dei Giubbonari).

c. Via del Pellegrino was formerly called 'Via Florea' (or 'Florida'). The current name derives from that of an inn—Osteria del Pellegrino ('Pilgrims' Inn')—that catered to the pious crowds for whom the street served as the major artery between the Vatican and the city.

Palazzo Spada: Façade

Leftmost Statue

Trajan,[a]

an emperor
of invincible
valor,
deserved
the name of
'Best'.

a. The emperor Trajan (r. AD 98–117) was recognized already in his own day as a model ruler. The title Optimus had by 114 been incorporated into Trajan's official style.

ii. Elogium of Pompey

MAGNO FORTVNAE

LVDIBRIO

VBIQVE VICTOR

INDIGNO VITAE

5   EXITV

SEPVLTVRA

CARVIT

CN POMP MA

1. FORTVNAE : *The cult of Fortuna as the bringer of military victory en-joyed a special vogue among the dynasts of the late Republic, most notably Lucius Cornelius Sulla, who took the* agnōmen *'Felix' in token of his unre-mitting good fortune.*

8. CN(aeus) POMP(ēius) MA(gnus) : *The abbreviation* CN *for* Gnaeus *is parallel to* C *for* Gāius *(see 1.1, line 1).*

iii. Elogium of Fabius Maximus

INVETERATAE

PRVDENTIAE

DVX

CVNCTANDO

5   RESTITVIT

[r]EM

FABIVS MAX

6. [r]EM : *The character enclosed in brackets is restored from context. The protean elasticity of the Latin word* rēs *is the despair of translators. Its sev-eral senses as proposed in* The Oxford Latin Dictionary *are: 'Property', 'supply', 'thing', 'physical phenomenon', 'fact', 'reality', 'deed', 'activity', 'material', 'affair', 'matter', 'purpose', 'concern', 'public business', 'the sum of human affairs', 'affairs of the state as a whole', 'situation', 'event' and 'influential circumstance'.*

7. MAX(imus).

Second Statue

Gnaeus Pompey the Great,[a]

though everywhere victorious,
by a great jest
of fate,
in a departure
unworthy of his life,
wanted for
burial.[b]

a. *Gnaeus Pompeius Magnus (106–48 BC) was treacherously slain during his war with Julius Caesar.*

b. *As in the case of St. Catherine of Siena, whose trunk reposes in S. Maria sopra Minerva but whose head is venerated at SS. Domenico e Sisto in Siena, the head and trunk of Pompey went their separate ways after his death. The former was delivered to his opponent, who caused it to be cremated and interred; the latter was cremated by a freedman and the ashes scattered on the grounds of Pompey's estate in the Alban Hills.*

Third Statue

Fabius Maximus,[a]

a commander
of firmly rooted
sagacity,
by delaying
restored
the state.[b]

a. *In the wake of Roman defeats at Lake Trasimene and Cannae, Quintus Fabius Maximus Verrucosus Cunctator ('the Delayer') employed delaying tactics against Hannibal during the Second Punic War (218–201 BC); hence the name of the Fabian Society, which advocated the gradual implementation of socialist principles.*

b. *The text quotes a verse from the* Annals *of the archaic Roman poet Ennius:* Unus homo nobis cunctando restituit rem *('By delaying, a single man restored the state to us').*

iv. Elogium of Romulus

AETERNAE VRBIS

FVNDAMENTA IECIT

MILITAREM DISCI

PLINAM DOMI

5   INISTITVIT

QVA IMPERIVM FELI

CITER CRESCERET

ROMVLVS

3. DISCI|PLINAM.

5. INISTITVIT : *Sic* (= instituit).

6–7. QVA . . . CRESCERET : *Rel. Clause of Purpose (the antecedent is* DISCI|PLINAM). — FELI|CITER.

v. Elogium of Numa

MARTIVM POPVLVM

RELIGIONI

ADDIXIT

VT PACE ET

5   BELLO

INVICTV[s]

[r]E[m]A[n]ERET

NVMA

7. [r]E[m]A[n]ERET : *The characters enclosed in brackets are restored from context.*

Fourth Statue

Romulus[a]

laid the foundations
of the Eternal City
and instituted
domestic military training
whereby her sovereignty
might auspiciously
increase.

a. Romulus, whom legend made the son of Mars and the Vestal Virgin Rhea Silvia, was supposed to have founded Rome in 753 BC and to have named it after himself (on the date, cf. 1.6A.i, note a).

Fifth Statue

Numa[a]

bound over
to religion
a martial race,
that in both peace
and war
it might remain
invincible.

a. Numa Pompilius, second king of Rome, was revered as the founder of the city's religious institutions.

vi. Elogium of Marcellus

BELLATOR

ACERRIMVS

OPIMA SPOLIA

IOVI

5   FERETRIO

POSVIT

M MARCELLVS

5. FERETRIO : *The temple of Jupiter Feretrius was reputed to be Rome's old-est. The etymology of the epithet* Feretrius *is obscure. Ancient authorities were divided as to whether it derived from* ferīre *('strike') or* ferre *('bear'). Instead of a cult image, the temple housed a flint—probably a fragment of a meteorite—used by priests called* fētiālēs *in striking treaties (which favors the derivation from* ferīre*). The temple was also where the arms of defeated enemy commanders were taken to be dedicated (which favors the derivation from* ferre*).*

7. M(ārcus).

vii. Elogium of Caesar

VNIVERSVM

TERRARVM ORBEM

HOSTILI CRVORE

REPLEVIT

5   SVO DEMVM

SANGVINE

CVRIAM INVNDAVIT

CAESAR DICT

2. TERRARVM ORBEM : *See 10.6.*

3–6. CRVORE . . . SANGVINE : *Latin makes a distinction, foreign to English, between blood that betokens death* (cruor) *and blood that betokens life* (sanguis).

8. DICT(ātor).

Sixth Statue

Marcus Marcellus,[a]

keenest

of warriors,

dedicated

the Spolia Opima[b]

to Jupiter

Feretrius.

a. Like Fabius Maximus, Marcus Claudius Marcellus played a decisive role in the war against Hannibal (see 13.5.iii, note a).

b. The Spolia Opima ('rich spoils') were those stripped from the corpse of an enemy commander slain in single combat by his Roman counterpart. The spoils were then dedicated in the temple of Jupiter Feretrius on the Capitoline Hill (see 1.6A.ii, note a). According to Roman tradition, the Spolia Opima were earned thrice only: by Romulus, by Aulus Cornelius Cossus (428 BC), and by Marcellus (222 BC).

Seventh Statue

The Dictator Caesar[a]

filled

the whole

world

with the shed blood of enemies

and ended

by bathing the Senate-house

in his own life-blood.

a. After defeating Pompey (see 13.9.ii, note a) and establishing himself as master of Rome, Gaius Julius Caesar (100–44 BC) was named Dictator Perpetuus ('Dictator for Life'). He was murdered at the opening of a session of the Senate, meeting that day not in the Curia on the Forum but in a hall of the portico attached to the Theater of Pompey (cf. 13.6, note b).

viii. Elogium of Augustus

IANO CLAVSO

FINEM

CIVILIBVS

ET

5   EXTERNIS

BELLIS IM

POSVIT

AVG CAESAR

6. IM|POSVIT.

8. AVG(ustus) : *On 16 January 27* BC *Gaius Octavius took the* cognōmen Augustus (*see 10.4A, lines 1–2*). *An initial proposal that he should style himself* Romulus *was rejected. According to the imperial biographer Suetonius, the surname* Augustus—*redolent of augury and divine consecration—had the double advantage of novelty and grandeur.*

13.6 Palazzo del Sodalizio Teutonico dell'Anima: Dedication

HEIC UBI IGNOBILES NUPER TABERNAE RUDERA ⌐

PREMEBANT PORTICUS CN POMPEII CUI CONTINENS ⌐

ERAT CURIA C IUL CAESARIS NECE INSIGNIS SODALITAS ⌐

TEUTONUM DE ANIMA NOBILIORES HAS AEDES ⌐

EXSTRUENDAS CURAVIT ANNO AB URBE CONDITA ⌐

MM DC XL VI A D M DCCC XC III

1. HEIC = hic : *On the spelling, see 1.6C, line 6.* — CN(aeī) : *On the abbreviation* CN *for* Gnaeus, *cf. 1.1, line 1.* — C(āiī) IUL(iī). — SODALITAS TEUTONUM DE ANIMA : *The Latin represents Ital. 'Sodalizio Teutonico dell'Anima'. On* Teutonēs, *see 1.4, line 2.* — MM DC XL VI : Bis mīllēsimō sescentēsimō quadrāgēsimō sextō.

2. A(nnō) D(ominī) M DCCC XC III : Millēsimō octingentēsimō nōnāgēsimō tertiō.

Eighth Statue

Augustus Caesar [a]

by the closure
of the temple of Janus,
put an end
to wars
both
domestic
and foreign.

a. *Adoptive son of Julius Caesar (cf. 1.8F, note c), the emperor Augustus (r. 27 BC–AD 14) was heralded by poets as bringer of a new Golden Age. His closure of the temple of Janus in the Forum signaled peace throughout Roman dominions—a state of affairs recorded only twice previously in the history of Rome.*

Via del Monte della Farina 18–19: Frieze

*Here, where tawdry shops lately encumbered the ruins
of the portico of Gnaeus Pompey,[a] to which was attached
the Curia famous for the assassination of Gaius Julius Caesar,[b]
the German Sodality of Santa Maria dell'Anima[c] undertook
the construction of this nobler palace in the year 2646
from the founding of the City,[d] in the year of the Lord 1893.*

a. *On Pompey, see 13.5.ii. The present structure rises on part of the site of the portico that extended some 180 meters to the east of Pompey's theater.*
b. *Annexed to the portico was the 'Curia of Pompey', in which Caesar was slain. See 13.5.vii, note a.*
c. *Santa Maria dell'Anima is the German national church at Rome.*
d. *The reckoning respects the Varronian era (see 1.6A.i, note a).*

13.7 Casa di Lorenzo Manlio: Dedication by Manlio

i. Dedication

1   VRBE ROMA IN PRISTINAM FORMA[m r]ENASCENTE LAVR MANLIVS ⌐
    [k]ARITATE ERGA PATRI[am gent a]EDIS SVO

2   NOMINE MANLIAN A S PRO FORT[un]AR MEDIOCRITATE AD FOR IVDEOR ⌐
    SIBI POSTERISQ[ue suis ipse] P

3   AB VRB CON M M C C XXI L AN M III D II P XI CAL AVG

1. FORMA[m r]ENASCENTE : *The portions of the text enclosed in brackets are conjecturally restored from context.* — LAVR(entius). — [k]ARITATE = cāritāte : *On the spelling, see 4.6C, line 3.* — PATRI[am gent(em)
a]EDIS : *Acc.Pl. (see 1.6H, line 12).*

2. MANLIAN(ās) A S(ōlō). — FORT[un]AR(um). — FOR(um) IVDEOR(um) = Iūdaeōrum : *On the spelling, see 1.8B, line 5.* — P(osuit).

3. AB VRB(e) CON(ditā) : *On the construction, see 1.7A, lines 2–3.* — M M C C XXI L : Duōbus mīlibus
ducentīs vīgintī novem. *In this notation, XXI is to be subtracted from L (cf. 4.6B, line 2). The case is Abl. of
Degree of Difference.* — AN(nis). — M(ēnsibus) III : Tribus. — D(iēbus) II : Duōbus. — P(osuit). — XI :
Undecimō. — CAL(endās) = Kalendās : *On the spelling, see* [k]ARITATE *(above, line 1).* — AVG(ustās) or
AVG(ustī) : *see 1.6G, line 11.*

ii. Name of Manlio

LAVR MANLIVS FVNDAVIT | LAVR MANLIVS A F[un]D POS

LAVR MANLIVS CVRAVIT | ΛΑΥΡΕΝΤΙΟΣ Μ[αυλιος εποιησεν]

1. LAVR(entius).

2. LAVR(entius). — F[un]D(āmentīs) POS(uit).

3. LAVR(entius).

4. ΛΑΥΡΕΝΤΙΟΣ Μ[αυλιος εποιησεν] : *Printed in accordance with modern typographical conventions, the text
reads:* Λαυρέντιος Μάνλιος ἐποίησεν.

Via del Portico di Ottavia 1–2: Frieze

Frieze

As the City of Rome was being reborn in its ancient aspect, out of affection
for his paternal family Lorenzo Manlio,[a] in keeping with his modest fortune,
built from its foundation the eponymous Palazzo Manlio on Piazza Giudea[b]
for himself and for his descendants.
He placed this 2,229 years, three months, and two days after the founding of the City, on 22 July.[c]

a. Lorenzo Manlio has been identified with one Rienzo Manei (1440s–1482), known from archival records. Like other early Renaissance enthusiasts of Antiquity, Manei assimilated his name to that of a famous Roman family—in his case, that of the Gens Manlia (see Names). Manlio's house is situated at the foot of the Capitoline Hill, scene of the heroic exploits of Marcus Manlius Capitolinus during the Gallic siege in 390 BC.

b. The house fronts what was formerly Piazza Giudea, the heart of Rome's Jewish quarter. On 12 July 1555, Pope Paul IV decreed the institution of the Ghetto, to which the Jews of Rome were to be confined from dusk to dawn. Its walls were finally pulled down in 1848.

c. Lit. 'on the eleventh day before the Kalends of August'. By the Varronian reckoning, the inscription dates to 1476 (see 1.6A.i, note a) and may be seen as an expression of the epigraphical enthusiasm of the Rome of Pope Sixtus IV (r. 1471–1484; cf. 1.6G, note a).

Above Sportelli

Lorenzo Manlio founded this. | Lorenzo Manlio built this from its foundations.
Lorenzo Manlio undertook this. | Lorenzo Manlio made this.

13.8 Portico of Octavia: Tribute of Fish Heads

CAPITA PISCIVM
HOC MARMOREO SCHEMATE LONGITVDINE
MAJORVM VSQVE AD PRIMAS PINNAS
INCLVSIVE CONSERVATORIBVS
5   DANTO

4. CONSERVATORIBVS : *See 1.6C, lines 5–6.*
5. DANTO : *Evidently modeled on ancient legal and religious formulae, in which third-person imperatives active are common.*

13.9 S. Gregorio della Divina Pietà: Inscription of Pius IX Rebuking the Jews

EXPANDI MANVS MEAS TOTA DIE AD
POPVLVM INCREDVLVM QVI GRADITVR
IN VIA NON BONA POST COGITATIONES SVAS
POPVLVS QVI AD IRACVNDIAM PROVOCAT
5 ME ANTE FACIEM MEAM SEMPER

EXPANDI . . . SEMPER : *The text quotes the Vulgate, Is. 65:2.*

13.10A Pons Fabricius: Dedication by Fabricius

L FABRICIVS C F CVR VIAR
FACIVNDVM COERAVIT

EIDEMQVE
PROBAVEIT

1. L(ūcius). — C(āiī) : *See 1.1, line 1.* — F(īlius) CVR(ātor) VIAR(um).
2. FACIVNDVM = faciendum. — COERAVIT = cūrāvit : *By the middle of the second century BC, the pronunciation of the diphthong /oe/ had progressed to /u:/. The older spelling tended to linger on in official formulae, such as this dedication, in which* FACIVNDVM *likewise constitutes an archaism (see 1.7B, line 2).*
3. EIDEMQVE = īdemque : *See 1.7B, line 3.*
4. PROBAVEIT = probāvit : *The desinence -eit/-īt is archaic (the reading on the S face is* PROBAVEIT *and on the N face* PROBAVIT*).*

Façade, R

The heads of fish
greater in length than this marble figure
must be handed over to the Conservators[a]
down to the first fins,
inclusive.

a. *Lit., 'they must hand over'. On the* CONSERVATORS, *see also 1.6C, note a.*
From the Middle Ages until the nineteenth century, the Portico of Octavia
was the site of Rome's fish market.

Façade

I have spread out my hands all the day
unto a rebellious people, which walketh
in a way that was not good, after their own thoughts,
a people that provoketh me
to anger continually to my face.[a]

a. *The text quotes the Vulgate, Is. 65:2. The church stands at what was once*
an entrance of the Ghetto.

Ponte Fabricio: N & S Faces of Large Arches & Central Arch

Lucius Fabricius, son of Gaius,[a] *Superintendent of Streets,*
undertook to have this built

and himself
approved it.[b]

a. *This Fabricius was probably Tribune of the Plebs in 62 BC (see* TRIBUNI-
CIAN POWER).

b. *According to the fourth-century historian Cassius Dio, the Pons Fabr-*
icius was built in 62 BC, the year following Cicero's celebrated consulship.
Horace alludes to it ironically as a place of suicide (Satire 2.3.36–38).
Because of its proximity to the Ghetto, in the Middle Ages the bridge was
also known as Pons Iudaeorum ('Jews' Bridge'). The name Ponte Quattro Capi *('Bridge of the Four Heads') derives from the four-faced herms*
mounted on the parapet.

13.10B Pons Fabricius: Dedication by Lollius and Lepidus

M LOLLIVS M F Q LEPI[dus m f c]OS EX S C PROBAVERVNT

> 1. M(ārcus). — M(ārcī) F(īlius) — Q(uīntus) LEPI[dus m(ārcī) f(īlius) :
> *The portions of the text enclosed in brackets are restored from the N face of*
> *the arch. The N face is identical to the S except that the names of the con-*
> *suls appear in the opposite order and the* T *of* PROBAVERVNT *is missing*).
> — c]O(n)S(ulēs) : *On the abbreviation, see 2.15, line 1.* — EX S(enātūs)
> c(ōnsultō) : *On the formula, see 2.8, line 2.*

13.11A Pons Cestius: Dedication to Gratian

GR[ati]AN[i tri]VMFALIS P[rin]CIPIS [po]NTEM AE[t]E[rnitati augusti ¬
nominis consecratum in usum senatus populique roman]I DDD NNN ¬
VAL[en]TINIANVS V[alen]S ET GRA[tia]N[u]S [uicto]RES M[aximi ¬
ac perennes augusti incoha]RI PERFICI DEDICA[rique iusserunt]

> GR[ati]AN[i : *The portions of the text enclosed in brackets represent restora-*
> *tions of lost text. The bridge was rebuilt 1888–1892 to accommodate the*
> *Tiber embankments. In the course of the work, the inscription was badly*
> *mutilated. Its poor condition and inconvenient location vexed the editor*
> *of the* Corpus Inscriptionum Latinarum: Ego propter locum incom-
> modum frustra conatus sum examinare (*'Because of the awkward site,*
> *my attempt at inspection was unsuccessful'*). *With the aid of field glasses*
> *and a raking sun, however, the surviving portions on the S side as here*
> *transcribed can with difficulty be made out.* — tri]VMFALIS : *On the*
> *spelling, see 2.1, line 2.* — DDD NNN = domīnī nostrī trēs : *On the prin-*
> *ciple that a doubled letter signifies a duo, a tripled letter signifies a trio*
> (*cf. 1.61, line 7*). — inchoa]RI : *On the spelling, see 8.8A, line 2.*

Ponte Fabricio: E Arch, S Face

*Marcus Lollius, son of Marcus, and Quintus Lepidus, son of Marcus,
Consuls, approved this in accordance with a decree of the Senate.*[a]

a. Marcus Lollius and Quintus Aemilius Lepidus, consuls in 21 BC (see
Consul), carried out repairs to the bridge, probably in consequence of the
inundation in 23 BC that destroyed the Pons Sublicius down stream from
the Tiber Island beyond the Pons Aemilius (today's Ponte Rotto). Analysis
of the letterforms has revealed that portions of the original dedication by
Fabricius were recut at the time of the reconstruction.

Ponte Cestio: Exterior Footing of Parapet, N & S

Our Lords Valentinian, Valens, and Gratian,[a] *greatest conquerors
and forever Augusti, ordered the bridge consecrated to the eternity
of the august name of Gratian, triumphant emperor, to be begun,
completed, and dedicated for the use of the Senate and People of Rome.*[b]

a. Valentinian I (r. 364–375) was acclaimed emperor at Nicaea after the
death of Jovian. Valentinian's younger brother Valens (r. 364–378) was
appointed AUGUSTUS in the E (364); he was killed in battle with the Visigoths at Hadrianople (378). In 367, at the age of eight, Valentinian's son
Gratian (r. 375–383) was appointed Augustus by his father.

b. The original bridge dated to the late Republic. It is likely that its builder
was either Gaius Cestius, Praetor in 44 BC (cf. 5.7A.i, note a), or his
brother Lucius, who had held the same office the previous year. The present
inscription commemorates the reconstruction and dedication of the bridge
as the 'Pons Gratiani' (AD 370). Stone for the project was quarried from
the nearby Theater of Marcellus. A longer inscription of the same date that
survives in situ on the interior of the N parapet features the last surviving
reference to an emperor as Pontifex Maximus.

13.11B Pons Cestius: Dedication by Benedetto Carushomo

[b]ENEDICTVS ALME

VRBIS SVMM SENATO

R RESTAVRAVIT HVN

C PONTEM FERE DIRV

5   TVM

1. [b]ENEDICTVS : *The character enclosed in brackets is restored from context.* — ALME = almae : *On the spelling, see 1.8B, line 5.*
2. SVMM(us) SENATO|R.
3. HVN|C.
4. DIRV|TVM.

13.12 Pons Senatorius: Dedication by S.P.Q.R.

EX AVCTORITATE GREGORI XIII PONT MAXIMI

S P Q R

PONTEM SENATORIVM CVIVS FORNICES

VETVSTATE COLLAPSOS ET IAM PRIDEM REFECTOS

5   FLVMINIS

IMPETVS DENVO DEIECERAT IN PRISTINAM

FIRMITATEM AC PVLCHRITVDINEM RESTITVIT

ANNO IVBILEI MDLXXV

1. GREGORI = Grēgoriī : *On the name, see 9.1B, line 2.* — XIII : Tertiī decimī. — PONT(ificis).
2. S(enātus) P(opulus) Q(ue) R(ōmānus).
4. VETVSTATE COLLAPSOS : *This formula, common in RL inscriptions, is found in an ancient dedication preserved in the Einsiedeln Catalogue:* S P Q R AEDEM CONCORDIAE VETVSTATE COLLAPSAM IN MELIOREM FACIEM OPERE ET CVLTV SPLENDIDIORE RESTITVIT *('The Senate and People of Rome, with more brilliant construction and ornament, restored to a superior aspect the Temple of Concord, ruined with age'). The formula occurs in a similar context at Suet.Aug. 30.*
8. IVBILEI : *See 2.12A, line 8. On the spelling, see 1.8B, line 5.* — MDLXXV : Mīllēsimō quīngentēsimō septuāgēsimō quīntō.

Ponte Cestio: N Parapet, Pilaster

> *Benedetto,*
> *Supreme Senator of the kindly City,[a]*
> *restored this bridge,*
> *which was all but*
> *ruined.*

a. *The bridge was restored in 1193 at the behest of Benedetto Carushomo, who governed Rome 1191–1193 under the title* Summus Senator. *The dissolution of the fifty-six-member Senate in 1191 was provoked by the attempt of Pope Celestine III (r. 1191–1198) to augment the body with pro-papal nobles (see* CONSERVATORS*).*

Ponte Rotto: Parapet, Inside

> *By authority of Gregory the Thirteenth,[a] Supreme Pontiff,*
> *the Senate and People of Rome*
> *restored to its former strength and beauty*
> *the Pons Senatorius, whose vaults,*
> *ruined with age and long since rebuilt,*
> *the onslaught of the river*
> *had once again overthrown,[b]*
> *in the year of the Jubilee 1575.[c]*

a. *Pope Gregory XIII Boncompagni (r. 1572–1585).*

b. *Known in the Middle Ages as the* Pons Senatorius, *Ponte Rotto (the 'Broken Bridge') occupies the site of the ancient Pons Aemilius. Partially destroyed in the disastrous flood of 24 December 1598 (see 10.1E), the bridge was never rebuilt. Of the three arches that survived the flood, two were demolished in the 1880s for the construction of Ponte Palatino, from which the present inscription is visible (with the aid of field glasses) on the interior of the N parapet. Before its reconstruction in the 1470s by Sixtus IV, the ancient Pons Valentiniani similarly bore the name 'Ponte Rotto' (see 14.1.i, note b).*

c. *See 7.4H, note b. As in the case of Ponte Sisto a century before (see 14.1.ii, note a), an impending Jubilee furnished the opportunity for improvements to the city's infrastructure. The bridge had been out of commission since the inundation of 1557 (see 11.5D).*

13.13A S. Cecilia: Dedication by Paschal I

1 HAEC DOMVS AMPLA MICAT VARIIS FABRICATA METALLIS ⌐

OLIM QVAE FVERAT CONFRACTA SVB TEMPORE PRISCO ⌐

CONDIDIT IN MELIVS PASCHALIS PRAESVL OPIMVS

2 HANC AVLAM D̄N̄I FORMANS FVNDAMINE CLARO ⌐

AVREA GEMMATIS RESONANT HAEC DINDIMA TEMPLI ⌐

LAETVS AMORE DEI HIC CONIVNXIT CORPORA S̄C̄A

3 CAECILIAE ET SOCIIS RVTILAT HIC FLORE IVVENTVS ⌐

QVAE PRIDEM IN CRVPTIS PAVSABANT MEMBRA BEATA ⌐

ROMA RESVLTAT OVANS SEMPER ORNATA PER AEVVM

> Nine HEXAMETERS

1. FABRICATA : *In* CL, *both* fabricāre *and* fabricārī *were in use.* — METAL-
LIS : *See 2.14, line 1.* — FVERAT CONFRACTA : *On the tense, see 1.6G,
line 7.* — SVB TEMPORE PRISCO : *In* ML, *the Prep.* sub *frequently appears thus in expressions of time (the scansion* sŭb *is however unmetrical).*
— PRAESVL : *See 3.3C, line 13.*

2. AVLAM : *See 2.14, line 1.* — D(omi)NI. — FVNDAMINE : *See 9.1B, line 1.*
— DINDIMA = Dindyma (Δίνδυμα) : *On the spelling, see 3.1, line 1. The
word is attested in* ML *in the sense 'mystery'.* — S(ān)C(t)A.

3. CAECILIAE ET SOCIIS : *Dat. of Reference.* — QVAE : *On the assumption that the antecedent of the Rel.Pron. includes* SOCIIS, *the Masc.Pl.* quī
would make better grammar. — CRVPTIS = cryptīs : *In older borrowings
such as this, Latin regularly assimilated Greek* Υ *to the native* V *(see 2.10,
line 2). Hence Greek* κρύπτη > *Latin* crupta > *Ital.* grotta. — PAVSA-
BANT : *The* LL pausāre *is 'to rest'.*

13.13B Statue of S. Cecilia: Testimony of Stefano Maderno

1 EN TIBI SANCTISSIMAE VIRGINIS CAECILIAE IMAGINEM ⌐

QVAM IPSE INTEGRAM SVO SEPVLCHRO IACENTEM VIDI

2 EANDEM TIBI PRORSVS EODEM CORPORIS SITV HOC ⌐

MARMORE EXPRESSI

1. EN TIBI . . . IMAGINEM: *The combination of the interjection* ēn
and the 'Ethical' Dat. is good CL *idiom, as is the Acc. that follows.* —
SEPVLCHRO : *On the spelling, see 8.8A, line 2.*

Apse

Constructed with variegated enamels, this spacious house
glitters which in former times had been broken down.
Paschal,[a] a munificent bishop, has founded in superior wise
this hall of the Lord, establishing it on a brilliant foundation.
These golden mysteries[b] of the Church resound with gems.
Rejoicing in God's love, he united here the holy bodies: here
youth glows ruddy in its bloom for Cecilia and her companions,
who formerly rested their blessèd limbs in the cemeteries.[c]
Adorned for aye, Rome ever exults in triumph.

Nine HEXAMETERS

a. Pope St. Paschal I (r. 817–824) took advantage of the peace afforded by
the papacy's alliance with Charlemagne and his heirs to revive the glories
of Constantine's Rome, distant by half a millennium. In addition to the
present BASILICA, Paschal rebuilt those of S. Maria in Domnica on the
Caelian Hill (6.3) and S. Prassede on the Esquiline (3.5). The mosaic represents Christ flanked by SS. Paul and Cecilia, with Paschal, and SS. Peter,
Valerian, and Agatha. Paschal wears the square nimbus of the living (see
3.5A, note b).

b. Lit., 'Dindyma'. The author airs his learning by an idle reference to the
Phrygian mountain that in Classical lore was home to Cybele, 'Mother of
the Gods'.

c. St. Cecilia was buried in the Cemetery of S. Callisto (see 6.10) and her
relics were transferred to the present church on the occasion of Paschal's
restoration. Although the paleo-Christian titulus has not been identified,
it is reasonable to suppose that its site was used for the basilica.

Pavement before the Statue

Behold for yourself the image of the most holy virgin Cecilia,
whom I myself saw lying uncorrupted in her tomb.
The same have I rendered for you by this statue in the very same
posture as her body.[a]

a. When her tomb was opened in 1599, Cecilia's body was found to be miraculously incorrupt. Its appearance was recorded in the present statue by Stefano Maderno (1576–1636), then in his twenty-third year.

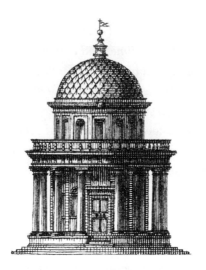

THE *TEMPIETTO* OF BRAMANTE

Following Classical practice, Bramante generated the proportions of his tempietto *(miniature temple) from a single dimension: the diameter of a column (referred to in technical parlance as the 'module'). Bramante's combination of a circular* cella, *a hemispherical dome, and a peripteral colonnade, though not without precedent in both Classical and Christian Antiquity, is executed with high originality and finesse. The coordinated deployment of the forms so as to suggest a heavenward impulse is particularly effective: the massive solidity of the Doric colonnade seems to melt away as it rises through the balustrade and the niches of the drum, above which it dissolves entirely in the airy weightlessness of the dome.*

XIV. From Ponte Sisto to the Acqua Paola

IN ROME'S EARLIEST DAYS, the territory *trans Tiberim*—'across the Tiber', whence came the modern name 'Trastevere'—was an outpost of the city on the hostile, Etruscan side of the river; the right bank was called the *litus Etruscum* ('Etruscan Shore'). It was connected to the city by the Pons Sublicius. Attributed in tradition to Ancus Marcius, fourth king of Rome, this earliest of Rome's bridges was the scene of the exploit of Horatius Cocles immortalized in Macaulay's *Lays of Ancient Rome*. By an ancient requirement of religion, the Pons Sublicius was constructed entirely of wood. This prescription, paralleled in other sacred structures of comparable antiquity, was regarded by scholars of former generations as evidence that the bridge dated from a period before the craft of ironworking was sufficiently advanced for technical application. The maintenance of the sacred fabric was entrusted to the College of Pontiffs. According to the Roman antiquarian Varro, it is precisely this charge that gave their office its name: etymologically, *pontifex* is a builder of bridges.

Trastevere was urbanized from the end of the republican period; its largest structures, mostly of a utilitarian character, were associated with the port on the opposite bank. Owing to its large population of sailors attached to the imperial fleet, headquartered at Ravenna, Trastevere was known for centuries as the *quartiere dei ravennati* ('quarter of the Ravennates'). The zone was formally incorporated into the city by the emperor Augustus (r. 27 BC–AD 14) as the fourteenth administrative region, which included the whole of the right bank from the Vatican to the zone opposite the port, including the Tiber Island. In the imperial period, communications were facilitated by several bridges, two of which—the Pons Fabricius and the Pons Cestius—formed a single crossing at the island. At the bridgehead of the Pons Aemilius, just below the Tiber Island, two important highways converged: the Via Aurelia, leading from the port at Centumcellae, and the Via Campana-Portuensis, leading from the ports of Claudius and Trajan at the Tiber's mouth.

Throughout Antiquity Trastevere was a popular and commercial quarter, notable for the cult places of the many foreigners who had brought their gods with them to the metropolis. To the north and south, villas and gardens occupied the lower slopes of the Janiculum; one of these belonged to Clodia Metella, bitter enemy of Cicero and purported lover of Catullus.

Because of its isolated situation with respect to the rest of the city, Trastevere long lacked an adequate supply of water; a branch of the Aqua Marcia reached the zone but was insufficient. Augustus introduced a new aqueduct, the Aqua Alsietina, which drew its waters from Lago di Martignano, near Lago di Bracciano. The chief purpose of the aqueduct, however, was to feed the emperor's *naumachia,* an artificial basin used for mock naval combats; the water was scarcely potable. Only in AD 109 did the emperor Trajan (r. 98–117) introduce a water supply of good quality, the Aqua Traiana, which would be reactivated in the early seventeenth century as the Acqua Paola.

The presence in Trastevere of a large Jewish community from early times perhaps explains the precocious diffusion of Christianity there. The quarter was home to three early *tituli*: that of Cecilia on the Via Campana-Portuensis and those of Chrysogonus and Callistus on the Via Aurelia. The present Basilica of SANTA MARIA IN TRASTEVERE rises on or near the site of the last, whose institution was credited to Pope St. Callistus I (r. 217–222). Callistus is the earliest postapostolic martyr in the *Depositio Martyrum*—a fourth-century catalogue of the church's feasts and martyrs—and is the unofficial patron saint of Trastevere.

14.2

It is unclear what relationship the *titulus* of Callistus bears to the basilica constructed in its neighborhood by Pope Julius I (r. 337–352). In the acts of the Roman synod of AD 595, the two appear jointly under the name *titulus Callisti et Iulii*. It is nevertheless possible that the older foundation—if indeed not altogether legendary—persisted in name only. The eventual dedication of the Julian basilica to the BVM is first attested in the latter half of the sixth century; it is the predecessor of to-day's basilica of Santa Maria in Trastevere.

The construction of the present church was likely initiated in the 1120s under Pietro Pierleoni, its titular cardinal, elected in 1130 as 'Anacletus II' and reckoned an antipope. The history of the Pierleoni makes a fascinating episode in the history of medieval Rome. Anacletus' great-grandfather was Baruch Pierleoni, a Jewish banker who in the reign of Pope St. Leo IX (r. 1049–1054) accepted baptism under the name 'Benedetto Cristiano'. Benedetto's son, Leone, baptized at the same time, became the leading financier of the Holy See in its struggle with the Saxon emperors. It is Leone's son Pietro who gave his name to the clan: 'Pierleoni' derives from 'Pietro di Leone' (Pietro, son of Leone). Of the family's many properties in Trastevere, the much restored 'Casa di Pierleoni' survives in Via di San Giovanni Decollato.

The Basilica of Santa Maria in Trastevere was completed in 1143 under Pierleoni's victorious rival, Pope Innocent II (r. 1130–1143). Although the bulk of the *spolia* with which the new basilica was constructed evidently came from the Baths of Caracalla, the capitals likely originated in the shrine of Isis in the Campus Martius. During the restoration of 1870, in a gratuitous act of vandalism, Pius IX (r. 1846–1878) ordered the Isiac cult emblems with which they were decorated to be chiseled off. A glorious MOSAIC depicting Christ enthroned with the Virgin and saints covers the vault of the apse. In the thirteenth century, Pietro Cavallini added a mosaic cycle on the LIFE OF THE BVM. Because according to tradition it was the first church in Rome opened to public worship—as well as the first dedicated to the Virgin—Santa Maria in Trastevere enjoys a primacy among the minor basilicas of the city. *14.3B*

14.3C

Isolated on the right bank of the Tiber, Trastevere was for centuries a city apart. From an early period, access to Rione Ripa and Rione Sant'Angelo across the river was restricted to the Pons Senatorius and the bridges of the Tiber Island. A fourth bridge, the ancient Pons Valentiniani, had been destroyed in a flood in 792. It was known for centuries as

'Ponte Rotto', a name that would be applied to the Pons Senatorius after it was ruined in the catastrophic inundation of 1598. When Trajan's port at the mouth of the Tiber was abandoned in the ninth century, Trastevere benefited from a growing volume of commercial river traffic. The quarter saw its era of greatest prosperity between the eleventh and thirteenth centuries. Towards the end of that period it became the thirteenth *rione* of Rome. With the departure of the papal court for Avignon at the beginning of the fourteenth century, Trastevere lapsed into the general stagnation under which Rome labored for a hundred years.

Medieval Trastevere was as crowded and unsanitary as the densest neighborhoods of the Campus Martius. Most of the quarter's houses were little more than shanties improvised amid the blackened ruins of ancient granaries and warehouses. As the majority lacked even a rudimentary stove, the streets were filled with the acrid smoke of cooking fires that burned at nearly every door. Livestock browsed on sickly flora that sprouted in odd corners protected from the tread of foot and hoof. Rainwater and filth stagnated in the muddy streets. The better dwellings were constructed of brick and equipped with defensive towers built of materials salvaged from ancient buildings; grander houses situated on opposite sides of a street might be joined by arched passageways, often slung so low that they impeded the passage of traffic. Because of the quarter's characteristic *mignani*—loggias that protruded aggressively into the street—its narrow and tortuous alleyways were virtually impassable for wagons and carriages; only at the end of the fifteenth century were these accretions systematically eliminated.

Communications between Trastevere and the city were substantially
14.1   improved by the addition of PONTE SISTO, constructed by Pope Sixtus IV (r. 1471–1484) on the foundations of the ruined Pons Valentiniani. The bridge gave direct access from Trastevere to Via dei Giubbonari and the network of recently paved streets that centered on Campo dei Fiori. By furnishing an alternative route between Trastevere and the central Campus, Ponte Sisto contributed perceptibly to the marginalizing of

Rione Sant'Angelo, which no longer served as the gateway for all traffic entering the city from the west.

In the following generation, Pope Julius II (r. 1503–1513) consolidated the link between Trastevere and the Vatican by rebuilding the ancient Via Septimiana as Via della Lungara. Near its southern terminus, Via della Lungara was connected by Ponte Sisto with Via Giulia, which followed a roughly parallel course on the opposite side of the river. We can only conjecture whether Julius intended to close the circuit at the northern end by rebuilding the ancient Pons Neronianus at the head of Via Giulia.

At the beginning of the seventeenth century, Pope Paul V (r. 1605–1621) undertook two projects of momentous importance for the future development of Trastevere. The first was the restoration of the ancient Aqua Traiana as the ACQUA PAOLA, which furnished the quarter with a copious supply of good water for the first time in a millennium. The second was the construction of Via di San Francesco. Since Antiquity, the fulcrum of Trastevere's street system had been the head of the Pons Senatorius (Ponte Rotto), where the Via Campana-Portuensis (the modern Via dei Vascellari) and the Via Aurelia (modern Via della Lungaretta) converged; after the loss of the bridge in 1598, these two principal arteries terminated on a void. Paul's Via di San Francesco established a new route across Trastevere from Porta Portese to Via della Lungara, redirecting traffic from northeast to northwest and thereby rotating the dominant axis of the quarter by ninety degrees. A few decades later, Urban VIII (r. 1623–1644) rebuilt the walls of the Janiculum, a point in the city's defenses that had proved disastrously weak in the assault and sack of the city in 1527.

In the second half of the nineteenth century, interventions on a large scale completed the urbanization of Trastevere at the expense of its antique atmosphere. In 1863 Pius IX installed the papal tobacco works between Santa Maria dell'Orto and Via di San Francesco; the *quartiere Mastai* was built to provide housing and services for the workers. One

14.2&5

of the first initiatives that the new government of Italy undertook after 1870 was the installation of the *muraglioni del Tevere*, the Tiber embankments. Reducing the width of the riverbed to a uniform 100 meters, this massive construction solved the age-old problem of flooding at the cost of severing the city from the river to which it owed its origins. Modeled on the boulevards of Paris and Turin, the ample Viale del Re of 1888— today's Viale di Trastevere—made an irreparable rent in the ancient fabric of the quarter. A new street, Via Garibaldi, facilitated access to the Janiculum from the south. The *passeggiata del Gianicolo,* on the other hand, which appeared in the late 1880s, is one of the handful of successful urban initiatives undertaken since the inauguration of 'Roma Capitale'—Rome in her capacity as the capital city of a united Italy.

On the southern height of the Janiculum rises the Church of San Pietro in Montorio. The toponym *montorio* is believed to derive from the Latin *Mons Aureus,* 'Golden Mountain'. The moniker alludes to the sand of yellowish hue that occurs in abundance on the hill. In the eighth or ninth century, a chapel had been built to commemorate a site that had a claim in legend alongside the Vatican as the scene of the crucifixion of St. Peter. The church that replaces it was built in the closing decades of the fifteenth century under the patronage of Ferdinand and Isabella, joint monarchs of Aragón and Castile, for a community of Spanish Franciscans. It is here that Beatrice Cenci was buried after her execution in 1599. Situated near the high altar, her unmarked tomb is said to have been desecrated during the French occupation of Rome. Boasting works of Peruzzi, Pinturicchio, Pomarancio, Antonazzo Romano, and Sebastiano del Piombo, the church is a treasure house of sixteenth-

14.4   century paintings. Its chief ornament, however, is the TEMPIETTO, that stands in the adjacent monastery on the reputed site of St. Peter's martyrdom.

Preoccupied as it was with the arrangement of geometrical elements on a two-dimensional façade, the architecture of the early Renaissance in many respects never transcended the art of the draftsman. It remained for Donato Pascuccio, called 'il Bramante', to revive the play of volume and void that had lent the edifices of imperial Rome their characteristic monumentality. The whole of Bramante's œuvre is informed by a robust sense of three-dimensional weight and mass. Despite its small size, the *tempietto,* built in 1502, embodies all the gravitas of its Roman forebears. Bramante's model was the circular temple of Hercules Victor in the Forum Boarium, with its colonnade of sixteen Corinthian columns. The sober Doric order that the architect employed for the *tempietto* better reflects the masculine austerity of the Christian saint. Ancient forms scarcely adumbrated in the architecture of the Quattrocento here achieve fresh currency; both the circular colonnade and the hemispherical dome are new to post-Antique architecture. Their combination in a single design proved as durable as it was inventive: the progeny of the *tempietto* range from the dome of St. Paul's Cathedral in London to that of nearly every capitol building in the United States of America.

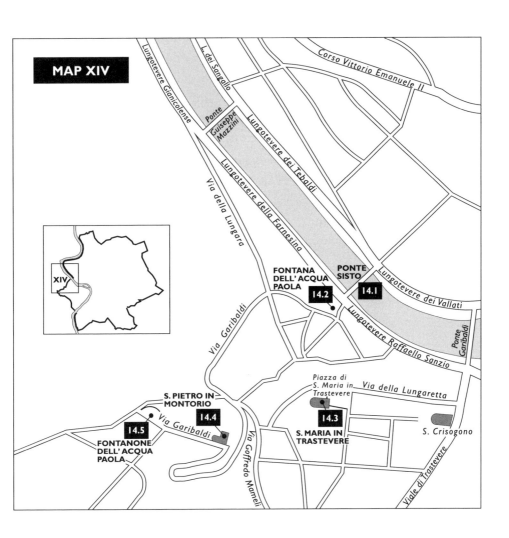

MAP XIV

Lungotevere Gianicolense

L. del Sangallo

Corso Vittorio Emanuele II

Ponte Guiseppe Mazzini

Lungotevere del Tebaldi

Lungotevere della Farnesina

Via della Lungara

XIV

FONTANA DELL' ACQUA PAOLA **14.2**

PONTE SISTO **14.1**

Lungotevere dei Vallati

Via Garibaldi

Lungotevere Raffaello Sanzio

Ponte Garibaldi

Piazza di S. Maria in Trastevere

Via della Lungaretta

S. PIETRO IN MONTORIO **14.4**

Via Garibaldi

14.3 S. MARIA IN TRASTEVERE

S. Crisogono

14.5 FONTANONE DELL' ACQUA PAOLA

Via Goffredo Mameli

Viale di Trastevere

14.1 Ponte Sisto: Dedication by Sixtus IV

i.

[xystus ĪĪĪĪ pont max
ad utilitatem p ro peregrinaeque multi
tudinis ad iubileum uenturae pontem
hunc quem merito ruptum uocabant a fun
5   damentis magna cura et impensa resti
tuit xystumque suo de nomine appellari
uoluit]

1. [xystus ĪĪĪĪ : Quārtus. *On the spelling, see 3.4D, line 4. The original in-scriptions were removed during restorations in the 1990s. Their beauty can be gauged better by the appearance of 13.4 than by that of the disappointing copies now* in situ. — pont(ifex) max(imus).
2. p(opulī) ro(mānī). — multi|tudinis.
3. iubileum = iūbilaeum : *See 2.12A, line 8.*
4. fun|damentis.
5. resti|tuit.
6. xystumque . . . appellari | uoluit] : *Cf. 4.5.i, line 2.*

ii.

[m cccc lxxv
qui transis xysti quarti beneficio
deum roga ut pontificem optimum maxi
mum diu nobis saluet ac sospitet bene
5   uale quisquis es ubi haec precatus
fueris]

1. [m cccc lxxv : Mīllēsimō quadringentēsimō septuāgēsimō quīntō.
2. xysti : *See 14.1.i, line 1.*
3–4. pontificem optimum maxi|mum : *Deriving ultimately from the cult title* IVPPITER OPTIMVS MAXIMVS, *this formula evokes the common humanist dedication* DEO OPTIMO MAXIMO. *The latter is itself based on the pagan model but used as a Christian substitute for* D(īs) M(ānibus), *a formulation frequent in ancient epitaphs.* — bene : *With* uale (*line 5*).
5. precatus | fueris] : *On the tense, see 1.6G, line 7.*

E Bridgehead, Parapet

Right

*For the convenience of the people of Rome
and of the multitude of visitors bound for the Jubilee,[a]
Sixtus the Fourth,[b] Supreme Pontiff,
with great care and at great expense rebuilt from its foundations
this bridge, which in former times they justly called 'Broken,'
and willed that it should be called 'Sisto'
after his own name.*

a. See 7.4H, note b.

b. Pope Sixtus IV della Rovere (r. 1471–1484). Sixtus ordered the restoration of the ancient Pons Aurelius, probably constructed by the emperor Caracalla (r. 211–217), whence the medieval name Pons Antoninus. Rebuilt by Valentinian I (r. 364–375), the bridge was also known as Pons Valentiniani. The name Pons Ruptus ('Broken Bridge') dates to 792, the year in which it was partially destroyed in a flood (cf. 13.12, note b). Sixtus' architect, probably Baccio Pontelli, incorporated into his structure the single arch that remained.

Left

1475

*You who cross by the kindness of Sixtus the Fourth,[a]
pray God that he may long keep and preserve for us
our Supreme and most excellent Pontiff.
Farewell, whoever you be,
once you have offered this prayer.*

a. See 14.1.i, note a. By providing an alternative route from the central Campus Martius to the Vatican, Sixtus hoped to relieve the crowding of Ponte Sant'Angelo. In the Jubilee of 1450, some 170 pilgrims had died by trampling or drowning in a crush provoked by a panicked mule on that bridge. Similarities of phrasing between the present texts and the account of the bridge's reconstruction in the 'Life' of Sixtus IV by Bartolomeo Platina suggest that Platina himself dictated them (the unfinished 'Life' ends at November 1474, before the completion of the bridge).

14.2A Fontana dell'Acqua Paola: Dedication by Paul V

PAVLVS V PONT MAX

AQVAM MVNIFICENTIA SVA

IN SVMMVM IANICVLVM PERDVCTAM

CITRA TIBERIM TOTIVS VRBIS VSVI

5   DEDVCENDAM CVRAVIT

ANNO DOMINI MDCXIII

PONTIFICATVS OCTAVO

1. PAVLVS V : Quīntus. — PONT(ifex) MAX(imus).
2. AQVAM : *On this usage, see 9.5A, line 2.*
3–5. PERDVCTAM . . . DEDVCENDAM : *Note the force of the prefixes.*
4. VSVI : *Dat. of Purpose.*
6. MDCXIII : Mīllēsimō sescentēsimō tertiō decimō.

14.2B Commemoration of the Fountain's Transfer by S.P.Q.R.

NYMPHAEVM AQVAE PAVLLAE

E CAPITE VIAE IVLIAE

ADVERSAE FLVMINIS RIPAE LAXANDAE CAVSSA

S P Q R

5   HVC TRANSPONI

NOVISQVE OPERIBVS INSTAVRARI

CVRAVIT

A MDCCCXCVIII

1. NYMPHAEVM : *The* CL nymphaeum *denotes a shrine dedicated to the nymphs, ordinarily featuring a fountain or pool.* — PAVLLAE = Paulae : *The papal name is used as an Adj. with* aqua *('aqueduct', see 4.5.i, line 2). The present inscription affects the spelling of the ancient Roman* cognōmen *(e.g.,* Lucius Aemilius Paullus).
3. CAVSSA = causā : *The spelling in* SS *is archaic (see 1.1, line 2).*
4. S(enātus) P(opulus) Q(ue) R(ōmānus).
8. A(nnō) MDCCCXCVIII : Mīllēsimō octingentēsimō nōnāgēsimō octāvō.

Piazza Trilussa: Attic of Fountain

Paul the Fifth,[a] Supreme Pontiff,
through his generosity caused the aqueduct
which extended to the summit of the Janiculum
to be brought down to the hither side of the Tiber
for the use of the whole City[b]
in the year of the Lord 1613,
eighth of his office.

a. *Pope Paul V Borghese (r. 1605–1621). The eighth year of his pontificate ran*
   from 16 May 1612 through 15 May 1613.
b. *Completed in 1612, the Acqua Paola served Trastevere (see 14.5A, note b);*
   the present inscription commemorates the extension of its service into the
   Campus Martius via Ponte Sisto (see 14.2B, note b).

Piazza Trilussa: Niche of Fountain

For the purpose of widening the river's opposite bank
the Senate and People of Rome
caused the fountain
of the Acqua Paola
to be moved here
from the head of Via Giulia
and set up on new foundations[a]
in the year 1898.

a. *The fountain was dismantled and moved from its original site at the S end*
   of Via Giulia in order to accommodate the construction of the Lungote-
   vere, the twin roadways that crown the embankments on either side of the
   Tiber. Conceived as stately boulevards on the Parisian model, with the
   advent of mechanized vehicular traffic these ample and sinuous thorough-
   fares quickly assumed the character of automobile raceways that confront
   pedestrians—Roman and visitor alike—with the triple threat of noise,
   motor exhaust, and blunt-force trauma.

14.3A S. Maria in Trastevere: Commemoration of Fount of Oil

FONS OLEI

[hinc oleum fluxit cum christus uirgine luxit
hic et donatur uenia a quocumque rogatur

nascitur hic oleum deus ut de uirgine utroque
5   terrarum est oleo roma sacrata caput]

VERSVS QVI OLIM LEGEBANTVR AD FONTEM OLEI

Two Leonine HEXAMETERS *(lines 2–3), one* ELEGIAC COUPLET *(lines 4–5)*

2. christus : *See 1.6A.ii, line 6.*

3. a quocumque rogatur : *The indefinite pronoun* quōcumque *unites the functions of demonstrative and relative* (= 'to him by whomsoever').

5. oleo : *From its role in ceremonies of consecration, 'oil' is used by metonymy for 'anointing' (cf. 10.1D, line 6).*

14.3B S. Maria in Trastevere: Dedication by Innocent II

HEC IN HONORE TVO PREFVLGIDA MATER HONORIS

REGIA DIVINI RVTILAT FVLGORE DECORIS

IN QVA CRISTE SEDES MANET VLTRA SECVLA SEDES

DIGNA TVIS DEXTRIS EST QV̄A TEGIT AVREA VESTIS

5   INNOCENTIVS HANC RENOVAVIT PAPA SECVNDVS

CV̄ MOLES RVITVRA VETVS FORET HINC ORIVNDVS

Six Leonine HEXAMETERS *(lines 1–2 and 5–6 'Caudati', 3–4 'Rich')*

1. HEC = haec : *On the spelling, see 1.8B, line 5.* — PREFVLGIDA = praefulgida.

3. CRISTE = Christe : *On the spelling, see 8.8A, line 2.* SEDES . . . SEDES : *The verb* (sĕdēs) *is accurately distinguished from the noun* (sēdēs; *see 3.4D, line 4).* — SECVLA = saecula.

4. DEXTRIS . . . VESTIS : *In the ML of Italy,* XT *and* ST *were pronounced alike and thus rhyme (like* SEDES . . . SEDES, *line 3). The central lines of the present dedication feature internal rhyme (at the caesura and line-end); the outer couplets feature end-rhyme.* — QVA(m)

5. INNOCENTIVS . . . SECVNDVS : *I.e., Innocent II. Scans* Innŏcentius. — PAPA : *See 3.6A, line 2.*

6. CV(m).

Podium of Choir

The Fount of Oil.[a]

Hence flowed oil when Christ shone forth from the Virgin,
here too is granted pardon to whosoever asks for it.

Oil is born here as Christ from the Virgin,
and by each anointing Rome is consecrated as head of the world.

Verses which were once inscribed at the fount of oil.

Two Leonine HEXAMETERS (lines 2–3), one ELEGIAC COUPLET (lines 4–5)

a. *According to the* GOLDEN LEGEND, *a spring of water on the present*
site, occupied at the time by an inn, was changed to oil and burst into the
Tiber—a phenomenon predicted by the Sibyl as a portent of the coming of
the Messiah. The oleaginous eruption is attested by the Roman historian
Dio Cassius, who dates it to the year corresponding to 38 BC.

Apse

In thy honor, thou resplendent Mother of Honor, this royal hall
glows ruddy with the brilliance of a divine beauty.[a] *The seat*
in which thou art enthroned, O Christ, endures beyond the ages;
worthy of thy right hand is she whom the golden garment mantles.
When the ancient edifice was on the point of collapse,
Pope Innocent the Second,[b] *native of the quarter, made this new.*

Six Leonine HEXAMETERS (lines 1–2 and 5–6 'Caudati', 3–4 'Rich')

a. *Against a brilliant background of gold, Christ sits enthroned with the*
BVM; to the left and right, favorite saints of Rome and Trastevere flank
the pair: Peter, Cornelius, Julius, Calepodius, Callistus, and Lawrence (see
4.7B); Innocent II appears with a model of the church (cf. 3.5A, note b).

b. *Pope Innocent II Papareschi (r. 1130–1143). Scion of a wealthy Trastevere*
family, Gregorio Papareschi was irregularly elected under the auspices of
the Frangipane family as Pope Innocent II within hours of the death of
his predecessor. His reign saw the birth of the Roman Commune: in 1143,
angered by Innocent's refusal to authorize the destruction of Tivoli in the
wake of that city's abortive bid to set up an autonomous municipal gov-
ernment, the petty aristocracy of Rome occupied the Capitol and set up a
government of its own.

14.3C Legends to Cavallini's Cycle of the Virgin

i. Nativity of the Virgin

HVMANI GENERIS SATOR ET QVI PARCERE LAPSIS

INSTITVIS MACVLAS VETERIS RVBIGINIS AVFER

ARGENTO THALAMVS TIBI SIT QVO VIRGO REFVLGENS

> Three HEXAMETERS

2. RVBIGINIS : *In* EL, *rūbīgō can denote 'corruption'. The language of the epigram recalls Prov.* 25:4 (Aufer robiginem de argento et egredietur vas purissimum).

3. VIRGO : *Scans* virgŏ (*cf. 3.4*D, *line 5*).

ii. Annunciation

TVQ' SVPER CVNCTAS BENEDICTA PVERPERA SALVE

VIRGVLA QVE SPONSVM NESCIS QVAM GRATIA SACRI

FLAMINIS IRRADIAT COELO MARIS ANNVE SYDVS

> Three HEXAMETERS

1. TVQ(ue).

2. VIRGVLA : *An allusion to Is.* 11:1, *interpreted as a prophecy of Christ's birth* (Et egredietur virga de radice Iesse et flos de radice eius ascendet). — QVE = quae : *On the spelling, see 1.8*B, *line 5*. — SACRI | FLAMINIS : *In* EL, flāmen *is used of the Holy Spirit.*

3. COELO = caelō. — SYDVS = sīdus : *On the spelling, see 3.1, line 1, and cf.* SYDERA *at 9.1*B, *line 2*.

iii. Nativity of Christ

IAM PVERVM IAM SVMME PATER POST TEMPORA NATVM

ACCIPIMVS GENITVM TIBI QVEM NOS ESSE COEVVM

CREDIMVS HINCQ' OLEI SCATVRIRE LIQVAMINA TYBRIM

> Three HEXAMETERS

2. COEVVM = coaevum : *On the spelling, see 1.8*B, *line 5. The* LL coaevus *is 'coeval'.*

3. HINCQ(ue). — SCATVRIRE = scaturrīre : *Both* scaturrīre *and* scatūrīre *are attested in* CL; *in the present verse, neither scans.* — LIQVAMINA : *The* CL liquāmen (*'liquid'*) *rarely appears outside the pages of the agricultural writer Columella.* — TYBRIM = Tibrim : *On the spelling, see 3.1, line 1, and cf. 11.5*D, *line 2*.

S. Maria in Trastavere: Apse Wall

Leftmost Panel

Thou creator of the human race, who likewise undertake to redeem
thy fallen creatures, remove the stains of the ancient corruption from
the silver wherewith the Virgin is to be thy gleaming bridal chamber.[a]

Three Hexameters

a. *The text alludes to Prov. 25:4, understood as referring typologically to the*
BVM who, according to Roman Catholic teaching, was conceived without
taint of original sin (see 4.2M, note e).

Second Panel

And thou, hail, mother blessèd above all women, maid[a]
who know not thy spouse, whom the grace of the Holy Spirit
in heaven illumines. Nod thy assent, thou Star of the Sea.[b]

Three HEXAMETERS

a. *The Latin word is* virgula, *diminutive of* virga *('rod'). Used of the BVM*
in medieval hymns, the title Virgula Iesse *makes another typological*
reference: 'And there shall come forth a rod out of the stem of Jesse, and a
Branch shall grow out of his roots' (Is. 11:1).
b. *The moniker* Stella Maris *is generally thought to have its origin in a tex-*
tual corruption of the phrase stilla maris *('drop of the sea'), St. Jerome's*
explanation of the Hebrew name Miryam.

Third Panel

Now, highest Father, now we apprehend that the child born
in due course is thy son. We believe that he is thy co-eval[a]
and that from this place a Tiber of oil bubbles forth its floods.[b]

Three HEXAMETERS

a. *That the godhead comprises three equal, distinct and coeternal persons*
forms the cornerstone of Nicene orthodoxy (cf. 3.3A, note b).
b. *In the mosaic, the miraculous flood of oil is seen to issue from the door of*
the inn that stood on the site of the future church (see 14.3A, note a).

iv. Adoration of the Magi

GENTIBVS IGNOTVS STELLA DVCE NOSCITVR INFANS
IN PRESEPE IACENS CELI TERREQ' PROFVNDI
CONDITOR ATQ' MAGI MYRRAM THVS ACCIPIT AVRVM

Three HEXAMETERS

1. STELLA DVCE : *Abl.Abs.*
2. PRESEPE = praesaepe : *On the spelling, see 1.8B, line 5.* — CELI = caelī.
   — TERREQ(ue). — PROFVNDI : *Qualifies* CELI.
3. ATQ(ue). — MYRRAM = myrrham : *On the spelling, see 8.8A, line 2.* —
   THVS = tūs.

v. Presentation in the Temple

SISTITVR IN TEMPLO PVER ET SIMEONIS IN VLNAS
ACCIPITVR CVI DANDA QVIES NAM LVMINA SERVI
CONSPEXERE DEVM CLARVM IVBAR OMNIBVS ORTVM

Three HEXAMETERS

1. SIMEONIS : *The Latin name is* Simeōn, -ōnis (*Greek* Συμεών).
2–3. LVMINA . . . ORTVM : *The language draws on the Vulgate, Luke 2:29–32*
   (Nunc dimittis servum tuum, Domine, secundum verbum tuum in
   pace, quia viderunt oculi mei salutare tuum, quod parasti ante faciem
   omnium populorum, lumen ad revelationem gentium et gloriam
   plebis tuae Israel). — CONSPEXERE = cōnspexērunt.

vi. Dormition of the Virgin

AD SVMMVM REGINA THRONVM DEFERTVR IN ALTVM
ANGELICIS PRELATA CHORIS CVI FESTINAT IRE
FIILIS OCCVRRENS MATREM SVPER AETHER PONIT

Three HEXAMETERS

2. ANGELICIS : *The* EL *Adj.* angelicus *corresponds to* angelus (*see 4.2J, line*
   2). — PRELATA = praelāta : *On the spelling, see 1.8B, line 5.* — CHORIS :
   See 4.2H, line 9.
3. FIILIS : *Sic* (= fīlius). — AETHER : *Both meter and sense require*
   AETHERA. *On* aethēr, *see 2.14, line 6.*

Fourth Panel

Unknown to the nations, the infant creator of earth and high
heaven, lying in a manger, is made known under the star's guidance
and receives the myrrh, frankincense, and gold of the Magus.[a]

Three HEXAMETERS

a. *All three magi are in fact depicted in the mosaic, each holding his gift. The*
six epigrams of the present cycle are attributed to Giacomo Stefaneschi
(c. 1270–1343), Cardinal Deacon of S. Giorgio in Velabro. Stefaneschi's
brother, Bertoldo, commissioned the cycle from Pietro Cavallini (fl. 1273–
1308), the Roman painter and mosaicist.

Fifth Panel

The child is brought to the temple and is taken up into the
arms of Simeon, to whom rest is to be given, for 'The eyes
of thy servant have beheld God, a bright light risen unto all.'[a]

Three HEXAMETERS

a. *The text follows Luke 2:29–32, known as the* Nunc Dimittis *from the first*
two words of its Latin text: 'Lord, now lettest thou thy servant depart in
peace, according to thy word, for mine eyes have seen thy salvation, which
thou hast prepared before the face of all people; a light to lighten the Gen-
tiles, and the glory of thy people Israel'.

Sixth Panel

Preceded by choirs of angels, the Queen is borne aloft
to the highest throne. Her son hastens to go to her.
Meeting his mother, he sets her above the heavens.[a]

Three HEXAMETERS

a. *Although the Assumption of the BVM—conventionally called her 'Dormi-*
tion' (falling asleep)—and her subsequent coronation as Queen of Heaven
are not recorded in the NT, *the authenticity of these events is confidently*
asserted by Roman Catholics on the basis of allegorical interpretation of
scriptural texts.

14.4 Tempietto of S. Pietro in Montorio: Dedication by Juan Carlos I

ANNO MDCCCCLXXVIII

REGE IOANNE CAROLO

HOC AEDICVLVM

OLIM FERDINANDI REGIS ET

5   ELISABETHAE REGINAE IVSSV

AB ALTO BRAMANTIS INGENIO

EXSTRVCTVM

PETRO APOSTOLORVM PRINCIPI

DICATVM

10   ET AEVI LONGA VETVSTATE LABEFACTVM

HISP NATIONIS PVBLICIS IMPENSIS

NE TEMPORIS INIVRIA DIVTIVS FATISCERET

SVB AVSPICIIS EIVSDEM HISP CATH REGIS

CVRA ET LIBERALITATE

15   RESTITVTVM EST

1. MDCCCCLXXVIII : Mīllēsimō nōngentēsimō septuāgēsimō octāvō.
2. IOANNE CAROLO : *The Latin name is* Ioannēs Carolus. *The Abl.Abs. has temporal force (see 5.8B, line 1).*
3. AEDICVLVM : *The LL* aediculum *is 'small building' (the CL word is* aedicula).
6. BRAMANTIS : *This Gen.Sg. form presupposes a Nom.* Bramāns (*on the Latinization of the name, cf. 12.3B, line 8*).
8. APOSTOLORVM : *See 1.61, line 7.*
11. HISP(ānae).
13. HISP(ānī) CATH(olicī).

Cloister, N Wall

In the year 1978,
during the reign of Juan Carlos,[a]
this Tempietto,
built in times past
at the bidding of King Ferdinand
and Queen Isabella[b]
through the lofty genius of Bramante,[c]
dedicated to Peter,
prince of the Apostles,
and weakened by great age,
lest it deteriorate further under the assault of time,
was restored
at the public expense of the nation of Spain
with care and generosity
at the initiative of the same Catholic king of Spain.

a. *King Juan Carlos I (r. 1975–) assumed the throne of Spain on the death of Francisco Franco, the nation's de facto ruler from 1939. Son of Don Juan de Borbón and grandson of King Alfonso XIII, Juan Carlos was appointed heir to the throne by Franco in 1969 and designated his successor.*

b. *The tempietto was commissioned by Ferdinand II the Catholic of Aragon (r. 1479–1516) and Isabella I of Castile (1451–1504). It was constructed 1502–1510 to commemorate a site identified in medieval legend as that of the martrydom of St. Peter.*

c. *Called 'il Bramante', Donato di Pascuccio d'Antonio (1444–1514) came to Rome from northern Italy in 1499. With the election of Julius II in 1503, he was given charge of all papal construction projects, most notably the Belvedere Court and New St. Peter's. The Doric order employed by Bramante for the tempietto is that prescribed by the Roman architect Vitruvius for temples of male deities (cf. 3.4D, note d).*

14.5A Fontanone dell'Acqua Paola: Dedication by Paul V

PAVLVS QVINTVS PONTIFEX MAXIMVS

AQVAM IN AGRO BRACCIANENSI

SALVBERRIMIS E FONTIBVS COLLECTAM

VETERIBVS AQVAE ALSIETINAE DVCTIBVS RESTITVTIS

5   NOVISQVE ADDITIS

XXXV AB MILLIARIO DVXIT

ANNO DOMINI MDCXII PONTIFICATVS SVI SEPTIMO

2. BRACCIANENSI : *The Adj.* Bracciānēnsis *corresponds to the toponym* Bracciānum (*mod. Bracciano*).

4. ALSIETINAE : *The Adj.* Alsiētīnus *forms part of the toponym* Lacus Alsiētīnus. — DVCTIBVS : *In addition to its other senses,* CL ductus *denotes the channel of an aqueduct.*

6. XXXV : Trīcēsimō quīntō.

7. MDCXII : Mīllēsimō sescentēsimō duodecimō.

14.5B Fontanone dell'Acqua Paola: Dedication by Alexander VIII

ALEXANDER VIII OTTHOBONVS VENETVS P M

PAVLI V PROVIDENTISSIMI PONT BENEFICIVM TVTATVS

REPVRGATO SPECV NOVISQVE FONTIBVS INDVCTIS

RIVOS SVIS QVEMQVE LABRIS OLIM ANGVSTE CONTENTOS

5   VNICO EODEMQVE PERAMPLO LACV EXCITATO RECEPIT

AREAM ADVERSVS LABEM MONTIS SVBSTRVXIT

ET LAPIDEO MARGINE TERMINAVIT ORNAVITQVE

ANNO SALVTIS MDCLXXXX PONTIFICATVS SVI SECVNDO

1. ALEXANDER VIII : Octāvus. — OTTHOBONVS : *For the inauthentic* H, *see 9.1A, line 2.* — P(ontifex) M(aximus).

2. PAVLI V : Quīntī. — PONT(ificis).

3. SPECV : *The* CL specus *is used of the conduits of aqueducts.*

8. MDCLXXXX : Mīllēsimō sescentēsimō nōnāgēsimō.

Via Giuseppi Garibaldi: Attic and Frieze

Paul the Fifth,[a] Supreme Pontiff,
by the restoration of the ancient channels of the Aqua Alsietina[b]
and the addition of new ones
brought the water in the territory of Bracciano,
gathered from most wholesome sources,
from the thirty-fifth milestone

in the year of the Lord 1612, seventh of his office.

a. *Pope Paul V Borghese (r. 1605–1621). The seventh year of his pontificate ran from 16 May 1611 through 15 May 1612.*

b. *The Aqua Alsietina was brought to Trastevere in 2 BC by the emperor Augustus to supply his* Naumachia, *a vast artificial basin used for staging naval combats. Because the water of the Alsietina was of poor quality, the sources used for the Acqua Paola were instead those of the Aqua Traiana, dating to* AD 109.

Central Niche

Alexander the Eighth Ottoboni[a] of Venice, Supreme Pontiff,
preserving the benefit conferred by Paul the Fifth, most provident pontiff,
the channels having been cleaned anew and fresh sources tapped,
gathered in one and the same extensive basin, newly built,
the streams once narrowly confined each within its own margins,
reinforced the surroundings from below against landslide,
and finished and embellished it with a stone brink
in the year of Salvation 1690, second of his office.

a. *Pope Alexander VIII Ottoboni (r. 1689–1691). The second year of his pontificate ran from 6 October 1690 through 1 February 1691, the date of his death. His reign of sixteen months is notable chiefly for the unseemly haste with which he enriched his relatives (cf. 11.3D, note d).*

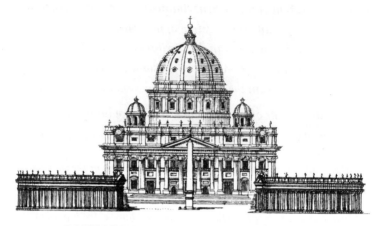

BASILICA DI SAN PIETRO IN VATICANO

The Italian word for the wholesale demolition of an urban quarter to accommodate new construction is sventramento—*properly, a 'gutting'. Rome's first* sventramento *of modern times took place under Pope Alexander VI, who in 1499 inaugurated a new 'Via Alexandrina' (today's Borgo Nuovo) extending 450 meters from Castel Sant'Angelo to the gates of the Apostolic Palace. In an instance of historical compensation that would do credit to Heraclitus, the Borgo Nuovo itself—with the whole of the surrounding zone—was annihilated in the city's latest* sventramento, *carried out for the construction of Via della Conciliazione (1938–1950) so as to open an impressive perspective on New Saint Peter's.*

XV. The Borgo & the Vatican

THOUGH IN THE DIMENSIONS OF HIS MAUSOLEUM Hadrian re-
frained from challenging the Divine Augustus, the emperor eclipsed his
predecessor's monument in every other respect. Clad in gleaming Carrara
marble and crowned with a mighty bronze *quadriga,* the tomb set a fitting seal on that emperor's extravagant genius. Over the subsequent century and a half, it would receive the ashes of the Caesars from Hadrian
himself through Caracalla. The stones bearing their epitaphs survived
until July of 1579, when they were destroyed at the order of Pope Gregory XIII to obtain decorative materials for the Cappella Gregoriana in
the Basilica of St. Peter. Their texts survive in transcription thanks to the
compiler of the Einsiedeln Itinerary, a pilgrim of the Middle Ages who
proved more solicitous for posterity than the pontiff of the Renaissance.

The massive fabric of the mausoleum was early incorporated into the
city's defenses. A natural fortress, it held against the Visigoths of Alaric in AD 410 and the Vandals of Genseric in 455, as it did against the
Ostrogoths of Vitiges in 537—though on that occasion its Byzantine
defenders, desperate for ammunition, were reduced to breaking up the
abundant statuary with which the parapets were adorned. In 590, the
monument was the scene of an event famous in Roman legend. In the af-
termath of a terrible flood that had provoked famine and plague, Pope St.
Gregory I (r. 590–604) led his flock in an expiatory procession through
the streets of the city. As the suppliants approached the mausoleum, they
were greeted by a vision of the Archangel Michael hovering atop the battlements and sheathing his sword in token of divine mercy. This apparition lent the monument the name by which it has been known from
at least the tenth century: *Castellum Sancti Angeli* or *Castel Sant'Angelo,*
'Fortress of the Holy Angel'.

In the Middle Ages, Castel Sant'Angelo was the prize in the struggles
of the local nobility, passing from the control of the family of Theophylact to that of the 'Crescenzi' and later the Orsini. Pope Boniface IX

(r. 1389–1404) transformed it into a papal stronghold; Nicholas V (r. 1447–1455) fortified it with a tower and bastions and installed a papal apartment. Following the occupation of Rome by Charles VIII of France

15.2A in January of 1495, the defensive works were improved by ALEXANDER VI (r. 1492–1503); the perimeter wall and the corridor giving access from

15.5A the Vatican—the PASSETTO—were restored. The *passetto* would soon come in for urgent use: on the morning of 6 May 1527, Pope Clement VII traversed it in hot haste, zealous to avoid capture at the hands of the imperial forces besieging Rome. On that occasion, though the fortress held, Clement spent four weeks pent up inside with thirteen cardinals. The events inspired a pasquinade employing an untranslatable pun: *Papa non potest errare* ('The pope cannot err/travel'). Two decades later Pope Paul III (r. 1534–1549), who had shared Clement's cheerless

15.2 sojourn, installed a lavish suite of apartments, including the SALA PAO-
B–D LINA, a handsome audience hall.

15.1A   The Pons Aelius, known from the early Middle Ages as 'PONTE SANT'ANGELO', linked Hadrian's mausoleum with the Campus Martius. As the tomb of Peter was the principal goal of medieval pilgrims, the streets leading from the Vatican basilica to the other great pilgrimage churches were heavily frequented. These routes all had their head at Ponte Sant'Angelo, which was to remain Rome's most important bridge into modern times. The bridge was subject to dangerous overcrowding. During the Jubilee of 1450, some 170 pilgrims were crushed and drowned in a panic. To ease the flow of traffic, Pope Nicholas V cleared the bridge of shops and demolished an arch of the emperors Gratian, Valentinian and Theodosius that stood at its head. The arch was replaced by a pair of chapels dedicated to the victims' memory. The site is now occupied by

15.1B STATUES OF SAINTS PETER AND PAUL.

    In the first century, the zone between the Tiber and the slopes of Vatican Hill was occupied by the gardens of the elder Agrippina. Here the emperor Gaius ('Caligula', r. AD 37–41), Agrippina's son, laid out a private circus for horse races. According to the historian Tacitus, numerous

Christians were executed on this site after Nero's fire in AD 64. Within a few decades, the circus fell into disuse and was encroached upon by the necropolis that extended along its northern flank; in the first half of the second century a large mausoleum was constructed directly over its *spina* ('central partition'). Amid the grander monuments of the necropolis rose an inconspicuous *memoria* ('funerary monument') that already in the second century was venerated as the resting-place of St. Peter. On this site, following the defeat of his rival Licinius in AD 324, the emperor Constantine I (r. 306–337) decreed the erection of a great church.

Constantine's foundation was first and foremost a memorial basilica intended for celebrations in the apostle's honor. Like the later churches of San Lorenzo, San Sebastiano, and Sant'Agnese, it was also a cemetery basilica, burial place of the faithful, and scene of the commemorative meals into which the church had transmuted the funeral banquets of their pagan ancestors. One important respect in which St. Peter's differed from other Constantinian foundations was its situation directly above the martyr's tomb. To accommodate this peculiarity, it was necessary to excavate the lower slopes of Vatican Hill and to level the necropolis. So that the dawn of the vernal equinox might flood through its portals to bathe the shrine of the apostle, the basilica faced due east. As late as the fifth century, the imperfectly Christianized Romans, prey to an understandable religious confusion, had to be instructed not to perform obeisance to the rising sun from the steps.

The basilica constituted a triune monument to the Savior, his apostle, and their champion—Constantine. The parallel between the emperor's military victories and the spiritual triumph of Christ was made explicit in the dedicatory inscription: QVOD DVCE TE MVNDVS SVRREXIT IN ASTRA TRIVMPHANS HANC CONSTANTINVS VICTOR TIBI CONDIDIT AVLAM ('Because under Thy guidance the world has risen in triumph to the heavens, Constantine in victory has founded for Thee this church'). As for St. Peter, his centrality in Rome's claim to ecclesiastical primacy is reflected not only in the basilica's situation but also in its magnificence. In size and splendor it exceeded the bishop's seat at the Lateran; from the outset, St. Peter's enjoyed an unofficial standing as Rome's second cathedral.

Old St. Peter's was preceded by a stair that led to a monumental porticoed atrium. Called the *Paradiso,* this was carpeted with the tombs of popes and monarchs. In the center stood the colossal bronze pine cone admired by Dante and now displayed in the Cortile della Pigna. At the western end rose the basilica. Covered in brilliant mosaics, the high façade sparkled in the sunlight; five portals gave access to the interior. Within, the cavernous nave was illuminated by the blaze of a thousand oil-lamps. Its magnificent colonnades, composed of ancient *spolia,* had no two bases or capitals alike; fragmentary dedications of Titus, Trajan, and Gallienus, incongruously juxtaposed, were plain to read on the blocks of the entablature. Beneath the glittering apse, spiral columns of curious workmanship screened the shrine of the apostle. The glow of marble and glint of gold were everywhere muted by a pungent pall of incense; the mesmerizing moan of liturgical chant reverberated in the gloom.

In the early Middle Ages, seafaring Arab marauders known in Europe as 'Saracens' began to harry the coasts of Sicily and southern Italy. Situated outside the wall of Aurelian, both the Basilica of St. Peter and whole of the *Borgo*—the crowded quarter that had grown up around it—were wholly unprotected from this threat. In August of 846, a Saracen raiding party overran the weak defenses at Ostia and sailed up the Tiber to Rome. All the extramural basilicas, including that of Saint Peter, were desecrated and sacked. Though the invaders were soon driven off, the need for a defensive circuit to protect the Vatican and Borgo was plain. Labor for the project was recruited from the *domuscultae,* fortified 15.5C   agricultural estates in the Campagna. According to surviving DEDICATORY INSCRIPTIONS, parts of the fortifications were constructed by the *militia* ('manpower') of the *Domusculta Capracorum* (situated near ancient Veii) and of the *Domusculta Saltisina* (located some fifteen miles from Rome on the road to Ardea). Named for Pope St. Leo IV (r. 847–855), the Civitas Leonina was dedicated on 27 June 852. In the sixteenth century, the fortified quarter was enlarged to the north with the Civitas Pia of Pope Pius IV (r. 1559–1565).

The first pope to take the Vatican as his residence was Nicholas III (r. 1277–1280). An Orsini, he preferred to reside within the territory controlled by his clan, which included the right bank of the Tiber. Not until the fifteenth century did Nicholas V (r. 1447–1455) permanently transfer the papal court to the Vatican from its ancient seat at the Lateran. A product of the new humanism, Nicholas proposed an ambitious program of architectural and urban projects patterned on ancient precedents. At St. Peter's, the head of Constantine's basilica was to be reconstructed with a vaulted dome *all'antica*. The Vatican obelisk—Rome's only such monument remaining *in situ*—would be relocated at the center of Piazza di San Pietro, a latter-day 'Forum' of Christ. Further, Nicholas envisioned the full-scale redevelopment of the Borgo with a trident of rectilinear streets converging on Ponte Sant'Angelo, counterparts to the three great arteries of the Campus Martius (the Via Papalis, Via Peregrinorum, and 'Via Recta').

Owing in part to the Turkish threat, intensified after the fall of Constantinople in 1453, Nicholas' initiatives went largely unrealized. After a lapse of 130 years, Pope Sixtus V (r. 1585–1590) implemented the Nicoline plan for the OBELISCO VATICANO. Its transfer to the center of the piazza was effected between April and September of 1586 under the direction of Domenico Fontana, who designed an elaborate machinery of winches, trusses, and rollers for the purpose. Legend maintains that Fontana kept a saddled horse at the ready for the duration of the risky undertaking in case he should have to flee the wrath of the famously irascible pontiff. The obelisk's dedicatory inscriptions blaze with the harsh piety of the former inquisitor.   *15.3*

Before Sixtus V, at the dawn of the sixteenth century, the plans of Nicholas V for the modernization of the Vatican had been taken up with ferocious vigor by Pope Julius II (r. 1503–1513) and his architect, Donato Bramante. Julius' program for the Vatican was threefold. Abandoning the apartments of Alexander VI Borgia, his hated predecessor, Julius engaged Raphael to decorate a suite of rooms on the floor above. These are the celebrated Stanze. A second initiative was the construction of the Belvedere Court, a monumental terraced garden enclosed by a double portico that connected the Vatican palaces with the villa of Innocent VIII (the Belvedere) on the brow of Vatican Hill. Most portentously, Julius was emboldened to order the replacement of Constantine's basilica, by then approaching ruin. Bramante undertook the labor of destruction with such relish that contemporaries dubbed him *Mastro Ruinante*, 'Master of Demolition'.

Rising within the deliquescent carcass of its predecessor, New St. Peter's for many years resembled a vast and disturbing ruin open to the sky. The labored history of the building's construction over twelve decades seems to vibrate in sympathy with that of the sixteenth-century papacy. There is a terrible irony in the fact that the tremendous cost of a monument conceived to represent the Church's renewal promoted a traffic in indulgences that fueled the fires of the Reformation. The very shape of the building emerged under the hammer blows of ideological debate. Bramante's original design for New St. Peter's, respected for a century, involved a central plan based on the Greek cross. The decision taken in 1605 to adopt a new design, based on the Latin cross, reflects the reactionary fervor of the Counter Reformation. Whereas the Latin cross unambiguously figured Christ crucified, the Greek was felt to connote, if not pantheism, at least an unwholesome ecumenism.

The basilica's monuments are legion. Among the few relics preserved from Old St. Peter's is the tomb slab of Pope Hadrian I (r. 772 –795), produced at Aachen by order of Charlemagne and transported to Rome (the prolix and uninformative epitaph is not included in the present collection). The new basilica bears dedications of PAUL V (r. 1605–1621), UR-BAN VIII (r. 1623–1644), and INNOCENT X (r. 1644–1655). Conspicuous

15.4
A,B,D

among its numerous tombs are those of JAMES STUART, pretender to   15.4F
the throne of Great Britain, and of his wife MARIA CLEMENTINA. The   15.4G
latter, Christina of Sweden, and MATILDA OF TUSCANY are the sole   15.4E
women granted the distinction of a monument in St. Peter's. Among the
more recent tombs is that of Pope JOHN PAUL II (r. 1978–2005), laid to   15.4L
rest in the Sacre Grotte in April of 2005. (That pontiff is responsible for
one of the most unusual Latin inscriptions to be found in the Vatican,
and indeed in the city at large: the dedication of an elevator.)

The modest PORTA DI SANTA ROSA is the first public work of John   15.7
Paul's successor, Pope Benedict XVI (r. 2005–). That it features an inscription in Latin augurs well for the vigor of the city's native tongue into
the twenty-first century.

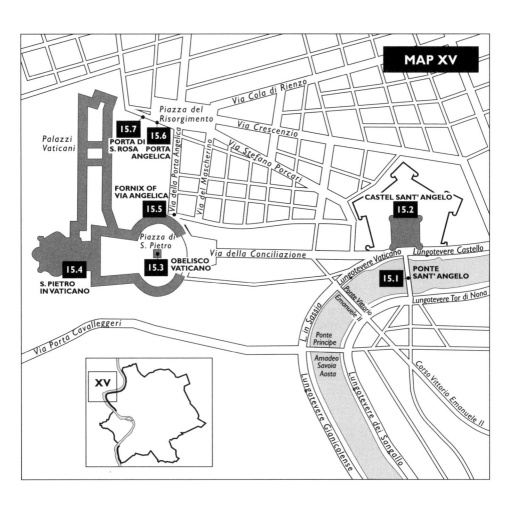

MAP XV

Palazzi
Vaticani

Via Cola di Rienzo

Piazza del
Risorgimento

Via Crescenzio

15.7 **15.6**
PORTA DI PORTA
S. ROSA ANGELICA

Via Stefano Porcari

FORNIX OF
VIA ANGELICA

CASTEL SANT' ANGELO

15.2

15.5

Piazza di
S. Pietro

Via della Conciliazione

15.4

15.3

OBELISCO
VATICANO

Lungotevere Castello

PONTE
SANT' ANGELO

15.1

S. PIETRO
IN VATICANO

Lungotevere Tor di Nona

Via Porta Cavalleggeri

Ponte
Principe

Amadeo
Savoia
Aosta

Corso Vittorio Emanuele II

XV

Lungotevere Gianicolense

Lungotevere del Sansallo

15.1A Statues of SS. Peter & Paul: Dedication by Clement VII

i.

CLEMENS VII PONT MAX

PETRO ET PAVLO APOSTOLIS

VRBIS PATRONIS

ANNO SALVTIS CHRISTIANAE

5   M D XXX IIII

PONTIFICATVS SVI DECIMO

1. CLEMENS VII : Septimus. — PONT(ifex) MAX(imus).
2. PETRO : *On the name, see 3.2A, line 2.* — APOSTOLIS : *See 1.6I, line 7.*
4. CHRISTIANAE : *See 1.7A, line 8.*
5. M D XXX IIII : Mīllēsimō quīngentēsimō trīcēsimō quārtō.

ii.

BINIS HOC LOCO SACELLIS

BELLICA VI ET PARTE PONTIS

IMPETV FLVMINIS DISIECTIS

AD RETINEND LOCI RELIGIONĒ

5   ORNATVMQ' HAS STATVAS

SVBSTITVIT

1. BINIS : *The distributive numeral* bīnī *('two each') is used also of things that form a pair.* — SACELLIS : *In* EL, sacellum *is 'chapel'.*
4. AD RETINEND(am) LOCI RELIGIONE(m) : *On the construction, see 1.6H, lines 11–12.*
5. ORNATVMQ(ue).

Ponte S. Angelo: E Bridgehead, Parapet

Left

> *Clement the Seventh,[a] Supreme Pontiff,*
> *to the Apostles Peter and Paul,*
> *protectors of the City,[b]*
> *in the year of Christian Salvation*
> *1534,*
> *tenth of his office.*

a. *Pope Clement VII de' Medici (r. 1523–1534). The tenth year of Clement's pontificate in fact ran from 19 November 1532 through 18 November 1533. Peter and Paul are venerated as the twin founders of Christian Rome.*

b. *See 15.4I, note b and 5.7E, note b.*

Right

> *In order to preserve the sanctity of the place[a]*
> *as well as its beauty,*
> *he replaced with statues*
> *the pair of chapels on this site,*
> *laid in ruins by the violence of war,[b] and,*
> *in the direction of the bridge, by the onslaught of the river.[c]*

a. *The chapels commemorated victims of an incident on Ponte Sant'Angelo in 1450 (see 14.1.ii, note a).*

b. *During the sack of 1527, imperial troops fired on Castel Sant'Angelo from the shelter of the chapels.*

c. *Viz., in the inundation of 1530 (see 10.1D and 11.5C).*

15.1B Legends on Statues of SS. Peter and Paul

i. St. Peter   *ii. St. Paul*

HINC   HINC

HVMILIBVS   RETRIBVTIO

VENIA   SVPERBIS

i.2. HVMILIBVS | VENIA : *Note the chiasmus (see 2.11A.i, lines 3–4).*

ii.2. RETRIBVTIO | SVPERBIS : *The language evokes Verg. Aen. 6.853:* Parcere subiectis et debellare superbis.

15.1C Legends on Statues of Angels

i. Column

TRONVS MEVS

IN COLVMNA

1–2. TRONVS . . . COLVMNA : *The text is quoted from the Vulgate, Ecclesiasticus 24:7. —* TRONVS = thronus : *In LL, the aspirated plosive represented by Greek Θ was assimilated in pronunciation (and often in spelling) to the native* T *(cf. 8.8A, line 2). In RL, conversely, inauthentic aspirates were not infrequently introduced by hypercorrection (cf. 9.1A, line 2).*

ii. Scourge

IN FLAGELLA

PARATVS SVM

1–2. IN . . . SVM : *The text is adapted from the Vulgate, Ps. 37:18.*

iii. Crown of Thorns

IN AERVMNA MEA

DVM CONFIGITVR SPINA

1–2. IN . . . SPINA : *The text is adapted from the Vulgate, Ps. 31:4.*

iv. Veronica's Veil

[respice in faciem
christi tui]

1–2. [respice . . . tui] : *The text is quoted from the Vulgate, Ps. 83:10.*

Ponte S. Angelo: Bases of Statues, L & R

Left

Hence
pardon
for the humble.[a]

Right

Hence
retribution
for the haughty.[b]

a. *St. Peter holds the keys of the Kingdom of Heaven.*

b. *St. Paul holds the sword of the Word of God. The language evokes* Aeneid *6.853, 'To spare the vanquished and conquer the haughty'.*

Ponte S. Angelo: Bases of Angels' Statues

First Statue E

My throne
is on a pillar.[a]

a. *The text is quoted from the Vulgate, Ecclesiasticus 24:7. The order in which the statues are arranged presupposes a 'zig-zag' itinerary from E to W. The iconology of the ensemble evidently takes its inspiration from the* Spiritual Exercises *of St. Ignatius of Loyola, the third stage of which is devoted to meditation on Christ's Passion.*

First Statue W

I am readied
for scourges.[a]

a. *The text is adapted from the Vulgate, Ps. 37:18.*

Second Statue W

In my agony,
while it is pierced with thorns.[a]

a. *The text is adapted from the Vulgate, Ps. 31:4.*

Second Statue E

Look upon the face
of thine anointed.[a]

a. *The text is quoted from the Vulgate, Ps. 83:10.*

v. Seamless Garment

SVPER VESTEM MEAM

MISERVNT SORTEM

1–2. SVPER . . . SORTEM : *The text is quoted from the Vulgate, Ps. 21:19.*

vi. Nails

ASPICIANT AD ME

QVEM CONFIXERVNT

1–2. ASPICIANT . . . CONFIXERVNT : *The text is adapted from the Vulgate, Zech. 12:10. On the spelling of* ASPICIANT, *see 8.2, line 7.*

vii. Cross

CVIVS PRINCIPATVS

SVPER HVMERVM EIVS

1–2. CVIVS . . . EIVS : *The text is adapted from the Vulgate, Is. 9:6.* — HVMERVM = umerum : *On the spelling, see 8.8A, line 2.*

viii. Titulus

REGNAVIT

A LIGNO DEVS

1–2. REGNAVIT . . . DEVS : *The text is quoted from the hymn* Vexilla Regis Prodeunt *of the Christian poet Venantius Fortunatus.*

ix. Sponge

POTAVERVNT

ME ACETO

1–2. POTAVERVNT . . . ACETO : *The text is quoted from the Vulgate, Ps. 68:22. In* LL, potāre *is used as a Trans. verb in the sense 'to give to drink'.*

x. Lance

VVLNERASTI

COR MEVM

1–2. VVLNERASTI . . . MEVM : *The text is quoted from the Vulgate, Song of Songs 4:9.* — VVLNERASTI = vulnerāvistī.

Third Statue W

*They have cast lots
for my garment.[a]*

a. *The text is quoted from the Vulgate, Ps. 21:19.*

Third Statue E

*Let them look upon me
whom they have crucified.[a]*

a. *The text is adapted from the Vulgate, Zech. 12:10.*

Fourth Statue W

*Whose lordship
is upon his shoulder.[a]*

a. *The text is adapted from the Vulgate, Is. 9:6.*

Fourth Statue E

*God has reigned
from a tree.[a]*

a. *The text is quoted from the hymn* Vexilla Regis Prodeunt *of the sixth-century Christian poet Venantius Fortunatus.*

Fifth Statue W

*They have given me vinegar
to drink.[a]*

a. *The text is quoted from the Vulgate, Ps. 68:22.*

Fifth Statue E

*Thou hast
wounded my heart.[a]*

a. *The text is quoted from the Vulgate, Song of Songs 4:9.*

15.2A   Castel S. Angelo: Dedication by Alexander VI

ALEXANDER V̅I̅ PONT MAX

INSTAVRAVIT

AN SAL M CCCCLXXXXV

1. ALEXANDER V̅I̅ : Sextus. — PONT(ifex) MAX(imus).
2. INSTAVRAVIT : Cf. 5.7B.
3. AN(nō) SAL(ūtis) M CCCCLXXXXV : Mīllēsimō quadringentēsimō nōnāgēsimō quīntō.

15.2B   Castel S. Angelo: Dedication by Paul III

ΠΑΥΛΟΣ ΤΡΙΤΟΣ Ο ΜΕΓΙΣΤΟΣ ΑΡΧΙΕΡΕΥΣ

ΘΕΙΟΥ ΑΔΡΙΑΝΟΥ ΜΝΗΜΕΙΟΝ

ΕΙΣ ΑΙΠΥ ΚΑΙ ΘΕΙΟΝ ΑΝΑΚΤΟΡΟΝ

ΜΕΤΕΒΑΛΕΝ

1–4. ΠΑΥΛΟΣ . . . ΜΕΤΕΒΑΛΕΝ : *Printed in accordance with modern typographical conventions, the text reads:* Παῦλος τρίτος ὁ μέγιστος ἀρχιερεὺς | θείου Ἀδριανοῦ μνημεῖον | εἰς αἰπὺ καὶ θεῖον ἀνάκτορον μετέβαλεν. *The wording implies some such draft as:* PAVLVS TERTIVS PONTIFEX MAXIMVS DIVI HADRIANI MONVMENTVM IN ARDVAM SACRAMQVE REGIAM TRANSFORMAVIT.

15.2C   Castel S. Angelo: Dedication by Paul III

1 QVAE OLIM INTRA HANC ARCEM COLLAPSA ⌐
IMPEDITA FOEDATA ERANT EA NVNC A PAVLO TERTIO

2 PONTIFICE MAXIMO AD SOLIDAM

3 FIRMITATEM COMMODAM VTILITATEM

4 SVBTILEMQVE VENVSTATEM EXTRVCTA DISPOSITA ⌐
ORNATA CONSPICIVNTVR

1. COLLAPSA IMPEDITA FOEDATA : *The three participles in asyndeton (cf. 1.2.i, line 4) are paired with three abstract nouns modified by adjectives* (FIRMITATEM, VTILITATEM, VENVSTATEM) *and a second trio of participles* (EXTRVCTA DISPOSITA ORNATA).
4. EXTRVCTA = exstrūcta : *On the spelling, see 4.2A, line 7.*

Façade

> *Alexander the Sixth,*[a] *Supreme Pontiff,*
> *restored this*
> *in the year of Salvation 1495.*

a. *Pope Alexander VI de Borja y Borja (r. 1492–1503). Alexander engaged the elder Antonio da Sangallo to make improvements to the defenses of Castel Sant'Angelo, including a moat, bastions on the perimeter wall, a tower and reinforcement of the* passetto *(see 15.5A.i, note b).*

Center of Ceiling, L and R Sides

> *Paul the Third,*[a] *Supreme Pontiff,*
> *transformed*
> *the monument of the divine Hadrian*
> *into a lofty and sacred palace.*

a. *Having as* Cardinal *shared the enforced sojourn of Clement VII in the primitively appointed Castel Sant'Angelo during the sack of 1527, Pope Paul III Farnese (r. 1534–1549) installed a suite of apartments that included the present audience hall. In allusion to the pope's Christian name (Alessandro), the frescoes depict scenes from the life of Alexander the Great. They are the work of Perino del Vaga and assistants.*

Frieze

> *Now built up, well ordered, and embellished by Paul the Third,*[a] *Supreme Pontiff, to a standard of firm strength, useful convenience, and refined grace,*[b] *what within this citadel was once fallen, impassable, and disfigured has become the object of admiration.*[c]

a. *Pope Paul III Farnese (r. 1534–1549).*
b. *The text is an elaboration of the principle prescribed by the Roman architect Vitruvius for the design and construction of buildings (De Architectura 1.3.2).*
c. *Lit., 'is gazed upon'.*

15.2D Mottoes of the Sala Paolina

i. Four Corners

FESTINA LENTE　　　ΔΙΚΗΣ ΚΡΙΝΟΝ

FESTINA LENTE : *The Latin translates Greek* σπεῦδε βραδέως, *quoted at Suet.Aug. 25.* — ΔΙΚΗΣ ΚΡΙΝΟΝ : *Printed in accordance with modern typographical conventions, the text reads:* Δίκης κρῖνον. *The thought appears to be condensed from John 7:24* (μὴ κρίνετε κατ' ὄψιν, ἀλλὰ τὴν δικαίαν κρίσιν κρίνετε).

ii. Over Moderation with Scales

SIT MODVS

IN REBVS

1–2. SIT . . . REBVS : *The text is adapted from Hor.Sat. 1.1.106.*

iii. Over Shrewdness with Snake

ANTE CONSVLAS

POST AGAS

1–2. ANTE . . . AGAS : *The thought is essentially the same as Sall.Cat. 1.6:* priusquam incipias consulto . . . opus est.

iv. Over Bravery with Lance and Lion

MANVS FORTIVM

DOMINABITVR

1–2. MANVS . . . DOMINABITVR : *The text is quoted from the Vulgate, Prov. 12:24.*

v. Over Justice with Sword and Scales

DISCITE IVSTITIĀ

MONITI

1–2. DISCITE . . . MONITI : *The text is quoted from Verg.Aen. 6.620.* — IVSTITIA(m).

Corners and Upper Walls

Corners

> *Make haste slowly.*[a]   *Judge in accordance with right.*[b]

a. *According to the imperial biographer Suetonius, a favorite motto of the em-*
peror Augustus ('Life' of Augustus 25). The sense is clarified by a quotation
from Euripides' Phoenissae ('For a safe general is better than a rash').

b. *The thought echoes John 7:24 ('Judge not according to the appearance, but*
judge righteous judgments').

E Wall, N End

> *Let there be*
> *moderation in things.*[a]

a. *The text is adapted from Horace, Satire 1.1.106.*

E Wall, S End

> *Think*
> *before you act.*[a]

a. *The wording recalls Sallust, Bellum Catilinae 1.6: 'Before you begin, there*
is need of counsel'.

W Wall, S End

> *The hand of the brave*
> *shall rule supreme.*[a]

a. *The text is quoted from the Vulgate, Prov. 12:24.*

W Wall, N End

> *Having been admonished,*
> *learn justice.*[a]

a. *The text is quoted from Virgil's Aeneid 6.620.*

15.3A Obelisco Vaticano: Dedications by Caligula & Gallus

⟨DIVO CAESARI DIVI IVLII F AVGVSTO

TI CAESARI DIVI AVGVSTI F AVGVSTO

SACRVM⟩

1a ⟦iussu imp caesaris diui f

2a c cornelius cn f gallus

3a praef fabr caesaris diui f

4a forum iulium fecit⟧

1. F(īliō).

2. TI(beriō). — F(īliō) : *Of the duplicate inscriptions, that on the E side is the better preserved.*

1a–4a. ⟦iussu . . . fecit⟧ : *The double brackets indicate that these words were effaced and replaced with those between angle brackets (cf. 2.2, line 10). The text is conjecturally restored on the basis of traces that survived the inscription's obliteration.* — imp(erātōris). — f(īliī).

2a. c(āius) : *See 1.1, line 1.* — cn(aeī) : *On the* C, *see* c(āius). — f(īlius).

3a. praef(ectus) fabr(um) = fabrōrum : *The original desinence in* -um *(cf. Greek* -ων*) was replaced by* -ōrum *on the analogy of* -ārum. *The older form persisted in religious, legal, and poetic diction.* — f(īliī).

15.3B Obelisco Vaticano: Dedication by Sixtus V

i.

SIXTVS V PONT MAX

OBELISCVM VATICANVM

DIS GENTIVM

IMPIO CVLTV DICATVM

5   AD APOSTOLORVM LIMINA

OPEROSO LABORE TRANSTVLIT

ANNO M D LXXXVI PONT II

1. SIXTVS V : Quīntus. — PONT(ifex) MAX(imus).

3. GENTIVM : *See 2.12A, line 3.*

5. APOSTOLORVM : *See 1.61, line 7.*

7. M D LXXXVI : Mīllēsimō quīngentēsimō octōgēsimō sextō. — PONT(ificātūs) II : Secundō.

Piazza di S. Pietro: Foot of the Obelisk, E & W Sides

⟨*Sacred*
to the Divine Caesar Augustus,[a] son of the Divine,
to Tiberius Caesar Augustus,[b] son of the Divine Augustus.⟩

⟦*At the bidding of Imperator Caesar, son of the Divine,*
Gaius Cornelius Gallus,[c] son of Gnaeus,
chief engineer of Caesar, son of the Divine,
built the Forum Julium.⟧

a. *The emperor Augustus (r. 27 BC–AD 14).*
b. *Tiberius Claudius Nero (r. 14–37). Tiberius was never formally deified*
and thus does not share the designation 'Divine' (see 2.4, note a).
c. *Though best known to classicists as the pioneer of Latin love elegy, Gaius*
Cornelius Gallus (c. 70–26 BC) was also the first Prefect of Egypt, annexed
by Rome in 30 BC (cf. 10.4A, note b). The Forum Julium was situated in the
neighborhood of Alexandria. Owing to his insolence, Gallus was recalled
to Rome and driven to suicide. Presumably in consequence of his damna-
tio memoriae (see 2.2, note d), Gallus' inscription (here enclosed in double
brackets) was removed from the obelisk, leaving only the tell-tale holes by
which the bronze letters had been affixed to the stone.

Base of Obelisk

South

Sixtus the Fifth,[a] Supreme Pontiff,
by a toilsome labor transferred
to the threshold of the Apostles
the Vatican obelisk,
dedicated in unholy reverence
to the gods of the heathen,
in the year 1586, second of his office.

a. *Pope Sixtus V Peretti (r. 1585–1590). The second year of his pontificate ran*
from 24 April 1586 through 23 April 1587. The dedicatory texts were dic-
tated by Cardinal Silvio Antoniano (see 7.1.i, note a); the letters and layout
were drafted by Luca Orfei (see 8.6, note e).

ii.

SIXTVS V PONT MAX

CRVCI INVICTAE

OBELISCVM VATICANVM

AB IMPVRA SVPERSTITIONE

5   EXPIATVM IVSTIVS

ET FELICIVS CONSECRAVIT

ANNO MDLXXXVI PONT II

DOMINICVS FONTANA EX PAGO MILI

AGRI NOVOCOMENSIS TRANSTVLIT

10   ET EREXIT

1. SIXTVS V : Quīntus. — PONT(ifex) MAX(imus).

7. ANNO MDLXXXVI : Mīllēsimō quīngentēsimō octōgēsimō sextō. — PONT(ificātūs) II : Secundō.

8. MILI : *The Ital. toponym Mili, here in App. to* PAGO, *is not Latinized. The present name of the town is* Melide.

9. NOVOCOMENSIS : *See 12.11, line 3.*

iii.

ECCE CRVX DOMINI

FVGITE

PARTES ADVERSAE

VICIT LEO

5   DE TRIBV IVDA

1. ECCE CRVX : *Its conventional English translation ('behold') notwithstanding, ecce is an interjection; it does not govern an Acc. case.*

4–5. VICIT . . . IVDA : *The text quotes the Vulgate, Rev. 5:5.* — IVDA : *The Latin name is* Iuda, -ae, *m.*

North

Sixtus the Fifth,[a] *Supreme Pontiff,*
in fitter
and more auspicious wise
consecrated to the Cross invincible
the Vatican obelisk,[b]
purified of unclean superstition,
in the year 1586, second of his office.

Domenico Fontana,[c] *of the town of Mili*
in the territory of Como, transferred
and erected this.

a. See 15.3B.i, note a.
b. Believed in the Middle Ages to have been the funeral monument of Julius Caesar, the obelisk was in fact brought from Alexandria by Gaius ('Caligula', r. 37–41) and erected in his circus, which is supposed to have lain parallel to the basilica.
c. See 7.1.ii, note c.

East

Lo, the Cross of the Lord!
Take flight,
hostile ranks;

the Lion of the Tribe of Judah
has conquered.[a]

a. The second section of the text alludes to the Vulgate, Rev. 5:5: 'Behold, the Lion of the tribe of Juda, the Root of David, hath prevailed to open the book, and to loose the seven seals thereof'. The language was adopted from the office of exorcism.

iv.

CHRISTVS VINCIT

CHRISTVS REGNAT

CHRISTVS IMPERAT

CHRISTVS AB OMNI MALO

5   PLEBEM SVAM

DEFENDAT

1. CHRISTVS : *See 1.6A.ii, line 6.*

v.

SANCTISSIMAE CRVCI

SYXTVS V PONT MAX

SACRAVIT

E PRIORE SEDE

5   AVVLSVM

ET CAESS AVG AC TIB

I L ABLATVM

M D LXXXVI

2. SYXTVS V : Quīntus. *The name* Sixtus *appears in various spellings (see 3.4D, line 4).* — PONT(ifex) MAX(imus).

6. CAESS = caesaribus : *See 1.61, line 7. The Dat. of the person is regularly used with verbs of depriving.* — AVG(ustō) — TIB(eriō).

7. I(ūre) L(icitō) : *The asyndeton is typical of legal and religious formulae.*

8. M D LXXXVI : Mīllēsimō quīngentēsimō octōgēsimō sextō.

15.4A S. Pietro in Vaticano: Dedication by Paul V

IN HONOREM PRINCIPIS APOST PAVLVS V BVRGHESIVS ¬

ROMANVS PONT MAX AN MDCXII PONT VII

APOST(olōrum) : *See 1.61, line 7.* —PAVLVS V : Quīntus. — BVRGHE-SIVS : *On the Latinization, cf. 12.3B, line 8.* — *Some such expression as* FRONTEM TEMPLI IN HANC ALTITVDINEM EXTVLIT *is to be understood as predicate.* — PONT(ifex) MAX(imus) AN(nō) MDCXII : Mīllēsimō sescentēsimō duodecimō. — PONT(ificātūs) VII : Septimō.

West

Christ conquers,
Christ reigns,
Christ commands:
May Christ defend
his people
from all evil.[a]

a. *This invocation served among other things as a battle cry of the Crusaders.*

Top of Shaft, W Face

Sixtus the Fifth,[a] Supreme Pontiff,
consecrated this
to the Cross most holy,[b]
torn from its
former foundation
and legally and licitly expropriated
from Caesars Augustus and Tiberius[c]
in 1586.

a. *See 15.3B.i, note a.*
b. *The obelisk was moved during the months of April through September of 1586. But for unanticipated delays, it would have been dedicated on 14 September 1586, Feast of the Exaltation of the Holy Cross.*
c. *See 15.3A, notes a and b. Alone of the City's obelisks, the Vaticano had remained* in situ *through the centuries.*

Façade

Paul the Fifth Borghese[a] of Rome, Supreme Pontiff, in honor of
the Prince of the Apostles, in the year 1612, seventh of his office.

a. *Pope Paul V Borghese (r. 1605–1621). The seventh year of his pontificate ran from 16 May 1611 through 15 May 1612. The prominence of Paul's name with respect to the phrase 'Prince of the Apostles' provoked a* PASQUINADE: *Angulus est Petri, Pauli frons tota, quid inde? Non Petro sed Paulo est dedicata domus ('Peter has a corner, Paul the entire façade: What must we conclude? The church is dedicated not to Peter but to Paul').*

15.4B   S. Pietro in Vaticano: Dedication by Paul V

PAVLVS V

PONT MAX

VATICANVM TEMPLVM

A IVLIO II INCHOATVM

5 ET VSQVE AD GREGORII ET CLEMENTIS

SACELLA

ASSIDVO CENTVM ANNORVM

OPIFICIO PRODVCTVM

TANTAE MOLIS ACCESSIONE

10   VNIVERSVM CONSTANTINIANAE

BASILICAE AMBITVM INCLVDENS

CONFECIT

CONFESSIONEM B PETRI EXORNAVIT

FRONTEM ORIENTALEM ET PORTICVM

15   EXTRVXIT

1. PAVLVS V : Quīntus. The text of Paul's original dedication read thus: ⟦paulus v pont max sacrosanctam beati petri principis apostolorum basilicam quam iulius ii pont max inchoauerat aliique pontifices maximi prosequuti fuerant ut uniuersum constantinianae basilicae ambitum religione uenerabilem includeret chorum sacrarium ac porticum benedicendo populo exaedificaret grandi accessione adiuncta opus amplissimum ac magnificentissimum absoluit anno m dc xv pontif x⟧ (*'Paul V, Supreme Pontiff, that he might comprise the whole extent of Constantine's basilica, august with sanctity, and that he might build the choir, sacrarium, and porch for blessing the people, by the addition of a mighty annex finished the basilica of the blessèd Peter, prince of the apostles, a vast and majestic work, which Julius II, Supreme Pontiff, had begun and other supreme pontiffs had furthered, in the year 1615, tenth of his office'*).

2. PONT(ifex) MAX(imus).

4. IVLIO II : Secundō. — INCHOATVM : *On the spelling, see 8.8A, line 2.*

6. SACELLA : *See 15.1A.ii, line 1.*

8. OPIFICIO : *See 3.4A, line 4.*

10. CONSTANTINIANAE : *See 8.3B, line 5.*

13. CONFESSIONEM : *See 15.4I, line 1.* — B(eātī).

15. EXTRVXIT = exstrūxit : *On the spelling, see 4.2A, line 7.*

Entry Wall, L

Paul the Fifth[a]
Supreme Pontiff,
completed
the Vatican church—
begun by Julius the Second[b]
and through the unceasing construction
of a hundred years,[c]
carried as far as the chapels
of Gregory and Clement,[d]
now by the increase of so great a fabric
comprising the whole extent
of Constantine's basilica—
embellished the Confessio of the Blessèd Peter[e]
and raised
the east façade and portico.[f]

a. Pope Paul V Borghese (r. 1605–1621).
b. Pope Julius II della Rovere (r. 1503–1513).
c. The cornerstone of the new basilica was set in 1506 and the façade completed in 1614.
d. The Cappella Gregoriana beneath the NE pier of the dome had been built under Gregory XIII (r. 1572–1585) and the Cappella Clementina, beneath the NW, under Clement VIII (r. 1592–1605). The decision at last to demolish the Constantinian nave was made shortly after the election of Paul V (16 May 1605). Paul's reign saw the completion of the head of Maderno's nave to the W and of the façade and portico to the E; the intervening portion was finished only in 1626 (cf. 15.4C, note a).
e. See 15.41.
f. The present text was composed by Pope Urban VIII to replace Paul's original dedication, which had been mounted in 1605 above the central portal. Urban had it placed above the left portal so as to form a pendant to his own inscription above the right portal (see 15.4C). Urban tactfully reduces his predecessor's achievement to its proper dimensions in the context of the building's history: Paul is credited with augmenting the plan of New St. Peter's so that it matched the dimensions of Constantine's basilica.

15.4C S. Pietro in Vaticano: Dedication by Urban VIII

VRBANVS VIII

PONT MAX

VATICANAM BASILICAM

A CONSTANTINO MAGNO EXTRVCTAM

5   A BEATO SYLVESTRO DEDICATAM

IN AMPLISSIMI TEMPLI FORMAM

RELIGIOSA MVLTORVM PONTIFF

MAGNIFICENTIA

REDACTAM

10   SOLEMNI RITV CONSECRAVIT

SEPVLCHRVM APOSTOLICVM

AEREA MOLE DECORAVIT

ODEVM ARAS ET SACELLA

STATVIS AC MVLTIPLICIBVS OPERIBVS

15   ORNAVIT

1. VRBANVS VIII : Octāvus. *Like many popes of the Renaissance and Baroque periods, Urban VIII was the last to bear his papal name. Other popes whose names have so far had no successor include Martin V (r. 1417–1431), Eugenius IV (r. 1431–1447), Nicholas V (r. 1447–1455), Callistus III (r. 1455–1458), Hadrian VI (r. 1522–1523), Sixtus V (r. 1585–1590), Julius III (r. 1550–1555) and Marcellus II (r. 1555). The names Clement, Leo, Paul, Gregory, Benedict, and Pius, by contrast, have proved very durable.*

2. PONT(ifex) MAX(imus).

4. EXTRVCTAM = exstrūctam : *On the spelling, see 4.2A, line 7.*

5. SYLVESTRO = Silvestrō : *On the spelling, see 3.1, line 1.*

6. TEMPLI : *On the diction, cf. 1.8G, line 5.*

7. PONTIFF = pontificum : *On pontifex, see 3.3C, line 13. On the abbreviation, see 1.6I, line 7.*

10. SOLEMNI = sollemnī.

11. SEPVLCHRVM = sepulcrum : *On the spelling, see 8.8A, line 2.* — APOSTOLICVM : *See 3.4D, line 4.*

13. ODEVM : *The CL ōdēum (transliterating Greek ᾠδεῖον, 'music hall') here furnishes a Classicizing alternative to chorus ('choir' in the architectural sense; see 4.2H, line 9).*

Entry Wall, R

Urban the Eighth,[a]

Supreme Pontiff,

in a solemn ceremony

consecrated the Vatican basilica,

built by Constantine the Great,[b]

dedicated by Saint Silvester,[c]

transformed

through the pious magnificence

of numerous pontiffs

into the aspect of an imposing temple,

adorned the tomb of the Apostle

with a massive monument of bronze,[d]

and embellished the choir, altars, and chapels

with statues

and manifold works of art.

a. *Pope Urban VIII Barberini (r. 1623–1644) dedicated New St. Peter's on 18 November 1626, reckoned the 1,300th anniversary of its dedication. The present inscription forms a pendant to the inscription of Paul V over the opposite portal (see 15.4B). Both were composed by Urban VIII, an accomplished Latinist. Taken together, the two texts furnish a précis of the basilica's whole history. In Urban's arrangement, the area over the central portal was occupied by Bernini's large marble relief depicting Christ's injunction to Peter 'Feed my sheep' (pasce oves meas). In the following decade this relief was removed to the portico by Innocent X, who wished to place his own dedicatory inscription (see 15.4D).*

b. *The emperor Constantine I (r. 306–337) founded St Peter's following his defeat of Licinius at Chrysopolis on the Bosporus in 324, much as he had founded St. John Lateran following his defeat of Maxentius at Ponte Milvio twelve years before (see 2.11A.i, note a).*

c. *The dedication of the basilica by Pope St. Silvester I (r. 314–335) belongs to the realm of legend (as does his baptism of Constantine, see 7.1.iii, note a).*

d. *The baldacchino (canopy) of Gianlorenzo Bernini, which towers over the high altar of St. Peter's, was manufactured of bronze taken from the portico of the Pantheon (see 11.3B.i, note c).*

15.4D   S. Pietro in Vaticano: Dedication by Innocent X

BASILICAM

PRINCIPIS APOSTOLORVM

IN HANC MOLIS AMPLITVDINEM

MVLTIPLICI ROMANORVM PONTIFICVM

5   AEDIFICATIONE PERDVCTAM

INNOCENTIVS X PONT MAX

NOVO CAELATVRAE OPERE

ORNATIS SACELLIS

INTERIECTIS IN VTRAQVE TEMPLI ALA

10   MARMOREIS COLVMNIS

STRATO E VARIO LAPIDE

PAVIMENTO

MAGNIFICENTIVS TERMINAVIT

2. APOSTOLORVM : *See 1.61, line 7.*

6. INNOCENTIVS X : Decimus. — PONT(ifex) MAX(imus).

15.4E   Epitaph of Countess Matilda

VRBANVS VIII PONT MAX

COMITISSAE MATHILDI VIRILIS ANIMI FOEMINAE

SEDIS APOSTOLICAE PROPVGNATRICI

PIETATE INSIGNI LIBERALITATE CELEBERRIMAE

5   HVC EX MANTVANO SANCTI BENEDICTI

COENOBIO TRANSLATIS OSSIBVS

GRATVS AETERNAE LAVDIS PROMERITVM

MON POS ANN M DC XXXV

1. VRBANVS VIII : Octāvus. — PONT(ifex) MAX(imus).

2. COMITISSAE : *The* ML *comitissa serves as Fem. counterpart to* comes
('count'). — FOEMINAE = fēminae : *On the spelling, see 1.8B, line 5.*

3. PROPVGNATRICI : *The* CL prōpugnātrīx *is 'champion', 'defender'.*

6. COENOBIO : *See 9.9.i, line 4.*

8. MON(umentum) POS(uit) ANN(ō) M DC XXXV : Mīllēsimō
sescentēsimō trīcēsimō quīntō.

Entry Wall Center

By new relief work,
by the embellishment of the chapels,
by the insertion of marble columns
in either aisle of the church,
and by the laying of a pavement
of variegated stone
Innocent the Tenth,[a] Supreme Pontiff,
completed with all due magnificence
the basilica
of the Prince of the Apostles,
brought to such massive grandeur
by the manifold construction
of the Roman pontiffs.

a. *Pope Innocent X Pamphilj (r. 1644–1655). The decorative work was completed in anticipation of the* Jubilee *of 1650.*

R Aisle, First Pilaster, N Side

Urban the Eighth,[a] Supreme Pontiff,
in gratitude set up this well-deserved monument
of her everlasting glory to Countess Matilda,[b]
a woman of manly temper, champion of the Apostolic See,
remarkable for her piety, renowned for her generosity,
after her bones had been brought to this place
from the Convent of Saint Benedict at Mantua,
in the year 1635.

a. *Pope Urban VIII Barberini (r. 1623–1644).*
b. *Betrothed at the age of ten to Duke Godfrey the Hunchback of Lotharingia, Matilda, Countess of Tuscany (c. 1046–1115), eventually returned to Italy to govern the extensive lands to which she was sole heir. Perhaps the most memorable episode of Matilda's career took place in January of 1077 at her ancestral fortress of Canossa, where the emperor Henry IV made his celebrated submission to Pope St. Gregory VII.*

15.4F Epitaph of the Stuarts

IACOBO III

IACOBI II MAGNAE BRIT REGIS FILIO

KAROLO EDVARDO

ET HENRICO DECANO PATRVM CARDINALIVM

5   IACOBI III FILIIS

REGIAE STIRPIS STVARDIAE POSTREMIS

ANNO M DCCC XIX

BEATI MORTVI

QVI IN DOMINO MORIVNTVR

1. IACOBO III : Tertiō. *The Latin* Iacobus *transliterates Greek* Ἰάκωβος, *a Hellenized form of* Ἰάκωβ. *The latter in turn transliterates Hebrew* Yaʿaqōbh, *associated by folk etymology with* ʿāqēbh *('heel', see Gen. 25:26). The original form of the name was in fact probably* Yaʿaqubh-ʾēl *('May Yahweh Protect').*

2. IACOBI II : Secundī. — BRIT(anniae).

3. EDVARDO : *On the name, see 6.5A, line 2.*

4. DECANO : *See 12.6, line 10.*

5. IACOBI III : Tertiī.

6. STVARDIAE : *On the Latinization, cf. 12.3B, line 8.*

7. M DCCC XIX : Mīllēsimō octingentēsimō ūndēvīcēsimō.

15.4G Epitaph of Maria Clementina

MARIA CLEMENTINA M BRITAN

FRANC HIBERN REGINA

1. MARIA : *The Latin* Marīa *transliterates Greek* Μαριάμ *or* Μαρία *(the latter a Hellenized form). Both represent the Hebrew* Miryam, *the sense of which is probably 'the corpulent one'.* — M(agnae) BRITAN(niae).

2. FRANC(iae) HIBERN(iae).

L Aisle, First Pilaster, S Side

To James the Third,[a]
son of James the Second, King of Great Britain,
Charles Edward[b]
and Henry,[c] Dean of the Cardinal Fathers,
sons of James the Third,
last representatives of the royal line of the Stuarts,
in the year 1819.

Blessèd are the dead
who die in the Lord.

a. Son of the Catholic King James II of Great Britain, deposed in the Glorious Revolution of 1688, James Francis Edward Stuart ('James III' of England and 'James VIII' of Scotland, 1688–1766) is called the 'Old Pretender'. He conducted an unsuccessful rebellion in 1715.

b. Charles Edward Louis Philip Casimir Stuart ('Charles III', 1720–1788) is called the 'Young Pretender' or 'Bonnie Prince Charlie'. His rebellion of 1745 came closer to success than that of his father thirty years before.

c. Younger son of 'James III', Henry Benedict Maria Clement Stuart (1725–1807) served as Dean of the College of Cardinals. On the death of his brother, he was proclaimed 'Henry IX' of Great Britain. The construction of the present monument was chivalrously sponsored by King George III.

L Aisle, Opposite Preceding

Maria Clementina,[a] Queen of Great Britain,
France,[b] and Ireland.

a. Maria Klementyna Sobieska (1702–1735), wife of the 'Old Pretender' (see 15.4F, note a), was granddaughter of the Jan III Sobieski of Poland who had driven the Turks from the gates of Vienna in 1683.

b. The claim of the English monarchs to the throne of France dated to the time of Edward III (r. 1327–1377). It was renounced by George III in 1801.

15.4H Commemoration of Pius IX

PIO IX PONT MAX

QVI PETRI ANNOS

IN PONTIFICATV ROMANO

VNVS AEQVAVIT

5   CLERVS VATICANVS

SACRAM ORNAVIT SEDEM

XVI KAL QVINT A MDCCCLXXI

1. PIO IX : Nōnō. — PONT(ificī) MAX(imō).

2. PETRI : *On the name, see 3.2A, line 2.*

5. CLERVS : *The* EL clērus *transliterates Greek* κλῆρος (*'lot', whence 'sphere of competency', then* EG *'clergy'*).

7. XVI : Sextō decimō. — KAL(endās) QVINT(īlēs) : *The completion assumes* CL *usage (see 1.6G, line 11). On the name* Quīntīlis, *see 1.61, line 16.* — A(nnō) MDCCCLXXI : Mīllēsimō octingentēsimō septuāgēsimō prīmō.

15.4I Dedication of Confessio

☧

SACRA BEATI PETRI CONFESSIO

A PAVLO PAPA V EIVS SERVO

EXORNATA

ANNO DOM MDCXV PONT XI

1. PETRI : *On the name, see 3.2A, line 2.* — CONFESSIO : *In the strict sense,* cōnfessiō *in* EL *is the place where a martyr 'confessed' Christ and suffered; it refers by extension to the resting-place of his or her relics, usually beneath the altar of a church.*

2. PAVLO PAPA V : Quīntō. *On* papa, *see 3.6A, line 2.*

4. DOM(inī) MDCXV : Mīllēsimō sescentēsimō quīntō decimō. — PONT(ificātūs) XI : Ūndecimō.

Central Nave R, Fourth Pilaster

The Vatican clergy
embellished the sacred seat
for Pius the Ninth,[a] Supreme Pontiff,
who alone
in the Roman pontificate
has equaled the years of Peter,
on 16 June 1871.[b]

a. *Pope Pius IX Mastai-Ferretti (r. 1846–1878). Pius completed the twenty-fifth year of his pontificate on 15 June 1871. According to tradition, the reign of St. Peter had lasted for twenty-five years (reckoned from his arrival in Rome in 42 to his martyrdom in 67). The fact that St. Paul makes no mention of St. Peter in his epistle to the Romans, written in the late 50s, implies that the truth is not as simple as tradition suggests.*

b. *Lit., 'on the sixteenth day before the Kalends of Quintilis' (i.e., of July; see 1.61, note c).*

Confessio

☩

The sacred Confessio of the Blessèd Peter,[a]
was embellished
by Pope Paul the Fifth,[b] his servant,
in the year of the Lord 1615, eleventh of his office.

a. *According to tradition, the Basilica of St. Peter rises on the site of the apostle's tomb, which was located in a necropolis to the N of the Circus of Caligula (see 15.3B.ii, note b). Archeological investigation has produced corroborative evidence including a remarkable specimen of ancient graffiti that reads: ΠΕΤΡΟΣ ΕΝΙ (i.e., Πέτρος ἔνι, 'Herein lies Peter').*

b. *Pope Paul V Borghese (r. 1605–1621). The eleventh year of his pontificate ran from 16 May 1615 through 15 May 1616.*

15.4J Basilica di S. Pietro: Dedication of Reliquary Shrines

i. St. Veronica

SALVATORIS IMAGINEM VERONICAE SVDARIO EXCEPTAM

VT LOCI MAIESTAS DECENTER CVSTODIRET

VRBANVS VIII PONT MAX CONDITORIVM EXTRVXIT ET ORNAVIT

ANNO IVBILEI MDCXXV

5–7   SANCTA | VERONICA | IEROSOLYMITA

1. SALVATORIS : *See 7.4B.*
3. VRBANVS VIII : Octāvus. — PONT(ifex) MAX(imus). — EXTRVXIT = exstrūxit : *See 4.2A, line 7.*
4. IVBILEI = iubilaeī : *See 2.12A, line 8.* — MDCXXV : Millēsimō sescentēsimō vicēsimō quīntō.
7. IEROSOLYMITA : *The* EL Ierosolymita *is 'native of Jerusalem' (Greek* Ἱεροσόλυμα).

ii. St. Helen

PARTEM CRVCIS QVAM HELENA IMPERATRIX E CALVARIO IN VRBEM AVEXIT

VRBANVS VIII PONT MAX E SESSORIANA BASILICA DESVMPTAM

ADDITIS ARA ET STATVA

HIC IN VATICANO CONDITORIO COLLOCAVIT

5–7   SANCTA | HELENA | AVGVSTA

1. CALVARIO : *The usual form of the Latin name is* Calvāria *or* Calvārius Mōns. *The* CL calvāria, *'skull', represents Aramaic Golgotha (Greek,* Γολγοθᾶ).
2. VRBANVS VIII : Octāvus. — PONT(ifex) MAX(imus).

Four Piers of the Crossing

SW Pier

Urban the Eighth,[a] Supreme Pontiff, constructed and embellished the reliquary,

that the dignity of its situation might in seemly wise preserve

the image of the Savior received on the kerchief of Saint Veronica,[b]

in the year of the Jubilee 1625.[c]

Saint Veronica of Jerusalem.

a. *Pope Urban VIII Barberini (r. 1623–1644).*
b. *Veronica's veil, which bears the visage of Christ (including the crown of thorns), has been venerated in the Vatican since the eighth century.*
c. *See 7.4H, note b.*

NW Pier

Urban the Eighth,[a] Supreme Pontiff,

took from the Sessorian Basilica[b] and deposited here in the Vatican reliquary,

with the addition of an altar and statue,

the portion of the Cross that the Empress Helen[c] carried off from Calvary to the City.

Saint Helen, Augusta.

a. *See 15.4J.i, note a.*
b. *'Sessorian Basilica' is another name for the Basilica of S. Croce in Gerusalemme.*
c. *Helen was the mother of the emperor Constantine I, who entitled her* AUGUSTA.

iii. St. Longinus

LONGINI LANCEAM QVAM INNOCENTIVS PONT MAX
A BAIAZETE TVRCARVM TYRANNO ACCEPIT
VRBANVS VIII STATVA ADPOSITA ET SACELLO SVBSTRVCTO
IN EXORNATVM CONDITORIVM TRANSTVLIT

5–7   SANCTVS | LONGINVS | MARTYR

1. PONT(ifex) MAX(imus).
2. BAIAZETE : *The Latin name is* Bāiazētēs, -is. — TVRCARVM : *See* 1.7A, *line* 5.
3. VRBANVS VIII : Octāvus.
7. MARTYR : *See* 2.10, *line* 2.

iv. St. Andrew

SANCTI ANDREAE CAPVT QVOD PIVS SECVNDVS
EX ACHAIA IN VATICANVM ASPORTANDVM CVRAVIT
VRBANVS VIII NOVIS HIC ORNAMENTIS DECORATVM
SACRISQVE STATVAE AC SACELLI HONORIBVS COLI VOLVIT

5–7   SANCTVS | ANDREAS | APOSTOLVS

1. ANDREAE : *On the name, see* 11.5A, *line* 2.
3. VRBANVS VIII : Octāvus.
7. APOSTOLVS : *See* 1.6I, *line* 7.

NE Pier

*With the addition of a statue beside and the construction of a chapel below,
Urban the Eighth [a] transferred to an elaborate reliquary
the lance of Longinus,[b] which Innocent, Supreme Pontiff,
received from Bayezid, tyrant of the Turks.[c]*

Saint Longinus, Martyr.

a. See 15.41.i, note a.

b. According to tradition, Gaius Cassius Longinus was the name of the soldier who pierced the side of Christ with his lance (John 19:34).

c. In exchange for the relic and a yearly ransom, in 1489 Pope Innocent VIII (r. 1484–1492) agreed to hold hostage in Rome Zizim, rebellious brother of the Ottoman sultan Bayezid II.

SE Pier

*Urban the Eighth [a] willed that the head of Saint Andrew,[b]
which Pius the Second undertook to have brought from Greece to the Vatican,
should be venerated here, adorned with embellishments
and the sacred honors of a statue and chapel.*

Saint Andrew, Apostle.

a. See 15.41.i, note a.

b. In 1462, Pope Pius II Piccolomini (r. 1458–1464) received the head of St. Andrew. Thomas Palaeologus, Despot of Morea—younger brother of the emperor Constantine XI, who had died at the fall of Constantinople (cf. 7.1.i, note d)—presented the relic in exchange for permanent hospitality at Rome.

15.4K Basilica di S. Pietro: Dedication of Nave and Cupola

i.

S PETRI GLORIAE SIXTVS PP V A M D XC PONTIF V

s(ānctī) PETRI : *On the name, see* 3.2A, *line 2.* — SIXTVS P(a)P(a) V : Quīntus. *On* papa, *see* 3.6A, *line 2.* — A(nnō) M D XC : Mīllēsimō quīngentēsimō nōnāgēsimō. — PONTIF(icātūs) V : Quīntō.

ii.

O PETRE DIXISTI TV ES CHRISTVS FILIVS DEI VIVI ⌐

AIT IESVS BEATVS ES SIMON BAR IONA QVIA CARO ET ⌐

SANGVIS NON RELEVAVIT TIBI

O PETRE . . . TIBI : *The text is adapted from the Vulgate, Matt.* 16:16–17. — CHRISTVS . . . IESVS : *See* 1.6A.*ii, line 6.* — IONA : *The Latin* Iona *transliterates the Greek* Ἰωνᾶς, *itself an abbreviated form of* Ἰωάννης (*cf.* 6.4). — QVIA . . . REVELAVIT : *See* 1.8F, *line 2.*

iii.

TV ES PETRVS ET SVPER HANC PETRAM AEDIFICABO ⌐

ECCLESIAM MEAM ET TIBI DABO CLAVES REGNI CAELORVM

TV ES . . . CAELORVM : *The text is excerpted from the Vulgate, Matt.* 16:18–19. — PETRAM : *The* CL petra *transliterates Greek* πέτρα ('*rock*').

iv.

QVODCVMQVE LIGAVERIS SVPER TERRAM ERIT ⌐

LIGATVM ET IN COELIS ET QVODCVMQVE SOLVERIS ⌐

SVPER TERRAM ERIT SOLVTVM ET IN COELIS EGO ⌐

ROGAVI PRO TE O PETRE VT NON DEFICIAT FIDES TVA ⌐

ET TV ALIQVANDO CONVERSVS CONFIRMA FRATRES TVOS

QVODCVMQVE . . . TVOS : *The text is adapted from the Vulgate, Matt.* 16:19 *and Luke* 22:32. — COELIS = caelīs : *On the spelling, see* 1.8B, *line 5.*

Frieze of Nave and Ring of Cupola

Continuous around the Lantern

Pope Sixtus the Fifth,[a] to the glory of Saint Peter,
in the year 1590, fifth of his office.

a. *Pope Sixtus V Peretti (r. 1585–1590). The fifth year of his pontificate ran from 24 April 1589 through 23 April 1590. The final stone of the vaulting of the cupola was set on 19 May 1590; Sixtus died on 27 August.*

Frieze of Right Transept

O Peter, thou hast said, 'Thou art the Christ, the son of the living God.' Jesus said, 'Blessed art thou, Simon bar Jonah, for flesh and blood hath not revealed it unto thee.'[a]

a. *The text is adapted from the Vulgate, Matt. 16:16–17. This and the following text constitute the famous 'Petrine Commission', the most explicit scriptural basis of the spiritual primacy of the popes in Roman Catholic teaching.*

On the Ring of the Cupola

'Thou art Peter and upon this Rock I will build my church, and I will give unto thee the keys of the Kingdom of Heaven.'[a]

a. *The text is excerpted from the Vulgate, Matt. 16:18–19. It exploits a pun on the Greek word πέτρα ('rock') and the name Πέτρος ('Peter').*

Frieze of Nave

'Whatsoever thou shalt bind on earth shall be bound also in Heaven and whatsoever thou shalt loose on earth shall be loosed also in Heaven. I have prayed for thee, O Peter, that thy faith fail not: and when thou art converted, strengthen thy brethren.'[a]

a. *The text is adapted from the Vulgate, Matt. 16:19 and Luke 22:32.*

v.

DICIT TER TIBI PETRE IESVS DILIGIS ME CVI TER ¬

O ELECTE RESPONDENS AIS O DOMINE TV QVI OMNIA ¬

NOSTI TV SCIS QVIA DILIGO TE

> DICIT . . . TE : *The text is adapted from the Vulgate, John 21:17.* — IESVS :
> *See 1.6A.ii, line 6.* — NOSTI = nōvistī. — QVIA DILIGO : *See 1.8F, line 2.*

vi.

O PASTOR ECCLESIAE TV OMNES CHRISTI PASCIS ¬

AGNOS ET OVES ΣΥ ΒΟΣΚΕΙΣ ΤΑ ΑΡΝΙΑ ΣΥ ΠΟΙΜΑΙΝΕΙΣ

ΤΑ ΠΡΟΒΑΤΙΑ ΧΡΙΣΤΟΥ

> O PASTOR . . . ΧΡΙΣΤΟΥ : *The text is adapted from the Greek text and
> the Vulgate version of John 21:16–17.* — ECCLESIAE : *See 1.7A, line 6.* —
> CHRISTI : *See 1.6A.ii, line 6.* — ΣΥ . . . ΧΡΙΣΤΟΥ : *Printed in accordance
> with modern typographical conventions, the Greek text reads:* Σὺ βόσκεις
> τὰ ἄρνια, σὺ ποιμαίνεις τὰ προβάτια Χρίστου.

vii.

HINC VNA FIDES │ MVNDO REFVLGET │ HINC SACERDOTII │

VNITAS EXORITVR

15.4L Epitaph of John Paul II

IOANNES PAVLVS PP II

16 X 1978 – 2 IV 2005

1. P(a)P(a) II : Secundus. *On papa, see 3.6A, line 2.*
2. 16 X 1978 – 2 IV 2005 : *Although it is immediately comprehensible to modern eyes, the notation does not lend itself to easy verbal expression in Latin*
   (ex diē sextō decimō mēnsis decimī annī mīllēsimī nōngentēsimī
   septuāgēsimī octāvī ad diem secundum mēnsis quārtī annī bis
   mīllēsimī quīntī).

Frieze of Left Transept

*Peter, Jesus saith unto thee three times, 'Lovest thou me?' Thou,
O chosen one, sayest in answer unto him him, 'O Lord, thou who
knowest all things, thou knowest that I love thee.'* [a]

a. *The text is adapted from the Vulgate, John 21:17.*

Frieze of Choir

*O shepherd of the Church, thou feedest all the lambs and sheep
of Christ: Thou feedest the lambs and thou pasturest the sheep
of Christ.* [a]

a. *The text is adapted from the original Greek of the Gospel and from the
Vulgate of John 21:15–17. In Roman Catholic teaching, just as Christ conferred the supreme government of the Church on St. Peter (Matt. 16:17–19,
ii–iv above), here he confers upon the apostle the supreme pastorate, or
'cure of souls'.*

Frieze of Crossing

*Hence a single Faith shines throughout the world. Hence arises
the unity of the Priesthood.*

Sacre Grotte

Pope John Paul the Second [a]
16 October 1978 – 2 April 2005.

☩

a. *Pope John Paul II Wojtyła (r. 1978–2005). Setting aside the prescribed
lapse of five years, Pope Benedict XVI (r. 2005–) formally opened the
Cause of Beatification for his predecessor on 13 May 2005. John Paul's profound and multifarious impact on the world of the late twentieth century
led to a widespread demand that he should be designated 'the Great', an
honor currently held by only three popes, all of the first millennium and
each the first to bear his papal name: Leo I (r. 440–461), Gregory I (r.
590–604), and Nicholas I (r. 858–867).*

15.5A   Fornix of Via Angelica: Dedication by Urban VIII

i.

VRBANVS VIII PONT MAX

DEDVCTVM IN ARCEM LATENTI FORNICE

TRANSITVM

A VATICANO RVINAM MINANTEM

5   CONSTABILIVIT TECTOQVE MVNIVIT

ANNO M DC XXX PONT VIII

1. VRBANVS VIII : Octāvus. — PONT(ifex) MAX(imus).
5. CONSTABILIVIT : *See 1.7A, line 11.*
6. M DC XXX : Mīllēsimō sescentēsimō trīcēsimō. — PONT(ificātūs)
VIII : Octāvō.

15.5B   Fornix of Via Angelica: Dedication by Pius IV

i.

PIVS IV MEDICES PONTIFEX MAX VIAM ANGELICAM

TRIBVS MILLIBVS PASSVVM AD CASSIAM DVXIT

ANNO SALVT M D L X III

1. PIVS IV : Quārtus. — MEDICES : *See 1.8G, line 2.* — MAX(imus). —
ANGELICAM : *See 14.3C.vi, line 2.*
2. TRIBVS MILLIBVS PASSVVM : *The usual* CL *construction would be* trīa
mīlia passuum (*Acc. of Extent in Space*). *Note also the late spelling* mil-
libus *for* mīlibus (*cf. 3.6A, line 5*).
3. SALVT(is) M D L X III : Mīllēsimō quīngentēsimō sexāgēsimō tertiō.

Attic above W Portal

South

> *Urban the Eighth,[a] Supreme Pontiff,*
> *stabilized and furnished with a roof*
> *the passage[b] leading by a covered arcade*
> *from the Vatican to the citadel,*
> *which was threatening collapse,*
> *in the year 1630, eighth of his office.*

a. *Pope Urban VIII Barberini (r. 1623–1644). The eighth year of his pontificate ran from 6 August 1630 through 5 August 1631.*

b. *The* passetto *('passage') connecting the Vatican palace with Castel Sant'Angelo, was begun by Pope Nicholas III Orsini (r. 1277–1280), who wished to link the Vatican with what was at the time an Orsini stronghold.*

Frieze above W portal

South

> *Pius the Fourth Medici,[a] Supreme Pontiff,*
> *brought the Via Angelica three miles to the Via Cassia[b]*
> *in the year of Salvation 1563.*

a. *Pope Pius IV de' Medici (r. 1559–1565).*

b. *The Via Angelica facilitated the approach of pilgrims arriving from the N by the Via Cassia. Pius IV developed the zone N of the* passetto *as the Civitas Pia (cf. 15.6, note a); at this period, seven openings were made in the old defensive wall on which the* passetto *was constructed. The quarter was enclosed by a new wall, demolished at the end of the nineteenth century.*

15.5A   Fornix of Via Angelica: Dedication by Urban VIII

ii.

VRBANVS VIII PONT MAX

GEMINAS HASCE INSCRIPTIONES

QVAE OLIM A S LEONE IV

IN LEONIANAE VRBIS MVNIMENTIS

5   POSITAE FVERANT

EX OBSCVRIORIBVS LOCIS

HVC TRANSTVLIT

ANNO SALVTIS M DC XXXIV

PONT XII

1. VRBANVS VIII : Octāvus. — PONT(ifex) MAX(imus).
3. S(ānctō) LEONE IV : Quārtō.
4. LEONIANAE : *The Adj.* Leōniānus *answers to the name* Leō.
5. POSITAE FVERANT : *On the tense, see 1.6G, line 7.*
8. M DC XXXIV : Mīllēsimō sescentēsimō trīcēsimō quārtō.
9. PONT(ificātūs) XII : Duodecimō.

15.5B   Fornix of Via Angelica: Dedication by Pius IV

ii.

PIVS I̅I̅I̅I̅ MEDICES PONTIFEX MAX PORTAM

ANGELICAM IVXSTA CASSIAM APERVIT

1. PIVS I̅I̅I̅I̅ : Quārtus. — MEDICES : *See 1.8G, line 2.* — MAX(imus).
2. ANGELICAM : *See 14.3C.vi, line 2.* — IVXSTA = iuxtā : *The spelling in S is phonetically redundant (cf. 4.2A, line 7).* — CASSIAM : *Often in the case of roads and aqueducts the noun is left implicit (here* VIAM*).*

Attic above W Portal

North

Urban the Eighth,[a] Supreme Pontiff,
transferred here
from their little-known sites
these twin inscriptions[b]
which once upon a time
were set by Saint Leo the Fourth[c]
on the fortifications of the Leonine City,
in the year of Salvation 1634,
twelfth of his office.

a. See 15.5A.i, note a.
b. The inscription pertaining to the Militia Saltisina (*see 15.5C.ii*) was discovered during improvements to the passage made under Urban VIII (*see
15.5A.i*). That pertaining to the Militia Capracorum (*see 15.5C.iii*) was
found in 1633 in the pavement of the Church of S. Giacomo at Settignano.
c. Pope St. Leo IV (r. 847–855).

Frieze above W Portal

North

Pius the Fourth,[a] Supreme Pontiff,
opened the Porta Angelica by the Via Cassia.[b]

a. See 15.5B.i, note a.
b. Via Angelica is so called from the pope's Christian name. This represents a
departure from the traditional nomenclature of the same pope's Porta Pia
(8.7A) and an anticipation of that adopted by Sixtus V for his Acqua Felice
(4.5).

15.5C   Civitas Leonina: Dedication by Leo IV

i.

CIVITAS

LEONIANA

2. LEONIANA : *See 15.5A.ii, line 4.*

ii.

TEMPORIBVS DOM LEONIS Q P P HANC PAGINE ET DV

[as t]VRRES SALTISINE MILITIA CONSTRVXIT

1–2. DOM(inī). — Q(uārtī). — P(a)P(ae) : *See 3.6A, line 2.* — PAGINE : *The word has the sense 'defensive wall' and appears to be attested only in this text and the next.* — DV|[as t]VRRES : *The characters enclosed in brackets are restored from context.*

2. SALTISINE = Saltisīnae : *On the spelling, see 1.8B, line 5.*

iii.

HANC TVRREM

ET PAGINE VNA F

ACTA A MILLITIAE

CAPRACORVM

5   TĒM DŌM LEONIS

QVAR P̄P̄ EGO AGATHO EI

1. HANC TVRREM : *The syntax is opaque* (TVRREM *functions with* PAGINE VNA *as the Sub. of* F|ACTA [sunt]).

2. PAGINE : *See above, line 1.* — F|ACTA.

3. MILLITIAE = mīlitiae : *The syntax is opaque (the word functions as an expression of agent with* A).

5. TEM(pore) DOM(inī).

6. QVAR(tī) P(a)P(e) = papae : *See 3.6A, line 2; on the spelling, see 1.8B, line 5.* — EI : *The stone is evidently damaged.*

Attic above W Portal, N Face

Above

The City
of Leo.[a]

a. *I.e., the defensive compound constructed by Pope St. Leo IV (r. 847–855).*

Center

In the times of the Lord Pope Leo the Fourth [a]
the Militia Saltisina constructed this wall and two towers.[b]

a. *See 15.5C.i, note a.*

b. *Works commenced in 848, using the manpower (militia) of the domus-cultae, large agricultural estates maintained in the Roman Campagna by the papacy. The domusculta Saltisina was probably located on the Via Ardeatina to the S of Rome.*

Below

In the time of the Lord Pope
Leo the Fourth [a]
this tower and a wall
were built by the Militia
Capracorum [b]
I Agatho ...[c]

a. *See 15.5C.i, note a.*

b. *The* domusculta Capracorum *was located on the Via Cassia N of Rome. Anastasius Bibliothecarius recounts the consecration of the walls on 27 June 852 by Pope St. Leo IV who, his head covered in ashes, led a procession of barefoot bishops and cardinals around the length of the enclosure, sprinkling it with holy water and pausing to bless each of its three gates with a special prayer.*

c. *Agatho was presumably foreman of the* militia Capracorum.

15.6 Porta Angelica: Fragments

ANGELIS SVIS MANDAVIT DE TE VT CVSTODIANT TE ⌐
IN OMNIBVS VIIS TVIS

ANGELIS . . . TVIS : *The text is quoted from the Vulgate, Ps. 90:11.* —
ANGELIS : *See 4.2J, line 2.*

15.7A Porta di S. Rosa: Dedication by Benedict XVI

BENEDICTVS XVI PONT MAX ANNO DOMINI MMV PONT I

BENEDICTVS XVI : Sextus decimus. — PONT(ifex) MAX(imus). —
MMV : Bis mīllēsimō quīntō. — PONT(ificātūs) I : Prīmō.

15.7B Porta di S. Rosa: Dedication by Benedict XVI

BENEDICTVS XVI P M
CIVITATIS VATICANAE OFFICIALIVM COMMODITATI
OSTIVM
APERIRI IVSSIT
5   A D MMVI PONT I

1. BENEDICTVS XVI : Sextus decimus. — P(ontifex) M(aximus).
2. OFFICIALIVM : *The* CL *Subst.* officiālis (*'official attending a magistrate'*)
is used broadly in LL *of any official.*
5. A(nnō) D(ominī) MMVI : Bis mīllēsimō sextō. — PONT(ificātūs) I :
Prīmō.

Vatican Bastion at Piazza del Risorgimento

He hath instructed his angels concerning thee
that they may guard thee in all thy ways.[a]

a. *The Porta Angelica was one of two gates in the bastion of Pius IV (see 15.5B.i, note b). The text is quoted from the Vulgate, Ps. 90:11. The choice of text reflects the influence mentioned at 15.5B, note b.*

Vatican Bastion at Piazza del Risorgimento: Gate

Benedict the Sixteenth, Supreme Pontiff,[a]
in the year of the Lord 2005, first of his office.

a. *Pope Benedict XVI (r. 2005–). The first year of his pontificate ran from 19 April 2005 through 18 April 2006.*

Vatican Bastion at Piazza del Risorgimento: Inside Gateway

Benedict the Sixteenth, Supreme Pontiff,
ordered an entry to be opened[a]
for the convenience
of the employees of Vatican City,
in the year 2006, first of his office.

a. *The Porta di S. Rosa, which provides access to Vatican City for pedestrian and vehicular traffic, is located on the site of a gate opened in 1929 but subsequently walled up. The bronze panels are by Gino Giannetti. The gate was inaugurated on 10 February 2006.*

Glossary

ARCHPRIEST. Formerly the senior presbyter (priest) of a diocese, empowered to perform the duties of a BISHOP in the latter's absence or during an episcopal vacancy.

AUGUSTA. Feminine form of *Augustus* (see IMPERATOR CAESAR AUGUSTUS). The first to bear the title was Livia Drusilla, wife of Augustus, on whom it was conferred after the death of her husband.

AUGUSTUS. The imperial title par excellence (see IMPERATOR CAESAR AUGUSTUS). The first to share the title was Marcus Aurelius (r. 161–180), who conferred it on his brother, Lucius Verus. Under the 'tetrarchy' established by Diocletian in 293, the Empire was governed by two *Augusti,* each of whom had a lieutenant designated *Caesar.*

BABYLONIAN CAPTIVITY. Originally, the sojourn at Babylon enforced on the population of Judah by Nebuchadnezzar of Babylon in the sixth century BC. The expression was used by Petrarch and others to refer to the residence of the popes at Avignon 1309–1377.

BASILICA. In architecture, a hall consisting of a central nave with two or more aisles. In ecclesiastical law, 'basilica' is a title assigned to certain important churches and conferring certain honorific privileges. The major (or 'patriarchal') basilicas are San Giovanni in Laterano, San Pietro in Vaticano, San Paolo fuori le Mura and Santa Maria Maggiore. San Lorenzo fuori le Mura may also be counted a major basilica. Among other distinctions, the major basilicas possess a 'Holy Door' opened on the occasion of a JUBILEE.

BISHOP. The highest order of clergy in the Roman Catholic Church. Archbishops, the highest in rank, are either 'metropolitan' or 'titular'. A metropolitan archbishop oversees an ecclesiastical province—a group of two or more dioceses—while simultaneously administering his own diocese (the 'archdiocese' or 'metropolis'). The dioceses of a province excluding the archdiocese are called 'suffragans'. Metropolitans are directly responsible to the pope, PATRIARCH of the West. Titular archbishops possess a see in name only. Next in rank to archbishops are 'ordinary' bishops; they exercise ecclesiastical jurisdiction over a geographical region, their see. The ordinary bishop is responsible to his metropolitan.

BVM. *Beata Virgo Maria*, the Blessèd Virgin Mary, Mother of Christ. The cult of Mary acquired considerable momentum after the Council of Ephesus (AD 431), at which the legitimacy of the title 'THEOTÓKOS' (Mother of God) was affirmed.

CAESAR. Properly a *cognomen* of the Julian clan. 'Caesar' was used by the emperors in place of a gentilitial name (see NAMES). When Hadrian (r. 117–138) designated Lucius Aelius Verus as his successor, he conferred on him the title 'Caesar'; henceforth the title served to designate the imperial heir.

CANON. One of a body of clergy attached to a cathedral or collegiate church and organized in a 'chapter'. Secular canons, who do not observe a common life, are to be distinguished from the Augustinian (or 'regular') canons, who live under a semimonastic rule (Latin *regula*).

CARDINAL. A member of the College of Cardinals, the body of high clergy that assists the pope in administering the church. Cardinal bishops are the titular bishops of the seven 'suburbicarian' sees of Rome: Ostia, Palestrina, Porto and Santa Rufina, Albano, Velletri, Frascati, and Sabina-Poggio Mirteto. The Titular Bishop of Ostia serves as Dean of the Sacred College of Cardinals. Cardinals appointed from episcopal dioceses are made cardinal priests, while those appointed from within the CURIA are made cardinal deacons; the *titulus* (see TITULAR CHURCH) is the prerogative of the cardinal priest, the DEACONRY that of the cardinal deacon. In 1587 Pope Sixtus V limited the number of cardinals to seventy (six cardinal bishops, fifty cardinal priests, fourteen cardinal deacons). Pope John XXIII abandoned this limit, expanding the cardinalate and raising the number of titular churches.

CENSOR. Under the Roman Republic, one of two magistrates whose office was established to relieve the consuls of the duty of holding the census. From the late third century BC, two censors were elected every five years and held office for eighteen months.

CONGREGATION. (1) A group of monasteries united under a single superior (e.g., the Benedictine Cassinese Congregration, taking its name from the Abbey of Monte Cassino). (2) An ecclesiastical society whose members take 'simple' vows as opposed to solemn (i.e., the vows are not irrevocable).

CONSERVATORS. Civil magistrates of the city of Rome from the fifteenth through the nineteenth centuries. The Roman Commune established in 1143 had as its principal organ of government the Senate, comprising fifty-six members. Progressively restricted by agreements with the papacy, the 'free' commune finally collapsed. In 1398, control of the City was formally ceded to Pope Boniface IX. Under the new system, the sole senator was a mere figurehead; the government was in the hands of the conservators, who headed the municipal bureaucracy and administered justice, and the *caporioni,* responsible, as heads of Rome's thirteen RIONI, for maintaining public order.

CONSUL. The highest magistracy of the Roman Republic. The consulship was an annual office held jointly with a colleague and was assumed on 1 January. Under the Empire, the emperor appointed consuls, often holding the office himself. The 'ordinary' consuls, whose names were used in citing the year, often served for only six months, making room for others to share the honor as 'suffect' consuls (under the Republic, a suffect was elected to replace a consul who had died in office). The last ordinary consul in the West held office in 527.

CONSUL DESIGNATE. A consul-elect. Under the Roman Empire, the emperors usually had themselves designated CONSUL towards the end of the year preceding that in which they wished to hold the office. Until 31 December, they bore the title 'Consul Designate' accompanied by a figure corresponding to the number of their future consulship (e.g., *Consul II Consul Designatus III*).

CURIA. The papal court through which the government of the Roman Catholic Church is administered. The Curia is organized in departments or 'dicasteries': These comprise congregations, tribunals, pontifical councils, offices, agencies, commissions, vicariates, and the secretariat of state.

DEACON. The lowest ordained clerical rank, below priest and BISHOP. In the early centuries of the Roman Church, seven deacons assisted by subdeacons administered ecclesiastical property and collected money to distribute to the needy. Their activity was coordinated within the city's seven ecclesiastical districts, established in the third century. Over time, the chief deacon ('archdeacon') came to be the leading administrative officer of the bishops of Rome. With the establishment of dioceses throughout western Europe, the archdeacon served as a bishop's principal lieutenant, supervising deacons in the administration of church property and enforcing discipline in the diocese.

DEACONRY. In this context, any of the numerous welfare centers operated by the early church in Rome (see DEACON). Many deaconries occupied sites that had been associated with the distribution of grain under the Empire. They were not churches, but featured an oratory, storehouse, bath, and hostel. In the course of the eleventh century, the seven ecclesiastical districts established in the third century became obsolete and the traditional duties of the deacon passed to the ARCHPRIEST. The honorary charge of the ancient deaconries is now assigned to cardinal deacons, as that of the TITULAR CHURCHES is to cardinal priests (see CARDINAL).

DIVUS. Under the Roman Empire, the title of a deceased emperor who had been formally deified by act of the Senate. The precedent was set by the divinization of Julius Caesar in 42 BC. In the five centuries from the death of Augustus to that of Anastasius, nearly sixty emperors were so honored. Inasmuch as it indicates that a given emperor was dead, the designation *divus* furnishes information useful in dating inscriptions.

EINSIEDELN CATALOGUE. A collection of inscriptions, both pagan and Christian, transcribed late in the eighth or early in the ninth century from monuments that in many cases no longer exist. It forms an appendix to the Einsiedeln Itinerary, a guide to Rome compiled by an anonymous pilgrim from northern Europe around the year 800.

GOLDEN LEGEND. A collection of saints' lives compiled in the thirteenth century by the Dominican Iacopo della Voragine (Iacobus de Voragine). It enjoyed an enormous vogue in the late Middle Ages; its popularity is attested by the fact that some 1,000 MS copies of the text survive. Though conceived as a source book for preachers, the collection is today best known for having furnished a wealth of subjects for the religious painting of the Renaissance.

IMPERATOR. Under the Roman Republic, the designation of a military commander vested with *imperium* (the quasi-sacral right of command), later used as an honorific title. Julius Caesar was the first to adopt *imperator* as a permanent part of his titulature. Caesar's heir took the title as a *praenomen:* IMPERATOR CAESAR AUGUSTUS. In inscriptions, in addition to forming part of the sovereign's name, the term ordinarily appears again with a numeral indicating the number of times he had been formally saluted as *imperator.*

IMPERATOR CAESAR AUGUSTUS. The name conferred in January of 27 BC on Gaius Julius Caesar's homonymous great-nephew and heir, the former Gaius Octavius. It consists of the title *imperator* as *praenomen,* the *cognomen Iulius* as *nomen* and the adjective *augustus* as *cognomen* (*see* NAMES).

INDICTION. A fifteen-year cycle used in citing dates. In the reign of the emperor Diocletian (r. 284–305), the term 'indiction' was used of an annual assessment of levies in kind. From 287, the indictions were numbered in cycles of five years; from 312, in cycles of fifteen. At Rome, three systems were in use at various times. The earliest was the 'Greek' or 'Constantinopolitan' indiction, reckoned from 1 September (the first day of the Byzantine year); it was in regular use at the papal chancery 584–1147. In the mid-twelfth century the 'Bedan' indiction, beginning on 24 September, was introduced alongside the Greek. Finally there was the 'Roman' or 'Pontifical' indiction, introduced under Urban II (r. 1087–1099) and reckoned from 25 December; it eventually superseded the other two. The ordinary practice was to cite the number of the year within the indiction rather than that of the indiction itself: for example, the years 312/13 and 1347/48 are both counted as the first indiction.

JUBILEE. Under Mosaic Law, a year in which land reverted to its former owners and slaves were freed (it occurred at the conclusion of a cycle of seven sabbatical years, so every fiftieth year); in Roman Catholicism, a special indulgence granted under certain conditions during a Holy Year to those who visit Rome. The latter was instituted in 1300 by Pope Boniface VIII, who meant it to be observed every 100 years. The interval was reduced to fifty years, then to thirty-three (to conform to the span of Christ's earthly career). The present term of twenty-five years was fixed by Pope Paul II in 1470.

LIBER PONTIFICALIS. A collection of early papal biographies. The life of each pope is written in formulaic language to a uniform scheme. Though the early entries are very brief, by the eighth and ninth centuries they assumed the dimensions of small books. The work was continuously edited and reissued through the pontificate of Martin V (1417–1431).

MAGISTRI VIARUM. In the Middle Ages, two municipal officials responsible for the maintenance of the streets of Rome. Pope Martin V brought the office under papal authority. In the 1450s, Nicholas V made the *magistri* papal appointees; and in the 1470s, Sixtus IV gave them powers of expropriation. In the sixteenth century the office was made a lifetime appointment and Pope Sixtus V raised their number to twelve.

NAMES. The name of a freeborn Roman male consisted of a *praenomen*, a *nomen*, and a *cognomen*. The *praenomen* was the given name; the *nomen* was the name of the *gens* or clan; and the *cognomen* frequently denoted a subdivision within the *gens*: e.g., Quintus Lutatius Catulus. More fully, the father's—and even grandfather's—name might be included: Quintus Lutatius Quinti Filius Quinti Nepos Catulus (i.e., Quintus Lutatius Catulus, son of Quintus, grandson of Quintus; in inscriptions, Q LVTATIVS Q F Q N CATVLVS). Under the Republic, following a victorious military campaign, a general might assume an honorific surname known as a *cognomen ex virtute* (name granted for valor) based on the name of the vanquished foe. Quintus Caecilius Metellus, for example, was known as 'Creticus' after his conquest of Crete; some such names became hereditary.

PASQUINADE. A witty and often scurrilous genre of lampoon. In 1501, the battered trunk of a Hellenistic sculpture group representing Menelaus recovering the body of Patroclus was mounted in Piazza Pasquino. The statue quickly became a venue for the posting of commentary critical of the authorities.

PATER PATRIAE. A title ('Father of his Country') accepted by Augustus in 2 BC and taken by all his successors except Tiberius, Galba, Otho, and Vitellius. It implied that the emperor stood in the same protective and chastening relationship to the Roman people as a *paterfamilias* to his *familia*.

PATRIARCH. A BISHOP who governs metropolitans as metropolitans govern suffragan bishops. In order to ease tensions between the Roman and Orthodox Churches, in 1964 Pope Paul VI abolished the titular patriarchates of Constantinople, Alexandria, and Antioch, which dated from the period of the Crusader kingdoms.

PRINCE OF THE YOUTH. A title (*princeps iuventutis*) first bestowed on Lucius and Gaius Caesar, adoptive sons of Augustus. The title was later taken by princes of the imperial family—the emperor's sons, brothers, and, in particular, his heirs. During the third century it became a general style of the future emperor.

PROCONSUL. Under the Roman Republic, a magistrate who held the authority of a CONSUL without the office so as to command an army or province. Under the Empire, the title was taken at times by Trajan, Hadrian, and the Antonines, especially when they were outside Italy. Septimius Severus and his successors held it almost always, even when they were resident in the city.

RIONI. Administrative quarters of medieval and modern Rome. The *rioni* are first attested in the eleventh century. The original twelve were augmented by the addition of Trastevere (beginning of the fourteenth century) and Borgo—the zone to the E of the Vatican (1586). New *rioni* were added after the establishment of the kingdom of Italy (1870), for an eventual total of twenty-two.

S.P.Q.R., Senatus Populusque Romanus ('Senate and People of Rome'). The formula refers to the chief repositories of political authority under the Roman Republic, the Senate and the people. As a shorthand expression for the sovereignty of the city and its political institutions, the abbreviation continued to appear on coins and in public documents—including dedicatory inscriptions—even after the establishment of the empire. When a new republic was declared in AD 1143, the formula S.P.Q.R. was revived as a stamp of political legitimacy. After the popes had succeeded in absorbing the communal authorities into the papal government, it was used as the official signature of the municipal administration (see Conservators).

Station Churches. The eighty-seven Roman churches having a note in the Missal: *'statio ad'*, followed by the church's name. The custom of the *statio* ('gathering'), in use by the fifth century, facilitated contact between the bishop and his flock. By the time of Pope Gregory the Great, its liturgy was fully developed. The people gathered at a given church (the *collecta*) and walked in procession to the station church. Over time, the participation of the pope was restricted to the most solemn feasts.

Supreme Pontiff. An honorary title of the pope (*pontifex maximus*). The pope is Supreme Pontiff of the Roman Catholic Church as well as Bishop of Rome, Patriarch of the West, Primate of Italy, and Metropolitan of the Province of Rome; he is in addition sovereign of Vatican City. In ancient Rome, the title belonged to the head of the College of Pontiffs, the leading figure in the state's religious hierarchy. Although in the Christian Church the term *pontifex* was in use as a synonym of *episcopus* ('bishop') from the fourth century, the full title was not adopted by the popes until the middle of the fifteenth.

Theotókos. 'She who gave birth to God', a title of the Blessèd Virgin Mary. In the early fifth century the title was rejected as Christologically incorrect by Nestorius, Patriarch of Constantinople. The matter was taken up in 431 by the Council of Ephesus, which substantially accepted the position of St. Cyril of Alexandria: the divine and human natures of Christ were perfectly united in his single Person, as mother of whom the BVM is fully entitled to veneration as *Theotókos*.

Titular Church. Any of the churches traditionally dated to the ordination by Cletus, St. Peter's successor as Bishop of Rome, of twenty-five presbyters for the Christian congregations of the city. Most in fact date to the fourth century and later. The *tituli* were originally semiautonomous foundations furnished with an income to support their clergy. When in the early Middle Ages the presbyters of the principal churches of Rome came to be designated 'cardinals' (see Cardinal), they were identified by the names of their titular churches. Before the sixteenth century, their number never exceeded twenty-seven or twenty-eight. In the Renaissance, impecunious popes erected new titles to sell to the highest bidder; in 1587, their number was limited to fifty by Pope Sixtus V. Popes since John XXIII have disregarded this limit, raising the number of titular churches as required by the expanding cardinalate. As of 2005, there were at least 150 titular churches in Rome.

TRIBUNICIAN POWER. Under the Roman Republic, the tribunes were in theory the champions of the rights of the people. They possessed the right of enforcing the decrees of the people and the right of veto against acts of magistrates and decrees of the Senate. Although as a patrician he was ineligible for the tribunate, in 23 BC Augustus assumed the power of a tribune (*tribunicia potestas*) and held it annually for the rest of his reign. The tribunician power was granted to all his successors on their elevation. The power was renewed at the beginning of each year of the reign (with a corresponding increase by one in the citation of the emperor's tribunician power in public documents, inscriptions included). From the reigns of Tiberius through Nerva, the imperial year was reckoned from the day of accession. Trajan reverted to the republican custom of entering the office on 10 December; this practice was followed by his successors. Hadrian—who assumed the tribunician power on 11 August 117, the date on which he was proclaimed emperor—assumed it for the second time on 10 December of the same year. The tribunate disappeared from the *cursus honorum* in the third century.

URBAN PREFECT. The holder (*praefectus urbi*) of an office instituted by the emperor Augustus in 16 BC for the purpose of maintaining order in the city of Rome. The responsibility of the office comprised not only the fourteen Augustan regions of the city but also a 100-mile zone including Ostia and Portus. In late Antiquity, the prefect commanded the three urban cohorts. His tasks were to publicize and apply the laws, provision the ports, and supervise the maintenance of the urban infrastructure. The office survived well beyond the Gothic period: Iohannes, the last Urban Prefect of whom we have knowledge, served in 599.

VIR CLARISSIMUS. The basic title of the senatorial aristocracy of the later Empire. From the time of Constantine, the aristocracy was divided into three categories: *clarissimus,* conferred on all members of the Senate; *spectabilis,* mostly deputies and lieutenants of the *illustres;* and *illustris,* a select circle that included the Prefect of Rome, the Master of the Foot, the Master of the Horse, and a number of others. During the Gothic Wars in the mid-sixth century, many members of the senatorial order fled to the East. Nevertheless, as late as 573 the Senate is recorded as convening under the presidency of the URBAN PREFECT.

Metrical Schemes

Unlike modern English verse, Greek and Latin poetry is quantitative. It depends for its structure on patterns of long and short—or, more precisely, of 'heavy' and 'light'—syllables:

   —   syllable is long (whether vowel is long or short)
   ◡   syllable is short (vowel is perforce short)
   ⏓   *syllaba anceps* (syllable may be long or short at the end of a verse)
   ⏕   either a single long or two short syllables may occur in the position

Syllables are combined in units called *metra* ('feet'), of which the following appear here:

Dactyl	Spondee	Iamb	Trochee
—◡◡	——	◡—	—◡

Four metrical schemes appear in this book: The Hexameter, the Elegiac Couplet, the Iambic Senarius, and Hendecasyllables:

The DACTYLIC HEXAMETER features six dactylic feet:

$$—⏕ \mid —⏕ \mid —⏕ \mid —⏕ \mid —◡◡ \mid —⏓$$

A spondee may replace the dactyl in any foot except (ordinarily) the fifth. The sixth foot is always a spondee or a trochee. In ML, pairs of end-rhyming hexameters are called 'Leonine'. Those featuring pairs of rhyming syllables are called 'caudati'; those featuring rhyming syllables at both the caesura and the line-end are called 'rich'.

The ELEGIAC COUPLET consists of a dactylic hexameter verse followed by a verse made up of two units, each comprising two and a half dactyls:

$$—⏕ \mid —⏕ \mid —⏕ \mid —⏕ \mid —◡◡ \mid —⏓$$
$$—⏕ \mid —⏕ \mid — \parallel —◡◡ \mid —◡◡ \mid ⏓$$

No spondees occur in the second half of the second verse of the pair.

The IAMBIC SENARIUS features six iambic feet:

$$⏓— \mid ◡— \mid ⏓— \mid ◡— \mid ⏓— \mid ◡—$$

A spondee may replace the iamb in the first, third or fifth foot.

HENDECASYLLABLES consist of eleven syllables (whence the Greek name) in five feet, of which the second is a dactyl and the last three are trochees:

$$⏓⏓ \mid —◡◡ \mid —◡ \mid —◡ \mid —⏓$$

The first foot ordinarily consists of a spondee but may instead be a trochee or an iamb. The final foot may be either a trochee or a spondee.

Index of First Lines

Entries are indexed by the first legible character on the stone irrespective of whether it is original or a copy.

549

Index of Sites